# THE WORLD AS POWER

# The Selected Works of Sir John Woodroffe (Arthur Avalon)

**The Dance of Shiva:** *Fourteen Indian Essays*

**The Garland of Letters:** *Essays on Tantra/Mantra Śāstra*

**The Great Liberation:** *Mahānirvāṇa Tantra*

**Hymns to the Goddess and Hymns to Kali:** *Karpūrādi Stotra*

**Introduction to Tantra Śāstra**

**Is India Civilized? :** *Essays on Indian Culture*

**Kamakalavilasa**

**Mahamaya:** *Cti-Shakti or Power as Consciousness*

**Principles of Tantra**

**The Serpent Power:** *Shat-Chakra-Nirūpana and Pādukā-Panchakā*

**Shakti and Shakta**

**The World As Power**

SIR JOHN WOODROFFE

*(At the Konarak Temple of Sun-god in Orissa)*

Courtesy : Mr P. K. DUTTA

# THE WORLD AS POWER

Sir John Woodroffe
*(Arthur Avalon)*

New Age Books

THE SELECTED WORKS OF SIR JOHN WOODROFFE
(ARTHUR AVALON)
THE WORLD AS POWER

ISBN: 978-81-7822-421-3
First NAB Edition: Delhi, 2013



**Library of Congress Cataloging-in-Publication Data**
Woodroffe, Sir John
The Garland of Letters: Essays on Tantra, Mantra Sastra/
Sir John Woodroffe—Ist Ganesh & Company edition
ISBN 978-81-7822-421-3 (pbk.)

*Published by*
**NEW AGE BOOKS**
A-44 Naraina Industrial Area, Phase-I
New Delhi (India)-110 028
E-mail: nab@newagebooksindia.com
Website: www.newagebooksindia.com

*Printed and published by*
RP Jain for New Age Books
A-44, Naraina Industrial Area
Phase-I, New Delhi-110 028. India

# INTRODUCTION

**There** is a Supreme Reality which is Eternal and Indefinable. It is an Absolute, inconceivable and ineffable—the Brahman. Unknowable in its utterness, this Reality presents itself to us in three supreme terms of its Truth : an absolute Existence, *Sat*; an absolute Consciousness, *Cit*; and an absolute Bliss, *Ānanda*. This is the poise of Brahman turned towards self-revelation.

It perceives itself as an infinite Existence; not a mere existence but a Being with a full awareness of all that It is, an infinite Consciousness. This Consciousness inherent in the supreme Being is no static awareness it is instinct with a Power, a Force dynamic with all the content of the Consciousness. And the nature of this self-conscient Existence is an inalienable Delight. All is a manifestation out of this triune status of the Eternal, *Sat-Cit-Ānanda*.

All is contained in the infinite Being of Brahman; it is brought out and released into a plenitude of manifestation by the Consciousness-Power innate in Himself for the sheer Delight of His Becoming. It is His own Consciousness as Power, the *Cit-Śakti*, that pours out the potentialities held in the infinitude of Brahman, throws up Forms from out of the Formless depths of the Eternal. The Seers of the Veda speak of it as *Māyā*, the power that measures (*miyate anena iti māyā*) out of the Immeasurable, the Force by which all is shaped out. This is the same "self-force of the Divine Being" which the Ṛṣis of the Upaniṣads beheld "deep hidden by its own conscious modes of working". All is a Play, *Līlā*, of this Power of the Divine in manifestation; all the forms and names that people the universe are self-deployings of this Ādya Śakti. Each is a diverse self-formulation of the Supreme Śakti, brought into being, maintained and withdrawn in the process of Her Cosmic Play with the Eternal Being, Her Lord, Śaktimān.

This is the theme of the present book by Sir John Woodroffe. Sir John has written numerous volumes on Indian Religion and Culture; but of all of them this series on the Doctrine of Consciousness-Power has a special importance providing as it does a closely reasoned basis for the subsequent development of his unsurpassed exposition of the philosophy and practice of the Śākta Āgama. At a time when the curve of Indian Civilization had reached the very nadir of the loss of its spirit and degeneracy of forms after an eventful life-period unparalled for its duration and expance; when the true visage of the Soul of India was so completely obscured that even the leaders of her renaissance movement were fumbling in their steps, apologetic of their past and ignorant of their true heritage, it was given to a few men of vision to see through the debris of the receding past and recover the priceless gems of her ancient bequest. Among the foremost of these selfless savants was Sir John Woodroffe who devoted the labour of a life-time for the reclamation of the profound truths of the most misunderstood and much maligned tradition in Hindu Religion, the Tantra Śāstra. A well-known member of the Judiciary, he specialized in Sanskrit studies, approached the sacred texts of the Āgamas with a becoming reverence with the aid of indigenous scholarship and guidance of Gurus, even delved into the arcana of the Sādhana Śāstra deep enough to emerge as an inspired champion of this hoary religion, astounding everybody by the amazing industry, the brilliance of mind and sympathy of understanding he brought to bear on his single-handed endeavour towards the resuscitation of the glory of the Tantra Śāstra, particularly the Śākta Vedānta. He wrote, translated, edited, annotated, lectured and did everything he could to present the teaching and practice of the Āgamas in their true original intention and laid India under a deep debt of gratitude for awakening her sons to a living sense of this great inheritance of theirs.

Coming to the present series of his writings (now happily brought together by the Publishers, uniform with their other famous publications on Tantra): We have here a detailed examination of the contribution of the six major Systems of Indian Philosophic Thought, the *Ṣad Darśanas* towards the understanding of the nature of the Reality, the Universe and the Individual. It is shown how each of the systems, Nyāya, Vaiśeṣika, Sāṅkhya, Yoga, and the schools of the Vedānta, lead one step by step towards a spiritual Monism as the ultimate Truth of Creation. It is noteworthy that Sir John does not deal with these thought-systems as things of the past but treats them as living stages in the progress of the human mind towards fuller and fuller Knowledge and relates them at every step to the march of modern Science. He is convincing when he discusses how most of the truths perceived by the Seers of old are now being confirmed by the progress of Science. This is not to say that all that is being discovered by Science today is there already known in the ancient thought of India and in the same form. The fact is that the fundamental truths of the Universe which were seized upon directly by the fresh and intuitive mind of the Seers of the Veda and Upaniṣad are now being confirmed by physical and psycho-physical sciences from the other end. Their method—the experimental method—is necessarily different but the conclusions at which they arrive are substantially and strikingly the same as posited by the Vedānta.

The author describes how the entire universe and its constituents is a spread-out, *prasara*, of the Supreme Power, the Ādya Śākti, the Divine Consciousness as Force. Spiritual and transcendent in its pristine station above, it bursts forth as and in the Universe, constituting or becoming the several orders of creation by a graded self-formulation and modification of itself in denser and denser forms of existence. Matter, Life, Mind, are each of them different terms of the self-manifestation of the One Divine Consciousness and are found to be as such in their depths when scrutinised with appropriate means. This basic unity, this oneness of origin that underlies all forms in creation is a fact of spiritual experience which is being increasingly corroborated by the results of the advance of Science. The Cartesian dualism of mind and matter no longer holds good. It is recognised that the 'missing links' pertain only to the superfices of the process of Evolution, and probed deeper, the Universe reveals an unbroken Continuum over all the several tiers of existence. Even Time and Space are categories of the Self-extension of this Consciousness-Power, terms which refer back to its original truths of Eternity and Infinity. All creation ultimately resolves itself into a vibrant manifestation of a Supreme Consciousness-Force, the Divine Śakti, in the ebullience of Her native Ānanda. It is One Līlā. The Play is Real. The Player is the Real of the reals. And man too has a part to play. Whether he will live in ignorance and be a puppet or, growing in Knowledge and Consciousness, he will liberate himself into an identity with the Dynamic Śakti and thus freely participate as a conscious player, is the choice before each individual.

*Sri Aurobindo Ashram*
*Pondicherry*
*July* 30, 1957

M. P. PANDIT

# CONTENTS

# POWER AS REALITY

(*Tattva-śakti*)

# FOREWORD

THE present book[1] is the first of a series which I hope to be able to complete, explaining succinctly some general philosophical principles of the Doctrine of Śakti or Power from the Śākta Vedānta standpoint. A correspondent once asked me—what was that? The answer is, that it is that Doctrine which is to be found, expressly or implicitly, in the Tantras of the Āgama-Śāstra of the Advaita Śākta and Śaiva communities of worshippers. The two have points in common in (amongst others) their Doctrine of Śakti and its evolution as the 36 Tattvas and so forth. Thus the latter are explained in both the Gandharva-Tantra, the Kashmirian Tattva-Sandoha, and other works. In the Prātah-Kṛtya as set out in the Mahānirvāṇa-Tantra (V. 39) salutation is made to Ātma-tattva, Vidyā-tattva, and Śiva-tattva, these being the three-fold divisions of the 36 Tattvas.

In what way another enquirer asks—is it to be distinguished from Viśiṣṭādvaita ? The answer is that according to the latter the Universe is the Body of the Lord, both now and in dissolution, that is always, whereas according to Śākta views though we may speak of the existing Universe as the Body of the Mother-Power (in Herself or *Svarūpa*, infinite and pure Consciousness or *Cidrūpiṇī*) yet in dissolution the Universe, the Power whence it proceeds and of which it is a transformation, and the Changeless Real or Śiva are one.

The books will be short but with much condensed substance. My object is to state general principles with reference to the thought of the day. The present counts. It is because Indian Philosophy and Religion are too often treated in an archaeological way, as things which have been and are gone, and as wholly unrelated to, and without value for, current thought, that they do not often receive the attention and respect which is their due. My own conviction is, that an examination of Indian Vedāntic Doctrine shows, that it is, in important respects, in conformity with the most advanced scientific and philosophic thought of the West, and that where this is not so, it is Science which will go to Vedānta and not the reverse. This is not necessarily proof that it is true, for the teaching

[1] All the six books of the series are brought under one cover in this volume.

of Western Science may or may not be well founded, and has certainly undergone revolutionary changes from time to time. What is laughed at to-day is accepted tomorrow and *vice versa.* But if Western Science is deemed of value, so must be the Vedāntic teaching which is in conformity with it.

This series will illustrate more fully what is here stated, but in a general way some examples may be given in support of it. The primary doctrine of Advaita-Vedānta is Unity. The world is not a heap of entirely disparate things thrown together by chance. All are connected, the one with the other and suffer and enjoy through one another. Some gain this truth through their reason, others through their heart and others again by the stick. Thus the late war[1] has discovered the truth to those ignorant of it—that each people and each man is dependent the one on the other. So that if we harm others we harm ourselves immediately or in the long run. Practical Science is charged with the same mission. Railways, steamers, aeroplanes, the telegraph, the telephone, all help to establish the idea of the unity of mankind, to diminish particularism and to foster a wide view of the Universe and its meaning.

India has ever held views which are both wide and of the deepest. Her infinities may bore or appal some. But who will deny that Her ideas have been the most colossal the world has known ? Her fearless logic has stayed at nothing, until reaching the last barriers of thought, man transformed by *Sādhana* and *Yoga*, has attained That which is alogical. By thinking and direct experience, unity is known. Western Science is working towards the same or similar conclusions by its own objective experimental method. In this process it is destroying the difficulties and contradictions, which itself had created. It has set up partitions which it now pulls down. Some of them may be pragmatically useful, for thinking would be fluid unless we controlled the continuous flow of phenomena by divisions, labels and so forth. Some are indeed imposed on us from without, for this power to impose itself on the mind is a test of our Reality. But others are the product of imperfect observation and gratuitously erroneous thinking. None according to Vedānta is essentially justified.

Unity and Continuity are metaphysical concepts. The forms which we observe are, as forms, breaches of both. Nevertheless from their gradations and relations the unity of Power of which they are manifestations is inferred. Union by *Sādhana* with such essential Power gives direct

[1] World War I (1914-1918)

experience (*Veda*) of the unitary essence which is displayed as Mind and Matter. Though the notion of Cit as the basis of all psychical modes is still peculiar to India, Western Science and Philosophy are now commencing to distinguish between Mind and Consciousness, holding that below and above the surface Consciousness there is yet another. There is in us much more than that of which we are aware. The unity of Mind and its action as a whole is now recognised, as also that Mind is a Force. This is well established in Indian Doctrine which teaches its activity in perception, actually *going forth* to its object and its creative power as shown in the so-called occult faculties or *Siddhis*.

Speaking of this Mind-ray reminds me of a recent announcement that an instrument in the nature of an electroscope is to be shown at a forthcoming medical congress in proof of the statement that in vision a ray proceeds from the eye,—an old Indian notion. The hitherto supposed gap between Mind and Matter is closing, thus rendering a transition from physical to psychical concepts easier. It is an ancient Indian Doctrine that both Mind and Matter are modes of one and the same Substance, and as such related to and akin to one another thus rendering all knowledge possible. Cognition is recognition.

Of the greatest importance is the change of ideas regarding the nature and constitution of Matter. India in the person of her great thinkers has never held to what Sir William Jones called the "vulgar notions of matter". Western Science now dematerialises Matter. The notion of real and lasting partitions between various forms of elementary matter is passing. The present tendency of science is towards the revival of the ancient Doctrine of one Substance-Energy, the Mahāśakti of the Vedāntic Śākta and the Prakṛti of the Sāṃkhyas. All material forms are passing modes (*Vikṛti*) of this one Power. *Māyā* becomes a possibility and not the absurdity which some have supposed it to be. Sāṃkhya is not a "chaotic impertinence" as the English Samskritist Dr. Fitz Edward Hall, with the usual depreciation of things Indian, called it. On the contrary, here as elsewhere the rational character of Indian doctrine is justified. The hitherto supposed gap between "living" and "non-living" substance is now by many denied. Both are forms of the One Power which in this aspect is *Prāṇah Prāṇasya*, the Life of all lives. In so-called "inorganic" substance that Form displays itself in certain restricted ways and in organic substance in other ways of increasing freedom. As regards the evolution of "living" substance, the Indian notion has always been that the various forms of it differ only in degree and not in kind.

In future numbers of this series I hope to deal with Cit, the unchanging principle of all changing experience. Its Power (*Cit-Śakti* and *Māyā-Śakti*), Unity, Causality, Continuity and the various manifestations of Power (Śakti) or modes of its Substance-Energy as Mind, Life and Matter.

But it is to be remembered that the Indian Quest has been and is a practical one—the quest of Happiness which all men seek. If it be true, as *Yoga* holds, that Man can by the appropriate method think and otherwise work himself *out* of the dualistic system of which he is a part, yet whilst he is in and of it, on the path of Enjoyment (*Bhoga*) his thinking has its end in some form of action. In Śākta teaching, *Yoga* and *Bhoga* are unified (*Yogo Bhogāyate*). Man gains every end in and through the finite yet real world—even those which are unworldly, in the striving for unity with the *Ens Realissimum* of which the world is an act of will. That action in the world will be powerful to effect his aims (and who does not want that ?) if he worships the infinite Mother Power, the Supreme and complete "I" (*Pūrṇāham*) of which he is according to this teaching a contraction (*Saṃkoca*) or form. By *Sādhana* he makes contact and then unifies himself with the fundamental Grand Will. This Will reinforcing his own individual and contracted will, the "Little Doer" achieves all success.

Another and most important matter to be remembered is this.—It has recently been said (Hoernle "Studies in Contemporary Metaphysics," 75) that "the Eastern doctrines of the veil of illusion over reality and of the elaborate ascetic regimen for Mind and Body by which the student must discipline himself for penetrating to the Reality behind the veil, have never profoundly affected the main current of Western thought. Most of the great Philosophers of the West, certainly since the time of the Renaissance, have been men of the world as well as students and thinkers. They have never tried to be 'holy' men set apart from their fellows and the problems of contemporary life. They have not, even when they were professors, spent their days in meditation and mortification of the flesh in order to achieve individually the blessedness of Union with the One."

These statements do not apply to the Middle Ages in the West. With the supposed "Veil of Illusion" this book deals. Śākta doctrine does not favour an "ascetic regimen", except by "ascetic", we understand a self-controlled and ordered life. Says the Kulārṇava-Tantra (Ch. I-V, 75, *et seq*) "Fools deceived by Thy *Māyā* hope to attain liberation by eating one meal a day, by fasting and other acts which emaciate the body. What liberation can such ignorant ones get by the torture of the body ? Donkeys go about naked, are they therefore *Yogis* ? If liberation is to be had by smearing oneself with mud and ashes then village dogs who roll therein are *Yogins*. Deer and other animals live on grass leaves and water, are they therefore *Yogins* ? Hogs are exposed to cold wind and heat. To them all food fit and unfit are alike. Are these then *Yogins* ? Oh Kuleśvari, all such practices deceive. The only direct cause of liberation is knowledge of the Truth (*Tattva-jnāna*). It again affirms that, in Kaula-Dharma, *Bhoga* (Enjoyment and Suffering) is converted into Yoga (*Yoga bhogāyate*) and the *world is made the seat of liberation* (*Mokṣāyate saṃsārah*).

The end which is beyond the life of earth is achieved in it. It is not the fugitive but the *Vīra* (hero) who meets life face to face, who conquers all vain fears and ignorance and achieves. He is *Vīra* who struggles with *Avidyā*. By what man falls, by that he rises. But in common with other Indian systems, it holds that by reason and speculation alone Reality, in its sense as the Supreme Experience, is not attained. For this, *Sādhana* as physical, intellectual and moral purification, self-control, discipline, and worship are necessary. Without these the doctrine is not, even in an intellectual sense rightly apprehended, still less is the Truth realised. Man must *transform* his nature to attain it. This involves right activity (*Kriyā*) with awareness of, and self-identification in all functions with, the indwelling Mother-Power: "She I am" "*Sa'haṃ*" he says.

It has been said in the West (and this is Indian doctrine) that there is no end to what the trained and tutored will can do; and that because if a man puts himself in line with the Forces of Life he can tap reservoirs of Power, the contents of which are bottomless, because they are co-extensive with the Universal Life. This is the meaning of two terms common in the Tantra, namely, *Yoginīpriya* (Beloved of the *Yoginīs*) *Yoginī-paśu* (slave of the *Yoginīs*). The *Yoginīs* are *Devatā* aspect of the Forces of Nature or *Āvaraṇa-Devatās* of the *Mahā-yoginī*, the supreme *Mahāmāya-Tripurasundarī*. Work with them and success is attained. Work against them and ill-fortune follows. Identify the self with the partial aspects which are the *Yoginīs* and then various Powers (*Siddhis*) are attained. Identify the self with the *Mahā-yoginī* Herself and Man is liberated, for He is no longer man but She. This is the Śākta teaching, come down from days when India was a *Siddha-Bhūmi*. With what a man should identify himself, depends upon what he wants. But whatever, it is, he gets the Power, if he but wills and works for it.

In conclusion, I wish to express my thanks to my friend Professor Pramathanātha-Mukhyopādhyāya[1] for the help he has given me in the preparation of and in revising this and the forthcoming volumes, in which latter I hope to include some valuable notes of his on their subject.

*Calcutta*, 14th July 1921 **J. W.**

[1] Now Swāmi Pratyagātmānanda Saraswati.

# THE WORLD AS POWER:

## POWER AS REALITY

### I

It is a common notion concerning the Hindus that they are an unpractical people, without "grip on reality," believing life to be a "dream." This estimate is supposed to receive corroboration from the fact of their political dependence[1] and to be in some degree the justification of it. Their Religion and Philosophy is said to be accountable for these alleged defects and their results. False philosophies and religions have (it is supposed) impeded India in the path of what its critics consider to be self-realization. That there has been a lack of dynamism is obvious enough, for otherwise things would not be what they are. Therefore is needed the worship of Śakti or Power. There has been in some quarters a lack of faith, of belief, of self-confidence which is life and the issue of Life. How wonderful is the saying of that unnamed sage (to which I will in another volume return) which is quoted by Puṇyānanda and Bhāskararāya in their Commentaries on the Yoginī-hṛdaya, and Nityāṣodaśikā-Tantras.

*Apūrṇaṃ manyatā vyādhih kārpaṇyaika-nidāna-bhūh*

"Sense of imperfection is disease and the sole source of every misery." But does not the Vedānta speak of the *Pūrna*, the *Whole* which is both Health and Life lasting ? Is it the fact that Indian philosophy and religion are responsible ? This is a large question, the answering of which would involve very many inquiries extending over a large field. Here I am concerned with one only. To me the Hindu typal-mind has a profound sense of reality, both as universe and its ground.

The power of ideas is immense and the greatest of all powers. But we must not over-exaggerate the influence on man at large of the technical discussions of professional philosophers. This is above all true of the philosophical issue, so long and even now agitated, namely as to the reality of the world of objects, as to the real nature of the "Real," as to what is

[1] Written in 1921 when India was not independent.

real and unreal in experience, and so on. The reality of the universe is imposed even on philosophers notwithstanding their arguments. For both they and the common folk form part of and perceive it. The difference between these two classes, in India as elsewhere, lies in this, that the reality of the world, in the technical sense of "Reality" as understood in the West, is taken for granted by the latter, who pursue their avocations unworried by self-created difficulties, whilst some at least of the former in the West have been engaged in the task of endeavouring to show that the things which we perceive are not really what we perceive them to be. Indian philosophic thought preserves the reality of the object experienced, whilst making full allowance for the influence in the act of perception of individual mental characteristics and tendencies called *Saṃskāras*, until that stage of cosmic consciousness (called Hiraṇyagarbha) is attained in which Reality as the Universals or Generals of the sense-particulars (*Tanmātras*) is experienced. Beyond this is Perfect Experience as Īśvara and then Pure *Saṁvit* Itself. In the Hiraṇyagarbha subsumed by Īśvara there is still the limiting Saṃskāra which while allowing perfect experience of the universals, yet precludes a perfect experience of the whole cosmic dynamism of things and their relations. This limitation is removed in the stage of Īśvara in which there is not only a perfect experience of effects (kārya) as they are but of causes as they are. There is no question of noumenal and phenomenal aspects but rather of casual and effectual aspects; nor is there a question of an unknowable background as in Western Science. Both aspects are actually known by us imperfectly; the effectual by Hiraṇyagarbha perfectly; both causal and effectual by Īśvara perfectly.

Western thought has endeavoured to show that things are not what they appear to be, that is, they are in fact other than what they seem. We are thus said to live in "appearances" of "things in themselves," unknowable yet existing in their own right. The sense-data are mere effects, produced in a perceiver's mind by the action on the sense organs of material objects, conceived in terms of imperceptible and hence hypothetical particles and forces. According to the Indian idea here described, it is affirmed that things are *as things* what they appear to be. There is no "thing in itself" and therefore no appearance of it. The individual's perception of a thing is however subject to the limitations of his sense-capacity and of his *Saṃskāras*. The Western view is—"What I see as green is objectively not green at all, but an hypothetical vibration of an hypothetical Ether." But according to Indian doctrine greenness is objective: though this greenness may be perceived by me subject to my *Saṃskāras* or prenatal tendencies and conditions of sense-capacity. The standard thing or the standard quality is not an unknowable extra-mental X, but the standard experience of a perfect Experiencer, Īśvara or Hiraṇya-garbha. Īśvara's experience is the "thing in itself" and of the "thing in itself"; my experience is an actual participation in His subject to my own limitations. There is thus no difference (as in the West) between "thing in itself" and "appearance" (which latter does not resemble the former), but between standard or perfect experience on the one hand and varied individual experience, subject to limitations, on the other. The Vedānta says that things are forms of, or appearances backed by, a Spiritual Reality which is not a thing at all. But so far as anything is a thing, we know it, subject to our limitations, for what it is. The Real has three bodies causal, subtle, and gross of which the former is the common source of the other two, which constitute the world of subtle and gross objects. Experience in each of these bodies is direct and real. Scientific doctrine has not this reality of experience. For the perceived is substituted the inferred, and some of this inference is (when not unsound) either based on slender evidence or mere hypothesis. Inference is not the experience of the real. It may be wholly error. In applied science we live in a real world. But theoretical science and metaphysics may, as regards the inferred ultimate nature of things, be without truth, the correspondence of the real. In such matters an idolatry of Science is amongst the most foolish. Nevertheless it is a fact that Science is putting forward to-day theories which, if without meaning as applied to the physical world alone, nevertheless tend to establish the truth, which gives them meaning. Thus when it attributes unity, conservation, and continuity to Matter, Energy, and Motion in an universe of obvious plurality and discontinuity (since every form is a real breach of it) what it is in fact doing is to show that none of its conceptions have any meaning, except on the assumption of the unity and unmoving continuity of Consciousness in the sense of the Vedāntic Cit.

Indian thought affirms the truth (in its grade) of experience whether empirical or transcendental. Mere speculation as to the nature of either as inferred by reasoning or sense data leads at best to a conclusion of probability. The only certitude is in direct Experience itself. Nothing useful is gained in attempting to prove that experience is in itself not real, or is an appearance of something unperceived. If we would know what some other than ordinary experience is, we must actually shift, not our speculative thought on to it but our being into it. In other words, we must have that experience directly. When we have made the shift, the experience which we have left is of no concern to us. But even if it were, it would not appear to be false but to be the relative truth of the stage at which it was had. It is "corrected" only in and for the next experience of the Real. Whilst on the plane of material experience, sense-data, inference, and reasoning take their part in raising the self to its own higher Self and its experiences. There is no magic carpet which wafts the self from one stage to the other. But it is only a part of the *Sādhana* as moral conduct, self-discipline and ritual worship which are the necessary preliminary of Yoga through reasoning (*Jnāna*), feeling (*Bhakti*) or action (*Karma*). Truth is given us in our awareness of the world, for as we see it so it really is for us. There are higher experiences than this. But if they are to be had, the whole subjective being and its material body must be so actually *transformed* as to enable such experiences to be had. In other words we must experience reality whatever be its aspect—and not merely discuss it.

Contrary to common belief, Hindu thinkers have been and are (in an epistemological sense) not only Realists but Realists of a thoroughgoing type. There is no trace of the Subjectivism which may be found in the Buddhist schools. I have used the term "Realism", because it can be described, for the present purpose, in a clear way as the doctrine which holds that the world of objects is real in the sense that they exist independently of the consciousness of the person who experiences them. The vast bulk of the people of India are as "naively realistic," as the rest of the world. Nor have they the mental malady which doubts the obvious and seeks for anything but a plain account of things. Theirs is the great common-sense which means man-kind-sense; even though like everything which is human, it is not free from error. Common-sense is the sense of Reality in its material form. I am not however here concerned with popular but with philosophic Indian thought. By "Indian" I mean Brahmanical or, to use a popular term, Hindu. In fact one of the great cleavages between Brahmanical and Buddhist thought concerns this philosophical question of Reality, either as the Constant Centre of experience, or the universe which is the object of its experience. If the charge made can be laid at the door of any philosophy or religion, it is at that of some forms of Buddhism. For the very mark of Brahmanism is reality and practicality in doctrine and discipline. "Realism" in the Western sense is the doctrine that reality exists apart from its presentation to, or conception by, consciousness. The realist believes that in sense-perception we have assurance of the presence of reality distinct from the modifications of the perceiving mind and existing independently of perception. *This is the Hindu position.* In Epistemology or theory of knowledge the Idealist asserts, after the manner of the Buddhist, that the reality of the world is its perceptibility. *This the Hindu denies.*

With this definition of "Realism" no harm is done by the employment of a technical Western term. Descriptive names given to Western systems of thought are not seldom in themselves ambiguous and often actually misleading when applied to Indian doctrine. They have their utility as a species of short-hand for the description of Western systems and serve a purpose when we endeavour to compare Western and Eastern thought. But care must always be taken in their use. "Realism" even in Europe does not always connote the same thing. Idealism again is a vague term. In the metaphysical sense, Idealism is the name given to any theory which maintains the Universe to be throughout the work or the embodiment of Reason or Mind.[1] In this metaphysical sense of the term, that is as opposed to materialism, all the Six Philosophies may be described as idealistic, for none of them is materialistic.[2] In an *epistemological* sense the Hindus are *Realists.* In the *metaphysical* sense, some of their systems, such as the Sāṃkhya and Vedānta have been called Idealistic. The former may perhaps be so described, if a system which derives matter from things mental can be so called. It is certainly not (as has been said)[3] materialistic. It sounds strange to call a system materialistic which derives matter from thoughts and ideas and such an estimate is[4] absolutely against the universal tradition of Hindus who, notwithstanding their assiduous critics, may be at least allowed to know what their own systems mean. For this reason, the Indian author last cited calls it Psycho-dynamism, inasmuch as the Principles which it regards as the origin of things are both psychical, that is, in the nature of feelings, thoughts and ideas, and dynamic,

---

[1] See Baldwin. Phil. Dict. *sub. voc.*

[2] The first standard or Nyāya-vaiśeṣika has been called "Hindu Realism" and in several senses it is so. It is however not materialism and cannot be called Idealism in so far as its creation is a conjunction of previously existing realities.

[3] By Prof. Garbhe. Samkh. Phil. 242: *et seq.* Prof. Max Muller called it a system of Idealism, *Six Systems.* X.

[4] As pointed out by J. C. Chatterjee in *Hindu Realism,* 14.

that is of the nature of forces or powers. The Vedānta again differs fundamentally from such idealistic Western stsyems as those of Fichte, Schelling and Hegel, in that (amongst other things) the Vedāntic Cause of the universe is not Mind or Reason as those terms are understood in the West but *Cit* (of which Mind is only a limited *mode*) and its Power or Śakti. It is better then in all cases to avoid Western terms except where they are nearly adequate, or comparison calls for them. We can most accurately describe Indian systems by avoidance of labels, and by stating what in fact they say, leaving others to docket them in their Histories of Philosophy, if they will.

The belief to the contrary of that which I have expressed is I think in part due to the fact that the most talked-of system in the West is the Monistic Vedānta of the School of Śaṃkarācārya, and in part to a lack of understanding of this system, which presents some difficulties to the European mind. Even in India there are, I believe, at the present day but few who are really masters of it.

## II

THE chief orthodox systems of Brahmanism are known as the Six Darśanas or "Means of seeing",[1] because what the West calls Philosophy is that which gives men sight of sensible verities and enables them to understand in the light of Reason the super-sensible Truth attainable only through Veda, that is, the super-sensible *standard* experience of the Ṛṣis[2] or Seers. Philosophy habits this experience, so far as may be, in its rational dress.

These six systems may for the purpose of metaphysics be grouped into three, *viz.*, (1) Nyāya-vaiśeṣika, (2) Sāṃkhya-Yoga, (3) Vedānta.[3] This last term means Upaniṣad. As such, it must be distinguished from the various interpretations of it which are given by the Vedāntic philosophical schools.

All these systems teach the empirical reality of the external world. In fact Śaṃkarācārya to whom the doctrine of the "unreality" of the world is attributed, emphatically affirms, in his polemic against the Subjectivism of the Buddhists, that matter is every whit as real as the mind which perceives it. The first of these groups teaches the absolute reality (that is, independence of the universe) of its nine eternally existing ultimate entities,[4] with their properties, relations and so forth; the second, the absolute reality or the independence of the universe of its ultimate root as the evolving Material Cause[5] associated with Efficient Cause[6] or Consciousness, the two Realities of this system; and the third, which is subdivided into two general divisions, teaches in the first of these divisions that the universe in ultimate resort is real, not as independent, but as part of the *one* ultimate Reality or Brahman; whilst the Māyāvāda Vedānta, which is the sole system of the second division and is regarded by its adherents as the crown of all doctrines, teaches that the universe, whilst empirically real, is in the transcendental sense neither "real" *nor "unreal"*, nor partly either, but is backed up and made apparently substantial by

---

[1] Darśana comes from the root "*Dṛś*", "to see" that is to know.

[2] Ṛṣi also comes from the same root "to see" for they saw as Seers, that is had experience (Jñāna) of supersensible truths.

[3] This is the Uttaramīmāṃsā. The Pūrva or Dharma-Mīmāṃsā's metaphysical basis belongs to the first group.

[4] Dravya : post.

[5] Mulaprakṛti: v. post.

[6] Puruṣa which is Cit.

this one Reality; which, though It is (relative to us) Being-Bliss-Consciousness[1] and Lord,[2] is in Itself beyond all mind and speech (which, however, does not make It *unknowable*).

These Six Systems are really One System,[3] containing three chief presentments or Standards of Indian Thought suitable to various types and grades of mind, which Standards, in themselves, mark stages of advance towards the understanding by the mind of the beyond-mind standard experience of the Seers or Ṛṣis. Those who regard them according to notions of historical succession only will not accept this. They will also further point to the controversies of the adherents of each of the philosophical and religious schools. It is however the Indian notion which is expressed by Śiva who says[4] "The Six Doctrines[5] are My Six Limbs[6] (that is they form the unity of His Intellectual Body). He who separates them one from another severs my limbs (that is the unity of His Body). These also are the Six Limbs of Kula."[7] Śiva is the all-knowing Supreme Consciousness,[8] and Mind[9] is a mode of it. The Six Philosophies are the Six Minds or six Ways in which *intellectual* approach is made to that Full or Whole Experience,[10] a state which transcends mind and its operations. This Indian notion is essentially a true one. It is unaffected by succession in time, or by the fact that each adherent of a system is taught[11] and believes that his system is the truth and would argue others out of theirs. It is necessary that this should be so, because only that can be received which the particular mind is capable of receiving. That is *its* truth. And that only can be held and lead to practical result in which one has faith. One stage is not contradictory of another, because they are stages complete and true in themselves, as representative of particular psychic development, of which the doctrine held is the corresponding expression. Absolute truth consists in this, that it is impossible of correction. But the stages being relative are in a sense corrected; not in the sense

[1] Saccidānanda. [2] Īśvara.

[3] Some correspondences between the Six Systems are given in the following notes with a view to explaining the statement that they are each a presentment of the one standard Truth.

[4] *Kulārṇava-Tantra,* II-84, 85.

[5] Darśana : commonly called the Six (orthodox) Philosophies.

[6] Two legs and feet, belly or trunk, two arms and hands and head.

[7] The community and doctrine of the Tantrik school called Kaulas. Kula—Śakti. Akula=Śiva. He who is Līna in both is Kulīna or Kaula.

[8] Cit. [9] Antahkaraṇa or inner instrument.

[10] Pūrṇa; which is the Immense or Brahman which is theologically God.

[11] See my Essay "Alleged Conflict of Śāstras" in *Śakti and Śākta*.

that they fail according to a standard applicable to the stage of particular development for which they are appropriate; but because the mind, enriched and transformed in its continuing advance, moves towards another and truer attitude and standpoint.

The Six Systems then are not wholly separate and mutually contradictory as commonly supposed, but are a graduated series in which the three groups form three great Standards suited to different types or grades of mind—different intellectual capacities and temperaments.[1] What system any individual should follow depends on his competency or *Adhikāra*, a very fundamental doctrine of Brahmanism. To each is given the truth of his stage. When acquired, the mind naturally ascends to the next until, by the elimination of all which is accidental, it passes into the one essential stageless Reality.[2] When therefore it is said that the Six form one system, reference is not made to their historical genesis. The relation is not temporal but logical. They are stages in a process of immanent logic of the Reason realising itself as the true expression (so far as may be) in mind of supermental experience. The former cannot truly represent the latter, but some systems of thought make nearer approach to it than others. Classification by time is superficial. One system may ante-date or post-date another but what is essential is its character as being more or less advanced in the process of self-realisation.

In all these systems the world as a combination of elements is a passing thing, it being a common Hindu notion that nothing which is produced (and the universe as we know it is that) lasts for ever. Into what is it resolved ? What are or is its fundamental Realities or Reality ? This leads to a short survey of the teachings of the Six Systems on this point.

[1] See *Hindu Realism*, 5, *et seq.*
[2] See my Essay "Alleged Conflict of Śāstras" in *Śakti and Śākta*.

## III

If we reflect on the nature of ultimate Reality or Realities, the most obvious division which suggests itself is that of the Experiencer and Experienced, of the conscious Selves and the world of objects together with their various properties and relations.

On the subjective side there is Consciousness and Mind, for none of the Indian systems fails to distinguish the one from the other. We know ourselves as conscious beings. Consciousness is recognised by the First Standard[1] as a property and as such must inhere in some Reality which is independent of the body, since it is not the latters' property for several reasons which this *Śāstra* develops. We may only note here the view that if Consciousness cannot be the property of the body as a whole, neither can it be a mere function of the brain, the brain theory of Consciousness being open to the same objections as the one which maintains that consciousness is a property of the body as a whole.[2] In fact consciousness belongs to what feels itself to be the possessor of the body and makes use of the body. But as in all the other Standards, a distinction is drawn between Consciousness and Mind.[3] The Ātman or Self is the basis of Consciousness and experience. It is not limited but is all-pervading and present everywhere. But we observe that the Self does not always perceive an object, even when the latter is in relation with a sense or senses by which it is perceived. Therefore the Self requires something else for perception, namely, attention in which case only perception of the object takes place. Moreover mind is wanted to enable the self to have experience, not simultaneously of all things at once but in succession. For these and other reasons the necessarily limiting function of moving atomic mind in relation to unmoving all-pervading Self, and the separate real existence of mind is shown. As consciousness is not the property of the body, neither is it the property of and one with the senses, life or mind.

[1] As to what follows the English reader may consult *Hindu Realism* by J. C. Chatterjee and others. To those who know Bengali, Rajendra Ghose's work on this System is recommended.

[2] See Chandrakānta-Tarkālankāra *Lectures on Hindu Philosophy*, II. 174.

[3] Manas. In this case between Manas and the Self or ātman whose property is consciousness and mind.

Mind and senses are instruments of Consciousness. Thoughts, ideas and feelings are generally called Mind in the West, but the Self as sustainer of consciousness is not any of these. For they are in continual change and are known and experienced as changing things in much the same way as the body and its changes are known and experienced. Being so experienced they are not the experiencer. We are here on ground common in general to all the Standards, the main distinction being that in this Standard the Self or Ātman is the Reality in which all consciousness inheres, and consciousness is not its essential characteristic as in Sāṃkhya and Vedānta. We thus get two ultimate Realities on the side of Perception for the senses are made up of the four minima[1] of discrete things perceived by the senses, and though real are not original ultimate realities.

Then what is perceived ? What is perceived is Matter with its properties and relations and so forth, now moving, now held in position in space. Matter is real, its properties and relations are real, and so are time, motion and space. The sensible world is thought to be five-fold, for it affects our senses in five different ways. As the Standard does not admit a common Substance with varying form, matter is constituted by a number of separate independently existing Realities. Matter has certain general qualities[2] which correspond to a certain extent to what European Philosophy calls the primary qualities which may be perceived by more senses than one: as also certain special qualities[3] which can each be perceived by a certain sense only and correspond to some of the so-called secondary qualities of Western Philosophy. But if external things exist, they must do so independently of the percipient, for that is their Reality. Their qualities are really inherent in them and not in the percipients. Nor can it be said, as some do in the West, that some properties are inherent and objective and others subjective. For the arguments which prove that some properties are objective will also prove that the rest are so. As further explained later the theory of perception is fully "realistic." The four special qualities which affect the four corresponding senses are odour, taste, colour, and the touch sense. Sound in this standard is not regarded as a property of the discrete sensible things, there being no such thing from which sound cannot be entirely eliminated; yet sound as a quality can have no independent existence of its own, nor is it purely subjective. It inheres in the Reality called Ether (*Ākāśa*)

[1] Paramāṇus.
[2] Sāmānya-guṇa. [3] Viśeṣa-guṇa.

though not possessing exactly the same qualities as the Ether of modern Western science. Things move in it and produce sounds not in themselves but in the medium in which they move. There are thus four classes of Minima of those moving things which are discrete and are perceived by the senses, each of which is eternal and changeless and a fifth Reality the ethereal motionless *Ākāśa* in which they are. These Minima or Paramāṇus have been called[1] misleadingly "Atoms." For the latter have in Western chemistry some magnitude, whilst the four classes of Paramāṇus are non-spatial and absolutely without any magnitude whatever. Unlike many, if not most, schools of Realism in the West there is no Hindu system of realistic thought which has ever held that the essential basis of the sensible world is a something or somethings which must have magnitude and extension. The ultimate constituents of sensible things are real but not hard solid particles with magnitude —a conclusion towards which Western investigation with its "dematerialization" of Matter now tends. The Minima combine to form sensible matter, the pure points standing themselves away from one another but being united mediately through the intervening ether which is itself a non-discrete Reality or continuum in touch with all discrete things. Each of these four classes of Paramāṇus, as the origin of a special quality perceived by a special single sense, is also the origin of the particular sense itself, namely, the senses commonly called touch, sight, taste, and smell. That is the special senses are essentially of the same nature as the ingredients or originators of the qualities themselves. It is thus important to remember that according to the Hindu theory of Perception the senses are essentially of the same nature as the originators of the qualities which are perceived by them. These senses perceive all perceptible things as moving, changing, coming into existence, and passing out of it. This standard has no such notion of inherent causal efficiency as is held by the second. It holds that the things themselves as things cannot do all this. Motion is communicated by the First Mover who is separate from that which He moves. Discrete things have no power of self-origination and movement—even if they had, we should not see the orderly movement which is in the universe unless there were some Power which makes this orderly movement and seasonable origination and distinction of things possible. But we not only see things moving and changing, but they hold relative positions to one another, that is, are held together in their positions and must therefore be conceived

[1] As pointed out in *Hindu Realism*.

as being acted upon by a Power which works in a direction opposite to that in which the power of movement works. This movement or *Kāla* produces all relations which are called temporal and so is in this sense Time. The other principle or *Dik* by which discrete things are held in relative position produces notions of spatial direction. Space and Time have an objective existence irrespective of the mind thinking about them. The relations which they produce are as the things related. They are relations of the real separate things.

Of Entities (*Dravya*) or as they are sometimes translated Substances, there are thus (both subjective and objective) nine.[1] These with their qualities or properties, movements or actions, species, particular, inherent inseparable relation and negation are known as the seven *Padārthas*[2] or Categories under which everything which can be imagined are classed. All these entities, properties, relations and so forth are real.

Dealing with the Entities (*Dravya*) there are in the Nyāyavaiśeṣika, the first and simplest of the three stages of philosophical development, on the one hand the Selves,[3] the basis of consciousness and experience, or that in which consciousness inheres, together with the Mind or instrument of their experience,[4] and, on the other hand, the four essential subtile objects of experience[5] from which are produced the gross perceptible objects of experience together with the ethereal medium[6] in which all discrete and separated things exist. To these it adds *Kāla*, the Principle of universal movement bringing, according to general Hindu ideas, things into existence, subjecting them to change and carrying them out of existence

---

[1] Ātman, Manas, Paramāṇus (4), Ākāśa, Kāla, Dik.

[2] Guṇa Karma, Sāmānya, Viśeṣa, Samāvāya (as of quality with substance, action with substance, part with whole) Abhāva. Guṇas are 24 in number and are Nitya and Anitya, Karma 5, Sāmānya (3), Viśeṣa many, Samāvāya 1, Abhāva 2 again divided into three. According to Kaṇāda there were only 6 Padārthas, Abhāva being omitted. That in which they inhere (ādhāra) are Dravya in the case of Guṇa, Karma, Viśeṣa; Dravya, Guṇa, Karma in the case of Sāmānya and Samāvāya; and Abhāva may be related to anything in Svarūpa-Sambanda. According to Vedānta, Śakti is different from these. The Nyāya includes Śakti or Power in Abhāva as the negation of obstruction, hindering production of effect (Prati-bandhakābhāva). Īśvara has Nitya-jñāna, Nitya-icchā, Nitya-kriyā. These three properties are called the Śaktis of Īśvara.

[3] Ātmans. These correspond (when I use this word here or elsewhere I do not imply that the notions are identical: on the contrary) to the Puruṣas of the Sāṃkhya-Yoga and to the one Ātman of the Vedānta.

[4] Manas. This, as an instrument of experience, corresponds to the Antahkaraṇa of the other systems of which Manas is one particular function.

[5] Paramāṇus. Their place is taken in the other system by the Tanmātras or supra-sensible matter.

[6] Ākāśa: given as such medium in all the schools.

giving rise in the percipient to the notion of Time;[1] and *Dik* the Principle which, notwithstanding the impulse of the former, holds things together in their various relative positions giving rise in the percipient to the notion of relative position as "here and there," "near and far" in Space.[2] In this system however neither Time nor Space are mere notions. They are *Dravya* or Entities that is something independently real, and self-subsisting. Confusion has arisen from the supposition that *Kāla* and *Dik* mean Time and Space in the general Western sense of those terms.[3] Western Realists have also maintained that Time and Space have an existence irrespective of the mind thinking about them, with the result that all necessary relations drawn from knowledge may also be regarded as having a reality independent of the mind reflecting on them. This does not mean according to Western Realism that they have existence as individuals or independent of the things related. But they have just such reality as we are intuitively led to believe them to have; that is, they exist as necessary relations of the separate things.[4] According to the Nyāya-Vaiśeṣika-Darśana, *Kāla* is a general principle of movement and *Dik* is a power which acts in exactly a contrary way, that is, by holding things together in a particular position. It is not Space in the sense of room[5] and is in the nature of spatial direction. Each Reality has only general relation with everything which moves or is held in position. They are both, as realities, distinct from the things in and upon which they operate: but as so operating they give rise in the percipient to the notion of relations called Time and Spatial position.

The imperceptible *Paramāṇus* or things of no magnitude produce perceptible things with magnitude.[6] In this system the World as a compound of these lasting eternal elements is real since it exists independently

[1] Kāla. In the Pāncarātra-Tantras also time is defined as "the mysterious power which urges on and matures everything." It is three-fold as Supreme, Subtle, Gross. Transcendental Time is traced back to Veda and is referred to in the saying Kālah kāle nayati mām "Time leads me in time." This is Akhaṇda Kāla or Time without sections. See Dr. Schrader's Introd. *Ahirbudhnya-Saṃhitā* 65. As to time as a form of perception (Anschauungs form) in the Pāncarātra see Schrader (*Op. cit.*—71) where also he says that the idea of spatial transcendence was known to them and others. As to the two higher standards v. post.

[2] It is a part of the function of Niyati in the 36 Tattvas accepted by Śaivas and Śāktas, *v. ib.* and my *Garland of Letters*. Dik is spatial position as to which see *post.*

[3] See J. C. Chatterji's *Hindu Realism*, 54 *et seq.* where the point is discussed.

[4] See Dr. J. McCosh. *First and Fundamental Truths*, 185.

[5] This is Ākāśa in which Dik operates. Space as extension or locus of finite body (Sthityādhāra) is called Deśa.

[6] Just as the infra-sensible Tanmātras of the other standards give rise to the Bhūtas and their compounds as sensible matter.

of experience. Its ultimate constituents are self-subsisting and independent of all perceiving entities or selves.

During dissolution[1] there exist all the *Padārthas*[2] except non-eternal compounded substance, non-eternal quality or properties and action or motion.[3] Where there is more than one thing there must exist some sort of relation.[4] The Selves or Ātmans[5] (in whom is their *Adṛṣṭa*)[6] and their *Manas*[7] exist unconsciously, that is, without experience. The Paramāṇus with their *Adṛṣṭa*[8] exist without motion in *Ākāśa*[9] and *Kāla* and *Dik* are inoperative. Īśvara alone is eternally conscious, willing and active but without production of the universe. At creation[10] Īśvara makes the *Adṛṣṭa* of the Ātmans operative and conjoins the *Ātmans*, ever associated with their Manas[7] in such wise that the Selves become Conscious and have experience of sensible Matter,[11] the *Adṛṣṭa* of which is also made operative, upon which they are active after their nature, have motion, combine as Dvyaṇukas and then as Trasarenu, that is, combinations of the Dvyaṇukas or six "atoms" which is the smallest sensible matter of three dimensions.

The second and more advanced Standard or Sāṃkhya-yoga asks whether, in an analysis of the World, we cannot reduce it to a lesser number of Realities than the nine entities with their properties and relations, namely Consciousness and Mind on the one hand, and on the other the four elements of matter in space, now moved, now held in position ? It answers that we can. We can keep Consciousness and Mind and include the rest under the common heading Matter and attribute the latter's motions and positions to its own inherent energies. We thus get three things—Consciousness, Mind and Matter. In the World we see constant change and we experience a continuity of consciousness as an unchanging

[1] Pralaya.

[2] See p. 21. Including Abhāva there are seven categories or Padārthas here spoken of, but different schools of Dārśanikas classify Padārthas differently. The Māyā-vādins say two (Cit, Acit), the Rāmānujas three (Cit, Acit, Īśvara), the Mādhvas have two (Svatantra, Paratantra), Nākuliśas three (Pati, Paśu, Pāśa).

[3] That is the Nitya-Dravya, Nitya-guṇas, Sāmānya, Viśeṣa, Samāvāya. There is Abhāva of Kārya and no Karma; Anitya (non-Eternal) Dravyas are everything beginning with the Dvyaṇuka of Pṛthivī, Āpah, Tejah, Vāyu. The rest are, including the Paramāṇus, Nitya (Eternal).

[4] Here called Saṃyoga-viśeṣa-saṃbandha.

[5] See p. 21.

[6] The product of past Karma and the cause of future Karma. Adṛṣṭa as a Guṇa cannot be ever separated from the Ātman.

[7] See p. 21.

[8] These have their Saṃskāras. All Matter has its appropriate behaviour due to inner tendency or Saṃskāra.

[9] See p. 21.

[10] Sṛṣṭi.

[11] Compounded of the ultimate Minima or Paramāṇus.

Self. We see and experience both Consciousness and Unconsciousness. The two chief concepts then which claim our attention are Consciousness, Unconsciousness, Changelessness, and Change. Examination shows the first differs fundamentally from the second and belongs to a category of its own, that is, it must be regarded as a separate and different reality from the rest. Why ? Because our intuition of Consciousness is of its continuity. It is true that some speak of the "stream" of consciousness, but examination shows that it is not unlimited consciousness which moves but the limited mind which is associated with it and is its instrument. Notwithstanding all apparent change, we are conscious of a persisting spaceless and timeless Self which gives meaning to all our notions of motion, change, space, and time. But whilst we know ourselves as consciousness we are aware of limitations upon it. Consciousness cannot as such limit Consciousness. It must then be something unconscious which does so. This something then is Mind. Mind certainly appears to be conscious, but this is so not because it is in fact Consciousness but because it is associated with, and backed by, Consciousness. Mind is a play of dark unconscious force which is lit up by Consciousness. Again Consciousness in itself is unlimited, but everything else which is not Consciousness, or so far as it is not so, is limited. Consciousness then is distinct from Mind and Matter in that the former is changeless, timeless, spaceless, unlimited, whilst Mind and Matter are changing things and (being things) limited in Time and Space.

The next question is—Consciousness being a distinct reality from Mind and Matter, are these last two separate realities or can they be reduced to one ? They can be so reduced if shown to have qualities in common bringing them under one general concept. We have seen that there are two such qualities. Each is *per se* unconscious. Consciousness is unlimited and all-pervading and therefore immanent (however veiled) in Mind and Matter. But abstractedly considered and by themselves, Mind and Matter are unconscious. Again they are both changing. We observe matter in constant change. So also the mind changes, its instability being compared to mercury. In fact motion, as both Aristotle and the Hindus say, is the essential characteristic of Nature. For this reason the world is called in Saṃskrit "*Jagat*" which means the "moving thing". The universe is Mind and Matter in constant movement (*Spanḍa*), not a single particle being even for one moment at rest. Throughout all this movement the Self remains as the one unchanged Consciousness, the static centre of this other Reality which is many, changing, and unconscious. Both Matter and Mind, which move in and around it are two aspects, the first gross and the second subtle, of one common Ground and Reality.

The Second Standard then reduces the many realities of the first into two, namely, the *Puruṣas* or Selves as Consciousness and *Prakṛti* the source of both the mental and psychical as subject on the one hand[1] and the material as object[2] on the other. *Prakṛti* the source of the world of mind and matter is self-subsisting Entity independent of the Selves which, as being in themselves Consciousness, lighten and give the similitude of consciousness to its dark unconscious operations. She is active before Him because Nature always works for the Consciousness directed towards it. As Prakṛti is real so also are its derivatives Mind and Matter, the latter including the whole universe of objects and the former all empirical subjects.

In this system the nine Realities of the previous one are dealt with as follows: The place of the eternal, infinitely numerous selves or *Ātmans* is here taken by the eternal, infinitely numerous *Puruṣas* or Selves. But whereas the Vaiśeṣika *Ātman* is a Reality of which consciousness is not an essential, inalienable characteristic but is that in which Consciousness is only sustained, the Puruṣas are Pure Consciousness (Cit) Itself. All the other eight Realities of the former system are assigned to, and included within *Prakṛti*, the non-conscious Principle. The place of *Manas* is taken by the inner instrument or *Antah-karaṇa*[3] by which infinite experience is had;[4] and the place of the four *Paramāṇus* and *Ākāśa* is taken by the five *Tanmātras* or forms, of supersensible "Matter" or universals, which in combination produce the particulars which are sensible matter.[5] *Kāla* as "Time" has no objective existence apart from the Moment[6] or ultimate and absolute unit of change, namely, the instantaneous[7] transit of a *Tanmātra* from one point in space to the next succeeding point. The

---

[1] The Antah-karaṇa working with the aid of the senses or Indriyas. Consciousness is reflected on these because the natural Principle (Prakṛti) and all its products are in themselves unconsciousness.

[2] Compound matter made up of the five forms of sensible matter (Bhūta) derived from the super-sensible Tanmātra.

[3] This term includes Buddhi, Ahaṃkāra, Manas which operate with the aid of the outer instruments, the senses, between which and the first two Manas is the link.

[4] Through a form of catalytic activity: that is by the reflection of consciousness on it.

[5] Bhūta. [6] Kṣaṇa.

[7] Lotze says "Nothing could conceivably have the power to interpose an interval of time, vacant as in that case it would be between cause and consequence."

moment is real, being identical with the unit of change in phenomena and the Time-relation thus shares in this reality. *Dik* as the totality of position, or as an order of co-existent points, is like order in time relative to the understanding, being constructed on the laws of actual relations of position intuited by empirical consciousness. Spatial position results from the different relations in which the all-pervasive Ether or *Ākāśa* stands to the various bounded objects in it. The category of Causality is mediated through the scheme of order in time. In short, Space, Time, and Causality are empirical relations of things having objective empirical reality but not independent of the things so related.[1] This standard teaches the efficiency, as inherent dynamism, of the world of things, since the Universe in all its forms is a manifestation of the Supreme Causal Energy-Substance Itself.

[1] See Dr. Seal's "Positive Sciences of the Hindus." 18-22.

## IV

THE third stage opens with the question whether it is possible to reduce the two Realities to one. At this point reason alone fails to establish the necessity of any such resolution. Perceiver and Perceived can only be unified in something which transcends both and therefore all empirical experience is something alien to it. Reason may doubtless establish conclusions of some probability, but it cannot be shown with certitude that the ultimate Reality is single whilst we still rest in present world experienc. If we assume one of two Realities only we may reasonably fix on Consciousness which is self-directing rather than on unconscious matter, but that there is only one remains to be proved. Supreme unitary experience is known only by consciousness divested of those conditioning limitations which are the very constituents of ordinary limited world experience, and which consciousness has thus expanded into that Immensity which is the meaning of the word Brahman. To know this One Reality directly is to be It. To know of It is learnt from those who have had unitary experience or have received the traditional teaching of such experiencers. Therefore it is that the Vedānta is essentially a *Śruti-pradhāna* or revealed *Śāstra* as opposed to a *Yukti-pradhāna* or reasoning *Śāstra*. That there is one ultimate Reality is known by most only secondarily as the revelation of the Seers or Ṛṣis who have "seen" this Truth, that is, have had direct[1] experience of it in *Samādhi* or ecstasy; and primarily by such direct experience which is open to all who are qualified and strive to attain it. Spiritual experience varies. It may be of a more or less dualistic character or (for so long as it endures) Monistic. The great Vedic saying (*Mahāvākya*) "That thou art" (Tat tvam asi) has thus received varying interpretations. The word *Tat* (That) in Sanskrit may stand for any case.[2] It may be read in the nominative, then meaning the identity of the Māyāvāda school or of Rāmānuja.[3] It may stand for other cases. *Tat* may mean *Tasmāt* as in Vallabha's school—"the one from Whom all proceeds." *Tat* may mean *Tasya*, as in Mādhva's school—"you are His."[4] "He is

[1] Aparokṣajñāna.

[2] See Bhāmatī Kalpataruparimala of Appaya Dīkshita, sūtra 1. No school stands for the accusative or instrumental, each school puts forward its own Veda-mantra.

[3] Tvam = here Aṃśa, "You are part of the whole."  [4] Svāmitva-saṃbandha.

your Lord, you belong to, and depend on Him." Tat may mean *Tasmin, Tasmai* as in the case of other dualistic teachers (*Dvaitavādins*) and devotees (*Bhaktas*). "He it is in Whom you live, with whom you must unite through devotion or It is for Him you are." "For him you are produced and for Him you must work being in His service." Out and out dualists like the Naiyāyikas say "You are not That (*Atat tvam asi*)".

In the system taught by Rāmānuja, Nimbārka, Vallabha and Mādhva, the world in each case is real, but the Principle of which it is the manifestation is not independent and self-subsisting but dependent on or present in God as the *Ens Realissimum* in various ways, as either the Body of the Lord,[1] within His Lordship,[2] or as different[3] from the Lord as the possibility of distinct and dependent existence,[4] and yet not different as impossibility ofeindependent existence,[5] or as one with God without recourse to any principle of *Māyā*,[6] such as Śaṃkara teaches, being a part of Him, as it were a spark thrown out by fire.[7] In all these systems[8] God is the *Ens Realissimum*, and all other realities are in one way or another dependent on Him, though independent of the mind of the creature who perceives them. Being part of the Lord they share in His Reality. For a knowledge of this ultimate Reality all depend on *Śruti* or *Veda* the teaching of which is interpreted in various ways. The interpretations differ and so do the spiritual experiences, but they are none the less true for that. They have the reality of all actual experience and the truth of their stage of experiencing. In spiritual progress man passes from out the lower to the higher experience, that is, an experience of greater unity. The *standard* spiritual experience is that of the Ṛṣis as embodied in the Vedas.

---

[1] Rāmānuja. God thus stands to the world in the same relation as man's soul to his body.

[2] Svāmitva-saṃbandha. The three real entities in this system are the Supreme who controls (Niyāmaka), the enjoyer (Bhoktri) and the objects of enjoyment (Bhogya). This system, in that it denies that God is a material cause of the universe, makes nearest approach to Christian theology. Union consists in making approach to and becoming like God. [3] Nimbārka. [4] Para-tantra-sattā-bhāvah.

[5] Svatantra-sattā-bhāvah. Hence the doctrine is known as Bhedā-bheda "different yet not different." In the Śaiva-Tantras of the Kashmir school (such as Svacchanda-Tantra, Netra-Tantra and others) and other Śāstras, Unity (Abheda), Diversity (Bheda) and Diversity in Unity (Bhedābheda) are also taught. Every Indian Śāstra shares ideas to be found in others (See "Kashmir Śaivaism" by J. C. Chatterjee, 6.)

[6] Vallabha.

[7] Śaṃkarācārya denies absolute identity in this sense, for according to him the identity of the Supreme and individual self is only established after eliminating Māyā from the first and Avidya from the second.

[8] The Western reader who desires a short summary of these different schools may consult V. S. Ghate "Le Vedānta E'tude sur les Brahmasūtras."

# V

THE third Standard or Vedānta consists of two main divisions. In the first is contained every school but that of Śaṃkarācārya. His Māyāvāda is the sole system of the second division. The ground of distinction consists in this, that he alone distinguishes between conventional and transcendental reality and truth. All Vedāntic schools are at one in taking up the analysis at the point at which it was left by the previous standard. They do not altogether discard its findings but hold that one of its two Realities, *Prakṛti* the Unconscious Form-principle, is not wholly independent of the other or Formless Consciousness or *Puruṣa*. Reality of the universe as the complete independence of that second Standard is denied, but another reality is given to the universe according to the first division, namely, the reality of that of which it is a part or with which it is connected. According to the Vedānta of the second division this reality of the universe is empirical only, and from the transcendental standpoint is denied. The Vedānta thus in the continuous approach to unity reduces the two Realities of the Second Standard to one Reality only.

The final step is taken by the Māyā-vāda Vedānta on its transcendental side. Empirically it admits a real material causation by *Māyā* as the Power of the Lord, who is Being-Consciousness-Bliss, as also the reality of the world of Mind and Matter. If the cause be real the products must be so. Matter is every whit as real as Mind, is not the creation of the latter. The order of evolution of the *Jīva* or individual differs from that of the Sāṃkhya. But from the transcendental aspect, which is the standpoint of God, the world is without reality. The ultimate experience is not a world-experience. From the view-point of the former's persistence, what comes and goes is unreal. There is here no infringement of Realist doctrine which affirms that matter exists independently of mind. This is fully recognised. But it is clear that in a state which transcends both, that is, in which there is neither Matter nor Mind, the question whether matter exists independently of mind cannot arise. There is no denial of the realistic position because a further form of experience is assumed where Realism, Subjectivism and the like have from the nature of the case no meaning. "Realism" assumes both Mind and Matter. So does the Advaitin Vedāntist as regards World-experience. In the state which it assumes beyond World-experience the question does not arise.

It is this second division of the Vedāntic schools occupied by one System only, namely, the Monistic Māyā-vāda doctrine of Śaṃkarācārya which has given rise to the notion that the Hindus think the world is unreal, though the vast number of ordinary folk can have no such notion and every other Indian philosophical school combats his teaching on this point. By its followers this school is regarded as the crown of the whole series of thought-systems of which the Cārvākas and Lokāyatas, atheists and materialists, are at the other and the lowest end. The fundamental distinction between it and the other Vedāntic systems lies in this, that whereas they in ultimate resort give to the universe reality, though dependent on Brahman of which it is in one sense or other a part, in this last system the manifold of the universe consists only of "Names and Forms",[1] which are no true part of the one and sole Reality or Brahman, whose presence gives the world the appearance of substantiality it possesses. They are the product of an inscrutable Power[2] of the Lord,[3] who is Himself only the Immense or Brahman seen through the self-same veil of *Māyā*. In this way the sole Reality, in its sense of unchanging everlastingness, is affirmed.

The unreality of the world was the theme of some of the northern Buddhist schools,[4] who in this as in other matters deserted the path of good sense marked out by Brahmanism. The Tibetan word which answers to *Māyā*, when given the meaning of a magical and illusory show conjured up by a Magician, is *s-Gyuma*. It was Śaṃkarācārya's object to refute these Buddhists and he, in so doing, gave an interpretation of Vedānta which, whilst in opposition to Buddhistic Idealism on the empirical plane, in that it asserted that matter was every whit as real as the mind which perceived it (and was therefore not the creation of mind), yet conceded the "unreality" (as his school defines the term "Real") of the universe from the transcendental standpoint.

That there is some similarity between his doctrine and that of the Buddhist Māyā-vāda was long ago perceived, as in the Padma Purāna which speaks of his system as a "bad doctrine and a covert form of Buddh-

[1] Nāma-rūpa. [2] Acintya-Śakti. [3] Īśvara.

[4] See my Introduction to the Buddhist Tantra, Śricakra-saṃbhara, Vol. VII, Tantrik Texts, p. xv.

ism."[1] It is however equally obvious that there are also fundamental differences between the doctrines, some of which we will shortly examine. In the first place, Śaṃkarācārya held to the empirical reality of the world as existing independently of its percipient. Since the *Jiva* or Individual Centre produces his own *Saṃskāras* or tendencies, there is, it is true, a sense in which we each make our own world. But in another sense the world exists independently, as the actualization of the collective *Saṃskāras*. He conceded empirical reality to the waking and dreaming states and even to illusion[2] (strictly so called) whilst they lasted. They are, they are "had" or experienced. Moreover the object as experienced is for such experience true. A vivid dream is for the dreamer indistinguishable from waking experience, the sense-data of which it revives and combines after its own mysterious fashion. All that Śaṃkarācārya said was that the reality of one state was "contradicted," that is corrected, by another, the dream by the waking state, illusion by normal experience. Is there then any state which is not contradicted or corrected by another ? The answer is—Yes, there is—it is that which exists "uncontradicted" in all the "three times" (past, present, and future). This is *Parā-Vidyā*. The working of the senses and intellect are *Aparā-Vidyā*. These are neither contradicted nor even corrected by *Parā-Vidyā*. All contradiction is within the *Aparā-Vidyā* between attributes—the work of the senses and the intellect. But where these have no place and forms have no meaning, where duality does not exist—how can such Reality (itself uncontradicted) contradict ? Contradiction is possible when opposite attributes are applied to a thing assumed to be the same. But the same relation does not exist between the two forms of Knowledge. They do not give opposite versions of one and the same Reality. There is and can be nothing in common between the formal Knowledge of *Aparā-Vidyā* and the attributeless Immense which is *Parā-Vidyā*. There is no sameness (in which all contradiction is based) between the qualified and un-qualified, between the formal and formless. Even if it be said that the basis is the same in both, they are indistinguishable. The self never contradicts the evidence of the senses and intellect. All contradiction is relative to these, its instruments but never with it. There are thus no two standards of truth.[3] The "Real" then is defined as that which is the eternally enduring and

[1] Māyā-vādam asacchāstram pracchannaṃ bauddhaṃ, etc.

[2] Prātibhāsika-sattā.

[3] See G. R. Malkani's "Method of Philosophy" (Indian Institute of Philosophy, Amalner), 28 *et seq.*

changeless, and this is the Supreme. It has been said too by some Western thinkers that conservation and persistence are the criterion of the Real.[1] This is the Hindu view. *Māyā*, the Principle of change, itself is not unreal any more than it is real. It is an inscrutable Mystery[2] which is neither. The world is metaphorically described as a dream,[3] as a mirage and a falsity. But to whom and when ? Not to the world experience to whom it is in fact real whatever his philosophy may be. In a state in which no world is experienced no question of its reality arises. There are in short two conditions, one in which there is world-experience, that is, the gross universe, and another or *Yoga*-experience in which there is either the subtle or ideal universe or no object at all. If we would compare the passing ephemeral world of Humanity with that state which is Divinity, the former has only the reality of its transient stage, whilst the latter is the stageless, timeless, and spaceless Unchangeable, which is alone (in this sense) the Real. To speak (as is commonly done) of an esoteric and exoteric doctrine is to mislead. The doctrine teaches the reality which is conventional or pragmatic and the reality which is the true and transcendental real.[4] Those who follow it, hold to both realities. The doctrine however is a subtle one, only truly known to its *Sādhakas*.[5] That it is possible to hold to the reality of the world and yet follow this Monistic doctrine is shown by its *Bhaktas*,[6] for a *Bhakta* or worshipper must believe in the reality not only of the object of his worship but of himself and his worship and the World in and by which it is done. How to live in this and other antinomies is the secret of men of his temperament, capacity, and type.[7] It is not uncommonly but wrongly supposed that an adherent of Māyā-vāda Vedānta cannot be a devotee (*Bhakta*). This is not so, as an Indian author

[1] As in physics by Professor Tait. Herbert Spencer on biological principles defined pleasure as the index of the unimpeded flow of vitality. Hence Supreme Bliss is absolutely unimpeded (Akhaṇḍa). Reality=Persistence=Deathlessness (Amṛtatva)=Bliss (Ānanda).

[2] Anirvacanīya. All systems ultimately get back to inscrutable Power (Acintyā-Śakti) "Omnia exeunt in mysterium" as the Schoolmen said.

[3] This description is common to many schools in the sense of nonlasting. So in the ślokas by the Sikh Guru Tegh Bahadur he says: "It is a dream. Know nothing is real but Him alone."

[4] Vyāvahārika-sattā, pāramārthika-sattā.

[5] He who does Sādhana follows the religious discipline which (and not mere intellectual knowledge) qualifies one to be a Vedāntist.

[6] He who has Bhakti or devotion to God: a devotee.

[7] It is not everyone who is qualified (Adhikārī) for it. Each will follow that school of thought which suits him best. Each has its merits and its demerits, that of Saṃkara included, since no intellectual system can truly present the alogical or reconcile the opposites.

well points out[1] instancing the teaching of the *Śantas* of Mahārāṣtra and Jñāneśvara the author of the well-known Commentary on the Gīta, who was both a convinced Māyā-vādin and an ardent partisan of Bhakti. Numberless instances might be cited, as for instance the Śākta-Tantras which though practical Scriptures of worship, teach Vedāntic Monism, or to be more accurate, "non-dualism (advaita="not two"). What is affirmed is that there is no duality but what else there is, is not affirmed. To the Transcendental neither oneness nor any other attribute strictly applies.

Probably it is a correct conclusion to say that Śaṃkara adjusted his exposition of Vedānta to meet the original Māyāvāda of the Buddhists and so promulgated a presentment of *Māyā* different from that of the Buddhists,[2] and therefore without abandonment of what he believed to be the essential principles of Brahmanism. In fact he was by tradition a worshipper of the Supreme Mother or Śakti whose *Śrī Yantra*[3] may sometimes be seen in Vedāntic Maths.

After all what does the doctrine amount to ? The empirical reality of the world is fully affirmed; that is, as long as one is in the world, both mind and its object are equally real. Objects are realities independent of the experiencer. The qualities of things exist in them and are perceived. The limited Knower, in so far as he is limited, is as much of a product as limited Matter is. If our experience tells us that we see a world of objects we in fact do so. Commonsense cannot proclaim otherwise. But the next question is—is it or is it not the fact that there is an experience for which the world does not exist ? The answer is in the affirmative, given on the authority of *Śruti*—which the West calls Revelation—but which may be perhaps better described by what is there called Spiritual Experience. This is not for the Hindu *any* spiritual experience but the *standard* experience of the Vedic Seers. That experience may be had by any man who strives for it, not necessarily now in this life but in some stage of his future self-evolution. Is this last experience itself corrected ? Those who have it say that it is not. It is a state, permanent, without change, in all the "three times," past, present and future. If

[1] Ghate *Op cit.* "Remarquons quil est d'ailleurs possible de conserver la bhakti sans rénoncer á la doctrine de l'unité absolue ni á as consequence la doctrine de la Māyā." XXVI.

[2] The term is used by other schools as meaning the inscrutable power of God whereby He is enabled to do that which seems impossible to us.

[3] A diagram used in worship.

the true Real is (as this system affirms) That which changelessly and for ever endures, then This alone is True Reality and all else *relative* to it, is unreality. It seems to be thought that its adherents take the world to be unreal in the epistemological idealistic (one has to take breath with such long words) sense. This is not so. They say in effect "we are in a world which to us *is* real, but we aspire to the attainment of a state known by our Seers, in which the world of things and pains, the world of contingencies, the world of opposites is not. *Relative* to that, our experience, though in present fact real, is ultimately unreal. The reality of the world is a pragmatic truth."

## VI

SPEAKING in a general way we may convert the second Standard or Sāṃkhya system into the Śākta doctrine of Power or Śakti by substituting for the infinite *Puruṣas* one Śiva, and for *Prakṛti*, Śiva's Power or Śakti, and then affirmating that Śiva and Śakti are not, as the Sāṃkhya says, two independent Realities but one Reality in twin aspect, namely, static and kinetic. The Sāṃkhyan Puruṣa is changeless Consciousness (Cit). So is Śiva. *Prakṛti* is as unlimited cause the principle of Change, and as effect limited changing forms, which are, as effects, modifications of their cause. Śakti or Power is that which, in itself unchangeable, producss from itself as Material Cause the world of change. Common language speaks of the Power *of* Śiva but strictly Power or Śakti *is* Śiva. When the one Reality or Brahman is regarded as the Changeless Consciousness it is called Śiva: when it is regarded as the Power of Consciousness or Consciousness-Power which projects the Universe from out itself, it is called Śakti. It is fundamental doctrine that there is no Śiva without Śakti nor Śakti without Śiva. But this substantial unity with diversity of aspect involves a changed view of the nature of the cosmic process. In Sāṃkhya there are two Realities, in Śākta doctrine there is only one with dual aspect. According therefore to Sāṃkhya, evolution is from and of *Prakṛti* who is distinct from the *Puruṣas* but associated with them. The *Puruṣa* is the efficient and *Prakṛti* the material cause, the two causes existing not in one but in two entities. In Śākta doctrine, as Śiva and Śakti are one, it follows that the world is evolved from and by the one Reality, Śiva-Śakti, that is by a Reality which in one aspect does not change (for Consciousness never does so) and in another aspect is the Cause of Change and Change itself. As we are here dealing with the Power-aspect of Consciousness to recollect and imagine forth the Universe, we may for convenience speak only of Power or Śakti, if we are careful to remember that Śakti is only the active power of actionless Consciousness (Śiva). The Śākta Darśana reminds us of this fact when it says that the universe is the product of *Cit-Śakti* and *Māyā-Śakti*, that is, Cit or Consciousness in its aspect as power and efficient cause and Māyā-power or material cause. Cit-Śakti like the Sāṃkhyan-Puruṣa is by its presence the efficient cause and yet the actionless Witness, of all which goes on. What happens is by and in its aspect as Māyā-Śakti which like Prakṛti, is the ultimate Substance-Energy out of and through which the universe is evolved. There is thus one ultimate enduring absolute Reality of which all other relative realities as Mind, Life, Matter are transient forms. The world is real and must be so, for we are here viewing the problem from the world standpoint. The question of its reality only arises when the problem is viewed from the other end.

If we put this doctrine into modern form avoiding all technical terms it comes to this. Persistence is the criterion of Reality. The ultimate Reality is Eternal Being-Consciousness which in itself is changeless. Consciousness whether transcendent or immanent in the world never moves. If in the world-process it appears to do so, this is due to the play of mind of which it is the basis. But this Consciousness is nevertheless a true efficient cause, that is, one which moves without itself being moved. As such it is consciousness-power. But what is the patent and the material cause in the Cosmic Substance ? It can be only the one same Reality for there is no other. But what is this Substance-Energy which is the material cause of the universe ? The answer depends on the side from which we view it. If we look at it from the other world aspect, that is, the Reality which we call Power as it is *in Itself*, then the answer is that it is Consciousness.[1] If on the other hand we look at it on the world-side then it is the Root-Substance-Energy of the universe which appears as Mind and Matter. That root as cause is neither the one nor the other but the Power to produce in itself and to appear as both, when Consciousness on the arising remembrance of world-enjoyment becomes outer-turned (*Bahir-mukhī*) and sees, in its gradual awakening to the world, the "This" (*Idaṃ*) or Universe. Why and how ? In consciousness there is the seed of power to manifest itself as object to limited centres in it. That seed is the collectivity of all Tendencies (*Saṃskāra*) towards life and form acquired in an infinite number of past universes. In short it is the nature of this ultimate Reality to manifest itself. How ? Consciousness has two attitudes, inner (*Antarmukhī*) and outward-turned (*Bahir-mukhī*). In the first and in its fullest sense there is an experience in which there is no subject or object. In the second the object or "This" (*Idaṃ*) is gradually experienced at first as part of and then outside the Self. There

[1] Cidrūpiṇi Śakti.

is a polarisation in unitary consciousness of "I" (*Ahaṃ*) and "This" (*Idaṃ*) the experiencing subject and his world. The latter is as real as the former which perceives it but since both are transient and change, their reality is relative. Full, timeless, spaceless, endless Persistence is the Absolutely Real which is the Supreme Experience.

I have stated the matter in the simplest way hoping to recur to it in a discussion on the term Śakti or Power. The Advaita, Śaiva and Śākta-*Śāstras* however explain it in great detail and complication and in technical terms of their own. It what are called Thirty-six *Tattvas* or stages of evolution of Consciousness into Mind and Matter, their Scriptures show the origin of even Puruṣa and Prakṛti. This scheme I have explained elsewhere.[1] These are not, in such case, the ultimate reality but merely one of the principles (*Tattva*) or stages in a line Consciousness which extends upwards beyond them.[2] Puruṣa and Prakṛti *Tattvas* merely mark the stage when the "This" (*Idaṃ*) or object of the "I" (*Ahaṁ*) is thrown out of the Self and becomes an outer thing distinct from it. In other words they are the immediate Root of Empirical reality but that Root is itself grounded in the soil of Consciousness which is ultimately *Saṃvit* or the Supreme Experience Itself.

The relation of this system to that of Māyā-vāda Vedānta will be more fully explained in a discussion of what the Śākta understands by *Māyā*. Both are Monistic or rather non-dualistic (Advaita-vāda). The Sammohana-Tantra thus gives high praise to Śaṃkarācārya as an incarnation of Śiva (Śaṃkara) and describes his four disciples as the four *Mahā-preta*, who support the Throne of the Mother of the World, for such is *Māyā-Śakti* to the Śākta. She in one aspect is the ultimate Changeless Reality. She in another aspect does evolve into and appear in the forms of the World. These are in their essence the enduring Real that is Herself, and as forms of Herself the passing yet real objects of experience. There is thus a real yet transient diversity in a real and enduring unity. Doubtless this doctrine does not explain how logically God can be changeless and yet change. But the *Māyā* of Śaṃkarācārya, which is neither real nor unreal, also runs counter to logic. The highest truth is alogical. Better the Śākta says accept both the reality of the changing World which is imposed by *Māyā* on us in our ordinary experience, as also the reality

---

[1] See "Śakti and Śākta" and "Garland of Letters."

[2] Through Śuddha-vidyā or Saḍ-vidyā, Īśvara, Sadāśiva or Sādākhyā, and Śiva-Śakti-Tattvas.

of the Changeless which is experienced in Yoga, a state free of the coercive effect of *Māyā,* which is Mahā-māyā Herself. No logical argument will solve the Problem. In spiritual experience the Problem disappears. And so Śiva says in the Kulārṇava-Tantra (1-110) "Some desire Dualism (*Dvaita-vāda*), others Monism (*Advaita-vāda*). Such however know not My Truth which is beyond both Monism and Dualism (*Dvaitādvaita-vivarjita*).

## VII

An examination of all the Indian scriptures of worship leads to the same conclusions. Some are philosophically related to the first division of Vedānta and some to the second in various ways and degrees. The Śākta-Tantras are a form of Advaita-Vedānta. All worshippers are practical realists, whatever their doctrine may be. This does not prevent a Śākta from holding to the doctrine that the Supreme Experience is not an experience by a limited knower of a world of limited objects, external to a plurality of selves, themselves mutually exclusive. He prays to the Mother knowing that the form of the One as Mother is that in which She appears to him.

To sum up: No Brahmanical system countenances any form of subjectivism. All teach the empirical reality of the world and the perception of the physical non-mental qualities of things therein. All but one give it, besides this reality, an ultimate reality either as being the combination of several or of two everlasting Realities, or as in some sense a part of the one ultimate Reality or Brahman in its aspect as Power. We have thus Pluralism, Dualism and Monism in all its shades. That one exception says that the universe is ultimately neither real *nor unreal*, nor partly one and partly the other, but an inscrutable mystery which we must accept if we would hold to the changelessness and partlessness of God—which all admit. For only in this way, even though it be formally, is the Reality beyond Reason truly expressed in that high manifestation of Itself which is Reason.

Indian doctrine is realistic firstly in so far as it affirms the independent reality of objects in our daily experience, wherein the percipient is in presence of a reality existing independently of, and distinct from the *Vṛtti* or modifications of the Mind. This we have seen. It is secondly realistic in its treatment of the nature of that perception; thirdly because the sphere of reality is more extensive than that which is generally allowed in the philosophic West, and because experience in time is only a section of what is an eternal process without beginning or end. The first point has been sufficiently established. I will now add some further observations on the second point and deal shortly with the third.

## VIII

To deal fully with the nature of perception would take me beyond the scope of this paper. It will be discussed when treating of Śakti or Power as Mind. It is necessary however to make some further reference to it here from Vedāntic standpoint for the doctrines held are more thoroughly realistic than those of many Western schools.

Perception has not only a real object independent of the percipient (thus rejecting the Berkeleyan dictum *esse est percipi*), but (as already stated) the physical qualities we perceive are, according to the Indian view, in the object itself. No distinction is made of primary, secondary or tertiary qualities. The first two are in the object as well as in the mind, and the last has an objective basis in the Universal Mind of which the individual mind is only a special case. A so-called secondary quality is not a mere mental impression in the percipient. It is "out there" in the object perceived. Its[1] real, in the sense of basic quality, is quality as the Universal apprehended by the Universal and Collective Mind. Its quality as a variable sense-particular is perceived by the individual mind according to its manner of perceiving. This quality is therefore "there" in the object even when there is no individual mind perceiving it. For this Universal is always "sensed" by the Collective or Cosmic Mind. It has not however all the qualities which different percipients see in it from different points of view and at the same time. For, in this sense, individual sensation is "private." Indian thought does not hold that the object as perceived is an exact copy of the object as it is in itself. Though the object is always one and the same, all do not perceive it in one and the same way. Both mind and its object are active in perception and affect the one the other. The mind brings its own quota to the act of experience. What is this? These are the individual *Saṃskāras* or tendencies and aptitudes produced by former experience in this and previous lives. As the product of such previous lives they are innate. The variety of sensation is thus due to the imported subjective element or individual *Saṃskāra* and not attributable to the object. It is the percipient's manner of perceiving it. The Universals of *Tanmātra*, the Generals of what is

[1] I here answer, from the Vedāntic standpoint, some queries put in R.F.A. Hoernle's "Studies in Contemporary Metaphysics," 104, where the question is discussed.

apprehended as the sense particulars, are always objectively present. Hence sensation is both "private" through the individual mind and common through the Cosmic Mind. The Hindus therefore are more realistic than those who distinguish between the qualities as primary and so forth and make sensation merely "private."

The basis of these principles may be found in the doctrine that the quality of the object which is sensed and the constitution of the sense which perceives it are the same.

The same forces which go to make the subtle mental object also go to make the sense which perceives it. The gross material object is derived from a combination of the subtle elements. One and the same Causal Stress in the original Substance-Energy (Śakti) phenomenally appears as the sense on the one hand and the matter and its qualities on the other. The knowing is of like by like. The causal aspect of an Universal is a stress or motion (Spanda) in Universal Substance without reference to any percipient organ at all. From the phenomenal aspect the Universal relates to a percipient organ evolved co-ordinately with it which may be either absolute or relative, universal or individual. The object is apprehended as it is with all its qualities, subject to the particular *Śaṃskāras* or mental tendencies which merely affect the manner of knowing them. Western science thinks that it is concerned with a real world which persists independently of our experience but then, as has been pointed out,[1] we are committed to a division between the contents of immediate experience and its causes which division has become deeper and more impassable with every advance in physics and physiology. For the physical causes of perception are now inferred but not perceived. The real material world has been driven into the unseen and now lies (it is said) hidden behind the screen of its own effects. Perception becomes a remote psychological effect of a long train of causes, physical and physiological, originally set in motion by the external thing but in no way resembling it. It dissolves the thing perceived into a remote reality which is neither perceived nor perceivable: as in the case of the reduction of matter to the structure and motions of invisible homogeneous electric units. Thus we perceive for example in an object impenetrability, density, weight, configuration, colour, taste and so forth whereas we are told that the object is really constituted of vortices in homogeneous ether which is not matter at all. It turns the world of common sense into an illusion and on this illusion it rests its case.[1]

[1] Balfour. Gifford Lectures (1914), 159.

According to the Indian view we *do* perceive things as they phenomenally are. The physical causes of perception are perceived. What is not perceived and is not the object of any percipient is the creative activity of and in the fundamental Substance-Energy which is phenomenally presented to us as mind and senses on the one hand and objects on the other.

As sensible experiences do undoubtedly exist, so there must be, other than and outside of ourselves as individual experiences, things by which such experiences are produced. It is not the fact that what really exist are only our impressions and ideas. The sensible world exists apart from, and other than, our experience. The *Śāstra* puts forward many reasons in support of these commonsense beliefs.[1] Thus we deny the existence of things perceived in dreams precisely because we are certain of the existence of things experienced on waking. If the sensible did not exist, then dreams, which are the repetition of things already experienced when waking as existing outside, would be impossible. If sensible things had no existence of their own, there is no reason why we should not see them at will and continuously just as we can have our own ideas at will and for so long as we like. But on the contrary we perceive sensible things only so long as they remain in relation with us and this is because they exist independently of us. So again we distinguish between right perceptions and hallucinations, which we could not do if sensible things had no objective existence: all of which arguments are grounded on good realistic common sense with nothing "dreamy" about them.

These teachings are not merely confined to the Standard itself but are parts of the other Standards also, subject to the necessary modifications involved in the fact that advance is made to a new Standard. It is obvious that the teachings of all the Standards are not in all respects the same, otherwise there would not be several Standards. Nevertheless there are teachings which are common, correspondences, and similarities. The second Standard takes up the matter (whatever it be) at the point at which it was left by the previous Standard and carries it further. Thus both the first and second Standard treat Consciousness as distinct from Mind, but the first regards it as a property of the Self and the second as the Self's essential characteristic. The first Standard does not recognise recognise the faculties of Mind and which the second Standard calls

[1] See "Hindu Realism," 21 *et seq.*

'Judgment,'[1] 'Self-arrogation,'[2] as substantive principles at all. It would regard them as attributes[3] of the Self. Mind as Manas is in the first Standard a substantive principle but it is atomic,[4] that is without magnitude. It is so to say a point at which and through which, connection is established between the Self and objects for the purposes of experience. Hence all experience is necessarily serial. It is like a tap through which all experience whether internal or external must flow. The functions of Manas are generally recognised as the same. But the whole "Inner Instrument"[5] as assumed by Sāṃkhya and Vedānta will better explain life by their respective activities than the simple atomic *Manas* of the first Standard. Just as the senses are of the same nature as the *Paramāṇus* or originators of the qualities which are perceived by means of them, so in Sāṃkhya and Vedānta the senses and their subtle objects[6] have a common origin. These minima of sensible matter are in the first Standard non-mental, in the others they are the universals or generals of the sense-particulars which by the addition of mass appear as such particulars in the form of gross matter. In a general way there are similarities especially in fundamental matters as regards the theory of Perception, such as the reality of the object with its own physical qualities and the like. On the other hand principles peculiar to the system have their modifying effect. Thus in the Advaita-Vedānta Consciousness is the one Immanent Reality, and it is the discovery of the essential identity between Mind and its material object which makes the substance of perception according to Vedānta. The main realistic position is maintained throughout the standards for all empirical experience.

---

[1] Buddhi. [2] Ahaṃkāra. [3] Guṇa.

[4] Aṇu; in Vedānta Aṇu is created and therefore cannot be partless.

[5] Antaḥ-karaṇa involving Buddhi, Ahaṃkāra, Manas.

[6] Tanmātra which in Sāṃkhya derive with senses from Ahaṃkāra and in Vedānta the senses and their gross objects both derive from the Āpancīkṛta-Tanmātra.

# IX

As regards the third point it is to be noted that there are many more Realities than those experienced by the gross mind. The Real as object is not merely the material as that term is ordinarily understood. There is the world of the Subtle Real which is the object of the mind which had developed to that stage in which it can be experienced. The[1] originating sources of the sensible are themselves supersensible realities. These constitute, besides the sensible, other worlds which are supersensible. A world or sphere of existence is nothing but a condition of the experience on the part of experiencing Beings; and therefore there must be as many varieties of worlds as there are fundamentally different types of beings. In the sensible world are a great variety of beings who form a number of orders and grades. These grades form a series, at one extremity of which lies that order of beings whose experiences are the most limited. From this grade upwards to man there is an ascending series, each successive order of which has experiences wider in range than those of the beings of the preceding order. Man stands at the head of this series. But there is no reason to suppose that he is absolutely the highest order. In fact he is limited and helped by Unseen Powers, Beings more powerful than he who exist in unseen forms. If what is super-sensible in man can exist in an unseen form after death, why not other Beings who habitually exist in such forms ? And if these Beings exist in unseen or supersensible forms, then there are also states of existence or worlds which are also supersensible and quite as real, if not in a sense more so than the gross world of ordinary experience.[2] Experience reaches up to that of the Cosmic Mind which apprehends the world of universals as they exist in themselves.[3] The *Saṃsāra*, or wandering or world of birth and death, is thus constituted of different orders of experiencing beings, of which man is one, and there are worlds of experience beyond the *Samsāra*

[1] See "Hindu Realism," 101.
[2] See "Hindu Realism," 101, 102.
[3] This is not the Supreme but the Hiraṇyagarbha Consciousness for which experience the Universals are still mysterious stresses in Consciousness, the real nature of which is only known to the Lord Himself (Īśvara).

from which there is no return for the Beings therein. These supersensible worlds[1] are as real as the material and as much the body of and in correspondence with the Metaphysical Real as is the latter.[2]

The stages here are *lived* through as states in each of which nearer approach is (through the transformation of the experiencer and with him his world) made to That (*Tat*) which is the full and perfect Real, which stages at length pass and expand into It as that Whole or *Pūrṇa* in which all forms of determined experience are had, which sums them all up in Itself and which transcends them all. The stages may be thought of and in some degree described, but are in themselves the actual experience lived through of determined being evolving into the *Pūrṇa*, the Full or Whole. The stage is not a matter of subjective information but is objectively lived. It is not a mere matter of argument but is a transformed life. The Self gives testimony of Itself in various ways to the Self in the process or movement of the Self to the Self. That testimony again is not something communicated from one to another. It is a realisation of the self as the Self in each of its grades of manifestation. "To know is to be"; a Vedāntic maxim which has application not only as a description of the highest end but to every stage on the way thither.

---

[1] Each of these has its inhabitants or Experiencers. The Lokas or Worlds of experience are fourteen, seven above and seven below; supernormal, normal and subnormal. Thus also the Śaiva systems speak of various classes of beings (Jīvas) such as Mantras, Maheśvaras; Mantreśvaras, Vidyeśvaras and so forth, who exist in the descending and ascending stages of involution and evolution which are called the 36 Tattvas.

[2] H. Keyserling dealing with the Indian outlook in his Das Reisetagebuch eines Philosophen, 3rd Ed., says at p. 86: Ich weiss dass das Psychische ein ebenso objectives ist wie das materielle, dass Vorstellungen ein genau so entsprechender leib von metaphysisch-wirklichem sein Konnen wie feste Korper, dass es uberall moglich ist im Prinzip von Geiste her den stoff zu beeinflussen.

## X

Here we touch upon the practical bent of the Indian mind and its craving for reality which makes it satisfied with nothing but the most real foundation for its knowledge. To truly know is *to be.* I do not intend to work out the matter now as it forms a distinct subject with which I hope to deal on some future occasion. It is this: the teachings of Religion which Philosophy supports are not mere speculation. The knowledge of plurality is based on actual experience, that is, of the senses and reasoning thereon. If the reality and nature of the world requires to be established it is done here. But what of supersensible matters ?[1] Their nature and existence is not the subject of mere speculative reasoning which can at best establish a conclusion of probability only. Reasoning on such matters gives no certitude that we perceive the Real and the True. The warrant of authority again is actual experience (*Anubhava*) which is not a specific form of proof coordinate with other forms but the basis of all these—the Self itself[2] of a suprasensible kind. Just as the physical sense faculties are extended by the use of scientific instruments, so by *Yoga* there is an extension of natural faculties which gives experience on a plane beyond that of the ordinary daily earth experience. This Yoga-experience is of varying degrees leading up to Īśvara-experience or that of the Lord Himself who is the Great Yogī. If then the Vedānta affirms that notwithstanding apparent plurality all is one—"All this universe is Brahman"—it is not merely because argument leads to a Monistic conclusion (it may perhaps as well lead to the contrary), but because that unity has actually and really been experienced directly by those who affirm it. The truth of the doctrine is accepted by others on the faith of this experience which they accept. This is the twofold sense of Veda.

Two points are apt to be overlooked nowadays owing to Western influence. The first is that the Vedānta is not a mere system of philosophy in the modern Western sense. It is based on Revelation (*Śruti*). If not

---

[1] Atīndriya.

[2] See G. R. Malkani "Method of Philosophy" criticising Professor Zimmerman's article "Truth and its criterion in Śaṃkarācārya's Vedānta" in Indian Philosophical Review.

so based, it is worth no more and may be worth less than any other particular philosophy, seeing that it, in some respects, at any rate in its Monistic form, runs counter to our sense-experience. The second point is, that it is not to be understood by mere reading and study. He who would understand it must first worship and self-discipline himself by the Vedāntic *Sādhana*. The notion, that a man if clever enough can understand anything is not an Indian one. His must be not only a good mind but a pure and good character. Such an one alone will act rightly and will understand the Real. Understanding it, he will worship the Ground in its form. The Hindu may be right or wrong but he is obviously a greater "realist" when he holds that matter is not only an independent reality, but it is perceived as it is with its qualities, than even the modern scientist who makes matter as presented an illusory appearance produced by some reality no doubt, but one which is wholly different from what we perceive. To the former present experience is real but still more so is the persistent Ground of it, attainable by a practical and real transformation of the Self. From whatever point of view we examine the matter we find a realistic standpoint. One is at a loss to know how the notion that the Hindus were non-realists arose. For however Māyā-vāda may be ill-understood it is in no case a philosophic system adopted by all India. Perhaps some may have confused the questions whether the world is real, and whether in action due regard is had to the realities or circumstances under which it is to be taken. A man who in his actions does not take sufficient account of the real facts of the world is sometimes said to have no sense of reality. This may doubtless in some cases be mere foolishness. In others when noble ends are pursued in disregard of the sordid "realisms" of the day, the world is the better for it. However this be, I merely note the possible ambiguity and do not further discuss a question which has no bearing on my present subject.

Whatever be Indian capacity in ordinary affairs, the Indian mind has done its thinking with a practical end in view. Philosophy was not pursued from a mere curious desire to know, to found "systems," earn academic applause, and so forth but with a view to realise the practical end of all material being or Happiness. Every system posits that as its aim. The world and material ends are real, but spiritual experience is the truly Real. Philosophy worked hand in hand with religion as in Europe during the Middle Ages, though it was never *Meretrix Theologorum*. The Vedānta is really an Indian Scholasticism based on *Śruti*, or what

Westerns call Revelation, though we must not confound the two. There is in fact scarcely any important technical term of Western philosophy or religion which can be used without some qualification. Rather we should say Philosophy and Religion were not severed, the fundamental principle of Vedānta being to sever absolutely nothing. All knowledge was considered in relation to the whole. The notion held by some in the West that Religion and Science and Philosophy are antagonistic was unknown: such a notion having arisen in the West for historical reasons, Religion there being identified with Christian Dogma. Indian Religion teaches that Absolute Bliss is to be found only in That which is beyond the contingent world of opposites which is unimpeded and full Being. It not only so teaches but gives out the practical means or *Sādhana* whereby this state of Bliss may be attained which is the True and Real.

The only fruitful path is that of real striving, or *Sādhana*. Any *Sādhana* sincerely and diligently pursued will secure its fruit. The fruit of the highest *Śākta-Sādhana* (for *Sādhana* may be of various kinds) is the realisation of its fundamental *Śruti*, "All this is verily Brahman" (*Sārvaṃ Khalvidaṃ Brahma*). "This" is the Universe. Brahman the Immense or Immeasurable is as Power (*Mahā-śakti*) its cause.

That Power is real and so is the universe which is for the worshipper Its Body or Form.[1]

For if the material cause is real so is the effect. He affirms "I am real as body" for Matter is a form of the Great Power or Śakti. I am real as Mind"; for mind is another form of the same Power. *Sa'ham* "She I am" refers to the Mother of the universe. Again "I am the Real as Unchanging Consciousness vehicled by Mind and Body and transcending it." The forms come and go re-entering and again reissuing from the *Paramārtha* or Supreme Reality. *So'haṃ* "He I am", *Śivo'ham* "Śiva I am" the Śākta also says, when speaking of the *Kūtastha*-Śiva or Enduring Real. Those who thus worship Power become "Power."

Though the unreality of the universe is spoken of because of its being a passing thing, it is yet to be also remembered that the world-process is according to Indian ideas an eternal one. The world is not something which appears and is gone for ever. It reappears eternally. It is not the

[1] A correspondent has asked me how this view differs from Viśiṣṭādvaita-Vedānta. It differs in this that according to Rāmānuja, mind and matter not merely seem to be but are the body of the Lord distinct from Him; whilst in Śākta doctrine, the world is the body of the Lord so long as it lasts, but ultimately there is only the one Ātmā in which mind and matter are merged.

first and only one produced, but merely one of a beginningless and endless series.[1] The manifestation of the universe is thus an eternal process. It appears and disappears. This is the pulsing movement as the systole and diastole of the Cosmic Heart as Divine Power. Nothing can come from nothing, and something cannot vanish into nothing. It arises from the seed of Tendency (*Saṃskāra*) which is in the Great Womb (*Mahāyoni*) and is there in a potential state. The seed sprouts as the great *Aśvattha* Tree which is the manifested universe. It dies down again into the seed of potentiality to reappear again in endless succession. This appearance and reappearance is the *Saṃsāra* or the constant "moving on" or wandering in the worlds of birth and death.[2] There is thus an eternal series of Experiencers.

Man breathes forth and inbreathes. What is done "here" (*Iha*) is done "there" (*Amutra*). The Universe pulses forth and rests, and pulses back again. Breathing is a microcosmic representation of the macro-cosmic process.[3] And so the duration of the life of the highest being in the hierarchy of Being or Brahmā, for whose experience the universe as a whole exists, is the duration of that particular Universe. The duration of Brahmā's life is that of one outgoing breath[4] of Kāla[5] which is objectively a beat of Cosmic Time. Time is no magnitude for the Supreme. For Him the Immeasurable there is no measurer. But Time is attributed to His appearances. The Universe is dissolved and at rest for a period of the same duration when it appears again with, what the Pāncarātra-Tantra calls, the "Wheel of Dawn."

Ancient Hindu teaching is thus to be found in the following words of Professor Huxley:[6] "The faith which is born of knowledge finds its object in an eternal order bringing forth ceaseless change, through endless

---

[1] For the argument of this point, common to all the three Standards, see "Hindu Realism," 95.

[2] Called in the West re-incarnation. Transcendentally there is no *re*-incarnation. Empirically also *re*-incarnation is not an exact term. In say a series of three, viz., X—Y—Z, the first X does not *re*-incarnate as X but as Y nor Y as Y but as Z. The forms change but there is yet a continuity which is the cause of Z affirming that *he* was Y and before that X and so on. The Ātman being eternal, has no real birth or death. It is merely related to and dissociated from a body.

[3] As to the charge of Anthropomorphism which with Animism stampedes so many I will deal in another place. In Prāṇāyāma or Breath-control, appearance, stay, and disappearance are Pūraka, Kuṃbhaka and Recaka.

[4] Niśvāsa.

[5] Kāla, here the Time-aspect of the Supreme. Then follows the Great Dissolution (Mahā-pralaya). See Introduction to Prapancasāra-Tantra 8. Tantrik Texts, Vol. 3, Ed. A. Avalon and Schrader, *Op. cit.* 27.

[6] Evolution and Ethics, pp. 8, 9.

time, in endless space: the manifestations of Cosmic Energy alternating between phases of potentiality and spheres of explication. It may be as Kant suggests, every cosmic Magma predestined to evolve into a new world has been the no less pre-destined end of a vanished predecessor." For Cosmic Energy we may read Divine Power or *Daivī-Śakti*: for phase of potentiality *Pralaya*, when the world exists potentially in the Womb of the Immense:[1] and for sphere of explication, *Sṛsti* or production› therefrom.[2] The Power, the Process and the Result are real. Śaṃkarācārya from his transcendental viewpoint calls the world "false," but to the Śākta, and from his standpoint, it is real. It is the field of action and liberation "*Moksāyate saṃsāra.*" "The world is made the seat of liberation as the Kulārṇava-Tantra says—To him Māya is not unreal (*Avastu*). It is not a mere mist of ignorance connected, yet unconnected, with the Brahman and which screens the Real. It is an eternal Reality or Power appearing as the passing and changing worlds. For it is the World-Mother who is the Great Power Herself. What is unreal (in the sense of passing) are the Names and Forms which are yet, so long as they last as the objects of perception, also real. And so the Śākta can say of himself that not only in Spirit, but in Mind and Body, *Sa,ham*, "She I am'," "I am the Real and the Power of the Real."

---

[1] Brahman.

[2] In the same way Herbert Spencer speaks of the alternating states of homogeneity (that is Pralaya when all is undifferentiated mass) Heterogeneity (that is Sṛṣti when the generals and their particulars are produced) a state of relative stability (Sthiti) and then a lapse into homogeneity again (Pralaya).

# POWER AS LIFE

(*Prāṇa-śakti*)

# FOREWORD

I take the opportunity given by the publication of the second volume of this series to deal with a criticism on the first which affects all. I am therein described as an "adherent" of "Śāktaism" and as "commending" the acceptance of such doctrine to others. It is true that I think that this doctrine has been misunderstood and has been the subject (on the whole) of unjust judgments. I think also that it is, in its highest presentment, a grand and inspiring system (by which I do not mean that it is the only one, or that it is without defect); otherwise probably I should not have concerned myself with it. I desire however to say here that I do not write as an "adherent" of this, or any other philosophical system or religious sect whatever, but as a free thinker and free-companion; "Neither Burgundian nor Armagnac." *Nullius addictus jurare in verba magistri.* But, as I have said elsewhere in describing *Śākta* teaching and Vedānta I write from that standpoint. Nor do I, *pace* my critic, make light of, and still less deny, the utility of Reason or its efficacy to give us the truth within the system of which it is a part. But the Truth as it lies beyond that system is directly realised as it is in Itself, that is beyond Mind not by Reason but by a Full Experience (*Samādhi*) which is not a "sleep" except to the gross world and is an awakening in the supersensible world. Those who talk in this fashion show want of knowledge of their own Scripture. There the highest praise is bestowed on reason. See for instance the Chapter on *Vicāra* in the Yoga-Vāsiṣṭha. Moreover Vedānta does not accept the intuitionalism which discards intellect. On the contrary the Bṛhadāraṇyaka Upaniṣad says that the Self must be thought upon and deeply pondered (*Mantavyo, Nidi-dhyā-siṭavyah*). What else is the meaning of *Jñāna-Yoga*?

Nor, notwithstanding my personal views of the Scripture, do I "commend" it to anyone. What others choose to believe is their affair in which I have no desire to interfere unasked. One of the many notions, for which we are indebted to the profound thought of India is the fundamental doctrine of Competency or *Adhikāra* which I hope to make the subject of one of this series of volumes. That Doctrine involves this—that there is a mental as well as physical food—a mental as well as physical stomach and digestion.

Talking of food it is curious to note here (see Professeur Picard "La Science Moderne" 245) that all the characteristics of living Matter such as its equilibrium, chemical and anatomic organisation are now regarded by the great majority of Biologists as secondary qualities in comparison with nutrition which is considered by them to be the essential attribute of Life. It is noteworthy that in this ancient Indian doctrine also, emphasis is laid on the physiology of Nutrition, all the main *Vāyus* except *Udāna* being concerned with this function of "living" substance.

Indirectly and on the whole, man tends to the Truth, but directly and immediately what he holds to or seeks is not the truth, but the truth which he *wants*. It is the cravings of his psychical being which he satisfies. This is the meaning of the phrase "will to believe". If there be a really detached search for truth it is excessively rare. He is a foolish and inconsiderate man who would deprive others of the meal of food, material or intellectual, which satisfies them, though it may not please him. A celebrated German Theosophist was I believe commonly wont to commence his addresses with the observation "I am now going to tell you a story". Well I also am telling a story. It interests me but I am the last person to persuade others to accept it if they be themselves indifferent or unwilling. I am not seeking "converts" nor trying to "prove" that any one is "wrong". If, in answering an internal urge to write, I can please others besides myself so much the better. My account of the main Indian Concepts may be of use either to those who are disposed to think the same way, or to those who simply want to know the facts. If the books are of use to any one in either way that is enough for me. Should anyone think that they are of no use, that also is enough; for I will not dispute the point with him. If his own theories held in good faith really satisfy him, I will certainly not "commend" to him any other. Each will answer the speculative questions which all ask, particularly to-day, according to their general theoretic views, the product of their intellectual make-up and temperament. As regards this, all that is required is sincerity, good faith and that openness of mind which is necessary for a progressive self-development.

But all can with confidence become adherents of the Religion of Health, procuring it for themselves and others and relieving their sufferings. Health = Hale = Whole or *Pūrṇa*. To be *whole* physically, psychically, and spiritually is to be *well*. The contrary of wholeness (*Apūrṇa*) is Disease. And so it is said *Apūrṇaṃ-manyatā Vyādhi*—"the sense of imperfection, that is want of wholeness, is Disease". In, with, or as the Whole, man has life here and hereafter. So one of the *Cakras* in the great *Śrīyantra* is called *Sarva-rogahara* or the Destroyer of all Disease which is *Adharma*. Śiva is called *Mṛtyuṃjaya* or "Conqueror of Death." As such above his head is shown the Moon shedding streams of Nectar (*Amṛta* = Deathlessness) over His upright body. After all it is what a man *is* and *does* which counts. The notion that mere cleverness is enough is not a Hindu one. What is the use of talking of the *Ātma* and so on if one has helped no one. And so in the Śākta Scriptures, as in others, emphasis is laid on *Kriyā* (action) which however may be given a more extended sense than that in which it is there ordinarily used.

To pass to the subject matter of this book I personally (like indeed, I suppose, most people) do not believe that Life is merely as Claude Bernard said a "fermentation", or that a true theory of it can be based on the now (with some) fashionable "colloidal solution". It has been said that, for the majority of Biologists, vital phenomena are merely physico-chemical phenomena. Nevertheless the Vitalist School is on a true track. If I remember rightly it was an English Chemist who lately observed that the more Matter is studied the clearer it is seen, that it is *away* from Matter (as such) and in the opposite direction that the solution, if any, of Life will be found. As regards the subject of this volume I believe in the "simplist" solution that Life, as we know it, is a power (as the Life of all lives) of the Supreme Power (*Parāśakti*). J.H. Fabre, the celebrated Naturalist and incomparable observer (as Darwin called him)—said: "I can't say I *believe* in God. I *see* Him. Without Him I understand nothing: without Him all is darkness." The question is not so much the existence of God but what sort of God. Philosophers and scientists would less grudgingly give to this Power the name of "God" were it not for the crude, ridiculous and even hateful notions which the beliefs of some have associated with this word. Merely physical explanations have availed nothing and will avail nothing. The Vedānta has dealt with the question very profoundly in distinguishing the Vital Body (*Prāṇamaya-Kośa*) from the Physical Body (*Annamaya-Kośa*) and in making the lower Mind-Body (*Manomaya-Kośa*) which is the vehicle of all the animal instincts, essence of the former. Life and instinct are wondrous things the sight of which evokes the sentiment of worship. Neither results from Matter. The explanation must be sought not below but above it in the Supreme Intelligence which they emphatically proclaim. J.H. Fabre conceived the relation between instinct and organ as analogous to that between Soul and Body. Instinct is an incorporeal element characterised by a native, infallible and irresistible impulse, superior to the organism as well as to sensibility, though it is not separate from, or completely independent of, these.

As regards evolution also, he would I think say that the separate creation of species is a truer notion than the theory that a higher species evolves from a lower one. For each species is a form of Divine Power (*Daivī-Śakti*). If, for example, A,B,C, be three distinct species in an ascending scale from A to C, it is not A which produces B, nor B which produces C, but it is the one Power (*Mahā-śakti*) which produces A,B and C. That Power which has appeared as A, appears also as B, and will next appear as C. B as an ascending type does not owe its ascent to A the lower type, but is a fresh pulsing-forth (*Prasara*) of Power with a view to liberate Consciousness which appeared as A, now appears as B, and will appear as C. Some Christian writers claim to be "liberal" in repudiating what they call the "crude" view according to which the Creator is perpetually "interfering" with His work. But in my opinion it is more true to say that every act of creation, maintenance, and dissolution in past, present or future is directly His. In the same way it is futile to search for the "missing link" as a lost *form* intermediate between A and B and B and C. The real link is the Supreme Power which produces each. So in a tree, one main branch does not derive from another but from a trunk common to both. This view is not based on any disrespect for Matter, which is as much a form of the Supreme Power in this doctrine as is Life or Mind. As Professor P.N. Mukhyopādhyāya so well says in his Note appended to this volume—"to those who see the All (*Pūrṇa*) there is no difference, except formal, when Life is materialised or when Matter is vitalised, or when Spirit is materialised or again when everything is spiritualised." If there has been any People who, taking them all in all, have seen things as they are and seen them "whole" it is the Hindus.

It is not enough to dispose of a solution to say that it is "materialistic." The difficulty in the way of the acceptance of such a solution arises from the nature of Matter itself. If we say, as Professor Tyndall did, that Matter contains the potency of all Life, we are using the word "Matter" in a sense which is not the ordinary one and trying to say something which is stated much better in this Indian Scripture, according to which Matter *as such*, that is as the *crust* or end of the *involving* process is not as such potent to produce Life which is part of the *evolving* process. It is the Power, of which Matter is a gross manifestation, which is able to organise Matter into "living" form, which is the first stage on the way towards liberation from Matter and thus towards Pure Experience. One of the chief keys to an understanding of Indian Philosophy is to remember that all its schemes *begin with everything*. Creation, evolution or whatever else it be called, is only the appearance in subtle and gross forms of an inherent tendency in pure Being—Consciousness, as the *nidus* of all the manifested tendencies or *Saṃskāras*. One cannot get out of a bag more than has been put into it. It it is not put there in the beginning, it will not be got out in the end. Thus Life manifests in form. Life has no origin except as manifesting in a particular form. But Life has, in itself, no origin, for it is but a limited aspect of Eternal Being in all Its fullness. Consciousness again has not itself *evolved*. It is gradually *liberated* which is quite a different notion. It is not a product of Matter. If it be not assumed in the beginning it will not be found at the end. It is eternal. Its existence is as a contraction (*Saṁkoca*) through association with Mind and Matter. And so with these last two. As constituting shapes they appear and pass away. But in the form of a potency to appear as such—a potency in the Cosmic Will—they had never, according to Vedānta, a beginning as they will never have an end.

The practical effect of a philosophy or religion is of primary importance. In this case the aim is Wholeness and Power and that is the effect of practical working or *Sādhana* as distinct from mere theorising. The high *Sādhana* (for there are several degrees) is self-purification and the worship of God as *Śāktimān* or the Supreme Possessor of Power. I hope to deal with *Sādhana* in a future volume. *Śakti* means "Power" and a *Śākta* is a worshipper of it in Its Supreme form. Then following this, entry is made upon the highest stage which is *jñāna-yoga* or religious philosophising by him whose mind and body have been purified and perfected by *Sādhana*.

The Śakti-saṅgama-Tantra says that the doctrine of *Śakti* was promulgated to establish unity amongst worshippers. For whatever might be the name of the God of their particular form of worship, all admitted His "feminine" aspect as Power. A Bengali writer, now deceased, who is not so well known as he should be, namely Bhudeva Mukhyopādhyāya stated in one of his books (on what authority however I do not know) that Śākta teaching was also promulgated with the political aim of hardening the power of resistance in the Hindu to foreign aggression. However this may be the doctrine is in fact powerful and power-giving. It is not possible that those who truly realise that in their essential being they are the self-same Supreme Power which created the universe, or in actual contact therewith, can be ever weak. It has been said that it was Christianity which first told the individual man that he was of worth. But how can that be seeing that hundreds of years before the incarnation of the Christ the Rishi had said "That thou art"? That is, man is not only of worth, but he is *Devālaya* or abode of the Divine Power itself. Life itself is a power which is weakened or increased in the individual as he has ability to resist, and to increase through faith in, and progressive realisation of, his essential oneness with, the enduring Whole, which, while timeless in itself, is represented in time by a principle of conservation within the limits of the life of an universe. Abundant life is needed for the successful undertaking of all human activity. How to gain it is the work of *Sādhana*. But in rightly stressing the necessity of practice, it has sometimes been forgotten, in the reaction against "Dogma," that practice must be backed by a doctrine which supplies the reasons for it. I read for instance that auto-suggestion is now being practised by the mere repetition of the words "I am becoming better and better every day and in every way", and the like. But unless one believes this what is the use of saying it? Some appear to believe without reason but with good results. But others will not believe this without having been given first a reason to show why such belief is well-founded and will therefore have good result. Be they sound or not, Śākta doctrine does give its reasons when it says that the ultimate Reality and inner being of each self is the unlimited Whole (*Pūrṇa*) of which the individual is a contraction or form, deriving the limitation implied in all form by the operation of those Powers which are Mind and Matter and the function of which is to negate the Whole or Consciousness (*Niṣedha-vyāpāra-rūpā Śaktih*) as Yogamuni finely says in his Commentary on Abhinava-Gupta's Paramārtha-sāra. That Really Real is the Inner Self and unlimited Being of which life in Mind and Matter is a limited form. It is Hale or Whole. It is unbroken (*Akhaṇḍa*) Bliss of which all happiness in the world is a fragment. It is unlimited Power in itself as the Transcendent Will. Limited Power exists in the form of the individual wills of living forms and the physico-chemical powers of Matter.

But all these forms of contraction are due to, and take place in, Mind and Matter. The one Spirit, which is changless Bliss, is the essential being of all these froms. From this it follows that each form may make contact with, and then realise, the whole, is his own essential Self, which is Health itself, the Source, infinitely joyous, of all limited power and life—*Prāṇah prāṇasya* as the Upaniṣad says or the "Life of all lives"—with results all beneficial to itself. To understand this, however, it is necessary to know the nature of Mind and its operations and therfore the meaning of the old saying in the Upaniṣads "What a man thinks that he becomes." If this be doubted the answer is "try". If the objector refuses to try a system which promises particular results, he cannot complain that he has had no benefit from it. Just as in the West one finds advocates of the Cult of Power, so others, both here and there, are opposed to it because of its abuses. It is true that Power may be wrongly used but that need not be so. The objection is not to the Cult of Power (which is not the same thing as the Cult of material force) but the use of it when obtained. In the same way loose thinking makes a distinction between Might and Right as though Might was wrong. There is nothing necessarily wrong about Might. The true distinction is between Might in the service of Right and Might in the service of Wrong. In the same way objection has been taken to the Śākta doctrine because it teaches *Yoga* through Enjoyment or *Bhoga,* as distinct from *Yoga* by Renunciation which but very few are willing to try, and are still less capable of achieving if they did. *Bhoga* which is both Enjoyment and Suffering is not limited, in the former case, to "Beer and Skittles" or to be more up-to-date "Cinema and Dancing Teas". It is a sound principle but, like everything else, susceptible of abuse by the sincere but weak on the one hand, and the hypocritical pretender on the other. It is an old doctrine in this line of thought that perfection can best be attained if each seeker of it perfects himself in all common human functions, and in his own particular avocation whatever it be. However humble it be let him only place himself, his life with all its functions and actions with the Whole, when they acquire meaning and strength. The individual life is then lived in and with the Universal Life. But it must be known what Life is. To this question this volume attempts to give shortly the Indian answer.

What is called the "Philosophy of Life" and Doctrine of Power is now in vogue in the West. "New Thought" as it is called (so akin in some respects to Śākta doctrine) says "Within you is the Power". "Spiritual healing" is taught and practised by the followers of what is called "Christian Science" to whom man's mind is "mortal mind" and the world of matter is a kind of *Māyā*. Great changes are taking place in Psychology. The debt of Theosophy to India is well known as also (though in another sense) of India to Theosophy which re-called to the Indian the value of his cultural inheritance. In Medical science, Psycho-therapy is establishing itself. An American critic reviewing one of the books which I have published of Tantra Śāstra spoke of this Scripture as being "perhaps the most elaborate system of auto-suggestion in the world"—a fact which he did not consider to be to its credit—for auto-suggestion, in its Indian sense, was not understood by him.

All these western movements are further instances of the approximation, which is now taking place, of modern western and ancient Indian thought to which I have often referred, as in the first volume of this Series on "Reality". There is no reason however for any racial bumptiousness on either side. These doctrines and practices are based on notions which are it is true very old in India. They are the product of Ancient India, of that Great India which thought for itself and did not wait for cultural food of any kind to be spooned out to it by strangers. To-day it is the West which is great not only politically but in its intense original life, in its worship of Power and Beauty, in its Art, Science and Philosophy, and in its keen research and elaboration of fresh ideas. There, even the smallest peoples with no great past history are respected Selves. India has not yet recovered from the state which laid her open to the foreign invader. She is still learning how to say "I" which if it be said will be starting point of her activities. This is not to deny the existence of great evils or that the present European civilization carries within it, like everything else, the seed of its death. Moreover, though I think the East has influenced the West, as the West the East, it is possible that similar ideas may have sprung up independently. If a theory has any truth in it, it may be discovered without help from any other. It is in respect of the absurdities of others that we more often require to wait for information. Probably no really new "Truth" is true. There is much truth in the Ancient Wisdom which is being re-presented to-day, sometimes with a richer content and in most cases with an objective proof which was previously wanting.

The Upaniṣads (some of which are more than 2,000 years old) teach the essentials of the lines of thought to which I have referred, such as that man's essential being is the one Spirit: that that being is pure Consciousness and Bliss of immeasurable power, that Mind and Matter are two of its powers and as such one with it, for power (*Śakti*) and the possessor of Power (*Śaktimān*) are one, that man makes himself what he is and he can make himself what he will; that (to use the words of the Chāndogya Upaniṣad) "what a man thinks that he becomes", that the Power is within, being known as the "Inner Controller" (*Antaryāmin*), that Mind is active and goes forth as a Ray to meet the excitations of matter, that it has power over matter, and may possess various *siddhis* such as moving matter without physical connection and others, and that mind can influence mind by telepathy and hypnotism (*Vaśī-karaṇam*) and in other ways. The recent theory, for instance, of the American Dr. Abrams that there is vibration (*Spanda*) of the "ultimate" electric units of matter, that specific rates of vibration are associated with definite pathological conditions of the blood or tissues, and that these conditions may be cured by electric waves possessing a periodicity enabling them to control the vibrations of the disease from which the patient is suffering, is strongly reminiscent of the theory of *Mantra*, which by its sound-vibrations affects and regulates the psychical and physical sheaths. In a recent book by a Bengali author it is observed (not with approval for he rejects the Vedānta and adopts the notions of Modern Western Theism) that it appeared to him that "in these modern speculations the old philosophers seem to have been winning all along the line." He says: "An Indian may well feel proud that the speculations of his age-old philosophers so long ridiculed by Europeans are adopted by the newest science"; but he finds that it is "difficult to resist the smile which such speculations naturally give rise to." Let him not resist the smile. No one will begrudge him that, for smiles and laughter spell health, nor will he perhaps demur to the amusement of others for a reason quite contrary to his own. Naturally those Indians who do not think much of the religion and philosophy of their ancestors will be amused (though the kindly ones will be saddened) at the sight of those Europeans who (as they think) are picking up ancient Indian errors and putting them forward as new Western truths.

Others of a different way of thinking will likely be of opinion that if modern western scientific theories tend to square with ancient Indian teaching, then some case is made out for the latter.

But after all it does not matter who first said what. The question is—is it true and therefore useful—a question which we should approach without prejudice.

My friend Professor P. N. Mukhyopādhyāya has been good enough, at my request, to supply me with the valuable Appendix which will be found at the conclusion of this book which will be followed by two volumes, which I have prepared with his help, on *Śakti* as Mind and *Śakti* as Matter.

*Puri* J. W.

30th May, 1922

# THE WORLD AS POWER:

## POWER AS LIFE

## (*Prāṇa-śakti*)

## I

"He said "I am Life' " (Sahovāca, Prāṇo'smi). "The life of all lives" (Sa u prāṇasya prāṇah) "Adore Me who am Life." (Prāṇo'smi, Māṃ upāsasva).

*Kauṣītakī Up.*, 3—2; *Kena-Up.*, 2.

In the West, matter is commonly divided into that which is organised and unorganised, the former being called living, and the latter non-living, substance, "brute," "inert" and "dead" matter. As is so characteristic of Western Thought, emphasis is thus laid on difference and discontinuity, these being apparent. An absolute gulf was created between the two; the greatest of all gulfs namely that between what is dead and what is alive. "Organisation"[1] means more or less systematic arrangement of relatively separate parts in a whole suited to fulfil any sort of function. According to the old meaning of the term "organic", an organic body is one, whether living or not, in which heterogeneous elements make up a composite whole. After Leibnitz two elements in the conception (that of composition of parts and relation of means and end) are intimately connected and Kant welds them together in his definition of the organic, as that in which all the parts are reciprocally means and ends to one another and to the whole. Thus historically the identification of organic with the living comes last, and the term means that which has life whether animal or vegetable as opposed to inorganic or inanimate. Organism in biology means a discrete body of which the essential constituent is living protoplasm. The term originally indicated the recognition of organisation as essential to life and as opposite to unorganised or "dead" matter. An organism has the inherent principle of its own systematic process. It is thus common to speak of organised matter in connection with life. But all matter is now held to be in a state of organisation, that

[1] See Baldwin, Phil. Dict.

is systematic arrangement of relatively separate parts in a whole suited to fulfil any sort of function. It is said to be constituted of complicated structural elements, and the molecules and atoms are described in fact as miniature solar systems. The supposed, self-moving, electric units of these atoms constitute distinct structural arrangements, varying in number and position in the varied forms of so called elementary matter. And so it has been said[1] that "as soon as we lift the veil of appearances, matter so inert in its outward aspect is seen to possess an extremely complicated organisation and an intense life." So again mineral being is characterised by its beautifully geometrical crystalline form as the living being is characterised by its anatomical one. In short all matter, everything which exists is organised. It is therefore not organisation but degree and nature of organisation which distinguishes so called living and non-living substance.

Nothing again is inert. According to Sāṃkhya and Monistic Vedānta all matter is a compound of derivates from one primordial Substance-Energy called Prakṛti Māyāśakti. This and its modes are in perpetual movement. For activity is the essential characteristic of the ultimate Substance-Energy. For this reason the Hindus call the world "*Jagat*" which means the "moving thing" because everything is in movement in changeless Spirit or Consciousness, just as in the phenomenal world all is moving here and there in the ethereal continuum. It is true that a common distinction, in ordinary parlance, exists between moving (*Cara*) and unmoving (*Acara*). things, but this refers to the appearance only of gross matter and even to living plants without locomotive movement. This notion of the inertness of matter was due to superficial observation of molar masses apparently at rest and set in motion by force from without. As above stated, according to the views now held, the ultimate particles of the atoms of matter are in constant movement and the atom itself is a reservoir of tremendous energy. It has therefore been rightly observed that the whole question of motion, as related to living and not-living being, requires re-statement in view of modern ideas of an ultra-physical nature relating to intra-atomic activities and to molecular movement.

There is no Indian equivalent of the phrase "dead" matter. The term "*Jada*" generally means anything without locomotive movement (*Acara*) a stationary thing. In this sense a plant may be *Jada* though

[1] Le Bon "Evolution of Matter".

there is movement in the plant itself. A moving thing (*Cara*) may be relatively *Jada*. Thus a man who is numbed with cold is said to be *Jadasada*. One is said to be in the state of *Jada* when he feels incapable or disinclined for physical or mental action. *Jada*[1] means without movement (*Nihspanda*) effortless (*Nirudyoga*). It also means unconscious (*Acetana*). But a thing which is *Acetana* is not necessarily and absolutely without consciousness. In fact nothing is that. Everything in Vedānta is a form of consciousness (*Cit*). Everything again, as regards its material body, is Māyāśakti or the finitising principle, Creatrix of the world of forms or Power which in itself (*Svarūpa*) is Consciousness. Again Māyāśakti as ground of appearance is constituted of three Guṇas (*Triguṇa-mayī*).[2] That is in everything there is the Factor *Śattva* (for the three *Guṇas* or factors of the Natural Principle never exist apart from one another), and *Sattva* is that aspect of the Natural Principle which manifests Consciousness in any phenomenon, veiled though that Consciousness be in differing degrees. What then we call unconscious or as having the appearance of unconsciousness is only that in which Consciousness is most obscured to the finite observer. But there is nothing which does not manifest it in some degree. Thus the response of matter to stimuli is evidence of the *Sattvaguṇa* and of the *Cit* which it reflects. In popular language *Acetana* (unconscious) may be applied to man who is *Ạcetana* to some things and *Cetana* to others. What may be in one condition *Acetana* may be *Sacetana* (conscious) in another. Thus *Acetana* (unconscious ) may be applied to a man who is not expert or quick about anything, incapable, worthless, in a state of fascination, dumb, blind, an idiot, any one who remains without action and effort.[3] How little a Hindu looks on anything as being absolutely dead, and how words are used in an analogical sense is illustrated by the case of an Orissan sculptor who told me that he was unable to make a statue I wanted out of an old stone which I gave him because it was "dead"; that is it had ceased to be able to be worked upon.

From a philosophical point of view then all is essentially unmoving Consciousness veiled in varying degree by continually moving Mind and Matter, most veiled in gross matter, and less and less veiled in plants, animals and man, who in Yoga becomes complete Consciousness and nothing else. Again the vehicle of mind and matter is the manifestation of

---

[1] See Prakṛti-vāda Dict. of Rāmakamala Vidyalaṃkāra.
[2] See "Reality", *supra*.
[3] Dakṣatā, Satvaratā, Akṣamatā, Akarmaṇya, Mohita, etc., see Prakṛti-vāda Dict.

the Power (Śakti) of Consciousness, that is Consciousness as Power. The term Consciousness must be understood not in its ordinary Western sense but as an approximate term for *Cit.*[1] All matter again is composed o· Sattvaguṇa as well as of the other Guṇas which are the principles of efficiency, and resistance or inertia in a phenomenon. There is no vehicle of Consciousness which is not in perpetual movement. There is no vehicle which does not in varying degree display Consciousness.

Neither then organisation, motion, nor consciousness is peculiar to living substance. Motion exists in both forms of substance, though it is what is called mechanical and determined in one, and apparently free and undetermined in the other. Organisation exists in both cases, though more and more complex in living substance. Consciousness is the essence of both, though so obscured in what is called inorganic matter that the latter is deemed unconscious. Yet even here science corrects crude observation. This irritability was supposed to be a fundamental property of living substance. It is however now known that "non-living" matter reacts to external stimuli. Thus its reaction to acid is a spasm. For knowledge in this direction we are indebted, as all know to experiments of the distinguished Indian scientist Sir Jagadish Bose. By taking as basis the fact that the most general and delicate sign in life is the electric response, he has shown that this electric response is the reaction of an obscure form of Consciousness in matter. He has thus shown by his ingenious experiments the fatigue of metals and its disappearance after rest and the action on these same metals of excitants, depressants and poisons.

Whilst it is of course true that self-conscious mind exists only in high manifestations of Life, it is also the fact that in the response which inorganic matter makes to external stimuli we see the most rudimentary form of that which when developed is called sentiency—a form of Consciousness. Matter is of extreme mobility and it has been said[2] "endowed with an unconscious sensibility which cannot be approached by the conscious sensibility of any being." The author cited adds "This sensibility of matter so contrary to what popular observation seems to indicate is becoming more and more familiar to physicists. This is why such an expression as the 'life of matter,' utterly meaningless twentyfive years ago, has come into common use. The study of mere matter yields ever-increasing proof that it has properties which were formerly deemed the exclusive appanage of

[1] See "Śakti and Śākta," by the author. Chapter on Cit-Śakti.

[2] Le Bon "Evolution of Matter," 249 (1907).

living beings. The analogies discovered are, it is likely, due to the fact that nature does not greatly vary her procedure, and constructs all beings from mineral to man with similar materials, whence they are endowed with common properties.

Then is the substance we call matter different in what is living and not living? The answer is in the negative. It is the same matter which is in living substance as in non-living substance. There are not two kinds of matter. The chemico-mechanical school stands for the continuity of evolution between non-living and living substance. The Vitalists say that there is no difference as to matter, but that, when viewing life, we are in the presence of "something else" (not matter) in addition to what is found existing in non-living bodies. Nature in fact constructs all beings from mineral to man with similar materials. The difference exists in the manner they are worked up to display the Consciousness which is their essence. The greater the display of consciousness the more complex the structure.

The various "elements" of matter may by combination give birth to bodies of increasing complexity from the forms of inorganic matter to the compounds forming the tissues of living beings. A living being is made up of an aggregate of chemical compounds formed by the combination of a small number of elements[1] so associated as to compose molecular edifices of very great mobility. A particularly complex but structureless homogeneous undiffernatiated chemical substance known as Protoplasm[2] is the substance out of which all "living" things, whether Plants, Animals or Men, are formed. This elementary life-stuff possesses even in minute portions all the properties seen in the most complicated living structures such as assimilation, growth, contractility, sensitivity, reproduction. Of it is built up the cell, itself a complicated structure with its walls and nucleus. Inorganic forms constitute molecular edifices of small complexity in structure, whereas compounds elaborated within the tissues of living beings are admittedly extremely difficult of interpretation. So long as chemistry had only to study very simple mineral or organic compounds, elementary laws were sufficient, but closer examination showed that

[1] The human body is about 75 per cent water, rest jelly and bones. The nerves and brain cells are 80 per cent or 85 per cent water. The Colloids are, it is said, the underlying fabric of many of the processes of life.

[2] Contains carbon, hydrogen, oxygen, nitrogen and a minute quantity of other elements notably phosphorus. It is however so complex chemically as to defy exact analysis. Moreover it is dead protoplasm of which chemistry speaks.

substances existed to which none of the known laws of chemistry could be applied and these substances are just those which play a preponderating part in the phenomena of life. A great number of chemical compounds, of which the aggregate constitues a living being, possess a structure and properties to which none of the old laws of chemistry are applicable. No formula can express their composition and no theory explains their properties. On them depend the majority of the phenomena of life. The viscid albuminoid Protoplasm, which is the fundamental substance of the cells, never appears to change, though by its presence it determines the most complicated chemical reactions. The writer[1] from whom we quote the above speaks of the chemical edifices which the humble cells perform comprise operations, not only the most skilful in the laboratories, but many more skilful still which man is unable to imitate. By means unknown the cells construct complicated and varied compounds and decompose the most stable bodies. "All these operations so precise, so admirably adapted to one purpose are *directed* by forces of which we have no conception *which act exactly as if they possessed a power of clairvoyance very superior to reason.* What they accomplish every moment of our existence is far above what can be realised by the most advanced science."

A living being is, as body, the aggregate of these cellular lives. What then is that which we call life, be it in the cells or the cellular aggregate, as the plant, animal, and man? What is it which constitutes the distinction between what we call life and non-living substance? For it must be admitted that there are obvious differences between the two, otherwise man would not have made the distinction. It is sometimes forgotten, in the desire to unify all things, that it is the characteristic of phenomenal Reality that it is made up of differences and apparent discontinuities. For it is only these which can constitute a world. If all were static and homogeneous there would be no world at all. Continuity only exists as regards the original Substance-Energy (Śakti) of which all apparent diversities and continuities are, modes. Nevertheless, whilst admitting diversity, we may discern elements of sameness or correspondence which are the phenomenal indications of the unity of Creative Reality Itself.

Varying definitions have been given of Life such as "the special activity of organised beings" which tells us nothing. Life is generally defined as a process and we are told what Life does rather than what Life is.

[1] See Le Bon, *Op., cit.*, 293—295.

Thus living substance is said to be that which is born, breathes, moves, assimilates, grows, adapts itself to environment, repairs and reproduces itself and dies. Whilst it is true that these are fundamental properties of living substance it cannot be said that, at any rate all of them, are properties of what is popularly called "living substance" alone. Perhaps in some degree none are. To be born and to die are only particular ways of coming into and leaving a passing form of existence. We cannot equate the behaviour of bodies with that of artificial machines. Thus the atom of matter does not depend on external impulse for its movements. It is not provided from without with its gigantic store of energy which it carries within itself. It keeps itself going until it dissociates. This dissociation is the death of the atom for which there must have been, as regards any particular atom, a corresponding birth. Nor can we say that one is self-moved and not the other. In gross matter there is intra-atomic and molecular movements, though as a mass it is moved only by the application of external force. "Brownian" movement may be reaction of external molecular conditions upon a small mass of matter, resulting in mechanical motions, but it is yet a movement of transport. Even so-called "selfinitiated" animal movement may be a reaction to external conditions. Some are of opinion that there is no spontaneous or voluntary movement and that all movement is the result of tactisms in the nature of a chemico-physical reaction.

Then what of the admittedly living cell. Except as an independent organism it may be incapable of movement of transport. Thus only the white cells of the blood have amoebic movement. Some cells have ciliary movement only. Others, such as the living cells, have no movement of transport at all. These cells are yet living and form part of a living organism. All admittedly living substance breathes. And hence the word *Prāni* or breathing creatures. The plant does so through its leaves. Even in an animal, the Amoeba, we cannot see the process of respiration taking place. It is therefore supposed that the interchange of gases which constitutes the breathing process takes place all over the surface of the creature, there being no apparent special organ. It may not be too fanciful to suppose that some such interchange takes place, through attraction and repulsion, (principles of universal operation) in the interstices of matter. Whether "nonliving" matter can assimilate depends on the question whether it is capable of growth. The process is in some measure chemical, for chemical changes and operations take place during its progress.

All matter is capable of crystallisation, and matter is thus individualised by incorporation of elements borrowed from the medium with itself. Cells and crystals have been said to show evident affiliation. The crystalline form corresponds to the anatomical one. The material molecules go through successive transformations to assume the crystalline form, being a representation, in a way, of tissue in the course of evolution. All this of course is not to deny that there are differences between the growth of crystals and of so called "living" bodies. So again with self-repair which is a mark of living substance. Like the animal or plant a mutilated crystal can repair its mutilation. In fact this healing or righting tendency is not merely present in individual bodies, but is an essential characteristic of the universe as a whole—an aspect of the universal Law or *Dharma* under which all abnormality, injury and wrong are in due time righted. So again as regards generation. In certain conditions liquids only crystallise if they have first received a crystalline germ. In other cases spontaneous crystallisation appears to be observed. The crystalline bodies which are produced by vital activities are identical in composition and molecular structure with crystals of "inorganic" origin. Adaptation, that is meeting the various conditions with which any living being is confined, may ultimately be reduced to Attraction (*Rāga*) and Repulsion (*Dveṣa*), and response to changes in environment, whether the reaction be due to more chemical changes in the composition of a thing, or whether there is also an element of purposiveness in them. Matter responds by expansion to heat, and by contraction to cold under a rigid law. Lower organisms are also largely subject to such law but as they rise in the scale of being the element of freedom manifests. In all cases a purpose is served; in some only is the organism conscious of it. All forms of Matter and Mind act according *Saṃskāra* or innate tendencies to realise their ends, though only in some bodies is that tendency presented as object to its consciousness. The form is adapted to the end of accomplishing what the organism is by nature fitted to accomplish. In some cases the action is the realisation of a chemico-physical law, in others by instinct, in some others again by conscious willing process.

Every centre acts according to the degree of freedom which evolution has accorded to it. It is in fact in *freedom* that we find the distinguishing characteristic of living substance. It cannot be said that either organic or inorganic matter is altogether free. For each form exists and operates according to the laws which govern it. Each has its normal behaviour or *Dharma*. But living matter shows increasing will and purposive action.

If we then examine the differences which exist between so called inorganic and organic matter, we find that they may be summed up in the generalised statement that living-matter is endowed, in greater and greater degree, with *freedom* and *individuality*. External control is never wholly absent but there is increasing freedom from it. Instead of a rule imposed on simply-organised subject material, the forms of living matter are biologically described as an organism rich in organisation with internal self-regulating control. Chemical and physical processes are rigid and unvarying and a particular behaviour may be expected with accuracy. We do not anticipate any departure from the regular lines of events involved in any chemical or physical process. On the other hand an opponent of the Vitalistic theory[1] has said that an animal never does the same thing twice in the whole course of its existence. Freedom and individuality is thus the fundamental characteristic of living matter. And this we might expect, seeing that the initial creative process is an impulse towards individualisation—an impulse which continues to gain strength with the evolution of forms.

The fact that gross matter exhibits (though in rudimentary form) the properties of living substance is regarded by some as proof that all matter is either, in an obscure sense, alive or has within it the potency of life. Either view is apt to introduce confusion and obliterate real differences. Life is a term which expresses a distinction. If we call all matter alive we thereby give to the word life a meaning which renders it meaningless. If again we say that matter as such contains the potency of life, we are again giving to the term matter another sense than that in which it is ordinarily understood, namely a sense which places it in contrast with both Life and Mind. The position taken by Śākta doctrine is in this matter, as in so many others, sound. It recognises both difference and unity. To the holders of chemico-mechanical theories of the production of Life by Matter, it says that Matter as such is not the cause of Life. On the contrary Life is a Power, a form of Consciousness which directs matter. But it is right to say that the cause of Life is immanent in matter as the Power which manifests as both Matter and Life. To the Vitalist, whether old or new, it says that he is right in affirming that Life is not a product of Matter as such, but wrong when he says that there is "something else"

[1] See Le Dantec, "The Nature and Origin of Life".

in living substance which is absent in non-living substance. For the one Power is present in both, but manifests either as so-called "dead" matter with its regulated and calculable motions and behaviour, or in "live" matter in which the gradual freeing of consciousness and will introduces "self-initiated" purposive action which is less and less calculable, until for practical purposes it becomes incalculable. It is not, in short, to matter as such that we must look for the appearance of life, but to the Power (Śakti) which is the cause of *both* matter and life. This is so fundamental and important a point that it is examined later in greater detail, after a short historical review of the theories held in East and West as to the nature of Life and its so-called origin.

According to the Indian Materialists (Cārvākas, Lokāyatas) Life, as well as Consciousness, was spontaneously generated (Abiogenesis) as a result of the chemical combination, under the influence of heat and moisture, of the four kinds of matter[1] in organic forms, just as the intoxicating property of spirituous liquors is the result of the fermentation of unintoxicating rice and molasses. The instinctive movements of the newly-born organism were held to be mechanically due to external stimuli, as much as the opening and closing of the lotus at different hours of the day or night or the movement of iron under the influence of the lodestone. It is common ground however in the Nyāya-Vaiśeṣika, Sāṃkhya-Pātañjala and Vedānta schools that Consciousness[2] transcends and is not the product of matter. The Naiyāyikas held that psychical and vital processes are immaterial and could not be resolved into motion.[3] The two latter schools held that both Mind and Matter are, as all else, which is not consciousness,[4] forms of motion, but are distinguished from one another in that the Vedānta holds that Life is also a separate substantive principle which the Sāṃkhya, on the ground of economy of categories, does not admit. Both held that consciousness is not a motion and cannot be the resultant of the motions of inorganic matter. Nor is the consciousness of the self or of the organism as a whole, the resultant of supposed consciousnesses vested in the constituent particles of the body. There is one central abiding

[1] Vāyu, Tejas, Ap, Pṛthivī. The fifth Ākāśa was not admitted as not being subject of perception. See Seal, 239—91, Positive Sciences of the Hindus.

[2] Caitanya. This is *not* mind. The latter is intermingled consciousness and unconsciousness.

[3] Pari-spanda. Life. It is a Guṇa, jīvanoniyatna or activity of the Ātman.

[4] As either the Sāṃkhyan Puruṣa or Vedāntic Ātmā. Both are transcendent, immaterial, and at rest : all else moves.

Consciousness. Life[1] according to the Sāṃkhya is not a *Vāyu*[2] or bio-mechanical force nor any mere mechanical impulsion resulting from the impulsion of *Vāyu*. Life is a reflex activity, a resultant of the various concurrent activities of the mind and senses.[3] This, it is said, explains the disturbing effect on the vitality of pleasurable and painful emotions. The Sāṃkhyas accept the substantive existence of Mind[4] but resolve Life into a mere resultant activity of the mind and senses. Whilst therefore for them Life was not a bio-mechanical force nor evolved from inorganic matter[5] it was only a complex reflex activity resulting from the operations of the psycho-physical principles or forces in the organism. The Vedāntists[6] whilst agreeing with the Sāṃkhyas that Life is neither a biomechanical force, nor the result of its operation, deny that it is merely the result of the concurrent sensory-motor, emotional, and apperceptive reactions of the organism. Life is prior to the senses, for it regulates the development of the fertilised living ovum from which the senses subsequently develop. The sensations do not explain life. Moreover the deprivation of any one or more of the senses does not mean a deprivation of life. The Vedāntists therefore hold Life, which is called Prāṇa,[7] as a separate, substantive, quasi-material Principle, pervasive of the organism, which is not a gross natural force or material energy but a form of regulative activity or motion guiding such energy phenomenally and, as the western Scholastics said, immersed in Matter. In the Śākta system, everything which exists is a form of Supreme Power or Śākti which is in Itself Consciousness and manifests as Consciousness-unconsciousness.[8] That Power is either of Will, Knowledge or Action. The Life Principle is a form of active power (*Kriyāśakti*). But the Powers are never entirely separated the one from the other. Wherever there is the one, there is the other. In particular manifestations, one or other may be predominant.[9] Therefore there is

[1] Seal, 241.

[2] Vāyu comes from the root Vā=to move.

[3] That is Ego (Ahaṃkāra), the emotional (Manas) and sensory-motor (Jñānendriya and Karmendriya) relations of the organism.

[4] Manas, as derived, co-ordinately with the Tanmātra, from Ahaṃkāra or individualised Prakṛti.

[5] Bhūta.

[6] Seal, *op. cit.*, 242.

[7] This word comes from the root *An* "to breathe"+prefix Pra.

[8] Neither the 24 nor the 36 Tattvas give Life as a separate substantive Principle or Tattva, as does the Māyā-vāda scheme. Life is here, as in the Sāṃkhya, merely a complex activity resulting from the operation of the psycho-physical Principles. It is a form of the Supreme Power which products them, though possibly (for the point is at present not clear) after the manner of the Sāṃkhya. That is Life as Cause is Power, though the mode by which it works may be that which the Sāṃkhya indicates.

[9] Pradhāna.

present both Will and Knowledge and all these are manifestations of the Consciousness. The Vital Principle is ultimately as all else Consciousness, in this case active to produce and sustain living substance and all its functions. Living substance is a form of God as Power.

*Prāṇa* has been defined[1] to be "the special relation of the *Ātmā* with a certain form of matter which by this relation the *Ātmā*[2] (or Self) organises or builds up as a means of having experience." *Prāṇa* in its general sense as the "Life Principle" is not breath, nor is it breathing except in a secondary sense. Breathing is only one of the manifestations of Life, an attribute of living substance. It is a manifestation of the Life-Principle. Breath is simply the circumambient air inhaled and expelled. The form of the Life-Principle or *Prāṇa*, as manifested function, is breathing. Life, as the vital principle, bears the same name as its chief characteristic—the breathing which, in various forms, is the mark of vegatable, animal, and human nature. And thus the word "Spirit" literally means breath. Man must speak in terms of material existence, and he here selected what seemed to him the least material, the most unsubstantial. A breath may be felt. The physical action of breathing may be seen and known. When breathing ceases Life ceases: and so the Kauṣītakī-Upaniṣad calls *Prāṇa* "the Life-duration of all." But That which is unseen, of which its functioning is seen, is Spirit or Brahman as the Life and source of all lives, the *Prāṇā* of all *Prāṇas*.

*Prāṇa* is either individual or cosmic. The latter is the Brahman as *Prāṇa*. The special relation, above mentioned, constitutes the individual *Prāṇa* in the individual body. The individual *Prāṇa* is limited to the particular body which it vitalises, and is a manifestation in all breathing creatures called *Prāṇī* of the life-giving activity of the Brahman. The cosmic *Prāṇa* which pervades and vitalises all breathing creatures (*Prāṇī*) is the Brahman as the collectivity of all individual *Prāṇas*, and the source of the individual and collective life. Breathing is a microcosmic manifestation of the macrocosmic Rhythm to which the whole universe moves and according to which it appears and disappears. And so it is said that the life of Brahmā, the Creative-consciousness in any universe, is of the duration of the

1 "Hindu Realism," J. C. Chatterjee. In the Tantras the Devī as Life-Principle is depicted as of a red colour in a boat floating on a sea of blood.

2 This term is compounded of A+at+man. The root *At* means All-spreading just as Brahman does. According to some the root is As "to be" (Asmi, Sum, I am) or *An* to breathe—the "Spirit," which has the same significance.

outgoing breath,[1] of the Lord as Time.[2] With His inbreathing all worlds are withdrawn.

The body is divided by the Vedānta into five sheaths, which are less and less gross as we proceed inward, namely the sheaths of food or matter, life, lower and higher mind and of bliss.[3] The *Prāṇamaya* or life-body differs from the gross outer body or body of food[4] which it vitalises. The latter is heterogeneous,[5] or made up of distinct or well-defined parts. But the vital-self[6] which lies within the gross physical self[4] is a homogeneous undivided whole,[7] permeating the whole physical body.[8] It is not cut off into distinct regions,[9] as is the microcosmic cosmic physical body known as the Pinda. Unlike the latter it has no specialised organs each discharging a special function. It is a homogeneous unity, present in every part of the body which it ensouls as its inner vital self. A new life appears with the germination of the seed[10] in breathing creatures. Into this seed *Prāṇa* enters. When the *Prāṇa* goes, that is when the organism ceases to breathe, the organism which the Vital Principle holds together disintegrates, though for a time the cells may continue a sort of life of their own.

Prāṇa is metaphorically called *Vāyu* in the sense of universal vital activity. It is itself one, but on entry into each body manifests itself in ten different ways under ten different names, of which the five chief are *Prāṇa*, *Apāna*, *Samāna*, *Vyāna* and *Udāna* later explained.

*Prāṇa* or *Ayuh*[11] (Life) like all other constitutive principles of the Universe has two aspects namely as cause and as effect. In the first Prāṇa is a name for the Supreme Brahman as the Cause of, that is the Power (Śakti) which produces, the life of individual being. Numerous Texts establish this: "He said "I am *Prāṇa* (*Prāṇo'smi*)[12] "Thou art *Āyuh*" (*Āyuṣtvaṃ*)[13] "*Prāṇa* is Brahman" (*Prāṇo brahma*).[14] Here *Prāṇa* means

---

[1] Niṣvāsa.

[2] Kāla—See Introduction. Prapañcasāra-Tantra, Vol. 3. Tantrik Texts.

[3] Annamaya, Prāṇamaya, Manomaya, Vijñānamaya, Ānandamaya.

[4] Annamaya. [5] Pariccinna. [6] Prāṇamaya Ātmā.

[7] Sādhāraṇa. [8] Sarvapiṇḍavyāpin. [9] Asādhāraṇa.

[10] In the viviparous Placental (no a-placental animals were known) or Jarāyuja, the oviparous animals or Aṇḍaja, vegetable organisms or Udbhijja. It was commonly believed that the fourth class Svedaja or Uṣmaja were spontaneously or a-sexually generated from inorganic matter through the action of moisture and heat such as maggots in corrupting flesh. See Rāghava-Bhatta Comm. on Śāradā-Tilaka, 1,27, 29. But the view was also taken that inorganic matter without seed (Bīja) could not give rise to animal life. See Seal *Op. cit.*, 177, 181.

[11] Āyuh is Prāṇa. Kauṣītakī-U., 3—2.

[12] Kauṣītakī-Up., 3—2: Prāṇa is Brahman (Prāṇo Brahmeti). *Ib.* 2-1.

[13] Maitri-Up., 5—1. [14] Chāndogya-Up., 4—10—5. Kauṣītakī, 2—1, 2—2.

Para-brahman[1] beyond Mind and Speech.[2] Hence God is enjoined to be worshipped as Life. "Adore Me who am Life (*Āyuh*) and Eternal."[3] "He who worships Me as Life and Immortality obtains in this world all Life (*Āyuh.*)"[4] Worship of life is done with life.[5] It is this Prāṇa, as the Supreme Cause, which gives life as Effect.[6] He is thus the Life of all lives.[7] The Kāṇva[8] says "The Devas worship that which is the Deathless One (*Amṛta*), which is truly Itself Life, and the Light of Lights."[9] The Āgama also says "As we two (Śiva and Śakti) are the Self of the World,[10] We Two are one with it. By reason of Our oneness with one another we are at all times the Life of the World (*Jagatprāṇa*)".[11] What is vitalised is so vitalised by Prāṇa.[12] And He is the Vitaliser or *Prāṇa* in chief.[13]

It is from this Supreme Life that all beings issue, enjoy their individual lives, and then re-enter into it.[14] It is thus the Cause of the universe. As such, Life is eternal.[15] It is also this universe.[16] As Life eternal it is an endless, constant and changless Persistence itself. It is also eternal as universe, in the sense that whilst particular systems come and go, the universal process is eternal—now dropped and now resumed. *Prāṅa* is *Paramātmā, Antarātmā,*[17] that is Supreme Being beyond and in bodies as Controller and Director. It is *Kāla* the force which urges on all things and is viewed as Time,[18] "Fire" (*Agni*) (which is the builder of forms);[19] exhibited in matter,[20] though itself beyond matter.[21] Eternal Life is

---

[1] Bṛhadāraṇyaka-Up., 4—1—3.

[2] Kauṣītakī-Up., 2—2. Here Prāṇa is indicative (Lakṣaṇārtha) only. As the Parabrahmasvarūpa or transcendental Brahman *It* is beyond Prāṇa. Cf. "Thou art He who is other than Prāṇa and the Devatās and Who art both." Kauṣītakī-Up., 1—6.

[3] Kauṣītakī-Up., 3—2 (He who is Prajñātmā).

[4] *Ib.* Cf. "They get life (Āyuh) who worship Brahman as Prāṇa." Taittirīya-Up., 2—3—1. Prāṇa is the third Pāda of the Gāyatrī, Taitt. 1—5—3.

[5] "I do Tarpaṇa of Āyuh with Āyuh." Śiro-Up., 1.

[6] Prāṇah prāṇāya dadāti, Cha.-Up., 7—15.

[7] Sa u prāṇasya-prāṇah. Kena.Up.,2.

[8] One of the recensions of the Bṛhad.-Up.

[9] Cited in Comm. to v. 1 Kāmakalā-vilāsa.

[10] Jagadātmatvāt

[11] Cited by Natanānanda-nātha in Comm. to v. 12 of Kāmakalā-vilāsa.

[12] Prāṇena abhiprāṇitah. Āit.-Up., 3—11.

[13] Mukhyah Prāṇah. Cha.-Up., 1—2—3—; 1—5—3—. Prāṇa is the fourth Pāda of Brahman. Cha.-Up., 3—18—4.

[14] Cha.-Up., 1—11—5. Prāṇa is Ra because in Prāṇa all beings enjoy (Ramante) Bṛ.-Up., 5—12—1.

[15] Prāṇo vā amṛtam. Br. Up., 1—6—3.

[16] Prāṇo' sau lokah. Br.-Up., 1—5—4.

[17] Maitri-Up., 6—9, 6—1, 6—8 and 7—7.

[18] Maitri-Up., 4—5.

[19] *Ibid.*, 6—9. It (as Brahman) is Tejomaya. Br.-Up., 2—5—4.

[20] *Ibid.*, 6—11.

[21] It is Amṛtamaya. Br.-Up., 2—5—4 and Adhyātma, that is above Daiva and Bhūta. Prāṇo vā amṛtam. Br.-Up., 1—6—3.

the persistent and true[1] which is enshrined by all name and form.[2] It is formless.[3] All have form but It.[4] The Supreme Brahman is formless, and so also is the organising principle of bodies, though it takes on the forms of the matter in which it is immersed.[5]

Life then, in its causal sense, is a name for the Supreme Power (*Śakti*) in its aspect as the originator of individual lives. That Power is in itself Consciousness (*Cit*). This consciousness is immersed in matter and is there veiled and appears as the director, guide, regulator, and controller of its material energies.

It is not "material" in the English sense, that is, it is not matter. On the contrary, Life or *Prāṅa* is said to be so called "because it leads and guides (*Prańayanāt*) and moves about."[6] Leads and guides what? The answer is Matter; for this which is the last product of the involution of Consciousness cannot, as such, guide and direct itself. The Vedānta clearly distinguishes, in its doctrine of the sheaths (*Kośas*) of the Spirit, Matter which is the outermost and most gross sheath, from the vital body which is the next inner and more subtle sheath, within which again are the sheaths of lower and higher mind and within the last the Self. The gross body is the sheath of matter or food,[7] and within it is, the vital or Prāṇic sheath[8] which, with Mind, are the subtle body of the Self. This latter is Consciousness, and Mind, Life, and Body are forms of its Power (*Śakti*).

If it be remembered that all is in essence Consciousness, veiled in varying degree by its Power as Mind and Matter, the nature of Life will be clearly understood. In the higher mind[9] functioning as Reason, Judgment and so forth, Consciousness is least veiled and most aware of itself. The lower mind[10] which attends, directs and synthetises the functioning of the senses is more veiled. Animal instinct again is a veiled form of consciousness. Another form of the mental principle is *Prāṇa* or Life. Though not specifically called mind, it is nevertheless that aspect of mind which is wholly immersed in matter as the directing consciousness of the

[1] Prāṇā vai satyaṃ. Br.-Up., 2—1—20. [2] *Ib.*, 1—6—3.

[3] Atha amūrtaṃ prāṇah. Br.-Up., 2—3—5.

[4] *Ibid.*, 2—3—4. Idaṃ eva mūrtaṃ yad anyat Prāṇāt.

[5] Vāyu, by which name Prāṇa is metaphorically called (in so far as Vāyu is a form of gross material Energy which Prāṇa is not) belongs to the formless (Amūrta) division of the Bhūtas (sensible matter).

[6] Praṇayanāt prakramaṇāt prāṇa iti abhigīyate. (Prakṛti-vāda Dict.) The first word may also mean because it builds up (matter) which is also a function of Life.

[7] Annamaya-Kośa. [8] Prāṇamaya-Kośa. [9] Vijñānamaya-Kośa.

[10] Manas of the Manomaya-Kośa.

material energies of the body. For to limit, regulate, control in whatsoever way is the function of the mental principle, and that which is the patient of such operation is Matter. Consciousness is present and at work in all matter, whether we call it living or not living; but when it directs the material energies in such a way as to build up and sustain breathing creatures (*Prāṇī*) it is called *Prāṇa* or the Vital Principle or Force. And so the Maitri-Upaniṣad[1] sums up these relations in the statement that the Life-Principle is the essence of Matter (and of food, which is matter which sustains life), the Lower Mind is the essence of the Life Principle, the Higher Mind is the essence of the Lower mind, whilst the Self in its body of Bliss is the essence of the Higher Mind.[2]

The Vital Principle manifests itself in various functions. All movement in matter may be reduced to the centripetal and centrifugal, attraction and repulsion, which are psychically, like (*Rāga*) and dislike (*Dveṣa*) and physically cohesion and affinity on the one hand, and their opposites on the other. Cohesion which links together the elements of bodies manifests in the mutual actions of the molecules. Affinity operates between particles of different bodies determining the majority of chemical reactions. Gravitation is an immense form of attraction and volcanic action is a repulsion on a large scale. In osmotic phenomena,[3] molecular attraction and repulsion are most clearly shown, there being produced two currents in a converse direction called exosmose and endosmose. These simple molecular attractions and repulsions, acting in the bosom of liquids, govern a great number of vital phenomena and are, it has been said, perhaps one of the most important causes of the formation of living beings. All such attractions and repulsions can act only at a certain distance. The term "Field of Force" is given to the space in which they are exercised and that of "Lines of Force" to the directions in which are produced the attacting and repelling effects.

*Prāṇa*, as a general term for Life, manifests in various ways and is thus given various names according to the functions.[4] *Prāṇa* is also the name of the chief of these functions. *Prāṇa* in the latter sense is the specific vital function which is *appropriation* or *injection*. It is the vital representative

[1] Maitrī-Up., 6—13.

[2] Prāṇo vā annasya raso, manah prāṇasya, vijñānaṃ manasah, ānandaṃ vijñānasya.

[3] All substances which possess the property of dissolving in a liquid attract the solvent and are conversely attracted by it.

[4] The chief of these are five and so in Prāṇāgnihotra Up., 2. Prāṇa=Agni= Paramātmā surrounded by the five Vāyus—Prāṇa, Apāna, Samāna, Vyāna, Udāna.

of the *centripetal* movement of matter and of the psychical principle which is Like or Attraction or *Rāga*. Leading instances of appropriation or injection are inspiration,[1] swallowing food or drink, absorption by the skin, either naturally, or in the case of medication, by skin absorption. On the macrocosmic scale *Prāṇa* is gravity. Commonly *Prāṇa-vāyu*[2] is said to include the outgoing breath.[3] But treating *Prāṇa-vāyu* as appropriation and injection, it would seem properly to come under the next head or *Apānā*.

The latter is the specific vital function which is *ejection*, the vital representative of *centrifugal* movement in matter and of the psychical principle which is *Dveṣa*, or repulsion and dislike. The organism appropriates and injects what it likes and wants and by ejection or excretion gets rid of what is not needed. It is instanced by all forms of elimination, and expulsion such as defecation, urination, sweating, nasal and aural excretion, semination, parturition. Thus in the last case the seed is received in the womb by *Prāṇa-vāyu* and is expelled as the child by *Apāna-vāyu*. On the macrocosmic scale we see it in operation in volcanic eruptions and oozing of moisture from the rocks and the like. It would be possible to resolve all vital functions into these two—*Prāṇa* and *Apāna*, but with greater particularity, vital functions are classified under three additional classes.

The third *Vayu* is *Samāna*, the function of which is *assimilation*. By this food is selected and rejected, broken up, metamorphosed in digestion and then assimilated.

*Vyāna* is in general terms the function of *distribution*. What has been appropriated by *Prāṇa* and is not subject of ejection by *Apāna*; what has been assimilated by *Samāna*, is distributed by *Vyana*. It includes conveyance of fluid blood produced from digested food, as also bodily movements as a whole, such as jumping, throwing and any function not included in the foregoing or the next.

*Udāna-vāyu* is concerned in the exhibition of *voice-function*, utterance as talking, singing, shouting, utilising for this purpose the air inhaled by *Prāṇa*.[4] It is to be here observed that the physical air inbreathed is not

---

[1] Śvāsa. See Bṛhad.-Up., 1—3—7; 5—14—3.

[2] Vāyu which comes from the root Vā = to move is here moving vital force in the form of Prāṇa. So also with Apāna-vāyu and the rest.

[3] Naiśvāsa, as in Yājñavalkya where Prāṇa is described as Śvāsa-niśvāsa-rūpa.

[4] See generally Caraka (Śārīraka-sthāna, 1—3). Suśruta, Cakradatta, Śva-saṃhitā, Jñāna-saṃkalinī-Tantra and Gaurīkānjalikā-Tantra, Shāradā-Tilaka with Rāghava-Bhatta's Comm., 1—45.

*Prāṇa* nor is the breath expired *Prāṇa.* Prāṇa-vāyu is the vital function by which the air is indrawn.

Five subsidiary Vāyus are also enumerated, concerned in the functions of belching, eyelid movement, hungering and thirsting, yawning and hiccup,[1] the last of which is a tonic contraction or spasm whieh takes place if there is no corresponding expansion and may perhaps be also identified with the *rigor mortis.*[2]

Besides these gross Vāyus there are others, Yoga-Śāstra speaking of forty-nine.

The term Prāṇa is used also in a general way as being speech;[3] vitality in the limbs,[4] offspring,[5] the principle of movement,[6] food,[7] and the Sun which is the material source of all earthly life.[8]

The above-mentioned special vital functions have each a centre of operation which centres are commonly said to be, as regards the first five principal *Vāyus*, in the throat (*Udāna*), heart (*Prāṇa*), navel (*Samāna*), anus (*Apāna*) and the whole body (*Vyāna*). It is however a mistake to identify the seats of these vital forces with these gross physical bodily regions. What is thereby indicated are the five subtle centres or Cakras in the spinal column called Viśuddha, Anāhata, Maṇipūra, Svādhiṣṭhāna and Mūlādhāra of which the Tattvas are "Ether", "Air" "Fire," "Water" and "Earth," respectively these being names for various motions and densities of matter.[9] Thus, in utterance, the physical throat is involved but the subtle vital centre is in the spine. The physical heart is merely a pumping machine, not directly concerned in breathing, though energy expanded in utterance may affect the cardiac movements. The navel has nothing to do with assimilation, the centre of which is at that portion of the spine which passes through the navel region. *Apāna* is not in the

---

[1] Nāga, Kūrma, Kṛkara, Devadatta, Dhanaṃjaya. To these some add others.

[2] It is said not to leave the body even after death. On this account apparently it is called Laukika Vāyu (Rāghava-Bhatta, Comm. on Śāradā, 1—15) as it remains in the body when all the other vital forces have abandoned it.

[3] Br.-Up., 1—3—27. [4] *Ib.*, 1—3—19. [5] *Ib.*, 1—4—17.

[6] Vāyu, as in Bṛhad.-Up., 1—1—1. Vātah prāṇah; where it is said to be the third part of Puruṣa, the other two being Fire (*Agni*) and Water (*Jala*), these three being the Doṣas of the body in the Vaidya-Śāstra. See also Muṇḍaka Up., 1—2—4, Mahā-nārāyaṇa Up., 14—1.

[7] Maitrī Up., 6—13. By food Prāṇa and by Prāṇa strength; by the Prāṇas Manas: Mahā-nārāyaṇa-Up., 23—1. Anna is both food and matter.

[8] Āditya is Prāṇa. Praśna-Up., 1—5; it is the outer Prāṇa (Bahih prāṇa, *Ib.*, 3—8).

[9] See *The Serpent Power.* These are the five physical centres. We are not here concerned with the sixth or mental Ajñā cakra. The words "ether" "air" are not to be understood in the English sense of the terms. See *Op. cit.*

physical anus but in the Svādhiṣṭhāna-Cakra in the lower part of the spinal column. *Vyāna* is said to be "in the whole body" in the sense that its operation is over the whole body, from its seat in the lowest spinal centre, the Mūlādhāra. The production of the *Jiva* is from this centre, though the process of reproduction namely semination is from the urethra governed by the Svādhiṣṭhāna tract.[1]

The Tantras, on the Yoga side, give the colours of the several vital forces observable by Yogic vision.[2] These colours are (following the order of the *Prāṇa-vāyus* given) emerald (Prāṇa), red like evening sun (*Apāna*), milky (*Samāna*), white like Dhaturā flower (*Vyāna*), colour of fire and lightning (*Udānā*).[3]

It has been observed that the Yoga-Śāstra speaks of forty-nine *Vāyus*. The Six Cakras are seats of the Letters and Tattvas or Principles of Mind and Matter. The sixth is the subtle psychic centre, and the remaining are subtle centres of physical function. It is clear that the first is more subtle than the remaining five. It is also clear that these five are less and less subtle between themselves as descent is made from the fifth to the first centre or Cakra, for they are the seats of Ākāśa, Vāyu, Agni, Ap and Pṛthivī, the five forms of movement which go to make up sensible matter perceived by the five senses. Each of these is more material or gross than that which preceded it. This greater materialisation as we descend is due to the increase of Tamas or Mass. The pulse of movement slows with each increase of Mass and thus the highest number of vibrations is in the highest centre and these gradually decrease until the last or "Earth" centre is reached. In each of these centres there are certain letters, 50 in number if we include Kṣa, in the Ājñā or psychical centre, or 49 if we exclude Kṣa as being a letter compounded of two other letters (Ka and Ṣa) appearing in the subsequent series. The letters are themselves each forms of movement of varying intensity or rate of vibration of which we become sensible by reason of the *Dhvani* or Sound which is their revealer. Thus *Dhvani* is not the letter but its revealer[4] and is caused by the contact

[1] As regards the minor Vāyus, Nāga, Kūrma, Kṛkara, Devadatta, Dhanaṃjaya, their places are given in Rāghava-bhatta, Comm. to vv. 44, 45 of Ch. 1 Śāradā tilaka.

[2] Yoga-dṛṣti. Prāṇa-Tattva is in Vedānta derived collectively from the Rajas or activity aspect of the Tanmātras or infra-sensible "matter" one of such Tanmātras being colour and form. All Tanmātras except the first two are with form (Mūrta). Prāṇa is a form of Kryā-Śakti.

[3] The colours of the subsidiary Vāyus are dark cloud (Nāga), collyrium black (Kūrma), scarlet like the China rose (Kṛkara) white like crystal (Devadatta), white like Dhatūra flower (Dhanaṃjaya).

[4] See *The Garland of Letters*.

of the vocal organs and the surrounding air producing soundwaves in it. The letter (*Varṇa*) itself is eternal[1] movement, which is known as "the sound which is not produced by the striking of things together" (*Anāhata-Śabda*), and which is revealed as gross sound to the gross ear through *Dhvani.* The vibrations of the letters are the same as those of the *Tattva* of the centre in which they are—in fact the letter is the movement of the Tattva manifested to the Ear as Letter (*Varṇa*). For this reason, when on a proper[2] initiation, a Mantra is given, if the disciple is on examination, found to be constituted in such a way that any Tattva is in excess or deficient, then the Mantra of that Tattva is given to him with the instruction to repeat it, if in excess with the outbreathing (*Ucchvāsa*), when so much of the *Tattva* is ejected or if in deficiency with the inbreathing (*Śvāsa*), when so much of the *Tattva* is injected, a practice which proceeds on the lines that the Tattva and its Mantra are one and the same.[3] The object is to obtain an equipoise, as near as may be, of the Tattvas which are variously predominant in various bodies. At the same time *Prāṇāyāma* regulates the psychic movements (*Vṛtti*), for breathing and thinking-movements synchronise. The letters are distributed as follows, 2 (consonants), 16 (vowels), 12, 10, 6, 4 consonants in each of the Cakras respectively. After the first psychic centre the order of the five Prāṇas, relative to the Cakras, are, as stated, *Udāna* in the second, *Prāṇa* in the third, *Samāna* in the fourth, *Apāna* in the fifth, and *Vyāna* in the lowest or sixth. From this it follows that *Vyāna* should be (as is in fact the case) the grossest of the five *Vāyus*, and Udāna which is called the Supreme *Vāyu* is the most subtle, after of course the vibrations of the psychic centre which are more subtle than any of the vibrations and movements of physical functions. That these centres govern and regulate the vital functions assigned to them is obvious from the scheme. A matter however which requires enquiry is the answer to the query what is the significance of the number of the letters in each Cakra relative to the vital function governed by it. It will be observed that starting from the last Cakra the number of letters increases 2, 4, 2, 4. To perfect the above

[1] In this and other similar cases "eternal" means during the life period of each cosmic system; these being infinite it is eternal, though appearing and disappearing with the dissolution of the particular system. The true Eternal or Brahman does not appear and disappear.

[2] Apparently many, if not most, initiations mean nothing nowadays, owing to the ignorance and apathy of both Guru and disciple.

[3] The Bīja-Mantra ends with the Anuśvara breathing or the letter Ma (M) as in this the "Sun" of letters, the Tattvas or Principles, are considered to be in equipoise.

scheme it would apparently have to be shown that *Vyāna* had four forms of movement, manifested collectively or separately, in the functions assigned to it; *Āpāna* had six and so on. There are thus 49 forms of vibration in which Vital Force exhibits itself and the Letters are Life-forces revealed to us by gross sound. In short the "Garland of Letters" represents all the Forces which go to the making of the universe made known to us as *Dhvani*, just as they are manifest to us in other ways through other senses. The above account will also explain why there can be such a thing as medical and spiritual treatment, by sound and Mantra. We treat disease by touch, as in massage, and medication through the skin; through the eye by colour,[1] by the tongue through medicine placed on it and gross drugging; by the nose through chloroform inhalation and olfaction generally. The influence of harmonious sound as Music is invariably acknowledged. In the Yoga-Śāstra lettered sound is operative also, since it stands for a movement which exists also in the constitution of the person sought to be affected thereby. *Ākāsa* is operative in Māntric treatment, *Vāyu* in electric treatment, *Tejas* in that by radium heat and light, *Ap* in Hydropathy, and *Pṛthivī* in drugging with solids and liquids. This last is the grossest form of medical treatment. How gross and unnatural then is the modern treatment (if it be in fact such) by injection into the body of vaccines, serum, colloid preparations and the like?

The appended diagram will more clearly explain the matters described in the Text. The spiraline coil which gradually contracts, as matter becomes more and more gross, is Kuṇḍalinī-Śaktī.

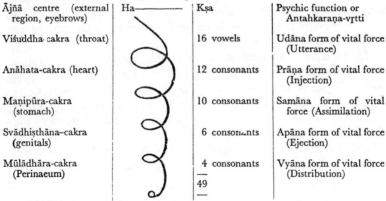

| | | | |
|---|---|---|---|
| Ājñā centre (external region, eyebrows) | Ha—— | Kṣa | Psychic function or Antahkaraṇa-vṛtti |
| Viśuddha cakra (throat) | | 16 vowels | Udāna form of vital force (Utterance) |
| Anāhata-cakra (heart) | | 12 consonants | Prāṇa form of vital force (Injection) |
| Maṇipūra-cakra (stomach) | | 10 consonants | Samāna form of vital force (Assimilation) |
| Svādhiṣthāna–cakra (genitals) | | 6 consonants | Apāna form of vital force (Ejection) |
| Mūlādhāra-cakra (Perinaeum) | | 4 consonants<br>—<br>49<br>— | Vyāna form of vital force (Distribution) |

[1] The colour treatment has been tried for several diseases and the effect of various colours on the mind is well-known.

The Āyurveda and other medical Śāstras treat of three Forces in the organism called Vāta or Vāyu, Pitta, Kapha, usually translated as "Air," "Bile" and "Phlegm" over which some merriment is made, as over so many other things by the non-understanding. The gross or physical body is composed of five forces and the forms of material substance which they constitute. The first of these five is Ākāśa or Ether, though the former term is not to be altogether identified as is sometimes done with the Western physical Ether. For the moment[1] it may be defined as the continuum in which the plurality of individual centres move. The last is Pṛthivī which is literally translated "Earth" but really means any matter in solid state. Āyurveda does not deal in this connection with Ether but with the centres which are interpenetrated by it, nor does it deal separately with Pṛthivī because, for its practical purposes, it regards both liquids and solids as solids. The remaining three are first Vāyu which is translated "Air". Many are under the error of supposing that the air we breathe is Vāyu. Air is composed of oxygen, nitrogen, carbon dioxide, vapour and various other things. It is not a gas or a chemical compound, but a mechanical combination of various gases and floating matter in mechanical combination. It cannot be accurately defined, for the nature of air, in this sense, varies at different places. It is not the same in a town as in the country, nor in the country as at the seaside, nor in a valley as on a mountain height. Vāyu is not air but the *menstruum* in which air, the mechanical combination, exists and by which it is held together. Vāyu comes from the root *Vā* which means "to move" and is, in its primary sense, motivity. Possibly as a substance constituted by such motivity it may be electric fluid just as Ākāśa or Vyoma may in the gross plane be ethereal fluid.

In the body it is exhibited as nerve force and as also any kind of electro-motor or molecular force and is in fact the power whereby the other principles of the body move. For without it they are said to be "cripples". In short it is as Suśruta says the force which sets the whole organism in motion.[2] It is the principal factor which determines the genesis, continuance and disintegration of the living body. This Vāyu is classified according to its function as Prāṇa, Apāna and the rest above described with five subdivisions of each. The other two principles are

---

[1] I deal with this subject in "Power as Matter" (Bhūta-Śakti).

[2] See Introduction by A. Avalon to Prapañcasāra-Tantra, Vol. 3. Tantrik Texts and the English translation of Suśruta Saṃhitā by Kavirāja Kunjalāla Bhiṣagratna.

Pitta which literally means Bile and Kapha which literally means Phlegm. But these are not either, except under those conditions in which they are transformed into Malās or fit to be ejected; but they are not Bile and Phlegm in those planes of their functions which determine the genesis, growth and continuance of the organism as well as its death, decay, and disintegration.

The function of Pitta or Agni (Fire) is, amongst others, metabolism and the bodily heat which is the product of the latter. One of its important functions is digestion, metaplasia, and assimilation. There are said to be 5 chief "Fires"[1] in the body each again of four subdivisions[2] as in the case of the next Principle or Śleṣmā. Kapha or Śleṣmā which is similarly divided is Apa, that is, the moisture principle. The watery principle keeps in check the last. The equipoise of these principles is essential to health. If Heat (Pitta) predominates the body dries up, if Moisture (Kapha) predominates heat is extinguished and if Motivity predominates there is irregularity everywhere. These three principles embrace the whole sphere of organic existence. These three principles are called Doṣas[3] and Duṣya is that which is affected.[4] All Life as movement arises under conditions of heat and moisture which as the manifestation of Divinity are the objects of worship in the Vedas.

There is as yet no general agreement on the fundamental problem of the nature of Instinct. Instinctive behaviour has been defined by Dr. Lloyd Morgan as that which is, on its first occurrence, independent of prior experience, which tends to the well-being of the individual and preservation of the race, and which is similarly performed by all the members of the same group of animals, and which may be subject to modification under the guidance of experience. Instinct is also not uncommonly described as race-habit. Instinct is an organised expression of what goes on in the unconscious. It is, however, now thought that animals are not altogether perfect in theii instinctive functioning. Instinct is a Saṃskāra or tendency and aptitude manifesting as vital Power in Prāṇa. On its first occurrence in any individual it is independent of prior experience as had in that particular form, but it does not actually then

---

[1] See *Ibid.*

[2] Thus Pācaka Pitta which is digestive heat is divided into one digestive fire of the mouth, two digestive fires in the stomach namely peptic and hydrochloric acid and two in the intestines namely Pancreatic and Bile secretions.

[3] Literally Faults because of the diseases to which their disharmony leads.

[4] See Prapañcasāra 15, namely, the Dhātus or substances, skin, blood, fat, etc.

commence but is a tendency, now latent now patent, in the whole series of evolution to which the individual displaying instinct belongs. The behaviour of inorganic matter is apparently fixed and calculable and seems mechanical. This fixedness of behaviour though less rigid appears in living substance as instinct. But not only is there a relatively greater freedom but the instinct may become modified and from out of this basis of instinctive action, self-consciousness and self-directed movement arise.

Heat, light and moisture are the generating conditions of all life evolved by the life-giving principle. It is heat and moisture diffused throughout nature which fosters life in all its forms. This Heat and Moisture, like all else, exist in gross, subtle and causal forms. Agni, Varuṇa and Soma are with others, names of the One—"That which is one wise call it by various names."[1] When then it is said in Veda[2] that in the beginning there was the Causal Water in which the One developed by the power of, or out of, Tapas and Desire[3] reference is not made to material Heat but to that intensive creative brooding thought and will which projects the universe, in which one of its gross transformations is material Heat in many forms, some subtle, some gross. Fire is seen in the heavenly bodies, flaming masses of molten viscous or earthy matter, in lightning which liberates a kind of light and heat[4] latent in the aqueous particles and vapours[5] just as the ordinary domestic and sacrificial fire[6] liberates it from wood or fuel.[6] Fire is stored up in the igneous rocks and exists as the various stores of animal heat. There are thus said to be ten Agnis or fires in the body.[7] In short heat, light, moisture as everything else which is manifested are various modes of the motion or activity of the supreme source of all such activities or Power. For the Vedāntists resolve all activity, physical, vital, and psychical into modes of subtle cosmic motion. It is not however the heat or moisture which directly and alone generates life. They are merely the conditions under which Supreme Power as Prāṇa-Śakti manifests itself. That Supreme Power is manifested.

[1] Ṛg-Veda, I. 64.
[2] X. 129.
[3] Kāma that is Ichchā or creative will.
[4] Tejas.
[5] Agni is "Son of the Water". The lightning flashes from the celestial cloud-ocean.
[6] The flame of burning wood (Indhana) is not pure Tejas for there is chemical union with earth-particles acted on by energy when the light and heat particles latent therein come forth as flame. It is not that the fire which is seen is there unseen but the potential energy which, given the necessary conditions, manifests as the seen fire.
[7] Three are immanent in the Doṣas and seven in the Duṣyas (see Introd. Prapañcasāra-Tantra, Vol. III, Tantrik Texts Ed., by A. Avalon). Pitta is fivefold, *viz.* Pācaka, Rañjaka, Sādhaka, Alocaka, Bhrājaka as also Kapha, *viz.*, Śleṣmaka, Kledaka, Bodhaka, Tarpaka, Avalaṃbaka.

Whilst all manifestation is movement, whilst all manifestation is a transformation of one and the same material Cause, yet differing names are given to the differing manifested forms. These denote the functioning or Power. It is that Power which manifests as both organised and unorganised matter but the organisation of it is not by matter but by and as the Power Itself in Its aspect as the organiser of matter, to be the receptacle of all the grades of life. What then are these grades?

Given the fact that all beings and things have their origin in one and the same material cause of which they are transformations, it necessarily follows that all things are essentially and ultimately one. They are one as to the general Energy-Substance (*Śakti*) of which they are manifestations, which Energy-Substance is active to reveal the static Reality as Mind or to obscure it as Matter. But this Energy or Power has various modes. These are the varied forms of it, displaying the generic and specific qualities of things. The qualities of things are modes of Power (*Śakti*) acting in these collocations. These forms appear according to an order or law of succession under conditions of causality, space, time and mode and hence in the world all effects do not manifest themselves at once. So-called inorganic matter and organic matter as vegetable or animal organisms[1] however differing as forms are thus essentially and ultimately one—in respect of their Substance-Energy. Metaphysical continuity is indicated in the graded continuity of forms.[2] At each stage of evolution there is a going forth (*Prasara*) of Power (Śakti) which stores up its Energy in some relatively stable form. There is then another push of Power to form a fresh equilibrium. These points of relatively stable equilibrium constitute stages in the evolutionary process. The redistribution of mass and energy which occurs at each of such stages constitutes the various forms of chemical, vegetable and animal species. There is no matterless mind nor mindless matter. The question is whether (the Cause, being transformed into inorganic matter), the power to organise the latter so as to display the phenomena of life comes directly from the

[1] Organic compounds are either vegetable (Sthāvara or Acara-Bhūta or immovables) or animal (Asthāvara or Cara or Jangama Bhūta). Both are compounded of the five forms of sensible matter (Bhūta) in greater or less proportions.

[2] See Seal *Op. cit.*, 17, 55, on the Sāṃkhya, citing Pātañjala-Sūtras and Vyāsa-Bhāṣya. So it is said: Jalabhūmyoh parināmikam rasādivaiśvarūpam sthāvareṣu dṛṣtham. Tathā sthāvarāṇāṃ jagameṣuṅ jaṅgamāṇaṃ sthāvareṣu (the evolved properties of Rasa and the like are seen in immovables that is vegetables. And these properties of immovables or vegetables are seen in animals and these properties of animals are seen in vegetables that is immovables.).

inherent power of the effect as such, or must be attributed to the Cause as a special form of functioning which is Prāṇa or the Life Principle. All change is transformation of Energy due to collocations of the threefold tendencies of the material cause in its varied products. The potential energies of infra-sensible matter[1] are actualised as the five forms of gross sensible matter.[2] The latter is a compound of the former and undergoes a change of state. From the five forms, compound substances are made and so the variety of all substances in the world is produced. These material substances go to the upbuilding of the bodies of all forms of organic life. These show vital phenomena of birth, assimilation of food, growth, death, sentiency, waking and sleep, health, disease, reproduction, response and movement within limits.[3] Plants[4] have a sort of dormant or latent consciousness and are capable of pleasure and pain.[5] Cakrapāṇi in the Bhānumati speaks of such consciousness as being of a stupified sort, that is darkened or comatose;[6] as also Udyāna who speaks of their very dull dormant consciousness.[7] In a well-known passage from the Śāntiparva of the Mahābhārata, it is said that plants have a (rudimentary) sense of hearing, touch, sight, smell and taste.[8] They feel pleasure and pain and when cut down they die. "Therefore (it is said) I see Jīva, that is living organism, in it. There is no unconsciousness there."[9]

The next evolutionary stage (however brought about) is the lowest, lower, and then the higher forms of animal life and lastly man. The differences between plant and animal life have always been regarded by the Hindus as being one not of kind but degree.

Moisture and Heat are essential factors in the generation of all animated matter which is divided into four chief divisions of which the plant life is the first and lowest. It is born through moisture and heat[10]

[1] Tanmātra. [2] Bhūta.

[3] Seal, 169 where some authorities are given.

[4] See as to Hindu ideas concerning plants and plant life, Seal *Op. cit.*, 169.

[5] *Ib.* Antah-saṁjñā bhavantyete sukhaduhkha-samanvitāh (these have inner consciousness consisting of pleasure and pain).

[6] Vṛkṣāstu cetanāvanto'pi tamaścannajnā-natayā śāstropadeśaviṣayā eva. (Trees though possessed of consciousness by reason of their consciousness being overspread by Tamas are esteemed objects according to Śāstric teaching).

[7] Atimandāntahsaṃjñitayā iti (because vested with a low degree of inner consciousness).

[8] The illustrations given are:

It is affected by thunder; it dries up under the touch of heat; the creeper finds its way and is therefore not eyeless; it drinks through its root and knows whether water is healthy and has therefore taste. Various odours free it from disease so that it bears flowers and so it has sense of smell.

[9] Jīvaṃ paśyāmi acaitanyaṃ na vidyate.

[10] Svedaja or Uṣmaja. "Heat" not "sweat" as some absurdly translate it.

and is called Udbhijja that is that which "pierces up" from the ground such as grasses, creepers and other plant forms. These spring from seeds. Life-potentiality is not merely contained in the seed but in the seed and environing conditions. The animal seed is developed in the egg or in the case of viviparous animals the mother's body. The mother's body, in the case of the plant-seed, is the earth, subject to the play of air, warmth and moisture.[1]

The next class is called Svedaja or Uṣmaja, moisture or heat-born. These conditions are common to plant life and the following forms of animal life. It was supposed by some of the ancients both in the East and West that there was a sort of spontaneous generation of the lowest forms of life from moist and heated inorganic matter such as rotten wood and excreta. Not improbably the reason for this was the minute character of the seed or germ and lack of knowledge as regards generation by fissure or gemmation. The opinion however was also held that Svedaja animal must be included there under the oviparous or plant-seed class; the idea being that though vegetable organisms may pass off into animal there cannot be generation without seed,[2] or ovum, and inorganic matter without either of these cannot give rise to animated matter in any form.[3]

The next division was the Aṇḍaja or oviparous animals and the highest and last the Jarāyuja, the viviparous or placental. An ancient author's[4] classification is based on the number of senses possessed by animals, such number determining its place in the series. As none of the senses are wholly absent in any form of living matter, probably only well-developed and active senses were alone intended: rudimentary or dormant senses being not reckoned. This classification has the advantage of distinguishing man from other mammalia which like him are viviparous by the former's possession of five well-developed and active senses and all the mental operations based thereon.

The constituents of the physical body are called Dhātu, of which there are seven, namely, Chyle (Rasa) derived from food, Blood (Rakta)

[1] Rāghava-Bhatta (Comm. on Śāradā-Tilaka, 1.27) says that when the earth is thus prepared it gets the state of "seedness" (Bījatva). The seed is planted and watered and then the seed attains the root-stage (Mūlabhāva) and then sprouts and continues to grow.

[2] Bīja.

[3] Seal *Op. cit.*, 181, citing Cāndogya-Upaniṣad, Prapāṭhaka 6, Part 3 and Saṃkara, Comm. on same, where the classification of animals is on this basis of their Bīja, that is seed or ovum.

[4] Umasvati, the author of the Jaina work Tattvārthādhigama. Seal *Op. cit.*, 188.

derived from chyle, Flesh (Māṃsa) derived from blood, Fat (Meda) derived from flesh, Bone (Asthi) derived from fat, Marrow (Majjā) derived from bone, Seed (Śukra) derived from marrow.[1] The seed of woman is called Stri-śukra and sometimes Śoṇita—which in this connection does not mean menstrual blood which is Ārtava. All this development takes place by metaplasm or conversion of one tissue into another. By heat the Chyle becomes Blood which is built up into Flesh, and also by a reverse process it becomes Fat with its interstices in which, by deposit of calcium salt, the bone is formed. Marrow is formed by the tunnelling of the bones of the tissue of which it is the essence. Semen (Śukra) is the essence again of marrow and the most elaborated of the Dhātus, which exists not merely in the testicles but is spread in subtle form throughout the whole body in the subtile channels known as the Śurkravāhinī-Nādīs, and is worked up into the gross form in which it is ejected in the genital organs.[2] The tissues of the developed seed in the male (Śukra) and female (Strīśukra) generate the child. Ojah is not one of the seven Dhātus but a substance which may be said to be the essence of all, which gives vitality to all and which "when it dies, man also wishes to die." It gives glow to the body. The Devatās of these seven Dhātus are Dākinī and others situated in the seven Cakras or centres.[3]

Three principles are at work in the body namely Pitta, Kapha, Vāta, the rendering of which as "Bile," "Phlegm" and "Air" gives no idea of their meaning. They represent the principles of Heat (Tejas), Moisture (Ap) and Activity (Vāta or Vāyu) respectively. The first two, when in excess manifest abnormal states of Bile and Phlegm which are excretions (Malā) of substance of which the body is ridding itself.

These three are called Doṣas. Vāta is classified into Prāna, Apāna and so forth above mentioned. All metabolic processes are called Pitta which has also five subdivisions according to functions and locations.

---

[1] In some cases Tvak (Skin), Roma (Hair), are stated in lieu of, or in addition to, those above stated. Thus Bhāskararāya in his commentary on the seventh Ṛk of Bhāvanopaniṣad speaks of nine Dhātus, *viz.*, those given in the Text and Roma and Tvak.

[2] The extraordinary use to which some so-called "Tāntriks" put semen is founded on the theory that it is Soma which gives deathlessness in the physical body.

[3] Dākinī, Rākinī, Lākinī, Kākinī, Sākinī, Hākinī, Yākinī, which according to the Mahāyoginī-Nyāsa in the Saubhāgya-ratnākara are protective Devatās over skin, blood, flesh, fat, bone, marrow, seed, and all other Dhātus respectively situate in the Viśuddha, Anāhata, Maṇipūra, Svādhiṣṭhāna, Mūlādhāra, Ājñā, Shaasrāra respectively.

In the Ṣatcakra-nirūpaṇa (*Serpent Power*) Dākinī, Rākinī, Kākinī, Ṣākini are in Mūlādhāra, Svādhiṣthāna, Anāhata, Viśuddha respectively, the other three being the same.

Kapha or Śleṣmā is also of five kinds, the functions of which are to supply to the body its watery element. Vāyu, Pitta and Kapha are thus fundamental principles of the human economy when, in virtue of their correlative and sustentative functions, they ensure an equipoise among the different vital physiological processes essential to its health; for disease is a lack of harmony and of completeness. Hence the word "hale" which means "whole". When the equilibrium is disturbed, pathological conditions arise which form the *esse* of disease and then they are said to be transformed into Doṣas or morbific diatheses. As excretions of Apāna Vāyu they are called Malās. Thus Vāyu, Pitta, Kapha are not "Air," "Bile," and "Phlegm" except under those circumstances in which they are transformed into Malās. They embrace both the biological and pathological principles of the organisms.[1]

The whole body is intersected by channels or Nādis which are both gross and visible as nerves and arteries, and also subtile and invisible to ordinary, but visible to yogic, vision. The "Eye of Food" is not the only one. Thus recent mention has been made[2] of the extra-ordinary capacity of a man to discern through the clothed body the existence of morbific growths in it. This is only an instance of the Siddhi of clairvoyance which it is claimed laid bare to the Yogīs the numerous subtile channels though which the bodily Energy-Substance functions.[3]

In the highest, man—evolution on the material plane ends. Evolution takes place through the Power of God which as material cause is always transforming Itself into higher forms in order that Spirit may be freed of the bonds of Mind and Matter in which It has involved Itself. This is the Eternal Rhythm of the Divine Mother as Substance-Energy. He who "sees," that is, creates Otherness, resolves it into Herself again. That is His "Play" (Līlā). Those who enter into the spirit of it and follow its laws gather the fruits of the world. It is given to man alone to recognise the Player, to unite himself with Her and thus to free himself from the fields of play which are the eternally recurrent universes. The Devotee (Bhakta) of the Mother as She is in Herself—seeks not Her limited forms, but Her own unbounded Self. It is not life in forms that he wants, though he knows them to be the Mother-Power, but the Life of all Lives which is

---

[1] See my Introduction to Prapañcasāra-Tantra, Vol. 3. Tāntrik Texts and the Suśruta-Saṃhitā (English Trans.) Edited by Kavirāja Kunjalāla Bhiṣagratna. Like the old Western systems the Indian is a kind of "humoral" system.

[2] By Sir Conan Doyle in his "Wanderings of a Spiritualist", p. 137.

[3] See as to these Yoga-Nādī, *The Serpent Power.*

Her own Brahman-self. But there is also another form of Devotion, that is Devotion to Her as Form, as universe. Here too *Siddhi* of the so-called "lower form" is obtained when the form is recognised as Her form. For that recognition is itself strengthening of individual power. In Karma-yoga without attachment both ends and aims are served.

APPENDIX

# LIFE AND THE FIRST PRINCIPLES

BY PROFESSOR PRAMATHANĀTHA MUKHYOPĀDHYĀYA

LIKE many other terms such as 'Ākāśa', 'Jyotih, etc., the term 'Prāṇa' is used in the Śruti to connote, in the ultimate sense, Brahman. The Vedānta discussing certain texts (see Vedānta, I 1. 23, I 1.28, etc.) from the Cāndogya and Kauṣītaki-brāhmaṇa attempts to establish this.

In fact, any Principle which exists and acts as adhiṣṭhāna (ground) in relation to any bhūtas (created things) is a manifestation of Brahman.

Because the ground or Adhiṣṭhāna is everywhere Brahman; the part is always grounded in the whole (Pūrṇa), the particulars in the general.

If, for example, X exists as the ground of the things A,B,C, then X, in so far as it is the ground, is a manifestation of Brahman which is the Ground Principle.

Now, Prāṇa even in the ordinary sense is the ground of the Indriyas. The Indriyas work so long as the Prāṇa is there in the body; they cease to exist when Prāṇa leaves the body. In *Suṣupti* again, the sense-capacities are absorbed in the Prāṇa; in Jāgrat they reappear out of it again. "Yadā vai puruṣah svapiti prāṇaṃ tarhi vāgapyeti prāṇaṃ cakṣuh prāṇaṃ manah prāṇaṃ śrotraṃ; sa yadā prabudhyate prāṇādevādhi punarjayant iti."

Hence, Prāṇa as the ground of the senses is a manifesation of the Ground Principle (*i.e.*, Brahman).

But Prāṇa in the ordinary sense is not the ultimate ground—the Pūrṇa itself. So that Brahman is spoken of as "Prāṇasya Prāṇah"—the Life of life.

The matter may be stated otherwise:

The bodily functions including the sense-functions represent a stress-system (or system of acting and reacting forces).

Prāṇa is the root or ground of such functions; because without it they all cease.

Therefore, Prāṇa is the radix of a particular stress-system.

The radix of stress-system considered as a whole is Brahman (as Cit).

Hence, Prāṇa is an aspect or manifestation of the Ultimate Radix (*i.e.*, Brahman).

The question, however, is this:

How does the ultimate Ground Principle become (or appear to become) an individualised or circumscribed Ground Principle? In other words, how does Prāṇasya Prāṇah appear as Prāṇa? If we know the process and its stages, we know the mutual relations of Mind, Life and Matter which are all aspects of the Ultimate Principle.

To understand this, let us begin by analysing our world of experience (*i.e.*, Fact).

World of experience = Cit involving Stress ('Stress' meaning Power to evolve or appear as a varied order of phenomena) = Cit (Sattva, Rajah, Tamah); S,R,T, being the three partials into which stress can be decomposed. Now, what is the nature of Cit considered as Cidākāśa (Ether of Consciousness)?

On reflection on the nature cf this Ether of Consciousness, we find that it possesses three svarūpa lakṣaṇas—*viz.*, unity, wholeness and freedom: It is Eka; It is Pūrṇa; It is Abādhita (*i.e.*, uncircumscribed, unrestricted). The whole Stress-system operates *in* this Ether.

Though the Ether as Cit never really loses Its nature (anyathābhāva), it appears, by reason of the operation of the Stress-system (*i.e.*, S, R, T) in it, to move or change. As for example, the ākāśa which is contained or circumscribed by a jar *seems* to move from one place to another when the jar itself is moved.

Since, however, the Stress-system is really one with the Cit Itself, we may say that the latter has two aspects, *viz.*, static (Śiva) and moving or kinetic (Śakti); that is, Cit is kinetic (Saṃkara, from the transcendental point of view, will say—*seems* to be kinetic) without ever ceasing to be static: Śakti must ever play on the breast of Śiva. The relation stated is alogical. To speak of 'aspects' of what is an indivisible unity is pictorial thinking. We cannot however help this if we must think and speak at all about the unthinkable and unspeakable Fact.

Let us consider the Motion-aspect. How can we state the Movement? Stress is resolved into three factors—S, R and T (Sattva, rajah, tamah). Movement of the Stress-system is its movement between the two limits, *viz.*, S (manifestation) and T (veiling). That is, the Stress-system moves from maximum veiling to maximum manifestation (or minimum veiling), and *vice versa*. Manifestation of what?—Of the Essence.

The movement is rhythmic.

The movement of the world as a whole is rhythmic (alternate sṛṣti and laya); movement is rhythmic in the details also, *e.g.*, heavenly motions, seasons, etc., motions in the living cells and organisms, motions in the atoms, and so on.

To use a physical figure, the movement cannot be represented by a moving simple pendulum; it is rather spiraline, or coiling movement.

Since it is rhythmic also, the Stress-system is alternately coiled and uncoiled.

Movement, therefore, analysed gives us these two elements:

(1) A finitising process; (2) an uncoiling and coiling process (vikāśa and laya). By the former we have in the world an hierarchy of samaṣtis and vyaṣtis (genera and species) having at the one end Iśvara as the *Summum Genus* and at the other the "point charges" or Śakti-bindus which are the *infima species.*

On account of the existence of this hierarchy, we have a double set of world-derivates, *viz.*,—a Samaṣti principle and its vyaṣti mode, *e.g.*, we have both Samaṣti manas and vyaṣti manas; Samaṣti prāṇa and vyaṣti prāṇa. 'Samaṣti' does not mean 'arithmetical sum total'.

The two processes (finitising and coiling-uncoiling) are concurrent.

Now, let us treat the latter process—Evolution-Involution.

Evidently the process is a resultant of two tendencies—*viz.*, association and dissociation. In the case where the former tendency preponderates, we have this fact—*viz.*, a given point, A, more and more recedes from the centre X; this is uncoiling. Where the latter tendency is in excess, we have A more and more nearing X; this is coiling. Where the ratio of attraction to repulsion (Rāga to Dveṣa) is constant, we have simple rotation or revolution of A round X in a fixed orbit. Where the ratio is variable, we must have evidently either the coiling or the uncoiling diagram traced by the moving point. The two tendencies are opposite *saṃskāras*; and their ratio is the *adṛṣṭa* of the given point A in relation to X.

In mathematical analysis we commonly regard the adṛṣṭa of a material body or particle (*e.g.*, the earth or the moon in the solar system; the electrons in the atomic system) as constant, because that assumption simplifies the data of calculation. But really a constant, unchanging adṛṣṭa is an abstraction, not fact. Adṛṣṭa being determined by the relative dispositions of S, R, T, must change, for it is the nature of these latter to always change. Hence, the simple rotatory motion of physics is an abstraction: it is obtained by limitation of the actual data. The earth, for example, is not *exactly* revolving round the sun, but moving in an eddying sort of motion. This eddying (coiling) movement may be clockwise or anti-clockwise. When the former, the earth may be gradually drawn towards the central solar mass, and be ultimately merged in it. That will mean the laya of Pṛthivi (*i.e.*, of the planet). When the latter, the earth may be gradually receding from the solar mass, in which case again, after a certain critical stage has been reached, the earth may be dismembered from the solar system, and drift into space. In both cases we have a *critical stage*. Suppose the earth is eddying round and round *towards* the Sun; after a certain critical stage has been reached, it will cease to go round and round, but will be pulled to the centre and be merged in it; *vide* the career of a straw in an eddy in water. In eddying *away* from the centre there is also a critical stage, after which the body ceases to eddy, but flies off from the circuit. Orthodox Astronomy will now hardly accept this account of celestial motion, but it should be borne in mind that spiral nebulae have doubtless played a great part in cosmogenesis. Astronomy now regards the masses of the sun and the planets as being practically constant, so that, the gravitational stresses between them are supposed to maintain a permanent configuration; it also excludes all "extra-physical" forces as having anything to do with the working of the material order. But if we at all admit the view of cosmic evolution and involution, we must hold (on *á priori* grounds at least, so long as experimental or observed facts are not forthcoming) that the stresses in the solar system (or any other system) do not maintain a *permanent* scheme of bodies; that the configuration of the planets, etc., is but approximately and relatively fixed.

The parrallel of the atomic system is instructive. Here Science already recognises that the system is only relatively stable; that the electrons (unit negative charges) stepping beyond a certain "critical speed" may be dissociated from the atom and flung away; this is evidenced by radio-activity amongst other phenomena. There is nothing to prevent us from imagining that an electron moving round a central positive charge may not have an absolutely fixed orbit; that it too may either eddy towards or away from the central charge according to its adṛṣṭa; that in the former case, the electron, stepping beyond a critical rate of motion is dissociated with the result that the atom may be reconsituted (a different chemical substance may thereby be produced); and that in the latter case, the electron (negative charge) may, by curling round and round towards the central positive charge, be merged and unified with it (after a certain stage). This mingling of positive and negative charges means the "loss" or dissolution) of matter—matter lapses back into Ether of which it is a strained and polarised condition. This coiling motion which we attribute to the elements of the "atom" is not unscientific, *e.g.*, the vortex-motion theory of the prime atoms is still the most promising theory of its kind.

Besides the coiling-and-uncoiling movement, the important thing to note is the "critical stage". An operation in Nature is commonly of a certain type within certain limits, but beyond them it passes into another type. There is a critical temperature (32°F) at which water becomes ice; another (212°F) at which it becomes steam. In all physical operations we can recognise such critical stages which mark "new" transformations or appearances or directions. In vital and psychic phenomena also we have critical stages. Increased stimulation produces increased sensation (of a certain kind) up to a limit; beyond it, it produces either no sensation or sensation of a different kind. The Mutation Theory of the Origin of Species (by Hugo De Vries) holds that new species are born out of old species suddenly like "monstrosities"; implying that the motions in the germ-cell overstepping a certain critical value change the character of the germ-cell itself and thus produce a new species, just as under similar conditions a new atom may be evolved out of a given atom (*e.g.*, in radioactivity).

There is a further important thing to observe. In the operations of Nature, a new Principle of Control is introduced after each critical stage. When for example at 32°F water is transformed into ice, "something" appears amidst the molecules of $H_2O$ to bring about their new shuffling or configuration; when again the germ-cell of the "anthropoid ape" "mutates" into the anthropic germ-cell, a new Principle of Control appears which develops it, physically and mentally, into a man rather than into an ape which is the starting datum. I need not take further illustrations, but simply note that the new Principle of Control is a new disposition of Power (Śakti) by which an old Form is transformed into a new; when for example, by changing the "atomic number" the modern chemist hopes that he will be able to transmute a "base metal" (say mercury) into gold, he is searching after a new Principle of Control. Behind every stable special "form" in Nature there must be a special Principle of Control: a Principle of Control evolves and maintains a special rūpa and nāma in the Spiritual Ether which is in itself without rūpa and nāma. In the Veda we call each definite Principle of Control (in the sense of a Form of Citśakti) a Devatā. Thus, all the special sense-capacities have their Devatās. The śabdic means whereby a special Principle of Control may be introduced (or invoked), is Mantra. The visual representation or optical diagram of the actual disposition of stress (Power) which constitutes a given Principle of Control, is its Yantra. And the Kriyā in general (including Mantra and Yantra) whereby a Principle of Control may be brought about or called into play, is Tantra. Kriyā here means 'functioning', whether in the body or in the mind. When, for example, in home we produce fire by the mutual friction of āraṇi, we are invoking a Devatā.

Recapitulating we find that in the understanding of the world-process the following points are worthy of special note:

(1) It is a finitising process—differentiating and then integrating, and then differentiating again.

(2) It is rhythmic—moving from maximum veiling to maximum manifestation and back (coiling and uncoiling).

(3) In this process there are certain critical stages at which new forms are evolved.

(4) At each critical stage there appears a new Principle of Control.

(5) A Principle of Control is the builder and sustainer of a new form.

(6) Since the world-process runs on Samaṣti and Vyaṣti lines, we must have a graded series (hierarchy) of critical stages and Principles of Control on both the lines.

(7) A critical stage represents a "plane" in Nature; a devatā has his adhikāra corresponding to a given plane. Suppose we take three planes in descending order—A, B, C. Then, the Principle of Control corresponding to A, has adhikāra not only over A, but also over B and C; that of B, has adhikāra (jurisdiction or competence) over B and C; that of C over C alone. *Cf.* the relations of Īśvara, Hiraṇya-garbha and Virāt on the Samaṣti line.

(8) A Principle of Control on a given plane in the Samaṣti line has control over the Vyaṣti Principle of Control on the same plane.

These properties necessarily follow from the fundamental nature of Cit. Cit is Eka, Pūrṇa and Abādhita (Svādhīna). The less it is veiled, the more will this fundamental nature express itself. Now, veiling may involve this—the Whole is hidden and only a part displayed (finitisation); and the part displayed may be more or less obscured, *e.g.*, the jāgrat-mind of man is a Vyaṣti mind, but it is more articulate (vyakta) than his svapna-mind which in its turn is more articulate than his Suṣupti-mind. We have this principle: the higher the plane, and the less restricted the sphere, the more patent the essential nature of Cit. Therefore, the plane being the same, a Samaṣti Principle will have control over the Vyaṣti Principle (because the sphere of the latter is more restricted, so that there has been greater veiling); and the extent of sphere being the same, a Principle on a higher plane will have control over a Principle on a lower plane. Thus, Vyaṣti Prāṇa will control Vyaṣti-deha; Vyaṣti-Manas, Vyaṣti-Prāṇa. There may be also, in some cases, dual control or diarchy. For instance, my mind does not seem to have complete control over the *whole* working of Prāṇa in my body; only *a part* of such working appears to be voluntary. In this case, remaining part (which seems to be involuntary) is under the control of the Samaṣti-Manas (or Generic Mind), which control, may after sādhana be transferred to the Vyaṣti-mind in proportion as the latter assimilates itself to the Cosmic-Mind by pushing back its limitations.

Without further discussing the details we may note that the critical stages or planes are broadly *five—viz.*, the five koṣas of the Śruti (Ānanda-maya, Vijñānamaya, Manomaya, Prāṇamaya and Annamaya). They constitute a descending series of Controlling Agencies. The lower five cakras of the body as the seats of the five tattvas (kṣiti, ap, tejah, marut, vyoma) illustrate this principle of higher and higher control. As we have pointed out, a higher Principle, because it is essentially Cit, will display to a greater degree the essential nature of Cit (unity, wholeness and freedom) than a lower one. Thus, Prāṇa is more unitary, coherent and spontaneous than matter which it controls. But even matter, being essentially the same as Prāṇa, cannot be *wholly* discrete, disorganised and "determined" (inert): it is only *approximately* so. There must be a trace of unity, organisation and spontaneity (freedom) even in the material atom. The fact that the atom is a "system" is suggestive of this. Physical science works by abstraction or limitation of the data; *e.g.*, there is *really* no "rigid" body in Nature satisfying the definition of it given by Dynamics. Science deals with Fact-sections and not with the Fact. No matter-particle is therefore "dead" and *absolutely* inert.

Suppose we consider the mechanism of a matter-particle. It is like a Chinese puzzle-box—having various concentric sheaths. It *has* all the five kośas. But in it all except the annamaya (gross) kośa are yet coiled up (*i.e.* involved, potential). One kośa alone is uncoiled (evolved, actual), and we have motions proper to this kośa. Physical Science deals with some of these motions (approximately), and we have the "dynamical theory" of matter. Ordinarily we have no suspicion of the four other kośas involved in the material atom. Now, suppose the motions in the outermost crust or kośa of matter reach a certain critical stage (by reason of their adṛṣṭa or the assemblage of "subtle" stresses determining them, only *some* of which Physical Science can *approximately* compute); then, when this critical stage has been attained, the next inner kośa (*i.e.* Prāṇa) which had hitherto been coiled or involved, will "wake up" and begin to uncoil and evolve itself. The moment this happens, the so-called "dead" corpuscle will begin to appear as a living corpuscle. According to the principles explained before, a new Principle of Control, hitherto dormant (not absolutely dormant however) will appear on the scene. Its appearance will be marked by certain phenomena not clearly noticeable before—the vital phenomena. The living corpuscle will now seize upon the particles of C, H, N, O, build protoplasm, differentiate and integrate it in sundry ways, reproduce itself, and so on. In fact, by virtue of the uncoiling of the second kośa, a new set of motions manifests itself, which was unmanifest so long as *its* plane or "scene" was folded up. So far as the play of forces is concerned, this question of "scene" is important; *e.g.*, I have stored up in me the saṃskāras of 84 lacs of births (*i.e.*, kinds of birth) through which I have passed; but in my present human life, the scene is suitable for the play of only some of those countless saṃskāras and unsuitable for the Play of the rest.

In a similar way, the motions in the Prāṇic kośa, by virtue of their adṛṣṭa, may reach another stage at which the third or mānasic koṣa may evolve itself. Here again a new Principle of Control is introduced. In the plants, the mānasic kośa, though given is undeveloped; so that the vital processes of the plant do not appear to be controlled by the saṃkalpa of the plant itself; impulses and instincts as mental activities do not clearly appear to govern plant-life. In the animals the mind-kośa uncoils itself; in the man and other higher beings, the Buddhi-kośa also. They are Lower Antah-karaṇa and Higher Antaḥ-karaṇa respectively.

It should be observed, however, that the critical stages or kośas are not absolute boundaries in Nature.

Like the colours in a rainbow, they give us but "working" and approximate boundaries.

Nor is it correct to regard the kośas as absolutely "closed curves" without mutual influence. They do, and cannot but, influence one another.

Nor again should we restrict the scope of the transformation of energy to particular kośas only; *i.e.*, it should not be said that the energy in the material plane and that in the Prāṇic or Mānasic plane do never transform into one another. The theory of the fundamental unity of Energy will not justify it, nor will facts warrant it. When, for example, the Cāndogya says that the food eaten goes to build the mind, the water drunk to build the prāṇa, it is not speaking quite in a figurative sense. The doctrine of Conservation of Energy (as an *á posteriori* generalisation) did not take into account the vast magazines of energy now discovered in the atoms; the proof of the doctrine to-day is therefore far too difficult. We can hold the doctrine only by taking Energy *as a whole* in all its different forms (physical, prāṇic, mānasic, etc.) We hold it then as an *á priori* principle.

Suppose there is a material system consisting of the three atoms, A, B, C. Suppose also that the physical energy which they contain between them is 100. This amount excludes the vast energies which may be interned *within* the atoms themselves. 100 represents only extra-atomic energy such as heat etc. Now, suppose by any means I am able to draw upon the energy which is contained *within* A or B or C. Since the stock is practically inexhaustible, I shall be able to do a vast deal of "work" by such intra-atomic energy; but I need not touch any part of the 100. This 100 still remains 100, though out of the given material system I am taking vast amounts of energy. Physical Science till lately knew only the 100; and stated its doctrine of transformation and conservation of energy on that basis. In fact, when we dive down to the Ether-elements themselves which compose matter, matter practically becomes dematerialised, and there material energy and vital energy may lose their "castes" or class-distinctions.

The root of the whole matter is—To what extent does a given Form release or unveil the nature of the Spiritual Ether (Cit) of which it is a mode?

We have seen that Matter as a Form of existence is more completely than any other a veiling and binding Form—though even in it we must have clear traces of unity, organisation and freedom, as Science by her discovery of atomic systems and the spontaneous "evolution" of those systems is beginning to show. What it thus restrictedly manifests is the nature of the Immense (Brahman) and the Perfect (Pūrṇa) in which everything is grounded. Life manifests or reveals the Ground more unreservedly; and it is a controlling Principle in relation to Matter inasmuch as it is a Form more expressive of the unity, wholeness and freedom of That of which it along with Matter is a Form. For the same reason, also, Mind and Spirit are still superior controlling Principles. But they are all grounded in the one Immense Whole. Hence all the Forms, though distinct in their respective spheres, point to a deeper, essential unity by reason of which their operations form one common, cosmic stress-system. They can have no absolute boundaries. Not only do they condition but they transform, as regards their "matter" and "energy", into one another. They are alike in all essential respects. To take only one example: As in the atom, we have the polarity of the static and the moving charge of electricity, so in the living body, the static coiled Prāṇa-śakti at the Mūlādhārā exists (as the Tantra points out) relatively to the dynamic Prāṇa-śakti distributed over and working the bodily tissues.[1] To those who see the All, there is no difference except formal when Life is materialised, or when Matter is vitalised, or when Spirit is materialised, or again when everything is spiritualised.

[1] See *The Serpent Power* where this matter is more fully explained.

# POWER AS MIND

(*Mānasī-śakti*)

# FOREWORD

Reference is made in the Text to some similarities and differences between European philosophical systems and the Vedānta. It may prove convenient however to summarise here some recent tendencies in Western psychology and their bearing upon Indian doctrines on the same subject.

The fundamental peculiarity of the Advaita Vedānta, and therefore of its Śākta form, is the distinction which it draws between Mind and Consciousness in the sense of *Cit;* a word for which there is no exact equivalent in any European language. I propose to deal with this term in a future volume but will meanwhile describe it as the Unchanging Principle of all Experience, and which is the common source and basis of both Mind and Matter. *Cit* is the infinite Whole (*Pūrṇa*) in which all that is finite, whether as Mind or Matter, is. This is the Supreme Infinite Experience, free of all finitization which is Pure Spirit as distinguished from Mind and Body. Finite experience is that which is had through Mind and Body, which are the products of the finitizing principle of *Cit* which is called Supreme Power or Mahā-śakti. Because of this the World is Power, being the manifestation as Mind and Matter of the Power which is the dynamic aspect of the Fundamental Reality or *Cit* as Śakti, or Supreme Consciousness-Power. Power being the principle of negation or finitization of Consciousness, its product or manisfestation as Mind and Matter is unconscious (*Jaḍa*) for in so far and to the extent that anything is not Pure Consciousness (in the sense of *Cit*) it is unconsciousness or *Acit*. It is because Mind is a manifestation of a principle of unconsciousness that the Whole (*Pūrṇa*) which is without section (*Akhaṇda*) or a continuum as the Ether of Consciousness (*Cidākāśa*) is experienced by the individual centre or *Jīva* as the not-whole (*Apūrṇa*) and as a section (*Khaṇda*). This is pragmatic or conventional (*Vyavahārika*) experience as contrasted with the transcendental (*Pāramārthika*) experience or Experience-Whole.

The existence of a supreme unitary experience is not a matter with which Western psychology is concerned, though in metaphysics there have been Monistic Systems. According to Vedānta however the question whether *Cit* is a fact or not, is not a subject of speculation only but a matter of actual experience as the *Samādhi* of perfected *Yoga*.

I may note, however, here some tendencies or conclusions which favour the Vedāntic view.

As the reduction of Matter to *quasi*-material Ether and that of Energy to Stress in Ether is going on in Science, we notice a marked tendency in psychology (as in Herbert Spencer, Wundt, Ladd, etc.) to regard the common basis of Mind and Matter (psychosis and neurosis) as spiritual rather than material.

As above stated, the common basis in Indian doctrine (by which I mean that here dealt with) is spiritual, that is *Cit*, the Ether of Consciousness (*Cidākāśa*) from which Mind and Matter issue and in which they are. "Ether of Consciousness" (*Cidākāśa*) does not of course mean that *Cit* is Ether but that *Cit* is, like the physical Ether, in being an all-pervading Continuum in which all things are and which penetrates all things. In Vedānta, Mind and Matter spring from one source (*Cit*) and exist in parallelism, the one having the same reality as and being the co-essential of the other.

It is now commonly held that there is both an Unconscious and Conscious Mind. The first is described by Freud as consisting of all that realm of the Ego which is unknown and cannot be spontaneously recalled by the subject and which is made manifest, and then often in a disguised form only, in special psychic conditions such as dreams and trances and can be evoked only by special methods. It is now recognised that a large part of our psychic life remains and operates in the Unconscious so that we are perforce unaware of it. Conscious Mind consists of that part of our psychic life of which we are aware. Unconscious and Conscious Mind are but two aspects of the one Entity, the Psyche. It has been said (Bow "Psycho-analysis") that the term "unconscious" is open to certain objections. Since we can only be aware of anything by means of Consciousness nothing that we are aware of can be in any realm but that of the Conscious: hence the term "Unconscious Mind" becomes meaningless. That is so in this theory, but not in Vedānta to which it makes some approximation. This approximation consists in the admission that Mind can be unconscious though it is added that it is also in another aspect conscious. The Vedānta and Sāṃkhya say that Mind, as such, is always an unconscious force and operation. It derives its appearance of being conscious because of its association with the Conscious Principle or *Cit*. It finitises *Cit* for the individual consciousness. What is called in the West "unconscious mind" is that state in which Mind ever associated with Consciousness, is yet not in the field of awareness owing to the density of the veiling principle of *Tamas*. In this realm of the Western Unconscious Mind are all the *Saṃskāras* or tendencies acquired in the course of the life-history of the individual of which he becomes aware if and when the density of the veil is lessened.

According to Sāṃkhya-yoga a *Saṃskāra* is a sub-conscious or subliminal (*Sūkṣmarūpa*) continuation of what was once a conscious activity (*Vyāpāra*) whether cognitive, affective or conative. A conscious activity when gone through does not absolutely end there: It simply passes into a potential and hidden (*Avyakta* and *Sūkṣma*) condition below the threshold of consciousness. It goes on *ad infnitum* more and more below the level of the ordinary consciousness. This for pragmatic reasons lights up only between certain limits. Stimuli and brain excitements of certain degrees of intensity only evoke response. But the activities do not leave when pragmatic consciousness fails to notice them. They go on.

Thus the course of any activity (*Vyāpārā*) in mental life displays itself when above the threshold of consciousness as conscious activity and when it sinks below the threshold it is called a *Saṃskāra* or tendency or potential due to unconscious mental operations. But each term, whether tendency or potential, implies *Prati-bandhaka* or constraint for why should it be tendency or potential only unless some influence keeps it down? It requires to be released from restraint to come up again which release takes place through a stimulus (*Udbodhaka Vyañjaka*). If mental activity be regarded as a form of *Parispanda* or vibration in the Mind-stuff, the motion does not cease when it becomes hidden (*Avyakta*) to consciousness. It still continues, though not with sufficient intensity to evoke conscious response. It is easily understandable that the more recent the impression may be, the easier is its recall. Some forms of Western psychology at any rate now recognise that Mind may be unconscious. It will gain further consistency by regarding all mental operation as unconscious, deriving its apparent consciousness from association with the Spiritual Principle which is the one and only illuminator. Though psycho-physical parallelism (*i.e.*, between psychosis and neurosis) is maintained, the tendency is less to-day to regard consciousness as merely a function of the brain. Hence, many now think that there is a consciousness wider and deeper than cerebral consciousness. Thus the possibility of "ejective" consciousness, disembodied consciousness, etc., is beginning to be recognised by many.

The present tendency is to regard the "subliminal consciousness" as constituting the most important and active part of our mental life. Thus the "threshold of consciousness" is only a pragmatic limit and not an absolute boundary of consciousness. According to Vedānta, Consciousness *per se*, that is in the sense of *Cit* is boundless. The individual is a centre in that boundlessness whose limits are determined by the combination of Mind and Matter which constitutes it as such individual. The individual again is aware of certain mental functioning in himself and the greater portion at any moment exists as *Saṁskāras* not present to consciousness.

Again the continuity of Animal Mind and Human Mind (in point of development), and the possibility of the latter's further development into Super-consciousness are now recognised. In fact, the relations of normal, abnormal and subnormal mental lives are now more correctly understood. The study of these different species of Mind (genius, lunacy, childhood, criminality, hypnosis, trance, etc.,) is perhaps leading to the recognition of a Generic Mind (Hiraṇyagarbha) which is in different modes of manifestation. Using Consciousness in its popular sense there is sub-consciousness, consciousness and super-consciousness or Yoga consciousness. Super-mind is Brahman. Further, Mind can no longer be treated in water-tight compartments.

The "atomistic" view of sensations, etc., which go to make up complex perceptions, etc., is now discarded. Mental life is now recognised as a *continuum*. The distinct perceptions, ideas, etc., are only the pragmatic "fact-sections" of the undivided whole of experience. (W. James, Ward and others.)

Psychology again, on the whole, demonstrates the unity and continuity of all mental life. Psychic life is a continuity in the sense that at any given moment it is determined by all that has previously happened and is happening. This is well established Indian Doctrine. The whole doctrine of *Karma* and *Saṃskāra* is based on this continuity. Mental Life is again one. Thus "Faculties" cannot now be treated as quite separate. Instinct, Intelligence, Reason, etc., are now treated from a more organic point of view. The departmental view of Mind is out of date. The division into "faculties" has a practical use as had in the Indian system the classification of the *Tattvas* which constitute the *Antahkaraṇa*. But though the working of Mind shows various aspects the *Antahkaraṇa* is at base one.

The Cartesian dualism of Mind and Matter (with no possibility of interaction) is commonly discarded in Modern Psychology which tends more and more to regard them not as merely "parallel aspects" but as co-essentials. I have dealt with the subject of inter-action in the Text. The Cartesian position which denied to the finite Mind any effective control over Matter and which was developed by many nineteenth century physiologists into this position, namely that Man is an "automaton" (Huxley), his consciousness and will having no real control over his brain and nervous system, but only recording and registering what may be going on in the brain, etc., as the result of physico-chemical changes—this position, is now being steadily given up. The Causal efficacy of consciousness is now recognised as in Vedānta. The distinction of Primary and Secondary qualities in sense-perception is disappearing. Either all of them are actually in the Thing or none of them are actually in the Thing. One of the latest developments (*viz.*, Neo-Realism) tends to place all of them in the Thing, as the Vedānta does. This subject I have developed in the earlier section of this volume ('Reality').

The Mind at the time of birth is not a *tabula rasa*, but a store-house of tendencies and pre-dispositions. This is a common position now. This is also the Vedāntic position according to which Man is born with his inherent *Saṃskāras*.

Emphasis has rightly been laid on the pragmatic view of Reality. Thus Western Psychology is coming to recognise *three* orders of Reality (*a*) Transcendental, *i.e.*, what exists independent of this particular experience; (*b*) Pragmatic, *i.e.*, what is useful to us and serves a practical purpose (*Vyavahārika*); and (*c*) Phenomenal or Apparent.

Next, what is called "The New Psychology" in the West (cf. E. Boirac's "Psychology of the Future," and "Our Hidden Forces") is establishing Mind as a Force, capable of energising in uncommon ways, and hence ushering in the Philosophy and Practice of so called "occult powers" and Yoga.

Lastly the fundamental Cosmic Impulse to evolutionary movement is not to-day blind physical "force", but modern thought tends to regard it more and more as a spiritual stress. Thus the *elan vital* (Vital Impetus) of Prof. Henri Bergson is neither physical force nor vital force in the ordinary biological sense; it is something more fundamental. This Impetus is at the back of Creative Evolution.

This last Matter opens up an exposition of the whole Śākta Doctrine. According to this teaching the Universe is a Dynamism—an expression (and therefore necessarily finite) of Śakti and an infinite reservoir of Power or Śakti. It is Auto-dynamic as such expression of Power. The ultimate Reality has two aspects—one static (*Cit*) and the other Kinetic or *Sakti* which is both *Cit Sakti* that is efficient cause as Supreme Will and *Māyā-Sakti* or instrumental and material (*Upādāna*) Cause. Before the manifestation of the Universe, *Cit* and its Power or Śakti were as one. Power was the mere potency of a future Universe. This general potency, or tendency holds within itself all the particular tendencies or *Saṃskāras* which are both the product and the producers of *Karma*. The impulse to manifestation is the display of Supreme Will which arises on the "ripening" of those tendencies towards manifestation. The Ultimate Reality which is Pure Consciousness or Spirit—thus vests itself from out its Power with a psychical and a physical body which is the Universe consisting of the totality of the individual Minds and Bodies in which the Source of all Power is immanent. The whole machinery of *Prakṛti* in the Sāṃkhya is automatic and *Sakti* is self-acting both as to the original creative impulse as also as regards all in which this impulse manifests.

Calcutta — J. W.
20th July, 1922

# THE WORLD AS POWER:

## POWER AS MIND

## (*Mānasī-śakti*)

### 1

This subject resolves itself into a consideration of the nature of "Mind" as contrasted with Matter and their relation to one another.

The fundamental difference between Western and Eastern psychology is that the former *does not,* and the latter[1] *does differentiate Mind from Consciousness.* On the contrary Western psychology interprets Mind in terms of Consciousness, that is Consciousness is the distinctive character of Mind. Where Mind and Consciousness are used as equivalents the one of the other, ordinary experience is of course meant and not pure *Cit* or supreme unconditioned Consciousness.

The Western "Mind" is something for which there is no adequate Sanskrit equivalent since the notions are different. When I speak of Mind in Vedānta I refer to what is explained later as the "Inner Instrument" (Anthkaraṇa) as distinguished from the "outer instruments" (Bāhyakaraṇa) or senses on the one hand, and on the other hand from Consciousness of which both mind and senses are instruments.

The term Mind bears a narrower as well as a wider meaning in the *Śāstras.* Thus in the saying "from where speech together with mind (*Manas*) withdraws failing to reach" (referring to the Brahman) the word *Manas* (mind) is evidently used for the whole "Inner Instrument." In strictly philosophical literature however, the term *Manas* is almost always used in a defined sense so that it cannot be translated into "Mind" as understood by Western psychologists. It is only then one function of the inner instru-

[1] In Sāṃkhya and Vedānta. It is the unchanging principle of all experience in mind and body which are its modes. Nyāya-Vaiśeṣika, though distinguishing Manas as the instrument and Ātmā as the substratum of Consciousness, does not recognise Pure Consciousness as Cit. Even the consciousness of its Iśvara is not pure (Śuddha) in the sense of being Nirviśeṣa. It is Saviśeṣa, with infinitely rich content.

ment. Indian "Mind"[1] is distinguished from Western Mind in this that the former as such is not Consciousness but a material force enveloping Consciousness, the two in association producing the Consciousness-unconsciousness of Western Mind. Pure Consciousness (*Cit*) is not an attribute of Mind. It is beyond Mind being independent of it. It is immanent in Mind and is the source of its illumination and apparent Consciousness.[2]

In the older Western schools "Consciousness" was used in the more limited and personal sense of the mind's direct cognisance of its own states and processes; the perception of what passes in a man's own mind. But it was later and is now used in a wider sense and the question is now raised whether Consciousness is co-extensive with mind. In this wider sense it is used,[3] in general antithesis to Matter, to cover that phase of reality which does not permit of exclusive interpretation in terms of matter in motion, but allows or requires the hypothesis of something analogous to conscious process. It is further said that there may be even unconscious mental modification, in which case Consciousness is not co-extensive with mind. Here we have something, either intelligence, feeling, or will, not in personal individual consciousness, without which however the flow of consciousness would not be what it is. The recognition by present-day psychologists of two forms of mental life, conscious and subconscious (sub-liminal) seems to contain the germs of the distinction, which India has always held, between Mind and Consciousness. This belief in two forms of mental life—conscious and sub-conscious (sub-liminal) is held by many psychologists.

This view is in consonance with Vedānta which calls the latent and sub-conscious a *Saṃskāra* and adds a third, *viz.*, Super-consciousness that is beyond ordinary consciousness, whether latent or patent, which is pure *Cit*. In this view ordinary consciousness is latent or patent, below or above the threshold of ordinary experience, and pure Consciousness or Cit, though immanent, transcends both as the Supreme Experience (*Saṃvid*) in which the other two are held. As between Consciousness and Mind, Western psychology regards what Vedānta calls a condition[4] that is

[1] Western "Mind" is the Indian Antahkaraṇā-vacchinna Caitanya, *i.e.*, Cit (Consciousness) as (apparently) conditioned by Antahkaraṇa which as Jaḍa or unconscious Process is of and in the condition, *viz.*, Antaḥkaraṇa and not in that which seems to be conditioned, *viz.*, Cit. Manas which is sometimes translated 'Mind' is only part of Antahkaraṇa.

[2] That is in Sāṃkhya and Vedānta.

[3] Baldwin Dict., *Sub-voc.*, Mind.

[4] Upādhi, that is something imposed on consciousness.

mind,[1] as the more essential part, inasmuch as it holds that Consciousness may not be an inseparable property of the mind, many functions of which may lie in unconsciousness. Mind[1] is thus that of which consciousness is a separable condition—the opposite of the Vedāntic view according to which Consciousness is that of which Mind is a separable condition. Consciousness is *Cit.* It is more or less *veiled* by Mind to which, whatever unconsciousness (in whatever degree) there is, is due. To use one of the expressive metaphors of the Vedānta, Cit, is like a lamp which the Mind envelops as a screen, sometimes revealing it by its transparency, sometimes concealing it by its opaqueness, and thus always conditioning its illumination both as regards its quality and quantity.

According to many Western psychologists, who in this follow or approximate to the Buddhist theory, "Mind" means conscious process, that is the changing series of impressions (sensations) and ideas, a continuous flow or stream. Of what? We may leave the question unanswered, either because it assumes what is denied, or what at least is supposed to be unknown, or we may answer with the older schools that there is a simple mental substance or Soul which experiences in us—thinks, feels and wills and underlies all the varied modes of Experience. It is thus that which exists as a permanent unity behind the phenomena of mind or its processes. From the other and materialist standpoint a "Mind-stuff" and "Mind-dust" is postulated. In either case Consciousness is a function and attribute of Soul or Mind-stuff, the fundamental distinction between Consciousness and Mind not being recognised. J.S. Mill's view that mind is the permanent possibility of experience may be said to vaguely hint at a transcendental principle. According to the Vedānta, that principle is Pure Cit of which both mind and matter are limited *modes* of Its Power. All psychical functions therefore, whether as intellect, feeling, will and the like are limited modes. *Cit* is pure Consciousness itself. Mind is a real or apparent negation or limitation or determination of that. Mind in fact, in itself, that is considered as apart from Cit (from which in fact it is never separate) is an *unconscious force* which in varying degree obscures and limits consciousness, such limitation being the condition of all finite experience. *Cit* is thus Consciousness. Mind is Consciousness *plus* Unconsciousness, the intermingled Consciousness-unconsciousness which we see in all finite being. Mind is both substance and process. It is substance as the mind-substance or Antahkaraṇa, and it is process as the modifications

1 Antahkaraṇa,

or *Vṛtti* of that substance. The process takes place in and of mind. It is not a process of Consciousness. The substance again of both Mind and Matter is *Cit*, the Supreme Consciousness and Pure Experience Itself. Mental process is a veiling or (relative) unveiling of *Cit* which is itself unchanged. Consciousness appears however to undergo change because of the modifications of mind of which it is the changeless *substratum*.

2

It will be convenient here to discuss in greater detail the nature of *Śakti* or Power as Mind before dealing with the question of their relation to, and interaction upon, one another.

The European and Indian theories of the relation between, or interaction of, Mind and Matter may be thus summarised.

We may take first the dualistic theories. The Vedānta agrees with the Cause Theory in so far as the latter holds that conscious process and nervous process are causally related, provided we substitute for the word 'conscious' the word 'mental'. The process is not in Consciousness but in Mind.[1] The mental is a subtle quasi-material[2] process. It holds that both processes, psychical and material, have a common ground in Consciousness and thus escapes the difficulty in conceiving interaction between things of a wholly different nature as Mind and Body are commonly supposed to be. It differs, therefore, from psycho-physical parallelism in that the latter offers no explanation of the relation between psychosis and neurosis. It asserts, as stated, not a mere concomitance, the nature of which is unexplained, but a causal interaction between Mind and Matter rendered possible by their common ground. It differs again from any system of Pre-established Harmony in that there is not merely synchronistic change, but an action by Matter on Mind and by Mind on Matter which is possible for the reason stated. It therefore also differs from any theory of Occasionalism according to which no influence passes from one to the other, but on occasion God intervenes when the one changes to bring about change in the other. In this connection however it may be noted that Malebranche's theory that "we see all things in God" seems to adumbrate the Indian doctrine which says that the Mind is

[1] Process is of and in the condition, namely, Antahkaraṇa and not in that which seems to be conditioned or Cit.

[2] Bhautika. It is difficult to find a rendering of this. "Material" is used only in the negative sense as denoting something which is not wholly immaterial, which is Cit or Spirit alone.

enabled to perceive Matter because both are forms of Supreme Power (Mahā-śakti) which is an attribute of the Supreme Consciousness.

Turning then to Monistic Western theories—these hold that Mind and Matter are parallel manifestations of one underlying Substance. They are not two substances in interaction, but this interaction is the outer form of the inner ideal unity of consciousness. Each particle of matter has a mental aspect. "It is as if the same thing were said in two languages." Western science thus vaguely feels that there ought to be a unity behind mind and matter but does not yet *know* where that unity has to be found, and so uses metaphors and language which from the Vedāntic standpoint appear vague. From this standpoint we must first clearly distinguish between worldly experience and Yoga-experience. According to the former there is in fact duality. We cannot escape that. From this dualistic standpoint there must be an interaction because if we assume two things we must assume an interaction between them unless we put the problem aside. Yoga-experience transcends this duality, as Pure Consciousness, for which however we have no warrant short of experience of this state. Relatively there is the duality of Mind and Matter and their interaction. In the state beyond relations there is Pure Consciousness. In the mixed and graded Consciousness-unconsciousness which constitutes world-experience it is Consciousness (which, as above described, is 'the underlying substance' of which mind and matter are manifestations) which perceives according to the nature and workings of the unconscious Mind and Matter in which it manifests. Consciousness is the ground of Knower, Knowing and Known. The Double Aspect theory endeavours to avoid inconsequence by referring both series conjointly to the causation of a single substance.

But here again we must distinguish. Pure Consciousness[1] as such is neither efficient nor material cause but Consciousness-Power is both.[2] The former as pure *Cit* or Indian Consciousness is the changeless and processless background of all changes and processes. Though not itself changing, it contains the ground[3] and possibility of all change. This alogical position is expressed in Śākta doctrine by saying that in one aspect It remains what It is, yet in another It is changing to become the world. This is the Power or *Śakti* or *Vimarśa* aspect. The first is the Being, the

[1] Cit, Jñāna-svarūpa, Cidākāśa, Saṃvid, etc., the Śiva or Prakāśa as opposed to the Śakti or Vimarśa aspect.

[2] As Cit-Śakti the efficient (Nimitta) and as Māyā-śakti the material (Upādāna) cause.

[3] Adiṣṭhāna.

second the Becoming aspect. Therefore in world-experience, Indian Consciousness is the unchanging Principle of all changing experience. Through its power it appears as Mind and Matter. It is against this static background that all changes occur. Activity is in Mind and Matter, now veiling, now revealing unchanging *Cit* by their material processes as Psychosis or Neurosis. It is simpler, as stated later, to ignore these divisions and to say that Consciousness is the static aspect of Power (*Cit-śakti*), the kinetic aspect of which (*Māyā-śakti*) produces Mind and Matter, both in differing degrees being veilings by Unconsciousness of Consciousness.

According to Pan-psychism all matter has a rudimentary life, and mind and matter has thus a physical aspect. This is so. But in what sense? In so far as any thing or process is or can be an *object* of consciousness[1] it is *Jaḍa* or non-conscious. The term has a psychological basis. Thus an object of consciousness may be either objective or subjective. What Western science calls Matter or quasi-material is an instance of the former. But the "inner instrument"[2] or Mind (including the Self) can be an object of Consciousness and is therefore as such *Jaḍa.* In fact even Prakṛti-śakti as the Causal Stress which evolves the world is from this standpoint *Jaḍa.* Pure consciousness or *Cit* beyond mind, though manifesting in the operations of the latter, is in its transcendental aspect alogical. Thus the first polarity which appears in Consciousness is that of the Knower and Known.[3] When this polarity appears *Cit* splits up as it were into two parts or poles—one part still remaining *Cit* (*i.e.*, Knower) the other appearing *as though it were* not-*Cit*[4] or *Jaḍa* that is as the Known.[5] In the latter, *Cit* as it is in itself[6] is veiled. The veiling principle which is Power or Śakti is manifested as the various tendencies[7] of the material Cause[8] in various combinations. When Cit is enveloped by the material Principle[9] in what is mainly its revealing tendency,[10] we have the Inner Instrument[11] which corresponds to the Western Mind *minus* Consciousness. When it is enveloped by the material principle[12] in what is mainly its activity-tendency[13] we have Life;[14] when it is enveloped by the material Principle[15] in what is mainly its veiling tendency[16] we have Matter in the Western sense.[17] When

[1] Jñeya (object known) as opposed to Jñātā, the Knower.
[2] Antahkaraṇa. [3] Jñātā, Jñeya, knowing being Jñāna. [4] Acit.
[5] Jñeya. [6] Cit-svarūpa. [7] Guṇa. [8] Prakṛti-śakti or Māyā-śakti.
[9] *Ib.* [10] Sattvaguṇa or the Sattvika veil.
[11] Antahkaraṇa, *i.e.*, Buddhi, Ahaṃkāra, Citta, Manas.
[12] Prakṛti-śakti or Māyā-śakti. [13] Rajoguṇa or the Rājaśika veil.
[14] Prāṇa. [15] Prakṛti-śakti or Māyā-śakti.
[16] Tamoguṇa or Tāmasika veil. [17] Mūrtta jaḍadravya.

therefore we speak of Matter as *Jaḍa* we do not mean that it is unconscious in the sense that it is *in itself* unconscious and without mind or life, but in the sense that it is an *object* for consciousness, something in this sense other than it is as knower. The first primary (logical) operation by which *Cit* becomes so disposed as to remain *Cit* in one part and *appear* to cease to be *Cit* in another part is *Sṛṣṭi* or Becoming called "Creation,"[1] and that which is obtained out of *Cit*—the "Other" the *Jaḍa*, the object—is *Bhūta* or Matter. Therefore Mind and Matter are both in the general sense Bhūta.[2] *Cit* however never really ceases to be such, not merely in the pole which is still the Knower[3] but also in the other pole which is veiled so as to appear as non-*Cit*.[4] Thus the Tāntric rite called *Bhūta-śuddhi*,[5] is philosophically considered, the removing of the Veil by the realisation of the Mantra: "He I am,";[6] that is the Universe is first identified with the "I"[7] and then this with the Pure Consciousness or *Cit*. It is thus the placing of the Self in the return-current.[8]

From the above it follows that Western Mind,[9] Life and Matter are at the root one, firstly because the primary basis in all cases is *Cit* and secondly because the Veiling Principle[10] which works them out is composed of the same factors[11] in all cases though in different degrees. Matter is Cit heavily veiled and inert, Life is Cit more lightly veiled and active. Mind is still more lightly veiled and active,[12] and becomes in its developed and complex processes the revealer of the Self to the self on the mental plane, whence passage is made to the Self, beyond which there is nothing.[13] Both the life-aspect and mind-aspect may be the subject of direct perception by special means either of science or Yoga. A block of stone is perceived by the natural eye as inert lifeless matter. To that eye neither the signs of life nor mind are revealed. Both however may (given the appropriate means) be inferred from certain recognised signs of them. When these

[1] The term "Creation" is here avoided owing to its associations with dualistic systems as the creation of something new from nothing as opposed to development of the actual from the potential.

[2] Bhautika: and therefore "material" either in a gross or subtle sense. Specifically, Bhūta=sensible matter. [3] Jñātā or Cetana. [4] Acit.

[5] Literally, purification of the elements of "Earth", "Water", etc., in the body as to which see my "*Śākti and Śākta*" and "*Śerpent Power*".

[6] So'ham. [7] Aham.

[8] And not, therefore the idle and superstitious mummery which some have ignorantly supposed it to be. Before blaming-criticism is given, endeavour should first be made to understand. [9] Antahkaraṇa.

[10] Māyā-śakti. [11] The Guṇas Sattva, Rajas, Tamas of Māyā-śakti.

[12] The activity of mind is compared to mobile mercury the "Semen of Śiva".

[13] Puruṣāt na paraṃ kiṃcit sā kāṣṭha sā parāgatih.

signs are perceived, it is said that there is a living and thinking object presented to mind. The ordinary sense-organs may be insufficient to found an inference of rudiments of life or mind say in a stone. But science extending natural faculty by its delicate instruments, or Yoga by its process of Saṃyama[1] may enable the observer to perceive that on which the inference of life and mind is established. *A priori* the conclusion may be established by the ontological theory or *a posteriori* on the theory of evolution. Though at root Matter, Life and Mind are one, yet as Matter and Mind they are phenomenally different. One must assume therefore in all objects the same causal interaction of their psychic and material aspects, more or less rudimentary as it may be. as we find in man's nervous processes with their corresponding psychoses.

3

What then according to Indian views is the nature of Mind?

It may be defined, in the first instance negatively, as that part of our subjective life which in itself is not Consciousness, though it appears to be conscious through association with the latter. This distinction is maintained throughout the Standards. Whether there is such a state as Pure Consciousness which is Mindless is established secondarily by *Śruti* or Veda as authoritative proof,[2] or directly, by actual personal experience.[3] This is a matter with which I will deal under the heading of Consciousness-Power (*Cit-Sakti*). As Consciousness in Itself is immeasurable or Immense (the meaning of Brahman), and as man's consciousness appears to be limited, otherwise he could not have finite experience, what limits it is a Force which as such, is different from the Consciousness it limits. In the first Standard or Nyāyavaiśeṣika, Mind is an unconscious entity (*Dravya*) separate from the Self (*Ātman*) by conjunction with which and the senses, the Self has conscious experience of objects. In the second Standard or Sāṃkhya-Yoga, Mind is a Force separate from and independent of Consciousness which it apparently *finitises:* or as in the Śākta doctrine, it is a form of *Māyā,* which is one with and not independent of Consciousness, being a Power of Consciousness to remain what it is and yet to contract itself into being a centre of limited experience; or it is neither the first nor the second but a form of *Māyā* which itself is an inscrutable, unexplainable mystery.[4]

---

[1] Concentration (dhāraṇa, dhyāna, samādhi).
[2] Āpta-Pramāṇa. [3] Pratyakṣa as Aparokṣajñāna or Sākṣātkāra.
[4] As in Māyā-vāda-Vedānta.

However related to Consciousness, it *is* fundamentally a mystery. Taking it as a fact of which we are aware we can also analyse it into its functions and the mode of their working. These functions are fully explained in the Sāṃkhya which in this respect is the basis of Śākta doctrine. Mind is through the sense organs (*Indriya*) affected by the objects which it selects (as *Manas*), refers to itself the personal experience so enjoyed (as *Ahaṃkāra*) and then determines (as *Buddhi*). The one Mind does all this, but is variously named according to its various functions as separate principles or *Tattvas*. In actual experience or functioning of the *Tattvas* in the fully evolved world, the knowing process commences with the last evolved subjective principle or the senses. The object of knowledge first knocks at this gate to be introduced within and to become subject to the inner operating principles, the last of which to so operate is the determining faculty or *Buddhi*. But in the cosmic evolution of the Principles or Tattvas themselves, the order is reversed and the last to function in the evolved world becomes the first to appear according to either a temporal or logical *prius*. A logical analysis of experience establishes this. The general basis of experience, to which in the functioning of the individual mind reference is made last, must necessarily in the cosmic evolution appear first. It is also clear that the evolving principles have also a more abstract significance. Thus the I-making or individualising and centre-making Principle (*Ahaṃkāra-Tattva*) in individual experience is that aspect of the mind which refers its operations to that particular individual. Whereas in the cosmic sense it is the tendency to individualisation which manifests later as the individual centre.

Though the mode of evolution is given differently in the Sāṃkhya[1] and Māyā-vāda Vedānta[2] and there are other differences,[3] the description of the faculties generally holds good in Māyā-vāda Vedānta. Though Śaivas and Śāktas accept the twenty-five Tattvas of Sāṃkhya they add eleven others preceding Puruṣa and Prakṛti, the whole being known as the Thirty-six Tattvas, which are higher forms of Consciousness evolving

---

[1] The order of evolution is Prakṛti, Mahat or Buddhi, Ahaṃkāra. Then co-ordinately Manas and Indriyas (10) and their subtle objects (5) Tanmātras, and from the latter the five forms of gross sensible matter (Bhūta). These with the Puruṣa make 25 Tattvas.

[2] The evolution is from the Apañcīkṛta or unmixed Tanmātras or subtle matter: from the Sāttvik part of these, the Tattvas Buddhi, Manas and the five intellectual sense-organs; from the Rājasik part the five Prāṇas and the five active organs; from the Tāmasik part, gross sensible matter.

[3] *e.g.*, Memory (Citta) is a separate faculty in Vedānta and is included in Buddhi by the Sāṃkhya. The Citta of the Yoga-Philosophy=Antahkarana of Sāṃkhya and Vedānta. Prāṇa (Life) is a separate Tattva in Vedānta but not in Sāṃkhya.

for the production of Puruṣa-Prakṛti and will be dealt with under the title Power as Consciousness (*Cit Sakti*). The Mind (as *Anthakaraṇa* or the Yoga-darśana Citta) is neither all-pervasive[1] nor atomic and partless.[2] It is not therefore eternal,[3] has a beginning,[4] and has a limited extension,[5] that is, it is a thing of finite dimensions. It is radiant, transparent, light,[6] like the Solar rays,[7] right and mobile.[8] It is a kind of "Radiant Matter."[9] In Vedānta it is called *Bhautika* because it is a mode of the unmixed *Bhūtas*[10] from varying aspects of which are derived according to the Māyā Vedānta both Matter and Mind. Therefore these two are essentially similar.[11] Mind (Antahkaraṇa) is not rigid, that is, is having the same configuration always, but elastic.[12] *It actually goes out like a ray* (though not in the act of knowledge altogether leaving the body) to the object of perception, envelops it, and *takes its form.* Some may call this materialism, but the Vedānta holds not that mind is derived from matter in the physical sense but that they are fundamentally and essentially one, that is Pure Consciousness (Cit) stressing or energising one way or the other. They are different modes of the one Power (Śakti) as Substance-Energy.[13]

4

We may now consider in greater detail the nature of Mind, its functions and their process. According to the pluralistic first Standard or Nyāyā-vaiśeṣika, the *Ātman* or Self is all-pervading, immense,[14] the ground,[15] and agent[16] of knowledge. It is thus the seat of consciousness. Beyond this we cannot say. It has the attribute of consciousness when conjoined with *Manas* or "Mind," which is something quite different from it. It is an atomic[17] or infinitesimal unconscious instrument[18] of knowledge. The

---

1 Vibhu-parimāṇa.

2 Aṇu-parimāṇa. It is therefore Madhyama-parimāṇa.

3 Nitya. 4 Sādi. 5 Sāvayava, paricchinna.

6 Taijasa, having a predominance of Sattva-guṇa or the revealing aspect of Substance-Energy, the aspect in which it reveals consciousness.

7 Ravi-kiraṇa-vat. 8 Laghu and Cara.

9 To use the term of Sri W. Crookes, applied by him to matter in the fourth state.

10 Apancīkrita or Sūkṣma-Bhūta. It is derived from their Sāttvika or revealing aspect, as Matter is derived from their veiling or Tāmasika aspect. According to the Sāṃkhyan scheme, adopted by Śakti-vāda, both the senses and subtle objects (Tanmātra) derive from a common source (Ahaṃkāra) or self-arrogating and individualising principle.

11 See last note. The Chāndogya Up. says that the lowest units (aniṣta aṃśa) of the food (anna) eaten go to build up the "body" of the mind.

12 Saṃkoca-vikāsa-śīla.

13 The Māyā-śakti of Advaita-vedānta and Śaktivāda corresponding to the Mūla-prakṛti of the Sāṃkhya.

14 Vibhu. 15 Āśraya or Adhiṣṭhāna. 16 Kartā.

17 Aṇu. 18 Karaṇa.

Self, working with it, is conscious. It is the means whereby perception becomes possible and may thus be called the Inner Sense.[1] It works in co-operation with the outer senses which are made of the same material as the objects which are sensed. Like is known by like. The atomic character of *Manas* is inferred from the fact that perceptions or experiences arise serially and not simultaneously. Sensations are thus experienced, though several objects may be presented simultaneously to several sense organs. If *Manas* were all-pervading it would be always in contact with the different sense organs, and through them, with the various objects, so that it might attend to and admit all these objects at once. But experience shows (it is said) that it does not. On the contrary it acts like a turnpike gate through which only one sensation at a time can enter. It has been aptly compared[2] to a door-keeper, who admits one person at a time and keeps others out. It is thus conceived as concentrated into a point. It is true that one may seem to have a number of different sensations (induced by different sense organs) at once but there is here (it is said) only an appearance of simultaneous activity. Manas is not only very small but exceedingly light[3] so that it can pass very quickly from object to object, so quickly indeed that its successive attention and apprehension appear as a simultaneous activity.[4] It may be objected: May we not explain both serial and simultaneous apprehension by conceiving *Manas* as a substance with parts which may be contracted and expanded? In such a case when several sensations are to be apprehended at once, the Manas expands and thus puts itself simultaneously into connection with several sense organs. When however one at a time has to be received, it contracts itself into a point and connects with only one sense organ. In such a case we need not assume any mistake. This suggestion of an elastic mind is rejected on the ground that it gratuitously assumes a substance with many parts which increase in expansion and decrease in contraction. It is in the Nyāya-Vaiśeṣika partless and unextended.[5] This partlessness is inferred from the seriality[6] of attention and apprehension.

The process of perception is in a general way as follows: It is either internal[7] or external.[8] In external perception[9] these connections must

---

[1] Antarindriya. [2] See *The Serpent Power*. [3] Atilāghavāt.

[4] Thus a spark of light if made to rotate rapidly in a circle appears as a continuous circle of light.

[5] Aṇurūpa. [6] Ayaugapadyāt.

[7] *e.g.*, "I am happy" Ahaṃ sukhi. [8] *e.g.* Ayaṃ ghatah "here is the jar".

[9] Bāhya-viṣaya-pratyakṣa.

be successively established—(1) the contact of the object with the appropriate sense organ,[1] (2) the Manas or the inner organ of apprehension must attend, and (3) offer the sensations to the self or Ātman.

Because of its atomicity (*Aṇutva*) *Manas* can attend to only one at a time, but it can attend quickly in succession because of its lightness. As a gate in action, it introduces the sensations one by one to the Self to be known, felt, and owned by the latter. *Manas* is itself unconscious,[2] partless,[3] atomic[4] and hence eternal[5] and unchanging. It simply plays the part of the Usherer, either admitting or refusing. It is instrumental in the production of knowledge but is neither its ground[6] nor agent.[7] Without the third step or offer of the sensation to the Self there is no knowing, and in particular no referring, of an experience to the Self-apperception as Western Psychology sometimes calls it.

The Self according to this system is possessed of fourteen attributes[8] of which Cognition (*Buddhi*),[9] Feeling (*Sukhaduhka*; agreeable and disagreeable) and Will (*Icchā*) are counted first.[10] The Self has three kinds of activity as knowledge, will, and action.[11] Cognition is divided into experience (*Anubhuti*) and representation or collection (*Smṛti*) and the former into direct perception, inference, analogy, knowledge due to authentic testimony.[12] This Standard is distinguished by the multiplicity of its ultimate entities and its non-recognition of pure *Cit* as the essential nature of the Ātmā. Consciousness is an attribute of the Self. A close examination of this matter reveals a greater connection with the other Standards than thus appears on the surface. For according to them also, knowledge of objects only takes place through the contact of object, senses, and *Manas* with the *Ātmā*. The Self in itself is called by them *Cit* but that *Cit* is wholly different from the apparently limited consciousness and is in fact indescribable by the latter or any other term.

Mental life does not consist of conscious processes alone. Many states and operations of *Antahkaraṇa* exist and go on in sub-liminal consciousness. It is to the dynamism of the sub-liminal or sub-conscious states and operations of *Antahkaraṇa* that the name *Saṁskāra* is given. The Western Cerebralist would explain the dynamism of memory and sub-liminal

[1] Indriyārtha-sannikarṣa.
[2] Acetana.
[3] Niravayava.
[4] Aṇu.
[5] Nitya.
[6] Adhiṣṭhāna.
[7] Adhyakṣa.
[8] Guṇa.
[9] From *Buddha* = to know.
[10] Cf. G.F. Stout: Classification of experience into cognition, interest, and the latter into feeling-attitude and volition.
[11] Jñāna-śakti, Icchā-śakti, Kriyā-śakti.
[12] Pratyakṣa, Anumiti, Upamiti, Śabdaja or Expert, including Revelation.

operations by cerebral modifications or cerebral motions. But cerebral modifications or motions, though they may be the physical counterparts, are not the physical *bases* of those states and operations, since these can exist even when the *Antahkaraṇa* becomes dissociated from the body. Modern Spiritualists claim that disembodied Spirits can put themselves into rapport with ourselves, and thus prove that they carry recollections of the life they lived as ordinary men on earth. How can this be possible if the brain be the physical basis of memory, etc.? The Śāstras claim that it is possible (and modern instances of such psychic phenomena are in evidence) that one can remember, whether spontaneously or through special voluntary effort, the incidents of one's previous births (*Jātismara*). How again could this be if the brain instead of the *Liṅgadeha* (Subtle Body which, according to Śāstra, leaves the physical body at the time of death) were the basis of memory, etc?. The dynamism of memory and subliminal processes in general will have therefore to be explained by the mechanism of the *Antahkaraṇa* itself, which mechanism is called the system of *Saṁskāras*. Since *Antahkaraṇa* (Mind), *Prāṇa* (Life) and *Bhūta* (Matter, are co-essential with one another, the latter two have also mechanisms corresponding to *Saṁskāras*. For instance, what are called Tendencies and Potential Energies of Matter may be called their *Saṁskāras*.

Now, in the First Standard (Nyāya-vaiśeṣika) the Saṃskāras inhere in the *Ātman* and not in *Manas*, which is simple and *aṇu*, and cannot therefore be the basis of a system of tendencies, subtle and potential energies. It also makes the *Saṁskāras* destructible: though unlike the Buddhistic systems it makes them *relatively* stable or persistent; time, disease or a last recollection (*Caramasmaraṇa*) can put an end to a *Saṁskāra*. But from the dynamic standpoint of the two Higher Standards, the *Saṁskāras* are Forces and as such must be persistent. From the standpoint of Sāṃkhya, a *Saṁskāra* is Tendency, while a *Vṛtti* is Action: both are *Vyāpāra* (energising) of *Antahkaraṇa*. Between Tendency and Action, however, it recognises no distinction in *kind*; it is only a distinction of *degree* and of relation with respect to normal consciousness. That is to say, when a *Vṛtti* sinks below the threshold of normal consciousness and *continues* as a subliminal action, it becomes a *Saṁskāra*. A *smṛti* or representation is thus the coming up on the level of consciousness (subject of course to temporal and other conditions) for a past presentation (*vṛtti*) which has never ceased to exist. The Second Standard makes the curve of life a *continuous* line which is, in parts, above and, in parts, below the normal line of consciousness.

Mental life = *Vṛttis* + *saṁskāras* + actual presentations + possible representations—actions + tendencies (which are *avyakta* or subtle actions). There is cyclic causation between *Vṛttis* and *Saṃskāras;* they cause one another. And this cycle is beginningless and endless, though at the time of the dissolution or creation or *Mukti* (liberation) the *Vṛttis* and *Saṃskāras* may lapse into *Prakṛti* or *Māyā* and so cease to have any *effect* on the *Puruṣa* or *Ātman*. With respect to the *Mukta-Puruṣa* or *Ātman*, they are effectively non-existent, they cease to exist. Bondage means subjection (through ignorance) to the causal cycle referred to above, Liberation means disengagement from the cycle. If bondage were based on *fact* as distinguished from *Avidyā* or ignorance of fact, then there could be no possible escape from the cycle for, in itself, the cycle can have no absolute beginning or end; hence both Sāṃkhya and Vedānta make the association of the Self with the cycle not a fact, but an ignorance of fact,—an ignorance of what It is and what the cycle is. The moment knowledge of this comes, the cycle goes. Śakti-vāda regards the *whole* as Fact that is Self and the Cycle; the ignorance of Self of what It is and what the Cycle is; Its knowledge; Its bondage and Its liberation. In any case, so long at least as liberation has not come, *all Saṃskāras* lie in *Antahkaraṇa* as latent activities, not only of this birth but of all previous cycles of birth. In a given type of birth (say, human), however, only those *Sāṃskaras* are called into play which are appropriate to that particular type; other kinds of *Saṃskāras* lie dormant then. Like forces, *Saṃskāras* aid or inhibit one another; as mutually aiding and inhibiting forces they constitute what is called *Vāsanā* (from *vas* to lie or inhere)—the very Background of our conscious mental life.

5

The second Standard or Sāṃkhya-Yoga recognises pure Consciousness or *Cit* as the *Puruṣas* who differ from the *Ātmans* of the last Standard, in that they are attributeless. *Puruṣa* is pure Being or Consciousness. He is not *Kartā* or agent. Experience is not his but another's. He simply manifests and without it there is no manifestation. With it is associated the changing Unconscious Principle or Nature of Prakṛti—*Natura naturans* as Spinoza would have called Her. Though associated with those *Puruṣas* or Spirits who are not freed from Her influence, She is yet separate from and independent of them. Consciousness and Unconsciousness (as mind and matter) are two distinct Realities, for the system is dualistic. This *Prakṛti* is constituted of three Factors and displays itself in three aspects and moments, as that which reveals Consciousness (*Sattva-guṇa*), that which veils Consciousness (*Tamoguṇa*) and as the Principle of activity which moves either to suppress the other (*Rajo-guṇa*). Prakṛti is primordial Substance-Energy in which the factors are in a state of Equilibrium. In creation the equilibrium is disturbed by a kind of catalytic action in which the *Puruṣa* or Consciousness does nothing, but Nature, eternally active, commences to play as various forms before him the Seer. The forms so produced are called *Vikṛti* or transformations and correspond to *Natura naturata.* Homogeneity of Substance-Energy becomes heterogeneous as various collocations of the one Substance Energy. In the first Standard the *Saṃskāras* or Tendencies inhere in the *Ātman*: in this Standard they inhere in the natural unconscious Principle or *Prakrti* and on creation are realised.

From *Prakṛti,* which is an ultimate and not a derivative principle, issues *Buddhi* the determining principle whether in thought or action. As a transformation of *Prakṛti* there first issues the Cosmic *Buddhi* or *Mahat Tattva.*[1] This is the stage at which Energy previously undifferentiated, assumes a definite direction[2] and posture[3] towards a defined line of evolution.[4] This condition of directedness is aptly expressed by the term determination (*Adhyavasāya*). Here, where we are dealing with the state of Energy prior to the appearance of the individual, it is in the nature of cosmic volition. *Mahat-Tattva* is the stage in which the tendency towards individualisation takes a direction or rather resolves (*Adhyavasāya*) to take a direction. But what direction? This is as yet implicit in *Mahat.* It is merely a determination as such to changing in a particular line, the line itself being still undecided. It is a massive (hence the term *Mahat*) cosmic resolution in which the "how" and the "what" of the operation are yet implicit. In cognition too a vague and massive experience commonly precedes a definite and articulated experience. It is as if *Prakṛti* says to Herself thus: "I shall no longer remain as equilibrated Energy, but I will change in a definite

---

[1] Sāmyāvasthā.

[2] Here and *post,* I refer to a paper on Mind by Professor P.N. Mukhyopādhyāya. See also Prof. J.N. Das Gupta's work on Yogaśāstra and as to the definition of the faculties J.C. Chattopādhyāya's Kashmir Śaivaism. In the Śākta system a posture, attitude or aspect of Power is Mudrā.

[3] Posture of Supreme Power or Mudrā (in the highest sense of the word). Mudrā in the Tantra-Śāstras such as Trikhaṇda-Mudrā also belongs to worhip as ritual gesture and posture.

[4] To borrow an analogy from mathematical language a scalar quantity (having magnitude but no direction) becomes a vector quantity (having both magnitude and direction).

direction: what this direction will be is seen later". *Buddhi* as this massive, inarticulate, cosmic resolution is not to be identified with the individualised will, though it is the ultimal basis of it. *Buddhi* is determination, decision[1] after deliberation in the nature of volition. Deliberation,[2] decision and volition are, from this standpoint, unconscious processes, which become conscious only by incidence thereon of the illumination of Consciousness as the *Puruṣa* or *Cit.* From the point of view of evolution, *Buddhi* is a state of mere presentation, consciousness of being only without thought of "I" (*Ahaṃkāra*) and unaffected by sensations of particular objects (*Manas, Indṛya*). In short, abstract from mind every other of the faculties hereafter stated and you have *Buddhi* as their basis. In the individual it is implicit in everything which is derived from it and includes all intellectual and volitional functions which are not theirs. It is thus the principal Tattva. It is the Basis of all Knowing, Feeling, Willing. Its special function is "determination" which is the last in the cognitional, affectional and volitional process. We must also include all three, the "dẹpartmental" theory in this matter being erroneous. Really there is one Mind with several functions, to which are given various names. A man is said to "determine" (*Buddhi*) who having perceived (*Manas*) and thought 'I am concerned in this matter' and thus having self-arrogated (*Ahaṃkāra*) comes to the determination 'this must be done by me".[3] "Must be done" here does not refer to exterior action only, but to mental action[4] also, such as any determination by way of forming of concepts and percepts ("It is so") and resolutions ('It must be done'). It is the thinking principle which forms concepts or general ideas and is in Sāṃkhya the seat of Memory.[5]

From Buddhi issues[6] *Ahaṁkāra-Tattva* or as Patañjali calls it *Asmitā*, the function of which is *Abhimāna* or self-arrogation. From the cosmic standpoint *Abhimāna* is the name for that stage of evolution in which Prakṛti first individualises Herself.[7] The tendency to individualisation, which

---

[1] Niścayātmika.

[2] Adhyavasāyātmikā buddhih (Sāṃkhya-Pravacana, II, 13). Buddhi is thus called Niścayakāriṇī.

[3] Kartavyaṃ etat mayā (Sāṃkhya-Tattva-Kaumudī, 23rd Kārikā).

[4] Mānasī-kryā. Action according to Indian ideas is not merely physical. The mind is constantly active.

[5] In Vedānta this is a special faculty as Citta.

[6] The earlier Tattvas are both Prakṛti (Producer) as regards what follows and Prakṛti or produced as regards what precedes.

[7] We may get an idea of what this is like by comparing with it the state of rising from sleep in which one has first a vague experience of mere being and then of an "I".

is the sum and substance of Ego, becomes explicit and a fact in the stage of *Asmitā*. To use physical analogies, it is the appearance of a centre or nucleus or axis of operation in the cosmic self. Thus in the nebular hypothesis, to explain the solar system, for example, we require either a centre of condensation (older hypothesis) or an axis of spiraline movement (new hypothesis). That centre or axis is the Ego of the nebular cloud. So long as this centre or axis has not appeared we have no beginning of actual evolution of the cosmic dust or vapour into systems of heavenly bodies.[1] Asmitā, as a creative cosmic principle, should not be identified with an individual Ego which is constituted of subsequently evolved principles in the form of sensorium and senses. It is the individualising Principle in nature, the Cosmic Ego which unfolds itself into a multiplicity of individual Egos. As a cause[2] is the subtle state[3] or potential condition of its effects and not merely their sum total,[4] Cosmic Ego is the subtle state of all the manifold Egos, conscious and unconscious, whether in sentient beings, or material things which make our world of experience.

The individual *Ahaṃkāra* is the personal consciousness which realises itself as a particular "I, "the experiencer. It arrogates to itself the experience offered by Manas and has the consciousness "I am so."[5] "I-making" is self arrogation,[6] that is that realisation of oneself in relation with the objects of experience as personal "I", affecting or affected by others. This is the "I" of empirical consciousness. Having so arrogated, it passes on the experience to be determined by *Buddhi*.

From *Ahaṃkāra* issues a double[7] stream of evolution namely *Manas* and the *Indŗyas* (lower mind and senses) on the one hand and the five *Tanmātras* or Generals of the Sense-particulars on the other, evolving in their turn gross sensible Matter. Here the Principles of the subject and its faculties of mind and sense having been developed, necessarily their objects, first as subtle and then as gross, appear over against them.

The functions of Manas are (*a*) attention, (*b*) selection, (*c*) synthesising the discrete manifold of the senses. Attention must co-operate with the

---

[1] Of course Prakṛti or Mahat do not correspond to Nebular Bodies. The latter appears on a lower plane. Previous to that Asmitā had already manifested itself in a superior plane. [2] Kāraṇa. [3] Sūkṣmāvasthā. [4] Samaṣti.

[5] Ahaṃkāra literally means "I-making" (faculty). [6] Abhimāna.

[7] One line dominated by Sattva whence issue Manas and Indŗyas, the other by Tamas whence issue the five Bhūtas; Rajo-Guṇa helping both the Sāttvika and Tāmasika evolutions (Parināma) by virtue of its impulsion. In the Tantras (cf. Śāradā-Tilaka 1-18) we find a threefold division of Ahaṃkāra into Sāttvika or Vaikārika which is the group of 11 Devas of the Senses, Rājasika or Taijasa which is the Manas and Indŗyas and Tāmasika or Bhautika which is the Tanmātras, the origin of the Bhūtas.

senses before the latter can "give" the experiencer anything at all.[1] Nextly, at one and the same minute the experiencer is subject to receive a countless number of sensations which come to, and press upon, him from all sides. If any of these is to be brought into the field of consciousness, it must be selected (*Saṃkalpa*) to the exclusion or rejection (presupposing *Vikalpa*) of others. The process of experience is the selection of a special section from out of a general whole and then being engaged in it so as to make it one's own, either as a particular object of thought or a particular field of operation. Thus its function is said to be *Saṃkalpa-vikalpa;* that is selection and rejection from the material provided by the senses of perception. When, after having been brought into contact with the sense-objects, it selects the sensation which is to be presented to the other faculties of the mind, there is *Saṃkalpa*. This presupposes a previous attitude of indecision, indiscrimination or oscillation which is *Vikalpa.* The activity of *Manas* cannot be revealed to the experiencer except through the operation of *Ahaṃkāra* and *Buddhi.* The images built up by *Manas*, through unconscious operation, cannot affect of themselves the experiencer, so as to move him in any way until and unless the experiencer identifies himself with them by *Ahaṃkāra*, that is by making them his own in feeling and experience. Lastly, as Western Psychology holds, the senses give not a completed whole, but a manifold—the manifold of sense. These "points of sensation" must be gathered together and made into a whole. These three functions of attention, selection or discrimination and synthesising the discrete manifold belong to the leader of the senses or *Manas*. It is leader, for without it the other senses are incapable of performing their respective offices—and as these senses are those of perception and action,[2] Manas, which co-operates with both, is said to partake of the character of both cognition and action. Just as *Manas* is necessary to the senses, the latter are necessary for *Manas*. It is the seat of will and desire as the desire to perceive and act, and therefore exists in association with the senses. Through association with them it appears as manifold, being particularised or differentiated by its co-operation with that particular instrument which cannot fulfil its functions except in conjunction with it. When *Manas* has functioned it passes its experience on to *Ahaṃkāra* which refers that experience to the individual Ego.

---

[1] See J.C. Chatterji's "Hindu Realism". And so in the Bṛhadāraṇyaka-Up., 13-2-7, it is said: "My Manas was diverted elsewhere therefore I did not hear".

[2] Jñānendṛya and Karmendṛya.

The function of *Manas* has to be understood in contrast with that of the intellectual organs[1] the function of which is simple apprehension of sound, touch, colour, taste and smell without conscious discrimination and assimilation or classification. When an object comes into contact with a sense organ we have at first simple apprehension like that of a child or one stupefied.[2] It is the sort of perception which can be expressed by an interjection like "Oh". It is undiscriminated and unassimilated (unclassed) knowledge.[3] Then the internal organ Manas attends, discriminates and classifies.[4] Manas is ranked with the ten sense-organs. It partakes of the nature of both kinds (*Jñāna* and *Karma*) of sense-organs. All the three (*Buddhi, Ahaṃkāra, Manas*) however are called *Antahkaraṇa*,[5] that is internal (*Antah*) organ or instrument of *Vyāpāra* or action (including knowing and feeling) in the most general sense of the term.[6]

Unlike the first Standard this view allows simultaneous as well as serial action of the inner organ and senses. On this Professor Pramathanātha Mukhyopādhyāya writes: "I think the Nyāya-vaiśeṣika view is only a first rough sketch of the ways of our mental life. Experience is a nameless unity, an alogical mass, an undefined universe to intuition. This is the "Fact". Then by the process of moving attention (attention moves because it is pragmatic) this mass is dissected into several elements which are the abstract "fact sections," that is colours, sounds, tastes, ideas, memories, anticipations and so on. Thus the Fact is *not* obtained by a synthesis of previously known and recognised fact-sections (that is by association) but the former is the original *datum*[7] out of which the sections are obtained

[1] Buddhīndrya or Jñānendrya. The term Indrya literally means a Linga of Indra or Ātman, an index or Upādhi of it. Here it means-Sāttvikāhaṃkāropādānatvaṃ indrya-tvaṃ—that is what is evolved from the Sattva-prevailing Ahaṃkāra. Buddhi and Ahaṃkāra though practically Lingas of Ātman are not themselves Indryas.

[2] Saṃmugdha. [3] Nirvikalpakaṃ.

[4] Its function as Vācaspati says, is indicated by "Idaṃ evaṃ naivaṃ," "It is this not that".

[5] Kriyate anena iti karaṇam. "Karaṇa" is that by which something is done. This something includes feeling and knowing. There are thus four kinds of Karaṇa according to function (Vyāpāra-viśeṣa) namely Buddhi, Ahaṃkāra, Manas and the ten Indryas (13 in all).

[6] Thus the function of Buddhi, Ahaṃkāra, Manas is Adhyavasāya, Abhimāna and Saṃkalpa-vikalpa respectively. These make the Antahkaraṇa or Inner Organ. Then there are the outer organs, *viz.*, organs of intellect (Jñānendrya) the function of which is Ālocana or sensation and the organs of action, the functions of which are speaking, grasping, etc.

[7] This is a fundamental notion of Vedānta according to which we start with everything *viz.*, the Pūrṇa or whole. As full Consciousness itself it appears as limited modes of experience. As the great Life (Prāṇa) it vivifies all particular breathing organisms. It is the original *nidus* of Power whence all varied forms of matter issue.

by moving and exploring attention impelled by *Saṃskāras*, that is obtained by dissociation. Most modern psychologists adopt this analytic view of experience. It follows therefore that the massive whole, the universe of fact can be taken in at once. It is a seamless but not a featureless unity. Scarcely can it be called an unity, for it is not a numerical fact at all. It is alogical, unreachable by the categories. We start therefore with the *whole* in which the parts are imbedded. Nor can we have this by means of a *Manas* which is atomic (*Aṇu*). The latter is set up to admit feelings and sensations one by one and piecemeal; but elementary feelings and sensations, sharply discriminated from one another, appear subsequently by an analytic operation upon an alogical whole of experience which intuition already has given. How did intuition give it? Could it have been intuited by an atomic partless Manas? Then again what is precisely meant by a single elementary feeling? Ordinarily a sound-sensation is regarded as one and as different from a colour sensation. Nyaya-Vaiśeṣika recognises atmospheric vibrations as the objective *stimuli* of sound-sensation. The vibrations are rapidly succeeding pulses of agitation. We have a great number of pulses in a short time.[1] Each pulse acting singly upon the ear will produce a shock of feeling. Hence when a sound has been heard for one minute only, there has been really heard a great number of individual sounds, each separately attended to and admitted by *Manas*. Theoretically of course the *Manas* can do all this. But this assumption if made to apply to the whole affair of experience, would put a needlessly fantastic appearance on it.[2] I think then on the whole that experience should not be limited to seriality alone: though in the economy of mental life we have certainly to recognise a distributive and discriminative principle. This principle of distributive (as opposed to collective or massive) attention prefers to address itself to the sections of experience one by one and when confined between two objects commonly oscillates between them.[3] Pre-

[1] The ether waves of modern physics would count several hundreds of billions in one second.

[2] Compare on this point the view of W.K. Clifford who posits an atom of feeling (not conscious) as the counterpart of each elementary nervous shock induced by each individual objective stimulus (*e.g.*, a single wave of luminiferous ether). These atoms of feeling do not aggregate and compound themselves below the threshold of Consciousness but each forces itself up into Consciousness where they all compound and blend together as one sensation. See his Lectures and Essays and for criticism W. James "Principles of Psychology", Vol. I.

[3] See Prof. Pramathanātha Mukhyopādhyāya's "Approaches to Truth."

ferential regard to one section is *Saṃkalpa* and the act of oscillation *Vikalpa.*[1] And this regarding and oscillating principle is *Manas*. Preferential regard is the bestowal of emphasis on a portion of a given continuum[2] by which the portion becomes especially vivid and interesting and the rest veiled. In such preferential regard therefore there is not absolute engagement with one to the exclusion of others. It is merely the apex of a curve of presentation. Similarly in oscillating, the objects only alternately rise and sink as regards emphasis, as attention vibrates between them: there is commonly no complete withdrawal from the other when attention dwells upon one. So much as regards common experience. In it there is undoubtedly a tendency to mono-valued (referring wholly and exclusively to one) attention: we require such attention in the interests of our practical life. The Nyāya view of *Manas* takes the limit of this tendency in the mathematical sense. In other words it conceives *Manas* as the perfection of this tendency: thus the normal *curve* of presentation dwindles into a point,[3] thus carrying to a theoretical limit a tendency that is certainly unmistakable in our normal experiences."

"Besides that distributive and oscillating principle (which may be called *Manas* though we need not go so far as to conceive it as literally *Aṇu*) we have to recognise in our mental life a principle of intuition or massive experience. The whole *Antahkaraṇa* or Inner organ (involving *Buddhi*, *Ahaṃkāra* and *Manas*, as assumed by Sāṃkhya and Vedānta) will better explain life by their respective activities than the simple atomic inner sense (*Antarindrya*) *Manas* alone as assumed by the Nyāya-vaiśeṣika. We have however, not wholly discarded the atomic view of *Manas*. We interpret it as the absolute limit of a tendency to distributive and oscillatory attention which normally operates in life but not to an absolute degree. Nyāya will apply the absolute limit itself to the explanation of ordinary knowledge (*Jñāna*) and has therefore to dismiss simultaneous apprehension as an illusory appearance."

---

[1] Manas is called Saṃkalpa-vikalpātmaka. In Vedānta, stress is sometimes laid on the *vikalpa* aspect: thus Vedānta-Paribhāṣā places the characteristic of *Manas* in *Saṃśaya*, and Pañcadaśī in *Vimarśa* (meaning doubt or indecision).

[2] *e.g.*, on the star Sirius in a clear sky.

[3] Professor P.N. Mukhyopādhyāya gives the following example: Thus instead of saying while eating an orange I have a massive experience of taste, smell, sight, muscular effort and sound together, in which the first two probably occupy the apex of the curve of presentation and the rest lie somewhere in the slopes, it says that I have and can have one sensation only at a time (Manas being Aṇu) and that the Manas on account of its lightness passes rapidly between the different succeeding sensations and thereby produces the illusory experience of co-existent apprehension.

The senses co-operate with *Manas*. Sensations aroused by sense-objects are experienced by means of the outer instrument (*Bāhyakaraṇa* as contrasted with the Inner Instrument *Antahkaraṇa*) which are the gateways through which the *Jīva* or individual receives worldly experience. Their function is *Ālocana* or sensation. An *Indṛya* or sense is not the physical organ such as eye or ear, but a faculty of the general mind, ultimately *Buddhi*, operating through that organ as its instrument. The outward sense organs are the usual means whereby on the physical plane the functions of hearing and seeing and so forth are accomplished. But as they are mere instruments and their power is derived from the mind, a Yogi may accomplish by the mind only all that may be done by means of these physical organs without the use of the latter. So it is said that a hypnotised subject can perceive things even when no use of the special physical organs, ordinarily necessary for the purpose, is made. By the instrumentality of the senses things are perceived and action is taken with reference to them. They are not however sufficient in themselves for this purpose. They cannot work unless in co-operation with their chief, the *Manas*. Thus unless there is attention there is no sensation at all. To be absent-minded, as the term is, is not to know what is happening. The mind is always and unconsciously being affected by what is happening, but these do not rise to a conscious level unless *Manas* functions as attention and selection and synthesises sensation.

The Senses are of two classes in which there are each five. The first class are organs of sensation and perception (*Jñānendṛya*), working through the sensory nervous system namely hearing by the ear, feeling as touch by the skin, seeing by the eye, tasting by the tongue and smelling by the nose.

The Antahkaraṇa together with its functions constitutes an organic unity, so that neither the different aspects of it, nor their respective functions are to be set in sharp contrast to one another. The fact that they derive from a common root precludes any exclusive scheme of partition. The question therefore is merely one of relative emphasis. In this way, the *Manas* presents and discriminates; *Ahaṃkāra* owns or arrogates to itself; and *Buddhi* decides and resolves. These are the three principal stages and forms of mental functioning: some object is presented; it is owned; and then action is taken with reference to it. Besides these, we may have a function by which past impressions are recollected: this is *Citta*, according to the Vedāntic classification. While this is clear it must be observed that, in a careful psychological analysis, the processes, *viz.*, presentation, apperception (self-arrogation) and resolution will be found to involve and presuppose one another. Just as *Sattva*, *Rajas* and *Tamas*, though always acting conjointly, are often referred to separately, according as one or either of the other two *predominates*, so also is the case here. *Manas* presents and discriminates, but it also does, though not prominently and consciously, what *Ahaṃkāra* and *Buddhi* do; that is to say, when *Manas* acts, the whole *Antahkaraṇa* acts through it, though its functioning may have its emphasis, during such action, upon discriminating presentation. That it is so can be shown by psychological analysis. Discriminating presentation does involve an element, though sub-conscious, of both owning and acting (*i.e.*, the functions of *Ahaṃkāra* and *Buddhi*). In other words, when *Manas* acts, we have the actions of the other two *implicit* in it, which analysis may bring out. What is true of *Manas*, is also true of *Ahaṃkāra* and *Buddhi*: while these latter act, the whole Antahkaraṇa acts. None can act in isolation. During the working of *Ahaṃkāra* and *Buddhi*, the places of emphasis have shifted; what was implicit in *Manas* has now become explicit. This follows *à priori* from the principle that they have a common root and have the same essential constitution; so that what is in the one is also, though in a different bearing, in the others;—an application of the principle that what is here is everywhere, and what is not here is nowhere. It follows also that one can be made to do the work which the others can normally do. Thus the sense-organs which *normally* exclude one another as regards their function, may be made to do the works of one another; *e.g.*, the sense of touch can be made to see.[1] In modern hypnotic experiments also, such *exchange* of sense function is sometimes observed. All this is possible because the sense-organs have a common root, and because the *Jīva*, in his entirety, functions through each, though the modes and emphases of operation are different in different organs. Much more is this true of the organs of the Antahkaraṇa. The second class of senses are senses of action, which are the reactive response which the self makes to sensation, working through the motor nervous system, namely mouth, hands, lips, anus, and genitals whereby speaking, grasping and holding, walking, excretion and procreation are performed, and through which effect is given to the Jīva's desires. These two classes are afferent and efferent impulses respectively. The fact of there being a variety of actions does

[1] Gautama, the compiler of the Nyāya-Sūtras did this, and accordingly he is also called Akṣapāda, *i.e.*, one who saw with his feet.

not necessarily involve the same number of Indṛyas. An act of "going" done by the hand (as by a cripple) is to be regarded really as an operation of the Indṛya of feet (Pādendṛya) even though the hand is ordinarily the seat of the Indṛya for handling.[1]

6

In the next part, I will examine exclusively the concept "Matter." Here however a few words are necessary. None of the six systems regards Matter from the Physico-chemical standpoint of science but from the psychological standpoint which regards its effect on the mind and senses. It has been said[2] that the division of matter from the standpoint of the possibility of our sensations, has a firm root in our nature as cognising beings, and has therefore a better rational footing than the modern chemical division of matter into elements and compounds which are being daily threatened by the gradual advancement of scientific culture. They carry with them (the author above mentioned observes) no fixed and consistent rational conception as the definitions of the ancients did, but are mere makeshifts for understanding or representing certain chemical changes of matter and have therefore only a relative value. Gross matter, as the possibility of sensation, has been divided into five classes according to their relative grossness corresponding to the relative grossness of the senses. These divisions are called "Ether" (*Ākāsa*), "Air" (*Vāyu*), "Fire" (*Tejas*), "Water" (*Ap*), "Earth" (*Pṛthivī*). The English names are merely literal translations of the Sanskrit words. It must not be understood that *Pṛthivi* is Earth in the ordinary English sense of the word, and so with the rest. Gross, that is sensible matter is, in all the systems, called *Bhūta*. All the systems posit certain elements of which it is composed. These are called by the First Standard *Paramāṇu* that is extremely small points of substance and, when massive enough, stimuli of sensation. Their place is taken in the second and third Standards by the *Tanmātra* or Generals of the sense-particulars that is Universals. The respective characteristics of these are compared later.

Philosophy has drawn a distinction between primary and secondary qualities, and regards in such case the former set alone as really inhering in matter and elements of matter, whilst secondary qualities are only effects produced upon a percipient subject by the primary set. The Indian

[1] Tantrasāra Āhnika 8. The Kashmirian work of that name and not the Compendium by Kṛṣṇānanda-Āgamavāgīśa.

[2] The Study of Patañjali by Prof. Surendranath Dasgupta, p. 178 (University of Calcutta).

systems recognise no such partition, holding that the arguments which prove that some of the properties are objective will also prove that the rest are equally so. If the external and sensible world exists it cannot consistently be maintained that any of its properties are subjective.[1] The material minima or *Paramāṇus* possess both sets of qualities. All the qualities, primary or secondary, are in the thing, and matter therefore is what it appears to us to be, subject to individual imperfections (*Doṣa*) in perception. It is seen perfectly as the Universals and combination of universals in yoga-consciousness. On this ground all the systems are thoroughly realist.[2] The minima again originate all these qualities in sensible matter because they themselves possess both.[3] The general properties[4] of sensible things are those which are never absent from any one of them. These may be perceived by more senses than one, and in masses of things only differ in degree and not in kind. These correspond to a certain extent with the so-called primary qualities of matter. There are however special qualities which are distinguished from the former in that they are perceivable by a single sense only, and they differ in masses of things not in degree only but in kind. They are therefore essentially different from one another and correspond to some of the so-called secondary qualities of Western Philosophy. These are touch and feel, colour and form, flavour and odour.[5] There are things from which one or the other of these qualities can never be eliminated so long as they exist as those things. The distinctive quality is of their essence.[6]

As the *Paramāṇus* are supersensible and non-spatial entities they are incapable of any distinction from one another in regard to size, shape, weight, density, or any other form of measure. But they may be and are classified with reference to the qualities which they produce in the different forms of sensible things that are themselves the product of the *Paramāṇus*.

The Naiyāyikas hold that the only differences (*Viśeṣas*) between the four classes of minima are their differing *Adṛṣṭas* (V. post). Therefore, according to the latter one Point of a particular class cannot have a form

---

[1] See *ante* "Reality". The Guṇas, Karmas, and Relations exist in the things themselves.

[2] Thus greenness is in the leaf and not in the perceiving subject. See "Reality".

[3] It is a fundamental maxim of this standard that the qualities (guṇa) in the effects (kārya) are due to the previous existence of them in the Cause (kāraṇa). So it is said (Vaiśe. IV—1—3) *Kāraṇa-bhāvāt Kāryabhavah*, which as the Upaskāra of Saṃkara Miśra explains, means *kāraṇaguṇa-pūrvakā hi kārya-guṇa bhavanti.*

[4] Sāmānya-Guṇa.

[5] Sparśa, Rūpa, Rasa, Gandha.

[6] Musk can never be imagined as without odour so long as it remains musk, while pure water need not have any smell at all.

(*Rūpa*) different from that of another *Paramāṇu* or Point of the same class. According, however, to the Vaiśeṣikas, each Point even, of the same class, is believed to have its own particular, individual characteristics (*Viśeṣas*). Thus to explain the actual particulars, Viśeṣas are put into the *Paramāṇus* themselves, thus practically robbing them of the universality which they ought, in theory, to possess. The partless Points of subtle matter like their gross aggregates or sensible matter, (for matter is throughout whether as molecular mass or atom the same) exist in the all-pervading continuum or Ether (*Ākaśa*) and are, therefore, subjected to the action of two other entities and forces, namely, *Kāla*, a general principle of movement, and *Dik*, a principle which holds things together in a particular position, which forces, by their operation, give rise in the percipient to the notions of relations called Time and Spatial Position. The *Paramāṇus* have severally no immanent dynamism though they have energy of position. They receive their initial motion from the First Mover or God: though as entities, they are eternal and are, therefore, not created by Him.

We here pass from the pluralism and metaphysical realism of the first standard to the Dualism of the second, and from it to the Non-dualism of the third standard which is that here adopted. These systems I have shortly described elsewhere,[1] and I deal here only with their concept of Matter. Both the second and third standards replace the *Paramāṇus* by what they call the *Tanmātras* which are five in number, namely, "Ether", "Air", "Fire", "Water", and "Earth", that is objective motions and forces which give rise to the five sensations of hearing, touch, sight, taste and smell. They are Generals of the Sense Particulars, or Types or Universals. *Tanmātra* means literally "that only" or "thatness". The "thatness" or General of the sense particulars is of each of the five classes. The mingling of these *Tanmātras* which like the *Paramāṇus* are super-sensible, and their combinations when so mingled go to make up gross sensible matter or *Bhūta* by the accretion of Mass or *Tamas*. The nature of the *Tanmātra* is little understood.

In order to understand what a Tanmātra is we may take this sheet of paper. 'What is it?' It is a particular form (*rūpa*) seen by the eye, a particular cause of sensation as touch (*sparśa*) and has a particular odour (*gandha*) and so forth. Subjectively, the paper = this particular form, touch and odour. But what is it objectively or in itself? Scepticism says it is unknown and unknowable. Agnosticism says the thing in itself is

[1] See "Reality".

an X which is unknown. Realism says the thing in itself resembles the paper as known or perceived. To what extent does it resemble? Scientific realism says that the resemblance holds only as regards what are called primary qualities. Hindu Realism in all the three standards does not restrict the resemblance to the so-called primary qualities alone, *i.e.*, the paper in itself has real form, real odour, real touch and so forth. But has the paper in itself a particular form and so forth which a subject may perceive in it? Different subjects may have different perceptions of the paper. The same object may be perceived differently under different circumstances. A Scientist by his apparatus may perceive in his way, what the ordinary man does not. A *Yogi* may have still another perception and so on. All these different perceptions of one and the same thing cannot be real. Hence it is said that the real form and so forth of the paper in itself are such as are perceived by a Standard Subject possessing an Absolute Eye and so forth. This standard or ideal subject is that aspect of Consciousness which is called Hiraṇyagarbha, a plane which Yogīs may reach. They see both the *Tanmātras*[1] and the combination of *Tanmātras* which when they become sensible or *Bhūta* constitute the gross bodies of all particular beings. These are then seen perfectly, that is without any defect (*Doṣa*) which is due to the action of inherited tendency (*Saṁskāra*) of any kind. For it is to be remembered that man's mind is never *tabula rasa* but a complex of impressions and therefore tendencies produced by previous actions (*karma*). The ordinary man's perception of the paper is of the paper in itself perceived subject to the limitations of the defects (*doṣa*) in him.

Examining this perception of paper we find (1) that it is gross (*Sthūla*) in the sense that it is patent; (2) that it is particular giving us mere sense particulars; (3) that it is a complexus of form, odour and so forth, *i.e.*, heterogeneous; and (4) that it is variable according to the circumstances and instruments of perception. A man's actual sense-datum possesses these four characteristics. Upon an analysis, however, with a view to discover the elements which underlie this sense datum, it becomes clear that the elements to be real, *i.e.*, to be real elements of the paper in itself, must present the following characteristics: (1) they must not be gross but subtle (*Sūkṣma*); (2) they must not be particular but generic or universal. Thus, if we take a particular form and colour such as whiteness of this paper, the very elements which make up this whiteness ought not to be

[1] The Tanmātras are seen by Yogis by that form of Yoga-dṛṣṭi which is called *Savicāra Saṁprajñāta-Samādhi*.

particular. The particularity must arise out of the particular grouping (*Saṃyoga*) of the elements. Particularity may also be due to the speciality of the instruments of a given subject's sense activity. If the elements themselves be particular, then they are not elements and they are not, as the Pātañjala-Yoga-Śāstra says, *Aviśeṣas.*[1] (3) They must not be complex; they must be simple or homogeneous in quality: otherwise, they are not elements. Thus each distinct species of colour must in itself be conceived as homogeneous in quality.[2] (4) They must not be variable, *i.e.*, they must be such as exist for a standard or ideal subject. It is these generic, simple, subtle and standard or ideal elements of our particular, complex, gross and variable sense-data which are the *Tanmātras* which again are the material causes of gross, sensible matter or the *Bhūtās.* Simplicity and subtlety, however, do not necessarily suggest that those elements are atomic. Being the elements of sense-data, they are necessarily of five kinds—sound, touch, form and colour, taste and smell—(*Sabda*, *Sparśa*, *Rupa*, *Rasa* and *Gandha*). But each is a family or class name. Thus, the sound universal or *Sabda-Tanmātra* means an hierarchy of generic sounds beginning with the *summum genus* or '*Om*'[3] down to the *infima species* (Ka, Kha, Ga, etc.). It excludes, however, the mere particulars, such as the sound Ka and other sounds as actually spoken by this man or that. The same applies to touch, form, taste and smell. There is a logical as distinguished from a temporal evolution from the *summum genus* to the *infima species.* The further evolution under the action of Consciousness as power (*Cit-Sakti*) of mere sense-particulars from the orders of the *Tanmātras* or Universals is the creation of gross sensible matter (*Sthūla-Bhūta*).

What, then, is the World of the Universals as experienced by those who attain to it[4] that is, to those whose mind is a Standard Mind? In the first place then, a thing really is as it appears. It is seen perfectly free

[1] See Pātañjala-Sūtra, II. 19.

[2] Thus "apple green" must always be of the same shade and the same shade throughout whereas the particular "apple greens" vary.

[3] The Mantra Oṃ is the approximate Natural Name and sound of the first general and massive movement in the evolution of the universe. From this come the particular heterogeneous movements; just as from Om come all the particular letters, which are themselves sound aspects of particular movements. See my "Garland of Letters".

[4] Śaṃkarācārya discusses the universals which he calls Ākṛtis or persistent Types under Vedānta-Sūtra, I, 3, 28. He speaks of Devatā Types, Sound Types, etc. From the Indian standpoint the universals are *ante rem* as existing in the creative "Mind" of God *in re* as the thing perfectly perceived and *post rem* as images of finite constructive thinking, as mental abstractions from the particulars.

from all the defects which attach to minds which are not Standard Minds. It is thus, in this sense, a perfect world. But from this perfect standpoint what are physical and moral ugliness, physical imperfection and vice? It must be remembered in the first place that 'ugly' and 'vicious' are terms of man's aesthetic and moral judgments which on account of his imperfections (*Doṣa*) are neither just nor correct measures of ugliness and vice. In the standard of perfect perception, the ugliness or viciousness of a thing or action must be absolutely just and in correct proportions. Thus from a man's standpoint, he may either over-estimate or under-estimate both. He may either see ugliness or vice where there is none. To a Standard Mind everything will be in the fulness of its bearings and therefore ugliness or vice seen perfectly is an absolutely just and correct estimate of either. From the perfect standpoint again, neither in the ordinary sense may ever exist, for from that standpoint everything is a play (*Līlā*) of the Perfect Consciousness (*Cid-Vīlāsa*) of the *Saccidānandamayī-Śakti.*

It must also be remembered that ugliness and beauty, good and evil are relative. What is beautiful to one pair of eyes may be hideous to another. One has only to remember in the former connection the varying ideas which exist upon the subject of woman's beauty and her fashions. The figure of Kālī-Devī is repugnant to the European. The Indian is drawn towards it. To him on the other hand the Christian's references to the "blood of the Lamp", the purification (of Mithraic origin) by blood, are sickening and repellent. As regards good and evil, what is fear and pain in the deer is joy and pleasure in the tiger, which devours it. The act of the assassin who stabs a Ruler in the dark may bring the light of liberty to his people. The betrayal of Judas, infamous as it was in itself, was yet for the Christian a necessary stage in God's scheme for the redemption of mankind and so on. Like the child's jig-saw puzzle what appears crooked, unintelligible in the part may be harmonious in the whole.

If we compare the *Paramāṇu* and *Tanmātra* we find certain similarities and certain differences. Whilst the first is an abstract and rigid model, the latter is a more concrete one and more easily usable. In fact the higher Standards attempt to complete and clear up what the First Standard leaves incomplete and implicit. Thus comparing the points enumerated in the description of the *Paramāṇu* (*a*) The *Tanmātras* are elements of sense experience regarded as objective, that is categories of sense experience objectified. (*b*) They are simple as elements of sense experience, but are not simple in relation to the individualising principle in consciousness

(*Asmitā* or *Ahaṁkāra*) from which or under the action of which they are derived. (*c*) They have origination (*utpatti*) and dissolution (*laya*), though there is no absolute destruction of them. They originate from the Principle named and are dissolved again into it which is again dissolved in the mental principle *Buddhi* and that again into the psycho-material cause of all (Prakṛti) or in the one Consciousness (*Cit*) according to the Sāṃkhya or Vedānta respectively. Therein they exist as potency. (*d*) Universality which is logically involved in the *Paramāṇus* is fully brought out in the *Tanmātra* which is manifestly a category. (*e*) A Tanmātra is not necessarily something "atomic" and "partless." To conceive it one need not conceive it as a Point. It may be extended or massive, only that mass must not be heterogeneous and variable in quality. It may thus have any magnitude varying from the point (*Aṇu*) to the infinitely great (*Mahat*). In fact a given magnitude, whether infinitely small or infinitely great, is not an inseparable proprium of a *Tanmātra.* Whilst we should not say that a *Tanmātra* has no magnitude, we should not also say that it has always a given magnitude. Thus whilst a *Paramāṇu* has no magnitude in the sense that it is only a point, a *Tanmātra* may be said to have no magnitude in the sense that it is not necessarily bound up with any magnitude.

It must be noted also that the Tanmātra has also objective magnitude, though not in the ordinary sense. A mental object (say an image) is not a subjective phenomenon only: it is in the mind but at the same time it is a real otherness as a condition of stress and strain in the universal ether or cosmic stuff. It can thus be transmitted from mind to mind.[1] Therefore as a stress and strain form it must have some magnitude, and regarded as a condition of the cosmic stuff this may be called objective.

An essential difference between the *Paramāṇu* and *Tanmātra* consists in the fact that the former is an eternal, independently existing, objective reality. It is as equally real as the Mind which perceives it and lasts as long as the Mind lasts. But the *Tanmātra* like the mind is not eternal but a product of the individualising principle of consciousness (*asmitā*) or (*ahaṃkāra*) which is again a product of that tendency in the Cosmic Consciousness (*buddhi*) which is realised in the next stage as a limited self-conscious centre, and which tendency again is a transformation of the Supreme Power (*Mahā-śakti* or God's Will) as both material and efficient cause, known in Śākta worship as the Mother. Since the Mother-Power is the material cause of the universe, all its effects as particular objects

[1] See "Reality" dealing with Perception and the Mind-Ray.

therein are, forms of Her power. She is present in, and as, all things, which are themselves possessed of an inherent Dynamism by which they are evolved, maintained and dissolved again into their Supreme Cause. As that Cause is Pure Consciousness and Experience (*Cit* or *Saṃvit*) all that exists is a form of that. Mind is a limited form of Consciousness as the finite subject. Matter is a limited form of consciousness as the finite object. At base they are one Power. In pure Consciousness a movement takes place which, at first knows itself as its own object, that is, as part of itself, and then as different from itself. This difference itself, as object, unfolds from within itself, on the rise of cosmic memory, the Generals of the sense-particulars and the particular sensible matter. Mind and matter are themselves ultimately twin aspects of the one Consciousness as Power: as *Cit-śakti* and *Māyā-śakti*.

The Mind or subject is one form of stress and strain in the cosmic substance. Matter or object whether gross or subtle is another. Both Mind and Matter are forms of the one Substance. In their ground they are one. Both subtle and gross matter are objective to the mind, in the sense that they are other than, and objects of, its operation. But the objects vary firstly, in that gross matter consists of particulars and subtle matter is the Universals. Secondly, gross matter is what its name means namely matter made massive by increment of *Tamas*. By reason of this massiveness it becomes perceptible to the senses which subtle matter as *Paramāṇu* or *Tanmātra* is not. The movement towards manifestation is throughout both a coarsening and a becoming more definite, particular, and heterogeneous. These characteristics are shown on both sides of the duality into which the one substance bifurcates, namely Mind and Matter. Popularly we think of gross sensible Matter as something occupying space outside the body. This attitude is the result of the increasing definition, particularity, and coarsening of both mind and matter. They thus recede more and more from one another. In the case of subtle matter the two sides make nearer approach.

Perception (*Pratyakṣa*) is explained in the second Standard as follows: The *Puruṣas* or Spirits are many and their nature is pure Consciousness. *Prakṛti* is one and is indescribable except as the unconscious Source of Mind and Matter, which are as unconscious as their origin. *Puruṣa* and *Prakṛti* are two separate independent realities. Experience is of two kinds. It is either the pure experience of the *Puruṣa* dissociated from *Prakṣti*, or the limited experience of the *Puruṣa* in association with *Prakṛti*. The result of such association is an apparent combination of consciousness and unconsciousness—"apparent" because Consciousness is ever unchanged and unaffected. The apparent combination of the two is the individual being or *Jīva*. Outer objects (*Arthas*) affect the sense-organs (*Indrya*). The *Manas* attends to and thus selects one or other from the field of objects and places it before the other faculties of the Inner organ namely the I-Making (*Ahaṃkāra*) and determining (*Buddhi*) faculties.[1] *Sattva* or the factor manifesting consciousness prevails in the latter and there is determination (*Adhyavasāya*.)[2] This modification (*Vṛtti*) of *Buddhi* is unconscious.[3] Hence for knowledge it is necessary that the illumination of Consciousness should fall on Buddhi and its function upon which they appear *as if* conscious.

A similar account is given in the Yoga-śāstra of Patañjali where *Citta* is the general term for the Inner Organ. The external object acts through the sense-channel on *Citta* and this occasions it to unconsciously evolve.[4] *Sattva* is said to be "transparent" and manifesting.[5] Hence it takes on the form of the external object,[6] a fact of importance to remember when dealing with the rationale of the rituals which are concerned with the transformation of *Citta*. But as evolution of *Citta* is unconscious, the light of *Puruṣa* is reflected on the state of *Citta*: or the reflection of *Citta* is cast on *Puruṣa* or they cast reflection on each other.[7] By such reflection there is an *appearance* of the state of *Citta* looking like a conscious state, a state of *Puruṣa* himself. As long as there are modifications (*Vṛtti*) of the *Citta* or Mind the *Puruṣa* becomes falsely identified with *Vṛtti* which is not his own. This is a virtual and not real identification. In non-yoga state the *Puruṣa,* though still really pure, appears to be impure on account of the virtual image of *Citta vṛtti* or mental modification falling on it. Yoga therefore is the stoppage of all modifications of the Mind,[8] when the witness or *Puruṣa* shines in this own pristine purity.

---

[1] Antahkaraṇa, that is Buddhi, Ahaṃkāra, Manas.

[2] *e.g.*, In a dim light my sight merely apprehends an object I know not what. Manas attends and makes it out to be an enemy aiming his weapon at me (here discrimination and classification have been made). Then I refer this to the self (Ahaṃkāra) and see that I am the object of his intention. Then finally I make up my mind (Adhyavasāya) by Buddhi to avoid his weapon by moving away. As to the nature and trueness of perception, see "Reality".

[3] Acetana.

[4] In Sāttvika-pariṇāma as Vācaspati has it.

[5] Svaccha and Prakāśaka.

[6] Bāhya-vastūparāga.

[7] According to various views, the latter being that of Vijñāna-bhikṣu.

[8] Yogash citta-vritti-nirodhah (Patañjali).

In modern parlance Consciousness and Mind are not two different things. This Standard assumes them to be two separate and independently existing things. "Reflection" and so forth merely means that interaction between Consciousness and unconscious Mind and Matter takes place without affectation of the former. Consciousness never ceases to be what it is, but its association with unconscious mind gives the latter the appearance of consciousness, and at the same time Consciousness seems to be limited as the object which it illuminates. We are conscious but know that our consciousness is limited. There is some force which apparently limits it and which appears as mind and matter. A more attractive view is that taken by the Monistic Śākta doctrine of Power: Being is one with twin aspects—as Consciousness and as the Consciousness-Power whereby it appears to contract consciousness as Mind which is then presented with its co-relative Matter. It is Consciousness which appears through its Power as unconsciousness and not unconsciousness which through reflection (*Ābhāsa*) appears conscious.

A modification or *Vṛtti* is in Sāṃkhya and Māya-vāda-Vedānta an *actual transformation* of the Mind-Stuff (*Citta*) but is only an imputation so far as pure consciousness (*Cit*) or *Puruṣa* is concerned.[1] The *Antahkaraṇa* of Sāṃkhya = the *Citta* of Yoga: and this bears no parallelism to the Nyāya *Manas*. The *Citta* is not partless and therefore unchanging. On the contrary being a transformation (*Vikāra*) of the Natural Principle *Prakṛti*, it is composite,[2] ceaselessly changing. Even in final dissolution[3] when it lapses into *Prakṛti*-stuff this latter has still homogeneous change as distinguished from heteropathic change.[4] The essential character of *Prakṛti* and all its derivatives is change and unconsciousness, just as unchanging consciousness is the nature of the Sāṃkhyan *Puruṣa* and Vedāntic *Cit*.

In later Vedāntic works a considerable part of the Sāmkhya doctrine has been assimilated. Thus *Prakṛti* of the latter appears as the *Māyā* of the former, though not of course as an independent principle, for the

---

[1] Cf. Yoga-sūtra (2.20) Draṣṭā dṛśimātrah śuddho'pi pratyayanupasyah. The witness, though only Seer and pure, appears to own and enjoy the Pratyayas or Vṛttis.

[2] As Sattva, Rajas and Tamas.

[3] Mahā-pralaya, and also in what in Yoga is Nirbīja-Samāshi.

[4] By the first or Sadṛśa pariṇāma is meant 'Change in its own given condition". The changed state is equivalent to the changing state, *e.g.*, in Mahā-pralaya, it is in the state of equilibrium (Sāmyāvasthā) of Sattva, Rajas and Tamas and changes so as to maintain this state of equilibrium: the change not upsetting the equilibrium. But in creation (Sṛṣṭi) Change is not of this character but Visadṛśa-pariṇāma. One relation of the Guṇas changes into another different from it and so on.

Vedānta of which we write is monistic. In the same way the notion of Prakṛti as constituted of three factors or *Guṇas* is accepted. Still more is this the case with Śākta doctrine, which is based on the Sāṃkhya with this difference, that it also denies that *Prakṛti* is an independent principle. There is one Brahman of two aspects static and kinetic. As pure unchanging Consciousness It is the one Śiva who takes the place of the plurality of liberated selves. Active Consciousness is the Power which effects change and appears as changing unconscious mind and matter. It is the One Supreme Power or Śakti (*Mahā-śakti*, *Ādyā-Śakti*) who takes the place of the independent Sāṃkhyan *Prakṛti*, though the name *Prakṛti* is retained. She is the Divine Mother (*Aṁbikā*) of all. As the Power of Consciousness or Śiva, or more strictly Consciousness *as* Power, She has two aspects—Her supreme or own (*Svarūpa*) aspect in which She is (as is Śiva) Pure Consciousness,[1] and an aspect in which She appears as the universe. As such She is *Māyā-Śakti* constituted of the three *Guṇas*.[2] It is She then who appears in and as mind and matter, who is both the Form which is these and the Spirit which ensouls them. The Sāṃkhyan Prakṛti has been personified but without ground. Rather is *Prakṛti* a dark impersonal form, a veil, a mystery, like the *Māyā* of Śaṃkarācārya's Vedānta.

To the Śākta on the other hand the Mother of the world is a Divine Person, the Supreme "I" (*Pūrṇāhaṁ*) in which all other limited Egos are. She is not and cannot be some independent Principle, for She is the Power of Śiva and Power and Power-holder (*Śaktimān*) are one. Man is three-fold as Spirit, Mind, Body. As Spirit he is Śiva who, in Himself, is pure Consciousness. As Mind and body he is Śiva as Power, or "God in Action" or Śakti. That Power contracts consciousness in those subject to it.[3] The same Power in the liberating aspect expands man's consciousness until it becomes infinite and one with Hers. *Māyā-Śakti* is the Mother Herself as the World-Creatrix. *Avidyā-Śakti* is the Mother in the form of man and all other beings and things. These are a mixture of Consciousness-unconsciousness, for in this world neither exists alone. There is no pure consciousness (for that means no world), except for the Yoga-Experience which transcends world-experience. Nothing on the other hand is absolutely

---

[1] Cidrūpā or Cinmayīśakti. This is Parā-Śakti.

[2] Triguṇa-mayīśakti. These Guṇas are gross forms of Her as the Powers of Knowledge, Will and Action.

[3] This is Avidya-Śākti (ignorance). The Devī or Mother as Māyā is not affected by the Power She wields. What is in Her called Māyā is in the individual, subject to it, Avidyā.

unconscious, for Consciousness is immanent in all beings and things. What seems to be unconscious is the Mother hiding Herself under the veil of forms: the thicker the veil (the more of Tamas Guṇa as the Hindu would say) the more apparently unconscious a being or thing appears to be. All is Consciousness. All is Brahman. All is the Mother whose power it is to obscure Her changeless Self in changing forms of Mind and Matter. Consciousness is the Mother-Power in Its supreme nature (*Svarūpa*). Mind is a veiled form of that Power. Matter is a more densely veiled form of the same. Throughout we are in union with the Supreme I (*Ahaṃ*).

Here we pass from the mere philosophising of Sāṃkhya to Śākta worship. So far however as its philosophical basis is concerned, it agrees, subject to modifications mentioned, with Sāṃkhya and generally with ordinary Vedāntic views as to the nature of Mind and its faculties and Matter and its properties.[1] Consciousness is of course distinct from Mind. The former is mindless Being. Mind however does not exist otherwise than in association with consciousness with which it is intermingled. Indian Mind—*Antahkaraṇa* or Inner organ—the three species of subjective activity of functioning, *viz.*, *Buddhi*, *Ahaṁkāra*, *Manas* above described, illumined by Consciousness.

Consciousness is the causal body, for out of it is evolved Mind and other elements of the subtle body, sheathed in Matter as the gross body. Between mind and matter there is no *essential* difference. They are each forms of the one Substance-Energy or Supreme Power, variously veiled and in differing collocations. There is no real partition[2] between "unextended" mind and "extended" matter. Both are abstractions of concrete experience which in itself is always extensive and even Immense (hence the term Brahman which is infinite Consciousness or Experience) and unbounded. One section of this we call subjective (Mind) and another section objective and external (Matter). But Extensiveness or Massiveness belongs to both. Experience is always extensive in the sense that experience

---

[1] I am here concerned only with the nature of Mind and its faculties. There are differences both as to essentials such as Māyā, Vivartta and Parināma (see as to the distinction, Vedānta-paribhāṣā, Vedānta-kalpataru-parimala in Sūtra 1—2—21" and Siddhantaleśa of Appaya-dīkṣita); cosmogony through Apañcīkṛta Bhūtas (See Rāghavabhatta Comm. on Śāradā-Tilaka, 1—27 as to this, Trivitkaraṇa and the nature of bodies of Devas, water and earth-dwellers, etc.) and details such as inclusion of Prāṇa amongst the Tattvas, Citta (memory) as a separate Tattva and so on.

[2] Professor P.N. Mukhyopādhyāya favours me with the following (summarised with some observations of my own) note on extensiveness and extension which represents views expressed in his "Approaches to Truth" and "Patent Wonder", portion of his work on Indian Culture.

is always an universe composed of many elements of feeling, ideas, and so forth in which our practical interest emphasises a few features and veils the rest though given.[1] The experience of the limited or Measured (universe) is actually (though not pragmatically) that of the Unmeasured (Brahman). Man is thus always experiencing Brahman without recognising it. (The teaching of Monistic Vedāntic and in particular Śākta teaching[2] is that we must ever recognise this. If man's experience is thus unified with Brahman then the world is a true source of enjoyment, and liberating timeless Bliss is in this way, and according to the perfection of such recognition, attained. It is said in the Tantras that the world was created in and by Bliss. The birth of the world gives no pangs to the World-Mother. It is the separation from and ignoring of Her which is pain in the creature.)

Apart from what was stated previous to this interposition, "Extensive" does not mean immense or unbounded necessarily. It means an experience that has a field having any magnitude and not therefore a point. Any experience (whether a mental image or an outer perception) has a field more or less wide. Experience is always *Vibhu* or all-extensive though by practical veiling or ignoring, this *Vibhu* appears to contract into more or less measured fields: and this sort of seeming or pragmatic contraction can even approximate to the other end of the pole, the *Aṇu* or atomic point which is an ideal limit. (The term "seeming" indicates the Māyāvāda view. According to the Sākta standpoint, there is a real contraction (*Saṃkoca*) as manifested Power of an unchangeable Power-holder. This antinomy it does not pretend to solve. This distinction does not affect the matter in hand.) For when a man thinks that he is attending to a point his experience is not really exhausted in that point.

Experience has ever then a field and perhaps an unmeasured field though this is practically ignored. By "field" is not meant an outer field always: it means a mass or tissue of experience which can be analysed into parts. A partless experience would be atomic or *Aṇu*: but this is an ideal limit only: ordinarily at any rate every experience has parts. An experience may be homogeneous or heterogeneous as regards its consti-

---

2 Thus when I say that I am seeing *a* star I am actually seeing many though one prominently. Besides at that moment I have also other kinds of sensations (sounds, smells, touches, etc.) which I ignore because they happen to be irrelevant to my present purpose.

1 "Particular" because to it everything *is* Brahman in the fullest sense. Its Māyā being Brahman itself as Power.

tution.[1] Psychology also attributes extensiveness to sensations.[2] Organic feelings such as headache, heart-palpitation are felt to be less extensive than feelings of general uneasiness such as fatigue, sleepiness, hunger and so forth. Thus extensiveness is a property regarding which sensations and also ideas may be compared with one another.

Summarising the above we may say that the ground of all experience is the Ether of Consciousness, or *Cidā-kāśa* as Vedānta calls the Supreme or Perfect Experience. The Experience itself is felt or intuited as an Universe to which no definite bounds can be set. Within this universe, we seize upon (swayed by pragmatic interests) a definite portion or section[3] and bring it into prominence and veil or ignore the rest, though given. Then we think and talk as though this selected part or section were the whole Fact. Thus I say "I am experiencing a particular pain now", and so on. This section also is a field in the sense explained: it is a definite measured field. This field may tend to contract more or less closely into a point.

Whilst extensiveness belongs to both mind and matter, in the latter case it takes a new form, involving as it does suggestions of muscular effort or rather of tactuo-muscular sensations. Here extensiveness becomes extension. Any mental state has its extensiveness or voluminousness besides intensity and protensity or duration. Its extensiveness is not essentially different from that of a material object, say a block of stone; the latter only explicitly involves suggestions of tactuo-muscular experience, such as up and down, near and far, right and left, inwards and forwards. *A priori* also this ought to follow. *Cidākāśa* is immensity of consciousness or awareness. All forms of existence, whether subjective or objective, are *Cidākāśa* or supreme, infinitely full, and entire Consciousness veiled variously by Māyā-Śakti. (From the Śākta standpoint it is Consciousness as Power veiling itself.) Hence all the products of Māyā can only be carved out of, and must be imbedded in, that Immensity.

And all, whether mind or matter are in essence one, for they are at root varying transformations of the one Power. Both the senses (*Indrya*)

---

[1] *e.g.*, I am sensing or imaging this white sheet of paper. This is homogeneous experience. It has parts or elements and therefore it is a field. An experience which is a mixture of sounds, colours, and smells, etc., is heterogeneous. This too has parts.

[2] *e.g.*, the roar of distant thunder is felt to be more extensive or voluminous than the screech of a parrot. The palm or the hand placed on the back of another is felt by that other as more extensive than the tip of a finger so placed.

[3] As Professor P.N. Mukhyopādhāyā appropriately calls it, since the Vedāntic name for the Supreme experience or Brahman is the Whole (Pūrna). It is *Akhaṇḍa* that is without sections.

and their chief *Manas* on the one side and the subtle matter, which by addition of mass (*Tamoguṇa*) becomes gross matter, derive from the same principle[1] of apperception or *Ahaṃkāra* which issues from *Buddhi*, as the latter does from the Finitising Principle or root of all things, which considered as a Force, is Prakṛti (and as a Personal Power an aspect of the Mother of the universe—Her Infinite Womb). Mind is that Immensity veiled in a way. Matter is also that same Immensity veiled in another way. It is true that mental activity has in some cases to be conceived as being focussed, as converging in a point and diverging from a point. So far as that is true, the Nyāya view of the inextended *Manas* which is atomic (*Aṇu*) is also relatively true. But this should not be taken to mean that *Buddhi* and *Manas* are essentially different from Matter and that their contrast is given by non-extension and extension respectively.

It has been supposed that the mind is not in space and that therefore it has neither extension nor motion. Space is regarded as something external to it. *Ākāśa* as Space is not essentially distinct from ultimate Reality or Brahman. The quasi-material Ether (*Bhūtakāśa*) is merely the Ether of Consciousness (*Cidākāśa*) veiled in a way. The immensity of the former is the immensity of the latter, though of course the immensity of Experience or *Cit* is the fuller Immensity (*Pūrṇa*) of the two.[2] Mind then exists, operates and moves in space,[3] a statement which has an important bearing on Yoga, and occultism, such as thought-transference.

7

All Psychology recognises the trinity[4] of Knower or Subject (*Jñātā*) Known or Object (*Jñeya*) and Knowing (*Jñāna*)[5] which is stress or interaction between the two. All these are however sections[6] of Consciousness,[7]

---

[1] So in the Vedāntic scheme both mind and matter are derived from differing aspects of one set of Tanmātras.

[2] See P.N. Mukhyopādhyāya's "Approaches to Truth" and "Patent Wonder". Śaṃkara in his Bhāṣya on the Vedānta-Sūtra *Ākāśastallingāt* distinguishes of course between the primary (Mukhya) and the secondary sense (Gauṇa) of Ākāśa and says that the Ākāśa of the Sūtrā is not Bhūtākāśa but Brahman Itself, but he says that the term in the secondary sense too is applicable to Brahman because the latter is similar to Ākāśa in many essential respects such as immensity (Vibhutva) and the like. Ākāśa is thus representative of Brahman, "Khaṃ Brahma" as the mantra runs. In some of the developments of Navya-Nyāya (Neo-Logic) too, Ākāśa, Kāla, Dik instead of being regarded as separate entities, are identified in substance with Paramātman or Parameśvara (*e.g.*, By Raghunatha Śiromani).

[3] Even Nyāya-vaiśeṣika which regards the Manas as Aṇu ascribes Vega or movement to it.

[4] Triputī.

[5] Mātri, Māna, Meya is the gist (Saṃkalitārtha) of Śakti.

[5] Avaccheda. [6] Caitanya.

so that in perception we have not to deal with foreign matter as common-sense thinks, but it is merely a transaction between one Fact-section and another: between one condition of Consciousness or Experience and another. The first is Consciousness conditioned by Mind (*Antahkaraṇa*); the second is Consciousness conditioned by the material object in relation to which the mind energises or functions: and the third is Consciousness conditioned by the functioning of mind. Consciousness being polarised into "I" (*Ahaṃ*) and "this" (*Idaṃ*) there is an interaction between the two. Mind (*Antahkaraṇa*) is with parts[1] and can move in space. Mind is a changing and differentiating thing. Mind is capable of moving from place to place and assuming the form of the objects of perception.[2] *This going out to an object and taking its shape*[3] *is actual.* The mind (I speak of Antahkaraṇa) is a radiant and transparent and light[4] Substance and can travel like a ray of light out through a sense organ. Mind is thus an *active force*, a form of the general Active Power or Śakti.[5] As the brain, the organ of mind, is enclosed in an organic envelope, solid and in appearance closed, the imagination has a tendency to picture it as being isolated from the exterior world, though in truth it is in constant contact with it through a subtle and constant exchange of secret activities.[6] These exist as unconscious psychological phenomena some of which rise to the level of consciousness.[7] The mind is not according to Indian ideas (as it has been sometimes regarded in the West) something static, passive, and merely receptive. It takes an active part in perception both by reason of its activity and the nature of that activity as caused by its latent tendencies (*Saṃskāras*). Cerebral activity further takes place not only in the mind itself, but radiates into space beyond the limits of the human organism where it makes for itself a sphere of action. This activity may display itself either in perception, the matter with which we are here directly concerned, or in such occult

---

[1] Sāvayava. Mind is created, that is, has a beginning. What is created is not partless, for creation is a putting together of parts.

[2] Artha, Viṣaya.

[3] Viṣayākārārita. See Bṛhad.—Up., 4-3-7; Śvetāśvatara, 3-18; Kaṭha—Up., 2-21.

[4] Taijasa.

[5] Every modification (Vṛtti) of the root Natural Principle is active and moving, just as its source is. There is nothing static in nature. The mind in particular is always undergoing conscious or unconscious modification (Vṛtti).

[6] See La realité du monde sensible par Jean Jaurés cited in Emile Boirac "La Psychologie Inconnue".

[7] Leibnitz appears to be the first in the West to formulate the conception of such phenomena or as he called them "insensible perceptions."

phenomena as thought-transference, magnetism, healing and so forth.[1] Here the mind not merely *knows*, but particularly through the faculty of all generates a motor force upon exterior objects. Consciousness (*Cit*) is everything:[2] but it has been veiled in the universe. It is revealed in those things in which mind is, or to which it goes out and which it illumines. Because Mind is the revealer of Consciousness it is the highest manifestation, in varying degrees, of the nature of the Supreme Power. Consciousness is eternally self-manifest. It is reflected however only by that which is capable of such reflection, just as the sun is reflected by a mirror. The Mind is thus a refiner of the veil,[3] which enables man to manifest consciousness in varying degree until by Yoga and elimination of mind, passage is made into Mindless Consciousness.

The following well-known passage from Vedāntaparibhāṣā gives an account of perception. "As water from a tank may flow through a channel into a plot of land and assume its shape (square, triangular or any other form) so the radiant mind (*Taijasa Antahkaraṇa*) goes cut through the eye or any other sense organ to the place where an object is and becomes transformed into the shape of that object. This modification of the *Antahkaraṇa*-stuff is called *Vṛtti*.[4] Such going out is subject to certain conditions. The object must be *Yoga*, that is must satisfy certain conditions in order that it may at all draw out the *Antahkaraṇa* to itself.

On this and in this connection Professor P. N. Mukhyopādhyāya observes: "Western psychology gives us a one-sided view of perception: an external stimulus acting upon a sense organ (*e.g.*, an ether-wave acting on the retina). The more vital side of the picture is however given by the above account quoted: the mind goes out as a radiant energy and takes the shape of the object. In the Vedānta view the stress is laid on this side of the affair, though the object's part is also recognised in the stipulation of *Yogyatā*. (For the mind does not go out everywhere and

[1] Here we may instance a form of initiation (Dīkṣā) to which I have referred in *The Serpent Power*.

[2] Sarvam khalvidam Brahma "All is Brahman" and the Brahman-Svarūpa is Cit. The form is Śakti or Power of Cit or rather Cit as Power.

[3] In Buddhi Sattva predominates and in Vedānta it is derived from the Sāttvikāṃśa of the Tanmātras.

[4] The movement (Saṃcaraṇa) and going out ("lelayate bahih") does not apply to Cit which never goes, but to an inner stuff, which though ordinarily connected with, and dwelling within, the gross body, can extend and contract and go out and take the shape of objects. In ordinary experience the connection with the body is maintained. In Yoga the body may be left altogether and entry made into another body. There is also an occult power or Siddhi of producing a projection of the self known as Cāyā-puruṣa.

always but only when certain conditions are fulfilled, among which we may suppose the tapping on the nerves by objective stimulation, the action on the body, to be one, the mind's *Saṃskāra* or predisposition or interest in a given perception to be another, and there may be other subtler conditions.) Thus the Vedānta view would appear to be a fuller view of the matter than the commonly accepted psychology of perception in the West. The 'jump' from the neurosis to the psychosis is a pretty long jump and an inexplicable one in Western psychology. The affair is explained only up to the stimulation of the *Annamayakośa* (the peripheral organs and the brain); but there is no suspicion of the really important steps in the process, *viz.*, the re-action of the *Antahkaraṇa* and the *Prāṇa* (vital principle) on the *Tāmasika* (veiling) crust of the object. Really, object = subject = the interaction = Consciousness differently encrusted or veiled. The *Antahkaraṇa* is believed to be a stuff that being *Sāttvika* (Consciousness-revealing) and *Taijasa* (radiant) can go out and invade the *Tāmasika* (veiling) crust of consciousness in the form of object (*Viṣaya-cāitanya*), envelop and infuse it by its own luminosity (somewhat like the X-rays which are themselves ordinary invisible, but make opaque things transparent) and thereby discover the essential identity between itself and the object: *it is the finding out of this essential identity* between Consciousness as the Knower (*Viṣayacaitanya*) and that between Consciousness as Knowing (*Pramāṇa-caitanya*) and Consciousness as object (*Viṣaya-caitanya*) which makes the substance of Perception according to Vedānta."

(In terms of Śākta doctrine *Mātṛ*, *Māna*, *Meya* or Knower, Knowing, Known are the gist (*Saṃkalitārtha*) of the term Śakti. It is these three which are referred to in the triplication of the Supreme Point or Bindu in which Consciousness commences to contract and thus subjectify itself as the Knower of objects.)

In perception there is a feeling of *directness* or *immediateness*. This feeling of directness[1] is and can be the import of *Cit* or Consciousness or Brahman only. Thus in any direct apprehension of objects we are really face to face with Consciousness or Brahman Itself.[2] All differences (*Bheda*) are so many barriers set up by the magic of the veil which is Śakti as *Māyā:* in each act of perception a barrier is momentarily removed so that the underlying and essential unity is recognised. As Professor P. N. Mukhyopādhyāya well says "*Perception is thus an act of owning:* the self owning another

[1] Aparokṣatva.

[2] *i.e.*, each perception is a Brahma-sākṣātkāra or realisation of Brahman in a way.

which it has disowned in practice (*vyavahāra*)". As however he is careful to point out this act of owning or identifying in common perception is rather a confused sort of recognition, not possessing the clear import of such ownings as "*Tat tvam asi*" (That thou art) "*Aham Brahma*" (I am Brahman), *So' ham* (He I am) or as the Śāktas also say *Sā'ham* (She I am). It is a kind of unconscious owning in actual fact, Philosophically recognised by reflection, but actually realised by the supreme experience of identity to which these sayings refer.

Immediacy or intuition or direct cognition[1] (*Sākṣātkāra*) may relate to two aspects of perception, *viz.*, the Knower, or to the object or the Known. How then is the sensation-complex on *Vṛtti* intuited? A sensation is a state of the *Antahkaraṇa:* how then do we become directly aware of it?[2]

The conditions of a direct perception or intuition of a sensation-complex or Vṛtti are (*a*) the *Vṛtti* must be *Yogay* (must satisfy the conditions), for every *Vṛtti* of the *Antahkaraṇa* is not that; (*b*) the object must also be *Yogya* in relation to its appropriate sense-organ in order that the particular sensation may be cognised; (*c*) there must be occupation of the same position in space[3] by the *Vṛtti* and the object; (*d*) lastly *Vartamānatā* or the object being present actually at the moment of the *Vṛtti* is another condition of direct cognition. Otherwise there is only recollection or anticipation. The Mind-Ray goes out to where the object is, envelopes it, takes its likeness and this objective double constituted of Mind-stuff (*Antahkaraṇa*) is the Vṛtti. Thus when a jar is seen, the double or *vṛtti* must also be projected and localised there: without such projection and localisation there is no sense perception, though there may be recollection or imagination. Such projection and localisation are also recognised by Western Psychology, but then it does not say that this going out and taking the shape of the object is actual. By actual going out, enveloping and so forth the essential identity between subject and object is recognised which is the essence of perception. Western Psychology leaves this essence of perception unexplained.

On this it is to be observed that *Antahkaraṇa Vṛttis* may be unconscious or rather subconscious. This corresponds to unconscious ideation or unconscious mental modification of some schools of Western Psychology. To engage the *Antahkaraṇa* and to be in it, is not therefore the same thing

[1] P.N. Mukhyopādhyāya.
[2] This is Jñāna-gata-pratyakṣa.
[3] Sāmānādhikaraṇya.

as being cognised. The revealing power of the *Antahkaraṇa* has its degrees. The *Antahkaraṇa* of an ordinary man can reveal matters, whether things or processes, only within certain narrow limits; but by *Sādhana*[1] these limits can be more and more widened and this process is called *Sattvashuddhi*. Thus *Yogyatā* or competency in (*a*) and (*b*) is relative to the state of purification of *Antahkaraṇa*. The ordinary experiencer does not cognise directly (though he can roughly infer) the *Saṃskāras* or tendencies laid in the *Antahkaraṇa*, but it is claimed that a Yogin can, and when he does he remembers his past and future cycles of birth. Again a colour-sensation for example of a certain requisite degree of intensity, duration and remoteness only rises into consciousness. We are blind to sensations (they are sensations in so far as they are modifications of *Citta* or *Antahkaraṇa* and not of the cerebral tissues only) lying beyond our normal limits of sensational intensity. But in clairvoyance and Yoga these subliminal sensations may be known. Referring to the third condition, it is necessary that the *Antahkaraṇa* should go out to where the object is, envelop, and pervade it with its own innate transparency and thus establish the equation between itself[2] and the object.[3] When the *Antahkaraṇa* does not go out to the object and establish the equation there is inference, but not direct cognition. This process may be compared with what Western Psychology describes as a localisation of sensation. 'Occupying the same position in space"[4] is laid down as an essential condition.

There are rules also for the direct perception (*Pratyakṣa*) of the object itself as distinguished from the mental state in relation, dealt with as above. It may be premised that Vedānta, though maintaining the essential unity (every-thing is *Cit*) of perceiver, perception, and perceived (the object in itself or the thing in itself as Kant would say),[5] yet distinguishes them from each other on account of their separate *Upādhis* or veilings. They are thus the same and yet are not the same. They are the same in so far as they are ultimately Śiva or *Cit*, and they are the same in so far as they are also the one Power or Substance-Energy which is *Śakti*. But as manifestations thereof they vary. Vedānta is not agnosticism because the thing as it is (not of course fully) is directly intuited by us: we do not simply know the *appearance* of a thing: we get at the underlying Reality

[1] Process by which the result desired (Siddhi) is attained.

[2] Antahkaraṇa-vṛttyavacchinna-caitanya.

[3] Viṣayāvacchinna-caitanya.

[4] Ekatrāvasthānaṃ.

[5] A Bauddha or modern sensationist would regard a thing as nothing but "a cluster of sensations" localised and objectified. Vedānta does not subscribe to this. See *Reality*.

which is *Cit* and which is the same as in us. It is however agnosticism in relation to the nature and working of *Māyā.*

The conditions under which the object itself is intuited are (*a*) the equation between *Antahkaraṇa* itself and not merely its modification (*Vṛtti*) and the object must be shown: that is the latter must be known as possessing an existence[1] not essentially distinct from that of the subject.[2] For this it is necessary that there should be a *Vṛtti* in the subject or *Antahkaraṇa* resembling the object: for this going out to the object is necessary; (*b*) the object must be *Yogya* or fit for the subject's intuition as before.

In plain language: when I a see jar and know that I directly perceive it, I must first have the object exciting through the physical[3] and vital[4] sheaths the *Antahkaraṇa* (which is the mental sheath),[5] which then goes out to it. The *Antahkaraṇa* temporarily removes, so to say, the gross (*Tāmasika*) crust or veil of the jar and thus brings out the essential unity between the consciousness "imprisoned" in that inert "other." It is thus the knowing (as perception and not in the Yoga sense) of the equation between self and other. In Consciousness (*Cidrūpiṇī*) there is a veiling which is Consciousness Power which again is *Māyā-Śakti* in association with *Cit-Śakti.* This veiling ranges from the slightest to the heaviest, according to the predominance of the Factors of Power. The former is Mind at its highest, that is consciousness lightly veiled: the latter is gross matter in which Consciousness is most veiled. Outgoing activity here slows down and becomes, so far as any further advance is concerned, a static crust. At each end and throughout there is the same Consciousness (*Cit-Śakti*) and Substance —Energy (*Māyā-Śakti*)—the one Mother of worship. But as we proceed from Buddhi to gross sensible matter through the various faculties and senses, *Sattva* or the Factor of Power as the Illuminator becomes less, and *Tāmas* the Factor of Power as the Veiler becomes predominant. The wholly veiled object is presented to the less and less veiled senses, *Manas, Ahaṃkāra* and *Buddhi,* when the Self which is in the form of *Buddhi* recognises itself in fact, though it is not consciously affirmed in the form of object. Cognition is then a kind of *recognition,* the self knowing its self-form. Ecstatic knowing (*Samādhi*) or spiritual knowing in Yoga is the experience by the formless Self of Itself. In the former both Mind and Matter are active. The latter is apparently inert but

---

[1] Sattā. [2] Pramātṛ.
[3] Annamaya-kośa. [4] Prāṇamaya-kośa.
[5] That is the two sheaths Manomaya and Vijñānamaya.

is only relatively so and is like all living forms a Magazine of Power. Both Mind and Matter are constantly active to affect one another. In 1842 Moser maintained that two bodies of whatever nature constantly imprinted their image one upon the other even when placed in complete obscurity.[1] For every manifestation of Power is active, Activity being the essential character of *Śakti*, as Rest is of Consciousness of which it is the Power. In fact the whole world is a criss-cross play of mutual influences, a fact the Hindu has long known.

As far back as 1914 before the more general recognition of occult as well as positive sciences to-day, Madame de Stael[2] when speaking of the rapports between metals and planets and the influence of these rapports on human life said "Why not give the experimental method a wider philosophical concept, which would embody the universe in its ensemble and would not turn up its nose to the 'nocturnal' side of nature, while waiting for more light." By occult phenomena we understand not something supernatural, something not related in a regular and constant form to the ensemble of the forces and laws of the universe which is throughout one, but as obeying one law governing all phenomena. It is in rapport to ourselves and not in themselves that they differ from the ordinary and constant sensorial phenomenon.[3] With these latter we are here concerned. But the obvious or gross (*Sthūla* and the occult or subtle (*Sūkṣma*) or Cryptoidal Phenomena are governed by the same law. It may be said that these views make of mind a material thing. That in a sense is what the Vedānta alleges it to be. The Śiva-Saṃhitā[4] in conformity with the Chāndogya-Śruti says that the finest part[5] of the food eaten goes to build or repair the *Liṅgadeha* or mental body.[6] Mind however is not material in the gross sense that "Matter" is, but in a finer and *quasi*-material sense. All is, in this sense "material" which is not Spirit (*Ātmā*).[7] Spirit does not interact. Mind and Matter which are forms of its Power do so. It is because they are at base the one and same Consciousness-Power that Mind can know Matter.

---

[1] Thus illustrated prints leave their image on glass made visible by the projection of vapour such as the vapour of mercury, iodine, chlorine tc.

[2] De L'Allemagne.

[3] Emile Boirac "La Psychologie Inconnue."

[4] V. Patala, 75-77.

[5] Sāratamah aṃśhah.

[6] Tatra sāratamo liṅgadehasya paripoṣakah.

[7] There are no degrees of or in Spirit. Difference exists between things due to their psychic and physical envelope. Brahman is therefore mindless (Amanah). This does not spell, as some have thought unconsciousness, but freedom of Consciousness from the limitation of mind.

The one formless Supreme Self (*Śiva-Śakti-Tattva*) in which subject and object coalesce in the Knowledge and Love of the formless Self of and for Itself appears, through its power, as the subject-form which has knowledge and ignorance, like and dislike for the object-form, both of such limited forms being aspects, subtile and gross, of the Supreme Self. That Self is known in world-experience in every act of cognition and feeling. The transcendental Self is realised in the ecstasy of Yoga (*Samādhi*) when the Self "stands away from" its limited vehicles of Mind and Body. This is the Experience-Whole of infinitely rich content. All other experience is of sections of that Whole. The experience of the Supreme I is "I am this universe." The limited I identifies himself with a particular mind and body in it. To the yogī the whole world is his body and therefore there is nothing outside him as in the case of those who experience through mind and body. This knowledge is bondage. They who surpass and are freed of it are mindless. But man must first use his mind. It is said "thinking of that which is nameless the stage is reached which is called Śākta":[1] that is the inner state of which Matter and Mind are the outward expression.

The Vedānta does not teach any intuitionalism which discards intellect. On the contrary the Upaniṣad says (Br.-Up., iv 5, "the self must be seen, heard, thought upon and deeply pondered. *Ātmā vā are draṣravyah, śrotavyo, mantavyo, nididhyāsitavyah.*" It is not by discarding any part of the limited self that the Full Self is known, but by the development of the limited self in every part *and as a whole* into the Whole.

8

All theory should suggest a practice whereby that which the former declares of value may be achieved through the latter. As I have elsewhere said the Indian quest is practical. Philosophising is not done because of mere intellectual curiosity but as part of a disciplinary system (*Sādhana*) enjoined for realization by the limited self of its own unlimited and essential nature. That nature has its intellectual aspect and is expressed as Reason. For what is irrational cannot be spiritually true.

From what has been stated it has been seen that Man's essential nature enjoys perfect experience. For it is the Whole which is unlimited Being (*Sat*), unconditioned Consciousness (*Cit*), and perfect and unbroken Bliss (*Akhaṇḍa-Ānanda*). Mind and Body are an expression of its Divine Power whereby Consciousness is finitised in the individual centres. It

[1] Śiva-Sūtra-Vimarśinī, X.

is the essential characteristic of Power as such (*Śakti*) to negate or veil infinite being and infinite experience so that it becomes finite being and finite experience.[1] But the negation or veiling exists in degree. It is much less in the case of Mind than in that of Matter, which to the limited experiencer is that which is other than and apart from the experiencing subject. Again in the case of Mind the degree of veiling of Consciousness varies. There is not Matter in which Mind is not present, though patent or latent in varying degrees. This follows from the scheme of the involutionary principles (*Tattva*) from *Buddhi* downwards, and the doctrine that the effect is the cause modified. From *Buddhi* the first psychical principle of *Ahaṃkāra* is derived; that is *Buddhi* remains what it is as cause and is transformed into *Ahaṃkāra* as effect.[2] *Ahaṃkāra* or *Asmita* is the individualising and therefore centre-making principle. From it is derived subtle matter and from the latter gross matter. Therefore all matter is individualised or is a Self, in which the psychical principles from which it is evolved lie veiled. An atom of Hydrogen is a Self and a Man is a Self, though the latter is and the former is not, a developed Self with fully realised Self-Consciousness. In the effect there is the cause and therefore in gross visible matter (*Bhūta*) there is that from which it is produced, *viz.*, subtle matter and the I-making principle (*Ahaṃkāra*) from which the latter is derived. In *Ahaṃkāra* again there is *Buddhi*. Mind however is so hidden and undeveloped in inorganic matter that its only expression is an extremely rudimentary response to stimuli made apparent by scientific experiment, such as those, now well-known, of the distinguished Indian Scientist Sir Jagadish Bose. Yet even here it may be that one kind of "non-living" Matter may be more responsive than another.

All Matter as everything else is composed of the three factors (*Guṇa*) of the Natural Principle (*Prakṛti*) which is the source of both Mind and Matter. All Matter has then *Sattvaguṇa* in it, that is a Principle which reflects or manifests Consciousness. Differences however exist between the various kinds of Matter, "non-living" and "living", as regards the degree to which the *Sattva* or manifestation of Consciousness is veiled by *Tamas-Guṇa*, or that factor in Being which obscures Consciousness by

[1] So it is said "Negation is the function of Power" in Yogamuni's Commentary on Abhinava Gupta's Paramārthasāra (Niṣedha-Vyāpārarūpa Śaktih)—a very profound saying.

[2] This doctrine is explained by the simile of "light from light". A second torch takes light from the first which yet remains itself undiminished.

suppressing the *Sattva* which manifests it. The first stage of evolution or liberation of Consciousness is the organisation of Matter by the vital Principle (*Prāṇa*). As explained earlier in *Life*, *Prāṇa* is a guiding, directing, and, to such extent, intelligent principle which organises Matter into living forms with increasing degree of freedom and greater and greater display of Consciousness. There is Consciousness in the lowest living forms, but there it is greatly veiled by the aspect of Power (*Śakti*) which is the specifically veiling principle (*Tamas-Guṇa*). During the course of evolution, Mind which has been always present, however latent, is more and more developed until we arrive at the higher animals, the earliest primitive Men and then Man as he exists to-day.

The process is the *development* of Mind and *release* of Consciousness under the influence of what has been called the Vital Impulse, itself unexplained. According to the Śākta doctrine however, this evolutionary impulse is one form of the eternally recurrent rhythm which is observed in (amongst other things) breathing, namely an outgoing and indrawing breath. So in the Macrocosm, Being of its nature (*Svabhāva*) goes forth (*Sṛṣṭi*) as Power involving itself in Mind and Matter, and then evolves itself out of Mind and Matter, and again involves itself in a process which is Eternal. This is the throb of the Heart of Power (*Śakti*) who is called the Heart of the Supreme Lord.[1] As this process involves all dualities and therefore suffering, those who are liberation-seekers (*Mumukṣu*) strive to free themselves by various methods, some negative and others positive. The mass of men ignorant and careless are satisfied to enjoy the world and to take risks of suffering so unevenly distributed. With the former we are here concerned.

Mindlessness (*Unmani-Śakti*) that is experience unconditioned by Mind, and therefore Being in all its infinite freedom and fulness is the aim and end. Mind, owing to the predominance of *Sattva-Guna*, reveals Consciousness more than Matter does: for the latter is dominated by the Veiling Factor of Nature (*Tamo-guṇa*). But Mind reveals Consciousness by degrees, some minds more than the rest. The purer the mind the more it reflects or manifests (whatever simile we apply) Consciousness. The object then of the self-realising discipline or Sādhana is to purify the Mind so that it may manifest Consciousness. Purity of Mind is therefore to be sought. "Pure" and "Purity" are not used in their sexual sense only. This is only one and an elementary form of purity. It is

[1] Hṛdayaṃ parameśituh.

obvious that if a Mind is dominated by sensuous desires and images, it cannot reflect or show Spirit. For this reason the Tantras in specifying the qualifications of the proposed disciple exclude the lewd (*Kāmuka*) and the glutton. It must be pure also in respect of other matters, and therefore free of greed, anger, envy and all else which is the mark of the impure Mind. Such a Mind is incapable of understanding spiritual things. But the Mind must not only be pure in the sense of freedom from what is bad, but must be positively kind and good and free from error. Purification of Mind is called *Citta-śuddhi*. The Mind must be an efficient and trained instrument of knowledge which is its appropriate food, and should if necessary be sharpened by the study of logic and the practice of debate. It should be made capable in this and other ways of understanding the highest metaphysical ideas. And so the disciple is recommended to study the sacred texts, Logic and Metaphysic. At the same time there should be devotion to and worship of God as the Mother-Power (one with Śiva as unchanging Consciousness) who is called Lalitā, Mahākālī Mahā-tripurasundarī, Mahākuṇḍalinī and by other names which denote only aspects of the one Reality as Power.

Ritual is the art of religion. The rituals are designed to secure realisation of Unity with Her. *Śākta-Sādhana* which term includes what is called in English "ritual", is based on sound psychological principles with which I will deal in another volume. The ritual is an expression in action of the philosophical principles above described. Thus the whole evolving cosmic process is imagined in the rite called *Bhūta-śuddhi*, in which each of the lower principles is merged in the higher, until in imagination the abode of *Śiva-Śakti* is reached.[1] So also the *Śrī-Yantra* or Diagram represents both the body of the Sādhaka as the Microcosm and the whole universe.[2] All ordinary acts and functions become worship by dedication to the Mother-Power, and self-identification with that Power in all physical functions and acts. The *Sādhaka* then realises himself as the Mother—Power in the form of himself.

A type of the worshipper's self-dedication is given in the *Mahānirvāṇa Tantra* (VI. 178-181).[3]

"Om—Whatever ere this I have done through the Mind, Vital Airs and Body, whether when awake, or in dream, or dreamless sleep, whether

[1] So Pṛthivī is dissolved in *Ap*, *Ap* in *Agni* and so on in the special centres or *cakras:* in *Sādhana* imaginatively, in Yoga actually.

[2] See my *Tantrarāja Tantra;* also my translation of the *Kāmakalāvilāsa* which deals with the Śri-Yantra.

[3] See "*The Great Liberation.*"

by mind, word or deed, whether by my hands, feet, belly or organ of generation, whatsoever I have thought or said—of all that I make an offering to Brahman. I and all that is mine I lay at the lotus feet of the Ādya-Kāli, *Om Tat Sat*."[1] After saying this, dedication is made of the Self.[2] The instructed worshipper knows that the self is dedicated to the Self, and that the Self, in the person of the worshipper, has thought, said and done all that is offered.[3] The unity of the self and Self is well brought out in the Mantra which is said over the elements in the circle of worship: "The act of offering is Brahman. The offering itself is Brahman. Into the fire which is Brahman offering is made by him who is Brahman. By him alone who is absorbed in the offering to Brahman is unity with Brahman attained.[4]

Not only must the Mind be purified, but care must be taken as regards what is offered to it. The Mind, as such, is never without an object. Care is therefore taken in the ritual to supply it with a good and divine object. As already stated the Mind goes out and shapes itself into what it knows. Therefore a divine object is presented to the Mind, so that it may shape itself into that. The Mind is, in its essential Nature, Consciousness. Mind as Mind obscures it. Endeavour is made by *Sādhana*, or worship and discipline, to lessen this obscurity by purification of the Mind as an obscuring force. *Sādhana* is external and internal or mental (*Mānasa*). When Mind is purified so as to manifest in high degree Consciousness, then the *Sādhaka* enters *Yoga* by the practice of which the Mind so increasingly reflects Consciousness that it disappears as the stars of the midnight sky in the blazing light of the sun at midday.[5] If it be asked how this is possible, the answer from the worshipper's standpoint is that all is possible by the co-operation of the individual and supreme Self. By worship there comes what is called the "Descent of Power" (*Śakti-pāta*) or Grace (*Anugraha*) which strengthens the individual effort.[6]

---

[1] Om. That (Brahman) Being or Reality (Sat).

[2] Ātma-samarpaṇam. This is vilomārghya or offering of the Self as Arghya at the feet of the Devī.

[3] Thus when the Śākta-Vīra takes the Consecrated Wine, he offers it to the Mother residing in himself in Serpent form in the Mūlādhāra Centre at the root of the Spinal Column. But how does She drink it? By and through him who is a representative (*Pratika*) of Her.

[4] *Mahānirvāṇa*, VIII, v. 215.

[5] One of the questions is—does it, as a limited centre remain in fact, even if it disappears to view. According to some it does, the saying being "Like a bird in the forest".

[6] In the same way the Sādhana-śakti of the worshipper is strengthened by the Mantra-śakti or power of the Mantra which he practises in Mantra-sādhana.

In monistic Yoga the Self works without another. In both cases the Self is working and because it is the Self which works, and because that in which it works or its vehicles is a form of the Self, it is capable of modifying and transforming them. For the result of all successful *Sādhana* and *Yoga* is transformation. From the *Sādhaka's* or worshipper's standpoint there is worshipper, worship and worshipped. From the Yoga standpoint the transaction is wholly between the self and the Self and none other. The result (*Siddhi*) which is the attainment of the Experience-Whole (*Pūrṇa*) is gained by the use of all men's faculties of knowing (*Jñāna*) feeling or devotion (*Bhakti*) and good disinterested action (*Karma*). In each case one or other of these operate in greater or less degree. All lead to the same end.[1] But men are of differing temperament and their faculties vary in power. Some men will be drawn to the path of action, others to that of devotion and those whose intellect is highly developed may follow the path of knowledge or religious philosophising (*Jñāna-Yoga*). But whether it be one or another, the One Consciousness is at work through the will of the individual to transcend the limitations of the Mind, at length passing from the highest state of mental experience (*Samanī-Śakti*)[2] to that of *Unmanī-Śakti*[3] which is Mindless or full unlimited Experience, unrestricted by the limiting forces of Mind. This is *Cit* or Pure Consciousness—the Kūtastha-Śiva which is full pure and Perfect Experience.

---

[1] And so it is said that there is no difference between Supreme Devotion (Parābhakti) and Jñāna.

[2] These terms mean "with Mind" and "without Mind" and are two aspects of Consciousness-Power. See *The Serpent Powers* and *Garland of Letters*.

[3] *Ibid.*

# POWER AS MATTER

( *Bhūta - śakti* )

# PREFACE

THIS part treats of an important subject, for many persons find a difficulty in understanding the Vedāntic doctrine as regards Matter. Others affirm that there is no such thing as Matter. It can be easily understood if we remember that Matter like Mind is potentially in, and is actually a form of, the ultimate Reality which is the *Pūrṇa* or the Complete, the Full, the Whole, the infinite reservoir of Energy which appears as the Universe. It is there, as it is here. How ? Not of course as the gross Matter which is the object of the finite experiencer. Such matter has no existence apart from the finite centre which experiences it. Then again it is asked "how and in what way ?" Scientific or conceptual matter as now understood in the West is reduced to electrons and protons or units of electric charge which again are, according to some, strain forms in, and of, an ultimate substance or Ether, and which in any event are forms of Universal Energy. But what we objectively perceive as Energy is subjectively Will. Each limited centre is a manifestation of Energy and a source of it within the universal scheme of which it is a part. But that whole scheme is a manifestation of the Supreme Will, Power or *Śakti* appearing as the Universal Energy in all its various forms. Ultimately then Matter is Supreme Power or *Mahāśakti*. In dissolution Matter, whether gross or subtle, resolves itself into potentiality or tendency (*Saṃskāra*). It then is in the Power of the Supreme Reality as a tendency towards manifestation. Tendency of what ? Of *Cit-Śakti* as the Supreme Experience. The tendency is Power which is then one with *Cit*. What we call Matter is then the Self as its own object. The Self is subject and the Self is object. The object or matter is not, as in the case of the limited centre, something other than, outside of, and separate from, the subject. When the Self knows its object as other than itself there is creation or *Sṛṣṭi*. But "Creation" is not for the first time. It is eternal and recurrent. Matter then is eternal, though it has two forms as seed and fruit. The seed is tendency in the supreme and infinite Reality to appear as Matter to the finite centre. It is potential energy or unmanifested Power. The fruit is that tendency realised as Matter and the Mind which experiences it. It always *is* as the power to become of Being, and recurrently *exists* as that Power manifested as psychic, vital and physical Energy in the form of Mind, Life and Matter. We do not thus let go of Matter (in one sense or another) at any time. The Finite Centre senses it now as something other than the Self. The Infinite Whole in which these centres exist experiences it as Itself. For the Power to appear as mind and matter is one with the Power-holder (*Śaktimān*).

In the same way Mind ever is as seed or fruit. As fruit it is limited *Cit* or Consciousness which has, as its objects, Matter and all forms constituted of it. As seed, it is the Power (*Śakti*) which is then one with unlimited Consciousness (*Cit*). The complete I (*Pūrṇāham*) is Experience as the Whole in which there is no separate subject and object but the Self knows and feels, that is loves, the Self, in which Self as Power is the potency of limited experience as the finite selves and their separate objects. The experience of the limited "I" (*Aham*) is an experience of a self as separate from its object or Matter which it knows and feels through Mind —a limiting force constituting the individual Consciousness.

Science by "dematerialising" "matter" has made a long step towards the acceptance of Vedānta : for gross matter is reduced by some to Energy of and in some substance which is not gross Matter. Nevertheless it remains a quasi-material object. Vedānta says that both it and Mind are forms of the one Power or *Śakti* which existing in those two forms is, in itself, one with the Power-Holder who is the Supreme Consciousness or *Cit*. Consciousness then as Consciousness-Power or Energy is at the back of everything. Since this book was written the English edition of Professor Lewis Rongier's "La Materialisation de l'Energie" has come to my hands. This is a lucid resume of recent physical investigations in which the view is taken that Energy is a substance which materialises as the sensible Universe which does not on that account lose the reality of the substantial characteristics which external perception and common sense have attributed to it.

There are some who disparage and condemn Matter and regard it as something evil and sometimes as unreal. From the following pages it will appear clear that this is not the Śākta View. For, in the first place, what is it according to such views ? It is the Gross (*Sthūla*) form of the Mother-Power which evolves the Universe. It is the form in which the Ultimate Reality is *touched* and handled. In the second place, is it real ? The answer developed in "Reality" (see *ante*) is, that it is real, for it is a form of *Daivī Śakti* or Supreme Power which is real, being one with the Ultimate Reality itself (*Kūtastha-Śiva*) who is the possessor of such power. But neither it, nor any other form (and Form implies finiteness) has the reality of the Ultimate Real—*Ens Realissimum*—for the latter endures changelessly in past, present and future, whereas Matter as such is in each universe developed from Power, and at the end of the Universe is absorbed in the Power from which it issued. Matter is real in the sense—that it is a reality independent of human appreciation, that is, it is not merely a creation of the human mind. Dematerialisation means the reduction of gross, so-called ponderable Matter into points of stress. What has been called ponderable Matter on the other hand has been described to be a form of Energy enormously accumulated in a narrowly circumscribed region of space. Nor again does Matter become unreal because recent Science has dematerialised it. It is not "illusion." "Illusion" is a misleading rendering of the word '*Māyā*' by those who did not know sufficiently Sanskrit or English or were possibly—misled by other phrases, *e.g.*, '*Mṛgatṛṣṇā*' ('Mirage')—a term to be found in *Advaitavāda* relative to the reality of the Supreme Brahman as compared with the passing Universe. *Māyā* comes from the root *mā*—to measure. *Māyā* is not "illusion" but power by which things are measured. *Mīyate anena iti Māyā*, *i.e.*, the principle of form or *finitisation.* But finitisation is not illusion. What is experienced by all normal experiencers cannot be an illusion in the English sense of that term.[1] Then is it Evil ? Essentially it cannot be so, for it is a manifestation of *Daivī-Śakti* which is Supreme Consciousness as Power. Nor even considered abstractedly as Matter, *i.e.*, apart from its combinations—is it so ?

As regards such combinations, it must be noted that according to Hindu views the gross material universe is a duality (*Dvandva*) of good and evil, of happiness and sorrow and of all other opposites which are themselves each relative. They are never absolutely separated from one another. Thus nothing is entirely good nor bad. Some physical things and events and some living entities are injurious and others favourable to man, and to some men and not to others or may be not favourable to any man but to some other living creatures, and so on. We do not complain of the matter of our body when in health. But we may do so

[1] Illusion is prātibhāśika sattā. Let it be here noted that the Vedānta does not speak of even this illusion as a form of unreality but as a form of Sattā or being for it is real while it lasts.

in disease. The same ship which makes shipwreck in a storm to the misery and death of its passengers has probably swiftly, safely and comfortably carried many others. Much evil is the cost price which we have to pay for what is good. Matter *per se* is neither good nor evil, but particular forms of it, or uses to which it is put, may be either good or evil relatively to some subject. In such case, it is the Mind which gives the direction which spells goodness or evil. The Universe of Mind and Matter is neither good nor bad. A Hindu is neither a pessimist nor an optimist in the ordinary sense of these terms. He sees that the world is a world of opposities, that duality involves such opposities and those who desire freedom from such duality, its risks and pains, seek liberation. This liberation is not, according to the method of the School, an "escape" from Matter, but a knowledge of what Matter really is and a Yogic transformation of the Self whose gross Vesture it is. By *Sādhana* and *Yoga*, Matter is recognised for what it really is, and thereafter there is, in consciousness, sublimation of Matter into its Essence.

I will in conclusion repeat what I have said elsewhere (*Śakti and Śākta*).

"And yet as extremes meet, so having passed through our present condition we may regain the truths perceived by the simple, not only through formal worship but by that adoration which consists of the pursuit of all knowledge and science after the husk of all material thinking has been cast aside. By this adoration, intellectual approach is made to the Brahman. For him who sees the Mother-Power in all things, all scientific research is wonder and worship. The seeker looks then not upon mere mechanical movements of so-called "dead" matter but at the wondrous play of Her Whose form all Matter is. As She thus reveals Herself, She induces in him a passionate exaltation and the sense of security which is only gained as approach is made to the Central Heart of things. For as the Upaniṣad says "He only fears who sees duality." Some day, may be, one who unites in himself the scientific ardour of the West and the all-embracing religious feeling of India will create another and a modern "*Caṇḍī*" with its multiple salutations to the sovereign World-Mother. (*Namastasyai namo namah.*) Such an one seeing the changing marvels of Her World-play will exclaim with the Yoginī-hṛdaya-Tantra "I salute Her the *Samvid Kalā*[1] who shines in the form of Space and Time, words and their meanings, and in the form of all things which are in the Universe."

[1] That is the Supreme and Perfect Consciousness.

*Deśakālapadārthārthātmā yad yad vastu yathā yathā,*
*Tattadrūpeṇa yā bhāti tāṃ śraye saṃvidaṃ kalām.*

This is however not mere "Nature-worship" as it is generally understood in the West, (see observations at p. 7 of Dr. Helmuth Von Glasenapp's recent book "Der Hinduismus)", nor the worship of "Force" as the Bengali "reformer" of Hinduism, Keshub Chunder Sen wrongly took the Śākta doctrine to be. All things exist in the Supreme Consciousness which, in Itself, infinitely transcends all finite forms. It is the worship of God as the Mother-Power which manifests in the form of all things, which are, in the language of the Śākta Scripture, but an atom of dust on the Feet of Her who is Infinite Being (*Sat*), Experience (*Cit*), Bliss (*Ānanda*):[1] and Power (*Śakti*).

This part was commenced by me with the help of my friend Professor Pramathanātha Mukhyopādhyāya, but during its progress and at its conclusion, I found myself to be so greatly indebted to him that it has became a joint work and is issued as such. I mention this to explain why some portions of the work are written in the singular as also to exempt him from responsibility for views (if there be any) which may not be his, and explanations of the subject which he might have bettered. In connection with the subject matter of this part I may refer to his essay on the Radioactivity of Matter, as also to Prof. Lewis Rongier's work "La Materialisation de I' Energie" the English edition of which ("Philosophy and the New Physics") only came to my hands after this work had been written. Prof. Rongier's general conclusion is—"abandoning the ether" (which is endowed with contradictory properties and which is declared defunct, without estate, a matter which has been here dealt with to some extent) "we are" (he says), "led to an entirely different theory, that of the materilization of Energy, emerging from the phantom realm of imponderables, to take substance, appearing as endowed with inertia, weight and structure and manifesting itself in two forms, one of which is called by virtue of long prescription, Matter and the other, Radiation." Here Energy (*Śakti*) is the principal concept.

The next part of this volume deals with the concepts of Causality and Continuity. It is followed by "Mahāmāya" dealing with the highly important subject of Consciousness (*Cit*), and its Power

---

[1] This Bliss is the Supreme Love of the Self for the Self. *Niratiśaya-premāspadatvaṁ ānandatvaṁ.* She is worshipped in Madhura-Bhāva.

(*Śakti*). Unless this term (*Cit*) is understood nothing in Vedānta or in its particular form—the Śākta-*Ā*gama—will be understood.

*Bormes, Var*

15th Feb., 1923 J. W.

# THE WORLD AS POWER:

## POWER AS MATTER

(*Bhūta-śakti*)

1

To begin with, we must distinguish between *Perceptual Matter* and *Conceptual* or *Scientific Matter*. Perceptual Matter is what possesses the sensible qualities of motion, impenetrability (that is limiting resistance or the limit where absolute resistance begins), weight, extension in space, colour, taste, smell and so forth. This is, for the psychologist, a certain group of sense-impressions objectified and localised in space. It implies a substratum of those sensible qualities (*i.e.*, a thing which supports sensible qualities and presents them to our senses), or an exciting cause of that group of sense-affections. Whether this implication of a substratum or thing as distinguished from (or as underlying) the sensible qualities or of an exciting cause as distinguished from a group of sense-effects, be ligitimate or not, we do commonly review in thought Perceptual Matter in the manner described above. That is, when we *think* of Matter which we have *perceived*, we think of it as a thing which underlines certain qualities corresponding to certain sense-impressions and as an exciting cause of these latter. This is commonly how the perception of Matter appears when it is passed in review. In itself, the actual perception of Matter or Matter as *presented* is alogical (*anirvacanīya*), admitting of no such logical categories or thought construction as Subject and Object, Cause and Effect, Thing and Attribute and so on. But upon the *presentation* of Matter, thought construction[1] begins, the categories of the understanding (as Kant would call them) are set in operation, and out of this operation (mostly instinctive) the *presented* Matter emerges as *re-presented* Matter, *i.e.*, what we think, believe and describe as perceptual Matter. Thus we know presented Matter as a *substance* existing in *space*, *objectively* to us, moving in *time*, possessing certain *attributes* and *causing* certain impressions in us. All the ideas involved are

[1] Antaḥ-Karaṇa-Vyāpāra.

logical forms or moulds into which the presented matter is cast by us, and the Matter thus informed or moulded is taken by us as the Matter of Perception. It is clear, however, that *this* Perceptual Matter involves conceptual elements. Whether these conceptual elements or thought-forms are or are not subjective forms only—*i.e.*, whether or not there are realities beyond our thought corresponding to these forms (Time, Space, Substance, Cause, etc.) is a question which is not here discussed. Thus, so far, we get two stages in the experience of Matter:

(1) The original, intuitive, alogical experience of Matter apart from the incidence of the thought-forms; this is Matter as we actually feel or apprehend it.

(2) Then we have that original datum of experience as treated by the Subject with his thought-forms: this treatment giving us what we believe, think and describe as the Matter of our perception.

This latter is believed by the Indian systems to possess, both the so-called "primary" and the "secondary" qualities.[1] The metaphysical reality of these is not here discussed, nor do we discuss whether the second or logical was already implicit in the first or alogical so that the second is only the "lighting up" of the first.

After the second stage, the psychologist would put in "images" or mental rehearsals of the things perceived, *e.g.*, the mental reproduction of the smell, taste, colour, size, weight, etc., of an orange which has been actually handled and eaten. It is clear that in such images the primary as well as the secondary qualities of the originals perceived are copied, though with loss of vividness and the like. As these images are not relevant to our present purpose they are passed over.

But let us suppose that the so-called primary qualities (or some of them) alone are retained in ideation, and colour, taste, smell and sound are abstracted in thought. This would give us a sort of Conceptual Matter of which we have no perceptual equivalent. We now have, for example, a Matter which occupies space, moves in space and time, possesses mass and weight, resists movement, and so on. But *in itself* it may be without colour, taste, smell, heat and cold, sound and so forth. These last result from its stresses upon our sense-organs. The effects wrought in us may be for aught we know wrongly (we are here simply stating the scientific position) fastened by us upon the exciting external cause.

[1] See discussion in *Reality*.

Now, this Conceptual Matter is Scientific Matter. Whether such Matter exists or not, we have commonly no perception of it. The Ether, Atoms, Centres of Force, Lines of Force and the rest with which Physics attempts to write a description of the mechanism of the world sensed by us are not objects of perception. And yet they are said to underlie and cause all our sense-experiences, and thus are at the root of all our sense-phenomena.

Physicists, again, are not impartial to all the so-called primary qualities. Some, like Descartes, would regard extension as being the essence of Matter. As Professor Tait, (in his book "The Properties of Matter") did, so one might give as a working definition of Matter; "Matter is whatever can occupy space." Others, following in the footsteps of Leibnitz, might put the essence of things in Dynamism, *i.e.*, power to exert, and resist the action of, force. This Dynamic view is steadily gaining ground in modern scientific thought—Sākta doctrine is also a pure and universal theory of Dynamism. Śakti is Power; all is Śakti. Matter is now that which *moves*, as indeed were things to Heraclitus, the ancient Greek Philosopher ("All things flow") and to the Hindus to whom the world was *Jagat* or "the moving thing" or again as they are to one of the philosophers of our day, Prof. Henri Bergson.

A comparsion of the notions held concerning Matter by Modern Western Science and the six orthodox Philosophies of India[1] must take account both of fundamental differences as well as similarities. The former are apt to be overlooked by those who estimate Indian Philosophy (whether such estimates be high or low) by its conformity or non-conformity with Western Science. At the outset therefore some of the main points which should be borne in mind are noted.

Ancient India had its Chemistry and Alchemy[2] and most important among these were the so-called Tantrik and Mercurial[3] Schools. But all this is part of Science[4] as it was then known. The six philosophies dealt with the subject matter from a philosophical and religious standpoint.[5]

---

[1] See *Reality*.

[2] See Sir P. C. Ray's Indian Chemistry. Both Indian Chemistry and Medicine are indebted to the Tantras. It was these latter which added the metallic medicines to the vegetable drugs of the Āyurveda.

[3] Mercury is the semen of Śiva as Mica is the bija or seed of Śakti. 'Ārtava' or menstrual flow is Red Sulphur. According to Hindu notions not women only menstruate, but the whole earth menstruates in its season.

[4] Vijñāna.

[5] Jñāna.

From the latter standpoint it is of the first importance to remember that the Indian notion of Matter is based upon a *psychological* analysis of the actual experience of Matter, the element thus obtained being substantialised, and not upon a *psysico-chemical* analysis such as that of Western Science. Start is made with the actual perceptions of gross sensible Matter. The mind divides and subdivides until it arrives at the minimum psychosis which, objectively considered, may be called, to use an expressive term of a recent English work, "Psychon" which in Indian terminology is a Paramāṇu or Tanmātra, the supreme power producing both the sensible and the senses and the sensations which the former stimulates in the latter.

As regards Matter, the first standard agrees with Western Science in so far as the latter makes it or treats it as an extramental reality. There are however, important points of disagreement between the two also. In the first place, Western Science draws a distinction between primary qualities and secondary qualities and regards the former set alone as really inherent in Matter and elements of Matter, whilst according to it, the secondary qualities are only effects produced upon a percipient subject by by the primary set. No one of the three standards recognises any such partition. In these standards things are as things what they appear to be. The qualities, primary or secondary, are in the things themselves. This question has been discussed earlier in *Reality*. The Hindu orthodox systems are, therefore,. in an *epistemological* sense realist, under whatever class they may be said to come metaphysically.[1]

The second standard (Śāṃkhya-yoga) is metaphysically realist in so far as it affirms the reality of Mind and Matter in both gross and subtle form.[2] In the Monistic Vedānta both Mind and Matter are as such real but are forms of That which is neither.".[3]

What then is Matter? It is of importance to note that former Western notions concerning Matter have been completely reversed in recent years. As we proceed backward in the later history of Western Science, we find less and less co-ordination between the Sciences and between the facts of any particular Science. The Universe presented the appearence of a heap of miscellaneous unconnected facts. Latterly, there has been an increasing

[1] A reviewer of the latter book has thought that "its object was to defend all the Hindu systems against the charge of philosophical idealism". This of course is not so. I dealt with the theory of knowledge. I was there contrasting Hindu doctrine with Buddhist subjectivism and referring to the reality of Matter to the individual experiencer.

[2] Both are forms or vikṛtis of the one Prakṛti.

[3] This ultimate Reality is mindless (amanah). We have therefore here no concern with systems which regard Matter as Mind.

tendency to the establishment of continuity and unity: and this is but natural, for the Scientific Mind working towards unity is, whether conscious of it or not, a step in the progress towards the realisation—"I am Brahman" (*Ahaṃ Brahmāsmi*). This unity of all things and the immanence of the Spirit in all things has ever been affirmed by India and represents one of the most valuable parts of its colossal philosophic and spiritual achievements. The general tendency is now towards some form of radical monism as a result of greater and greater co-ordination and unification of sciences and of science with Philosophy and of Philosophy with Religion. Summarising the main result of this scientific revolution, we may say that it consists firstly, in the teaching of the destructibility and *dematerialisation* of sensible matter existing in an *ethereal* medium; secondly, the *unification* of Matter and Energy in the sense that these are no longer considered different things but aspects of one and the same thing; and thirdly, in the acceptance of the doctrine which places the essence of matter in its *dynamism*. Matter in this latest view is not something inert merely occupying space but essentially dynamic with mobility as its fundamental trait.

Each of these affirmations which are considered later in detail were made by ancient Indian doctrine. To it gross sensible Matter (*Bhūta*) issues in and from, and is again dissolved in, the Ether in the sense of *Ākāśa* and is in its ultimate sense not material at all. It is, to use the words of the Poet, "such stuff as dreams are made of". Matter (*Bhūta*) and Energy (*Karma*) are two aspects of the Ground Power (*Mahāśakti*). Matter is only a variety of Substance-Energy; what are called imponderable things are mere forms of energy being a subtle rapid mode of function whilst ponderable matter is a gross and slow mode of function of Universal Substance-Energy. The essence of things is dynamism which, in its causal sense, is the Supreme Power or Will (*Parā Icchā Śakti*) and, in the sense of effect, psychical (*Mānasa-Śakti*), Vital (*Prāṇa Śakti*) and physical (*Bhūta-Śakti*) manifestations of such Will. What we know and are consicious of in ourselves as Will-Power is objectively observed as energy. We may measure energy as it is manifested within the universal system: but the sum total of energy is not as in the doctrine of "Conservation of Energy" a limited constant. There are no absolute bounds to the magnitude of energy which is the manifestation of the Infinite Power of Becoming (*Śakti*), of Being itself (Śiva). This dematerialisation and dynamic view of matter and unification of matter and energy as aspects of one substance together with the recent revival, though with added proofs, of the old doctrine of

Relativity makes the notion of *Māyā* at least intelligible even to those who have hitherto derided it. But *Māyā* covers both Mind and Matter. Some have regarded extension as being the essence of the latter. Mind in its antithesis was said to be unextended. The allegation that Matter is extended and that mind is not, is only a metaphysical theory. When dealing with any metaphysical or scientific theory, it will be useful to remember that the Vedānta does not admit of any absolute partitions whatever. The realisation of its standpoint in this respect is one of the chief keys to an understanding of that system. The doctrine of the macrocosm (*Bṛhat-Brahmānda*) and micrososm (*Kṣudra-Brahmānda*)—expresses the same principle, so well-defined in the Viśvasāra Tantra in the words "what is here is elsewhere, what is not here is nowhere". (*Yad ihāsti tad anyatra, yannehāsti na tat kvacit.*) In each centre everything is in some manner, be it explict or implicit. Thus, it is said in the Mantra-Śāstra that all the letters of the Alphabet are in each of them. Thus, mind and matter are both Fact sections (as they have been aptly called) of Experience as a whole (*Pūrna*).[1] Matter is said to be that which occupies space which space, considered as substance, is the Ether in which the material world is. Mind, considered as a centre of stress and strain, postulates also a continuum in which it also energises, *i.e.*, the Ultimate Plenum (Pūrṇa or Pleroma) which is Infinite Consciousness and unlimited Experience. Mind and matter are two aspects as subject and object of one and the same Whole (*Pūrṇa*) which is neither and yet inclueds both. Matter and Mind are one in this that neither is *as such*, Spirit, since both are principles of unconsciousness. Mind can be said to be immaterial only in the sense that it has not the materiality of ponderble matter which is a gross and slow mode of energy-function. It is not, however, immaterial in the sense that Spirit as such is: that is absolutely so. Just as the recent experiments on Matter speak of emanations less and less material, semi-material, quasi-material and so forth between gross ponderable Matter on the one hand and the Ether which is not "Matter" on the other,[2] so we may say that since neither Mind nor Matter are as such Spirit, both are in essence "material", ponderable matter being wholly so and Mind being quasi-material in the sense of its being like Matter an unconscious principle or Force veiling Spirit or Consciousness (*Cit*) but not grossly material as

[1] By Prof. P. N. Mukyopadhāya in his "Approaches to Truth".

[2] That there is a substance intermediate between Matter and Ether is said to be shown by the variability of the mass ascertained.

ponderable Matter is. Ether in the Indian sense of *Ākāśa* is derived from what may by called a "Psychon"[1] or an element of Psychosis as sense-experience regarded as objective. This Psychon again is a projection of certain fundamental psychic cosmic principles[2] which are themselves rooted in the fundamental Power of Becoming which is the Cosmic Will (Mahā-śakti).

2

It will be useful here to shortly survey the immediate past and present notions of Matter held by Western Science, even though some conclusions are yet of an hypothetical character only. I refer to currently accepted and orthodox scientific teaching. For there have always been, as elsewhere Alchemical and Mystical schools and lately systems of scientific monism which affirm unity in the form of a Fundamentsl Substance and its development into various modes of itself. As the great Giordano Bruno, who was burnt because of his doctrine, said in his treatise "Della Causa Principio Ed Uno"—"What in the principle is unseparated, single and one appears in externality in things, sundered, complex and multiplex".

Firstly, let us consider the *de-materialisation* of Matter. Formerly the material universe was regarded as made up of compounded bodies, themselves constituted by the aggregation of simple bodies. These last were the so-called irreducible, chemical elements some eighty in number. The ultimate factors of compound bodies were the molecules or the smallest particles subsisting of those bodies which exhibited the properties of those bodies. The molecule again is a group of atoms. The atom was according to Newton, a hard, geometrical, impenetrable,[3] solid body incapable of deformation. Though infinitesimally small and indivisible, it was yet regarded as spatial and as having some magnitude. Like gross sensible matter of which it was the ultimate factor, it was held to be extended and to have mass or amount, weight[4] and was characterised by Inertia. There were as many different kinds of atmos as there were different elementary substances. Each of these substances was regarded as a separate chemical species which, like species in living beings, were invariable. An absolute break was thought to exist in each case between the different

---

[1] Or Tanmātra: to borrow a term of an English author whose name I forget.

[2] Asmitā, Ahaṃkāra and Buddhi, see *post* and *Reality*.

[3] This was believed to be true not because it was demonstrated but because it seemed reasonable, as it was on the assumption of hardness. Clerk Maxwell called it nevertheless "a vulgar opinion".

[4] The elements in the order of their atomic weights arranged from the lightest or Hydrogen to the heaviest Uranium.

species of so-called inorganic matter, between non-living and living matter, and between Matter, whether organic or inorganic, and Mind. Carrying disunity and discontinuity further Theology postulated the greatest break of all between the universe of Mind and Matter and its ground as God.

The Hindus have, for at least some two thousand years, postulated a continuum in which discrete material things exist, *viz.*, a subtile substance and plenum called *Ākāśa.* This as Ether was put forward in the 17th century by the Scientist Huygens in order to explain the Phenomena of light. Some now accept it and some do not. Those who do so have regarded it commonly as a third thing distinct from Matter and the supposed Forces which animate the latter, though Energy exists both in Ether and in Matter which lies immersed in Ether and cannot be isolated from it. There were thus three separate indestructible and constant things, *viz.*, Matter itself, Ether itself and Energy in Matter and Ether. The duality of Matter and Energy, the indestructibility of the former and the conservation of the latter were generally accepted doctrines.

It was then however observed that, as in living beings, there were both genus and species. Certain forms possessed a family likeness and therefore possessed similar properties. They can be divided into their respective families by their atomic weights. And so by what is called the Periodic Law of Mendeleef and Meyer the properties of an atom may be known from its weight. This law was established before the dissection of the Atom. Since then it has been suggested that the atomic weight of an element is proportional to the number and form of arrangement of the electrons or units of electric charge, of which the atom has since been conceived to consist. The arrangements according to the Periodic Law almost suggested, it has been said, a genealogical tree. Predictions of the properties of new elements which would fill up the missing links in the scale were subsquently verified by actual discovery. Earlier Chemistry noted the existence of bodies of seemingly identical nature, though differing in properties, called allotropic. These allotropic states may be classed as different species of the same genus. The same metal presented itself in forms which could not be confused. On the other hand nearly a quarter of the simple bodies known are so similar, that without special investigation they could not have been isolated. Further investigation with instruments of greater precision showed (it was said) that between chemical as between living species there were transitional forms. There is a genus with several species, and there are some species so alike that chemical action could scarce distinguish them. Colloidal metals may even resemble in some ways organic substance. All this pointed to the same variability of chemical species as biologists affirmed as regards living beings. When it was discovered that the atom was not invariable or indestructible, it was affirmed that simple bodies may be transformed even more easily on account of their greater simplicity than animal species. If Matter, as it is now held to be, is no longer indestructible and fixed, then the invariability of chemical species no more exists than of living species. We thus return to the transmutation of substances of the old and derided alchemists.

Spectrum analysis showed that the materials of the universe were throughout the same whether on earth or in the remotest stars. It was also by the same means observed, that the hottest stars are constituted of very much fewer chemical elements than the colder ones—a fact which suggested that the elements in the latter were evolutionary transformations of the former. These observations alone, however suggestive were insufficient to prove the actual transformation of chemical elements into others with different characteristics which they possessed at certain relatively fixed states for so lengthy a period as to almost disprove evolution as the continuity of change in the elements. Then Sir William Crookes discovered the Cathode Rays. He called it a fourth state of matter and named it Radiant Matter, now considered by some to be electricity. To the three conditions of matter solid, liquid, and gaseous in which there is decreasing cohesion in the molecules was added a fourth state which was said to be as far removed from a gas as gas is from a liquid. Later on, the particles were called Corpuscles or Electrons or units of Electric charge. The latter made up the atom which was then regarded as a cluster of electrons varying in number and arrangement but identical amongst themselves, building up by such number and arrangement the different kinds of matter—the "elements" known to the chemist. Professor Crookes was then led to put forth the ancient idea (to which man has returned again and again) of a Primitive Stuff called Protyle from which all the elements were derived. The Phenomenon of the dissociation of matter was then more fully investigated. Certain stages in the process of the dematerialization were noted. Radio-activity was established as regards all forms of matter, though most manifest in some radio-active substances such as the heavy Radium, Thorium, and Uranium. The first emission was a non-electrified product called by Professor Rutherford the "emanation," which to him was material gas and has also been said to be (le Bon)[1] semi-material. From it are produced the Alpha, Beta and Gamma rays. The Alpha rays are positive Ions of which the electron or atom or unit of negative electricity is the Nucleus. The Beta Rays are radiations of electrons formed of negative electric atoms which are identical with those of Cathode Rays; and the Gamma rays are said to be analogous to the Rontgen or X-rays the nature of which is not known but which are neither Cathode, nor ether waves in the nature of light but which are (it has been suggested) pulses of electric and magnetic force manifested in the breaking up of the electron itself. These Rays are said to be less and less materialistic, the first being invisible atoms of matter or an intermediary having properties in common with a material body: the second being pure electricity freed of matter and the third as above described. As regards the unit of positive electricity there is more ignorance but the opinion has been expressed that it also is freed of "matter". That there is a substance intermediate between matter and ether is said to be shown by the variability of mass ascertained. One property of matter remains invariable namely the mass measured by the weight. But variability of mass or "mass-acceleration" is ascertained as regards particles emitted by radio-active bodies. The mass varies with the speed showing (it is said) that substances exhibiting such a property are no longer "matter", the mass of which is fixed and invariable. The Atom of matter has been described to be no longer an indestructible mass, but is a sort of solar system formed by a central group of nucleus charged with positive electricity around which negative electrons gravitate in closed orbits. The electrons are the same from whatever source they are obtained. Thus, it has been said, we find that the infinitely small which had been thought to be final has itself grown into a world. And naturally so, for each form of existence is a microcosm (*Kṣudra-brahmāṇḍa*) as the Śāstra teaches and the Brahman is both greater than the great and more minute than the little. (*Mahato Mahīyān Aṇoraṇīyān.*)

To sum up, Matter has been defined as that which possesses inertia, weight and mass. As so defined, matter is what is ponderable, but inertia in the ordinary sense is now denied. No matter is at rest since all is in continual movement (*Spanda*). On the contrary the atom is now said to be a reservoir of stupendous energy. Everything must be that if it be a

[1] L'Evolution de la Matiére. See also the same author's "L'Evolution des Forces".

form of infinite Power. The notion of inertia we get from superficial observation of molar masses. There is no rest anywhere beyond (in some conditions and for a time) an apparent absence of relative change of conditions between one particular molar mass and another. Even here each molar mass itself is disintegrating and its atoms are in continuous movement and dissociation. There is continuous molecular birth and death.[1] Whether again Matter has weight depends on certain conditions. It would cease to have weight if taken to the centre of the earth or placed at a suitable distance between the sun and moon. The attraction of the earth depends upon where it is. Would it, if so placed, cease to be matter? A measure was therefore sought independent of position namely division of the weight of the body at a given place by the value of gravity at that place, the quotient being called the "Mass". Moreover matter is said to dissociate into the imponderable Ether which cannot be weighed. In other words matter is ultimately something not weighable. It can be weighed only so long as it remains in that state in which it can be weighed. Mass again is the measure of inertia, that is to say of the property which enables matter to resist motion or changes of motion. In the case of ponderable matter this mass is not permanent. Variability of mass that is of inertia has been noted in the particles emitted by Radio-active bodies during disaggregation. The mass varies with their speed and this variation is relied on to show that substances which exhibit such a property are no longer "matter". The particles produced during the dissociation of matter possess a property resembling inertia, and in this are akin to matter, but this inertia instead of being constant in magnitude varies with the speed, and on this point the particular particles, though issuing from matter, are differentiated from its atoms. It has also been supposed that the corpuscle or electron which is said to be the ultimate element of matter is quite free from it. Moreover Ether into which matter is said (in disaggregation) to ultimately lapse, is, according to some theories, without mass, therefore Matter in its ultimate basis is without it. In other words the first law of motion which may also be expressed by saying that all matter has inertia or inability to move, or to change velocity or direction if it already has motion, only appears to be experimentally true of bodies whose magnitude and state we can ordinarily see. The notion is due to superficial observation of change of position of

---

[1] Both Brahmā and Rudra are continuously at work. It is an error to suppose that Brahmā created some years ago and is now doing nothing. See chapter on "Om" in my *Garland of Letters*.

gross bodies. But further knowledge of the constitution of Matter itself has shown that the ordinary notion of the inertness of matter is not true. For Energy, called sub-atomic, is now found to be locked up in the atoms and if they have energy they must have motion of some sort, and are shown to be in motion even when the molar mass of which they are the atoms appears to be in rest. In the same way it has been said that potential energy must in some way depend on motion. A French author (L. Houllevigue) after describing this process of dematerialisation asks "Are these things certain? One must beware of believing it. Tomorrow perhaps the wind of a new theory may sweep away all these hypotheses. We are upon scientific ground of too recent a date, for it to be possible to build solid structures." Since this was written, subsequent investigation has confirmed in considerable part what had previously been affirmed. It is however a fact that some parts of the theories set forth are regarded from a scientific standpoint as doubtful or as semi-certitudes or mere hypotheses. In some matters the "wind of theory" to which the author refers has veered towards older and rejected doctrines such as regards light the corpuscular doctrine of Newton, and as regards electricity that, whatever it be, "it is a thing and not a mere form of energy". In other points the movement is towards a new outlook. Thus there is a school of chemists such as that of Franz Wald and Oswald who would give account of chemical processes not in the language and according to the ideas of the atomic theory, but in terms of Energetics, according to which matter is but a Centre of Force or a Complex of Energies found together at the same place. The former view is more akin to the Nyāya-Vaiśeṣika system with its lasting "atomic" Paramāṅus deriving ultimatley their motion from a First Mover and the latter to the Vedānta doctrine of Śakti which as immanent Power in and as all things is the source of their auto-dynamism.

But can the Mind stop at the electron? It cannot rest until it has become the whole[1] beyond which there can be nothing as it is all. Electricity itself is now believed by some to be granular or atomic in structure. The electric condition is regarded as a condition of stress in Ether which is not in any sense Matter according to its scientific meaning and is that which is the subject of stress and strain. The Electrons are points of centres of energy in the ethereal continuum constituted by stress and strain centres not only in, but also composed of, the ethereal substance—vortices of and

[1] Pūrṇa.

in the ether as it has been suggested. Regarded as such, they might be considered as the infinitely small:[1] but the stress when considered as an attitude of the universal system taken as a whole is infinitely great.[2] The infinitely little from one aspect is from another the infinitely great. Everything which lies between these two limits exists in varying grades of magnitude.[3] But the ideal limit or perfection of the continuum[4] is not Scientific Ether but is in Vedānta the Cidākāśa or Ether of Consciousness, of which as Power, in the form of efficient and material cause[5] all the psychical and physical universe is composed and in which its movements take place. Science however is not concerned with Matter other than as objective extra-mental Reality. Vedānta resolves both it and Mind into forms of expression of the Supreme Cosmic Will containing latent tendencies (*Saṃskāra*) towards manifestation as centres of limited will and experience.

What, then, is Energy? This is defined as 'capacity' for work. The ability which one body has to move another is sometimes called its energy. The energy which a body has, depends on its own amount of motion. Motion, again, is of two kinds—*viz.*, motion in a body of its constituent elements, motion which makes it what it is. Then there is motion of the body as a whole from one place to another, that is, locomotive movement. This last may be communicated from without by another body in movement or may be self-initiated. The inner movements and self-initiated locomotion of living bodies is well-known. But molar masses of inorganic matter were observed to be at rest. They did not move unless something moved them, *i.e.*, motion was communicated to them from without by means of other bodies themselves in motion. It was assumed then that the ultimate constituent of Matter, the atom, was also at rest and incapable by itself of quitting the state of repose. The interior constitution of the Matter as a system of moving units was unsuspected. Inorganic Matter was then held to be inert—dead or brute Matter as it was called. Of itself it could not move.

Inertia was a property which enabled it to resist motion or change of motion. This had to be overcome by the application of energy in action or force. Matter might possess energy but for this it must have motion and this motion must be communicated to it from without through the motion of

---

[1] Aṇu. [2] Mahat.

[3] The supreme exemplar of these two limits is the all-pervading Cidākāśa and the Point of Power or Bindu Śakti which the Śāstra describes as ghanībhūtā śakti that is condensed concentrated Power about to manifest.

[4] Mahat. [5] Cit-śakti and Māyā-śakti.

other moving bodies which had thus either received and passed on these movements or, in the case of living bodies, had generated them. All this was true enough as applied to molar masses of inorganic matter without power of self-initiative locomotive movement. But it ignored intra-atomic movement, the self-generated perpetual movement of the particles constituting the atomic system. There were thus two different things, however linked together, namely Energy in work or force and the inert Matter which it moved. Language was sometimes used in which energy was spoken of as if it were an entity or something which might exist though there was no substance to move. This, of course, is not so; for the two, namely, Matter and Energy are never dissociated. By the forms of our thinking we cannot conceive of one without the other. We think of matter which moves and is moved. In a transcendental sense, substance in its ultimate meaning is that which is common to all which is and which acts. It has two modes, namely, the rapid mode of function which manifests as the imponderable energies called light, electricity, magnetism and the slow mode of function which manifests as ponderable matter. Matter the ponderable is a gross and relatively stable form of it. Heat, light, electricity and other imponderables represent suitable unstable forms of it. Both are forms of substance-energy in perpetual motion and manifesting such motion in organic matter as in all else. Matter is not, as formerly thought, incapable of possessing any energy but that transmitted to it and is on the other hand now held to be not inert but a reservoir of colossal intra-atomic energy or *Śakti*, and this must be so to the Śākta who believes that the minutest particle of inorganic matter is a limited form of the Mother-power, the potentialities of which are unlimited. All is in motion and though matter as a self may and does resist, yet mobility (Spanda) is its fundamental trait.

It has been said:[1]

"It would no doubt be possible for a higher intelligence to conceive of Energy without substance for there is nothing to prove that necessarily it requires a support but such a conception cannot be attained by us. The essence of energy being unknown we are compelled to materialise it."

Both Substance and Energy however are necessary concepts of dualistic thinking. It is not possible to resolve either, as we understand them, into the other. It is only when they are transcended that their unity is found to be grounded in the Supreme Will as both efficient and material cause. It appears both as energy and matter, *i.e.*, energy inseparably associated

[1] Le Bon, L'évolution de la Matiére 17.

with matter and matter inseparably associated with energy. Similarly in the same way mind is inseparably coupled with matter and matter with mind, their unity being found in the Power of Consciousness which is neither and which transcends both.

Energy has been divided into many forms such as kinetic, potential, chemical, magnetic and so forth. It was first thought that all the various forms of energy were subdivisions of the first two and then that all energy was kinetic, even potential energy being in some way dependent on motion. What have been called "Forces" are various forms of motion of matter, or the Ether each embodying energy. The ability which one body has to move another is sometimes called its energy, the energy which a body has depending on its own amount of motion. One form of physical motion or energy may be transformed into another, all being correlated. None of the forms is necessarily prior to any other. The various forms of Energy have been described as a closed ring of inter-relations within which motions are being exchanged by contact and radiation. If energy is conserved, so also is motion and matter, all three being constant. Physics which formerly counted several energies which it distinguished from each other welded them all into one great concept "Energy" of many forms and of which constancy was predicated.

Professor Emile Picard says[1] that for one school of scientists, Energy is not merely an abstract conception, without objective reality, but it has objective reality as much as and perhaps more than Matter and cannot be created or destroyed. Whether from the equivalence of different forms of energy one can draw the conclusion of their identity is for the experimenter a question which will be answered by each according to his different theoretic views.[2]

The result of recent investigation is summed up in the following words by a writer in the "Times" reviewing recent theories of the nature of Matter:

"A monistic interpretation of matter has displaced the older view. And what are electrons, these new symbols of the physical conception of

---

[1] "La Science Moderne et son état actuel," 136, 137.

[2] "Pour toute une école de savants, l'énergie n'ést pas seulement une conception abstracte sans existence ré-elle a pour eux, comme la matiére, plus peut être que la matiére, une existence objective et, nous ne pouvons ni la créer ni la détruire. De l'équivalence des diffèrentes formes de l'energie peut on conclure ā leur identité. La question pour, l'experimentayeur, n'a pas de sens... Et chacum peur y répondre diversement suivant ses vues théoriques." According to the Śākta standpoint there are phenomenally various kinds of Energy which are forms of the Divine Power (Daivī-Śakti) as the one Supreme Will.

the material universe? They are spoken of as positive and negative, the one with a mass two thousand times that of the other and with a two thousandth part of its diameter. They are mathematical abstractions, their properties inferences from mathematical reasoning. In the last resort, matter has become a number, a measure, not a thing. *The metaphysician expelled from the physics of the last century has come back to his own.*"

In the result Matter in its ultimate form ceases to be the gross thing which it was formerly thought to be, and is not in such form, "Matter" in its ponderable sense at all. On the contrary, it is at base a subtile thing yet with some, however minute, degree of magnitude. This is not however to say that because Matter is subtile it is any the less real.

Indian Scripture carries the matter still further backwards. The First Standard to which Matter is also an objective extra-mental reality reduces however sensible Matter to Elements (*Paramāṇus*) which have no magnitude whatever.[1] In the Second and Third Standards both Matter and Mind are modes of one and the same Principle, Cause of the Psycho-physical (Prakṛti, Māyā). Form the Vedāntic standpoint they are modes of the Supreme Power (Mahāśakti) which, while it is in Itself pure unlimited Consciousness, is for the limited centre the fundamental Substance-Energy from which the limitations of Mind and Matter are derived. Matter then is the manifestation of the Power of the Supreme Will to appear as an *object* to a limited experiencing subject or Mind. But Matter does not appear all at once in the form of Gross, particular, sensible Matter. It appears first as the Generals of the sense particulars, that is as the world of the Universals and then, with the development of the gross physical senses, Matter, is experienced as the gross sensible particulars.

Both the world of the Universals and particulars[2] have their origin in a common Psycho-Dynamic Principle which is itself a product of the Cosmic Will.

3

Before recurring again to the Matter of Western Science I will make a short resume of Indian Doctrine according to the three standards. For those who would understand Vedānta must also know both Sāṃkhya-Yoga and Nyāya-Vaiśeṣika. What is here described as Śākta doctrine is a form of the Monistic (Advaita) Vedānta of the Third Standard.

---

[1] They have neither length, breadth or height. The smallest particle of tri-dimensional and therefore theoretically perceptible, Matter being a Trasarenu *vide post.* The "magnitude" of a Paramāṇu is Pārimāṇḍalya or a mathematical point.

[2] See as to these *Mind.*

To Western Science, Matter is an extra-mental objective reality in the sense of that which exists in its own right independent of mind: that is experience or no experience it exists. This is akin to the view taken by the First Standard (Nyāya-Vaiśeṣika) though according to the latter the ultimate elements of matter (Paramāṇu) which have been called "atoms" have no magnitude whatever.[1]

The "element"[2] of matter (the Tanmātra[3] of the second and third standards[4] is not an objective reality in the same absolute sense in which the true elements the (Paramāṇus)[5] of the first standard are believed to be. Taking objective reality, in its fullest sense, to mean that which is independent of experience, "experience" may mean either finite individual experience, whether conscious or unconscious,[6] or Cosmic Experience namely that of that Infinite Individuality (Parāhaṃtā). The *Paramāṇus*, as external are independent of both. On the other hand the *Tanmātra* according to Sāṃkhya-Yoga is derived from mental functioning (*Buddhi-vyāpāra*) which need not be reflected on individual consciousness in all cases and is therefore independent of experience in that sense, for if it is not reflected in any particular consciousness, there is no *Tanmātra* produced for it. In Vedānta the *Tanmātra* is not independent of the Lord's experience, nor is it independent of mental functioning (*Buddhi-vyāpāra*) in the sense of the cosmic process of Māyā. It may, however, be independent of individual experience both conscious and sub-conscious.

Metaphysical Realism can therefore be predicated of the First Standard in which Matter as such, though in its subtle form, is eternal. The second has been called both a form of Materialism,[7] of Idealism,[8] and of Psycho-

---

[1] And therefore differ from the atom or electron of science which have some magni tude however minute.

[2] In inverted commas because the Tanmātra is not a simple ultimate but a derivative from higher psychic principles.

[3] Lit. "thatness only"; they are generals of the particulars or universals of which the Types (ākriti) are constituted.

[4] Sāṃkhya-Yoga and Vedānta.

[5] Lit. "supremely little"; the constituent minima of sensible matter.

[6] That is conscious functioning of the mind (Buddhi-vyāpāra or Buddhi-vyāpāra reflected in consciousness or Cit; or unconscious or sub-conscious Buddhi-vyāpāra that is functioning of mind (Buddhi) not reflected in Consciousness or Cit.

[7] Garbe "Sankh." Phil. 242 *et seq.*

[8] Max Muller "Six Systems" X. It is neither "Materialism" nor "Idealism" for both Mind and Matter are phenomenally distinct and have their ultimate basis in Prakṛti which is neither but the source of both.

dynamism;[1] and the Vedānta a system of Idealism, though it is not exactly Idealism in any Western sense of the world. Western labels are apt to mislead. It is better therefore to use the Sanskrit descriptions which are correct, namely the doctrine of an absolute new creation out of discrete pre-existing ingredients[2] in this case the minima of matter; the doctrine of the existence of the product in a potential form prior to its actual manifestation,[3] and the doctrine of the reality (in its truest sense)[4] of only the Originating Source of things, a doctrine in which the originating reality remains what it is but yet brings about and appears through its power as the result. In the first standard, matter in its gross sensible form is transient and its subtle constituent minima are eternal. There is no inherent dynamism. In the second and third both gross sensible and subtle matter are transient and dynamic, but in the second matter is eternal only in the sense that in the dissolution of the universe it is in potential form as the Fundamental Substance from which it really evolves. In the third standard from a pragmatic standpoint it potentially is as a Tendency in Being to which manifestation is given by the Divine Will; whilst from the transcendental standpoint, there is no actual manifestation at all but the changeless Consciousness or Spirit alone. Thus even when matter as such as a mode of substance disappears it has the eternality and reality of its Cause.[5] All appearance as a form, action as such form, disappearance into some other form, is according to Śākta views due to the inherent dynamism of matter attributable to it because of its being an expression, though of a gross kind, of the Supreme Power (Mahā-śakti) which is both the material and efficient cause of all.

The dynamic view of Matter which makes mobility the fundamental trait of Matter, would seek to deduce all the other "primary" properties of Matter out of this fundamental one. Matter occupies a certain volume of space, and resists movement in and through this volume; not because it is "inert" but because its essence lies in its power of self-conservation.

---

[1] J. C. Chatterjee "Hindu Realism", 14; inasmuch as the principles which it regards as the origin of the things are both psychical, *i.e.*, of the nature of feelings, thoughts, ideas; and dynamic that is of the nature of forces or powers. But here too a caution is necessary in that the psychical is the association of the natural psychic and physical principles with Consciousness which is not psychic in the sense of mental at all.

[2] Ārambha-vāsa or Asat-kārya-vāda that is the non-existence of the produced before actual production.

[3] The evolutionist standard (Pariṇāma-vāda) or Satkārya-vāda, *i.e.*, existence of product in potential form prior to actual manifestation.

[4] That is as changeless.

[5] Vivartta-vāda or Sat-Kāraṇa-vāda.

An outside object is pressing against it; why does it resist? Why does it not absolutely yield? Because it exerts forces counteracting or seeking to counteract the action of the forces exerted by the pressing object. Only force can oppose force. A push or stroke is given to a thing; it resists; does not quite yield; and even returns the push which is felt as muscular reaction and possibly pain. According to Newton's Third Law of Motion, the force with which the thing has reacted is equal and opposite to that with which the push or stroke acted. The lump of Matter which is the thing, is therefore really capable of exerting and resisting force. It occupies a certain volume of space precisely because it can maintain itself in its own sphere. Without such power, it would have no sphere, no *locus*, and no existence at all. All individual things must posses such power to conserve themselves as they are, even though it be for a moment. To be an individual I must be able to hold my own, not only philosophically but practically in the life of the world. So life; so also Matter. A piece of iron is an individual object and self because it is able by its cohesive forces to hold together its molecules against the action of heat and so forth; a molecule is so because it is able by its cohesive forces to hold together the constituent atoms; an atom is so because it is able by its cohesive forces to hold together the electrons or "electric charges" which are supposed to be in it, revolving in their orbits; and so on; for, even the electron cannot be the absolute unit of Matter. It is clear therefore that every form of Matter has its boundary (*i.e.*, extension) determined by its own stresses acting against the stresses of the enveloping Order. Its essence is Stress or Power (Śakti). The Stress operates in and is a condition of, Ether—says Western Science; it operates in and is a condition ultimately of, Cit or Ether of Consciousness—says the Vedānta. Philosophers in the West too (as Herbert) have recognised that the essence of Thing-hood is in the power of self-conservation; and idealists such as Hegel, Green and others have seen in it the power of self-realisation. Indian Thought (Śruti) says that the 'thing'is Brahman and is realizing itself as such, by its energising (*Karma*,) through enjoyment (*Bhoga*) and ultimately through liberation (*Apavarga*) from the veil of ignorance (*Avidyā*). This "ignorance", so much misunderstood, is knowledge. Knowledge of what? Knowledge of the world as mundane experience. And hence the Śaiva Scriptures say "*Jñānaṃ Bandhah*" that is knowledge is binding. But what is knowledge in this sense is ignorance (*Avidyā*) in another; for it is just knowledge as a state of experience which is ignorance of pure spiritual experience as it is in itslef. Power which, as mind and matter, cuts the full experience into sections gives sectional experience which necessarily shuts out full experience.

The very fact that Matter occupies space shows therefore that it is a system of stresses. The *form* of a material substance, again, is a *function of its motion*, *i.e.*, varies as this latter varies. A thing which is spherical when at rest will become an oblate spheriod when it moves in a certain manner. H. A. Lorentz has shown that an electro-magnetically constituted body which has a permanent configuration when at rest, when set in motion with a certain velocity, will contract in the direction of the velocity to a certain fraction[1] of its original dimension; distances at right angles to the direction of the velocity remaining unaltered. Now, since according to modern ideas, all Matter is electro-magnetically constituted (*i.e.*, made up of electrons or moving unit charges of electricity), the above result applies to all material things. We cannot therefore have a rigid body the spatial extension of which is permanent and independent of its velocity. A measuring rod, for example, will shorten in the direction of its length in a given ratio when it moves in a given manner. Spatial dimensions are thus the functions of, and relative to, the motions of things. Temporal dimensions or time-measurenemts also depend on and are relative to, the motions of bodies. This is the modern (though in fundamentals very ancient) theory of Relativity at which Dr. Einstein and others are still working. Space and Time relations are thus determined by the mutual stresses of things. What a thing apparently is, is determined by how it moves or by how it stresses. According to Hindu notions, the stress, or constituent forces of a thing as heard by the Absolute Ear is its Natural name, *Śabda or Bīja Mantra* which evolves and sustains its form.[2]

Not Form alone is the function of Motion (*i.e.*, varies as this latter does). Mass also is so. In Newtonian physics Mass was regarded as a physical constant. Howsoever Matter may move, its Mass was believed to be independent of its motion. A thing is at rest; it is moving with a moderate velocity; it is moving with a prodigious velocity; in every case, its Mass was believed to remain constant. But the electro-magnetic constitution of Matter does not warrant this belief. In the Electron Theory the property of Mass is explained as an effect of electricity in motion. Suppose an electric charge (*i.e.*, electron) is moving; that charge has its lines of force;

---

[1] ($\sqrt{1-v^2/c^2}$ where $v$ is the velocity of the moving body, and $c$ a constant, *viz.*, the velocity of light.)

[2] See *Garland of Letters*.

so that when the charge moves, it carries its lines of force with it. Ether through which these lines of force are carried is dragged forwards by them (as explained by Sir J. J. Thomson); hence the momentum of the charge (*i.e.*, product of Mass and Velocity) is due to the inertia of the ether. It possesses a given momentum because it drags forwards ether by its moving lines of force. A moving charge has therefore something analogous to mass in virtue of its motion. The scientists Thomson, Heaviside, Searle and others have calculated how much mass is due to how much motion. Kaufmann has also given definite experimental evidence that the ratio of the charge to the mass for the corpuscles projected from radium decreases as velocity increases. That is, the fraction $e/m$ (ratio of charge to mass) decreases as velocity increases. But since the charge (*i.e.*, the numerator of the fraction) is constant, the mass (*i.e.*, the denominator of the fraction) must increase in order that the fraction itself may decrease *pari passu* with the increase of velocity. Hence it follows that the Mass of the charge is a function of its velocity, *i.e.*, varies as this latter varies. It is true that for a slow-moving corpuscle, the Mass of the electric charge remains unaffected by its velocity; but when its velocity becomes comparable to that of light (nearly two hundred thousand miles per second), the electric Mass increases very rapidly. Nor must we imagine that such high velocities are exceptional in the case of the moving charges. The ejected corpuscles from radium move with velocities comparable to that of light; in the "atom" itself where the unit charges or electrons are "bound" instead of being "free," they have orbital motions compared with whose velocities, those of the planets in their orbits round the sun would seem to be far too small. In the Ṛgveda the *Devatā Vāyu* or *Marud-gana* has for his chariot-animals packs of spotted deer which stands as the symbol of fleetness; and *Vāyu* in the Veda is, in its physical aspect, a subtle universal fluid in movement[1] of which gross "air"[2] is a coarser derivative. In the Anāhata-Cakra too in the Tantras, where the *Vāyu-tattva* is located, the *Yantra* (or graphic representation) includes the symbol of a deer. However that be, the electric charges or electrons which, in various configurations, are now believed to constitute all Matter, are not slow of foot: their high velocities are not exceptional. And we have seen that their Masses are the functions of their velocities.

[1] From *vā*—to move.
[2] Pañcīkṛta—Marut.

And physicists now generally believe that the *whole* of the Mass of Matter is electro-magnetic Mass. That is to say, Matter does not possess a mechanical mass ultimately different in kind from its electro-magnetic Mass. The scientists Abraham, Thomson and others have calculated on the assumption that an electron is, *nothing but* a spherical charge of electricity, and their calculations tally with experimental results so far obtained. Matter now is thus not something which merely carries an electric charge or charges with it, but it *is* electric charges (positive and negative) somehow configurated together. The greater bulk of the Mass of atom is, according to some views, concentrated at the nucleus which is represented by the positive charge, and the swarm of negative charges moving round the nucleus have also their small masses; and the total mass of the atom is only the aggregate of the masses of its constituents which are positive and negative charges. This is the Electron Theory.[1]

We have therefore a Syllogism. The Mass of a moving charge is a function of its velocity; the Mass of Matter is wholly the masses of the charges by which it is constituted; therefore, the mass of Matter is also a function of velocity (velocities of its constituent parts). Mass of a thing is thus dependent on its stress-system on what may by called in Sanskrit *śakti-kūta* or *śakti-vyūha.*

Because the mass of a body is a function of its underlying stress (Śakti), or what is the same thing, of the motions of its ultimate units, it follows that by changing or otherwise controlling those motions it is possible to change or otherwise control its Mass. Gold and iron have different masses because in each the stress-system is different. Or because in each the ultimate units (the electrons, to wit) are configurated and are moving differently. If we can equate these motions, gold and iron will be equated as regards Mass. Alchemy thus becomes possible by what the modern Chemist would call the change of "Atomic Number". Mass can be reduced or increased by controlling the domestic economy of the motions of the corpuscles. Many *Siddhis* or Powers will follow from such ability to control them.

The Bindu (or Metaphysical Point of which so much is said in the Mantra-Śāstra)[2] as the concentrated or *ghaṇibhūta* condition of Śakti is an important stage in the creative evolution of the world according to the Śākta-Vedānta view. Mass (Tamas Guṇa) follows as a consequence of

[1] See Sir J. J. Thomson's "Matter and Electricity," or any other similar work.
[2] See *Garland of Letters.*

such concentration of Śakti or Power. I revert to this when further discussing the Ether and its stresses.

We have seen that extension (together with Form) and Mass are Energy-functions (*Śakti-Vyāpāra*) according to the teachings of Modern Science as they are in Śākta-Vedānta. Other properties are also traceable to the same *activity* which is at the basis of Matter. Take for example, resistance and rigidity of form. A substance which is non-resisting and without any shape, (*i.e.*, "a perfect fluid") may in virtue of rotational movement, come to offer resistance and present a definite shape. Rings of smoke illustrate this. A top at rest can hardly be balanced on the palm of the hand; if it be, its condition is most unstable; the slightest touch will upset it. But if an attempt is made to balance a top while spinning rapidly, on the palm of the hand, that can be easily done; the rotation of the top will counteract the effects of gravity—it will now stand on its point. If the spinning top is slightly pushed it will become disturbed and will oscillate about its position of equilibrium to which it will speedily return after a few oscillations. The rotating top resists (as is felt when attempt is made to stop or disturb it) any movement which seeks to disturb it. Thus it shows resistance and rigidity of form *on account* of its rotational motion. If we take a perfect (*i,e.*, frictionless) fluid such as Ether and somehow[1] set up a vortex movement in it, it will possess, in that eddying portion, permanence, resistance and rigidity of form—all on account of the curling motion. This was the basis of the theory of Helmholtz and Lord Kelvin, that atoms of matter may be vortex-rings in Ether. This we shall see later. We find now that the "primary" qualities of resistance, rigidity and so forth are also Energy-functions or effects of movement.

Gravitation, or the mutual attraction of Masses of Matter has proved a stumbling-block to many otherwise successful theories. The effects of all other forces (such as heat, light, electricity, magnetism) are propagated through space in finite time; *i.e.*, they have their finite rates of velocity. If, for example, a distant star be now extinguished or rekindled, we should be aware of that phenomenon through light or loss of light, many years hence. Light takes so much time to travel from there. But suppose the lump of Matter which we call that star be now annihilated or a new lump be now created; then, this fact will instantaneously affect the gravitational system throughout the whole universe of matter. That is, its effect will be instantaneoulsy felt (or produced) here. This *prima facie* makes the case

[1] It requires what is called a super-natural agency to set up a vortex in a *perfect* fluid.

of gravitation a different one. Nevertheless physicists have worked at it; and attempts have been made to explain gravitation as a resultant of the attractions (*Rāga*) and repulsions (*Dveṣa*) of the positive and negative charges which are believed to constitute Matter in conglomeration; in terms of pressures and pulls exerted through the ether; and as (by Le Sage) a result of the battering of "Ultra-mundane corpuscles" on the atoms of matter.

So all the "primary" qualities may be reduced to and expressed in terms of Energy, Stress or *Śakti*. Energy or Movement is thus the fundamental principle in Matter.

That the secondary qualities such as colour, smell, etc., are effects wrought on us by the action of the primary qualities has been long recognised in science.

4

We have seen, how all the "primary" qualities believed to reside in "scientific matter" are modes and functions of energy which is of the essence of Matter. That is, Matter possesses mass, extension, resistance, weight, etc., *because* it is *something* which is *dynamic* and energises. Now, what is that *something*? How and why does it become dynamic? And what is the nature of the Energy which operates in and through it? These are the three fundamental queries regarding Matter.

As regards the second and third questions, Science confesses that she is not in a position to answer. It is true that Electricity is not uncommonly regarded as the most fundamental kind of physical energy, but physicists are not sure about the nature of Electricity. We do not yet know what it *is*, though we know much about how it works. Can it be traced to something more fundamental than itself? Physicists no longer look upon Electricity as a continuous fluid flowing in and out of conductors; it is now believed to be granular or "atomic" in structure; that is, we have now grains, "atoms" or corpuscles of electricity entering like "companies", "battalions", "armies," etc., into substances and leaving them. These units of Electricity were called by Sir J. J. Thomson "corpuscles," and by Johnstone Stoney "Electrons". But what is this unit charge? Can we regard it as a vortex in Ether? How does it then take a positive and negative character out of vortex-motion? Is it only a difference in the *direction* of motion? The difference between a positive charge and a negative charge appears to be fundamental. Likes repel and unlikes attract each other.

How is that effected? These questions probing to the very root of the matter still remain unanswered.

The common hypothesis, however is to regard the electric condition as a condition of stress in Ether. The *something* which is stressed and strained is Ether, all forms of energy (Electricity included) are forms of stress in Ether, and Matter with all its properties is the manifestation of such stress-and-strain in Ether. In this conception, we have only substituted the word "stress" for the word "energy"; but we are still far from clearly understanding its nature. What is this stressing in Ether, why and how does it stress? This is not known.

Energy is commonly stated to be the capacity for doing work; and Work is commonly expressed in terms of motion or change of configuration. In this way a 'formula' of Energy or work may be given; but it is a description and not a definition; it never tells us what Energy or Capacity for doing work *is*. Clerk Maxwell, one of the greatest of British physicists, in his "Matter and Motion" said: "We are acquainted with Matter only as that which may have energy communicated to it from other Matter, and which may in its turn communicate energy to other Matter."

So, according to him, it becomes necessary to understand 'Energy' in order to understand 'Matter'. But what is Energy? "Energy" on the other hand, he says, "we know only as that which in all natural phenomena is continually passing from one portion of matter to another." As a definition of Energy it involves the vicious circle. The inscrutable "that which" appears in both the statements. Taking again the famous Treatise on Natural Philosophy by Sir William Thomson (Lord Kelvin) and Professor Tait, we read (S.207)—"we cannot, of course, give a definition of *Matter* which will satisfy the metaphysician, but the naturalist may be content to know matter as *that which can be perceived by the senses, or as that which can be acted upon by, or can exert, force*. The latter, and indeed the former also, of these definitions involves the idea of *force*, which in point of fact, is a direct object of sense; probably of all our senses, and certainly of the "muscular sense." The idea of force is the essence, and it is claimed by these authors, as indeed it has been claimed by all realistic philosophers, that force is a *direct* object of sense experience—that in muscular activity in particular we directly apprehend what force is. Empiricists from Hume and Mill down to the physical empiricists such as Ernst Mach, Poincaré, Karl Pearson and others, have objected to these definitions of Matter as being too metaphysical or even as being unpsychological. The inscrutable "that which" which occurs in these definitions refers to the metaphysical "thing-in-itself" as distinguished from phenomena; and force or energy which these definitions suppose to be a direct object of sense, is nothing of the kind at all: we are only aware of *changes* in our groups of sensations and *infer* objective causes of such changes (*i.e.*, things and forces). According to this psychology, then, Matter is for us only a "complexus of sense-experiences"; it will not even allow us to say with J. S. Mill that "Matter is a permanent possibility of sense impressions" (System of Logic, Bk. i, Chap. iii). For, the unwary may take even this to imply a supersensuous entity at the base of the sense-impressions!

Whether right or wrong, this view which apparently would not permit us to go beyond groups and series of sense-experiences and their changes to search after 'realities,' is, if consistently held, the *reductio ad absurdum* of all thought and all science. What we directly and immediately experience is a universe, and this universe of experience is the Fact which is alogical and unspeakable.[1] It is by Thought (*Buddhi*) that we treat this universe of experience variously: this treating principle being, of course, immanent, and not transcendent, in relation to the universe of experience which is treated. How is it treated? It is treated by being veiled, by being changed or moved, and by being presented. If we call the treating operation, Stress, then clearly it has three partials as just indicated — presentation (*Sattva-guṇa*), movement (*Rajo-guṇa*) and veiling (*Tamo-guṇa*). For example I think I am now hearing the cooing of a bird; *really* this phenomenon is the emphasised part or section in a whole universe of experience which I now have; but this whole has been more or less veiled, so that I *appear* to have a particular sensation only (*viz.*, the cooing sound) at this moment. And the veiling of the whole, the prominence of a part, its passing away and coming into prominence of another, presuppose movement. From this short analysis it will appear that the Empiricist can get his "clusters of sense-impressions" and "series of sense-impressions" only *after* his mind or *Buddhi* has treated, in the manner above indicated, the logical Fact-Whole, and cut it up into segments and rearranged them according to certain basic *Saṃskāras* (laws) of his Buddhi. His Empiricism is not *radical;* he is a dealer in second-hand articles—the so-called 'impressions' and 'ideas'. Radical Empiricism must bring us face to face with the

[1] This is the position of Prof. P. N. Mukhyopādhyāya in his "Approaches to Truth" and "Patent Wonder" to whom I am indebted for the exposition of his case in this and other sections. — J. W.

Fact; and when it does so, it becomes *Radical Realism*, for then the Ideal and the Real become one. *This is the position of Vedānta.*

The Empiricist would have us believe that his "cluster" and "series" (*i.e.*, co-existence and sequence) of "sensation" are native to actual experience while the Realist's "thing" and "attribute," "cause," "force" and "effect" are only thought-constructions foreign to actual experience. But this is an untenable position. Either say with Kant that all these (co-existence, sequence, thing and attribute, cause and effect, etc.) are thought-forms or categories only and are therefore foreign to the "thing-in-itself" which we do not know; or say with the Realist that these are thought-forms *as well as* actual forms of the thinkable itself — that Thought thinks in these forms and ways *because* the thinkable has in reality these forms and ways. We cannot admit truths by halves.

The Vedāntic position is as follows:

Reality is Experience. Experience is a Universe. This Universe lives, moves and has its being in Consciousness[1] or *Cit*. *Cit* therefore is Reality and the foundation of Reality. There is no inscrutable "thing-in-itself" beyond or behind Consciousness.[2] Far from being unknowable, Reality is Cognition itself. Now, the Universe of Experience which is, and appears in Cit, may be regarded by us from *three* stand-points. (A) As it is, without any limitations; this is the Alogical Fact which cannot be circumscribed by any category. (B) As the quiescent and transcendent as well as immanent ground of what we have; this is *Cit* as such or Śiva as the worshipper personifies it; or the same in its dynamic or stressing aspect—which is Śakti which is theologically the Devī or Mother. The two aspects put together, Śiva and Śakti identified with each other, give us the Alogical Whole or Fact. (C) The Universe of Experience is treated with reference to particular centres in it and their pragmatic interests. Time, space, causal relation, the relation of thing and attribute and other categories do *not* apply to *Pūrṇa* or Absolute Whole; they arise and have their application when the *Pūrṇa* has by Its own stress finitized Itself into centres distinguishable from one another. So that when a Centre reviews the universe of Experience from its *own* point of view (*i.e.*, the Self) its review casts itself into the forms of certain categories: it thinks of a world existing objectively to itself in *Space*, consisting of *Things* and their *Attributes*, *causing* phenomena in itself, and changing

---

[1] That is pure Consciousness unaffected by the operations of unconscious mind. See *Reality*. [2] *ib.*

in *Time*. And this is a *necessary* treatment of experience by a Centre: it cannot but do it. A Centre treats its experience in this fundamental way and in no other, because experience has *in reality* the basis of all these relations. That is to say, Space, External Order, Time, Cause, Substance and the rest are no mere subjective dreams of the Centre: these *relations are objective arrangements as well as subjective representations of those arrangements* — which is Realism. The Vedāntist, therefore, differs from Kant in two essential respects: (1) He offers no unknowable "Thing-in-itself" beyond phenomena or Experience. His Reality is Experience. (2) Within this Experience certain fundamental operations go on: a particular Centre itself born of those fundamental operations in it, reviews those operations from its own standpoint; by its review it frames its own "scheme" of the universe; and this "scheme" is *not essentially unlike the real scheme of the universe* because the universe is nothing else than experience; a Centre is nothing else than a "Point-of-view" in it, and a Centre's review and thought of existence, evolved out of and governed by, the fundamental operations in experience itself, cannot be essentially unlike what experience, and therefore Reality, really is. The Laws of Thought are thus justified. These Laws cannot belie those fundamental disposistions and operations of Reality which make them possible.

We need not therefore be shy to speak of a real Space, in which real Matter energises in real Time and really causes sense-affections to a given Centre. Only it should be clearly understood that the basis of all this is consciousness and the stressing in consciousness. The Śākta Vedāntist offers no Substance separate from its Energy, no *Śaktimān*[1] separate from *Śakti*,[1] but Indian Substance which is Cit *is* Energy. Man as a given centre, knows it in both the aspects (Substance-Energy), and as a member of the universal stress-system, he *directly* apprehends Energy in other Centres or the world for the matter of that. Action and reaction are correlative; there is no idea of the one without an idea of the other. When therefore he acts and feels that he is acting, he feels at the same time that something other than himself is reacting on him; *e.g.*, when he gives a blow to a thing, he feels his own force, and he feels that of the thing. It is a single feeling presenting two poles like a magnet.

Nor is the Hindu driven to look upon Conceptual or "scientific" Matter as something essentially unlike Perceptual Matter, or this latter as something essentially unlike real Matter or real Thing-in-itself. There is a

[1] Possessor of Power and Power.

tendency in science to regard Ether, Atom, Lines and Tubes of Force, etc., as "convenient fictions" or "conceptual models" only which have no perceptual equivalents; perceived Matter is also believed to be unlike the real Thing-in-itself. Thus "Scientific Matter" is *doubly* removed from the world of realities. This, however, need not be the fact. Since no "dark" world of things-in-themselves exists, a given Centre's *resume* of the universe is a *resume* of the world of experience from its own standpoint (and therefore subject to its own Saṃskāras or tendencies which may veil to a degree the Reality which is Experience or *Cinmaya*);[1] but its *resume* of Experience, and therefore, of Reality must be true as regards the fundamentals or essentials. For example, its *resume* so far as it postulates a real Space, a real Time, real centres of force stressing upon one another, a real Ether as the medium through and by which the mutual stresses are exerted, and a real universal Energy which is *Cit-śakti* (*i.e.*, of the nature of Will), is valid. Man's fundamental commonsense is not therefore common non-sense. However much science has sophisticated, Man's *essential* beliefs as regards the universe he lives in are *true*.

And what are the essentials of our *resume* of Matter? In the first place, we postulate some sort of a continuum (*Vibhu*, *Vyāpaka*) whether that be a *vacuum* (*i.e.*, Space) or a *plenum* (*i.e.*, Ether); the *continuum* appears in two forms — static and dynamic; the first is Space or Ether, the second is Time; for Time is the continuum regarded as a drift or flow. Both are forms of Substance-Energy which is *Cit*. In the second place, we postulate discontinuous, discrete "sections" (which may be reduced to points or *Bindus*) in the *continuum*; that is to say, the *continuum* must also be known and conceived by us as finitised, broken into discontinuities which are centres or points in it. This finitisation is the work of *Māyā-śakti* whereby the unlimited is experienced as limited. In third place, these centres of discontinuity imbedded in a *continuum* are stressing upon one another, so that they are bound to one another as members of a universal stress-system. These being the three fundamental postulates of our *resume* of Matter, we have a sufficient warrant for Ether, Energy and Centres of Energy (which appear as the "chemical atoms") which sum up Matter.

Because we cannot be mistaken as regards the fundamental postulates involved in our *resume* of experience, it does not follow that our ideas about Matter, Life and Mind must all be the same and all be true. Each of us is a Centre and a particular standpoint; hence though we all agree

[1] That is essentially consciousness as *Cit*.

as regards certain inalienable essentials of existence, we must differ as regards the forms in which those essentials may express themselves. For example, we cannot but be right as regards the continuum itself; it exists. But what is it? Is it a *vacuum* as was supposed by generations of physicists or is it a *plenum*? If the latter, what is its nature? How is Ether to be conceived? As an elastic Solid? As a perfect Fluid? As a perfect Jelly? Then again, we cannot but be right as regards the centres of discontinuity in the *continuum*. But what are they? Chemical Atoms? Ether-elements in vortex-motion? A centre of strain in Ether? A centre of force? Lastly, we cannot but be right as regards the mutual stressing of the centres. But how is it exerted? Through wave-motion? By actual Lines and Tubes of Force as supposed, for example, by Faraday ? So, the actual *forms* may be more or less veiled to a given conscious Centre; another may be better enlightened than he is; and so there is need of Science, Philosophy and Realisation by *Sādhanā*.

Further, our placing the foundations of Matter in Cit-Substance-Energy has relieved us of the necessity of partitioning Reality into Matter, Life and Mind and then trying hopelessly to link them up again. We have nothing else than Experience. Matter, Life and Mind must be modes of Experience. The Essence of each is Cit-Substance-Energy or Śakti. If, therefore, Matter be spiritualised, and Mind be materialised and both be vitalised, we merely solve an equation. The fundamental laws of Matter, Life and Mind are not exclusive and peculiar (*sui generis*).

All Energy is *Cit-śakti* or Consciousness-energy. This Energy has two forms—the agent which does work; and the instruments with which, and the material upon which, work is done. Energy appearing as agent (*Kartā*) is technically called *Cit-Śakti*; and Energy appearing as instrument and material (*Kāraṇa* and *Upādānā*) is *Māyā-Śakti*. In every form of existence, sentient or "insentient", living or "non-living," Energy must appear in both forms. Thus there must be *Cit-Śakti* or Energy as agent in a so-called "atom" of Matter also. It cannot be wholly *inert*, *i.e.*, moved by external impact alone like a billiard-ball. It must have (as Śākta doctrine holds) its own stock of spontaneity. It must have its own domestic economy of intra-atomic energy, which is controlled by the "Self" or *Ātmā* of the atom. And does not the Science of to-day recognise this? She now puts a tremendous amount (almost limitless) of Energy into the tiny atom; and She recognises some sort of domestic government in the atom, by which the "sub-atoms" move in a certain order according to certain velocities, are sometimes pitched off (as in Radio-activity) when they overstep a certain "critical" velocity; by which the atom itself may evolve into a different kind, and may even dissolve into the sea of Ether and its stock of universal and fundamental Energy. The basis of this arrangement in, say, an atom of Hydrogen, is the "Self" of that atom of Hydrogen — its Energy appearing as agent. And this is *Cit-Śakti, its Abhimāni Caitanya* or *Adhiṣṭhātrī-Devatā*, which, as appearing in H, may be more veiled than as appearing in a "living" corpuscle (C.H.N.O.), or as appearing in the cave of Intelligence (*Buddhiguhā*) of a rational animal; but still it *is* and *works* in the atom of Hydrogen. So in the unitary system of existence, there is perfect fraternity between man and the "meanest" particle of Matter. What is here in him is also *really* there in that, and *vice versa.* Like him that also has its action (*Karma*), its enjoyment (*Bhoga*) and its release from all bonds (*Apavarga*) through *Abhyudaya* or progression in the course of upward evolution into man and from man to God.

Hence the three fundamental queries regarding Matter with which we opened the present section can be briefly answered according to Vedāntic Doctrine in this way: (1) The *something* which affects our sense as Matter is *Cit*-substance-energy (Śakti). (2) It is *essentially dynamic* and its dynamism works eternally in certain lines, so that we cannot justly speak of its acquiring a dynamic character or dynamic tendencies at any time. It works, and *this* is what is meant by saying that it is Energy. Laws of Work (*Karma*) are the Laws of Energy. Energy works as an atom of Hydrogen rather than as an atom of Oxygen, *because in the former case its Karma has been, is and will be different from that in the latter case.* Its being H is therefore determined by its *Karma.* It is however not immutable, as was thought by the older generations of physicists. All Matter is slowly radio-active—which means that all Matter is slowly transmuting, evolving; a conclusion which must inevitably follow from Sāṃkhyan and Vedāntic principles. It transmutes by its stresses, *i.e.*, by its *Karma.* (3) And this "Material" Energy is Consciousness-Energy analogous to what we experience in attention and will.[1]

The *whole* operation goes on in *Cit* which, regarded as a quiescent background or frame, is the *Cidākāśa* or Ether of Consciousness. Man has direct experience of this too in the *Samādhi* or ecstasy of completed Yoga.

---

[1] Energy, though mutable, is indestructible. "She who sports on the breast of Mahā-kāla has neither beginning nor end—neither birth nor death".

6

We have seen that Continuity and Discontinuity have both their base in our universe of experience; Thought therefore is not fanciful when it conceives a *continuum* in which discontinuous or discrete centres (*Jīvas*) are in action and reaction. The need of a continuous *plenum* or Ether (*Ākāśa*) and that of the Atom (*Aṇu*) are therefore real needs; we cannot do without either. Those physicists who discard the Ether cannot discard the *continuum* of Space and Time. Those again who looked askance at the "atom" or "corpuscle" cannot do without "centres of force" or "points where given *quanta* of Energies operate."

The continuous and the discontinuous must have no rigid limits set to them. The ideal limit or perfection of a continuum is not Scientific Ether (about which the scientific doctors differ), but is in the Vedānta the Ether of Consciousness (*Cidākāśa* which the Chāndogya calls *Jyāyān* and *Parāyaṇam* (*i.e.*, greater than the greatest—*Mahato Mahīyān* as also *aṇoraṇīyān* smaller than the smallest) and the ultimate Ground and Support of all things or God. Similarly, the ideal limit of the discontinuous is not the scientific atom or electron, but the *Bindu* which is a focussed condition of Śakti or Energy of God or more strictly God as Energy. The Nyāya-Vaiśeṣika *Paramāṇu* which is a point of stimulation is also as already stated not so crude as the scientific atom or electron.

In the search after the ideal limit in either direction (*viz.*, continuity and discontinuity—*Mahat* and *Aṇu*—), it is necessary to pass through a series before the ideal is reached—Ether of Consciousness on the one hand and the ideal Śakti-Bindu on the other. In other words, we must have a *Continua*-series and a *Discontinua*-series of largeness and a series of smallness. The upper limit of the first is *Cidākāśa* and the ultimate limit of the second is *Bindu-śakti*. It is always well to remember these two series and their limits; if we do not, we shall not understand the search after Ether and Corpuscles in Science, nor the genesis of the sensible world as given in the Vedānta Book of Genesis. The latter starts with the ideal limits; hence its First Principles cannot be *completely* rendered in terms of Scientific Ethers and Electrons. Nevertheless these serve a purpose as far as they go. They give us a sort of rude "first sketch" of Nature as, in the words of Dr. Bertrand Russell, Newton's Physics gave of the ways of Nature some two centuries ago.

Between the uppermost limit and the lowermost we have a series of *continua* and *discontinua* arranged in ascending and descending orders; and all these intervening orders of largeness and smallness, continuity and discontinuity are susceptible to strain and stress in a varying degree. The *Bhūtas* or "Elements" arise out of this variable stress-and-strain attitude. A Śāstric parable may be taken to represent the birth of this series. Aditi, the Vedic mother of the Devas, literally means that which cannot be divided or cut: She is as such the continuum in the limit or perfection. She is the Perfect Ether. In her womb, Vāyu or Maruts are born. Vāyu means, in the world-aspects, the (relative) continuum in movement. It is the Moving Ether. Now, Indra, jealous of the strength of this Devatā about to be born, enters Aditi's womb and cuts it up into segments. Let Indra represent here *Cit-śakti* by which the undivided continuum in movement is divided into a number of "components" of the movement. In this way, Vāyu becomes in fact the Maruts (plural) which are said to be 49 in number.[1] The single continuum in movement thus evolves, under the action of *Cit-śakti*, a series of moving *continua* which are the *Marud-gaṇa*. Every Devatā, it should be remembered in this connection, has a physical aspect. For all that is, is an Epiphany of the Divine.

The problem before Physics as well as Metaphysics is this: Assuming that the Absolute Continuum is X and the Limit of Discontinuity is Y, how and where shall we place, between these two Limits (*Cidākāśa* and *Bindu*), Sky, Air, Water, Earth, Life, Mind (*Antahkaraṇa*), and the rest? How shall we fit our actual order of experience into his frame-work? Science in the West is solving, though hardly as yet suspecting the Ideal Limits, this Problem; Philosophy in India has also attempted to solve it. One solution of Science is that Matter is non-matter (*i.e.*, Ether) in motion. What does it mean and how near to Truth does it bring us? This we shall next see.

7

No one of the Six Standards or Points of view of Indian philosophy[2] looks at matter from the physico-chemical point of view. They consider it from the standpoint of its effect on the mind and senses. Matter in this view is *that* which, affecting the mind and senses, produces therein the sensations of hearing, touch, form and colour, taste and smell. The first Standard differs from the rest in its treatment of sound and hearing (v. post), but they agree also in this, that matter is both gross (*Sthūla*) that is, sensible, and subtile (*Sūkṣma*), that is, unperceivable by the senses but by mind alone. What then is *that* which produces these sensations? Here the standards

[1] See *ante Life.*
[2] See *ante Reality.*

differ. It is necessary, in the first place, to understand the Indian classification of magnitude.

There are four kinds of magnitude—small (*Aṇu*), large (*Mahat*)—terms relating to solid or three dimensional magnitude; short (*Hraṣva*), long (*Dīrgha*)— terms which relate to linear magnitude. The first standard also considers (VII.1.11.14.17) these two pairs of categories as giving rise to two series (*Dhārā*), *e.g.*, A is smaller than B, B than C, etc., one series. A is shorter than B, B than C, etc. There are six possible combinations of these four magnitudes, *viz.*, (1) *Aṇu-Mahat*, small-large; (2) *Aṇu-Hraṣva*, small-short; (3) *Aṇu-Dīrgha*, small-long; (4) *Mahat-Hraṣva*, large-short; (5) *Mahat-Dīrgha*, large-long; (6) *Hraṣva-Dirgha*, short-long. The first and sixth combine contraries (VII.1.10) and are, therefore, cancelled. The third is also untenable, because a thing which is small in dimension cannot be long. Similarly, a thing which is large in dimension cannot be short and the fourth goes out leaving only the second and the fifth as logically tenable combinations. Each of these magnitudes has its degrees. Thus *Aṇu* which is small and atomic may represent several degrees of which the extreme limit or infinitely small than which there is nothing smaller is Paramāṇu.[1]

According to the first standard (*Nyāya-vaiśeṣika*), gross, transient, sensible matter, is that matter which is large (*Mahat*) and consists of many parts and has form in itself. Compound matter is constituted of certain aggregates called Ternaries (*Tryaṇuka Trasareṇu*) which are the smallest tridimensional, and therefore theoretically perceivable, aggregates consisting of three couplets or Binaries of two points each; such points being called *Paramāṇus*. The single Ternary though theoretically perceivable is in practice not so. The Binaries and Points are unperceivable. Perceivable matter is of three dimensions and infra-sensible matter, or matter unperceivable by the senses exists as a Binary of two dimensions or as a Point without magnitude. The smallest particle of tri-dimensional matter is theoretically perceivable,[2] that is provided the requisite sense-capacity is there. In any case it can be actually imaged, and since it possesses both primary and secondary qualities it can be concretely imaged. The annotators who in some cases possessed neither the Yogic vision[3] of the ancient Seers,[4] nor the knowledge of modern science, often represent the Particle or *Trasareṇu* as a moving particle visible to the eye, such as a mote seen in a sun-beam as a pencil of light, let through an aperture into a dark room. It is said to

[1] Parama (supreme) and Aṇu.
[2] Pratyakṣa-yogya.
[3] Yoga-dṛṣṭi.
[4] Ṛṣis.

be composed of three Binaries (*Dvyaṇuka*) and broken up into six "atoms" (*Paramāṇus*). But this cannot be so, as even a microscopic particle must according to Western science contain multi-millions of corpuscles. A particle or *Trasareṇu* is an "element" of solid dimension in sensible matter. It has a magnitude of three dimensions namely length, breadth and thickness. It is thus the solid element of matter. The Particle or *Trasareṇu* is composed of three Binaries or *Dvyaṇuka* which have neither breadth nor thickness and which are "elements" of linear dimension.[1] The Binary again is composed of Points. Two Points, not touching, make a short line of which the breadth and thickness or solid dimension are nothing. Next, two such elements of linear dimension (*Dvyaṇuka*) are combined. From a common origin or point of reference two short lines are drawn in two different directions thus producing a very small surface or "element" of surface dimension.[2] If again three such short lines are drawn from a common origin at say right angles to each other there is produced an element of solid dimension or volume.[3] Three binaries make in this way a perceivable Particle or *Trasareṇu* or Ternary, the magnitude of which is much greater than that of a Binary, for the former has breadth and thickness which the latter has not. Hence compared to a Binary it is large (*Mahat*). Again many lines must be bundled together like slender wires, twisted into a rope, to produce even a very small volume; each of the constituent lines is short but the aggregate of these short lengths is comparatively long (*Dīrgha*). Hence the magnitude of the Ternary or *Trasareṇu* is large and long (*Mahat-Dīrgha*) just as the Binary is small (*Aṇu*, because lacking solid dimension) and short (*Aṇu-hrasva*).

We have next to consider the ultimate Points or Atoms which go to make up the Binaries, the Ternaries and the combinations of these which, as molar masses, form sensible matter (*Bhūta*). I call it an atom, not because it is like the atom of Western Science, but because it is the true atom that is an indivisible partless point of substance without any of the three dimensions and relative to its effect a Point of Force, whereas the atom of Science and even its electron has some magnitude, however minute. Without this

---

[1] Dl in mathematical notation.

[2] Ds in mathematical notation.

[3] *Dv* in mathematical notation. It appears to me that this scheme of the Nyāya-Vaiśeṣika is referred to by what in the Tantras are called the crooked or bent line (Vakra-rekhā); the straight line (Ṛjurekhā) and the prismatic form (Śṛngātaka) of which the Devatās are Vāmā, Jyeṣṭhā, and Raudrī. See Yoginīhṛdaya-Tantra, p. 167. From the curved line said to be in the form of an elephant-goad (Aṅkuśa) representing surface dimension, a line is drawn upwards into another plane and the tridimensional figure is formed.

explanation the translation of the Point or Paramāṇu as atom is misleading. The "measure"[1] of the *Paramāṇu* or true atom is called *Parimaṇḍala* which means literally a "sphere." It is therefore an infinitely small sphere or Point (*Bindu*). Each series (*Dhārā*) of the four categories of magnitude has a superior[2] and inferior[3] limit. If A in the series is the inferior limit, and if it be absolutely small, then it is the Atom or *Paramāṇu* just as Z may be the superior limit and absolutely great,[4] such as the Self (*Ātmā*) and Ether (*Ākāśa*). Between these two limits there are several orders relatively great or small. If the *Paramāṇu* or point had any finite magnitude, however small, like the scientific atom or electron then it would not be the inferior limit—the partless unit. Hence the infinitely small unit is nothing greater than a Point (*Bindu*). The same reasoning will apply to the other pair "Short-long". The infinitely short thing is again a Point. If it had any finite length it would be divisible. So the inferior limit of the second series is also the *Paramāṇu*. It is a *Parimaṇḍala* because it is a sphere of which the radius is infinitely small, that is a Point. Things of perception are seen to be divisible into smaller and smaller particles. All these are spheres of finite, however small, radii. So are even the electrons of science. Pushing however to the limit we get a sphere of which the radius is infinitely small and this is *Pārimāṇḍalyā*. In all physico-mathematical analysis of things in Science, we have to imagine and deal with the "volume elements". A mere Point or mere Line cannot be an object of concrete imagination for us—we cannot perceive it even with the eye of imagination. Such perception becomes possible only when we take a solid element. Neither the Point (*Paramāṇu*) nor Line (*Dvyaṇuka*) are that, and are therefore unperceivable. The smallest solid element is the *Trasareṇu* which is theoretically perceivable, if there be the requisite sense capacity which ordinarily there is not. The chemical atom, electron and so forth, being larger or smaller solid elements, fall under the generic category of the Ternary or *Trasareṇu* for they cannot be either the Binary or *Dvyaṇuku* or the unit or *Paramāṇu* which are not thus perceivable or imaginable by us. They are supersensible[5] or transcendental, not in the sense that while too small (such as a *Trasareṇu*) to be perceived by the unassisted senses or aid of instruments hitherto invented they could be perceived by the senses with the aid of ideally perfect instruments, but in the sense that they can never under any circumstances be perceived by

[1] Parimāṇa. See Vaiśe., VII. 1. 20.
[2] Utkarṣa.
[3] Apakarṣa.
[4] Parama-mahat.
[5] Atīndṛya.

the senses. They can only be conceived by the Mind. The Points are also non-spatial that is to say they cannot occupy space or localised position.[1]

Before describing their nature it is necessary to enquire how from the points as things of no magnitude, things of magnitude are produced.[2] The sensible is either visible or invisible, such as the aerial atmosphere which is limited and consists of discrete parts, otherwise there could be no movements in it, for in an all filling continuum no parts of it can move from their places, nor can other parts come in from some other quarter. All sensible things are of limited extent and as such discrete, consisting of parts. A thing of limited magnitude may be produced by things already having magnitude, or by a number of things without magnitude, standing not contiguously but at distances from one another and then entering into a combination or unification so as to form a single unit which, as a whole, may behave as one individual, and in which the originating parts are no longer entirely independent of the whole, in which case the originating parts or factors need not have any magnitude whatever. The unified wholes are secondary or produced units or individuals.[3] The constituents are not contiguous but have spaces between them for the discrete sensible is never an absolute solid.[4] A Point which is contiguous to, and thus coinciding with another Point remains a Point, but standing apart produces a Line. A number of pure lines that is having only length, which are not less than three, can produce a thing of solid tri-dimensional magnitude that is length, breadth, and thickness. Contiguous lines produce only a line just as the contiguous Point is nothing but a Point. But if the lines stand apart and in two planes, their combination produces a figure which is a thing of tridimensional magnitude (*Trasareṇu*) which by the addition of Mass becomes perceivable to all.

Why it may be asked should the ultimate constituents of matter be without magnitude? Because in the first place thought cannot rest there and will subdivide again and again as long as any magnitude is assumed· And next it is seen that things with magnitude may be produced from things without magnitude. Thirdly if the ultimate constituents of sensible things were composed of solid, hard, and extended particles with magnitude, however small, then the Ether could not be all-pervading. The Points without magnitude which are the ultimate constituents of matter being

[1] Pradeśātīta.

[2] See "Hindu Realism" by J. C. Chatterjee, 25 *et seq*.

[3] That is a new thing, an individual (Avayavin) other than a mere aggregate.

[4] Things can be operated upon by heat and can be compressed.

partless cannot, like discrete things composed of parts, be produced or destroyed and are eternal.[1] Gross sensible matter is non-eternal. What then is *Paramāṇu* the ultimate constituent of sensible matter but itself beyond the senses? In the first place it is not an infinitely small element of what we actually experience which are all compounds, but it is an infinitely small partless Point of Substance (really existing and entering variously into compounds) which is the ground and cause of four classes of sensation, *viz.*, touch, form and colour, taste and smell.[2] It is a real and independently existing Force and self-subsisting stimulus, producing both the sensible and sensation.[3] As sensation is fourfold, they are, as the cause of it, of four classes technically and symbolically called "Air," "Fire," "Water," "Earth".[4] This does not mean that they are what we call such, which is gross compounded matter because they are respectively and in particular manifest in pure air which may be felt through its motions and temperature, which may be seen in all fiery substances, tasted in watery form (for the flavour of a thing is only had when it is dissolved into liquid form) and which may be smelt as solid matter.[5] The aerial *Paramāṇu* is the ultimate constituent of the form of Matter from which all other sensible special qualities can be eliminated except Touch; the fiery, watery, and earthy Paramāṇus are the ultimate constituents of those forms of matter from which all other sensible qualities can be eliminated but not colour and form, taste and smell. Therefore the Vāyu-Paramāṇu is a material point which produces gross measurable matter sensible as touch and the sense of touch, just as the rest *Tejas-Paramāṇu*, *Ap-Paramāṇu*, and *Pṛthivī-Paramāṇu* produce gross matter sensible as colour and form, taste and odour. V.P. has the quality of touch and feel only; T.P. has this and colour and form; A.P. has the two last and the property taste, whilst P.P. has the last three and as its own inalienable characteristic the quality of odour. V, T, A, P, exist in two forms, one subtle and eternal[6] and the other gross and non-eternal.[7] The former is the

[1] Destruction means division into component parts.

[2] In Sanskṛit Sparśa, Rūpa, Rasa, Gandha.

[3] Paramāṇus originate both sensible matter and the particular sense. The senses are of the same nature as the stimuli which provoke them.

[4] Vāyu, Tejas, Ap, Pṛthivī.

[5] Water may be smelt, but if so it is due to the presence of solid matter in it. Pure water is without odour. "Earth" does not mean only what is popularly so called but any solid substance, *e.g.*, flesh, flower, fruit in so far as the same are solids. Both earthly, that is gross sensible, fire and air are compounds.

[6] Sūkṣma and Nitya: existing even during the dissolution of the world.

[7] Sthūla, Anitya; arising only on the "creation" of the world.

ultimate supersensible unit or minimum[1] and the latter is sensible matter formed by the aggregation[2] of the ultimate units according to a definite order of combination, *viz.*, binaries or couplets (*Dvyaṇuka*) and Ternaries (*Trasareṇu*). At this last stage matter becomes theoretically fit for perception,[3] or as it is called *Bhūta*, though in practice it only becomes perceivable when it becomes large and consists of many parts.[4] Thus as we have seen the subtle *Pṛthivī-Paramāṇu* itself possesses and produces the four kinds of qualities in gross *Pṛthivī* or *Pṛthivī-Bhūta*[5] (P.B.) It has therefore colour and form (*Rūpa*) and the rest, but its form is not such as can be apprehended by the senses.[6] When the object becomes large and has many parts, and has form in itself, it becomes an object of visual perception. For the mere existence of form in a thing is not enough for its being perceived by the eye. To be perceivable it must possess such form as brings it within the range of our normal sense-capacity.[7] The Paramāṅus or Material Minima have infrasensible mobility, form, taste, and smell, which originate these qualities in sensible matter as the gross object of perception.

The first Standard in its description of the *Paramāṇus* omits one quality namely Sound (*Śabda*) which is also perceived by a single and special sense namely hearing. For it does not regard sound as a property of discrete sensible things. It may be eliminated from all of them for they all may be conceived as absolutely silent. Sound may be said to be common to all things, in that it may be produced by means of any of them but at the same time there is no sensible thing which cannot exist without it. But though sound is not a property of the discrete sensible it must, as a quality which is not subjective, inhere in a Reality and that Reality is the Continuum or Ether (*Ākāśa*). The sense of hearing is essentially of the nature as Ether itself, and so with the other senses which are essentially the same as the stimuli themselves. The sensations produced by these stimuli existing in the Continuum (*Ākāśa*) are taken up and co-ordinated by the Mind which is here called Manas and passed on by it to the Self (*Ātmā*) in which Consciousness inheres.

8

In the second Standard (Sāṃkhya-yoga), Matter is not, as in the preceding Standard, something which, either in gross or subtle form, is

[1] Carama Avayavī or Paramāṇu. [2] Saṃyoga. [3] Praytakṣa yogya.

[4] Mahat and has many Avayavas. Vaiśe., IV. 1. 6.

[5] Bhūta is the nearest expression for the sensible matter of science.

[6] Udbhūta.

[7] That is Rūpa-viśeṣa or Udbhūta-Rūpa. Thus the pollen dust of scented flowers floating in the wind excite the sense of smell but not that of sight.

eternally separate and distinct from Mind. In the second Standard Mind and Matter are phenomenally distinct, but are in their ground and during the dissolution of the universe, one. That is, they are each transformations[1] and modes of the one Natural Principle[2] from which both evolve when such Principle is associated with the Selves[3] who are Consciousness. According to this doctrine of evolution[4] the cause evolves into the effect and yet, as cause, remains what it is. As effect it is modified that is the effect is the cause modified. All which exists is a transformation of one substance, their cause. Causation is transformation; cause and effect being different positions of the same thing in the time sequence, the antecedent position being the cause and the consequent position the effect. The Natural principle as the source of Mind and Matter has three factors or *Guṇas—Sattva*, *Rajas* and *Tamas*. The meaning of these is simple but has been obscured. The Natural Principle, which is a principle of unconsciousness, works in association with Consciousness which is itself quiescent. What is its effect? it may do one or other of two things. It may obscure Consciousness, in varying degree, or it may similarly reveal Consciousness. When it is said that *Sattva* "reveals" Consciousness what is meant is that it does so relative to the operation of Tamas. Consciousness is self-revealing.[5] The Natural Principle is an obscuring and negating one (for the *Guṇas* are ever inseparate) but not always in the same degree. In so far as and to the extent that it suppresses the specifically obscuring factor (*Tamas*) it reveals Consciousness and is called *Sattva Guṇa*. In so far and to the extent that it suppresses the revealing factor (*Sattva*), it obscures Consciousness and is called *Tamas*. But both these actions involve activity and this is the *Rajas Guṇa*.[6] As all which is in the effect is in the cause, and as the effect is the cause modified, it follows that these three Factors are factors of Mind and Matter and the whole universe is composed thereof. In some things one factor prevails more and in varying degree than in others. Thus *Tamas* most prevails in what is called gross inorganic matter, and yet also even here in varying degree. But even in such former Matter *Sattva* is not altogether absent, for *Sattva*, *Rajas* and *Tamas* never exist separately from one another. It follows then that this inorganic Matter also reveals consciousness in its degree. When we pass to the lowest forms of vegetable life there is a greater display of *Sattva* though there is *Tamas* in very great degree. As ascent is made through

[1] Vikṛti. [2] Prakṛti. [3] Puruṣas.
[4] Pariṇāma. [5] Svaprakāśa.
[6] Rajas makes Tamas active to suppress Sattva and makes Sattva active to suppress Tamas.

higher vegetable, lower animal and higher animal forms until we arrive at Man, *Sattva Guṇa* (revealing Consciousness) more and more increases and *Tamas Guṇa* lessens. In Man the increase is observed to range from the rudest of primitive men to the Yogin whose consciousness is united with the Supreme Consciousness.

The order of evolution of what are called the Tattvas shows the development of the various mental and material principles. The evolution is not a temporal but a logical one. All the evolved principles are immanent but latent in the ultimate Natural Principle. By evolution they become manifest. In this Standard start is made with the association of the two Principles of Consciousness (the many *Puruśas*) and Unconsciousness (the one *Prakṛti*), the first of which is inactive and eternally changeless, and the second is eternally active. Change actually takes place in the Natural Principle though owing to the association of Consciousness with the latter, change seems to be observed there also. What is evolved? The experience of past worlds. Everything which will appear is already there potentially in the Natural Principle. On the dissolution of the previous universe all is merged in the Natural Principle and becomes a mere *Saṃskāra* or tendency, which, in its most fundamental form, is a disposition towards manifestation as the world of finite experience. In this general disposition lie implicit all the particular tendencies and experiences which manifest as the world of man, animal, vegetable and inorganic matter. How and in what manner does the evolution of tendency into manifested form take place? In the first place by the autodynamic evolution of the Principles (*Tattva*) which constitute all manifested being. The first production of the association of Consciousness and Unconsciousness and therefore the first transformation of the Natural Principle is the Principle (*Tattva*) called *Mahat*[1] or *Buddhi*. To understand this state most easily we should go to our own individual experience which is a microcosmic form of what appears in the world at large. When a man (say X) drops into dreamless slumber he is in the state of dissolution (*Laya*).[2] Let us suppose that he very gradually awakes from his slumber and slowly regains his waking consciousness. The first experience is a vague one of *mere being*, with a sense of limitation no doubt, but as yet without defined *centre.* Thus the sleeper has first the experience of being without the experience that it is *he* X who is that being. He is not

[1] Mahat=great or massive: a good description for the experience is a massive one. Another derivation however of the word is from Maghas or Light.

[2] This dreamless state (*Suṣupti*) is not as some suppose the same as Liberation (*Mokṣa*).

yet to himself an "I" (*Aham*). There is a vague sense of awareness without reference to a conscious self. Then it comes to him "It is I (X) who went to sleep and am now awaking. The sense of limitation is deepened. Then he X observes with greater and greater details the *things* around him and takes up to-day the thread of experience from yesterday, interrupted by sleep. And so with the universe. It falls into dreamless sleep in the Natural Principle and passing through the dreaming state awakens again to the world. It is again to be remembered that in the first state or *Buddhi* there is in addition to *Buddhi* as it is in itself all other principles and experiences in a latent state. A person in the first state of awakening from dreamless slumber has only a vague sense of being. But therein lies implicit the experience of all particulars which that person has had or will have.[1] So in the second state in which the sense of I (*Ahaṃ*) emerges—a principle called the "I—maker" (*Ahaṃkārā*) there is patent both *Buddhi* and *Ahaṃkārā* and there is latent all other principles and experiences and so on with the rest of the Principles (*Tattva*) to which I now turn and which have both a cosmic and individual, or macrocosmic and microcosmic aspect.

The first sprouting of the seed of Tendency in Substance as the Natural Principle (*Prakṛti*) is that transformation of it which is called *Mahat* or *Buddhi*. Here the cosmic tendency *Saṃskāra* as *Avidyā* or the ignorance of the whole which renders knowledge of the section possible is actualised.[2] This form of Cosmic Energy is the first manifested form of volition towards definiteness of being and direction of evolution. There is at this stage no finite centre but a mere undefined experience of being (the first mere awareness of the awakening sleeper) containing within it the potency of every definite form which is ultimately to evolve from it. It is as if the Will to Become assumes definite shape and direction and decides on a definite line of evolution. *Mahat* however as a state of Cosmic volition is merely a massive determination to change in which the "How" and the "What" of the operation are still implicit. Substance then transforms Itself into a Centre. This is the stage of the individualising principle, the self-arrogating[3] "I making" principle called *Ahaṃkāra* or *Asmitā Tattva*. This Cosmic Ego

[1] There is a particular experience which Western literature might call "hypnagogic" but to me real in which the world is known and understood without being seen in its form as particulars. It may occur "accidentally" but I was told of a Yogī who knew how to bring it about.

[2] The Bhāṣya quotes Bārṣaganya Ṛṣi as saying that the true or whole view of the Guṇas that is Cosmic Power is not had in ordinary experience. What we call the present view of a thing is only a cross-section of the whole in which past, present and future unite.

[3] Abhimāna.

or centre of operation in the Cosmic Stuff must be distinguished from the individual Ego, who only appears with the completed evolution of all the psychic and physical principles. From the individualising Principle in which the self as *Buddhi* and *Ahaṃkārā* or psychic functioning have as their object an experience of limited general being in which all particulars are implicitly contained, we pass to the stage in which those particulars become explicit. There is evolved first and together that aspect of mind (*Manas*) which is the chief and controller of the senses (*Indrya*), the ten senses of perception and action (*Jñānendrya* and *Karmendrya*) and the five *Tanmātras* which are generals of the sense particulars or universals. These *Tanmātras* take the place in this system of the *Paramāṇus* of the first. They will be found compared in detail earlier in the section "Mind". They are the subtle forms of matter and from these by compounding and accretion of mass, gross matter (*Bhūta*) is produced namely that fivefold form[1] of the one Substance when sensible, and which affects the senses in five different ways as Sound, Touch, Colour and Form,[2] Taste, and Smell[3] through the corresponding senses of hearing, touch, vision, taste and smell. From the subjective standpoint each form of Matter is the corresponding psychosis objectified. From an objective standpoint the five forms of Matter are five forms of motion. "Earth" and the rest are at the lowest or gross end of the scale. Earth (*Pṛthivī*), the characteristic of which is obstruction, is that form of motion which produces cohesion, whilst at the highest end Ether (*Ākāśa*) the characteristic of which is non-obstruction, being the medium in which all other things and motions are, is non-obstructive all-directed motion, radiating in all directions. Between these is first locomotive motion (*Vāyu*) upward motion giving rise to expansion (*Tejas*) and downward motion giving rise to contraction (*Ap*).[4]

As previously stated the Śākta system may, in a general way, be understood if we accept the Sāṃkhya scheme of the evolution of the 24 Tattvas but in a Monistic sense. In lieu of the many selves (*Puruṣas*) there is one Supreme Self who is Śiva the God of Good, and in lieu of the Natural Principle or Prakṛti there is the Power (*Śakti*)[5] of God or Śiva represented

[1] As Ākāśa ("Ether"), Vāyu ("Air"), Tejas ("Fire"), Ap ("Water"), and Pṛthivī ("Earth").

[2] The two go together. No form is perceived unless there is colour.

[3] Śabda, Sparśa, Rūpa, Rasa, Gandha.

[4] In the Tantra-Śāstras each of the Bhūtas is symbolised by a colour and form. Thus earth (*Pṛthivi*) is yellow and is represented by a square cube to denote the notion of solidity. The same notion of solidity is denoted by the elephant who upholds the cube.

[5] As Cit-Śakti that is Consciousness as Power and Māyā-Śakti that is Power as Māyā or as instrumental and material cause.

under feminine form as His Consort. The "tender"[1] Prakṛti, as the Sāṃkhyas called Her, was separate from and independent of the Selves, but Power (Śakti) and the Possessor of Power (Śaktimān) or Śiva are one. Even the phrase Possessor of Power is an accommodation for in their ultimate sense,[2] Śakti = Śiva. Each therefore of the Principles (*Tattvas*) and forms or *Vikṛti* of *Prakṛti* in the Sāṃkhya are forms of power (*Śakti*) of the supreme power (*Mahā-śakti*). Therefore the universe which these principles compose is self-evolving Śakti or Power. God in one aspect, that is as Consciousness-power (Śakti) evolves as the Universe, and yet in another as Consciousness (Śiva) remains unchanged.[3] What is further peculiar to this system is that it adds twelve further Principles or Tattavas to the twenty-four. It explains how both Prakṛti and Puruṣa, as understood in this system, were themselves evolved. But as these earlier Tattvas deal with the evolution of consciousness before and as a preliminary to the manifestation of the world of duality it is dealt with in the section Maha-Māyā as Consciounsess (*Cit*). The nature of Matter as above described is not affected. Matter is a form of the Supreme Power and as such is composed of the five forms of motion above described.

As already explained[4] Śākta doctrine or the Doctrine of Power (Śakti) is a form of Vedāntic monism which possessing elements of its own uses also others drawn from the Sāṃkhya. As regards these elements Nyāya-Vaiśeṣika teaches *Yaugika-sṛṣṭi;*[5] Sāṃkhya-yoga teaches *Yaugika-sṛṣṭi*[5] and *Pariṇāma-sṛṣṭi;*[6] Vedānta teaches *Yaugika-sṛṣṭi,*[5] *Pariṇāma sṛṣṭi*[6] and *Vivarta-sṛṣṭi.*[7] Śākta doctrine teaches in its own way also all three though being a practical system of Theology and Ritual its own *Vivarta-sṛṣṭi* is conceived in a different manner[8] and it adds an *Adṛṣṭa-sṛṣṭi* up to the appearance of Puruṣa and Prakṛti Tattvas according to the scheme of the thirty-six Tattvas.[9] Its conception of "Matter" however is not substantially different from the Sāṃkhyan and Vedāntic views above described.

---

[1] Komala.          [2] That is as Consciousness: Śakti as Cidrūpiṇī.

[3] Just as in Sāṃkhya one Tattva evolves into another and remains what it was as cause. Thus Buddhi produces Ahaṃkāra and yet remains Buddhi.

[4] See *Reality* earlier.

[5] Creation by combination of previously given Elements.

[6] Creation by evolution; the product existing in a potential form prior to actual manifestation.

[7] Creation where the originating Reality remains what it is and yet brings about the effect according to Advaita Vedānta apparently; according to Śākta practical doctrine, really.

[8] See last note.

[9] See *Śakti and Śākta* where this scheme is explained.

9

We have seen that in the search after the ideal limit of discontinuous (*i.e.*, granular) matter, we must pass through a series (*e.g.*, "body", "particle," "molecule," "atom," "subatom" (or Electron) and "prime atom"), and also that we have to pass through another series in our search after the ideal limit of continuous matter (i.e., homogeneous, nongranular, seamless) through Ethers of increasing subtlety until we come to the Cidākāśa or Ether of Consciousness itself. The physical unit in Science (as distinguished from the chemical unit which is the "atom") is now the Electron (as unit charge of Electricity); but Electron has a definite mass and dimensions as compared, for example, with those of an atom of Hydrogen; and since it is so (*Sāvayava* and *parimita*), it cannot be the ultimate unit. G. Johnstone Stoney, who invented the name 'Electron' says[1] "Here, then, the electron is introduced to us as a new entity. Is not it, too, a complex system within which internal events are ever taking place; And when this question can be answered shall we not be in the presence of the inter-active *parts* of an electron? And do not the same questions arise with respect to these? For there is no appearance of there being any limit to the minuteness of the scale upon which Nature works. Nothing in Nature seems to be too small to have parts incessantly active among themselves." So the Electron need not be partless.

Coming then to the other series, we note this that since scientific Ether is a medium which is capable of being stressed and strained (*i.e.*, changed in form or configuration), we must be able to conceive "grains" or elements in this so-called continuum itself; for, change of configuration presupposes the existence of parts which *have* a configuration or relative positions with respect to one another. Thus it is impossible to conceive a vortex-strain in a sea of Ether otherwise placid, unless this sea is composed of grains or elements which can change their places. There can thus be no halt at scientific Ether, just as there can be no halt at the scientific Electron. In fact, physicists have sometimes imagined a granular structure for Ether; as Professor Osborne Reynolds who in his "The Sub-Mechanics of the Universe" conceives Ether as a sea of indefinite extent composed of uniform spherical grains (smaller than the electrons) which are in relative motion with one another. Strain-forms pass through them as waves pass over water. A Commentator on this theory says:[2] "Matter is a persistent strain-form

[1] See Preface to "The Electron Theory", by E. E. Fournier d'Albe (1909), p. XX.
[2] W. C. D. Whetham, "The Recent Development of Physical Science" (1904), p. 294.

flitting through a universal sea of æther: we have explained matter in terms of æther. Æther in its turn is described as a fairly close-packed conglomerate of minute grains in continual oscillation: we have explained the properties of the aether. So be it. But what of the grains of which the aether is composed? Are they "strong in solid singleness" like the one-time atoms of Lucretius? Or have they parts within which opens a new field of complexity? Of what substance are they made? Has a new aether more subtle than the first to be invoked to explain their properties, and a third ether to explain the second? The mind refuses to rest content at any step in the process. An ultimate explanation of the simplest fact remains, apparently for ever, unattainable."

An ultimate explanation in terms of science of That Power Whose ways are inscrutable (*anirvācya*) is not to be Thought of. But, on the other hand, in seeking after the ultimate ground of things, it is best not to be groping in the dark or chasing after elusive theories. The Ether of Science, for example, has now become something of which it is not possible to form a physical conception.[1] What is it like? Is it stagnant or moving? What are its properties? These questions cannot now be answered; the only conception of Ether as a medium is this that it satisfies a number of differential equations associated with the names of Clerk-Maxwell, Lorentz, Larmor and others. Some physicists are therefore seriously asking if such an Ether is not a mathematical fiction only. Even the positive evidence of the Hertzian electric waves and wireless telegraphy does not convince some minds as to the real existence of Ether. At any rate, if a real Ether should exist, it is a hopeless task to give a rendering of it in mechanical and physical terms. The same difficulty meets us in the other direction. The Chemical atom has now been weighed and measured; the Kinetic Theory of Gases as well as other means now enable us to count the number of atoms or molecules in, say, a cubic inch. The number of particles in a cubic inch of air in the ordinary state of the atmosphere is represented by a number which is approximately 3 followed by 20 cyphers. Now, these particles having definite weights and dimensions cannot obviously be the physical minima; in fact it has now been possible to go beyond the chemical atoms

[1] Prof. Emile Picard, "La Science Moderne," 134, after pointing out that bizarre theories and contradictions have lessened the enthusiasm and provoked some discouragement amongst scientists says: "Il a pu mȇme paraitre ā quelques uns qu'il ètait ètrange d'expliquer le connu par l'inconnu, le visible par l'invisible, d'imaginer par example, comme on l'a dit, un èther que nul aeil humain ne veera jamais." Then in the usual way he refers to it as an useful image provided that we do not pretend to have attained reality. But its utility if real is a guarantee of its reality.

and discover the sub-atoms which also in their turn have been weighed and measured. We are therefore impelled to push farther. The common tendency in science to-day[1] is to regard the Prime Atom as a sort of strain (probably, rotational, gyrostatic) in Ether. This, however, is something which has been dematerialised. According to this view, then, an electron or unit charge of electricity is a centre of intrinsic strain, probably of a gyrostatic type, in an aether, which is also the medium in which are propagated the waves of light and wireless telegraphy. Moreover, the electron is identical with the sub-atom which is common to all the different chemical elements, and forms the universal basis of matter. Matter, at any rate in its relation to other matter at a distance, is in this view an electrical manifestation; and electricity is a state of intrinsic strain in a universal medium. That medium is prior to matter, and therefore not necessarily expressible in terms of matter; it is sub-natural if not super-natural. Matter itself therefore becomes Non-matter in motion. But notwithstanding all the equations in Hydro-dynamics, it is not known why and how a Non-matter can move gyrostatically or otherwise. The physicist's enquiry or quest in both directions (*i.e.*, continuum and atom) therefore brings him sooner or later to a confession of ignorance; his attempt to explain matter in terms of Ether is only explaining the unknown by the still more unknown.

We therefore require a surer ground than theory and mathematical analysis to go upon in our quest. We find that surer ground in experience. We must start from and upon that and rest in that also. Theory and mathematical analysis have their use, but only if they proceed upon the firm ground of Experience. If it should posit any Ether, that Ether must have its warrant in Experience; if there be any strain-centres in it, our Experience must be able to vouch for them. If there be any stress or energies, these also must be such as our Experience can guarantee. In one word, Experience must be in a position to stand surety for all the essentials of any theory, pending its actual verification by Experience in all the details.

Now, we firstly ask this: Is a continuum *given* in our Experience? If so, what is it? Our Experience, as we have pointed out before, is a universe apart from the action of pragmatic interests which narrows it down to particular sections or segments such as (the noticing of the star Sirius in the sky on a clear night). Now, this world of Experience or measurable is felt by

[1] Recent Development of Physical Science, p. 282. See also Sir Oliver Lodge's "Modern Views on Electricity" where Electricity is regarded by him as a condition of Ether.

us as a manifestation in Cit. This Cit is the boundless *plenum* or *continuum* (the Brahman which means the Immeasurable, the Immense) in which and, of which, the whole manifestation is. This therefore is the basis of all *continua* that we may require and search for. It is the basis and prototype of the Ether (or Ethers) of Science, of Space and of Time. *Cit* is no theory; its being a continuum is not theory. It is the Fact.

We secondly ask this: Is any strain-centre given in our Experience? If so, what is it? How does it form? Is it permanent or passing? Does it change so long as it remains? The key to all this is in actual experience. I am directly aware of myself as a stress-and-strain centre or *Jīva* (strain presupposing stress), inasmuch as I know myself as a "point-of-view" distinguishing myself from the rest of my universe and yet as being its point of reference; and also, practically or dynamically, as a centre of power at which and through which forces converge and diverge (resulting in incessant actions and reactions) throughout the universe. Thus my being the unifying Principle of apperception, and a Centre of Power is a fact. It is also a fact that this Principle and Centre presupposes and accepts a universe in which operate similar other Principles and Centres. For, there can be and there is no stressing for a solitary Centre in a perfectly homogeneous continuum. Plurality of correlated centres is therefore a necessity. Nay; I directly experience it. Whenever I function, I feel that my functioning has relation to, is addressed to, and conditioned by the functions of other Centres. In other words, my being a member of a joint stress-system to which others also contribute is a direct experience. Whether or not those other Centres all live, feel and think as I do, is another matter; but *all* are stress-centres; my having a universe of Experience means my finding myself as one in a system of stress-centres; and each stress-centre or point of Power (Śakti) is also necessarily a strain centre, *i.e.*, a point that has, through that Principle in Being which is *Asmitā* or *Ahaṃkāra*, individualised and distinguished itself somehow on account of its manner of stressing.[1] What therefore impresses me as Matter must ultimately be such stress-and-strain centres in rapport with me as a centre. The atoms of Chemistry, the "sub-atoms" and so forth of physical theory are only more or less crude guesses or approximations to these Centres. These guesses may be invalid in part; but there cannot be any doubt about the Centres of Stress in *rapport* with

[1] That every person or thing including the minutest coherent particle of matter is regarded as a self follows from the fact that everything which exists including both subtle and gross matter is derived from and is a product of the individualising or centre-making cosmic Power which is called Asmitā or Ahaṃkāra.

us which our Experience directly gives. *Cit* as the Primary Continuum, and *Bindu-Śakti* as the Primary Individual, are not therefore unknown; with respect to them, we cannot pretend to say "we are ignorant".

Further, to make joint partnership and co-ordinate interaction possible, all the centres in my universe must be like me in all the essentials. In this sense, there is a fundamental truth in Leibtnitz's theory of monads. Any two monads, A and B, are alike if we into take account both what is latent (potential) and what has become patent (kinetic) in each. Dynamically, it could not be otherwise.

Take a particle of dust here on earth and an incandescent gaseous particle in a distant star. They seem to be unconnected. But really each expresses in its way the entire stress-system which the universe is. So it is said that man and all other centres is a microcosm (*Kṣudra-Brahmāṇḍa*). A passage from the Viśva-sāra-Tantra says *Yad ihāsti tad anyatra*—"what is here is elsewhere" —*Yannehāsti na tat Kvacit*—"what is not here is nowhere" To understand this passage we must include both the latent and patent power as potency, and power as manifested. The given position, composition, properties and relations of the one cannot be *completely* understood without taking into account the entire stress-system of the universe. In this way, the whole universe is given in a particle. A given particle, however, in virtue of its peculiar position in the universal stress-system has or appears to have a given set or round of operations which constitute its own *Karma* and determine its separate individuality. These are its patent or kinetic *Karma*. But in virtue of its peculiar position in the universe-system, it has also the potentiality of other operations which are its latent or potential *Karma*. A load which is lifted from the ground and placed at the top of a building, has a potential energy by virtue of its position;[1] so when the load again falls to the ground it does work on account of that potential energy. A string put to the bow has thus potential energy by virtue of its position. So on and so forth. Hence, any particle or any centre in the universe has, besides its kinetic or patent *Karma*, a store of potential energy by virtue of its place in the cosmic system. As in the examples of the load and the bow-string, the stock of potential energy is determined by previous kinetic actions, *e.g.*, lifting of the first and stretching of the second. The potential energy again determines future *Karma*. The potential energy which is not patent until it expresses itself in kinetic action, is called *Adṛṣṭa* (lit. what is not seen). Every Centre

[1] Kinetic Energy is Energy of Motion, while Potential Energy is Energy of Position or Configuration.

has thus its *Karma* and *Adṛṣṭa*, which both completely considered, give us the entire cosmic Energy. Hence, any Centre, A = any other Centre, B; because, A's whole kinetic energy + A's whole potential energy = B's whole kinetic energy + B's whole potential energy = whole cosmic energy = Brahman (the Immense, the Whole or *Pūrṇa*).

It follows from the above analysis that the difference between me (as a Centre or *Jīva*) and a particle of dust is *not* in the *sum* of the Energy which I represent and it represents, but it is in the peculiar *distribution* of that sum-total between kinetic energy and potential energy; that is, I divide the sum-total into a certain proportion of kinetic energy and potential energy which is *not* that of the particle of dust; my *Karma* and *Adṛṣṭa* are thus *distributively* different from those of the particle. And this special proportioning of *Karma* and *Adṛṣṭa* on my part and on its, depends on, or is incidental to, our respective positions in the cosmic system. Position again is determined by *Karma* and *Adṛṣṭā* (*i.e.*, their proportion); *Adṛṣṭa* is determined by *Karma*, and *Karma partly* by *Adṛṣṭa*. And this cyclic causation is beginningless. The Vedāntists says that *Karma* is *partly* determined by *Adṛṣṭa*, because, contrary to the rigid determinism of Science, the Vedāntic position is this that *Karma*, even in a so-called material centre, cannot have its essential freedom or spontaneity completely veiled and suppressed. *Cit-Śakti* is free, and through every centre of its operation, its essential freedom must also vent itself, as also the other fundamental aspects of it, *viz.*, Being-Feeling-Consciousness-Bliss; such expression may however be, and commonly is, subject to the operation of its own correlate *Māyā-Śakti* or *finitising* principle by which its essential nature may be variously veiled and treated, but never completely suppressed or negatived.

Position in the cosmic scheme is position in Space, position in Time and position in the tissue of Causality. In one word, it means place in the curve of the life of the world. And this, as we have seen, is determined by *Karma* which produces *Adṛṣṭa*. *Karma*, as already mentioned is ultimately of *Cit-Śakti* and as such its freedom or spontaneity can in no case be completely veiled or effaced. An atom, for example, was formerly treated as a hard particle which moved in obedience to external forces only and had no choice of its own, no energy of its own (*i.e.*, apart from external impacts or impressed force). But the atom of modern science is a complex system of sub-atoms, and in virtue of the motions and positions of these latter within itself, it possesses an almost limitless stock of kinetic and potential energy in a state of relatively stable equilibrium; the energy thus stored up, and as evidenced by radio-activity, is so great that if we could make it available to us and control it, then we should be able to do all the work of the world by its means alone, without requiring to burn coal to produce steam, electricity, etc., or to make chemical explosives. Control over the intra-atomic energy is a tremendous *Siddhi* or Power. We may illustrate by a Vedic parable which says that Indra (*i.e.*, for illustration let us suppose *Cit-Śakti*) let loose the cows which had been shut up in a cave by the Aśura (Pani, *i.e.*, Māyā-Śakti). The cows are the forces which are stored up and concealed in everything (by the Veiling Principle in Nature) which is therefore like a cave. Now, what about this vast amount of intra-atomic energy? Does not an atom possess spontaneous action on account of its own store of power? Can it not choose to move and work in a manner which is *not* determined by the external influences alone? That it can is proved by the evidence of radio-activity which, as Sir E. Rutherford and others define it, is a *spontaneous* activity on the part of the atom which apparently does not depend on, and cannot be influenced by, the ordinary chemical and physical means (chemical action, great heat and cold and so forth). Precisely by such spontaneous activity, the atoms give out their radiations and emanations which are of enormous dynamic value, and they evolve and transmute. It appears therefore that the atom has its own work (*Karma*) and tendency or *Saṃskāra*. It is describing its curve of life according to the equation of its *Karma* (including *Adṛṣṭa*) as I am doing. It may be that on a future day, it will be possible to give a mechanical account of the atomic system in terms of the motions and positions of the sub-atoms in it, just as we now give a mechanical account of the solar system. But even then the question will only be shifted. In the first place, that mechanical account (*i.e.*, account in terms of Newton's Laws of Motion and their corollaries) will be possible only by "Limitation of the actual data" or by abstract analysis. The concrete, the actual always baffles attempts at a mechanical explanation; it is only the abstract, the conceptual obtained by "limitation of the data" which has so long been amenable to mechanical or deterministic treatment (which begins by assuming that things are inert in themselves and have therefore no spontaneity). It should be remembered that the machine made "things" of Physics are not exactly the things as they exist and as they act. In the second place, supposing that Physics is able to prepare a mechanics of the intra-atomic system in terms of the motions and positions of the sub-atoms, the question of "inertia or spontaneity?" will still arise with regard to the sub-atoms themselves *i.e.*, with regard to the total activity of the components of the sub-atoms (for, the sub-atoms cannot be the ultimate units). There cannot be rest until we come to the *Bindu-Śakti* which, as a centre of operation of the *Cit-Śakti*, must be essentially a centre of spontaneous or free energising. Man's own experience of himself gives him, it is said, the warrant for so thinking. The appearance of intra-atomic energy has, it is true, disturbed the quiet faith of the physicist in conservation of Energy, for it has upset all his calculations so far made, as it has come as a new factor never before suspected. But the doctrine in so far as it maintained that the sum-total of energy in the universe always remained constant[1] was unpsychological and therefore untrue; no absolute bounds can be set to the magnitude of Energy in the universe which is *Cit-Śakti*; e.g., we cannot draw a line and say that the sum-total of Energy can only be so great as that, but can never exceed that. The Mother Power (*Mahā-Śakti*) cannot be circumscribed and measured; and the symbol pictures Her as nude.[2] 'Unmeasured' and 'immeasurable' are Her true characteristics. Man's Will, for example, is a tap through which new Energy is being continually drafted into the universe: He is no more "points-man" on the cortex of the brain switching off and directing existing energies therein: He is in Vedānta a creator. At any rate, he draws upon a Bank which Physics was not prepared to charter.

Lastly, if he interrogates his own experience he finds that the generic and homogeneous condition precedes the particularised and heterogeneous condition (though the recognition of the former may be a later phenomenon). He finds also that particularised and heterogeneous states of experience have a tendency (which is sometimes periodic) to lapse back into the undifferentiated state from which they sprang. A *Sāmānyāvasthā* (undifferentiated condition) giving birth to a *Viśeṣāvasthā* (differentiated condition), and this again returning to its ground—is a fact of experience, and a fundamental fact. Empirical psychologists in the West of the last generation were too busy with their "atoms" of sensation, their "laws of association and synthesis" to recognise this order. To-day, however, we know better. Now, what does the fundamental fact referred to mean? It means this: Man as well as every other

1 See Emile Picard, La Science Moderne, 133 *et seq.*

2 The Mother is said to be space-clad (Digaṃbarī) because She is Herself free from the covering of Māyā though wielding that Power: Her Body is dark blue because She pervades the World. See *Hymn to Kālī*. In Kamalā Kānta's Sādhakarañjana it is said that "Māyā is the Ākāra (form) of Nirākara (formless) Brahman. The Śūnya or 'void' is formless until encircled by Māyā".

centre is a system of tensions or tendencies (*Saṃskāras*). These may periodically (or at times) be (normally or by effort) in equilibrium (*Sāmyāvasthā*). What does *this* mean again? It means not that the tensions themselves have severally vanished (so that energy then becomes a sum of zeros), but that their resultant ("algebraic sum" as the mathematician would say) then becomes in-effective. This again means that then his dynamic system lacks a special direction of doing work. This is its *Sāmyāvasthā* which is an undirected (or "scalar") condition.[1] But presently by the "catalytic" action of Cit-Śākti this spell of equilibrium is broken.[2] It is to be noted that without such spontaneous action or *Saṃkalpa* of the Cit-Śakti, there is no reason why *Sāmya* or equilibrium of the entire cosmos once established should again be broken, and also why *Vaiṣamya* or dis-equilibrium once set agoing should again revert to equilibrium.[3] By the breaking of the spell, lines of force or directions of tendency effectively manifest themselves. These are the Jatājāla of Vyomakeśa beginning His cosmic dance. These directed tendencies are in mathematical parlance "vector" quantities doing work in definite directions.

Now, this fundamental of Experience is a fundamental of the universe also, for the latter *is* the former. Taking Matter, therefore, we can say that the grains of Matter of various grades (prime atoms, sub-atoms, atoms, molecules, etc.) are born out of an homogeneous or undifferential Substance; that all their differing tensions arise out of the dis-equilibrium of that primordial stuff; and that after their varied *Karma*, *Adṛṣṭā* and *Saṃsṛtī* (evolution), they at last come under the influence of the Cosmic Cit-Śākti or Lord as the Supreme Self (*Parāhantā*) to equilibrate their tensions, and thus return to their starting ground. Modern Physics too in working out its Law of Dissipation of Energy contemplates such periodicity in cosmic equilibrium and dis-equilibrium.[4] Hence Matter is a periodically appearing and disappearing, (and evolving while in appearance), strain-form in "non-matter". The first undirected condition of the stress-system is called, in the Mantra-Śāstra, *Nāda*; which passes into that which is called *Bindu* in which it is

[1] *e.g.*, in Suṣupti, or dreamless sleep, Samādhi or Ecstasy, the state of just waking, the state just before falling asleep, etc.

[2] *Cf.* the meaning of the Gāyatrī-Mantra in which Cit is thought of as impelling our Buddhi (*i.e.*, stress-system) in all its states. In catalytic action one thing affects another by its presence without itself being affected. And this is the action of Puruṣa in the Sāṃkhya.

[3] In this respect the Sāṃkhyan doctrine of Prakṛti and Vikṛti is rightly criticised by the Vedānta.

[4] See Herbert Spencer's work in this connection.

about to manifest itself in definite directions or lines of force, (for, without points, directions or lines have no meaning), and its manifestation on its threefold division into Knower, Knowing, and Known is the multiple varied and finite universe, the limited expression of infinite Power. Modern Physics too, it may be noticed, cannot do without super-natural agency (*i.e.*, miracle) in explaining the appearance of dis-continuities in the homogeneous continuum and their disappearance in it (if indeed they should disappear.)

The existence of polarities (*e.g.*, that between the positive and negative charges of Electricity) by which attractions and repulsions in the universe are sought to be explained, are grounded in Experiencc as the fundamental *dvaita* (dichotomy) in Consciousness as Śiva-Śakti, Static-Kinetic, Cit-Māyā, Subject-Object, "*Ahaṃ-Idaṃ*".[1] Attraction between the dissimilar poles means their tendency to return to the condition of Whole (*Pūrṇa*) whose aspects they are and yet from which they appear to have become separate. Attraction (*Rāga*) is thus the return current tending to lead to the *Pūrṇāvasthā*: in the "conscious" plane it appears in its form as *Rāga* in the sense of Love. So Love makes us whole (*Pūrṇa*). By reason of this coalescing tendency, the Subject ("I") draws towards itself in perception and volition its Object ("This"), so that perceiving and willing is really an act of equating and owning. Śakti in the universe is always tending towards satisfaction (*Ānanda*) and *Ānanda* being Śiva Himself, this cosmic tendency is only the love of the "Divine Pair" (*Divya-Dampati*):[2] the Supreme *Haṃsa* or "Bird" swimming in the Lake of Consciousness. Static and Kinetic Energies also pre-suppose, require and "complete" each other. But if this return-current or coalescing tendency were not retarded by an opposite current, the universe would at once sink all its distinctions and polarities and there would be no difference or *Bheda*. The world's very existence therefore pre-supposes a *prati-bandhaka* or obstacle to complete union. This *prati-bandhaka* is *Dveśa* (repulsion). In the "conscious" plane, it appears as Hate or Resistance. Similar centres of the same pole thus repel one another. *Their* attraction would give but one pole, one aspect or "half" of Reality; while the meeting of two centres from the opposite poles would give a complete centre of Reality. So one "I" ejects another "I" (*i.e.*, cannot *directly* make an object of it),[3] but readily attracts "this" or "that";

[1] See *Kāma-kalā-vilāsa* and *Śakti and Śākta* where the development is shortly given.
[2] See *Kāma-kalā-vilāsa*, V.
[3] In the sense that I cannot *directly* know and feel your thoughts and feelings *as such* in your Mind. I have to infer them from what you say or express by your bodily expressions. This is the sense in which "ejecting" is used here.

in Biology similar sexes are rivals; in Physics similar "charges" repel each other.

So starting on the ground of our "given" Experience, we are enabled to establish on a sure footing the essentials of a right conception of Matter. To sum up:

(1) The unit of Matter is a stress-and-strain centre ultimately in *Cit* which as Pure Experience is the Perfect Continuum.

(2) The Perfect Continuum of its own power or Śakti becomes first a massive undifferentiated Continuum (*Nāda*).

(3) And then *Bindu* as the condition of Power which mainfests as centres or points of differentiated mass.

(4) The mass of a given centre is a function of its motion (*Karma*) which, though subject to position (*Adṛṣṭa*) is also spontaneous.

(5) Consequently, by *Karma* the mass of a centre may accelerate (*i.e.*, change), and it may thus become a different kind of centre, *e.g.*, one kind of Matter may evolve into another kind, into "living" matter, into "feeling" matter, into "thinking" matter.

(6) The 'point-charges" have polarities on account of which they attract and repel one another.

(7) Periodically, these strain-centres have a tendency to dissolve in the continuum (*Nāda*), which is their *Pralaya.*

(8) Strain presupposes Stress (Energy), and this is fundamentally *Cit-Śakti* or *Cit* as Power and is unmeasurable.

10

Summing up the teaching of the six systems, the First Standard (Nyāya Vaiśeṣika) proposes nine *Dravyas* or Entities, *viz.*, *Kiśti*, *Ap*, *Tejas*, *Vāyu*, *Ākāśa*, *Kāla*, *Dik*, *Ātman*, *Manas*. Of these, the Ātman or Self is the substratum of consciousness (*caitanya*) and experience (*jñāna*). Hence, if, we define an 'objective' reality as that which exists in its own right beyond consciousness and experience, then all the other eight *dravyas* are objective realities. That is, experience or no experience, they exist. They (including mind as *Manas*) are unconscious Principles. So as regards Matter, the First Standard agrees with Western Science in so far as the latter makes it or treats it as an extra-mental reality. There are, however, important points of disagreement between the two also. In the first place, Western Science draws a distinction between Primary qualities and Secondary qualities and regards the former set alone as really inhering in Matter and elements of Matter, whilst, according to it, the Secondary qualities are only effects produced upon a percipient Subject by the Primary set. The first Standard recognises no such partition.[1] The *Guṇas*, *Karmas* and relations exist in the things themselves. For example, Pṛthivī, or matter stimulating the sense of smell, possesses fourteen qualities (*Guṇas*) and these fourteen include what in Western parlance are primary and secondary qualities. Its material *minima* or *Paramāṇus* also possess both sets of qualities, and they originate both these sets in sensible matter because they themselves possess both.[2] One of the fundamental maxims of the First Standard is this: *Kāraṇa-bhāvāt Kārya-bhāvah.*[3] This, as the *Upaskāra* of Śaṃkara-Miśra explains, means —*Kāraṇa-guṇa-pūrvakā hi kārya-guṇa bhavanthi*—the *guṇas* in the effect are due to the previous existence of them in the cause.[4] Now Pṛthivī in its gross, or compounded sensible form possesses *Rūpa*, *Rasa*, *Gandha* and *sparśa* or luminous, flavoury, odoriferous and thermal matter.[5] *Pṛthivī* is either eternal (*Nityā*)[6] or non-eternal (*Anityā*). The former is the ultimate unit (*carama avayavī* or *Paramāṇu*) of *Pṛthivī*; the latter is *Pṛthivī* formed by the aggregation (*saṃyoga*) of the ultimate units according to a definite order (*Dvyāṇuka*, *Trasareṇu* and so forth). Though the different schools of interpretation of the First Standard differ as regards the unchangeability or otherwise of the *Guṇas* in the *Nityā Pṛthivī* or *Pṛthivī-Paramāṇu*, yet all agree as regards the possession of the four kinds of *Guṇas* by it. This therefore is *prima facie* an important point of difference between Western Science and the First Standard.

In the second place the primordial motions and aggregations (*i.e.*, at the time of creation) of the eternal *minima* are explained by the First Standard by an extra-material influence (*i.e.*, by the ripening of the *Adṛṣṭa* of the selves of *Ātmans* and those of the *Paramāṇus* themselves). Hence though regarding the *Paramāṇus* as the material cause of the world, it postulates a spiritual efficient cause also. Western Science has not so far made up its mind as regards this great question. "Uniformitarianism" is becoming an exploded creed not only in Boilogy and Geology, but in Physics also. That is to say, the physicist can hardly maintain now that the cosmic order has

[1] See *Reality, ante.*

[2] The Paramāṇus originate the corresponding senses: thus the Pṛthivi-Paramāṇu produces the sense of smell.

[3] Vaiśeṣika-Darśanam, IV. 1. 3.

[4] Also, Vaiśeṣika, II. 2. 24.

[5] "Rūpa-rasa-gandha-sparśa-vatī Pṛthivī"—Vaiśeṣika, II. 1. 1.

[6] "Sada-Kāraṇa-vannityam" (Vaiśeṣika, IV, 1. 1.) A Nitya object is defined as a "Sat" or being which has no Kāraṇa or cause. It is self-existent, if a Dravya or Entity; if a Guṇa or property or a Karma, it must be unalterable as existing in its Dravya. Alteration presupposes causation or Kāraṇa.

practically existed in the same form from eternity and will continue to do so for ever. He can hardly maintain this creed even as regards what he calls his "fundamentals". By the Law of Dissipation of Energy all the higher forms of Energy are being dissipated into Heat; and Heat also by its universal radiation is tending to a condition of equilibrium which, when established, will render all flow or radiation of Heat impossible. Heat is believed to be a motion or quiver (*Spanda*) of the "molecules" of Matter; perfect equilibration of Heat throughout the universe will mean therefore the equalisation of the motions of the molecules of Matter. That is, the molecules will *all* move or quiver equally when perfect equilibrium has been established. But Physics cannot stop at the moving molecules. It must go farther and consider the motions of the Atoms, Sub-atoms and Prime-atoms. In the so-called "atom" of Chemistry there is a vast store of energy due to the motions of the Sub-atoms, which Energy is also (as is evidenced by Radio-activity) being more or less slowly dissipated. Hence, taking these into account, we come at last to Ether in which certain "strain-forms" (*i.e.*, the electrons, etc.) are moving equally; that will be the state of equilibrium of Ether. Then there will be undifferentiated (*Sajātīya* or *Samāna*) motion, but no differentiated *Vijātīya* or *Viṣama*) motion.[1] But can the Mind stop here too? What is a 'strain-form'? How is it produced? Does not a strain imply an in-equality or heterogeneity in the stuff? The motions of the strain-forms are equalised; but the very *existence* of the strain-forms in different positions in a continuum will imply non-equal motions at the basis of the strain-forms themselves.[2] Hence, either of two positions is possible: (*a*) Say either that cosmic equilibrium is established when the motions of all the elements in the universe *severally* vanish, so that all movements stop; (*b*) or say that equilibrium is established when the component motions, without severally vanishing, produce a resultant which is nothing or practically so. We say "practically nothing" because the resultant of the cosmic motions (or forces), without being zero, may be an effective something, but a constant—an invariable something. When the resultant is zero, the cosmic system as a whole will not move at all—it will have no evolution

[1] In the Mantra Śāstra in the four states Parā, Paśyanti, Madhyama and Vaikharī of Śakti as Śabda, located in the centres or Cakras (see *The Serpent Power*.). Motion is first general and undifferentiated (Sāmānya) of which "Om" is the Mantra expression, then special (Viśeṣa) and lastly fully and clearly particularised (spaṣṭatara) as Vaikharī.

[2] Though the strain-forms may be otherwise identical, yet the very fact that they exclude one another and keep to different positions in the Continuum implies that the forces behind them cannot be the same; they have differing *adṛṣṭas* within the meaning of the previous sections.

(*Pariṇāma*). When the resultant is effective but an invariable something, the cosmic system will continue to move in a given state, which is *Sadṛśa-Pariṇāma*; and so long as the resultant is invariable, the system will not deviate from its given state. This is about the cosmic system as a whole. But what about the component things and elements in it? These being the component forces of the system must also either continue unaltered, or so alter relatively to one another that their resultant may remain unaltered. But this latter alternative will not give us dissolution or *Pralaya*, (to which the scientific principle of Dissipation of Energy also points), for then also, *ex hypothesi*, particular things and groups of things will continue to move and move in varied manners. There will therefore still be an universe (*Saṃsāra*). Hence true dissolution of an universe (*Pralaya*) will imply either the stoppage of all motions distributively and collectively in the universe, or the continuance of all motions, distributively and collectively, in the universe in the same given state of non-manifestation or potentiality (*Avyaktā-vasthā*). The first is called *Pariṇāmābhāva*, the second is *Sadṛśa Pariṇāma*.

Now, so far as the *Paramāṇus* are concerned, the First Standard adopts the first view. The second Standard (Sāṃkhya) adopts the second. The Third Standard (Vedānta) adopts the first view, but dispenses with the *Paramāṇus* as the persistent elements of the universe. It distinguishes between the static (non-moving) and dynamic (moving) aspects of the world, and believes that Motion may proceed out of Non-motion and lapse back into it. The basis of this belief is Experience.

Western Science is also now dimly conceiving the possiblity of the cycle of Appearance (*Sṛṣṭi*), continuance (*Sthiti*), and Dissolution[1] (*Laya*); but its ideas are still unsettled on the subjects. It deals with Ether and strain-forms in it. But if there should be dissolution (*Laya*), what would become of these? Would Ether be the undifferentiated itself, and therefore without the strain-forms? If so, how can strain-forms arise again? How again can perfect homogeneity be effected in Ether? Does not the final reduction of all strains or heterogeneities in Ether imply a super-natural action —a "miracle," in short? Does not again the appearance of strains in a perfectly homogeneous Ether imply a miracle? Or, in order to avoid the miracle, will it say that the tendency of the existing world is towards perfect equilibration of all energies; but that such perfect equilibration is an infinitely distant

[1] The Devatās of which are Brahmā, Viṣṇu and Rudra and their Śaktis. Sṛṣṭi and the other two are not merely applicable to the first appearance of the universe but, during its continuance as a whole, manifest as molecular birth, life, and death.

event, so that dis-equilibrium and heterogeneities will always continue, though gradually becoming evanescent? Or again, will it take up a position like that of the Second Standard?

For Science these questions are still unanswerable. But She must note this that if, in tracing out the world's curve of life, She makes the curve double upon itself—*i.e.*, if the curve going in a certain manner and in a certain direction should turn back and retrace its course—then, to explain such "critical" changes of direction or "nodes" at least, She must invoke the "miracle" She is so anxious to ban. Nothing short of "miracle" or spiritual actions will enable her to get heterogeneity out of homogeneity and *vice versa*, disequilibrium out of equilibrium and *vice versa* and evolution from involution and *vice versa*. Spiritual action is a miracle to Her, because She still makes Matter and Spirit *two*; but if they be *one*, then the action of the former is really the action of the latter, and then there is either no miracle or all is then miracle, for the commonest of experiences is so.

The First Standard believes in this commonest "miracle" of spiritual action upon Matter, though for it Matter is a substance different from the Spirit or Ātman. During *Laya*, the *Paramāṇus* are dissociated and stationary (*acala*). For their first *Priyā* (*i.e.*, motion) they require *Prayatna-vadātma-saṃyoga*, *i.e.*, the association of Ātman energising. *Kusumānjali*, a celebrated work on the First Standard, argues that at the time of *sarga* or creation the *Paramāṇus*, which are inert and disconnected, require the causal activity of *Ātman* energising in order to move and come into contact with one another, because such moving and associating is *Karma*, and *Karma*, as in our bodies, requires the causal energising of Ātman to be produced. '*Ātman*' in the case of creation means '*Paramātman*' or *Īśvara* (Lord), and 'causal energising' means '*Prayatna*' (Volition). The association of *Paramāṇus* into *Dvyaṇukas* (couplets) requires therefore *Īśvara-Prayatna* or the Lord's Will. But then the question arises: Why should A couple with B and not with C or D? Why is there such preference in coupling when the creative action is just beginning? The Lord's will which is the efficient cause of such coupling cannot have preferences of its own. Therefore there must be intrinsic though latent differences or tendencies in the material itself. These tendencies are the *Adṛṣṭa* of the *Paramāṇus*. As explained in a previous section, an *Adṛṣṭa* is the Energy of Position in the universal configuration. Even during dissolution (*Laya*) the discrete *Paramāṇus* have certain positions relative to one another. But they do not move then, and therefore they have then a static configuration. Where are they configurated? In Ether (*Ākāśa*) which is eternal (*Nityā*); and *Kāla, Dik*[1] and the Self or *Ātmā* also remain then. What therefore God's Will as efficient cause does is this—it realizes or actualizes the tendencies (*Adṛṣṭa*) of the *Paramāṇus* themselves; it helps their release or manifestation (*i.e.*, the translation of their static energy into kinetic energy). Then again a 'tendency' implies a relation; it presupposes duality (*Dvaita*); for a solitary thing (whether *Aṇu* or atomic or *Mahat* or immense) in the universe, there is no tendency. There must be actually two or more things; or duality (or Plurality) must be latent in the given solitary substance, or else it must be assumed to have power to appear as many (*Cf.* "*Eko'haṃ bahu syām prajāyeya*" "One am I, May I be many"). Now, the *Paramāṇus* of the First Standard are always many, and therefore they have their tendencies (*Ádṛṣṭa*) always in relation to one another, and also in relation to the "Selves" or *Ātmans* which, in this Standard as well as in the Second, are also many.[2] In relation to the Self, bodies, and therefore the *Paramaṇus* which are their ultimate constituents, are objects and instruments of enjoyment;[3] and the Self is the enjoyer.[4] Hence the *Adṛṣṭas* of the *Paramāṇus* are partly, if not wholly, determined by the *Adṛṣṭas* of the non-liberated Ātmans. In fact a given *Adṛṣṭa* as a given relation between A and B, has two correlatives; so that, if for example it is the *Adṛṣṭa* of A to be the enjoyer (*bhoktā*) of B, then by virtue of the same fact it is the *Adṛṣṭa* of B to be the enjoyed (*bhogya*) of A. An *Adṛṣṭa*, as we have seen is but a tendency, a static or potential condition of what is to be (*dṛṣṭa*); therefore, it requires an impetus, an efficient cause to be realised or actualised. So long as the universe is in movement, and *Paramāṇus* and groups of *Paramāṇus* are in movement, a particular *Paramāṇu*, or body, or self finds or may find such an impetus for the realisation of its *Adṛṣṭa* from the movements of others; but on the eve of creation when, according to the First Standard, there is no movement at all, the impetus can come only from a transcendent source. This transcendent Source is the Lord's Will, and by it, as the analysis has shown, the *Adṛṣṭas* or arrested tendencies of the *Paramāṇus* and the rest are released and become effective. This is creation (*Sṛṣṭi-Prakṛya*) according to the First Standard: the primordial motions and associations of the *Paramāṇus* are due to *Adṛṣṭa-sahakṛta-Īśvara-prayatna*.[5]

---

[1] That is the forces which move things on and hold them in position giving rise to the notions of Time and Space, see *Reality*.

[2] (Vaiśeṣika, II. 2. 19, 20, 21).

[3] Bhogya, Bhogāyatana, Bhoga-sādhana.

[4] Bhoktā.

[5] See also the summary of the process as given by its critics, *e.g.* Vācaspati's Bhāmatī under Vedānta, II. 2. 10, and also Saṃkara's Bhāṣya under Vedānta, II. 2. 11.

Points to be noted are: (1) *Adṛṣṭa* of the components of the Cosmos presupposes the pre-existence of an *active* cosmic order before *Laya* or dissolution; there is no absolute beginning. (2) God's Will is the efficient cause but it acts as the releasing force upon the latent tendencies in the dissolved cosmic order. (3) The expression of this moving force is *Kāla* or Time which is the scheme or succession of phenomena. The First Standard however, makes it a *Dravya* that is something which is independently real and self-subsisting and it is such an one not only in which, but by which, things are moved in their temporal relations, *i.e.*, 'A before B'; and 'B after A'; 'B and C together'; and 'D quicker than E'; 'E slower than F'; and so forth. Vaiśeṣika, II. 2. 9 and also VII. 1. 25 make *Kāla* a *Kāraṇa* in relation to all things that begin and end; II. 2. 7 and 8 make it *nitya* and *eka* (*i.e.*, eternal, one, undivided). To make *Kāla anitya* (non-eternal) is to say that it has a beginning and an end. But where? In a larger Time?[1] Therefore it must be eternal *nitya*. Again, the "sections" of Time (Hour, minute and so forth)[2] are not really sections of Time itself, but they are our representation of Time according to certain conventions (Vyavahāra), *viz.*, the Sun's motion, or those of the motions of the hands of a clock. The difference and division (*Bheda* or *Khaṇḍa*) is ascribed or imposed (*Aupādhika*).[3] *Dik* is the scheme of Co-existence or configuration, and is a Dravya, according to the First Standard. *Dik* like *Kāla* is a *Dravya*, *nitya* and *eka*.[4] *Dik*, therefore, is neither space nor the spatial directions, distributively or collectively. It is that by which things are made to form a definite scheme of co-existence in Space or arranged in positions in definite directions of one another. Similarly, *Kāla* is neither "Time" nor the temporal relations, distributively or collectively. It is that by which things form a definite scheme or succession. The two are thus obviously opposed to each other. By the former, the *Paramāṇus* are held together in a static configuration; by the latter they become dynamic, *i.e.*, are displaced and go on being displaced from their given configuration. By the first, the *adṛṣṭas* are conserved; by the latter their static energies are rendered more and more kinetic, and the ratio of these two continually changed. Physics studies the first in its Statics the subject matter of which is Equilibrium; it studies the second in Dynamics the subject matter of which is Motion or Displacement. Biology studies them in the anabolism

[1] This is Mahā-kāla and Kāla as which it manifests is time as the individual centre knows it. The Kālavādins deal with the universe in terms of time. Supreme Time is a name of the Lord. And so Veda says "Time leads me in time" "Kālah kāle mām mayati"

[2] Which come in with the Sun, Moon, Stars and Seasons, all forms of the Supreme Lord.

[3] See *Upaskāra* under II. 2. 8.

[4] II. 2. 11, 12, 13.

and katabolism of the living tissue.[1] The First Standard, in its analytical method, sets up *Dik* and *Kāla* as separate entities, and each distinct from the Self or Ātman; but it will be a more critical view to regard them not as separate things, but as manifestations of the Lord's Will by which as the efficient cause, *Paramāṇus* are arranged in relative spatial directions as well as moved in definite succession in relation to one another. Between God's Power and the *adṛṣṭas* of the *Paramāṇus* and *Ātmans* we need not interpose *Dik* and *Kāla* as separate entities. *Dik* and *Kāla* simply express a polarisation (or an opposition involved) in the way the Lord's Power seizes upon the *adṛṣṭas* of the cosmic elements and makes them effective upon the stage of action. By one 'Pole' or aspect of that Power, those which *tend* to appear on the stage *together* at a given time are actually led so to appear, and those whose tendency to appear together then is not "up to the mark" are held back. The first set have their right (*Adhikāra*) to appear, and God willing, they do appear; their precedence is not in the preference of God as before explained; it is in the degree of force with which their tendencies press themselves. This aspect of God's Power is in Śākta Doctrine *Dik-Śakti*; its correlate pole, *Kāla-śakti*,[2] is that aspect of it by which things which *tend* to follow one another on the stage are made to do so, and things whose time is not yet are held back. These two *Śaktis* imply, condition and oppose each other. Yet like the First Standard, we need not "Substantiate" them. Nor can the "tendencies" alone be left alone to fight out their cases. They require so to say an universal "vitaliser" and "prompter".[3] Comparing the cosmogenesis of Science with that of the First Standard we note that the latter admits (*a*) cyclic creation (*sṛṣṭi*) and dissolution (*Laya*); (*b*) *Adṛṣṭas* of *Paramāṇus* and *Ātmans* during *Laya*; and (*c*) the change of this static system of stresses into a dynamic system under a transcendent act, *viz.*, God's volition. Science is dimly feeling her way to the possibility of *Sṛṣṭi* and *Laya*, and therefore to the cosmic alternation of static and dynamic conditions; but beyond this She now hardly ventures to go.

As Biology seeks to explain the rate of change (*i.e.*, growth and decay) of a living tissue by the *ratio* of Anabolism to Katabolsim, so one might conceive the rate of change of the cosmic order as being determined by the ratio of *Dik* and *Kāla* which are concurrent, though variable, "forces."

---

[1] See the account of them in *Reality*,

[2] "Kālo'smi Loka-kṣaya-kṛt"—Gītā; "Kalā-kāṣṭhādi-rūpeṇa pariṇāma-pradāyinī" —Caṇḍī.

[3] The subject of Tendency and Activity, the passage from one to the other, and God's Power as leading and effecting the passage will be discussed in *Causality*.

Thus during *Laya,* the former factor prevails, owing to which *Paramāṇus* and *Ātmans* remain in equilibrium: it gives a static order. During *Sṛṣṭi,* the latter factor prevails, so that *Paramāṇus,* etc., move from their positions of rest, mingle in varied groups, and so on. During the continuance of the universe or *Sthiti,* the latter still exceeds (sometimes to a greater and sometimes to a lesser extent) the former, so that though the cosmic order generally persists, it moves and changes.

Next, we come to this. '*Karma*' from the standpoint of the First Standard means '*Spandana*' (Motion or displacement). Vaiśeṣka, I. 1. 7 classifies Motions or displacements into five kinds. Three kinds of effects are produced by Karma, *Saṃyoga* (association), *Vibhāga* (dissociation) and *Vega* (momentum).[1] Thus two *Paramāṇus* A, B associate or dissociate and receive a momentum in virtue of their motions. Now, question is this: Is motion (*i.e., Karma*) *always* produced by motion? That is, is a given motion *M* necessarily produced by another and that by another, and so on? This raises an important issue between Physics and the First Standard. The former is disposed to explain motion of one thing (say, of a ball) by that of another (*viz.*, the stick's motion), this again by another (*viz.*, the hand's motion), and so on. But it is not necessarily so, according to the First Standard. Vaiśeṣika, I. 1. 11 and 24 lay down that motion (*Karma*) is not necessarily the cause (*Kāraṇa*) of motion (*Karma*). It recognises that volition (*Prayatna*) is a cause of Karma, and volition, according to the First Standard is not a motion itself. *Prayatna* is a function of the self (*Ātmā*), and it produces motion in the muscles of the hand, and so forth (V. 1). V. 2. 21 forbids action '*Kṛyā*' in the sense of *Spandana* (vibration) in the continua—*Dik, Kāla, Ākāśa* and Ātmā. It pertains to what is discontinuous, discrete. The first creative act of the Lord on the *Paramāṇus,* etc., is not therefore, according to this Standard, a '*Karma*': it is an extra-physical action.

Next we ask this: Do the *Paramāṇus* involve an immanent dynamism? Severally they are not believed by the First Standard to contain immanent or intrinsic energies; but collectively they do even during the time of dissolution (*laya*). The aggregate of discrete *Paramāṇus* possesses energies (static) in virtue of their positions. These as we have seen, are the sum of their *adṛṣṭas.* When, as explained later, by the Lord's Will,[2] their relative positions change, their static energies become kinetic. We may compare the Nebular Hypothesis of the physicists which contemplates such translation of potential energy into kinetic, and also Helmholtz' theory of the

[1] Vaiśeṣika, I. 20. [2] Īśvara-prayatna.

contraction of the solar mass by which the potential energy of the sun is rendered kinetic (*i.e.*, heat), and supplies in part the heat which the sun loses by radiation. Vaiśeṣika,[1] assigns certain movements (*e.g.*, that of iron to magnet, etc.) to *Adṛṣṭa*; the leaping up of flames is also so explained; the movement (*spandana*) of *Paramāṇus* at the time of creation is also due to *Adṛṣṭa*. Comparing the examples we may infer that what is meant by '*Adṛṣṭa*' is that it is a not-commonly-apparent stress. Magnetic stresses, gravitational stresses, chemical stresses and so forth are subtle forms of stress which Yoga (including Science) may partly reveal or discover, but in all analysis an undiscovered and unexplained residuum must remain which is then the *Adṛṣṭa*. In a dissolution (*laya*) the *Paramāṇus* must have tendencies or tensions which do not produce actual movement. What it may be asked are these tensions? *Adṛṣṭa* says the First Standard, and does not go farther. But what are they in reality and how can they exist? The Second and Third Standards conceive them as energies of position. Evidently enquiry cannot stop even here; for, how can A be conceived to have energy by virtue of its position alone in a scheme A, B, C? It requires an explanation. Ultimately however an unexplained residuum must remain, because the *fact* is alogical. In the meantime, the Second and Third Standards carry the investigation further than where the First has brought it.

What is a *Paramāṇu*? From the realistic standpoint of the First Standard which does not partition the Primary and Secondary qualities, a sensible object really exists as we sense it. It *has* form, taste (*rupa*, *rasa*), and so forth. Western Science does not admit in its atoms of matter *Rūpa* (in its colour aspect), *Gandha* or odour, *Rasa* or taste: these being secondary qualities. Now, this sensible object is made up of parts (*e.g.*, a piece of cloth). The parts have also form (*Rūpa*) and so forth. The parts have parts again. And so on. Ultimately we have the thing divided into "points". In mathematical language, these ultimate[2] parts are the infinitely small elements of the real thing. Since they are infinitely small elements of the real thing, (*a*) they cannot have a finite magnitude capable of being sub-divided (in fact or in imagination); and (*b*) they, being the *minima* of the real thing, must possess the fundamental qualities (*Nitya guṇas*) of the thing.[3] We sense a lump of earth or a piece of ice. Is that the real thing meant here of which the *Paramāṇus* are the minima? The lump of "earth" perceived is a compound of *Pṛthivī*, *Ap*, *Tejās*, *Vāyu*; it is not pure *Pṛthivī*. Hence *its* minima

[1] V. 1. 15. [2] Carama.

[3] These are not however the Primary qualities of Science only.

are not *Paramāṇus* of one kind but P's of different kinds. Pure *Pṛthivī* is not earth which is a compound. So pure *Ap* is not water as we find it. And yet they are not mere ideals or abstractions. They really exist and mix variously. Our senses give us complexes of sensations; we find that these sensations fall into five groups—form, taste, smell, touch, hearing;[1] our sense-experiences also give us certain permanent combinations of the first four (leaving out the fifth for the present). *E.g.*, certains objects being there, we invariably experience (provided our instruments of knowledge are normal) all the four; in other objects (*e.g.*, water or air) we may sometimes experience all of them,[2] but not always. Hence we think that in the former set of objects the combination of four is natural,[3] whilst in the latter such combination is due to the admixture of adventitious elements.[4] Eliminating smell (*gandha*) we have a combination of three, and these with two others added (*viz.*, *Dravatva* or liquidity and *sneha* or adhesiveness) make *Ap* in which the combination is permanent. We here omit the *propria* and *differentia* of *Pṛthivī*, *Ap*, etc., and note the general characteristic, *viz.*, that each stands for a "permanent possibility" of a certain combination of sensations, and is a *dravya* or independent entity. Thus *Pṛthivī* is not earth but the permanent possibility[5] of a kind of combination of the four. So with *Ap* and the rest. It is not obviously a chemical analysis of Matter, but the classification is based upon a psychological analysis and synthesis: so the *Bhūtas* are not "Elements" of Physical Science.

Suppose now that the required combination of all the four kinds of sensations, founded in a Substance, be called P; the required combination of 3, A; that of 2, T; and that of 1 (*i.e.*, sparśa), V. Then in all ordinary experiences of the senses, we have mixtures of P, A, T, V. But the experience of the mixture is an experience of the components. Thus we do experience P, we do experience A, and so on, though ordinarily not in freedom from the company of the others. By their mixing, which the Third Standard explains by *Trivṛtkaraṇa* or *Pañcī-Karaṇa*, their qualities (guṇas) variously commingle, and sometimes may inhibit one another. Vaiśeṣika[6] forbids, however, the mixing called *Pañcī-karaṇa* in the sense of Vedānta. But still according to it the Bhūtas mix in a way. We shall not pause to discuss the

[1] Rupa, rasa, gandha, sparśa and śabda.

[2] *e.g.*, when water is perfumed, and when glowing sparks and scent-dusts move in the air.

[3] Or sāṃsiddhika.

[4] Āgantuka.

[5] *i.e.*, dravya or samavāyi-kāraṇa.

[6] III. 2. 2 and 3, and VIII, 2. 4.

distinction between the two, but only note that some sort of mixing[1] is allowed by the First Standard.

Hence a *Paramāṇu* of *Pṛthivī* is not an infinitely small element of what we actually experience as earth, stone, body, etc., which are all mixtures, but it is an infinitely small element of a substance (really existing and entering variously into compounds) which is the ground and cause of a certain permanent combination of four classes of sensation, *viz.*, smell, taste, form and colour, and touch. The infinitely small element possesses and produces the four kinds of qualities in gross (*Sthūla*) *Pṛthivī*. It has *Rūpa* (form, colour)[2] etc., therefore; but its *Rūpa* is not *Udbhūta*, *i.e.*, such as can be apprehended by our senses. Vaiśeṣika, IV. 1. 6 says that *Rūpa* is apprehended when an object is *mahat* (large), consists of many *Avayavas* (parts) and has *Rūpa* in itself; then it becomes an object of visual perception. A *Pṛthivī-Paramāṇu* has the *third* quality, but neither the first nor the second; hence its *Rūpa* is not seen. IV. 1. 7 and 8 go on to show why *Vāyu*, in spite of its being large and constituted of many parts, has no visible *rūpa*, and how the mere existence of *rūpa* in a thing is not enough for its being perceived by the eye—that to be thus perceivable it must possess *Rūpa-viśeṣa* or *Udbhūta rūpa* or such *Rūpa* as would bring it within the range of our normal sense-capacity. In this way, the minute pollen-dusts of scent-flowers floating in the wind excite the sense of smell but not that of sight. The *Paramāṇus*, according to this Standard, possess in this way *infra*-sensible *Rūpa*, *Rasa*, etc., which originate sensible *Rūpa*, *Rasa*, etc., in the gross objects of perception.

The four kinds of *Paramāṇus* are different as regards their qualities from one another. But the question may be asked - Are *Paramāṇus* of the *same* class (say, *Pṛthivī*) absolutely identical? Vaiśeṣika[3] says—No, each *Paramāṇu* has its generic or class characteristics and also its own individuality.[4] If, therefore, we take the *Paramāṇus* A, B, C belonging to the same class, we cannot say that A=B=C. It is for ascribing such individuality to *Paramāṇus* that the Vaiśeṣika has been so called. Nyāya differs in this. Each *Paramāṇu*, by virtue of its position alone in the universal configuration, must possess, or be associated with, a stock of static, potential energy which cannot be identical with that possessed by another *Paramāṇu* in a different position. These distinct separate stores of static energy are

[1] *viz.*, as samavāyi-kāraṇa of one and as upaṣṭambhaka or nimittakāraṇa of others.

[2] According to Indian notions all form is coloured: by its colouration it is seen as form; the colourless is also formless.

[3] II. 2. 6.

[4] Viśeṣa.

*adṛṣṭas*. This word means "that which is unseen" and which for practical purposes[1] is synonymous with *Saṃskāra* or tendency and aptitude in its unmanifested form which is the product of previous action or *Karma*. We shall see also that the first movement[2] of the *Paramāṇus* is due to *Adṛṣṭa*.[3] Now the *Adṛṣṭa* of a given *Paramāṇu* constitutes in a way its individuality;[4] but has it (say, A) also an individual form or taste[5] as compared with another *Paramāṇu* of the same class (say, B)? The parallel case is that of the allotropic modifications in Chemistry. Coal, Graphite and Diamond are all allotropic modifications of carbon—they contain nothing else than carbon atoms. And yet their physical properties are so markedly contrasted. How can that be if the matter in them be the same? Now, in order that two things, A and B, may be the same, we must have (1) A's matter equal to B's matter, and also (2) the arrangement of A's matter similar to the arrangement of B's matter. Charcoal and Diamond are not the same because though the first condition of similarity is there fulfilled, the second condition is not; matter is differently *arranged* in them. But why and what does that presuppose? Ultimately the difference must be explained in terms of the dynamisms of A and B; the forces (*śakti*), static and dynamic, which operate in the one are different from those which operate in the other; their stress systems are different. According to modern Chemistry, all forms of Matter are really the allotropic modifications of one another, since they are now believed to be only different arrangements of a fundamental Matter—"Protyle" or Electron or Ether or whatever else we may call it. Oxygen and Hydrogen, for example, are only different arrangements of Electrons. These different arrangements are the individualities (realtively stable) or *Viśeṣas* of the chemical 'atoms'. And these are ultimately determined by the immanent stress systems of the atoms. Science denying the "secondary qualities" in the atoms and corpuscles cannot say that O has a form or taste[6] different from that of H; but it does say that it has a different weight, mass and constitution. But suppose we take two atoms of O itself. Is there any difference between them as distinguished from that which they must have on account of their different positions in the material system? Science is not yet ready with an answer; but if it be true, that atoms are complex systems and not simple, partless units, then, *a priori*, two atoms of the same element ought to have their individualities (*Viśeṣas*) over and above their

[1] Sometimes the terms are used synonymously, in others a distinction is made. Postponed *Adṛṣṭa* is Saṃcita-Karma.

[2] Ādya-Karma.

[3] See V. 2. 13.

[4] Or Viśeṣa.

[5] Viśeṣa-rūpa or rasa.

[6] Rūpa or rasa.

typal or generic similarity. We are all individual men though belonging to the same type, Man. So it ought to be with the atoms of the same "element" (say, Oxygen). Nor can we avoid such individuality in a sub-atom or electron, for even this, having a definite mass and dimensions, cannot be an absolutely simple thing; it is likely that they are also systems in their turn. Hence Science cannot avoid the *Viśeṣa* or individuality in her current units of Matter.

But the *Paramāṇus* are partless points of Substance. Hence it may be argued (as it has been argued by the Naiyāyikas and others) that their only *Viśeṣas* can be their differing *Adṛṣṭas*, but that otherwise they must all be equal; *i.e.*, one *Paramāṇu* of *Pṛthivī* cannot have a form[1] different from that of another *Paramāṇu* of *Pṛthivī* (earth). The Vaiśesika Text does not appear to make the point clear but, since the Vaiśeṣika conception of *Bhūta* is based upon a *psychological* analysis of our actual experience of Matter (the "element" thus obtained being substantialized) rather than upon a physico-chemical analysis, it ought to follow that the irreducible minima of Matter thus obtained are really the counter-parts of the actually perceived forms of Matter on a miniature scale. Now, some of the actually perceived forms of Matter have not only form (*Rūpa*) in general but individual forms (*rūpa-viśeṣas*), *e.g.*, this white paper and that green leaf.[2] Suppose a *Paramāṇu* of the paper be A and that of the leaf be B. Suppose also that they are both *Pṛthivī-Paramāṇus*. Then, since A and B are the irreducible minima of the paper and the leaf as actually perceived by us, the *Rūpa-Viśeṣas* of A ought to be that of the leaf. Though both are *Pṛthivi-Paramāṇus* they have their special forms (*Rūpas*), and the different *Rūpas* of the paper and the leaf are caused by the special *Rūpas* of A and B respectively. Such representation is psychologically correct. We start with the actual perceptions of paper and leaf; we go on dividing and subdividing until the mind halts at the *minimum Psychosis* (or "Psychon" to use the expression employed in the Text and in a recent English work); and then this Psychon is treated objectively; and so we get the *Paramāṇu*. *Pari passu* with such analysis, a physico-chemical analysis of the paper and the leaf may be attempted; and in the progress of this latter analysis we soon come to a stage when the subdivisions or segments ceasing to possess *perceptible* colour, taste, smell, etc., disappear, and only *indirect* evidence is left of the existence of weight, resistance, motion, etc., in the particles. Now, when this stage in the analysis has been reached,

[1] Rūpa.
[2] Papers and leaves also may be of different shades of whiteness and greenness.

there are evidently two ways of proceeding: (*a*) We may either say that the subdivisions which come beyond our limit of perception are similar to those which are perceived by us—that the ultimate particles are therefore our minima of Psychosis objectified, and hence each having its own *Viśeṣa*; (*b*) or we may say that since colour, etc., disappear in the progress of the analysis but evidence of weight, inertia, etc., is still left, these latter alone are the real properties of Matter, so that if, for example, paper and a leaf are visually sensed by us differently, that is not because the atoms of the two (*i.e.*, A and B) actually possess the different colours or any colour, but because the former atom (A) is moving in a way different from that in which B moves and excites our sensibility. The former is the concrete, psychological view and it is that of the Vaiśeṣika. The latter is the scientific view which, in so far as it stows apart Primary and Secondary qualities, is abstract and unpsychological. But even after spiriting away the secondary qualities, Science has got to consider this: A and B (say, atoms of the same "element") possess weight, inertia, etc., but do they not possess differing weight, inertia, etc.? That is, has not each its own *Viśeṣa* as regards the primary qualities at least? *Prima Facie*, it ought to have—even the Electron.

Next comes the difficult question of the magnitude of the *Paramāṇu.* To meet this question one has to free one's mind of the notion that the *Paramāṇu* is something like an "atom" or an "electron." These latter, as we have seen, have definite magnitudes. But *Paramāṇu's* magnitude is infinitely small. Vaiśeṣika, VII. 1. 20 calls the measure (*Parimāṇa*) of the *Paramāṇu* "*Parimaṇḍala,*" and this magnitude is permanent (*nitya*). But what is this *Parimaṇḍala*? Literally it means a "sphere." It is therefore an infinitely small sphere, or a "point". As already stated, this Standard contemplates, *four* kinds of Magnitude- (1) Aṅu, (2) Mahat, (3) Hraṣva, and (4) Dīrgha. The first is 'small', the second 'large', the third 'short', the fourth 'long'. It also considers (VII. 1. 11 and 17) these two pairs of categories as giving rise to two series (Dhārā, *e.g.*, A is smaller than B, B than C, C than D, and so on. This is one series. A is shorter than B, B than C, an so on. This is another series.) Now, obviously, each series has a superi r limit (*utkarṣa*) and an inferior limit (*apakarṣa*) *e.g.*, in the first series, A may have the smallest magnitude and Z the largest. A then is the inferior limit, and if it be absolutely small magnitude, than it is the *Paramāṇu.* Similarly Z is the superior limit and *Parama-mahat* (*e.g.*, Ākāśa, Ātman—VII. 1. 22.) Between these two limits we shall have several orders which are relatively great or small. If the *Paramāṇu* had any finite magnitude, however small, like the scientific atom or electron, then it would not be the inferior limit—the "partless" unit. Hence the infinitely small units is nothing greater than a Point (Bindu). The same reasoning will apply to the other pair "short-long". The infinitely short thing is again a Point. If it had any finite length, it would be divisible. So the inferior limit of the second series is also the *Paramāṇu*. It is a "*Parimaṇḍala*" because it is a sphere of which the radius is infinitely small *i.e.*, a Point. Things of perception are seen to be divisible into smaller and smaller grains or particles. All these are spheres of finite (however small) radii. So are even the Electrons. Pushing to the limit we get a sphere of which the radius is infinitely small, and this is *Parimāṇḍala*.

'Anu' and 'Mahat' are terms which relate to solid or three-dimensional magnitude, and '*Hrasva*' and '*Dīrgha*' to linear magnitude. Now, there are as already stated *six* possible combinations of these four terms taken two at time: (1) *Aṇu-mahat*, (2) *Aṇu-hrasva*, (3) *Aṇu-dīrgha*, (4) *Mahat-harṣva*, (5) *Mahat-dīrgha*, (6) *Hrasva-dīrgha*. Of these the first and the sixth combine contraries,[1] and so they are cancelled. Third is also untenable, because a thing which is small in dimension cannot be *Dīrgha*. Similarly, a thing which is large in dimension cannot be *Hrasva*, and therefore the fourth combination is also untenable. Only the second and the fifth are logically tenable combinations.

Now, suppose we join together two Points or *Paramāṇus*. What do we get? A short *line* of which the breadth and thickness, (*i.e.*, solid dimension) are infinitely small. Yet the thing thus obtained is not a *Paramāṇu*. Because the magnitude of two points put together must be greater than that of a single one. By combining the two points (not coinciding them, however) we get a very short line (of which the solid dimension is nothing)—the "element" of linear dimension, as it is called in Mathematics (*Dl* in mathematical notation). How shall we characterize it? It is *Hrasva*, as well as *Aṇu* (because lacking solid dimension)—*Aṇu-hrasva*. This is the magnitude of the binary or *Dvyaṇuka*. It is an "element" of linear dimension.

Suppose next we combine two such elements of linear dimension—two binaries or *Dvyaṇukas*. From a common "origin" or point of reference, we draw two short lines in two different directions. What do we get? An "element" of *surface* dimension—a very small surface (*Ds* in mathematical notation). If we draw from a common origin *three* such short lines (say, at right angles to each other), we get an "element" of solid dimension or

[1] VII, 1. 10.

volume (*Dv* in mathematical notation.) Three *Dvyaṇukas* make in this way a *Trasareṇu* (lit. a moving particle.) Its magnitude is much greater than that of a *Dvyaṇuka*, for the *Trasareṇu* has a breadth and a thickness whilst a *Dvyaṇuka* has neither. Hence, compared with the *Dvyaṇuka*, it is *mahat.* Again, many lines must be bundled together (like slender wires twisted together into a rope) to produce even a very small volume; each of the constituent lines is short, but the aggregate of these short lengths is comparatively *Dīrgha.* Hence we may say that the magnitude of the Trasareṇu is *Mahat-dīrgha.*

In all Physico-mathematical analysis of things in Science we have to imagine and deal with the "volume-elements." A mere point, or a mere line cannot be an object of concrete imagination for us—we cannot "perceive" it with the eye of imagination. Such "perception" becomes possible only when we take a solid-element. If we had the requisite sense-capacity, we could actually perceive such a solid element however small. The *Trasareṇu* therefore is the true "corpuscle" or "particle" of Matter. It is perceivable provided the requisite sense-capacity be there. At any rate it can be actually *imaged*, and since according to Hindu Philosophy it possesses both primary and secondary qualities, it can be *concretely* imaged by us. The chemical "atom", "electron", etc., being larger or smaller solid-elements fall under the generic category of *Trasareṇu.* They cannot be either Paramāṇus or Dvyaṇukas. They are theoretically perceivable by us, provided the secondary qualities are also left in them. *Paramāṇus* or *Dvyaṇukas* are not *thus* perceivable or imaginable by us. This is the meaning of the teaching of the First Standard that when the Trasareṇu stage is reached, the combination becomes fit for perception (*Pratyakṣa-yogya*). The combination as we have seen is geometrical and not chemical—it is the putting together of the three dimensions.

It has been observed in a previous section that this has not been quite well grasped by the latter-day annotators of the First Standard who in some cases possessed neither the Yogic vision (Yoga-dṛṣṭi) of the seers (Ṛṣis) nor all the advantages of modern Science. In some cases, their common-sense treatment has missed the real points. Similarly[1] a profound scientific wisdom has been said to underlie the matter presented in the Veda-mantras even in the ritual section (*Kryā-Kāṇḍa*). But it lies concealed, and later interpreters have not always uncovered it. In the annotations, the *Trasareṇu* is often represented as a moving particle of matter visible to

[1] See P. N. Mukhyopādhyāya's Bengali Lectures on Veda and Vijñāna.

the eye when, for instance, a pencil of sun-beam is let into a dark room through an aperture. Like a larger ball made up of six smaller ones, it can be broken up into six *Paramāṇus* or three *Dvyaṇukas;* so it is said. But this is absurd, and this is not the position of the First Standard. Even a microscopic particle must contain multi-millions of "corpuscles"—says Science. It may be so, says the First Standard; its *Trasareṇu* being, as we have seen, only the "element" of solid dimension which embraces the scientific corpuscles, etc. The First Standard then proceeds to analyse Matter from the *psychological* stand-point, though the elements thus obtained by it are treated objectively and rigidly by it. This should be remembered when one has occasion to compare it with Western Physical Science.

Vaiśeṣika[1] in a number of Sūtras indicates the natures of *Pṛthivī*, *Ap* and the rest. We have seen that each is a permanent possibility of a certain combination of sensations (or objectively, qualities or *guṇas*). Later commentators have taken pains to show that *Pṛthivī* is nearly what we know as earth, that *Ap* is water, and so on; and so the definitions or *Lakṣaṇas* have been complicated. *E.g.*, *rūpa*, *rasa* and *sparśa* in *Pṛthivī* are given special meanings.[2] We need not here discuss the details. We may simply observe that we cannot be far from the mark if we say that *Pṛthivī* (earth) stands for (*a*) Rigidity (or relative definiteness and stability of form), and (*b*) a certain combination of the four kinds of *guṇas* (*gandha* or odour being its speciality). *Ap* "water" stands for (*a*) Liquidity and Adhesiveness, and (*b*) a certain combination of the three kinds of *Guṇas* (omitting *Gandha*).[3] *Tejas* stands for (*a*) Radiations (Heat, Light and Electricity)[4] and (*b*) a certain combination of *Rūpa* and *Sparśa*. *Vāyu* stands for (*a*) Fluidity and Mobility, and (*b*) a certain kind of *Sparśa*. *Ākāśa* stands for (*a*) continuous *plenum*, and (*b*) Śabda which[5] cannot be an intrinsic *proprium* of those objects which have 'touch'.[6] *Śabda* however is here used in the sense of 'sound' and not *Spanda* or motion which is *Karma* according to the First Standard.

To sum up: *Pṛthivī* ("earth") is *rigid* matter; *Ap* ("water") is *liquid* matter; *Tejas* ("Fire") is radiant matter; *Vāyu* ("air") is *fluid and mobile* matter; Ākāśa ("ether") is ethereal matter. These may be taken as broad

[1] II. 1 and 2.
[2] Aneka-rūpa-vattva, aneka-rasa-vattva, pākaja-sparśa-vattva.
[3] II. 2. 5 adds "śītatā" or 'coolness' also saṃsiddhika Guṇa to Ap.
[4] V. 2. 9 and 10. As the Vyāsa-Bhāṣya on Pātanjala-darśana (III. 44) says: "Mūrtir bhūmih, sneho jalaṃ, vahniruṣṇatā, vāyuh pranāmī, sarvatogati-rākāśa iti."
[5] As II. 1. 25. explains.
[6] Sparśa-vatam.

*lakṣaṇas* or definitions. *Ākāśa* or ether in the First Standard is not conceived as space, but as an infinitely continuous *plenum* of which the quality or *guṇa* is sound (*śabda*).[1]

If we remember that Vaiśeṣika makes sound (*śabda*) the *guṇa* and not the motion (*karma*) of Ākāśa, then the apparent discrepancy between it and Science as regards sound will disappear. *Karma* is motion (displacement), vibratory or otherwise. Science, explaining sound as being caused by the vibrations of Air, makes it motion (*Karma*) of Air. Now, sound being a secondary quality is subjective from the standpoint of science; the vibration of Air being the cause of sound, but not sound itself. But suppose we objectify or externalize sound itself—we take it as existing outside of us as sound. Doing so we find that like form, touch (*rūpa*, *sparśa*), etc., it is not confined to particular limited objects. *Rūpa* or *Sparśa* is where the object itself (*e.g.*, a conch-shell) is; it is not where the object is not. Odour travels away from the object (*e.g.*, of a flower), but then we have positive evidence there that minute particles of the object itself have travelled and carried the smell along with them; so in smell too we may say that it is where the object is (the flower or its particles). But the case of sound is different. The sound of a conch-blown is *not* necessarily where the conch-shell is; it may be heard in different directions and in different positions; several people in different positions may hear it together or nearly together. There is no evidence that, as in the case of smell, particles of the conch-shell themselves have travelled; and even if they did, they could not carry the sound of the shell; for, as is rightly pointed out,[2] the sound of a lyre or flute is not in the particles of them taken distributively, as the smell of a flower is. Hence if we accept the maxim that the qualities of a thing cannot be where the thing is not, we must say that sound must be the quality of a substance which is large and continuous. That sound takes time to travel and therefore persons at distances from one another do not hear a sound at the same moment, proves only that sound has an efficient cause[3] which is the propagation of atmospheric vibration.[4] But the material[5] cause of sound is the *continuum Ākāśa*. *Śabda* is thus the quality (*Guṇa*) of *Ākāśa*, but is revealed and propagated by the *Karma* (*i.e.*, *Spanda*) or motion of *Vāyu* or air.

Concluding we observe this: If like Western Science we define Matter as that which moves (in the sense of displacement), then, from the view-

[1] That Ākāśa is not mere space is indicated in II. 1. 20, etc.
[2] II. 1. 25.
[3] Nimitta-Kāraṇa.
[4] This is recognised in the First Standard; see Bhāṣāpariccheda and other works.
[5] Samavāyi.

point of the First Standard, all *Dravyas* or independent entities which have *Karma* (*i.e.*, *spandana*) or movement are Matter; and they are—*Kṣiti* (earth), *Ap* (water), *Tejas* (fire), *Vāyu* (air), and *Manas* (mind). V. 2. 12 and 13 say that all these (including *Manas*) have Karma. And V. 2. 21 says that *Dik*, *Kāla*, *Ākāśa* and *Ātman* are *Niṣkrya* (*i.e.*, do not have *Karma*). V. 2. 14 also separately assigns *Karma* to *Manas*; this can be moved by effort (*Prayatna*) and also by external stimuli. The *Indryas* or senses are also material. VIII. 2. 5 and 6 show that the sense of smell is *Pārthiva* ("Earthy"), that of taste is *Jalīya* (watery), that of vision is *Taijasa* (fiery) and that of touch is *vāyavīya* (aerial). *Śrotra* or that of hearing is simply a portion of Ākāśa cut off by the ear-membrane, such cutting off in a given manner being due to *Adṛṣṭa.*[1] It is not therefore a *pariṇāma* (transformation) of a substance like the eye, etc., but it is the pure substance itself (*i.e.*, *Ākāśa*) bounded by the ear-membrane.

11

All philosophies attempt to trace the causal series in the world to the ultimate root or roots. Of these some proceed on the straight path which is the psychological method (*i.e.*, analysing actual experience), and others choose a round-about path. The method of all the three standards of Hindu Philosophy is *psychological*; their difference lies in the *extent* to which the investigation has been pushed. The First Standard carries its investigation to the *Paramāṇus*, *Dik*, *kāla*, *Adṛṣṭa*, and *Ātman*. By it these are (except *Adṛṣṭa*) presented as separate entities. Indeed so we must take them if we do not or cannot push our investigation farther.

But suppose we are able to go farther. We ask this: A *Paramāṇu* is a Point of Substance, which though simple and partless, possesses a cluster of permanent *Guṇas* (*Rūpa*, *Rasa*, etc.,), has its own *Viśeṣa* or individuality, and has also its *Adṛṣṭa*. Is it conceivable that a *thing* which is absolutely simple and partless can have a *Rūpa-viśeṣa*, a *Rasa-viśeṣa*, a *Gandha-viśeṣa*, a *Sparśa-viśeṣa*? Its *Guṇas* and *Karmas* form a complex whole; can the *basis* of this complex whole be a simple point of substance? Śaṃkarācārya in Vedānta, II. 2. (11-17), gives an exhaustive and able criticism of Paramāṇukārana-vāda. His criticism principally relates to (a) the possibility of *first* motion in the *Vāyavīya* (aerial) *Paramāṇus* at the time of creation (*sarga*); (*b*) the manner of their association; and (*c*) their simplicity inspite of the complexity of their *Guṇas*. We need not go into the details, but only

---

[1] "Viśiṣṭādṛiṣṭo-pagṛhīta-karṇa-śaṣkulyavacchinno nabho-deśa eva śrotram."—Upaskāra.

observe that the complexity of *Guṇas* and *Karmas* in a *Paramaṇu* renders it impossible that the basis can be but a Point-Thing. On similar grounds Western scientists felt dissatisfied with the "simple and hard" atoms even when positive evidence of the electron was not forthcoming. Difference in weight, valency and other chemical properties, spectrum analysis and various other things suggested the complexity of the atom.

Therefore, why not say this—A *Paramāṇu* is a complex thing whose elements (*Avayavas*) are the *Rūpa*, *Rasa*, *Gandha*, etc.,? Instead of saying that Paramāṇu is a simple X possessing the complexus of guṇas A, B, C, D with all their *Viśeṣas*, we say that *Paramāṇu* is a whole of which the elements are A, B, C, D. The Paramāṇu = A + B + C + D. In this way (1) simplicity in the thing and complexity in the *Guṇas* and *Karmas* as postulated by the First Standard vanishes; (2) the necessity of an extra-mental support of *Rūpa*, *Rasa* and the rest is obviated; and (3) the method becomes more psychological, and new vistas of psychological analysis open before us beyond the *Paramāṇus*. The elements of *Rūpa*, etc., which constitute the *Paramāṇu* are the *Tanmātras* or Generals of the sense particulars of the Second Standard. So instead of saying *Kāla* and *Dik* are *entities* which make the *Paramāṇus* and their aggregates appear in orders of succession and co-existence, we may simply say that the former is the sum of the moments ($m^1$, $m^2$, $m^3$, etc.,) or *Kṣaṇas*[1] of the Tanmātras, and the latter is the sum of their relative positions ($p^1$, $p^2$, $p^3$, etc.). The mystery why things move variously and occupy various positions is not cleared up merely by saying that there are entities to make them do so. Thus, the Second Standard simplifies matters by these three equations: (1) P (Paramāṇu) = A + B + C + D; (2) K (Kāla) = $m^1+m^2+m^3$—......; (3) D (Dik) = $p^1+p^2+p^3+$......

But by these Equations the Problem itself is not solved. By them we have merely shaken off needless encumbrances, which however *are* useful frame-work for arranging the world-phenomena in the first instance. The *Tanmātras*, their nature, distribution and change, give us a complicated whole which *prima facie* cannot be the ultimate order, and which therefore requires and stimulates further enquiry. Such enquiry is undertaken by the Second Standard by making us pass through *Ahaṃkāra*, *Mahat-tattva* and *Mūla-Prakṛti*.[2]

---

[1] A 'Kṣaṇa' or Moment is a partless unit of time and is measured by the transit of one Paramāṇu (or Tanmātra) from one position in Space to another. See Pātañjala, III. 52.

[2] The I-making principle derived from the mind in its fundamental aspect as Buddhi again derived from the Root of both the psychical and material.

It is not necessary here to deal in full with *Ahaṃkāra* and the rest.[1] But the trend of the investigation of the Second Standard is clear: (*a*) Having reduced Matter to complexuses of *Tanmātras* which are Generals of the Sense-particulars or Universals, it recognises the basis of Matter in the Mental Principle, or rather a Principle which, in having to evolve as sensible Matter, has first to evolve as the Mental Principle. (*b*) The first Standard had left even at the beginning a heterogeneous order *viz.*, *Paramāṇus*, their *Guṇas*, *Adṛṣṭas*, *Dik*, *Kāla*, *Ātman* and the rest. But the Second Standard is able to trace all this heterogeneity to a homogeneous unconscious Root (*Prakṛti*) which, however, it still leaves tripartite (as being constituted of *Sattva*, *Rajas* and *Tamas*[2] and *Cit* or *Puruṣa*). This tripartite "homogeneous" Root as being the object "seen" by Consciousness, is the Primordial "Mind" and Primordial "Matter" which first evolves as *Buddhi*, then as *Ahaṃkāra*, then as *Tanmātras* and lastly as the particles of gross matter or *Bhūta*. Thus this system makes the mental precede the material, the universal precede the particular, the homogeneous precede the heterogeneous. It also conceives the world-process as an unfoldment or Evolution.

Pātañjala Darśana, III. 44 speaks of the *five* conditions of the *Bhūtas*. (1) *Sthūla*. The actually perceived condition involving *Gandha*, *Sparśa*, etc., each perception gives a particular form of *Bhūta* with a particular set of qualities. (2) *Svarūpa*. The *generic* quality (*jāti*) of the five kinds of *Bhūta*; the generic quality of *Pṛthivī*, of *Ap*, *Tejas*, etc. (2) *Sūkṣma*. The *Tanmātras* which are the *units* or causes of the *Bhūtas*. (4) *Anvaya*. The three *Guṇas* (*Sattva*, *Rajas* and *Tamas*) which underlie and constitute ultimately all *Bhūtas*. (5) *Arthavattva*. The end for which each form of *Bhūta* exists and evolves; the *Bhūta* as an object or instrument of *Bhoga* or enjoyment. He who can do concentration or Samādhi on these five conditions of *Bhūta* can control it.

We have said that the *Tanmātra* is the unit of the *Bhūta*. In what sense? The *Tanmātra* is called *Aviśeṣa* (non-particular) in the Second Standard (*e.g.*, in Pātañjala, II. 19). It is called also the *Sūkṣma-Bhūta*. The etymology of the word would suggest that it is the unit, or standard, or archetype. I see whiteness in this paper or greenness in that leaf. Is that the *Rūpa-Tanmātra*? Is it any kind of sensation or quality apprehended ordinarily by the senses? No. To be *Aviśeṣa* it must not be any particular variation

[1] See *Mind ante*.
[2] Power (Śakti) as presenting, veiling consciousness and the activity in each.

of *Rūpa*, but the Rūpa as a Universal; to be a standard or archetype, it must not be *Rūpa* as apprehended variously by various limited sense-capacities but as apprehended by a perfect or "Absolute Eye."[1] To be *Sūkṣma*, it must not be *Rūpa* as seen by me in this paper but as existing in the "elements" of the paper. That is, it must be elementary *Rūpa* appearing, within the limits of man's sense-capacity and subject to his inherited tendencies or *Saṃskāras*, as the *Rūpa* of this paper.

Suppose we make this hypothesis. Let this paper be divided and subdivided till at last the non-magnitudinal "points" are reached; and let a Perfect Sense (*i.e.*, free from the limitations of varying tendencies or *Saṃskāras*) apprehend those points. Then, to such a sense (say, the eye) there will be presented standard "Rūpa-points". A Rūpa-point is an "atom" of *Rūpa* or an infinitely small element of *Rūpa* as apprehended by a Perfect Eye. Similarly, a Śabda-point is an "atom" of Śabda; and so on. Each is a sort of ideal or standard "Psychon"; and there are obviously five kinds of Psychons involved in the constitution of sensible matter. In the Second Standard we discard non-mental supports of the guṇas, *viz.*, the *Paramāṇus* of the First Standard. Hence, now, this paper, for example, is *just* the aggregate of *Rūpa*-points, *Rasa*-points, *Gandha*-points, etc. As the Physicist now explains Matter by "atoms" of Electricity (or Electrons which however, cannot be the ultimate units), so Sāṃkhya reduces Matter to an aggregate of Psychons which, from its view-point, are *standard* elements of *Rūpa*, etc., as presented to a Perfect Eye.

As Psychons they are obviously not reducible to one another. A *Rūpa* is not a kind of *Rasa* or a kind of *Śabda*. In synthesising from the psychological standpoint the world of sensible Matter we cannot come to a number of distinct classes less than five;[2] the five *Tanmātras* are the five irreducible minima of categories within which our experience of sensible Matter can be summed up. Though differing as *effects*, they may however agree as regards their *causation*, *i.e.*, they may *all* be deduced from the differing activities of *one* higher Principle (*e.g.*, *Asmitā* or *Ahaṃkāra*, the I-making or individualising principle by which a limited centre recognises itself as such).

In passing through the "refracting and defracting media" of our limited and varied individual *Saṃskāras* pertaining to our instruments of perception, these *standard Rūpa*, *Rasa*, etc., become in effect infinitely

[1] *Cf.* Plato's doctrine of Archetypes.
[2] As was recognised by J. S. Mill in his "Logic".

diversified; so we experience almost limitless kinds of *Rūpa*, *Rasa*, etc., which change and pass, and differ from case to case. Behind all this kaleidoscopic changes of form, etc., we have the standard *Tanmātras* themselves and their permutations and combinations. These are the "things-in-themselves". It is clear that the *Tanmātras* are the Generals or Universals of which *our* perceived *Rūpas*, *Rasas*, etc., are the aggregates and particular variations.

As, again the Electrons by their number and various arrangements are believed to constitute the atoms of Matter, so the *Rūpa*-units, *Rasa*-units, etc., by their various combinations make the *Bhūtas* or sensible matter. Whilst a *Śabda-Tanmātra* may exist singly, a *Sparśa-Tanmātra* is commonly a compound of *Sparśa* + Śabda; so a *Rūpa-Tanmātra* is = Rūpa T. + Sparśa T. + Śabda T.; so Rasa T. is a combination of 4; and Gandha T. is a combination of 5. By reason of such combination, they possess, in the above-mentioned order, 1, 2, 3, 4, 5 *Guṇas*.[1]

Whatever the original Datum or Stuff may be, whether *Cit* or *Prakṛti*, it is clear that we can have "points" of *Rūpa* etc., in it, only after some Individualizing Principle (*Ahaṃkāra*) has operated upon it; by such operation separated Centres of Action and Reaction appear in the Continuum. The Individualizing or Centre-referring Principle is *Asmitā* or *Ahaṃkāra*. The whole operation again pre-supposes, and is resolvable into, three concurrent activities which the Sāṃkhya calls *Sattva* (Presentation), *Rajas* (Movement), and *Tamas* (Veiling). *Cit* or Consciousness stands apart but lights up the whole show.

12

We need not further examine this doctrine here, but only observe that *its* investigation into the foundations of Reality is also halting. If we conceive the *Tanmātras* as ideal points of *Rūpa*, etc., then *where* do these points exist and operate? In *Ākāśa*? But *Ākāśa* as perceptual Space is not antecedent to the *Tanmātras*. *Dik* as a *nitya dravya*, and as a Principle of configuration, is not admitted. It is simply the aggregate of the directions in which the points stand to one another. What then is the required *continuum* for the points to exist and operate in?

Why not say simply with Vedānta that it is Consciousness (Cit) which in one aspect of Its Power (Māyā-Śakti) evolves as Object (*Dṛśya*) and in another aspect (Cit-Śakti) manifests and controls it as Subject (*Draṣṭā*)?

[1] See Pātañjala-Bhāṣya, II. 19.

Then this Cit Itself or Pure Consciousness will be the required Continuum, and one which is self-revealing (*svaprakāśa.*) All operations and all operatives and all operators will be then the conditions of Consciousness Itself.

Dik, Kāla, Ākāśa and Ātman will only be the *Cit-continuum* or Consciousness ( *Cidākāśa*) in different attitudes and relations. Cit or Pure Consciousness or Spirit is the subject of a future volume.[1]

As before pointed, the *Continuum* has a static (quiescent) and a dynamic (stressing) aspect. The second does not cancel or suppress the first. When the *Cit*-Substance as Energy (Śakti) evolves as the world, Its static or quiescent form is *also* maintained. This is the significance of the Kālī Mūrti—the figure of the moving Kāli-Śakti on the corpse-like (*Śava*) quiescent form of Śiva—a common symbol in the Tantras.

In Its evolution as Energy (Śakti) the Series (Dhārā) with its superior and inferior limits explained before applies. So that we have higher and higher continua and lower and lower discontinua. The perfect limit of the continua is Pure Cit, and the lowest limit of discreteness is the *Bindu* as a form of Supreme Energy. While Energy concentrates[2] into Bindus, Its continuous forms also exist as "fields" for the operation of the Bindus. Hence if Śakti to operate as and through Points requires Dik and Kāla, we have them already given for they are only modes of presentation of forms of *Cit* to *Cit* itself.

In fact, the *Nāda-Bindu* which concludes every mantra— the *Continuum* and the Point—are the correlates of each other. One is not without the Other. They are the two poles of Being, so that Brahman is at once "*anoraṇīyān mahato mahīyān*" "smaller than the smallest and greater than the greatest"—as Veda says.

Hence when at the one pole the "point" of Śabda as Tanmātra appears at the other pole the subtle continuum of Śabda or sūkṣma, apañcīkrita Ākāśa (ether) appears. They are aspects of the same appearance.

Psychologically it is so. The infinitely small element or unit of Śabda as presented to the "Absolute Ear" (an idea which is however *implicit* in the Second Standard), and therefore as *Aviseṣa* (universal), was the Śabda-Tanmātra considered before. But the "Absolute Ear" may "hear" bothwise—the smallest as well as the largest (*parama mahat*). Hence to It Śabda as Tanmātra or Universal will present both the poles—*Śabda as Point* and

[1] (*Now included in the present volume*)

[2] That is, becomes as it is Ghanībhūta.

*Śabda as Continuum* (both universal, because not, *ex hypothesi*, presented to this limited hearing instrument or to that). If, again, by 'Sabda' we mean not 'sound' only but '*spanda*' or movement then we have this:

(1) Sūkṣma-Ākāśa—Universal-*śabda-continuum* = *Cit-śakti* in a condition of *stressing in general*. Similarly,

(2) Sūkṣma-Vāyu—*Universal-sparśa-śabda-continuum*, and is a derivative from the first.

It is a condition of Cit in which there is (dynamically) mobility in general, and (psychologically) *Sparśa* or touch in general. Both the mobility-in-general and the *Sparśa*-in-general being as they are presented to an "Absolute Touch"; our experiences of mobility and *Sparśa* being limited, varied and particular. In (1) the stresses are considered as not producing actual motion. Then we have (3) Tejas—Universal-*śabda-sparśa-rūpa-continuum*, and is a derivative from (1) & (2).

It is not easy to present in a simple manner the special dynamical aspect of Tejas, Ap and Pṛthivī, but we may say that their dynamisms are such that they produce Radiation (Electrical or other), Liquidity and Rigidity in general respectively; psychologically, they are responsible especially for Rūpa, Rasa, Gandha (*all in general*). And it should be borne in mind that in the two higher standards (and more particularly in the third), psychism is = dynamism; they are only aspects.

We have taken the Absolute Sensibility and presented to It *Śabda as continuum, sparśa as continuum*, etc., and obtained pure *Ākāśa-Tanmātra*, etc. We might have as well begun at the other "pole" or the Point.

Because Prajāpathi or Hiraṇya-garbha as Absolute Sensibility knows *Śabda-Tanmātra*, etc., it must not be thought that His knowledge is restricted to the pure Universals only. He is *sarvajña* and *sarva-vit.*[1] His Sense is the Ideal Limit of our senses: He thus *transcends us*; His sense is the aggregate of our senses: He is thus *immanent* in us.

In explaining (2), (3), etc., we have seen that the higher principles necessarily enter into their derivatives, so that in Pṛthivī-Tanmātra, for instance, the characters of the four higher principles are involved. This is as it should be. But *further* compounding is necessary (which is called Trivṛtkaraṇa or Pañcīkaraṇa) to get the Sthūla-Bhūtas, or sensible matter, which is the subject of physico-chemical science.

---

[1] As Sarvajña He is knower of the Universals or generals of the sense particulars; as Sarvavit He is knower of the particulars.

# THE WORLD AS POWER:

## POWER AS CAUSALITY AND CONTINUITY

(*Kāraṇa-śakti and Sthiti-śakti*)

## PREFACE

The portion of this book which deals with Causality is my work in the carrying out of which I am indebted to Dr. Seal's learned work "Positive Sciences of the Hindus". The second portion, on Continuity, has been written by Professor Pramathanātha Mukhyopādhyāya with whose collaboration I intend to publish the next volume[1] of the series dealing with *Cit* or (to give this untranslatable word an English name) Consciousness. After a discussion of the essential terms, Reality, Consciousness, Mind, Life, Matter, Causality and Continuity, and possibly a few others such as Saṃskāra or Tendency, the ground will have been prepared for the treatment of such special Śāstric subjects as Adhikāra, Sādhana-Śakti, Mantra-Śakti, Ritual in general, Yoga and so forth. It is more than useless to attempt to deal with such matters unless the philosophical terms I have mentioned are understood.

*Bormes, Var*
16th February 1923 J. W.

[1] Mahāmāyā : Power As Consciousness. (The next section of the present volume).

# THE WORLD AS POWER:

## POWER AS CAUSALITY

(*Kāraṇa-śakti*)

1

It has been said[1] that causation has been involved in a denser dust of discussion especially since the days of Hume, than any other subject except Free Will which is intimately connected with cause and effect; and that there is no agreement among Psychologists as to the internal conviction nor among physicists as to the external relation. Many centuries however before Hume the same questions were discussed and it is to India that we owe the notable doctrine of the essential identity of Cause and Effect,[2] though we may read English works of Indian writers on Causation rich in references to Berkeley, Hume, Mill, Herbert Spencer and others without mention of what India has said on the subject.[3] I suppose Cinderella would not have minded neglect so much if it had not been that of her sisters. It will be found however that India has in its main heads fully dealt with the matter from the empirical, metaphysical, and absolute aspects of Reality according to the three Standards which constitute the Intellectual Body of Vedāntic Truth as Spiritual Experience.

First then as to the internal conviction as to the truth of the principle of Causality, namely that there is no phenomenon without its cause. Is it derived from the individual's generalisation from his experience? It is not; because it is always and from the beginning associated with it. Moreover universal propositions cannot be established by limited perceptions. Nor is it a form in the Kantian sense of the understanding considered as isolated from and independent of the things presented to it. Whence then does it come? It is one of the innate tendencies or *Saṃskāra* inherent in

[1] Dr. McCosh, "First and Fundamental Truths", 207.

[2] Dr. Sterling. Gifford Lectures 279—287, who says "I suppose we owe all this to the Hindoos".

[3] Therefore I would tefer these and English readers to Dr. Seal's "Positive Sciences of the Hindus" where the subject is summarised from the Indian standpoint and the authorities are given.

mind generated by its past experiences. These accumulated *Saṃskāras* are in Indian philosophy the source of all our irresistible assumptions and convictions. Thus Kant contended that the persistent reality of the causal order is as necessary an assumption for our knowledge of the external world as time and space. World-experience does not justify these assumptions. But they are there as (it is said) the product of an infinite number of experiences in an infinite number of worlds. Mind is never in any Indian system a Tabula Rasa but is on the contrary a mine of impressions and tendencies. There is a given form of experience because there has always been a similar experience under similar circumstances. There is a given state of facts because there has always been a similar state of facts under similar conditions. This is the principle of the Uniformity of Nature in its Indian form. The pre-existent experience so postulated, though not without rational proof in its favour, cannot be established with certitude by reason alone. In supersensible matters reason can only attain at the best conclusions of probability. The affirmation of pre-existence rests secondarily on *Śruti* or Revelation and primarily on actual experience in the form of that threefold supersensible knowledge (*Traividya*) which is concerned firstly with the cosmic history of the individual self and secondly with such history of others, both being effects in the general cosmic process, and thirdly with the cause of such process.[1] If any one says that he does not believe the possibility of such supersensible experience he is entirely within his rights and no one can possibly have any objection. But those who for any reason have satisfied themselves on this and other similar matters will not in their turn be affected merely by these doubts or denials unless they are of the class of persons who in this country are stampeded into immediate repudiation on hearing merely the powerful Mantras "Science", "Superstition", "Progress" and the like.

But India has not been without Her own sceptics. Indeed from the Womb of her Thinking She has thrown out every type of doctrine, Agnosticism, Scepticism, Materialism, Idealism, Atheism, Theism, Pantheism. May be that like a woman who has borne too many children Her fecundity has tired Her. The ancient sceptical school of Cārvākas held as against those who assumed the Principle of Causality as a ground of induction (*Vyāpti*) that it itself was an induction with the result that there was circular reasoning. Universal propositions cannot be established (they held) by

[1] Pūrvanivāsānuśmṛti, Parasattbānāṃ ca utpatti jñānam, and the Jñāṇa regarding Pratīyasamutpāda or the origination of things after having experienced another thing referring to the evolutionary process.

limited perception. Every inference is based on an unconditional concomitance which must itself be inferred. There is thus a *regressus ad infinitum*. The *nexus* between cause and effect was only (they held) a notion based on former perception which by accident is found justified by the result in a number of cases. In a similar way Hume held that we do not apprehend any efficiency in the causal order but only a certain regularity of sequence which contains no absolute guarantee of permanence. An 'effect' is only what habit leads us to expect. But a necessary connection that is possibility of inference between any two existent things cannot be based on a mere expectation which though it has never been falsified may yet some day be so. The Nyāya of the first Standard has produced in its later developments some of the greatest logic-choppers in the world, but in its earlier forms was both acute and sensible. Without assuming (as the Buddhists did) Causality as an *a priori* principle, and making deductions therefrom, and without holding (as they did) causal efficiency to be of the essence of empirical (relative) reality, the first Standard took its stand on observed concomitance. It admitted that strong objections might be urged on the basis of mere observation but held that they could not be answered by the canons of causality and essential identity proposed. Falling back on the rational practice of thinking persons it was content with a pragmatic certitude.[1] It was held that the internal conviction was sufficiently justified for all our practical purposes.

The Buddhists took another line of argument to the objection that whilst it is true that logical methods of induction may show how in particular cases the causal relation is to be established, yet this is only a method which itself requires a warrant. The Buddhists replied that pragmatic reasons assign a limit to doubt. If in any particular case the method was satisfied, the antecedent in question must be the cause, for there was no other to serve as such. If it is not the cause then there is none and this conclusion is in contradiction of the rational ground of all practice, since all volitional activity proceeds by implication on the principle of causality namely that there is no phenomenon without a cause. If things could happen without a cause, all motives to action would be baffled. The truth of the principle was held to be guaranteed by the same ultimate criterion of empirical reality as the truth of perception itself, namely, the correspondence between the rational and practical activity of the self.[2]

[1] See Seal, "Positive Sciences of the Hindus," 267—269.
[2] Seal, *op. cit.*, 259—261.

2

The second Standard fully accepts the principle of Causality and efficiency in the transcendent sense of an unmoved Reality disturbing the rest (as equilibrium) of the active source of mind and matter and their energies. Through this co-operation Nature is dynamic. The third Standard similarly assumes the Principle of causality and efficiency with this difference that in lieu of two Principles it posits One of dual aspect, static as Being-Consciousness, kinetic as the Power of Becoming in which Being-consciousness weaves the garment for Itself, which is the unconscious (in themselves) psychic and material forces. The first in the Śaiva and Śākta doctrines is Śiva and the second Its Power or Śakti. But the two are in the Monistic schools one. Māyāvāda Vedānta whilst accepting such a view as empirically valid takes the last step and holds that in the absolute sense the Principle of causality and efficiency is as much Māyā as the universe to which it is applied.

As to the external relation, the First Standard held that cause and effect were two distinguishable conditions of things in a relation of antecedence and consequence. Its doctrine of causation is that of the absolute non-existence of the produced before its actual production;[1] that is the effect is not latent in and essentially identical with the cause as in the next or Evolutionary Standard. As regards the relation of cause and effect it denies a nexus in the form of a supersensible power (*Atīndrya-Śakti*) in the cause to produce the effect, or an ultimate form which is supposed to be present whenever the effect is produced. For it such efficiency was neither a matter of observation nor legitimate hypothesis. A cause is thus the invariable, unconditional, immediately antecedent, sum of operative conditions, and the effect is the consequent phenomenon which results from the joint operation of the antecedent conditions. But it does not admit either as a matter of observation or legitimate hypothesis any transcendental *nexus* between cause and effect as supersensible Power:[2] that is such productive metaphysical efficiency as is affirmed by the second Standard[3] according to which the causal relation is one of identity. Causation takes place through kinetic operation in the nature of molar or molecular motion.[4] There is in each case of causation a redistribution of the latter. Whilst the first Standard thus repudiates the notion of Transcendental Power (*Śakti*) in the mechanism of nature and natural causation,

[1] Which gives it its name Asat-kārya-vāda.
[2] Atīndrya-śakti.
[3] See Seal, *op. cit.*, 262.
[4] Bhautika-parispanda.

it does not deny but affirms the Power (*Śakti*) of the Lord in His creation of the Universe out of the pre-existing realities,[1] nor does it deny the existence of metaphysical conditions like merit (Dharma) which constitute a system of Moral Ends which fulfil themselves in and through the mechanical system and order of Nature.[2] The creation of the world takes place as an absolutely new creation[3] by what is called Yaugika-sṛṣṭi or conjunction of the nine eternally pre-existing entities (Dravya) with all their properties and relations.

Motion (Karma)[4] is defined in the Commentary on the Vaiśeṣika Aphorisms as the unconditional cause of change of place in a particle which in its simplest form is instantaneous and as *Vega* or impressed motion, or momentum is a persistent tendency or physical *Saṃskāra* implying therefore a series of motions.[5] This motion is as we may see happening around us, conveyed from or communicated by one object to another. Final causality or motion is attributed by the First Standard to *Adṛṣṭa* (lit. "Unseen") which is resorted to in explanation of observed phenomena only when these cannot be derived in any way from the operation of known causes. Several classes of cases fall under this head such as the operation of the transcendental cause, Merit and Demerit[6] which explains the conjunction and disjunction of Souls (*Ātmans*) with their bodies, or according to the law of *Karma* or action or the operation of moral causation as superimposed on the natural order; and the first motions in the primordial elements of matter[7] at the beginning of creation. It is the Lord (Īśvara) who is, though Himself unmoved, the First Mover operating according to the law of the unseen causes or *Adṛṣṭa*. Motion therefore in this system is something communicated, and it is this communicated, as opposed to inherent motion or essential efficiency of the second standard, which constitutes the phenomenal cause of the first.

3

The first Standard conceived the matter under discussion in a simple fashion. The world is reducible to certain eternal realities. These are brought together by God and form everything experienced in the Universe.

[1] Īśvara in this system has the three śaktis: nitya-jñāna, nitya-icchā, nitya-kṛyā.

[2] Dr. Seal *op. cit.*, 265—266.

[3] Hence it is called Ārambha-vāda.

[4] See Seal, *op. cit.*, 129—152.

[5] Vega is either persistent tendency (Saṃskāra) to motion or tendency to restitution of shape in elastic bodies.

[6] Dharma, Adharma. That is an action in accordance with or contrary to the universal law.

[7] *Paramāṇu*.

The things so formed by the eternal realities are absolutely new productions which had no sort of existence whatever before their production. All moving things are moved by a force called *Kāla* which though different from and independent of other realities is in general relation with them. *Dik* again is the force of relative position. Final Causality or motion is attributed to *Adṛṣṭa* (*lit.* "Unseen") such as the first motions in the primordial elements of matter. *Adṛṣṭa* is only resorted to in explanation of observed phenomena when these cannot be derived in any way from the operation of known causes. In the universe so constituted causation takes place through molar and molecular Motion (*Karma*) which is the cause of change in place in a particle. This motion is conveyed by one body to another. Cause is one thing and effect is another. The former is the invariable, unconditional, immediately antecedent, sum of operative conditions and the latter or effect is the consequent phenomenon which results from the joint operation of the antecedent conditions. As already observed the power of movement is not lodged in matter itself. It is a distinct principle in general relation with it. There is nothing but the invariable unconditional time relation between the cause and effect. This Standard does not admit either as matter of observation or legitimate hypothesis any nexus between cause and effect as metaphysical power (*Atīndrya-Śakti*) or productive efficiency inherent in the cause to produce the effect as posited in the second Standard. The cause is nothing other than an unconditional, invariable complement of operative conditions and the effect nothing other than the consequent phenomenon which results from the joint operation of the antecedent conditions. The Nyāya however while repudiating transcendental power (Śakti) in the mechanism of nature and natural causation does not deny the existence of metaphysical conditions like merit (*Dharma*) which constitute a system of moral ends that fulfil themselves in and through the mechanical system and order of nature.[1]

In the next state or Second Standard we are introduced to the concept of efficiency. It is not the invariable or unconditional succession which constitutes causation but it is the power in the cause which produces the invariable succession. In other words the concept of efficiency is essential to the causal relation. This is based on the fact of the individual man's sense of power and the consciousness of it, or on the experience of subjective activity as such which has been regarded as a primary or the sole source of this concept of efficiency. This subjective consciousness of power as the

[1] Seal, *op. cit.*, 262 *et. seq.*

original experience from which the concept of efficiency is derived has been held to be a justification of its validity; that is there is in fact power in the cause to produce the effect. As so conscious we have the feeling that in human activity we are in the Power-house itself. It is objected that this is a mere ejective interpretation, a projection of our consciousness of power into the outside world. The world outside us does not give the concept of efficiency except we read what we are conscious of into it. We do not sense power or initiative force anywhere. In fact causation is a notion derived from our own conscious activity. This is true as also that it is Consciousness which makes the very change of nature intelligible to us.[1]

Nevertheless we may support the dynamic view of the universe on the Monistic principles of the Śākta system. Mind and matter are twin aspects of the Mother-Power (Mahā-Śakti). They are themselves forms of power in differing degrees of contraction (*Saṃkoca*). Power exists in either case, though in man's mind only it is revealed together with the consciousness of it. It is true that efficiency is discovered not outside but within us. But if it did not exist all would not make discovery of it. The charge of anthropomorphism only succeeds against those who altogether sever mind and matter, the intelligible from the sensible. It is however a formally valid criticism that the unity on which this argument is based is not itself established. This calls in question the truth of Monism itself. Śāṃkhyan dualism gives independent reality to motion or change. It may be objected[2] that these as absolute, objective, independent occurrences have in themselves no meaning, for their meaning is in Consciousness which by giving meaning to succession demonstrates its own persistence, which as conscious continuity by creating time and space proves its own timelessness and spacelessness, thus as the Monistic Vedānta says, giving testimony of consciousness as the Self being the sole basis or reality. But can reason establish anything more than that motion or change has no meaning independent of Consciousness? We make a further step when we say that there is in fact only reality namely Consciousness, a position for which we may argue but which cannot be established with certitude except by an actual or direct experience of unity. Those who seek to establish supersensible (*Atīndrya*) truths on any other ground must fail; just as those who

[1] See as to this and the concept of Energy generally the skilful criticism from the Advaita-Vedānta standpoint in Metaphysics of Energy by G. R. Malkani published by the Indian Institute of Philosophy, Amalner, (E. Khandesh).

[2] See "Metaphysics of Energy."

argue against the validity of the individual's experience must fail. It is his experience, adduce what facts and arguments you will against it.[1]

4

In the second Standard there are two ultimate Realities, existing independently the one of the other, namely the class of Selves (*Puruṣas*) whose nature is Consciousness and the psycho-physical Principle (*Prakṛti*). When the two Principles are associated as in world-experience there is consciousness identifying itself with its vehicles of mind and matter. Where they are dissociated then Consciousness is alone in its aloofness (*Kaivalya*). These two in association are the efficient and material causes respectively of the universe, whilst in Vedānta there is only one Reality which in different aspects is efficient and material cause. True efficiency is the power to initiate change that is the power of X to affect Y whilst X itself is unaffected and remains at rest. If the agent X is itself moved then it becomes a patient. This efficiency is transcendental and not the ordinary notion of efficiency of science which has no metaphysical support. Lotze says; "There cannot be an inner state of anything such as to be for that thing the condition of its being in another particular state." It is in fact impossible even to conceive X moving Y in the world of things without the former itself moving in the act of moving the latter. If X moves then it must be moved from outside. The agent which is moved and moves does not initiate but merely communicates an impulse which it has itself received from outside. In the phenomenal world the moving cause can only be conceived as part of an universe which by the configuration of its other parts helps to determine its movements. No element whether animate or inanimate can be conceived as moving itself because everything remains at rest until it is moved through a cause outside itself. And once recourse is had to outside causes the notion of efficiency is lost.[2] In the universe as it exists there is an unending change of cause and effect, each movement therein being the result of a previous one and the cause of that which follows. It is common doubtless to speak of the self-initiated movements of animate being. It is not affirmed that there is true efficiency in the case of such movements, but that the movement of living substance is not necessarily dependent on mechanical propulsion by something else from outside. In fact some altogether deny spontaneity of movement in living bodies attri-

[1] It is the truth *for him* however much others may refuse to accept such experience as truth for themselves. It is only alleged sense-knowledge which is capable of verification or refutation.

[2] See Metaphysics of Energy, by G. R. Malkani.

buting their movements to the colloid and chemical reactions of the mobile beings and the medium. But, however this be, no true efficiency, as above defined, is discoverable in any form of phenomenal being as such. True efficiency only exists in their ultimate Cause. In Sāṃkhya the Psycho-physical Principle is essentially active. It is never at rest. No cause is thus required to set it in motion. Consciousness (Puruṣa) is efficient in the sense that it determines the equilibrium of the former principle so that it deploys and manifests itself in the psychical and physical variety with which the unity of consciousness identifies itself.

The Psycho-physical principle is composed of three Factors, Moments, or Aspects[1] which are a tendency towards Activity, that is what is efficient in any phenomenon,[2] and which may work upon either of the other two factors[3] which are tendencies towards the Manifestation[4] or Veiling of Consciousness in that phenomenon[5] respectively. The very nature of Energy is Efficiency to do work, to overcome resistance and to produce motion. All energy is therefore kinetic, even potential energy being energy of Motion in imperceptible forms. And so it is said of the essentially active Root-Energy-Stuff of the universe or Prakṛti[6] that it has both homogeneous[7] and heterogeneous or heteropathic change.[8] By the former is meant 'change in its own given condition'. The changed state is equivalent to the changing state. Thus the threefold Factors of the Root which is the material cause of the future and still unmanifested universe are in a a state of equilibrium. The Root even then changes so as to maintain this state of equilibrium the change not upsetting the equilibrium. It changes because activity of some kind is of its essence. The reason is that the inherent tendency to manifeststion is counterbalanced by the resistance of the Factor which in produced nature is called mass resistance, stability, or inertia. Consciousness as the *Puruṣa* is the efficient agent for the destruction of this equilibrium and the manifestation of the universe to Consciousness

[1] Guṇa; translated as quality but which also means strand or thread. The Root is threefold like the twisted sacred thread of the Brāhmaṇa.

[2] Rajas Guṇa.

[3] Making one suppress the other.

[4] Sattva-guṇa. It is that in the Material Cause which serves as the medium for reflection of the Sat or Consciousness of the efficient cause, the Puruṣa. It is therefore the conscious element as mind in the Phenomenon.

[5] Tamas Guṇa, counteracting the tendency to conscious manifestation, physically manifesting as the mass and inertia of Matter which as such is the unconscious element in the Phenomenon.

[6] Pra+kṛti=before creation or She from Whom production begins or She by whom all actions (Kṛti) are done. Actions=Sṛṣṭi (production), Sthiti (maintenance), Laya (Dissolution).

[7] Sadṛśa or Sarūpa-pariṇāma.

[8] Visadṛśa or Virūpa-pariṇāma.

through the Mind with which the latter identifies itself. In manifestation however Change is heterogeneous. Manifestation involves varied collocations of energy. One relation of the Factors then changes into another different from it and so on with the result that Causation is a transformation of the homogeneous origin into the heterogeneous effects which are the varied universe of Mind and Matter.

As stated, consciousness as efficient cause of movement does not itself move. We may seek a physical analogy in the nature of catalytic activity. In a chemical substance which is possessed of catalytic action the latter effects something and yet does not itself (so far as we can see) get transformed nor lose anything of its mass or potential during that chemical activity. Such a substance does not combine with the others which it influences but it (by its presence) influences others in proximity to one another to combine and to become themselves the seat of chemical activity and transformation. All such bodies therefore lose nothing and gain nothing and so keep themselves what they were. They naturally cease to influence if isolated from material to act upon. Their activity in the sense of influence would have a final terminal should they be altogether and permanentaly isolated which is the meaning of *Kaivalya*.[1]

Action may thus be apparently caused or directed by a body which itself undergoes no change.[2] Whilst this example illustrates the changelessness of the Efficient Cause it does not bring out to view the apparent combination of the two Principles. In the Śāstra in order to explain the nature of this influence, recourse is had to the analogy of the reflection of a red flower in a crystal. The former and all its movements are reflected in the crystal but the latter is in itself unchanged. This illustration has the merit of showing both influence and apparent combination of both the Realities. Whatever analogy be applicable[3] the substance of the doctrine is that one Principle affects another without the former really combining with it and thus being affected and undergoing any change.

---

[1] As applied to the Puruṣa detached from Prakṛti, Kaivalya is isolation or Aloofness when Consciousness as Puruṣa dissociates Itself from Prakṛti.

[2] So platinum will cause action without itself undergoing any kind of change which can be detected by the chemist; and so with other bodies. This is without loss to itself just as from an initial magnet any number of others can be made without loss to the generating magnet.

[3] In fact the Scriptures declare that the matter is Apratarkya, that is beyond all human discussion and conception. Our analysis must from the nature of the case be limited and imperfect.

We may leave physical analogies which are necessarily crude, though not without effect, for those who live in the actions and reactions of matter, and endeavour to explain the subjects from the psychical standpoint. In this view we may say that Nature always actively "works for" that is shows Herself to the consciousness which associates itself with Her. To the consciousness which discovers its true nature and that it is other than and separated from mind and matter She withdraws herself. Until then Consciousness which identifies itself with Mind and Matter continues to be the efficient cause of their production. All Mind and Matter and their energies are contained in the Original Energy-stuff: so that manifestation is an unfolding. This is the doctrine of the existence of the product in a potential form in the cause prior to its actual manifestation as effect.[1] Things are not formed out of pre-existing materials as new creations, but products already exist in a potential form in the original productive principle. They simply unroll themselves out from this potential state as a tree unrolls itself from out the seed. The Cause holds within it the effect potentially. The effect is the cause modified. Cause and effect in the universe are different positions and states of conditionedness of the same thing in the time-sequence. The effect is in the cause and the cause exists in the effect which is only the cause manifested in a collocation.[2] The effect which is potential is actualised. Nothing which is produced is something entirely new. The manifestation or causation of an effect is only the passage from potentiality to actuality. Cause and effect are thus essentially (that is as to substance-energy as distinct from collocation) one. The X which is virtually the cause is the same X which is virtually the effect.

The Factors of the Root, notwithstanding their transformation into diverse forms, are neither created not destroyed and are eternal. The totality of Mass[3] and Energy[4] remains constant if account be taken both of the actual and potential. But the concrete phenomenal modes evolved in this process are subject to growth and decay, which are only due to changes of collocation and consequent changes of state from the potential to the actual. The course of evolution conforms to a fixed law inherent in the transforming whole, the transformation of which is constant and not arrested for a moment. There is thus both transformation and conservation of Energy. As the total Energy remains the same while the world is

[1] It is therefore called Sat-Kārya-vāda.
[2] Kāraṇasyaiva saṃsthānamātram. Cf. Seal, *op. cit.*, 89.
[3] Tamas. [4] Rajas.

constantly evolving, cause and effect are only more or less evolved forms of the same ultimate Root-Energy Stuff. The sum of effects exists in the sum of Causes in a potential or unevolved form. What is called the material cause or sum of material causes is only the Power which is efficient in the production, or rather the vehicle of that power. This Power is the potential form of the Energy set free in the effect through concomitant conditions necessary to call forth the so-called material cause into activity. There is liberation of potential Energy following on the action of the proximate efficient cause or concomitant condition. The causal operation of these lies in the fact that they supply the stimulus which liberates the potential energy stored up in a given collocation. Everything in the phenomenal world is a special collocation of the three Factors of the Root cause. The sum of material causes potentially contains the Energy manifested in the sum of effects: and in the passage from potency to actualisation the effectuating condition (concomitant, cause), when it is itself accomplished, is only a step in the evolutionary series which adds a specific stimulus and renders determinate that which was previously indeterminate. When the effectuating condition is added to the sum of material conditions in a given collocation, all that happens is that a stimulus is imparted which removes the arrest, disturbs the relatively stable equilibrium and brings on a liberation of energy together with a fresh collocation. Non-material (in the sense of subtle) concomitants like Merit and Demerit[1] do not supply any moving force or Energy of the sum of material conditions but only remove the arrest or state of relatively stable equilibrium in a given collocation.[2] The order of evolution follows a definite law inherent in the root-cause and its manifestations. The cosmic order is one and fixed but comprehends divers series arising from different combinations or original Factors which constitute subordinate or particular laws of cause and effect. The qualities of things are only modes of Energy acting in those collocations sometimes actual and at other times potential. The Original Energy is one and ubiquitous and everything therefore exists in everything else potentially[3] without prejudice to the generic and specific differences of things. Inorganic matter, vegetable and animal organisms are essentially and ultimately one, so far as mass and energy are concerned, but the varied forms of Energy and the generic and specific qualities or

[1] Dharma and Adharma.

[2] As the owner of a field removes the barrier in flooding his field from a reservoir of water.

[3] Sarvaṃ sarvātmakamiti.

properties of things (which are but modes of Energy) follow a definite and unalterable law (which we observe in the phenomenal world) in the order of their appearance and succession under conditions of space, time, mode, and causality and hence all effects do not manifest themselves at once.[1] The category of causality is mediated through the scheme of order in time. The empirical institution first superimposes relations of antecedence and sequence on changing phenomena and the understanding out of these relations creates order in time. The empirical intuition then intuits the phenomenal series of transformations of Energy in this Time-order and in so doing imparts the relation of cause and effect into Nature.[2]

It is to be noted that the Energy which Mind, Life, and Matter display is of a transcendental nature. That is, it is not the energy of forms of mind and matter considered in and by themselves, but it is the one infinite Energy of the Original Principle of which they are both limited psychophysical modes.

5

The Third Standard as Vedānta in its Monistic form holds that the measurable universe is reducible to one Reality alone, the Brahman, the Immeasurable or Immense. We may consider the matter first from the empirical standpoint of Śākta doctrine. Here in lieu of the plurality of Selves (*Puruṣa*), there is the one Changeless Consciousness of Śiva who, relative to the world, is efficient cause. The world is not something which has a reality independent of Consciousness. It is the transforming and transformed Power of Śakti of Siva who is the Divine Mother of the Universe. The Mother as Material cause is in Herself (*Svarūpa*) one with Śiva[3] who is Consciousness-being-bliss. The material cause is not thus, as the Śāṃkhyas affirm, something unconscious. The Mother-Energy is the Source of all mind, life, and matter and their energies which are all modes of Her as Substance-Energy. The Power which evolves the world is both Consciousness (*Cit-Śakti*) and *Māyā*[4] or the finitising power (*Māyā-Śakti*) which manifests as mind and matter. Neither Śiva nor Śakti in themselves, that is as Being-consciousness-bliss, change, but Śakti is the Principle of Change and assumes the changing forms which

[1] Dr. Seal, *op. cit.*, 13—18 which I summarise and in which the authorities are given.
[2] *Ibid.*, 22. [3] Cidrūpuṇī.
[4] Māyā means that by which a thing is 'measured' that is 'limited', (Mīyate anena iti Māyā) the principle which imposes forms on the formless. Some explain it as Mā (not) Yā (That) *i.e.*, that which is the contrary of the infinite That without attributes.

constitute the universe. Here also there is a relation of essential identity between cause and effect. Consciousness remains one and unchanged, immanent in all mind and matter: and the latter are essentially one as regards Substance-Energy. There is true causal efficiency in its transcendental sense. But the efficient and material causes are not two independent Principles but twin aspects of the one Reality in whom inhere both. Causal efficiency is the very essence of Reality in its Power aspect and it is this efficiency which is inherent and manifested in all things in the universe which are the transformations of the Mother-Energy-Substance (Mahā-śakti) one in Herself with Consciousness.

It is to be observed however that there is a difference between the modes of operation in the evolution of the world, that is of its constitutive principles and in the world so constituted.

In the case of transformation of Energy-Substance in the world itself the result of the cosmic process above described, the cause ceases to exist as cause immediately before and when the effect comes into existence. Thus as the Lakṣmī-Tantra says "in the world milk loses its nature immediately when it becomes curd (there is curd only not milk and curd)" but this does not apply to the Supreme Cause and Its process for the quality[1] of that Cause is Vīrya,[2] that is unaffectedness in spite of being the transforming material cause.[3] This principle is applicable in the case of both the second and third Standards or Śāṃkhyan and Vedāntic systems respectively. In cosmic evolution the cause when transforming itself into the effect remains what it is as cause. The effect (as effect) is the cause modified but the cause (as cause) remains what it was, is, and will be. This must obviously be so, otherwise with the evolution into effect the cause would disappear in it and so on until the last of the evolved principles was reached when all the antecedent principles would have disappeared in the last. But the universe exists as a combination of those constituent principles.[4]

The evolutionary process is also in both cases reversible, that is, cosmically. In manifested Nature there is continuous degradation until

---

[1] Guṇa. [2] This term here=Vikāra-rahita.

[3] Schrader, Ahirbudhnyasaṃhita, 33.

[4] Thus in Sāṃkhya, Prakṛti becomes Mahat and remains Prakṛti, Mahat becomes Ahaṃkāra and remains Mahat and so on. And in the 36 Principles (Tattvas) of the Śaiva and Śāktas, Śiva-Śakti Tattva evolves Sādākhya and remains as they were, Sādākhya evolves Īśvara-Tattva and remains Sādākhya. In the Māyā-vāda scheme there is not the same chain of development because Matter, Life and Mind are derived from the different Guṇa aspects of the Universal (Apañcīkṛta-Tanmātra.) But the Tanmātras themselves are evolved similarly from Māyā the material cause.

the terminal of activity as the whole universe is reached. Could the reversibility of the processes of life be discovered we might then see the adult organism led back through the successive stages of its development to the primitive germ whence it sprung. Hathayoga may in degree arrest degradation and give a reverse tendency to individual organic process.[1] But it is the work of Cosmic Power to withdraw as a whole what it has ejected as modes of itself. This is *Pralaya* or dissolution of the universe when the two Radical Principles alone are.

In this connection it may be observed that to Aristotle the "First Mover" must be functioning actuality, absolute *Energeia* for were it only potential *Dunamis* there were no reason so far as it was only that, it should become actual. It has absolutely actual being which moves out of itself and returns to itself. The potential presupposes preceding actuality. What is potential may or may not be. There is no absolute beginning of this process: and so it has been said "that no Theist can assign a first to Deity nor atheist a first to the systems of things in time."[2] The Sāṃkhyan Material Cause as Energy-Stuff is prior to manifestation a state of equilibrated inner activity[3] associated with the efficient Cause (*Puruṣa*), and in Vedānta the efficient and material causes are aspects of the One Reality, the Whole and Full (*Pūrṇa*), with all-mighty Power.[4] Neither in Sāṃkhya nor in this or other Vedāntic schools is the universe the production of something absolutely new: but there is an unfolding or development in the sense that what previously existed in a subtle form in the Cause is made explicit and gross in the effect.[5] In the Vedāntic schools the Lord is the efficient cause.

6

Before stating the doctrine of Vedānta from its transcendental standpoint in which all Causality is as much *Māyā* as the universe itself it is necessary to consider further the question of the relation of essential identity of cause and effect as held by the second Standard and by the third on its empirical side. Cause and effect may be complete or partial. By 'complete cause' is meant the attitude of the universe as a whole at the antecedent moment and the 'complete effect' is the attitude of the universe

[1] In Kuṇḍalini or Laya-yoga the individual actually retraces the stages of the cosmic evolution and becomes one with the initial Energy in its form as Consciousness. For this Yoga proceeds on a Monistic basis.

[2] Dr. Sterling. Gifford Lectures (1890), 126.

[3] Sadṛśa-pariṇāma.

[4] Sarva-śaktimaya.

[5] In Madhva's dualism it is exceptionally held that God is not the material cause of the universe.

as a whole at the subsequent moment. When dealing with the complete cause external influences are excluded, that is, influences not within the system itself.[1]

As to the treatment of Causality there are thus two standpoints namely the ordinary pragmatic standpoint which deals not with the universe of Fact but with Fact-sections[2] and the philosophic standpoint which tries to deal, so far as possible, with the universe itself. Thus from the first viewpoint the cause of an eclipse of the moon is the falling of the shadow of the earth[3] on her. From the second view-point the cause is the condition of the universe as a *whole* at the antecedent moment, that is the antecedent attitude of the universe, and the effect is the consequent attitude of the universe, that is the condition of the universe as a *whole* at the subsequent moment. In this case the cause and effect are not held apart and one set of things held to be the cause and the other the effect. The whole as cause is the cause of the whole as effect—the state of the whole which exists first being called the cause, and the other which follows the effect, though the two are essentially one, distinguishable by the specific arrangement of Matter and Force. In the instance given the physical universe as a whole must be in a certain attitude in order that the sun, moon, and earth may be in conjunction and thereby cause the eclipse. Neither sun nor moon can be torn apart from the physical system and treated in an isolated manner. The cause or "antecedent assemblage of conditions" is really the antecedent attitude of the system as a whole. The effect also is not circumscribed to the particular section which we care to notice. It is as wide as the consequent attitude of the universe as a whole. But the ordinary outlook is narrow. Science tries to broaden it; Philosophy to complete. From the ordinary standpoint the equality of the cause and effect relates to Matter and Force, though in some cases scientific analysis must supplement or correct ordinary analysis in the proof of such equality. But as regards their collocation and distribution it is evident that there is no apparent equality, a point with which I will next deal.

---

[1] Thus a seed is growing to be a plant. Here external influences are those external to the forces which constitute the seed such as soil, air, sunshine, rain and so forth. These are partial causes as is also the attraction of the earth producing the effect, namely, the fall of the apple.

[2] See Prof. P. N. Mukhyopādhyāya's "Approaches to Truth" and "Patent Wonder".

[3] Rahu who is said to "devour" the moon is called Bhūchhāyā or Earth-Shadow. All the ancients were not so infantile as is sometimes supposed.

It is obvious that if the cause is absolutely identical with the effect there is no efficient causation at all. But we do, it is said, see "Becoming" that is continuous natural process. Hence arises the notion of relative sameness through a series of changes, stages, positions. In so far as any of the determining conditions of an aspect of reality remains unchanged, in so far that aspect is said to be continuous. The reality of Becoming involves continuity of transition. All natural processes are conceived as continuous. Motion cannot be perceived without continuity. But this continuity again must be relative. For if there be continuity in its strictest sense the cause becomes coincident with the effect, all process becomes impossible and therefore all differences are abolished. Continuity of transition is a necessary presupposition without which Becoming is inconceivable. What however practically is our experience ? Objectively we only know successive positions, mere static points. Forms succeed one another in the natural process. Nextly differences of quality are shown in these successive forms. This diversity and succession of forms, discontinuous in themselves, set up the appearance of motion. The forms are many and mutually exclusive. Objectively then all that we know are successive static points which are plural, diverse, different in quality, discontinuous in themselves. The points as objectively given are discrete and unconnected. We do not see transition between one form and another, the melting of one form into another. If we accept process and with it real differences of form, continuity becomes meaningless, for that which exists as a limit only cannot become another limit continuously. Nevertheless the notion of continuity is imposed on us being involved in the notions of causation, energy and motion. Our experience is apparently not of simultaneity. The terms of reality are successive because mutually exclusive. The cause of the reality of X is not thought of as existing contemporaneously with, but has having arisen before, X. Motion cannot be constructed by any number of mere static points. For such points always involve a gap between them with the result that there is a series of discontinuous points but no motion. What is done by any experiencer is to fill in these gaps by a subjective content. Objectively there is apparently no place for continuity. As regards causation we conceive of an ideal abstraction of Substance-Energy which is the unchanged ground beneath all changes of form which take place in it and we give to the static points a sort of movement and construct the image of a line.[1]

[1] For a fuller treatment of Continuity see *post*.

The universe, it is admitted, evolves. Evolving is also changing in a sense. Something is evolving. If there was absolutely no difference in any respect the "what" which in fact evolves would not evolve at all, for it would ever remain what it is. Yet there is something which does so remain. What so remains is the substance, stuff or material and the total amount of energy or Śakti (kinetic or static) working upon or in the substance. Thus if the complete cause be X and the complete effect Y then X=Y as regards the matter in them (Śakti as material cause) and as regards the energy in them (Śakti as efficient cause). But as there is change, and the effect is the cause in some way modified, there is something in respect of which cause and effect in appearance differ, though as regards substance and energy they are the same. This is the collocation or distribution of the matter[1] in it and the collocation or composition or diagram of the forces in it. It is these which constitute what is called in Māyā-vāda Vedānta "Name and Form".[2] From the standpoint of this Vedāntic school, Name and Form, as changing things, are *Asat*, that is, the contrary of constant and permanent. Their Stuff and Energy are *Sat* as relatively (that is in the world) constant and permanent. If reality be determined by the possession of these characteristics then (according to this definition) the Name and Form are unreal and Substance-Energy are real. Hence X=Y.

The analysis of effect above given applies not only to material but to vital[3] and psychic effects.[4] An analysis of the Cause gives us the same scheme.

From the Indian philosophic standpoint the view taken is that the subsequent total attitude of the universe is the unfolding or evolution (as regards the types[5] at least) of the antecedent total attitude of the

[1] Viśiṣtarūpa.

[2] Nāma-rūpa: These produced changes or Vikāras such as a pitcher made of earth are names and forms and are Asat, a term which is better translated, non-persistent and not "unreal", whereas the Earth, *i.e.*, the substance is alone Sat (relatively) persistent. The degree of persistency a thing possesses is its Sat. Sat is that which eternally and for all time is Sat. Asat is that which is Sat for a time and becomes Asat at some time.

[3] Prāṇic.

[4] *e.g.*, in a mental effect say anger: the Substance=Mind stuff (Antahkaraṇa): Energy=force of the predispositions (Saṃskāra)+forces of exciting cause or causes. The form (Viśiṣta-rūpa) of that anger is its special form as a psychic state (it is not anger in the abstract but anger as a particular mental state in a particular person at a particular time) and the form of the Saṃskāras, etc., is the particular arrangement of them which represents that anger as an actual presentation into the mind.

[5] These generals or universals called Parajāti are held in the Cosmic Mind as Mahat which corresponds to the Buddhist-Saṃskāra in the chain of causation. These types are a form of pure being (Sattā) the correspondence of which in the rational world is the power to form and hold generals. But in this latter world the particulars are explicit.

universe. Putting aside for the moment the question of Types and their variations, that is whether there is any real variation at all, cause and effect are equal also not only as regards substance-energy but as to the collocation and distribution of matter and force. In what way ? If we imagine an evolving "what" as a solitary something evolving without external influence or environment, the general scheme of collocation or distribution may be the same in both[1] but it cannot be said that the *actual* collocation or distribution of matter and force in the cause is the same in the effect. If it were there would be no change. But evolution means change. From this it follows that the matter and force are redistributing themselves without however giving up the general scheme of distribution. As regards such redistribution there is a difference that is as regards particular forms.[2] Hence while basic matter-form (for the two may be regarded as one) together with their typical arrangements also persists, the actual form does not. If we take[3] persistence as the mark of the Real and the Real to be only that which does so persist, then we may eliminate the changing characteristics of name and form as unreal in which case again X=Y for the residue is constant. If however whilst we regard the ultimate Cause as the Ens Realissimum we give to change or non-persistence a relative reality of its own, then unity can only consist in the identity of the cause which remains the same as cause even when variously self-modified as effect. The Śākta view that a thing changes as regards appearance (collocation, etc.) and yet does not change, that is, persists as regards energy and substance can only equate X=Y by ignoring the difference in collocation or experience, and the reason why X and Y being identical in substance and energy still differ as regards experience. Not only the appearances of X and Y but also the reason of the difference in appearance is ignored. Without ignoring them we cannot equate X and Y. The identity is affirmed by reference to Revelation as direct spiritual experience without attempt to effect explanation in terms of reason. It is the inscrutable (Acintya) Power of God. Śaṃkara is formally able to ignore them by defining his reality or Sat as that which persists so that from this standpoint, X=Y because the collocation of X and that of Y and their reasons do not persist and are therefore the contrary of Sat or Asat.

[1] *e.g.*, when a small crystal forms into a large one in the solution the scheme of configuration of the molecules remains the same. Thus the cubic shape does not change though the size increases.

[2] Nāma-rūpa.

[3] As the Advaita-Vedānta of Śaṃkara does.

Thus the pluralism of the first Standard deals with nine independent entities, their properties and relations. Of these, matter is moved not by any inherent Energy but by another independent force called *Kāla*. The motion of one thing is communicated to another. All that is observed is this motion. Cause and effect are two things, and whether one stands to the other in the relation of cause and effect depends on its invariable unconditional, immediate, antecedence. Here we have the empirical notion of cause. The second Standard reduces these Realities to two only and introduces the notion of efficiency which is attributed to one of these namely Consciousness. The other, the Psycho-physical Principle, is inherently active and the cause of its movements is not to be sought outside itself. The relation of Cause and Effect is one of identity. Here we have the notion of causation as metaphysical efficiency. So also in Monistic Vedānta when viewed from the empirical standpoint: only here the efficient and material cause are aspects of one Reality. Lastly, from the absolute standpoint there is no causation at all: the notion having empirical validity only.

# POWER AS CONTINUITY

## ( *Sthiti-śakti* )

### 1

As the notion of Causality is based upon the more fundamental notion of Continuity, I propose to deal with the latter in this second part. In the present Series as well as elsewhere, Experience, Consciousness, Ākāśa have in many places, been described as 'Continuum'. Now, with regard to this, we have to satisfy ourselves, if we are to probe deeper into the matter, that *firstly*, the idea of Continuity is a fundamental and concrete idea (as distinguished from a mere mental abstraction); *secondly*, the idea is grounded in fact, or in other words, the Continuum really exists and is not only fabricated by the mind; *thirdly*, the idea as well as the reality of Continuity manifests itself in thought and in the world order in a variety of forms of which Causality is one. Our problem reduces itself therefore, in this second part, to three questions: (*a*) Is the idea of Continuity a native expression of the Given or Experience, or is it something constructed by imagination and superimposed upon the order of Experience ? In other words, Is it a datum of Experience or is it only a mental construct ? (*b*) Supposing that Experience involves this idea as its original presentation, the next query is: Does the Continuum *really* exist? Is existence really continuous? While the first is an epistemological question, the second is a metaphysical question. The first enquires as to whether the idea is *given* in Experience, the second as to whether it is *valid.* (*c*) The next question is—In what forms does Continuity evolve in thought and in reality ? *Prima facie*, the ideas of Uniformity and Causality amongst others seem to be forms of the idea of Continuity; are they so ? So also, Consciousness, Time and Space amongst others seem to be actual forms of Continuity; are they so ? Besides these three theoretical queries, we may have a practical one, *viz.*, (*d*) The Continuum, though it may be given in Experience and really exist, often seems to be veiled in the representation of Experience; now how can we realise what has thus been veiled ? In other words, How can we *live* in consciousness the Whole and the Perfect (*Akhaṇḍa* and *Pūrṇa*) which we perhaps really are ?

2

The first question then is: Is Experience continuous or discontinuous ? In seeking to answer this question we must avoid on one hand the mistake of Sensationist Philosophy, and on the other, the illusion of "common sense". The former is committed to the view that our perception can only give us "points of sensation" or the "manifold" of experience which are always discrete. Our mental life is thus a "series" of impressions and ideas (to adopt Hume's classification) which do *not* constitute a continuous flow or "stream" (as supposed by William James and others) of experience. The idea of continuity in Time and in Space is a mental construct—and may be an illusion like the notion of an objective causal nexus. Our sense-experience gives us "facts" which are discrete, discontinuous, finite, particular. This psychology of Hume, Mill, Bain and others, and taken up by many physicist philosphers, which would seek to explain the phenomena of experience by the association of atoms of sensation, involves a fundamental mistake. Experience is never built up in that way. Experience never begins with, and never is atoms, or points of sensation. It always is a continuum, a universe. As such it is the Given, the Fact.[1] The discrete points of sensation are obtained by dissociation, analysis, veiling or ignorance of the Whole.[2] The whole is always an undefined and undefinable universe of sounds, sights, smells, touches, tastes, organic sensations, ideas, feelings, hopes, fears, likes, dislikes, desires, etc. These constitute a seamless alogical mass. The "elements" surprise one another, are discriminated from one another, not in presentation but in representation, not in perception but in review. It is true that the distribution of attentive interest is not homogeneous and uniform over the whole field: that while some parts are on the apex of the curve of presentation, others lie more or less nearly on the slopes. By reason of such preferential and in-equal distribution of interest, there arises the distinction between what William James would call the "substantive states" and the "states of transition", the "warm and intimate" tracts of consciousness and the "fringe" of consciousness. It is the non-recognition of the states of transition, the fringe, etc., constituting the

[1] See Professor P. N. Mukhyopadhyāya's "Approaches to Truth" and "Patent Wonder."

[2] See *ante*, *Mind*—Extensiveness.

slopes of the complete curve of presentation, which is accountable for the fantastic psychology of the sensationist philosophers reducing our mental life to isolated, disconnected "points" of sensation only.[1] Mental life is never a manifold of discrete elements, a series: it is *always* a continuum. This continuum which is ever given is ignored for *practical* purposes, and only points of sensation which happen to serve some practical purpose or other are noted. The points or portions thus especially noted are regarded by us as constituting the *whole* experience of the given moment; the rest, though actually given, are ignored by us, and hence become veiled. When, for example, I am gazing at the star Sirius in a clear night, my whole experience is supposed to be concentrated for the time being at that particular star, while, really, my total experience at that time is a universe involving not only a more or less veiled presentation of many neighbouring stars, but of many imperfectly attended sounds, smells, touches, organic sensations, ideas, memories, etc. Experience at that moment is a continuum, seamless, indefinable, alogical: it undoubtedly involves many elements, but these are not yet logically discriminated *as* elements. This entire experience as given is the fact. But I am not ordinarily interested in the whole; I am interested in parts or segments. The parts I am especially interested in are especially attended to, and are emphasised: they constitute, so to say, the crests of the continuous waves of presentation. The experiences which connect together the points of emphasis, the slopes and hollows which lie between the crests of the waves, happen not to be interesting, and they are practically ignored by us—not indeed in intuition, but in review, representation and description. We *think* as though the points of emphasis were alone the whole of experience. This thought, as we have seen, is practically useful. Without preferential regard or distributive attention, life, as we ordinarily live it, would be impossible. Hence the points of emphasis, the "crests" of the waves of presentation, may be called Pragmatic Facts, and they are, as before explained, Fact-sections.[2]

It will be observed, therefore, that the continuum is an inalienable datum of our life of experience—it is a fundamental posture, an original attitude of the Given. It is *not* obtained by the putting together of originally discrete factors by imagination; in other words, it is not a mental construct, a result of abstraction.

---

[1] See *ante, Mind,* for a criticism of the Nyāya-Vaiśeṣika view of Mind making it *aṇu* or Point only. [2] See "Approaches to Truth" and "Patent Wonder".

Now, continuity has never been denied in India, except by some forms of Buddhistic thought. Continuity in its various forms will be studied in a later section, but here we may note three forms of it. In the first place, there is the distinction between ontological continuity and epistemological continuity. The former is continuity pertaining to Reality, apart from, and independent of, experience. It raises this issue: Is Reality or forms of Reality continuous, whether or not we experience or think it as such ? The latter is continuity pertaining to experience, and it raises the following two issues: (1) Is experience or forms of experience actually continuous ? (2) Has our life of experience a *basis* or ground which is continuous, though conscious experience in itself may not be so ? Keeping these two issues apart, therefore, we may have, in the second place, another distinction, *viz.*, that between psychological continuity and epistemological continuity. The former relates to experience as it is actually felt or intuited, the latter to what may be implied in experience, either as its basis or as its condition. Now, keeping in mind these distinctions, we may note that the First Standard or Nyāya-Vaiśeṣika apparently does not recognise psychological continuity, but it clearly and definitely recognises the two other forms of it. As regards ontological continuity, *four* of the fundamental Substances (*Dravyas*) postulated by the First Standard are not only continuous, but infinitely continuous, which is the meaning of the term *Vibhu*. Each of the four entities, *Ākāśa*, *Kāla*, *Dik* and *Ātman*, is *Vibhu*. We need not discuss here the first three continuities, but refer only to the last. *Ātman*, which according to the First Standard is the basis or ground (*āśraya*) of experience, is an infinitely continuous substance. Though experiences themselves are discrete and transient, the spiritual ground in which they inhere is a continuum. The fundamental basis or ground of experience always is and everywhere is. A given experience has *prāgabhāva* (*i.e.*, non-existence before actual appearance or presentation), and *dhvaṃsābhāva* (*i.e.*, non-existence at the third moment from its origination); but the Subject whose experience it is and wherein it inheres remains as a "permanent possibility" (to use the words of J. S. Mill). This permanent possibility of experience is always and everywhere. This conception of an eternal and all-pervasive continuum as the spiritual basis of experience is remarkable, and is characteristic of orthodox Hindu thought. According to this thought, which is clearly in evidence in the Vedas, the Spirit, whatever its fundamental nature be, is an infinite *plenum*, akin to the Æther of

Science, though purer and more perfect (as we shall see), whose individuality arises chiefly if not solely, from the circumstance of its being, associated with different Minds, Sensoria, etc., just as according to Science, the individuality of the physical atoms or corpuscles arises from the circumstance of the sea of ether being subjected in different places to different forms of stress and strain.

How for instance does, according to Science, the difference between an atom of Oxygen and an atom of Nitrogen arise ? Both are believed to be made up of and grounded in, the same continuous stuff—ether. But while O is a relatively stable stress-and-strain centre of a *certain* type in, and of, ether, N is a stress-and-strain centre of a different type. Owing to the difference in the disposition of *Śakti* (Power) in them, their properties apparently differ.[1] But two points, brought into relief by recent Science, are worthy of note. *First*, that assuming electricity to be, from the physical point of view, the fundamental mode of substance-energy (it is not a mere form of energy to-day), we are enabled to say not only that it exists where it appears to exist (as "free" electrons), but it exists, in a relatively static condition, even where it does not appear to exist, *i.e.*, in the so-called "neutral" atoms of O, N, etc. (as "bound" electrons).[2] The basis of substance-energy in Matter (whether as Ether or as Electricity which is by some believed to be a condition of Ether) is thus ubiquitous. *Second*, as a corollary to the above we have this that in spite of all the difference between O and N and the rest, a slow process of evolutionary transmutation is noticeable in the material world by reason of which O, N and the rest are changing and evolving, though this universal process (symbolised by the Vedic Ṛṣis as *yajña* in many places) may be especially noticeable in what are called the radio-active substances.[3] This universal radio-activity is evidence not only of the unity of the fundamental physical basis of Matter as substance-energy, but of the unity of the *law* of material being.

Now, this fundamental unity as regards substance, energy and law in the material world will serve not only as an analogy but an illustration of the fundamental unity in the world of experience. Life, Mind and Spirit are o a higher plane, and on a more comprehensive scale, what Ether and Electricity are, according to Science, on a lower plane and on a comparatively restricted scale. In other words, as we shall presently see, Life, Mind and Spirit are the ascending orders of a series of continua

[1] See *ante, Matter.*
[2] See *Ibid.* [3] *Ibid.*

of which Ether and Electricity are comparatively lower orders. The Ātman as Spirit is thus the Perfect Ether—*Ether in the limit.* Ultimately it is, as the Vedānta says, the *Cidākāśa.* The Chāndogya Upaniṣad makes it *jyāyān* (the highest) and *parāyaṇa* (the ultimate ground). It is the Immense—*Brahman.* It, therefore, underlies, and manifests as, Time, Space, Life, Cosmic Mind, Physical Ether, and in fact, as all other continua. It is *its* pervasive presence which makes anything appear as a continuum. To withdraw it is to withdraw the basis of continuity—nay, the basis of existence. This spiritual basis of continuity and existence in its pure forms (*viz.*, as *Cit*) will be studied in the next following section, but here we may note the point which is especially pertinent to the present discussion. It is this: All the three standards of Hindu Philosophy definitely recognise this spiritual basis of continuity, though its *nature* is seen with increasing purity and clearness as we gradually mount up from the First to the Third Standard.

It is thus remarkable that even the First Standard which, generally speaking, reviews the world from a commonsense and pragmatic standpoint, makes the spiritual basis of experience (*Ātman*) *vibhu*, *i.e.*, a limitless continuum. It thus makes *Ātman* similar to what Ether is to Science. As in Science the basis of Matter and he possibility of its physical or concrete manifestation is given everywhere, so according to the First Standard, the basis and possibility of experience is given everywhere. Far from making the *Ātman,* as some of the Cartesian philosophers did, the special proprium of man, Hindu thought, in all its stages, recognises it, as latent or patent, in *all* things and in *all* places. But then, as we have pointed out, the standpoint of the First Standard is pragmatic and we accordingly find it stopping short of the last limit to which the theory of continuity can be consistently pushed. The First Standard is, generally speaking, the first approximation, the first approach to Truth. We have, therefore, the following limitations or reservations left with regard to *Ātman* or the spiritual basis of experience. (1) Though *vibhu,* it is limited by the independent existence of other *vibhus* (or infinite continua), *viz.*, *Ākāśa*, *Kāla* and *Dik* (though in some branches of Neo-Logic there have been attempts to reduce to a common denominator which is *Iśvara* or *Paramātman*). (2) It is limited by the independent existence of a Chief *Ātman* (somewhat like the Arch-monad of Leibnitz). (3) It is limited by its own plurality, that is, by the fact that Spirits are many. (4) And as regards functioning, it is limited by the circumstance of its having to depend upon inner and outer instruments (*antarindrya* and *bāhyendrya*) and objective material in order to rise to a life of conscious experience.[1] Hence though it is the basis and possibility of experience, it has to depend upon the co-operation of other factors for the purpose of getting actual, conscious experience. It is only the Supreme Spirit whose knowledge (*jñāna*), etc., is *nitya* (permanent). All these limitations or reservations are made, as we shall see in the volume on *Cit*, on pragmatic considerations, as approximations or approaches to Truth. Closer approximations or nearer approaches are made by the two higher Standards, until at last in supreme experience the Fact is recognised as the *Pūrṇa* (Whole) itself of which the *Śruti* paradoxically says: Even if *Pūrṇa* be substracted from *Pūrṇa*, *Pūrṇa* remains.

Reverting, however, to the classification of continuity given before, we now see that the First Standard definitely recognises both ontological continuity and epistemological continuity. It recognises the latter inasmuch as, according to it, the spiritual basis of experience (*i.e.*, what is presupposed and implied in experience) is *vibhu*. But on account of the working of the atomic Mind, Sensoria, *saṃskāras*, etc., the actual experiences are, from the pragmatic standpoint of this standard discrete, transient, serial, and not continuous.[2] There is thus no psychological continuity.

Thus whilst the continuity of the spiritual basis of experience may be guaranteed by the experience of the Seers (Revelation), or may be *inferred* from the data given in our own experience, the First Standard is not prepared to say that our conscious experience itself directly gives us sufficient warrant for believing in such continuity. In actual feeling, we have a manifold, a series only, as the older generation of Empiricists would say. There is no immediate apprehension, no intuition, of continuity in our mental life. This, however, is, according to our showing, ignorance or veiling of the Given — the Fact. Such ignorance is practically useful : hence, commonly, we all thus ignore, select and emphasise. The Second Standard rends this veil of ignorance. It shows that the spiritual basis of experience and consciousness of which experiences are modes are not two, but one. In other words, consciousness or *Cit* itself is the spiritual basis of experience. If therefore that basis be continuous we must have an immediate feeling or intuition of it. That feeling or intuition may be, for practical reasons, obscured in our ordinary mental life, but it can never be altogether effaced, since

[1] See *Reality* and *Mind*. [2] *Ibid*.

the very essence of the life of experience is consciousness. Particular experiences may cast their "reflections" on *Puruṣa* (or *Cit*), just as fleeting clouds may cast their shadows on the surface of a lake; but as in the one case, so in the other, the "reflections," though themselves varied, discrete and fleeting, do not make that which supports or reflects them (*i.e.*, *Cit*) itself so. *Puruṣa* indeed owns those reflections, and they *appear* also as his own; but really he abides undiminished and unconditioned, while they come and go. It is the recognition of this felt or psychological continuity over and above the two other forms of continuity which makes *Sāṃkhya-yoga* a standard of closer approximation than *Nyāya-Vaiśeṣika*. But even this view is, as we have seen in the preceding sections circumscribed by pragmatic considerations. The continuity of the Spirit is still limited, firstly, by the fact that the number is plural, and secondly, by the fact that there is maintained a material or objective Principle of experience independent of Consciousness, which is *Prakṛti*. According to our nomenclature, therefore, the Sāṃkhyan *Puruṣa* like the Vaiśeṣika *Ātman* is still a Fact-section, a Pragmatic Fact.

The Fact is not reached till we come to the Vedāntic idea *Brahman* —the Immense and Whole in which everything is grounded and out of which everything is evolved. And what is this Immense, this Whole ? It is Experience when we take it without ignorance, and therefore, without any limitations or reservations. It is the recognition of what we are, and can never cease to be, except through ignorance or veiling of our complete Being.[1] It is certainly alogical being, the uncircumscribed intuition of life; but at the first effort of analysis, it presents two aspects to our thought *viz.*, a quiescent or static Being-aspect and a stressing or dynamic Becoming-aspect: the aspect of *Cit* or Consciousness as the ground and manifester, and the aspect of *Śākti* or Power of Consciousness to ignore, veil, circumscribe and variously evolve itself. In the Śākta view, the former is *Śiva* and the latter is *Śakti*, and they are in reality one, or rather, the Fact which they compose is an alogical Whole which in its perfectness is not expressible in terms of any logical category. This Whole is the perfection, "limit" and basis of all our continua, Time, Space, Ether, and so forth. And whatever may be said of Time, Space, etc., this alogical Whole is no *theory*; it is the Fact.

---

[1] See "Approaches to Truth" and "Patent Wonder" where the Doctrine of Fact is elaborated.

The well-known *Eko'haṃ bahu syāṃ prarāyeya* which describes the creative ideation of *Brahman*, clearly involves this idea of the Power of Consciousness or Consciousness as Power to evolve as the infinitely varied world of experience. The fundamental condition of undefined, uncircumscribed and therefore, alogical Being-experience is one of wonder[1] and almost one of awe.[2] In the Ṛg-veda itself the Fact is spoken of in many places as *Aditi* (lit. that which is not segmented; therefore, the Entire, the Whole). She is the mother of the gods, and particularly of *Dyauh* and *Pṛthivi* (loosely translated as Heaven and Earth). As *Aditi* means the Entire, the Whole, so *Diti* means the section, the part. In the Ṛg-veda itself we have unmistakeable evidence (as we shall see) to show that in the intuition of the Vedic seers *Aditi* was no other than what we have known as the Fact, so that *Diti*, her opposite, is the Fact-section. The former is the Fact accepted and manifested; the latter is the Fact ignored and veiled.

*Aditi*, therefore, is the vedic equivalent of what we have so long been speaking of as the continuum in the limit of Perfect Continuum. In Chāndogya-Brāhmaṇa it is *Ākāśa*, *jyāyān* and *parāyaṇam*. In many of the Upaniṣads it appears as *Brahman* or *Ātman*; sometimes as *Prāṇa*. In the Ṛg-veda itself, Indra, Varuṇa, Soma, Agni, Viśvakarmā, etc., are apparently dealt with as separate Devatās, but looking narrowly into the matter one cannot fail to perceive that beneath all this appearance of multiplicity, there runs not only a connecting thread of harmony and kinship, but one of unity. In other words, viewed from the deeper standpoint, the vedic gods certainly present the aspect of a unitary system. Indra, Soma, Agni and the rest each, in the ultimate sense, means the Perfect Continuum which is also Perfect Experience. It is not fair to say that such meaning or such metaphysics can possibly be *read* into the Vedas by us (and were in fact read into them by Sāyana and other commentators in many places), but that probably the vedic seers themselves had little or no suspicion of that meaning or that metaphysics; and that their minds had hardly yet been elevated above the level of natural animism, spiritism, etc., which represents the infancy of the human mind in every age and country.

---

[1] Kathopaniṣad and Gītā (Āścaryavat paśyati kaścidenam, etc).

[2] Bṛhadāraṇyaka, where the experience of unity or singleness is spoken of *as if* it were an experience of fear. The idea is—the Primordial One multiplies itself because it seems as if it were afraid of its own singleness.

To the penetrating and discerning eye, the vedic literature offers three stages or planes of interpretation, and these planes of understanding and interpretation were, as we shall see in another volume of the present Series, not foreign to the minds of the vedic Ṛṣis. In other words, there is ample internal evidence in the vedic literature itself to warrant the hypothesis that such lines of interpretation, instead of being later interpolations, were actually known and pursued by those who were first responsible for the vedic hymns. It is true that in the *Saṃhitā* portion of the Vedas, these lines are not clearly indicated, and that for a clear differentiation of these lines one must look into such Upaniṣads as the *Bṛhadāraṇyaka*, *Chāndogya*, etc., which mark the natural disengagement of thought from the ritualistic side of the vedas (*Karmakāṇda*), and its rise to the philosophy of life and its values and their realisation (*Jñānakānda*). But though not very clearly set forth, these lines or planes are unmistakeably given in the Vedas—as progressively higher standpoints of understanding, realising, and representing the subject-matter. These standpoints which as we have said, are definitely adopted in the Upaniṣads (in such matters as the *Udgītha*, *Yajña*, etc.,) appear also to be adopted, though not quite so explicitly, in the *Saṃhitā* portion of the Vedas, in the understanding and representation of such matters as the nature of Indra, Aditi, Soma, Agni, Yajña, etc. The standpoints are: *Ādhyātmika*, *Ādhideivika* and *Ādhibhautika*. The first interprets in terms of Experience or Consciousness; the second interprets in terms of forms of Consciousness-Power (*Cit-Śakti*) objectively treated; the third interprets in terms of objective things in which *Cit* is apparently veiled. The first is psychological; the second is psycho-physical; and the last is physical. The first gives us *Caitanya:* the second a *Devatā;* the third what appears to us a *jada.*

Now, Aditi, Indra, Agni, Soma, etc., have all been thought of and represented on these three lines. Aditi, for example, is according to the first standpoint, Perfect and seamless Experience which we have called the Fact. There is intrinsic evidence in the Vedas themselves to show that Aditi was actually so thought of by the Ṛṣis.[1] According to the second standpoint, she is the primordial manifestation of *Cit-Śakti* as Mother-Power in whose womb all forms of *Cit-Śakti* (called Devatās) are born.[2] In the evolution of the world, the manifestation of the forms

---

[1] For a full discussion of the subject see Professor P. N. Mukhyopādhyāya's Lectures on Veda and Vijñāna (in Bengali).

[2] The matter is dealt with in *Mahamaya, post.*

of *Cit-Śakti* (*i.e.*, forms of Consciousness working as agents) constitute an hierarchy of genera and species, of which the highest order or *summum genus* is Aditi (the undivided). She is therefore the most generic form of *Cit-Śakti*, as according to Mantra-Śāstra, the mantra *Om* is the most generic form of *śabda*.[1] From the third or physical standpoint, she is a subtle, continuous *plenum* (roughly analogous to Ether) in which the physical universe "lives, moves and has its being". In each case, be it observed, she stands for a continuum: as meaning that which is not divided, she represents the idea of continuity in each case. In each case again she presents the Mother-aspect. In the first, she is the Mother-Experience or Fact out of which all particularised experiences or Fact-sections are elaborated. In the second, she is the Mother-*Cit-Śakti* or Devatā which represents the original, conscious "vital impetus" which is the Root of all the Varied forms of conscious vital impetuses or urges in the world. Not only *Dyauh* and *Pṛthivī*, but *Indra*, *Agni*, *Vāyu* and the rest are her progeny; each is a special form of Consciousness working as an impetus in the world; if we generalise these specific forms, or take their generic character, we have the original or Mother-form which is *Aditi*. In the third, she is the Mother-stuff (call it Ether or Electricity or Protyle) in which the "atoms" and "elements" of Matter originate as strain-centres or centres of discontinuity.[2]

Not only Aditi, but Indra and the rest have been understood and represented in the Vedas on the three lines before explained. And what is more important and more pertinent to our present purpose is this that each Devatā has been dealt with specifically as well as generically from the three standpoints. Generically treated, each Devatā = Aditi = the Continuum in the limit: the progeny are thus reabsorbed in the Mother-Power; the Fact-sections in the Fact.[3]

These then are the cardinal principles of vedic (or śāstric) interpretation: (*a*) the subject-matter is dealt with according to the three lines or on the three planes before explained; (*b*) each matter is dealt with generically as well as specifically, so that the vedic treatment of it yields a series in the ascending and descending order; and (*c*) the Vedas often take the superior "limit" of the series (*caramotkarṣa* or *paramotkarṣa*), and thus reduce the specifically different matters (such as Indra, Agni,

---

[1] See *The Garland of Letters*.

[2] See the section *Matter*.

[3] See *The Serpent Power* for the Tāntric *Bhūta-Śuddhi*.

etc.) to fundamental identity. If, therefore, in our vedic (or śāstric) studies we lose these clues, we shall soon find ourselves lost (as many orientalists have been) in a jungle where there is no track leading to a system; and which abounds with dangerous pitfalls of hopelessly obscure paradoxes, difficult tangles and flagrant contradictions. In Ṛg-veda, X, 72, for example, we have the genesis of the Devatās. In that *Sūkta*, we have the following paradox: Prajāpati Dakṣa is born of Aditi and Aditi is born of Prajāpati Dakṣa. Aditi is thus the mother as well as the daughter of Prajāpāti. What can this mean ? Ṛg. I. 69. 1. (*Pariprajātah*, etc.), for example again, says that Agni, though he is the son of the Devas, is also their father. What is this ? Ṛg. I. 95. 4. also speaks of Agni in a similar strain : Agni, though son he be, has given birth to his mothers.[1] And there are similar paradoxes regarding Indra and the rest. The Ṛṣis used to record their experiences in a species of shorthand which we cannot hope to be able to decipher unless we carefully follow the clues above explained. We need not here attempt an explanation of these and many other paradoxes,[2] but may simply observe this that Aditi who is represented as the mother of the Devas cannot obviously be taken in the same sense as Aditi who is the daughter. So about Agni, Indra and the rest. In the light of the principles before explained, it will be readily perceived that Aditi, Agni, etc., are not conceived *rigidly* in the Vedas, but that each constitutes a series with a superior and an inferior limit spread over the three planes referred to before. Thus reviewed Aditi as Mother=Caramā or Paramā Aditi or Aditi (Continuum) in the superior limit=Indra=Agni taken in the superior limit. In the superior limit all specific or divergent manifestations (whether as Caitanya, or as Devata or as Bhūta) converge and meet in fundamental, undivided unity which is the Fact. Aditi as daughter is obviously a lower continuum or a continuum in the descending order of the continua-series. Suppose now Aditi as Mother=the Perfect Continuum of Experience, the alogical Fact; Prajāpati=Experience in which the Self has differentiated itself as the Subject and makes an object of that Experience, and wills to evolve that Experience into mutually distinguishable Fact-sections (the stage of the Prajāpati is itself a Fact-section as compared with the Fundamental Given which is alogical); Aditi as daughter=experience evolved and conditioned as Ākāśa (or any other lower continuum) by the

[1] "Vatsah Mātṛī janayata, etc."
[2] See "Veda and Vijñāna."

creative volition of Prajāpati. This is a solution of the paradox from the *ādhyātmika* or psychological standpoint. And it can be justly claimed that this solution is not simply *read* into the Vedas by later commentators or by ourselves.

Similarly, Agni, Indra, Vāyu and others in their ultimate sense stand for the Perfect Continuum. And there can be little doubt that they *were* taken in their ultimate sense (as well as in their relative senses) by the vedic Ṛṣis. In many places, Agni stands for ordinary fire or heat, though with respect to this also many hymns assert that it is universally present, both as latent and as patent.[1] There are many epithets applied to Agni which are quite applicable to what is ordinarily sensed by us as fire or heat. There are other epithets which can be applicable only to something universally existent—latently even in water—which is indestructible[2] and eternal. Some *Ṛks* make it unmeasured;[3] others make it immutable;[4] others again make it great or a continuum.[5] It is true that in some *Ṛks* Agni is described as the son of Force or Energy, *bala*[6] or Śākti; but there are others which clearly identify Agni with *Ātman* or *Brahman*;[7] and there are a few which are understandable only if Agni be regarded as a form of *Cit-Śakti*, the epithets used being *vidvan*[8] *vedhasah*,[9] etc. On the whole, if we carefully study Agni throughout the vedas, the conclusion seems to be irresistible, *viz*., that the vedic Ṛṣis realised Agni on all the three planes explained before and dealt with it generically as well as specifically—that is, as a continua-series with a superior and an inferior limit. Ultimately, Agni like Aditi is treated as the Primary Root and Basis of all Becoming.[10]

The vedic cosmogony starts, as we have seen, with a continuum which is commonly described as a sort of cosmic fluid.[11] Ṛg. X. 3. 8. asks: Where does this Water begin ? Where is its middle ? And where is its end ? Evidently, therefore, it is a boundless *plenum* symbolised as Water which again in later Śāstric works appears as *kāraṇa-salila* (the causal fluid). Ṛg. X. 82. 1. shows that what is first created by *Viśvakarmā* is a continuous cosmic substance not yet finitised into a granular structure. Ṛg. X. 72. 6. definitely, though metaphorically, outlines the process by

---

[1] Ṛg., I. 68. 1; I. 59; I. 95. 4; I. 65. 5, etc.
[2] Ṛg., I. 26. 9.
[3] Ṛg., I. 27. 11.
[4] Ṛg., I. 73. 2.
[5] Ṛg., I. 59; I. 68. 1, etc.
[6] Ṛg., I. 45. 9; I. 26. 10; I. 27. 2.
[7] Ṛg., I. 18. 7.
[8] Ṛg., X. 1. 3.
[9] Ṛg., I. 72, 1, etc.
[10] Ṛg., X. 5. 7.
[11] Ṛg., X. 82. 1; Ṛg., X. 190, etc.

which granules or centres of strain appear in the continuous cosmic stuff. It tells us how the Devatās begin to Dance in the cosmic all-pervasive Water; and how grains or particles (symbolised as dust) are formed by the dance of the gods. This important vedic parable is traceable in some of the other so-called mythologies of the world, and it represents a fundamental law of creative evolution. It shows the birth of centres of stress-and-strain in an otherwise placid and homogeneous cosmic substance; the birth of the "cosmic dust" from the "cosmic fluid". Almost all philosophic systems and almost all physical theoires which have ever ventured into metaphysics have had to deal with this fundamental riddle, *viz.*, how discontinuities first appear in the midst of continuity, heterogeneity evolves out of homogeneity. Modern Physics too is faced with this riddle. If, for instance, we take the Ether of Physical Science as the approximate equivalent on the physical plane of what is spoken of in the vedic parable as the Mother Fluid, then physicists are called upon, supposing they care to go to the very root of the matter, to explain how the Prime Atoms or Electrons or Centres of Intrinsic strain appear in a continuous Ether. And there appears to be a fundamental truth in the hypothesis of Lord Kelvin and others that, if Ether be something akin to a Perfect Fluid, vortex motion cannot be imparted to Ether in different centres except by a miracle, that is to say, by the action of an extra-physical agency.[1] Now, this extra-physical agency is, according to Indian conception, *Cit-Śakti* which, in various forms, appears in the vedas as the Devatās or gods. The dance of the gods, therefore, means the action of the Forms of *Cit-Śakti* upon the primordial and continous cosmic stuff, by which action "dusts" appear meaning discontinuities or centres of strain (gyrostatic or otherwise).

Practically the same truth is expressed in somewhat different terms by the Manu-samhitā which opens with a cosmogony. Here too the primordial cosmic substance is symbolised as *Ap* or water (which is peculiarly apt to express a condition of mobile continuity). In this water the Creator casts His seed.[2]

This of course means two things : (1) fundamental action of *Cit-Śakti* upon the given Datum of cosmic Matter; (2) by that action the cosmic Matter becomes, so to say impregnated, that is, informed with *Cit-Śakti*, instinct with Consciousness-Power. This is quite in consonance with

[1] See *Matter*
[2] *Tāsu Bījamavākṣipat.*

the Vedāntic doctrine that there is no evolution of *Prakṛti* or Cosmic Matter except by and through the action of *Cit* as Power.[1] In the Tantras this is spoken of as the co-operation of *Śiva* as Efficient Cause and *Śakti* as Material Cause in the creation of the world. By the action of *Cit-Śakti* the Mother Stuff (symbolised as *Āpah* or Waters) contains the seed, that is, potency of the Creator, and thus becomes the possibility of evolution as the world. This condition of potentiality or possibility is spoken of as the cosmic Egg or Ovum (*Brahmāṇḍa*). It should be noted in this connection that in the vedas themselves *Agni* is frequently described as being born in the womb of water and also as impregnating water—a symbol which on the physical plane means[2] the presence of *Agni* as Latent Heat in water (and not only in water but in all *Bhūtas—Sarva-bhūteṣu nigūrhah*), and the formation of rain-drops by *Agni* acting as electric corpuscles or Electrons as centres of condensation (a modern scientific truth founded upon experimental evidence and quite well-known to the vedic seers).[3] On a higher plane, however, *Agni* means *Cit-Śakti* and *Ap Māyā-Śakti*, and we have seen how the latter becomes instinct with the former, and how this is essential to creative evolution.

The fact ultimately is experience, and we may observe that this vedic cosmogony seems to be well-grounded in experience as we actually have it. We have direct knowledge of causal efficiency when by a volition we set in motion matter in the motor centres of the brain. We as forms of *Cit-Śakti* do upon the matter in the brain what in the vedic parable the gods are supposed to have done upon the primordial cosmic stuff or Water. As Indra assisted by the Maruts is supposed in another familiar vedic parable to have released the cows shut up in the caves by Pāni,[4] so every Centre of Consciousness (*e.g.*, I) releases by its activity power latent in matter. When again the Manusamhitā speaks of the dichotomous division of the Cosmic Ovum, and says that the upper half becomes *Dyauh* while the lower becomes *Pṛthvī*, and the intervening space *Antarīkṣa*, it draws upon a vedic source. Ṛg., X. 82. 1 tells us how Viśva-karma first creates a continuum in which *Dyāvā-Pṛithivī* are still indistinguishable from each other; then afterwards, they become separate and distinguishable from each other. *Dyāvā-Pṛthivī* are crudely interpreted to mean Heaven and Earth respectively; but there seems to exist enough internal

[1] See Vedānta, particularly the Sūtras, *Ikṣater-nāśabdam*, and *Racanānupapatternānumānam*.

[2] *Tāsu Bījamavākṣipat.*

[3] See "Veda and Vijñāna."

[4] Ṛg., I. 6. 5 and X. 108.

evidence in the vedas themselves to show that they were not so crudely understood by the seers, but that they, like every other matter, were understood in the three planes we have explained before.[1] *Dyāvā-Pṛthivī* is the symbol or short-hand description for any condition of existence which has become polarised, that is, which presents two opposite poles (*e.g.*, the positive and negative poles in Electro-magnetics). The polarised substance may be immense (*mahat*) or small (*aṇu*). For example, when two unit charges of electricity of opposite kind (called corpuscles or electrons in Science, particularly the negative ones) dissociate from each other and create by their stresses a gap between them, we have the truth of the vedic parable about *Dyāvā-Pṛthivī* illustrated on the physical plane. The mutually associated condition of existence is a neutral condition—*Dyauh* and *Pṛthivī* rolled together into one, so to say. There is then no *antarīkṣa* (inter-space) between them. They are indistinguishable: there is no manifested polarity. For polarity to actually manifest itself, each must dissociate itself from the other. And unless poles manifest themselves, there is no manifestation of kinetic energy, and therefore no work done. Hence the dichotomy of *Dyāvā-Pṛthivī* is essential to creative evolution. In the psychological plane, this means the polarity of Subject-Object, *Aham-Idam*, and our experience evolves precisely upon the appearance of this polarity.[2] In the evolution of living beings too appearance of polarity (whether in the shape of sexes or not) seems to be essential. This fundamental fact is symbolised by the parable of *Dyāvā-Pṛthivī*.

The Primary Basis of evolution (*i.e.*, from and upon which evolution starts) is like the Primary Basis of our exeperience, alogical, indefinable, inscrutable. This is variously described in the vedas as *Asat*,[3] *Rātri*,[4] etc. The Manusaṃhitā describes it as *Tamobhūtam*, and gives it such adjectives as *aprajñāta* (unknown), *alakṣaṇa* (indefinable), *apratarkya* (inscrutable, unthinkable). This *tamas*, however, is not darkness; it is a condition of being of which though we may have intuition, we cannot have any thought, any logical judgment. The approximate equivalent of this in our mental life is *suṣupti* or dreamless sleep. Ṛg., X. 72. 3—4 speak of the birth of *Diks* or Directions. This is important as it shows that the Primary Continuum from and out of which evolution proceeds, is an undirected, "scalar" condition of existence—one in which "lines" of force or tendencies to manifestation have not yet appeared. In the

[1] See "Veda and Vijñāna."
[2] See "Approaches to Truth". [3] Ṛg., X. 72. 3-4. [4] Ṛg., X. 190.

Mantra-śāstra, the undirected, massive condition of Power which precedes creative energising in definite directions, is called *Nāda.*[1]

To sum up: The Continuum has been understood in the vedas in what the Chāndogya calls *Parovarīyān* fashion; the result is that we have a series of continua, the superior limit of which is *Cit,* which is in the vedānta the Primary or Absolute Continuum (*Ātman* or *Brahman*); what are pragmatically regarded by us as continua such as Ether, Air, Water and so forth, are only relatively so. It is important to bear in mind the distinction between Primary Aditi and Secondary Aditi, between Secondary Aditi and Tertiary Aditi, and so on. Otherwise the Śāstra will appear, as it has in fact appeared to many, as a jungle in which there is no path.

3

In the preceding long section we have dealt with the meaning of continuity, its presentation in the Śāstra (and particularly in the vedas), and its psychological basis. In the remaining few pages we shall attempt to give only a synopsis of the subject-matter which, as regards some points or aspects, has already been discussed in the preceding pages, and which, as regards other points or aspects, will be discussed in some of the forthcoming volumes. Now, we have seen that we have sufficient warrant for the idea of continuity in our normal experience which is a universe in fact, but is veiled or ignored, and thereby reduced, for pragmatic reasons. The veil makes us take things by their contraries. Thus what is in fact a boundless *plenum* is practically accepted by us as a tiny "fact" of experience, *e.g.*, as a particular sound or colour, a particular feeling or idea. The real "Fact" is supposed by us to be an "abstraction" or a mental construct; while the pragmatic "fact-section" which in reality is abstract is taken as the "Fact". Thus sensation appears to be more real and more original than perception. It is therefore necessary for us to be able to lift the veil in order to have a full and complete view of Experience as it is. This is *Vidyā* which is opposed to *Avidyā* (ignorance). The lifting of the veil, and the consequent realisation of Experience as it is, is the work of *Sādhanā.* Evidence of continuity, though not lacking in ordinary life, is thus supplied by *Yoga.*

In what is called *Kuṇḍalini-Yoga Bhūtaśuddhi*, there is effected a progressive absorption of all limited and discrete forms of experience (*i.e.*, fact-sections) into the Primary Continuum which is *Śiva-Śakti* united

[1] See *The Garland of Letters.*

together. It is the merging of the finite into the Infinite, of the Part into the Whole, of the measurable and thinkable into the Immeasurable and Unthinkable. This is the realisation of *So'ham.* Then again, starting from this, the limited forms of experience are progressively evolved and in the reverse order (as compared with the order of absorption).[1] Yoga establishes the continuity of experience (*a*) as regards extensity, and (*b*) as regards protensity or duration. In *Samādhi* it reveals the *Cidākāśa* which is Cit manifested as extensity. It also shows the continuity of mental life (the nexus between actual presentations and possible presentations or *Saṃskāras*), by lighting up subliminal consciousness. It traces the complete and apparently infinite curve of mental life not only by showing how actual presentations persist in subtle forms when they sink below the threshold of consciousness, but also by tracing the curve out through previous cycles of birth.[2] It therefore shows that there is no void in *Cit*, and interruption in the flow of experience. Further, it is able to show that the life-cycle of the world itself is continuous not only in this sense that it has no absolute beginning and end, but in this also that the cycle of the life-history of the world continually repeats itself, as regards the Types at least, if not as regards their detailed manifestation. This gives us continuity of the World Form, and of the Law of its evolution.

4

In the earlier section *Matter* the physical basis of Continuity has been discussed. There reference was made to the search after the limit of the Continua-series and after that of the Discontinua-series made in Science. Search in one direction has now brought us up to Ether, and in the other, down to the Electron. But as we have seen, neither the scientific Ether nor the Electron can be taken as the limiting position. It is just possible that the Science of to-morrow will push beyond both. But in any case the need of "points" of charge or centres of stress-and-strain, and of a continuous medium (whatever that turns out to be) somehow linking them up, will remain. Particular *forms* of Ethers and Charges may be given up as being not fundamental; but Ether *as* Continuum, and Charge *as* Point of stimulation must abide. All the three standards of Hindu Philosophy recognise this and retain both, though in different forms. (1) The First Standard has *Ākāśa, Kāla* and *Dik* (over and above *Ātmā*) on the continua side, and *Paramāṇus* (as Points of stimulation) on

[1] See *The Serpent Power.*
[2] See *Mahamaya, post.*

the other side. (2) In the Second, *Pradhāna* (*Prakṛti*) and *Mahat* stand on the continua side, while by the action of the Centre-making Principle (*Aśmitā*), *Tanmātras* evolve out of the continua and work them out into discontinuities. (3) In the Third, *Cit* as the Primary Continuum progressively finitises itself by its own Power, and discontinuities appear as the result of this veiling and limiting operation. The Mantra-Śāstra contemplates the attitudes of Power as *Nāda* and as *Bindu*. The Physical Continua—Space, Ether and the rest—evolve out of this self-veiling and self-limiting and self-determining operation of Consciousness as Power. So do Cosmic Mind and Cosmic Life (*i.e.*, *Manas* and *Prāṇa* as universal, pervading all existence as latent or as patent).

As was pointed out under *Matter*, the tendency of modern Science is to treat the one-time constant *mass* of Matter as a function of Energy, so that the physical units of Matter (Atoms, Electrons, etc.), are no longer regarded as absolutely persistent. Continuity of Matter in that sense therefore no longer holds. Matter can be annihilated and also perhaps created. When annihilated it liberates an enormous quantity of stored up and "bound" (one could say, *Kundālākṛti*) energy which is the essence of Matter; it is created when *Śakti* becomes in a given manner "bound" about a nucleus or centre. When again one kind of Matter (Hydrogen) changes into another kind (Helium), we see this transference of Mass into Energy illustrated. The First Standard, it is true, lays down the indestructibility of the *Paramāṇus*, but the Second makes *Prakṛti* alone indestructible into which *Tanmātras* and the rest may be reabsorbed as they are evolved out of her. The Derivatives too are persistent, if we take into consideration their patent as well as latent conditions. In the latent condition, each Derivative becomes assimilated into its immediate Root or Cause. The Third Standard asserts absolute continuity in its *Cit* working as Power (*Śakti*).

5

We may briefly note also continuity in Life. Hindu thought has recognised the continuity of Life not in the crude sense in which Biogenesis holds the view that the germs of life have not been evolved by "non-living" matter, but in the deeper sense (now corroborated by the researches of Sir Jagadīsh Bose) that Life is latent in all being, since it is the one primordial *Cit-Substance* which by its own Power appears as Mind, as Life and as Matter. "*Ekāṃ sad viprā bahudhā vadanti*"—as the Veda says. In fact, the Upaniṣads study the *Prāṇa* in the *Parovarīyān* fashion, noticing different strata. *Prāṇa* may mean "breath"; it may mean "vital air" or "nerve energy"; it may mean *Hiraṇyagarbha* or Cosmic Life and Mind (*i.e.*, the substratum and synthesis of all forms of life and mind in the universe); and finally it means *Brahman* or the Immense itself. The last underlies all existence, since it is and manifests as all existence. So that there is no "non-living" matter—nothing in which there is not life. Hindu thought maintains further (1) continuity of the Types (*Ākṛti*), including the Types of living being. These Types may be, however, either latent or patent in a given age or locality. The Type Homo for example is persistent, though in a particular cycle of world-operations, it might have appeared as patent after certain geological strata had been formed and certain other anthropoid types had appeared. It maintains too (2) that the process of evolution (with reversions and retrogressions) of living beings is an infinite curve line without beginning and without end. This curve is *Saṃsṛti*, and is traced out on the map of infinite Time and Space in accordance with the Law of *Karma*. It maintains also (3) continuity in the life of the world in rhythm (creation and dissolution being compared to exhalation and inhalation of the Divine Mother—diastole and systole of the Cosmic Heart); in heredity; in tradition; and so on.

On the whole we may say this: The world starting from a common Root has, or appears to have, three divergent (and yet parallel) manifestations—as *Artha* (Object), *Pratyaya* (Thought) and *Śabda* (Name). Now, the Hindu position is this that each line is continuous, starting from the Origin and going back to the Origin again.[1]

6

Continuity may be regarded in different forms. Some have been discussed by us in a previous section. We propose another scheme here. In the first place, continuity may be of Substance or of Form, or of both. The substance of a Thing remains but its form varies; or its form remains but substance varies; or both the substance and form remain. Continuity of Substance may be of two kinds: continuity of stuff or Matter, and continuity of Energy. Continuity of Form may also be of two kinds: continuity of Types and continuity of Laws.

7

Now, Stuff or Matter in the universe appears in the four forms: Spirit, Mind, Life, Matter (*Bhūta*). We know that the Highest Standard regards these four as essentially one. Hence the stuff of the world is continuous

[1] See *The Garland of Letters*.

(*a*) as regards essence, and (*b*) as regards evolution and involution (from one to another).[1] In Nature there is no vacuum, no missing links. As regards Energy, it is maintained to be fundamentally *Cit-Śakti*; and though therefore transformation and correlation of the various forms of Energy are allowed, Vedānta is not prepared to circumscribe *Śakti* itself which is immeasurable, so that we cannot say that its sum-total always remains constant. Conservation of Energy in that sense is therefore only approximately and pragmatically true.[2] It follows also that energy which is fundamentally of the same nature operates in different planes—spiritual, vital and physical. It may be there as Static and as Kinetic. Absolutely static form of Energy (the limit of quiescence) is *Cidākāśa* which is *Śiva.* What ordinarily passes for static or potential Energy is really subtle Kinetic Energy. The definition of the former as Energy of Position and that of the latter as Energy of Motion are only pragmatic definitions. Now, operative Energy may be pragmatically analysed with respect to two co-ordinates: Succession, Co-existence. The former again may be variable and conditional or invariable and unconditional. If invariable and unconditional, it makes Causation, or Causal Operation. Power as *Kāla* moves things in succession; Power as *Dik* holds them in their relative positions; Power as Cause produces phenomenon. Whilst the First Standard makes the first two Powers separate entities (*viz.*, *Kalā* and *Dik*) and reduces causation to invariable and unconditional succession of one phenomenon upon another in which the former was non-existent (*Prāgabhāva*), the Highest Standard, as we have seen, makes ultimately *Kāla* = *Dik* = Consciousness as Power; and in both Sāṃkhya and Vedānta, Cause = Effect (each completely considered), as regards substance and energy, the only difference being the configuration or collocation of substance-energy in the latter which is not apparent in the former.[3] In Vedāntic parlance, it is merely the difference of *Nāma*, and we might add, of apparent *Rūpa.*

As regards Formal Continuity we have noticed two modes: the continuity of Types and continuity of Laws. The world is a cycle of operations which completes itself in a time which is technically called *Kalpa*. During the life-time of this cycle, Types and their variations down to mere particulars appear: Types of *Artha*, *Pratyaya* and *Śabda.*

---

[1] See *Reality.*

[2] Hence the stock of energy is not a closed curve; see the account in *Matter.*

[3] See *Causality.*

Now, it is a common position of Hindu thought that the cycle of operations in one *Mahā-Kalpa* repeats itself, at least as regards the Types in another *Mahā-kalpa* (hence it is called *cycle*), and that as a *Pravāha* or flow it is infinitely continuous (*anādi* and *ananta*). The question whether the particulars or details also reappear is a difficult one, and there seems to exist some ground for holding that the world-movement is *spiraline* (which combines upward motion with rotatory motion), instead of being merely rotatory with the result that there is progress in spite of the persistence and repetition of the Typal Forms. Types again may range from the *summum genus* to the *infima species*, in the three fields of *Artha*, *Pratyaya* and *Śabda*. Hence we have orders or Hierarchies. For example, on the cosmic plane we have the hierarchy of *Īśvara*, *Hiraṇyagarbha* and *Virāt*, and in ourselves that of *Prājña*, *Taijasa* and *Viśva*.[1]

We need not refer in particular to Continuity of Laws, and the question whether they are invariable or variable; nor discuss here the epistemological relations of Continuity to other concepts such as Homogeneity, Sameness, Infinity and Uniformity. These relations will be dealt with in "Cit". Here, however, we need only say a few words about certain forms of Continuity which will make its bearings somewhat clearer. In the first place, Continuity may be either absolute (*aikāntika*) or relative (*apekṣika*). The former is one which eliminates or is beyond all difference (*bheda*). *Bheda* may be of three kinds. (1) *Svagata* or intrinsic—as the difference between waves, eddies, etc., in a mass of water; it is that by which one part of a substance is discriminated from another. (2) *Sajātīya* is one by which one individual of a species (*jāti*) is distinguished from another (*e.g.*, the difference between one man and another). (3) *Vijātīya* is one by which objects of different kinds are constituted as such (*e.g.*, man and stone). Now, absolute continuity is free from these three kinds of difference. But this can be either real or pragmatic. It is *real* when difference does not exist at all. It is *pragmatic* when difference, though perhaps existing, is veiled or ignored by us. Real absolute continuity is Pure Consciousness or *Cidākāśa*. Pragmatic continuity which as we have seen, is veiled difference, is instanced by *Deśa* (Space), and *Kāla* (Time). Concretely, there *is* difference between one position and direction of Space and another—between here and there, up and down, and so on. Similarly, there *is* difference between temporal determinations—between past and future, now and then, for example. But abstractly, Space and

[1] See *The Garland of Letters.*

Time are conceived by us as though they were homogeneous, uniform and impartial. Such conceptual Space and Time are the veiled products of perceptual Space and Time. On the other hand, relative continuity admits of difference of one or other of the three kinds. It is therefore unity-in-difference. Thus we speak of a continuous mass of water though waves, etc. on it may constitute real difference. Our mental life is continuous (*i.e.*, like a stream) though the facts are infinitely various. The colours of a rainbow or a spectrum are in this way continuous. Thus also is Space continuous: so Ether; so Time; so Life. Now, this relative continuity may also be real or pragmatic. The former is illustrated by *ghaṭākāśa* (the Space bounded by a jar) and *maṭhākāśa* (the Space bounded by a temple). Here there is real (though not absolute) continuity, but this is veiled on account of certain practical determinations, *viz.*, those constituted by the jar and the temple. Pragmatic relative continuity is one in which real difference is ignored for practical purposes, and objects are thought of as being continuous. *e.g.*, the air we breathe: it is a mixture of different gases; and the particles of different gases have also their interspaces filled by a different substance. All our lower continua are thus pragmatic. What, for example, is the position of *Ākāśa*? From one standpoint, it is pragmatic or veiled continuity, *viz.*, from the absolute standpoint of *Cidākāśa:* there *are* real intrinsic differences in *Ākāśa* (whether as actual or as potential). Similar is the position of the Sāṃkhyan *Prakṛti.* From another standpoint, however, *Ākāśa* is real continuity, *viz.*, with respect to other "continua" which are inferior to it. If we rigidly define "real" as that upon which no "veil" has operated to any extent then, the "Fact" alone is real and all "Fact-sections" (*Ākāśa*, *Kāla* and the rest) are pragmatic. Thus rigidly defined, no *relative* continuity can be real continuity: relative and real become contradictories of each other.

Then, again, continuity may be either statical or dynamical. The former is continuity of Being (*sattā*); the latter is continuity of Becoming (*pariṇati*). Such analysis of Fact into Being and Becoming, Consciousness and Stress, *Śiva* and *Śakti*, is however, pragmatic. Adopting such analysis, Absolute Real Statical Continuity is *Cidākāśa* or *Śiva*; and Absolute Real Dynamical Continuity is *Cit* as Power or *Śakti*. *Cit* as Being and *Cit* as Power-to-become is real and is absolutely continuous. *Cit* is never *minus Śakti*, and *Śakti* is never *minus Cit.* The Power manifests Itself in infinite variety and such manifestation is generally cyclic; but Power *as* Power suffers no change. It is the identical Power to evolve as the varied world-order: Power as such never becomes other than Itself —in this sense the *Devī* is *nityā* and *vayaya.* In the evolution of the 36 Tattvas (see *Śakti and Śākta* and *The Garland of Letters*), Power never really becomes other than the Holder of Power, and never other than Itself. The symbol of *Cinnamastā* (a Form of the *Devī* which shows her cutting off her own head and drinking the hot blood sprouting out of the severed trunk) is a symbol of the creative process, but it is not a symbol of self-destruction which feat even Power Itself must be incapable of achieving.

Identity, Sameness, Homogeneity are modes of the idea of Continuity: they together with the last form one family of categories. We shall not study them here. Each, we may note however, may be classified on the lines of Continuity. In what sense, for example, can Self and the Supreme Self be identified with each other? *Tvam* with *Tat*? It is absolute real (though ordinarily veiled) identity, according to Pure *Advaitism* (the realisation being *So'ham* or *Sā'ham*). It is relative and pragmatic identity according to *Viśiṣṭādvaitism* and the various forms of *Dvaitism.* Man is only the image of God; His part; and so on: there is real difference between Self and Supreme Reality (or Fact) which *persists*, even when the former is without its veil. The Tantra, as a *sādhana* Śāstra, leads to the realisation of *So'ham* or even beyond (*i.e.*, the transcendental, alogical state beyond the polarity of *Tat* and *Tvam*), but in the discipline it provides, there is, to begin with, *practical* recognition of duality.

The Substance-Energy of the cosmic order being fundamentally the same, we cannot have absolutely one set of laws for Matter, another set for Life, and so on; all must be ultimately governed, in so far as they are governed, by one fundamental Law or set of Laws.

8

Another point should be finally noticed:

It is not enough in Philosophy to know continuity; by *Sādhana* we must *realise* it. As realised it is *Amṛtatva*—Blissful Deathlessness. There are Paths progressively leading to *Amṛtatva*—through Science, through Art; through Philosophy; and through *Sādhana*, when we realise *So'ham* or *Sā'ham* (He or She am I).

---

# POWER AS CONSCIOUSNESS
*Cit-śakti*

SIR JOHN WOODROFFE
&
PRAMATHA NĀTHA MUKHOPĀDHYĀYA

# PREFACE

The English reader is recommended to have recourse to the author's other published books for a better understanding of the present volume. Its subject is an exposition of some aspects only of the Indian doctrine of "World as Power" (Śaktivāda), as also a comparison between this and the better known Vedānta system called Māyāvāda. Both systems speak of Māyā, but understand the term differently as explained in the first and following Chapters. Consequences of prime importance follow therefrom.

All the known ancient religions of the world including those of what are called "lower culture" have believed in a universal fund of Power which cannot be defined and circumscribed. All imply a universal, indefinable, all-pervading Power, not necessarily in itself "personal," but of which personality is an expression. So Dr. Carpenter (Comparative Religion, p. 81) speaking of the concept *Orenda* "of the North American Indians" says that it expresses an incalculable Energy manifesting in and as the sun, moon, and stars, waters, plants and animals, and all other objects of nature, breathing in the winds and heard in the thunder. This belief commonly called Animism is a crude form of the doctrine of an *Anima Mundi* held by some of the greatest thinkers. It is the universal background of the doctrine of Power on which ancient faiths, higher or lower, have rested and out of which they have evolved. When all such faiths and conceptions are reduced to a common denominator, we find a doctrine of Cosmic Power itself unmeasured and undefined, but which "measures" out (the root meaning of *Māyā*), or makes finite forms in the formless infinite which together (form and formlessness) constitute one alogical Whole (*Pūrṇa*). That Power was called the *Magna Mater* in the antique West, and in India is named *Māyā* when it finitizes and *Mahāmāyā* when it liberates from the finite. The finite is conditioned Being, and that is the universe or *Samsāra*. *Nirvāṇa* is Being unconditioned. The two are at base one, since the finite beings spring from the infinite and re-enter it, the latter yet remaining unaffected.

The "World as Power" doctrine has grown from simple origins to which expression is given in sexual imagery. It, like all else, has been sublimated by the Vedānta of which as Śrīvidyā it is a form. Sex is here both the symbol and sensuous manifestation of a fundamental dichotomy or diremption evolving in Consciousness and of a fundamental polarity appearing in its Power. It is with the doctrine thus philosophically developed that we deal.

In this exposition of Consciousness-Power (Śaktivāda) reference is made to western philosophy and science. To anticipate criticism it may be said at once that it is not intended by the authors to assert that all the conclusions of such science and philosophy here mentioned were in the mind of the Indian sages. What is affirmed is that much of modern Western Scientific teaching is consonant with and follows logically from the principles laid down in Indian Scriptures dealing with Power or Śakti. These general principles implicitly contain more than the Indian texts explicitly state. Nothing, however, is here said which is not warranted by these texts and general Indian beliefs. Western philosophy and science may therefore be used to illustrate the Indian Principles and their applicability to many problems both ancient and modern. They do so illustrate precisely because the principles implicitly contain the scientific and metaphysical conclusions which are here found in them. This might seem to be too obvious for statement were it not our experience that mention of Western doctrine made by modern exponents of Indian Scriptures, frequently leads to the charge that an attempt has been made to read something into such Scriptures which is not there. On occasions this "something" is to be found expressly stated. In other cases it is the legitimate deduction from first principles which these scriptures do affirm. Whether the Vedānta in this or any other form, or for the matter of that, Western Science, shifting its position from time to time, are in all respects or at all true is another question. This book is written according to Indian practice from the point of view of an adherent of the system of the World as Power. Its object, whatever be its effect, is not to prove the truth of this or any other system but to give an exposition of Consciousness as conceived in the doctrine of Power (*Śakti*) — a hitherto little known system — and in such exposition to show that it is not a mere fossil in a museum of antique thought, but has practical utility to-day. It offers to Western philosophy a new conception of Consciousness and Mind, and brings to the controversies within the Vedāntic schools a profoundly conceived contribution, in its theory of Power and in its doctrine of the unity of conditioned and unconditioned Being, of the state of worldly experience which is *Samsāra* and of that superworldly experience which is *Mokṣa*.

*Oxford* J. W.
20*th April*, 1929 P. N. M.

# INTRODUCTION

As later and further explained, the Universe of Experience is said to be analysable into five aspects, namely, Being,[1] Consciousness,[2] Bliss,[3] Name[4] and Form.[5] These are called the Five Predicables.[6] For any object *is*, is *known*, is *pleasant* to some experiencer or another, in some relation or another, and has a *Name* and a *Form* or a defining set of qualities. Form is the defined object denoted by Name which is the idea of it expressed in word[7] of which the thing spoken of is the meaning.[8]

Of these five Predicables the first three are common to all object experiences. The last two terms, Name and Form, differ from object to object; the Name and Form of one are not those of another.

All five Predicables taken together stand for the Reducible Real or World-Order,[9] that is, Being-Consciousness-Bliss appearing as Name and Form, or the psycho-physical Universe of limited Selves. The Universe as the psycho-physical is the Reducible Real because it derives from, and on dissolution is resolved into, the Irreducible Real as God. The Universe is thus imaged as the super-imposition of Name and Form on the basis of Being-Consciousness-Bliss. In the words of one of the Tantras the Lord paints the World-Picture on this basis with the "Brush" which is His Will and with which He as the great Artist, the Poet or Maker, expresses Himself to be well pleased. If we abstract Name and Form, the three first Predicables, or Being-Consciousness-Bliss, stand for the Irreducible Real[10] whether as the thinkable Supreme Self or God,[11] or as the alogical Godhead.[12] The Irreducible Real as Power to evolve as the

---

[1] Sat.

[2] Cit, Samvid for which however no English term is an equivalent.

[3] Ānanda. These three terms make the compound Sachchidānanda.

[4] Nāma. [5] Rūpa.

[6] Asti, Bhāti, Priyam, Nāma, Rūpa.

[7] Śabda. See "The Garland of Letters".

[8] Artha. See *Ibid.* [9] Viśvarūpa-Brahman.

[10] Brahman-Svarūpa. It is said;
Asti, Bhāti, priyam, rūpam, nāma, chetyangsha panchakam.
Ādyam trayam brahmarūpam, jagadrūpam, tato dvayam.

[11] Sakala-Śiva, Sakriya-Śiva, Śiva-Śakti Tattvas, Īśvara or Īśvarī, Saguṇa or Apara-Brahman, the logical Paramātmā.

[12] Paramaśiva Tattvātīta, Niṣkala Śiva, Niṣkriya Śiva, or Nirguṇa or Para-Brahman, the alogical Paramātmā.

Reducible Real and involve it again (Itself remaining unreduced) is the Reality-Whole or *Pūrṇa*. It has an infinity of aspects of which 'irreducible' and 'reducible' are two, logically appreciated.

Being is Consciousness and Consciousness is Bliss. The Selves[1] are pragmatically limited Being-Consciousness-Bliss. The Irreducible Real is Being-Consciousness-Bliss unlimited by Name and Form whether as Supreme Self or as alogical Godhead, and is thus free of all limitations which characterise its manifestation, the Reducible Real. "Unlimited by Name and Form" may mean, as later explained, two things: (1) *excluding* Name and Form; and (2) *exceeding* Name and Form. The *Pūrṇa* or Reality-Whole, logically appreciated, involves three aspects: (*a*) a universe limited by Name and Form: (*b*) Being-Consciousness-Bliss unlimited by Name and Form; and of this latter we have two forms in the two senses of the term "unlimited".

There is no non-being as such. By 'nothing' is meant nothing, that is, no psycho-physical name and form. Such appearances or concrete forms may be thought away, but not being as such. Is-ness is never negatived. 'Nothing' then means only lack of form and name. These vary, but Being is everywhere and is always given, either as the alogical Real or God-head or as God, who is the highest logical construction placed upon the alogical, or as the limited beings or selves. Being is then both experience itself and the unalienable basis of all modes of experience.

The term being, however, does not tell us what Being is, which is learnt from introspection. Man then becomes aware that he not only *is* but that *to be* is to be *conscious*, and function as such. For his being is indistinguishable from his consciousness. All forms or modes of consciousness may be thought away, but not consciousness as such, for it is the changeless basis of such modes.

What is called 'subconsciousness' or 'unconsciousness' does not imply Being functioning apart from Consciousness as such, but (as later explained) apart from certain degrees and tones of consciousness which are pragmatically accepted as constituting consciousness.

There is no equivalent in English or any other language for the Sanskrit term *Cit*. The nearest rendering of "Cit" is consciousness because it is revealed as the empirical conscious self. But the term is not altogether apt, because consciousness in the English sense of the term

[1] Jīvātmā or Puruṣa.

requires an 'I', and a 'This', which is other than the self which has experience of it. Consciousness as God or Supreme Self is a consciousness of the unity of 'I' and 'This', and alogical consciousness or God-head being above all dualities, cannot be called a self. There is, however, no more appropriate term available. If we abstract from empirical consciousness all limitations, we have pure, that is, unlimited consciousness or *Cit*. As these limitations arise from the association of consciousness with mind and matter, we can say that pure consciousness is that which is dissociated from mind and matter and is mindless,[1] bodiless,[2] consciousness. Empirical consciousness is that which is associated with a psycho-physical body and the consciousness of the individual center or finite self.[3]

This (*i.e.*, Pure Consciousness dissociated from Name and Form) is the special sense in which the term *Cit* is sometimes used in Vedanta. But *Cit* is also the Reality-Whole or *Pūrṇa*.[4] In this extended sense It is Consciousness functioning as Perfect Power *to be* and *become* a Universe of Name and Form. In this sense the World is *Cit* in essence, in power and in manifestation.

Bliss is implied in Being-Consciouness. Wholeness and fullness as perfect Being-Consciousness, is perfect Bliss. As Śruti says[5] "the great and limitless is bliss not littleness and limitation." Pleasure and pain indicate expansion and diminution of being respectively. Bliss proceeds from the expansion of conscious life towards freedom and fullness of being. The ultimate real is then that which cannot be conceived as other than Being-Consciousness-Bliss, or fullness be conceived as other than Being-Consciousness-Bliss. or fullness of being which is the essence of all the existents which have the attributes of happiness and unhappiness according as, and to the degree that, essential Bliss[6] is revealed or veiled.

To the concept of Being-Consciousness-Bliss, we must add that of Power (*Śakti*). The former is Power-holder. Power and Power-holder are never separate from one another. Could *Śiva* as motionless Being be bereft of His Power, he would be but a corpse (*Śava*). The two (Power-holder and Power) are as such one, though the transformations of Power are many. We speak of transformation or evolution, because Power and its holder is held to be both efficient and material cause of

---

[1] Amanah. Unmanī Bhāva. [2] Videha. [3] Jīvātma, Puruṣa.

[4] See *post*. [5] Chhāndogya-Up., VII, 23.

[6] The Sanskrit term is "Ānanda," which like "Cit" is untranslatable. See *post*, however, for explanation.

the world. Power as the material cause is thus transformed in, and as, its effects, though the cause remains what it was. The cause contains its effect, and the latter is the cause modified as effect. The rule is pragmatically different in the evolved universe, where it is said "milk when it becomes curd ceases to be milk".

It has been said that, strictly speaking, creation ((*ex nihilo*) is not taught by any system of Hinduism, each system presupposing some "potential matter" out of which the world is evolved in recurring cycles, from eternity to eternity, and that the essence of that "prime matter" and its dependence on spirit or spirits at whose call or presence it evolves, varies according to the different systems. By "potential matter" in this statement must be understood that which in itself is not matter, prime or otherwise, but is the cause of the becoming, amongst other things, of the material world. That cause is the Power of Consciousness which, as the individual Centre, establishes a dichotomy of self and not-self in itself, as the Consciousness-Whole.

Moreover there is no first creation. The Universes come and go eternally. The present Universe, therefore, is not something entirely new, for it is the outcome of past worlds and their activities or *karma*. Not only "conscious" entities but *all* individual centres in the world have their *Karma* which is here conceived as essentially Play[1] out of Joy[2]—therefore, essentially free action, though pragmatically restricted.

Man in his essence is the Ātman or Being-Consciousness-Bliss, and in and as his bodies, he is a Power of the Ātman or Brahman. There is thus no impassable gulf between Divinity and Man, for he is already divine in his essence even though he may not have realised it. This Essence as Power works through mind and matter its forms, until that Supreme Experience which is the formless[3] Essence is reached.

Reality may be regarded from three aspects. The Universe is the reducible real since it derives from, and on dissolution is resolved into, the Irreducible Real as God. God or the Lord (Īśvara) or Divine Mother (Īśvari) as the Hindus call Him and Her, is the reducible Real regarded as in relation to the Universe of which it is the Creator, Sustainer and Ruler. It is the Irreducible Real considered as Being-Consciousness-Bliss-Power, and reducible real considered with respect to its own self-limiting Forms (Time, Space, Causality) by which it manifests itself as the Creator,

[1] Līla. [2] Ānanda.
[3] That is, beyond all limitations.

Sustainer and Ruler of the Universe. That aspect of the Irreducible Real in which it is considered as It is in Itself, beyond its aspect as in relation to the Universe, is the alogical Godhead.[1]

The terms "Absolute" and "Transcendental" also should be clearly defined; *the distinction between Māyā-vāda and Śakti-vāda hinges on these definitions.*

Both "Absolute" and "Transcendental" mean "beyond relation". But the term "beyond" may be used in two senses: (*a*) exceeding or wider than relation; (*b*) having no relation at all. The first does not deny or exclude relation, but says that the Absolute, though involving all relations within Itself, is not their sum-total; is not exhausted by them; has Being transcending them. The latter denies every trace of relation to the Absolute; and says that the Absolute must have no intrinsic or extrinsic relation; that relation, therefore, has no place in the Being of the Absolute.

Śakti-vāda adopts the first view, Māyā-vāda the second. From the first point of view, the Absolute is relationless Being *as well as* Manifestation as an infinity of relations. This is the true and complete Alogical Whole. Inasmuch as the Absolute exceeds all relation and thought, we cannot say that It is the Cause; though It is the Root of Creation; and so forth; but inasmuch also as It does involve relation and thought, we can say that It is the First Cause; that there has been a real creation, and so forth.

The Māyāvāda view by negating all relation from the reality of *Brahman* negates from its transcendent standpoint the reality of causation, creation, and so forth.

"Beyond" may, therefore, mean (1) "exceeding," "fuller than", "not exhausted by"; or (2) excluding, negating, expunging. By diagrams:

(1) 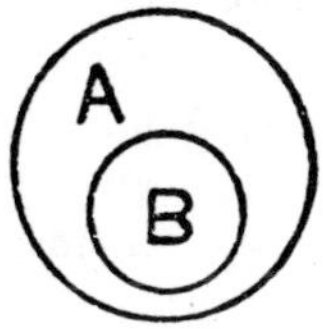


A is beyond B,
*i.e., exceeds* B.

(2) 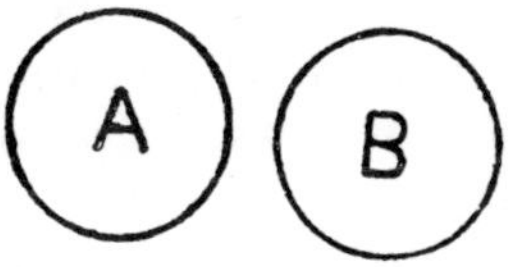


A is beyond B, *i.e.*,
*excludes* and is quite outside B.

In Śakti-vāda, the Supreme Reality is fuller than any definition (limitation) which may be proposed. It is even beyond duality and

[1] Both aspects (as also many others) combined give the *Pūrṇa* (Whole). See *post.*

non-duality. It is thus the Experience-Whole, the Alogical. The Māyā-vāda Pure *Brahman* is an *aspect* of it: but it is not the Whole (*Pūrṇa*).

The expression "wider than relation" may be thus illustrated. I am related in one way to my wife; in another way to my children; in yet another way to my brothers, friends, and so on. I am not fully expressed by any one of these relations, nor even by their aggregate; for, as a member of an infinite Stress-system I bear an infinity of relations. Pragmatically, most of these are ignored and it is thought that I am expressed by a certain set of relations which distinguish me from another person who has his own "set". But *Brahman* as Absolute can have no such "set". It is expressed, but not fully expressed, even by the infinite set of relations which the Cosmos is, because relations, finite and infinite, imply a logical, and therefore, segmenting and defining, thought: but *Brahman* as Absolute-Experience-Whole = the Alogical.

Since *Brahman* = Experience-Whole = *Cit* as Power-to-Be-and-Become, it is nothing like the unknown and unknowable being ("Thing-in-Itself") of Western Sceptics and Agnostics.

In all Indian systems the World is real in the sense that it has objective existence for, and is not a projection of, the individual mind. In all such systems Mind and Matter co-exist. And this is so even in that form of *Ekajīva-Vāda* which holds that *Brahman* by Its own veiling and limiting Power makes one Primary Self of Itself, and that all other selves are but reflexes of the Primary Self, having as reflexes no existence apart from that of the Primary one. The world of matter is not a projection of an individual mind, but its reality is co-ordinate with that of the individual mind, both being derived from the Self-veiling and Self-limiting operation of *Brahman* appearing as the one *Jīva* or Primary Self. *Brahman* in appearing as Primary Self also appears as its (logical) correlate or Pole—the Not-Self; and this Not-Self is the Root-Matter on which the Primary Self is reflected as multiple selves, and their varied relations. Matter, in this fundamental sense, is not, therefore the product of the First or Primary Individual (Self); it is with Self the co-effect (logically speaking) of a common fundamental activity which is the veiling and limiting action of the Supreme Being.

The version commonly given of Ekajīva-Vāda, namely that the one Primary Self is I, and that You, He and the rest, and the world of objects are its projection—is loose and unpsychological. In the first place, "I" cannot be there (logically conceiving) without its Correlate or Pole—the

"Not-I," so that, by the very act by which "I" is evolved from *Brahman*, its Correlate is also evolved and this Correlate is Root-Matter. In the second place, projection, reflection, and so forth presuppose not only the projecting or reflecting Being (that which projects or reflects), but also something on which the projection or reflection is cast. Projection out of nothing and projection into nothing will give only nothing.

Where then there is Matter there is Mind. Where there is no Matter (not necessarily gross) there is no Mind. One is meaningless without the other. Each is every whit as real as the other. But there is no Indian system which is Realist in the sense that it holds that Matter as experienced by man exists when there is no Mind of man to perceive it. Such a state is inconceivable. He who alleges it himself supplies the perceiving Mind. In the First Standard[1] Mind[2] and the so-called "Atoms"[3] of Matter are separate, distinct and independent Reals.[4] Matter does not derive from Mind nor the latter from the former. In the Second Standard[5] both Matter and Mind are equally real but derive from a common source, the Psycho-physical Potential[6] which, as such, is neither. 'Psychic' here means Mind as distinct from Consciousness in the special sense of *Cit*. This Psycho-physical Potential is a Real,[7] independent of Consciousness which is the other Real. In the Third Standard as non-dual Vedānta, the position is the same, except that the Psycho-physical Potential is not an independent Real but is the Power of the One Supreme Real as God. The world is then Real in the sense that it has true objective Reality for the individual Experiencers for the duration of their experience of it. No one denies this.

The next question is the problem of Monism. If ultimate Reality be One, how can it be the cause of and become the Universe? It is said that Irreducible Reality is of dual aspect, namely, as it is in relation to the World as Īśvara the Lord or God, and as it is in Itself beyond such relation which we may call Godhead or *Brahman*. According to *Māyāvāda*, *Īśvara* is *Brahman*, for *Īśvara* is *Brahman* as seen throuth the veil of *Māyā*,[8] that is, by the Psycho-physical Experiencer. But *Brahman* is not *Īśvara*, because *Brahman* is the absolute alogical Real, that is, Reality, not as conceived by Mind, but as it is in itself beyond (in the sense that it is exclusive of) all relations. The notion of God as the Supreme Self is the highest concept

[1] Nyāya-Vaiseṣika. [2] Manas. [3] Paramāṇu.
[4] Dravya. [5] Sāngkya-yoga. [6] Prakṛti.
[7] In Sāngkhya, one, in Śaiva darśana, many.
[8] Though this veil be of a refined "stuff" (Vimala-Sattva-guṇa).

imposed on the Alogical which, as it is in itself, is not a Self either supreme or limited. The Absolute as such is not a Cause. There is, transcendentally speaking, no creation, no Universe. The Absolute is and nothing happens. It is only pragmatically a Cause. There is from this aspect no *nexus* between Brahman as God-head and the World. In the logical order there is.

What then is the Universe? It is said by some to be an "illusion". But this is an inapt term. For to whom is it an "illusion"? Not to the Psycho-physical Experiencer to whom it is admittedly real. Nor is it an illusion for the Experience-Whole. It is only by the importation of the logical notion of a Self to whom an object is real or unreal that we can speak of illusion. But there is in this state of Liberation no Self.[1] More correctly we say that the World is *Māyā*. But what is Māyā in Māyāvāda? It is not real for it is neither Supreme Brahman nor an independent Real. Nor is it altogether unreal for in the logical order it is real. It is neither Brahman nor different from it as an independent reality. It is unexplainable.[2] For this reason some of the scholastics of this System call it the doctrine of the Inscrutable.[3]

In the doctrine of Power (Śaktivāda), Māyā is the Divine Mother Power or *Māhāmāyā*. The two aspects of Reality as *Brahman* and *Īśvara* are each accepted, as real. The Lord is real but that which we call 'Lord' is more than Lord, for the Real is not adequately defined in terms only of its relations to the Universe. In this sense it is alogical, that is "beyond Mind and Speech". As the one ultimate Reality is both *Īśvara* and, *Brahman*, in one aspect it is the Cause and in the other it is not. But it is one and the same Reality which is both as *Śiva-Śakti*. As these are real, so is their appearance, the Universe. For the Universe is *Śiva-Śakti*. It is their appearance. When we say it is their appearance, we imply that there has been a real becoming issuing from them as Power. Reality has two aspects. First as it is in itself and secondly, as it exists as Universe. At base the *Saṁsāra* or worlds of Birth and Death and *Mokṣa* or State of Liberation are one. For *Śiva-Śakti* are both the Experience-Whole and the Fact which exists therein as the Universe. Reality is a concrete unity in duality and duality in unity. In practice the One is realised in and as the Many and the Many as the One. So in the Śakta wine-ritual,

[1] As the Buddhists said — in Nirvāṇa even the knowledge that the phenomena have ceased to appear and are therefore unreal is not to be found. Das Gupta, Hist. Phil. 142.

[2] Anirvacanīya.

[3] Anirvacanīya — khyāti-vāda.

the worshipper conceives himself to be *Śiva-Śakti* as the Divine Mother. It is She who as and in the person of the worshipper, Her manifestation, consumes the wine which is again Herself the "Saviouress in liquid form".[1] It is not only he who as a separate Self does so. This principle is applied to all Man's functionings and is of cardinal importance from a Monistic standpoint, whatever be its abuse in fact.

Real is again used in the sense of eminence. The Supreme Real is that which is for itself and has the reason for its being in itself. The Real as God is the perfect and changeless. The Universe is dependent on the *Ens Realissimum,* for it proceeds from it and is imperfect as limited and changeful, and in a sense it is that which does not endure, and in this sense is called 'unreal'. Though however, the Universe comes and goes, it does so eternally. The Supreme cause is eternally creative. The Real is then both infinite Changeless Being as also unbeginning and unending process as the Becoming. In this system the Real both is and becomes. And the essence of is-ness is Activity or Power. It yet becomes without derogation from its own changelessness, as it were a Fountain of Life which pours itself forth incessantly from an infinite and inexhaustible source. Both the infinite and finite are real.

Real is again used in the sense of interest and value and of the 'worth while'. In this sense the worshipper prays to be led from Unreality to Reality, but this does not mean that the World is unreal in itself, but that it is not the supreme worth for him.

In whatever sense then the term Real is used, the Universe is not an illusion. All is real, for as Upaniṣad says "All this Universe is verily Brahman."[2] The Scriptural Text says "All". It does not say "This, but not that". The whole is an alogical concrete Reality which is Unity in Duality and Duality in Unity. The doctrine does not lose hold of either the One or the Many, and for this reason the Lord Śiva says in the Kulārṇava Tantra "There are some who seek dualism and some non-dualism but my doctrine is beyond both." "That is, it takes account of and reconciles both Dualism and Non-dualism. The natural and spiritual are one.

Reality is no mere abstraction of the intellect making jettison of all that is concrete and varied. It is the Experience-Whole whose 'object' is Itself as such Whole. It is also Partial Experience within that Whole.

[1] Tārā Dravamayī.
[2] Sarvam Khalvidam Brahma.

This union of Whole and Part is alogical, but not unknowable, for their unity is a fact of actual experience just as we have the unity of Power to Be and Power to Become, of the Conscious and Unconscious, of Mind and Body, of freedom and determination, and of other qualities of Man's experiencing.

What the term *Cit* means is expressed neither fully and adequately, nor univocally, by the English word "Consciousness".[1] Barring the case of the materialist who holds that consciousness is a "by-product" of matter specially organised as brain-substance, Western Idealists, Realists and Pragmatists are not agreed among themselves either as to the nature or as to the function of consciousness. They conceive it differently. None of these conceptions approach the Vedānta concept of *Cit* as the Supreme and Perfect Reality-Power, as regards the depth and amplitude of its import. In fact, in the history of Western Thought, Consciousness as such has been so far permitted to appear in a minor role even in Idealism. The chief part has been assigned to Reason or Thought, to Will, to Imagination, and as has recently been the more usual practice, to Experience. Commonly in these forms of Idealism, Consciousness is not the substance of Reality — which may be a Cosmic Idea, Reason, Will, and so forth. Commonly too, Consciousness is not a *proprium*, or even an inseparable accident, of Reality. The Cosmic Idea or Will may thus be with consciousness or without it; it may evolve into consciousness only in some places or positions and remain unconscious in others.

Recently there has been a tendency in Idealism to make Experience the basis of Reality instead of a specific aspect of it such as Reason, Will or Imagination. This bases Reality upon "Fact" instead of a "section" and abstraction of Fact. But such approximation to the Vedantic position has meant but little gain to Consciousness which is still commonly taken to be a separable accident of Experience; Experience can be, and often is, it is supposed, sub-conscious and even unconscious.

At the back of this supposition is the taking of Consciousness in a restricted sense making it either abstract "awareness," or else, coincident with normal, "fully awake" "conscious" experience only: the former

[1] Sometimes the substitute is "Intelligence" which is even more inappropriate. *Cf.* Dr. Carpenter, "Comparative Religion," pages 60, 157. Cit= "Thought" also "Understanding" and "Intelligence". (p. 158).

See also, R. G. Bhandarkar's "Vaishnavism, Shaivism and minor Religious Systems" (Encyclopaedia of Indo-Āryan Research, Vol. III. part 6), page 78—Cit = "Intelligence".

view showing it as a "torchlight" which makes us aware of the contents of experience; the latter making it the "lighted zone," the cognised contents of experience. In either case, Consciousness is not the equivalent of Experience which is supposed to be the larger fact. The "torch-light" is believed to reveal some or the actual contents of experience, while the rest lie outside the reach of its illumination. In the alternative supposition also, the "lighted up" contents of experience are believed to be a part only of the total content. And Consciousness is thus restricted not merely in individual experience, but also, commonly, in Cosmic Mind and Experience. This latter has been supposed to possess consciousness either as a separable or an inseparable *accident:* but, commonly, it has not been believed that consciousness is the essence and substance of the Cosmic Experience.

There is, however, no warrant for taking Consciousness (*Cit*) in the restricted sense of either a "torch-light" illumination, or as the "illumined zone" of Experience. The first alternative raises four issues: (1) Does the "torch-light" illumine the whole of an individual's experience or only part of it; in other words, does the circle of illumination coincide with that of experience, or is it included in the latter ? (2) Does it illumine individual experience always or only occasionally ? In other words, is individual experience conscious now, and unconscious then ? (3) Does it illumine the whole of cosmic experience or only a part of it ? And, (4) Is Cosmic Experience conscious now and unconscious then ? Now, taking these four issues together, they may be decided on the principles of the Doctrine in this way: Consciousness as the Illumination[1] illumines and never fails to illumine the whole of Experience, though in the case of individual Centres, the fact of experience being illumined may be ignored, that is unrecognised, pragmatically, often to a degree which reduces such illumination, for practical purposes, to be non-illumination as the subconsciousness or unconsciousness. Really, however, "subconsciousness" and "unconsciousness" are grades of Consciousness itself— that is, if what has been unrecognised and unaccepted for ordinary practical purposes be recognised and accepted. This Perfect Illumination is the Ether of Consciousness[2] which is unbounded and unrestricted. The total content or Object[3] of Experience is so also; and, while both (the Illumination and the Illumined) are infinite, the former is intuited

[1] Prakāśa. [2] Cidākāśa. [3] Vimarśa.

to be even a greater infinity (if infinities can be compared) than the latter;[1] and this reverses the position commonly taken in non-vedāntic views, eastern or western, that the circle of illumination forms a part only of the circle of experience.

Then, as regards the second alternative — making Consciousness, not the Illumination or awareness only, but concrete, conscious experience with a content — the criticism is this: This concrete experience with an object or content is a condition of Consciousness; but Consciousness has a transcendent condition also, which is immanent in the ordinary conditions; and this transcendent condition of Pure Consciousness or Pure Illumination is not an abstraction. It can be intuited in the ordinary experiences, and realised apart from the determinations of content or object, in *Yoga*. Consciousness, thus, may be with a content or without it;[2] and though, by Rāmānuja amongst others it has been contended that the Iluminator must co-exist with the Illumined as its logical correlate, Consciousness itself is alogical, beyond all antitheses or poles; and yet manifests by its Power all poles and correlations in experience. Pure Consciousness, immanent as the unchanging "ether" in ordinary changing experiences, and realizable as such in *Yoga*, is not therefore the Illuminator as distinguished from the Illumined (which as poles must co-exist); but it is Illumination itself which is its own content. The doctrine thus keeps clear of two unwarranted positions: (1) Experience with a content ("modes, "states" or "determinations" as they are called) is the only real, concrete fact, of which contentless, pure consciousness is an abstraction,[3] and is, therefore, unreal; and (2) Experience as contentless consciousness is the real Fact, upon which, the varied content of experience, that is, world-experience, has been laid as an unreal appearance as that of magic. On the contrary, Pure Consciousness is real, its Power to evolve as a world of varied content and to involve it again is real; and the world of varied content, which is the manifestation of Reality-Power, is also real.

Nor again does the Śākta view regard Consciousness as an "accident," separable or inseparable, of the Reality-Experience. Consciousness is not statical only as the "Ether"[4] but dynamic or stressing; it is not Being only, but it is Becoming also.[5] In fact, the essence of Being is Power and Func-

[1] Antarlīna-vimarśa. [2] Saviśeṣa or Nirviśeṣa.

[3] *i.e.*, Cit is saviśeṣa only; it is never nirviśeṣa cinmātra.

[4] Even this implies the Being-Power of Cit; see *ante*.

[5] *Cf.* Fichte, The Science of Knowledge, Preface p. iv, "The facts of Consciousness are not facts of mere being, but facts of activity." *Cf.* Also Gentile's idea of Being in his Philosophy of the Spirit.

tion to Be. So that Consciousness is the varied world-experience, as also, transcendent, pure Illumination. It is at the same time the Basis, the Evolver and the Content of Experience. This view does not recognise any ultimate duality between Substance and Attribute,[1] between Power and Possessor of Power,[2] between Power as Cause and Power as Effect or Manifestation,[3] however they may in the Logical order be so treated. Hence, if Consciousness as Power evolves as the World-Experience, the three terms involved in the process (*i. e.*, Consciounsness, Power and World-experience) must be ultimately identified with one another. It is dualism to maintain that Consciousness is one thing and its activity or Power is another; that the Power of Consciousness to be (*i. e.*, existential activity) is one thing, its Power to become or evolve is another. It is not possible in this view to regard Consciousness as an "accident" or even as a "proprium" only of something else—of any substance. Consciousness is the Substance,[4] the Power, and the evolutes and involutes[5] of Power. Philosophies, western or eastern, have often reduced it to an "accident," because they have taken it to mean limited, pragmatic consciousness only—that is, what in ordinary parlance passes as "normal consciousness" distinguished from both "sub-conscious" and "unconscious" and because they have taken it in an abstract way to mean "awareness' or "feeling' or "cognition," and not in a concrete way to mean *Reality functioning to be and yet to evolve as experience of a varied content.* Thus, in this view it has been wrongly supposed that feelings, thinkings and willings, which constitute the actual life of experience, are the facts of which consciousness makes us aware in part; and that, whether they be thus revealed and "shewn" or not, they happen, go on and change—in fact, the drama of mental life plays itself whether or not the stage be lighted by consciousnsess.

Limitation of the meaning of *Cit* or *Caitanya* is responsible for a view like, or more or less similar to, the above not only in Dualistic systems, but also in many Idealistic monisms. The *Nyāyā-vaiśeṣika* makes consciousness a separable feature of individual Selves, though in the case of the Lord, it is regarded by it as an inalienable, that is, permanent[6] feature. But it is a feature only, not the Substance. The *Bhatta* School of *Pūrva Mīmāmsā* makes Ātman conscious in one part and unconscious in other, thus anticipating the modern "floating ice-berg" conception of mental life "nine-tenths of which are buried in the depths of sub-consciousness." The

---

[1] Guṇa and Guṇī. [2] Śakti and Śaktimān. [3] Kāraṇa and Kārya.
[4] Padārtha. [5] Vyakta and avyakta products. [6] Nitya.

*Sāṁkhya* System, though it makes *Cit* the essence of *Puruṣa*, makes the psychodynamic Principle evolving "Understanding, ' Mind and so forth, unconscious, so that Experience is an unconscious process lighted up by consciousness. Consciousness, it is true, is there not merely as a lighter or reflector, its witnessing the process—unconscious in itself and casually a "closed curve"—somehow influences it, in this way that, it goes on with reference to the witnessing, and it stops where such reference ceases. And since, in this view, there are many witnesses, the process goes on with reference to other witnesses, though it may stop in respect of some, that is, those who attain liberation.[1] In this view, Consciousness is recognised as an independent Entity (it is no longer a mere property or accident of something); and the "catalytic action" which it exercises on the evolving Psycho-physical dynamic Principle[2] implies its Being-Power, as well as, Power to influence the Becoming of some other Being. This leads a considerable way to the *Śākta* Vedānta position; but it is a halting method in so far as (1) it does not make Consciousness the whole Being and Experience; and (2) it assigns practically the whole realm of dynamism (*i.e.*, evolving power) to a Principle alien to, and independent of, Consciousness, reserving to itself only a vague veiled suggestion of power expressed in its so-called "catalytic action".

Even Idealistic Monisms have sometimes stopped short of the final position here adopted. The attitude of such monisms towards Consciousness has commonly taken four forms: (1) Consciousness as Perfect Knowledge (that is, Knowledge of all general and particulars) is an element of the Supreme Reality which is also the Supreme Power; but it is not the whole of it, the sum and substance of it; so that if the Supreme Reality-Power is represented by a circle, Consciousness forms an aspect, part or element of that circle; it is but one attribute of the Supreme Substance which has an infinity of attributes,[3] and there is nothing to warrant the supposition that this one attribute is the basis and root of all others. Furthermore, Consciousness with an infinitely varied content is an aspect of the Supreme Reality; pure, contentless consciousness is not an actual state of experience either in the Supreme or in the individual realities; it is an abstraction and, therefore, unreal. (2) Another position, whilst

[1] Kaivalya.

[2] Prakṛti.

[3] *Cf.* the doctrine of Spinoza in the West which gives the Substance an infinity of attributes of which we know but two, *viz.*, Thought and Extension. See his Ethics; Proposition XI, read along with Def. VI and Prop. IX.

agreeing with the first as regards all other essential points, makes Pure Consciousness not an abstraction and unreality but the Illumination[1] of the Perfect Being or Lord which aspirants may actually realise as Pure *Cit* and nothing else at a certain stage of their spiritual approach to their final objective, but pushing beyond that stage, they realise that what was pure, featureless[2] illumination before is really the light radiating from a Perfect Being infinitely rich in power and content. Perception of the Light only — apart from the form and features — is, therefore, ontologically speaking, an abstraction, since Perfect Being is not Light[3] only; but psychologically speaking (that is, as an actual, though halting and imperfect, perception by the aspirant of the Supreme Being), it is not an abstraction. The intuition of Pure Light in what is called "non-polar meditation"[4] gives, accordingly, an approximate and subordinate view of Reality, transcending which the aspirant has a truer vision of Reality[5] as the Perfection of power and attributes. The vision of the Pure Ether of Consciousness is thus a stage, and not the goal of realization.

(3) Next comes the position of *Māyā-vāda* which reverses the above order or relationship between what has to be regarded a stage and what the goal of realization, what must be looked upon as Reality and what as an abstraction. Here, the "Pure Light" alone shines when the goal is reached, forms and features, powers and attributes appear but on the way to it; so that *Cit* as pure Light is the Supreme Reality of which "a varied content" is not, indeed, an abstraction, but upon which is laid as an ascription or imposition[6] due to *Māyā* which makes Reality appear otherwise than as it is in itself.[7]

The stress in the first position (1) is laid exclusively upon "infinitely rich power and content" nature of Reality, as it leaves no room for the "Pure Light" either in the scheme of Being (*i.e.*, ontologically), or in the actual experiences of Being (*i.e.*, psychologically). Consciousness is ever with content and never without it: this is the position. The stress in the second position (2) is laid as in the first, but Consciousness as Pure Light is recognised as a subordinate and imperfect (though actual) stage in the realisation of Perfect Being. In the third position (3), the stress is shifted on to what has been unreal in the first and subordinate in the second, so

[1] Jyotih. [2] Without Nāma and Rūpa.
[3] Nirviśeṣa Cinmātra. [4] Nirvikalpa Samādhi.
[5] *Cf.* the conception of the Vaiṣṇava placing the eternal Abode of the Lord (Vaikuntha and Goloka) beyond the Cidākāśa of Vedānta.
[6] Adhyāsa. [7] Vivartta.

that what is the real and ultimate in them (1 and 2), becomes unreal or only pragmatically real[1] in the third. In all these three positions the emphasis is laid now on this and now on that phase or aspect[2] of the Supreme Fact.

Hence (4), it is claimed, that if the Fact is to remain the Fact, no emphasis must be laid upon what is but a section or aspect of it, but it should be laid upon the Whole.[3] Pure Consciousness "without content" and Perfect Consciousness of infinitely rich content, are both logical aspects of the Whole which is alogical. The Whole can be approximately described in terms of its aspects (that is, as Pure and as Perfect), but, in itself it is fuller than such descriptions of it. Thus It is Pure in the above sense, but is not that only; It is Perfect in the above sense, but is not also that only. Again, it is only from a pragmatic and logical standpoint that of these two or other aspects of It, we can regard one as the primary and higher, and the other or others as secondary or lower. In fact, any aspect is as much real as any other: thus Perfect (*i.e.*, infinitely rich) Consciousness is as much real as Pure Consciousness; Consciousness as Power is as much real as Consciousness as such; and the Product or Manifestation of this Power is as much real as the Power itself. We disturb this even balance and co-ordination of the aspects by attempting to thrust them into pragmatic, logical moulds.

It is true that, in having to state an alogical Fact logically and to represent an extra-temporal and extra-spatial process temporally and spatially, the *Śākta* doctrine speaks as if *Cit* as Pure Consciousness[4] were alone "in the beginning," that this Consciousness then evolved into a Consciousness first of latent, then of patent polarisation between Self and Not-Self, between consciousness as Illumination[5] and that as the Illuminated or Object,[6] that this Object is then variously evolved; that all this is then involved back into Pure Consciousness; and that while this process of evolution and involution goes on, Pure Consciousness as such changelessly abides. This statement gives, of course, primacy to Pure Consciousness as compared with Its Power to evolve and involve, and also, as compared with the work which that Power does. Pure Consciousness is there whether or not It operates as Power to project out of Itself an Object of varied content, and withdraw that Object back into Itself. This reason coupled with the fact that the most fundamental ex-

[1] Vyavahārika sat. [2] Kalā. [3] Pūrṇa.
[4] Parā Saṃvit. [5] Prakāśa. [6] Vimarśa.

pression of existence, namely Being[1] and Joy,[2] is given in Consciousness as such[3] as it is given (that is, to the same ultimate degree and in the same fundamental way) in nothing else; the fact that liberation is not attained except by realisation of Pure-Being-Consciousness-Bliss, would seem, from a logical point of view, to ensure the primacy given to Pure Consciousness. But really, in the alogical complete Fact itself, in regard to which as the Whole we cannot make any statement in terms of Space, Time and other Categories, Pure *Cit*[4] is co-ordinate with and not superior or subordinate to, the Power[5] by which It evolves and involves; and this again is co-ordinate with Its manifestation as the total Product or Achievement; and these co-ordinate aspects (*viz. Cit* as Being, *Cit* as Power[6] and *Cit* as Product)[7] embraced by, and in, the mysterious Whole is Fact. Liberation cannot be attained except by realizing *this;* since bondage is due to the non-realization of this — which is but non-recognition, that is ignorance, of what the Fact is. There is, therefore no liberation by realizing what is an aspect only. Liberation is achieved by realizing that *Śiva* as quiescent Being-Consciousness-Bliss[8] (which also is Power-to-be), becoming as dynamic Being-Consciousness-Bliss[9] and evolving and involving infinitely varied Objects, that is, World Experience which, on the whole as also in detail, is Being-Consciousness-Bliss.[10] The World is *Śiva-Śakti*, and the Fact is not realized, and therefore liberation is not had, so long as it is looked upon as a product of *Māyā*, in the sense of that which is neither real nor unreal; as a "mirage," as an order in which there is actual, as distinguished from pragmatic unreality, unconsciousness and unhappiness.[11] Not only the World as a sublime whole, but the World in its minutest details (even in the so-called "stocks and stones") must be perceived to be nothing but Being-Consciousness-Bliss in Play.[12] It is the whole Being-Consciousness-Bliss Power (*Śiva-Śakti*, and nothing but that: It seems to be "small" only with reference to the province of Convention in which the particular Centres "consciously" live and move and bargain. Hence even a grain of dust is Perfect *Śiva-Śakti* incarnate, and must be realised as such by an aspirant before libera-

[1] Sat. [2] Ānanda. [3] Cit. [4] Śiva.

[5] Śakti; Śāstra makes Śakti the consort of Śiva, and they are in inseparable union and alogical unity. *Cf.* Devi Bhāgavata, IX, I, 10, 11, which make Śakti Brahma-Svarūpa nityā (eternal); and She is related to Reality as Being as the heat of fire to fire.

[6] Kāraṇa or Śakti. [7] Kārya Brahman.

[8] Saccidānandamaya. [9] Śakti Saccidānandamayi.

[10] Jagat Saccidānandamaya, which is the Play of Śiva-Śakti.

[11] That is, the opposite of Sat-Cit-Ānanda. [12] Līlā.

ation can be had. The Perfect Being thus really given in the "infinite" as well as in the "small" is a miracle, and the basis of this commonest of all miracles is laid in the primary act by which the Perfect Being-Becoming Power in order to evolve a world of correlated Centres potentialized Itself as the infinitesimal "Point".[1] And if the Infinite can thus according to the premises of this doctrine, live and operate in, and as, the Infinitesimal, It also can do so in, and as, the "finite" and "limited" being — which, in the fullness of fact, is not finite and limited at all except with reference to the conditions of the province of inter-central convention. That province begins when, and in so far as, the realm of *Māyā* begins in the evolution of the Thirty-six-Principles, in the form of the so-called "impure" Principles.[2]

In the *Śākta* view, therefore, there is no place for Unconsciousness,[3] except in a pragmatic and conventional way, relating either to Reality as being, or to Reality as Power, or to Reality as product or Manifestation. The "seeming" consciousness"[4] of *Sāṁkhya*, or of *Māyā-vāda* as it is commonly stated, has no place either : If there be any "seeming" in the scheme of world-manifestations, it will be found rather in the other way — Consciousness "seeming" to be unconsciousness, Joy "seeming" to be indifference or pain, free Play "seeming" to be necessity and determination. And yet this "seeming" as an actual element in the Play of the World-power by which the Divine Mother variously "screens" Herself in the form of interplaying Centres, is no "illusion". This "seeming" is no seeming, since both the Power and Herself — screening Play as interplaying Centres are real. It is seeming in altogether different conditions, *viz.*, (1) when that Power withdraws Her Play as Centres into Herself and plays with Her own Being;[5] or else (2) when to the eyes of a "fortunate" Centre She lets the screens and veils drop, and permits it to realise the identity between Herself and Itself.[6] A block of stone is really unfeeling and unconscious matter to an ordinary Centre whose total assemblage of conditions[7] is of a certain kind relatively to that of the stone; it is no "seeing" in that given tissue of relations; it is then an outcome of the real interplay. But the character of the play — the bearing,

1 Bindu.
2 See Chapter dealing specially with Māyā and the Kancukas or "Envelopes".
3 Acit or Jada. 4 Chidābhāsa.
5 Which is Śiva Saccidānandamāya, playing with Śakti Saccidānandamayī. This is Ātmarati.
6 Expressed in the experience — "Sā'ham" — She am I.
7 Karma and Adṛṣṭa.

impression and import of the one in relation to the other — is bound to change with the change in their total assemblage of conditions; — a circumstance which does not make the first "impression" unreal, and make the latter real, but makes each real in its own way and sphere. The term "seeming" as applied to such partial, conditional experiences of correlated Centres may be justified in one sense only — that Power as Being-Consciousness-Bliss never ceases to be such, in Itself or in Its manifestations, whatever be Its veiling and unveiling play. A block of stone as Perfect Being-Consciousness-Bliss (involving Play) is, therefore, the Standard Experience to which other experiences are more or less near approximations, constituting "grades" and "values", but each real in its way.

The above position keeps clear of both common Realism making things exist outside and independent of Consciousness and Experience, and common Idealism making them "ideas" or "clusters of sensations, actual and possible" only. Things do exist outside and independent of Centre-referred and Centre-owned Consciousness and experience;[1] but Consciousness, without such reference and limitation, is the Fact and the Power to evolve as facts. On the other hand, Consciousness, as the root Being-and-Becoming Power becomes real things as also real minds apprehending, judging and otherwise experiencing those things; this combines the truth in Realism and that in Idealism. Thus, a block of stone is not, from this standpoint, "matter" only: it is *Cit* as Joy and as Play — though the fact is veiled to ordinary Centres; on the other hand, it is not an "idea" or "mental construct" only: it is *Cit* as Power constituting it as much and as active a reality as the experiencing and reacting mind is. While pulling down the arbitrary wall erected by "Scientific Realism" between Primary and Secondary qualities of which the former alone are supposed to be real, the doctrine does not go to the other extreme of that "naive" Realism which regards this mental impression as a "copy" of the external thing. Things as "standard" realities exist in, and for, the Supreme Mind, other Centres' perceptions being gradual and partial reproductions of those "standards" or models—a circumstance which does not make their perceptions unreal, but approximations to the real; each Centre knows the reality subject to the limitations of its *Karma* and "cosmic situation".[2] There is need, therefore, for the education and devolopment

[1] Iśvara is not here included in the Order of Centres.
[2] Adṛṣṭa, the result of karma.

of man's "knowing instruments," giving him progressively higher and larger visions, through science and philosophy, through intuition and meditation, and, finally, "revelation"[1] and realisation. This view supplies what is deficient in naive Idealism also by (1) making Matter and Life every whit as real and active as Mind, and (2) forbidding exclusive emphasis on this or that aspect of Experience, such as Reason or Idea, Will or Imagination. Its *Cit* is not transcendent or empirical consciousness only; it is not being or becoming only; it is not quiescent or dynamic only; it is not undetermined or determined only; and it is not of this feeling-tone or of that only. It comprises all these and other alternatives, and, (from man's viewpoint) contradictory phases. Its fundamental being and expression is Joy[2] pulsating as Will-Power and manifesting Itself in an unspeakably sublime cosmic Play. It is not a mere "abstraction"—a "wilderness" of Pure Being or Pure Nothing as some critics of Vedānta[3] have imagined the abode of Reality to be.

This view concedes also the possesssion of an element of truth to "Pragmatism," ancient or modern. Philosophies in India have always recognised the Province of Convention,[4] the conditions of inter-Central "behaviour" by which the experiences and realities of the correlated Centres are determined. In Indian Thought, by *Karma* a Centre is what it now is, what it was, and what it will be; by *Karma* it determines not only its "cosmic situation,"[5] but its Cosmos also; since, to each centre the Cosmos and its realities are, and seen, as its Karma[6] has determined them to be for it; to another Centre, they are different more or less, and to the "same" centre also they change as its *Karma* changes. There can be no more thorough-going "Pragmatism" than this. "Pragmatic consciousness," "Pragmatic reality" has its place, but, in the Śākta view, however it is not "illusory". Pragmatic consciousness is Consciousness as Power limiting Itself as this or that mode or aspect of Experience for the purpose of *Karma* (*i.e.*, Play) in a particular line and manner,[7] and Pragmatic reality is the Reality-Whole determining and circumscribing Itself with

[1] Śruti and Āgama. Śiva, in the Kulārṇava Tantra, reveals, for example, five "Methods" by His five mouths, and a sixth by an esoteric sixth.

[2] Ānanda.

[3] This refers to the Māyā-vāda Reality, but is not appropriate, since in that system Pure Being=Pure Bliss.

[4] Vyavahāra. [5] Adṛṣṭa.

[6] The Pūrva-Mīmāṃsā in particular shews Karma itself as Īśvara or Lord "Karmeti mīmāṃsakāḥ".

[7] See *ante* for examples of "Pragmatic facts".

reference to the conditions of action and enjoyment[1] of the Centres and groups of Centres that have evolved or will evolve in It. When, therefore, the modern Pragmatist says that the "fact" or reality, for a given Centre, A, is constituted by the behaviour of A, or the "uses" to which A can put that reality, he has the support of non-dual *Vedānta* provided (1) the behaviour is primarily the play of the Reality-Whole to evolve and play as A, and also as B, C, D, and so forth, correlated with it; (2) the behaviour of A and each of the others is also play[2] (as *Karma*) subject to the conditions (a) the manner of A's play in the past,[3] and (b) the nature of B, C, D and the manner of their play relatively to it is understood; and (3) that by behaviour[4] again of the appropriate kind, A can release itself from being an individual Centre subject to limitations.

The Neo-Pragmatist very often builds his case upon biological besides psychological grounds. A.B.C.D. form a system of Centres (some living, and the rest "non-living") not only co-operating but in conflict with one another — in "the struggle for existence". In relation to A, B.C.D. constitute the "environment"; and A lives, and expects to live, by adjusting itself and the environment each to the other, adjustment meaning the adaptation of A to B.C.D. as much as that of B.C.D. to A. Thus A changes agreeably to a change in the environment, but also changes the environment agreeably to itself. Through Natural Selection and other long-continued processes, A's organism has been so constituted as to be, generally, a suitable "machine" for doing this work of vital adaptation. Generally the machine does its work smoothly and by a pre-established arrangement—represented by its stereotyped sets of reactions—the "automatic" actions — reflex, spontaneous, instinctive and habitual. These are supposed to have their nerve-arrangements in the spinal cord, medulla oblongata, cerebellum — that is, in regions below the cerebral cortex which is the organ and seat of consciousness, either sensory or motor. The automatic actions are, accordingly, not accompanied by consciousness, and are believed by some to have nothing to do with consciousness. Consciousness accompanies those actions which meet with a sort of "deadlock" in the centres of automatic action, and which therefore, cannot "rattle smoothly off". The cortical centres which are the centres of consciousness are the centres of selection (of "deliberation and choice") by which dead-

[1] Karma and Bhoga. [2] Implying Joy and Freedom.
[3] Constituting its tendencies and adṛṣṭa or cosmic situation.
[4] As Sādhanā.

locks are removed. All actions, whether automatic or deliberative, are "behaviour" framed with reference to what is of use and value to the individual or his race; and behaviour becomes "conscious experience"— knowing, feeling or willing — under special conditions, that is, when conditions are such that what is of interest (the end as well as the means) has to be represented as a future good or evil (therefore of use and value) in relation to which the attitude of the individual must be framed, if need be through deliberation and choice. A sensation of "hot" is thus the consciousness that that which is hot will more or less burn if touched; the sensation is thus the index of the results to which a certain behaviour *viz.*, touching, will lead, and also of the uses to which those results can be put. It is use which assigns to each Centre its province of behaviour, and out of this province only a fraction is assigned to consciousness when the conditions of use are of a special kind. The conditions and limits of a Centre's knowing, feeling and willing, are the conditions and limits of what is of use to that Centre or its group.

That there is a substantial element of truth in this statement of the case may be conceded by Indian Thought. Both the "world" and the experience of the world are fashioned for a Centre as the conditions of its own *Karma* and Enjoyment[1] — (the cumulative effect and resultant of those conditions) — require them to be fashioned. It is thus that the differing "Worlds" and experiences of one man and another, those of an ordinary man and of a Seer, those of stocks and stones and those of plants and animals, and so forth, are constituted; the differing organs and instruments of the different Centres are also due to the same factors, *viz.*, *Karma* and Enjoyment (presupposing special need and use).[2] Consciousness is thus limited and specialised in a particular Centre — which, therefore, has, ordinarily, no consciousness beyond certain limits, and has, even in the zones of its conscious life, varying degrees and tones of consciousness ranging from subconsciousness and semi-consciousness to "wide awake" consciousness.

But these limits and degrees of Consciousness are "pragmatic" only. Individual Centres, according to their varying needs and uses, have these limits and degrees practically settled for them; but these do not cut up and circumscribe Consciousness itself. Because (1) the Universe being one undivided stress-system, (a system of mutual actions and re-actions) the experience which takes the universe in, cannot really be a

[1] Bhoga. [2] Prayojana, Artha or Puruṣārtha.

fragmentary and parcelled out experience, though for the practical purposes of finite Centres it appears to be so; (2) that the so-called subconscious and unconscious are really inside Consciousness (not that normally accepted as such by a finite Centre), may be said to be shown by the fact that a Centre can more and more fully reclaim them as Consciousness or conscious experience by avowing what he has so far ignored, recognising, noting what he has "chaotically" felt; and from the fact that the whole universe (*i.e.*, the "fact") can be so reclaimed in, and as, Experience when that finite Centre is able at last to uplift completely the "veil" of ignorance and non-acceptance, and becomes, in consequence, one with the Immense Consciousness-Power. It follows from this that a Centre's ordinary experience is not the whole Experience because, though really having it and living it, he has been accustomed to ignore it as the whole and accept and avow it piecemeal; and he has been so accustomed because "the needs and uses" of his pragmatic existence as domicile in "the province of convention" have so required, and determined his experience to be pragmatic accordingly. Besides these two, there is also a third reason which requires that Existence and Consciousness coincide with each other: (3) the essential marks of consciousness-in-itself are Joy and Freedom (or Free-Will-to-be-and-become). There is no form of existence — even "material" existence — which is not an expression of, and in its turn does not express (however veiled the expression may be in relation to certain "cosmic situations"), Joy and Free Power. Now if both Existence and Consciousness possess the same essential marks, it is reasonable to hold that one is the other, or both are manifestations of a Common Root. But since a Root more fundamental than Consciousness cannot be imagined (everything being representable as a mode of Consciousness, but Consciousness not being representable as a mode of anything else), it must hold that Consciousness = Being = Reality.

The above position is strengthened by the fact that the aspirant is able, it is claimed, by pursuing the appropriate method of realisation, to go round the whole circuit of involution and evolution — starting from ordinary pragmatic World-experience, passing through progressively higher and fuller "universes," coming at last to Pure and Perfect Experience which sums up all Existence and then descending again to the ordinary pragmatic order of world-experience in the reverse order. In this an experimental proof is afforded as to the manner in which the common finite order of existence and consciousness thereof for a finite Centre, can be made to tend to, and ultimately become, Perfect and Pure Being-Experience, and, how again that Perfect and Pure Being-Experience, progressively evolves, and in evolving limits Itself as, the finite, pragmatic order of existence and consciousness which an individual Centre calls his "universe". The experiment is similar to that of a geologist (for example) who shows how a great rock or a layer of the Earth's crust has been formed by experiment with a small sample of it in his laboratory. The aspirant shews in his experiment that all the elements of his universe (Solid Matter, Liquid Matter and so forth) can be, without leaving a "residue", dissolved into Consciousness, and that all partial and pragmatic universes can be made to fall into a Perfect Universe which is Perfect Consciousness; and also in the reverse order, they can be made to evolve from It. This, it is said, shows that there is nothing ultimately but Being-Consciousness, and the Power of Consciousness to be and become.

## CONSCIOUSNESS AS POWER - HOLDER AND AS POWER

The concept *Cit* is unique.

Indian Thought in its highest form regards it as the fundamental Reality. In the West, there have been thinkers who have reduced the World to Idea, to Will, to Intention or to Imagination, but it is the Indian Vedānta — and other cognate doctrines based upon it — which makes the World *Cit*, in its root as well as in its manifestation. Cit as Power (*Cit-Śakti*) appears as the World but in so appearing never ceases to be in itself *Cit*. This is the essence of non-dualist doctrine. *Cit* is Being or Fact (*Sat*) and *Cit* is Bliss (*Ānand*). Veda says that the World proceeds out of Bliss, is sustained by Bliss and is reabsorbed into Bliss. Being is Bliss which is *Cit*. The latter as such, that is as distinguished from its Power, never *becomes* other than *Cit*. How Reality can change as the changing world and yet remain what it is — how in fact change and no change can be predicated of the same Reality — is a problem of which the Māyāvāda of Śaṅkara is one solution and Śaktivāda or the Doctrine of the World as Power is another.

*Cit* is, to use an English term, the Spiritual Principle in man in which his universe of experience lives, moves and has its being. Not only is it the static *basis* of such universe, but it is that which by and as its own power (*Śakti*) *becomes* or appears as that Universe. This Spiritual Principle, which in itself is immense[1] and immeasurable,[2] becomes by its own Power,[3] differentiated into a multiplicity of correlated Centres, some of which are the human selves. This Power by which the Immense and Immeasurable becomes *as such Centres* limited and measured, by which the "Fact" becomes veiled and ignored as "Fact-sections," is *Māyā* (which operates as a measuring, limiting or determining and therefore negating Principle).[4] Subjectively considered it is the sense of difference[5] by which the object of experience is seen as other than and different from the self. It is no Cosmic Material, *foreign* to and *independent* of the Spiritual Principle[6] in man which evolves as the Universe of Mind, Life and Matter, deriving its efficiency from the presence of the Spiritual Principle (whose action on "Matter" is comparable to catalytic action in chemistry). Non-dualism says, firstly, that the Universe is *wholly* a product of the Spiritual Principle as Power, which is not only the "catalytic" source or prompter of its *efficiency*, but which is its *ground* and its *material* as well; secondly, that It, in so becoming the varied universe, does not require the operation upon Itself of a Power *other than* Itself; and thirdly, that in such evolution it presents two aspects, nemely, a static, quiescent aspect or the 'Male' Śiva in which it remains the self-same Principle, and a dynamic, stressing aspect as the Mother-Power in which it moves and changes as the world of Mind, Life and Matter.

This reduction of the universe into a Spiritual Principle and its Power one with itself (or *Cit* working as Power), calls to mind the attempt of the modern physicist to reduce the mass of Matter to electromagnetic mass alone which is referred to by way of illustration.

Is the mass of a material particle, charged with an electrical charge, partly mechanical and partly electrical? Or, can its mass, in the last resort, be reduced to the electrical mass alone ? Is mass in its nature of one kind or two kinds — *non-dual* or *dual* ? Now, the answer of modern Science has been clearly pointing to the non-dual alternative. The Electron Theory of Matter makes the mass of Matter of one kind; its mass is constituted by the masses of the positive and negative charges, protons and electrons (whatever be their precise number and distribution) which constitute an atom of matter. But even after such reduction of material mass to electrical mass, duality persists in another form. How is electrical mass related to Energy ? Are they two and independent of each other ?

[1] Bhūman. [2] Brahman. [3] Śakti.
[4] Mīyate anayū iti Māyā. [5] Bhedabuddhi. [6] As in Sāṅkhya-Yoga.

An electron (or unit charge of negative electricity) is in motion in a varied manner; its kinetic and potential energies in a given system are thus different. Now, does it possess the same mass whatever be its velocity and energy? Will its mass remain unaffected when, for example, its velocity approaches that of light? Physicists have shown that velocity — particularly when it is high — changes the mass of the moving thing: this is what is called mass-acceleration. Mass and Motion (or Energy for the matter of that) are not independent of each other : Mass becomes a *function* of Motion, that is, it varies (may be beyond certain limits only) as the latter varies. This indeed points to the unity of Mass and Energy which, however, it still remains for Science to definitely establish.

Electricity is a substance, which many have thought, to be Ether which is *quasi*-material. What, therefore, Science is now called upon to investigate is the exact relation which subsists between this Substance and Energy (or Motion). It is practically confronted with the question: Are Power and Holder of Power[1] one or two? Translated into the language of Science, and restricted to the physical plane, this means; Is Ether (if we must separately retain it) and the Stress by which it is strained into various forms, which are probably the Prime Atoms, one or are they two? In other words, can we say this that the same substance, which considered in its static aspect is Ether, is *also* Energy when considered in its stressing or dynamic aspect? Or, to use the expressive language of the Śākta Tantra, can we say that the Ether-aspect is the *Śiva*-aspect (restricted to the physical plane), and that Energy at work subjecting Ether to various forms of stress-and-strain is the *Power* or *Śakti* aspect (restricted also to the physical plane) of the one fundamental Reality ! The next problem is, how *Power* and *Power-holder* are related not only on the physical plane, but beyond on the planes of Life, Mind and on that of Power as the Radical Potential of which Life, Mind and Matter are the evolutes. In other words, Ether and its Energy must be brought into *rapport* with Life and Vital Power, these again with Mind and Will Power, and so on, until all pragmatic limitations of the data are dispensed with, and Substance and Energy are seen in their alogical identity (which man's logical thinking splits into aspects) in the complete Fact itself which is *Cit*.

For a clearer understanding of the meaning of *Cit*, we should distinguish the different standpoints from which It can be regarded. In the first place, we must distinguish between the standpoint of the Whole[2]

[1] Śakti and Śaktimān. [2] Pūrṇa.

and that of the Part,[1] between the complete view of Reality and the partial view of it. There is the former when Experience is avowed and accepted without the least veiling or ignorance of what is given — when there is absolutely no limitation of the data. This is Perfect Experience.[2] It is an experience of All-presentation or No-veiling. Man's centralised or individualised life is commonly a life of greater or less veiling or ignorance of the Given. By tiying to remove the veil, or by trying to own and accept what has been disowned and ignored, he can more or less closely approximate to Perfect Experience which is the *Limit* (in the sense of consummation or perfection) of progressively higher and higher forms of experience; but which remains unattainable so long as his life, and therefore, his standpoint, remains centralised (*i.e.*, referring to a Centre such as the Ego) and individualised. Central reference or individualisation means a stressing and straining in a particular manner of Being and of Experience; by such stressing and straining Being and Experience are apparently limited, and circumscribed, so that this circumstance precludes the possibility of a complete avowal and acceptance of Being-Experience as it is in its entireness.

Man's view-point in therefore ordinarily partial, imperfect He may indeed extend his frontiers, and thus more and more closely *approximate* to the All,[3] but so long as central reference, conscious or sub-conscious, remains, he cannot reach out to the realisation of the Perfect Being-Experience itself. His essay is therefore an essay of approximation, of nearer and nearer approach. Ordinarily he stops more or less short of the Goal or Limit itself which gathers, subsumes and perfects all. He stops because he refers to a Centre; because he is an Individual; and has therefore to know, feel and act practically with reference to other Centres or Individuals in a correlated system or Kosmos or *Ṛta* as Veda calls it. Such knowing, feeling and acting in a correlated system is practical or pragmatic living, and it not only implies but requires limitation of the data, or ignorance of the given, or veiling of the concrete, which is called Ignorance.[4] For instance, life such as man ordinarily lives it would be impossible if at every moment he were to attend *impartially* to all that

[1] Kalā is a common concept in the Scripture dealing with Śakti and is graded as Pūrnakalāmūrti, Kalāmurti, Angshamūrti, Angshāngsamūrti. There are no Kalās in Unmanī in Śivatattva. The Kalās appear with Samanī śakti in Śaktitattva.

[2] Chhāndogya, III, 14, 1.

[3] Pūrṇa.

[4] That is relative to Vidyā or knowledge. Avidyā=na vidyate. This "ignorance" is a knowing of a limited kind.

he felt, accept and emphasise *uniformly* all that he knew, and frame his actions *indifferently* with respect to whatever he felt and knew. As a matter of fact, he selects, ignores and emphasises in what he feels and knows; he owns and accepts a section only as being of interest or practically useful to him, and ignores and disowns the rest though given. Actions too are framed with respect to *selected* sights, sounds, etc., in the "objective" world, and selected ideas, feelings, desires, and so forth, in the "subjective". And such veiling and acceptance, such rejection and selection, is made (not always voluntarily by men) in a universe of Being-Experience which is undefined, seamless and alogical in itself, and which, in itself, cannot be labelled exclusively as either objective or subjective.[1] It is by such practical veiling and acceptance that we *seem* to see only a particular star or cluster of stars when looking up to the sky in a clear night: it is thus that we *seem* to hear a particular sound only in a "situation" in which not only many other sounds but countless sights, smells, touches, organic sensations, etc., constitute our actual *Given* of experience; it is also thus that we *seem* to have a particular idea, memory or desire in the mind when the *actual* universe of the moment is an undefined and undefinable whole of countless "objective" and "subjective" elements (*i.e.*, perceptions and ideas), most of which happen, for the time being, to be not of interest, and are therefore silently ignored. In a given universe of experience, attention is, for pragmatic reasons, focussed at a paruicular point which happens to be of interest for the time being; around this point of clearest attention or emphasis, spread tracts of comparative inattention till they merge into the outlying realm of the unfelt or unknown.[2] The process is analogous tc the operation of turning the search-light of a vessel plying in a dark night upon different portions of the surrounding situation. The search-light is here Attention or Regard,[3] and the mechanism of its working is that of the tendencies or partialities[4] connected with a given Centre or Individual.[5] And it need be hardly pointed out that, like the vessel also, a Centre[5] cannot move to any definite purpose, if it be not provided with such special mechanism. It is useful and also indispensable in a certain sense.

We have therefore necessarily to select and refuse, accept and ignore in the midst of what we actually have. In all this a Principle of Limitation,

[1] Īsha. Up., 5.
[2] See P. N. Mukhopādhyāya's "Approaches to Truth" for fuller discussion.
[3] Selective Attention or Regard, "Pakṣapāta".
[4] Samskāras. [5] Jīva.

selection or contraction[1] is operative. Now, in so far as its operation can apparently be traced to, and therefore connected with, the energising of a given Centre, it is called Ignorance;[2] and in so far as this veiling, measuring, limiting operation is the expression of a Cosmic Tendency or Will-to-become, and in so far therefore as it not only transcends but underlies (as generating activity) the life of the individual Centres, it is called Māyā, power of finitization.[3] And whether we consider it cosmically or individually, it is patent that this Principle of finitization (which is the Power of Reality itself) is a limiting or contracting Principle — the Radical contracting force[4] by which the All,[5] without actually ceasing to be such, becomes Part,[6] by which Experience of Everything[5] without actually ceasing to be such, becomes Experience of something:[7] in brief, by which the "Fact" becomes "Fact-section".

The first distinction therefore, is that between Experience as whole,[5] and Experience as section or part.[6] The former remains for man a goal or "limit" only so long as there are central reference and selective regard in his experience. He can, however, more or less closely approximate to it. Nearer approach can be made to the All in proportion as the operation of the two conditions — *viz.*, reference to a Centre and selective attention — can be diminished. The All is realised when the operation of each ceases. To realise is to live and accept what has lived without being accepted. In realisation man does not veil or ignore what he has or rather what he is. His experience, therefore, does not *really* cease to be the All, when, on account of his having to refer to a Centre and bestowing his attention selectively, he has experience of parts or segments only; nor, on the other hand, does a previously non-existent All tend to be established and consummated, when, by making attention a-centric and impartial as completely as possible, man tends to come as near as possible to its realisation.[8]

## CONSCIOUSNESS AS THE WHOLE

THE preceding sections have introduced the distinction between Consciousness[9] as whole or entire[5] and as section or part.[6] The former is

[1] Saṁkoca; a common term in the Trika school of Māyā operating to produce the individual key. [2] Avidyā.

[3] It is that by which things are measured (mīyate), that is, formed.

[4] Kancuka. [5] Pūrṇa. [6] Kalā. [7] Kincit.

[8] It is Svarūpa-Viśrāntih or Svarūpa-Pratiṣṭhānaṃ.

[9] Cit.

Perfect Experience. Since all ordinary predicables or categories apply to only aspects or segments of experience, which are man's pragmatic facts, the Perfect Experience is beyond the reach of the predicables or categories.[1] That is to say, its nature cannot be adequately described by any of our concepts. Its description is therefore possible only by the mode of negation.[2] Those concepts are—to employ the classification of Kant — the forms of Time and Space, and the Categories of Quantity, Quality, Relation and Modality. By means of these forms and Categories, experience becomes thinkable, that is, logical. If these Forms of Thought (including the Categories) be withheld, the "Matter" or stuff of experience becomes formless, and therefore cannot be thought about and spoken of. By being cast into these moulds, the "Matter" becomes impressed with forms and thereby becomes thinkable and speakable.[3] That Experience becomes thinkable or logical by being circumscribed in review is a fact that can be readily verified by intuition. The entire universe of sensations, feelings, ideas, memories, and so forth, which constitute total[4] Experience at any moment, can never be thought about *as a whole;* the whole must be limited and measured before it can be thought about and described. Even what is taken as "experience at any moment" is a cross section of the Experience as the whole or Fact.[5] In itself the Fact is timeless. Similarly, it is neither cause nor effect. What is known as cause or effect is a portion measured out of the Fact. These and other categories are applicable not to the whole as a whole[6] but to the whole delimited as part.[7] Perfect Experience is thus alogical. But though unthinkable and indescribable,[8] it is not on that account unknown and unknowable. It is Experience itself, Consciousness itself: no "thing-in-itself" beyond Experience. It is the Supreme Intuition.[9] It is unthinkable as is the Kantian "thing-in-itself", but its essence is Consciousness itself;[10] it is inscrutable[11] Consciousness Power.[12]

Experience becomes thinkable or logical by being circumscribed or limited. Now, since Experience, Consciousness or Feeling is ever what

---

1 "Yatovāco nivarttante aprāpya manasā saha," Tait. - Up., II, 9.

2 Niṣeda; Neti Neti.

3 Padārtha and Vācya. The Forms and Categories are called—Nāma and Rūpa by which the Avyākṛta (undifferentiated) becomes Vyākṛta (differentiated).

4 Akhaṇḍa which means without sections.

5 Pūrṇa and Akhaṇḍa.

6 Pūrṇa as Pūrṇa.

7 Kalā.

8 Avāngmānasa-gochara.

9 Nija-bodha-rūpa.

10 Cit and Śakti Cidrupunī.

11 Anirvācya.

12 See P. N. Mukhopadhyāya's "Approaches to Truth" for further discussion.

it is, its limiting can only mean this that it is ignored or veiled as a whole, and accepted or attended to in a part. In other words, the two facts, *viz.*, that we have actually at this moment a universe of experience comprising many sounds, sights, smells, touches, organic feelings, ideas, etc., and that we have at the same moment the perception of a particular sound or sight only, can be reconciled with each other only if we believe that the "universe," though actually given at this moment, has not been avowed and accepted as such, and that the particular sound or sight of which alone we seem to have perception at this moment is the pragmatic section of the universe especially selected and noticed by us. The pragmatic point or section has not indeed displaced or effaced the universe; even when attention is very nearly concentrated at a point or section, it does not cease to be slightly diffused, like twilight, over the outlying tracts or indeed over the whole "universe" that is actually given. The point or section always remains imbedded in that universe; always set on a larger background of experience. [The psychologist William James would call it (that background of actual feeling) the "fringe" of experience.] It is always there. So that the universe and the pragmatic point or section are *both* given as *actual* feeling. They can be both given in actual feeling only if the former, though given, is more or less ignored (*i.e.*, not attended to), and the latter, given as it is as part of the larger experience, is, by reason of its special interest, especially attended to. Thus while we are especially attending to a point or section only, we have, and cannot but have, the "Universe" also. That it is not then attended to does not mean or constitute its ceasing to be an actual feeling: it does not become *no* experience. It then becomes or is an experience of a different tone or intensity—blurred, indefinite, confused. The pragmatic or interesting portion becomes lighted up, definite and discriminated. When, however, the experience of the moment, the "universe" involving the points of interest is passed in review or thought about, it is commonly represented as though it were confined to or exhausted by the points of interest only. This is pragmatic thought giving the pragmatic facts, but which should be carefully distinguished from the Intuition of Fact. Circumscription or limitation of experience commonly means its veiling or ignoring as a whole and its avowal or acceptance in the "points of interest".

Veiling or contracting may, therefore, be defined as the circumstance which limits Reality considered as one aspect—as Power[1]—without

[1] Śakti, the Divine Mother.

making it other than what it is in its other aspect as Power-holder:[1] by which the whole[2] appears as part[3] and yet remains the whole. When, and in so far as, this circumstance operates in relation to the experience of an individual Centre, and its operation is immanent in it it is called Ignorance.[4] When it operates cosmically and its operation is transcendent to a given Centre, it is called Māyā. Evidently a Centre as so constituted, becomes a Centre of individualised stresses (potential and kinetic) in Reality which is Perfect Experience, because Experience by its own Power[5] so finitises and individualises itself. Veiling may be of two forms: (1) that which is done by the stresses (potential and kinetic)—that is impressions, tendencies and volitions[6] in the case of an individual Centre; and (2) that which is done by the Stress or Power of Reality itself underlying and evolving as the world of finite forms. In both cases the general definition of veiling applies. That is to say, Experience, and therefore Reality. never ceases to be the whole[2] because it has been veiled or contracted in an Individual Centre, or because it veils itself in evolving and appearing as the world of varied forms. When, for example, we appear to see a star only or hear a sound only, we actually have, and cannot but have, an undefined and indefinable "universe" of experience which is ignored except as regards the star or sound: so also in the case of "subjective" experiences, *e.g.*, a feeling in the mind, a memory, an idea. The "universe" never ceases to be such by being veiled in these cases, and emphasised in the points of interest. If we provisionally call that universe too the whole, then the whole remains as such while it appears as part.[7] In the cosmic or universal case also, where veiling has been called *Māyā*, the Immense and Immeasurable remains so even when it is to the individual eye finitised and measured. This finitisation, this evolution of *Brahman* as world, of *Śivā* as Power determined in a particular way,[8] is not, however, "illusive."

We may note also that between the cosmic case and the individual case, there is a threefold distinction as regards the circumstance of veiling. In the first place, in the individual Centre veiling or ignoring is partly voluntary and partly involuntry. When, for example, a person looking up at night wishes to see a particular star, he voluntarily veils (but cannot altogether efface) his universe of experience at that moment, and by that veiling his universe is *apparently* reduced to the perception of a single star or cluster of stars. In many cases, however, his universe becomes thus

[1] Śaktimān. [2] Pūrṇa. [3] Kalā. [4] Avidya.
[5] Śakti. [6] Samskāras. [7] Kalā.
[8] The thirty-six Tattvas as taught by the Advaita Śaivas and Śāktas.

reduced not by an actual volition in his mind, but by the play of potential stresses in him which are his tendencies.[1] This is involuntary veiling. Such veiling may be either accidental or essential. It is accidental veiling when the total experience is ignored and a part accepted because of the working of a subliminal desire or subconscious interest in the mind which, for the time being, prevails most and vents itself in certain partialities. Thus even while we are not consciously attending to and selecting our experiences, we have our experiences apparently dealt out to us in partials: certain sounds out of a great many actually given, for example, are apprehended by us: these are apprehended by us because certain predispositions, working subliminally and possessing the greatest causal efficiency for the time being, make us partial to them. But there is also a deeper kind of involuntary veiling which pertains to the essence of a Centre *as such.* We have referred before to the fact that an individual Centre's universe of experience cannot be Perfect Experience (which is ultimate Reality) in so far as that universe is referred to and organized round that Centre. Reference to, and organization round a Centre is itself a limitation of Perfect Experience. In fact, Perfect Experience limits or finitizes itself in appearing as such centre of reference and organization. This is the working of *Māyā* by which the Immeasurable is measured, the Indefinable is defined, the Infinite is finitized. With respect to different Centres again, (*e.g.*, amoeba and man) stresses, potential and kinetic, are differently organized, so that what is ordinarily one Centre's universe is not that of another. Essential veiling means the limitation of Perfect Experience by reason of a Centre being a specialized centre of reference and organization.

It should be noted, however, that the difference between voluntary and involuntary veiling, and that between accidental and essential veiling, is a difference of degree and not one of kind. Ordinarily these differences seem to be fundamental like those between the voluntary and involuntary muscles, voluntary and involuntary nerve centres in the body. But by using appropriate means the jurisdiction of volitional control can be gradually extended over those centres which ordinarily lie outside it. The ganglia along the spinal axis, for example, which, according to some, are probably connected with race habits and instincts, can by proper discipline[2] be made amenable to voluntary control like the motor centres in the cerebral hemispheres. Such wakening of the spinal ganglia, is, it

[1] Samskāras. [2] Sādhanā.

has been claimed, a collateral effect of the piercing of the "Six Centres" by *Kuṇḍalinī Yoga*. It may be incidentally observed too that such extension, of the range of voluntary control over motor centres of the body which are ordinarily involuntary, has its parallel in the transposition and extension of sensory functions under hypnotism and *Yoga*. *E.g.*, a hypnotic subject may "see" by the sense of touch. In the Psychic literature of the West many examples of such transposition and extension of special sensory functions are to be met with.[1] By training and effort[2] it may thus be possible for a given Centre to extend and rearrange its universe of experience (1) by extending the range of its voluntary control, (2) by extending the range of its sensory functions, and (3) by lighting up what is dark and subliminal in consciousness. By this process his universe can be made to approach Perfect Experience. And ultimately Perfect Experience itself can be realized when a Centre is able to transcend itself as a specialized centre of reference and organization.[3] Then, what has been called essential veiling is done away with, and *Māyā* which measures and binds is transcended. A given Centre has *ordinarily* its universe of experience determined primarily by the Limiting Principle[4] by which it has been constituted a specialized centre, and secondarily by the circumstances of its own choice and control. Even ordinarily, his universe is thus partly at least an "intentional".

Now, let us turn to the cosmic case. It will be shewn later that the appearance of a primordial, generic cosmic Centre is a condition precedent to the appearance of a multiplicity of special individual centres. Perfect Experience (or full Reality) must first "divide" itself as a Self and its Object or Universe, in order that such division may be reproduced in a multiplicity of particular centres.[5] Perfect Experience is, it is true, alogical; but *within* this Experience the polarity of Subject and Object must appear in order that the veiling and limiting process producing the world of finite forms may start. In the *Upaniṣads* we accordingly read how the Supreme Self was alone in the beginning, and then, how He began to see Himself (*i.e.*, made object of Himself). In the *Kāmakalāvilāsa*,[6] *Śiva*, whose nature is illuminating Consciousness or *Prakāśa* is depicted as

[1] The Ṛṣi Gotama, in ancient India, it is said, saw the face of his disciple Vyāsa by transferring his sense of sight to his feet, and so Indian tradition has given him the name *Akṣapāda* (*i.e.*, one who has eyes in his feet).

[2] Sādhanā.

[3] This is "Laya Yoga" of which Unmanī (lit. transcending Mind) is a conspicuous type.

[4] Māyā. [5] Jīvas or Puruṣas. [6] Kāmakalāvilāsa, 1, 2.

seeing himself reflected in the "Pure Mirror" which is his Power as the *Vimarśa*[1] on which the latter evolves as universe.[2] The *Vimarśa*[3] or Self-reflection of the Supreme Reality, by which act It knows Itself as a perfect Universe, is the Perfect of Supreme Self.[4] Contrasted with this is the relative self,[5] whose object of experience is partial[6] compared with that of the Supreme Self whose object is All.[7]

Now, the Supreme Reality makes use of its own Power (*viz.*, *Māyā*)—(1) to appear as Supreme Self knowing Itself as a Perfect Universe, and (2) to evolve out of Itself a world of correlated finite centres. Unlike the finite centre, in which the operation of veiling is partly voluntary and partly involuntary, the Supreme Centre[8] exercises Its veiling power freely —that is to say, It is the Lord of Māyā[9] whose creatures the finite centres are. In the *Upaniṣads*, the Lord has accordingly been called wielder of Māyā.[10] To distinguish it from the *Māyā* of the Supreme, the "veil" in a finite Centre[11] has been called *Avidya* (Ignorance). In Vedānta, the former is constituted by the predominant and lucid principle of unveiling and presentation whilst the latter is dark, opaque veiling. This is the first distinction between the cosmic case and individual case.

The second distinction is that whilst in the experience of the Lord knowledge of the particulars[12] co-exists with knowledge of the universals,[13] in the experience of the finite Centre,[14] knowledge of particulars is commonly possible by the veiling of knowledge of the whole, and *vice versa.* Thus while we are attentively regarding a particular star, we do so at the cost of, that is by veiling, the universe of experience we actually have at that moment; conversely, if we wish to abandon ourselves to the "universe" or the entire "given," we must disengage ourselves from the particular star which especially binds our interest now. Partial, especially focussed intuition and impartial and non-focal intuition (in so far as such intuition may be possible to a *finite Centre*) do not co-exist in man with an equal degree of psychic intensity, which means that the one must be veiled (without being actually effaced) in order that the other may

[1] The objective side of experience.

[2] It should be noted that the order of evolution indicated, though stated as temporal, is really logical: it is not a question of *first* this and *then* that.

[3] See Kāmakalāvilāsa; and the Commentary of Natanānanda, where authorities are cited. See Kaṭha-Up., "Natatra suryo bhāti," etc.

[4] Pūrṇāhantā or Parāhantā.

[5] Aparāhanta.

[6] Kincit

[7] Kritsna.

[8] Pūrṇāhantā or Parāhantā.

[9] Māyādhīśa.

[10] Māyāvin.

[11] Aparāhantā.

[12] Viśeṣa.

[13] Sāmānya.

[14] Jīva.

rise to clearness and definiteness. In the Lord's Experience, on the other hand, the Fact, the Whole,[1] need not retire into the shade in order that the Fact-Sections[2] may come into the light, and *vice versa*. This is because *Māyā* which veils is His *Māyā* and *Māyā* does not veil for Him who is the controller of it.[3] The Lord[4] is both knower of universals[5] and of the particulars,[6] and both these forms of knowing are eternal[7] in Him.[8] Therefore they co-exist.

The third distinction is that while *Māyā* (the veiling and limiting Principle which is but Supreme Reality regarded *as* Power to evolve as the world of finite forms) is immanent in the Experience of the Lord, it is transcendent in relation to the experience of a particular Centre. The consequences of this are important:—(*a*) whilst a world of finite forms is "objectified" in the experience of the Lord, it is not ejected and localised as something alien and existing outside as with man; in other words, Space is not a form of that experience in the sense in which it is a form with man; accordingly, there is no foreign "matter" seeming to exist by its own right outside of that experience.[9] (*b*) Accordingly, there is no need for *gradually* knowing that foreign outside matter and extending control over it in that experience; the Lord is Possessor of Perfect knowledge and power.[10] In the finite Centre, on the other hand, the veil has operated in such a way that an alien objective world lies outside of it in Space, which it essays to know and control gradually and partially.[11] (*c*) Time also is a measure which is immanent in the experience of the Lord; that is to say, the Lord, His experience and His Creation are not subject to temporal determination; on the contrary, these transcend Time; and what is Timeless in the Lord becomes temporal in relation to the subordinate Centres. The Lord's experience includes ideas of Time and Space, but, unlike man's is not subject to them.

The Śāstric symbols (which are also claimed as real experience of the seers) which depict the Lord and His Power—the two being in reality

---

[1] Pūrṇa. [2] Kalā.

[3] There is, however, a distinction (as we shall see) between *Cit* as Pūrṇa and this "Pūrṇa" being objectified by the Supreme Self.

[4] Īśvara and as Divine Mother Īśvarī.

[5] Sarvajña. [6] Sarvavit. [7] Nitya.

[8] Even Nyāyā Vaiśeṣika makes jnāna nitya in Īśvara.

[9] The Lord knows the world as Himself and as man sees it, as non-self.

[10] Sarvajña and sarva-śaktimān.

[11] Bṛhadāraṇyaka, III, 7, shows the Lord as Antaryāmin (Controller) in respect of everything.

one—as unclad, or nude,[1] imply this (1) that Supreme Experience which is Supreme Reality is an experience of no veil; (2) that though it of course *involves* the veil, it is not applicable to the Whole,[2] and that therefore no veil can be drawn over it; and (3) that consequently the categories and forms of thought such as Time, Space, Causality and so forth by which our Pragmatic Facts are dressed up, though all born out of, and immanent in the Complete Experience, are not forms by which the whole itself can be dressed up or vehicled. In the above exposition, 'Lord' has been taken in the sense of the Supreme Personality[3] which knows Itself as the Complete "I"[4] : it is Perfect Experience making an object of itself. This object is Power as *Vimarśa.* Between Perfect Experience and this Supreme I[5] there is a distinction which will be dealt with again in our study of Perfect Experience and how the Tattvas are born out of it. Meanwhile, be it observed, that the distinction does not affect the position here stated, namely, that the Lord controls the veil, and that Perfect Experience. involving Time, Space, Causality and so on, may be described as Experience of *no* veil. It is experience from which nothing has been ejected, held back; in which nothing has been ignored.

## VEILING OF CONSCIOUSNESS

THOUGH the Supreme Reality is only realised in Yoga, the intellect gives, it is claimed, warrant in normal experience for the truth of the scriptural teaching. Let us then examine and reflect upon such experience. Recurring to the example already given let us suppose we have experience of a sound now. Commonly we think and say that our experience is, for the time being, of that sound only. This thought, though it does not represent to us the whole truth is practically useful. But evidently our whole experience at this moment is not confined to that sound. Several other sounds besides sights, smells, touches, organic sensations, feelings, ideas, desires and so forth, are in the universe of experience, though unattended, unnoticed, and therefore veiled and confused. Disengaging our interest from the sound which happens to lie on the apex of the curve of the presentation, and extending the range of attention, it is possible to explore this given universe. If we do that we shall discover two circumstances

[1] Digambara and Digambari or Mahāśakti or space-clad because being Brahman She is her own Māyā. See *Hymns to the Goddess.*

[2] Pūrṇa. [3] Parāhantā. [4] Pūrṇāham.

[5] Being Brahman.

connected with that universe. In the first place, it is indefinable, so that no positive bonds can be set to it; we shall never be able to say that it goes thus far and no further, that it includes so much and no more. Beyond what we have "explored" by the search-light of attention, outlying vistas of semi-attended or unattended, and therefore more or less veiled and confused, tracts of experience will always lie. In the second place, the veiled and confused zones are not exactly sub-conscious or subliminal; many of them are above "the threshold line", they constitute actual feelings; they, together with the sound which happens for the time being to be the point of interest, constitute our actual total experience (or "Fact") of the moment. But though they are above the threshold line, their curvature is low, the summit or apex of the curvature being represented by the sound now heard. When these two circumstances connected with the Fact have been discovered, the Veil drawn over the Fact has already been to some extent removed. Why not completely removed? We shall presently see.

Inspection of the Fact will further reveal to us two things. First, the whole "universe" involving as it does change, is sustained, "lives, moves and has its being" in a boundless and changeless "Ether of Consciousness".[1] In other words, the Fact *is* this boundless, changeless, quiescent background of Consciousness against which a Stress, infinitely various in its motions and forms, is at play. The Fact is thus static and dynamic.[2] The dynamic, stressing, evolving aspect does not displace the static and unchanging aspect. They co-exist; they blend together into an inexpressible alogical identity. Man is ever Consciousness *as* power though he commonly does not realize that he is so. He is commonly so much taken up with the "Fact-sections," the Pragmatic "Facts". When the veil of ignorance by which man ignores because of special interests in particular elements of Fact[3] has been so far uplifted as to give him a glimpse of the Ether of Consciousness and Stress playing in it,[4] then it is that he finds, in his own experience, a clue to the fundamental riddle of creative

[1] Cidākāśa. This is a familiar concept of Upaniṣad. It is not meant that the physical ether is consciousness, for it is a product of Cit, but that consciousness (as Cit) is like the ether an all pervading continuum. In a similar way the Śākta Tantras call the infinitely vast tract of consciousness the "Ocean of Nectar" set in which is the Bindu as the "Isle of Gems" (Manidvīpa) wherein is the Supreme Self as the highest concept in the logical order of the Alogical Real.

[2] "Guṇātīta" as well as "Gunāśraya" and "Guṇamaya".

[3] Or Pakṣapāta.

[4] Of Kāli standing and moving on the prostrate inert body of Śiva, to use a very familiar Śāstric representation of the truth.

evolution, *viz.*, how Reality[1] evolves as the world-order and yet remains eternally what it is;[2] how in other words, in one aspect appearing as all change it does not in the other aspect change; how, thus, its creative energising involves for logical thinking a contradiction—change and no change side by side. When man does not ignore himself, he knows that he is Consciousness which as the illumining Power[3] to *be* remains as placid, unchanging, sustaining and illuminating "Ether" of Consciousness, and as the becoming and illumined aspect[4] changes and evolves as a world of varied names and forms;[5] that the latter aspect, though opposite in character to the former, does not prevail by suspending or suppressing it. Man has warrant for this unthinkable, alogical blending of contraries in his own normal experience. The veil of pragmatic thought, when uplifted, will, it is claimed, show this to him.

The second point is this. The Stress or Power has a triple disposition in man. In the symbolic language of the Scripture, the Supreme *Bindu* (lit. Point)[6] which is fundamental, massive Potency to evolve, ready for actual evolution, becomes a triangle[7] when it attains the condition of primary manifestation.[8] Introspection will shew the "triangle" (the "Polar Triangle' as it may be called)[9] in the normal universe of experience. One fundamental disposition of Experience shews the polarity of Centre (*Aham* or "I"), its co-ordinate (*Idam* or "This") and their active correlation.[10]

Another fundamental of experience is this: There is the aspect of Pure Consciousness[11] in which man's universe appears, and by which it is revealed or manifested : and there is the aspect of Stress which evolves as that universe. The former is the aspect of Being-Consciousness;[12] the latter[13] is that of Stress-Becoming. By the former the universe is and is felt; by the latter it evolves and is determined. The former or revealing aspect is *Prakāśa;* and the latter or determining, "informing" aspect is

---

[1] Brahman, Śiva and Śakti.
[2] Cit. [3] Prakāśa-śakti.
[4] Vimarśa śakti. The word Vimarśa comes from the root Mriś to handle or pound. Vimarśa is that which is handled. It represents the objective side of existence and the power which produces it. It thus expresses a similar idea to that expressed by the terms Prakṛti and Pradhāna or that which as its product is placed in front of an object.
[5] Nāma-rūpa, that is the psycho-physical 'sheaths' or bodies of Spirit.
[6] In the Śākta symbolism, Bindu means 'a drop of seed'.
[7] Trikona or Śringāta-rūpa.
[8] Unchchūnāvasthā, lit. swelled state.
[9] P. N. Mukhopādhyāya — *Approaches to Truth.*
[10] Vyāvahāra. Matā Māna Meya is the gist (Saṁgkalitārtha) of Śakti.
[11] Cidākāśa. [12] Para-śiva, Parā Śakti.
[13] Śiva-Śakti.

*Vimarśa*. In the experience of a sound, for example, our analysis shews three elements: the sound *is;* it is *known*, it is *determined* or "informed" as sound and as a particular sound. These elements are of course aspects of one undivided *concrete* experience, and should not be taken as separate principles or entities. The aspects which analytic thought yields compose one indivisible unity of being. Hence Being and Becoming,[1] the placid Spiritual Ether and the point of Creative Stress,[2] Power Holder and Power,[3] *Brahman* and *Māyā* are not two, but one; or rather they are aspects, sundered apart by our analytic thought, of an alogical, ultra-numerical, Fact. Now, since the immensity of Fact or Experience or Being becomes circumscribed, and therefore veiled, in being determined (*e. g.*, when the total experience of a moment is represented as being that of a particular sensation or thought)', it follows that the two aspects,[4] though connected with each other, are yet opposed to each other: the former being the revealing aspect of Consciousness, and the latter the determining, and therefore veiling, aspect of Consciousness. But determining or "informing," though it involves veiling, is not only that. When, for example, our experience is determind as that of a particular sound, the given, ineffaceable immensity of experience has undoubtedly been veiled or ignored, for the Universe in itself is still undefined and undetermined; and not only has that universe been veiled, but the emphasis of attention has moved from elsewhere to the place of the particular sound which, accordingly, now occupies the apex of the curve of presentation. The aspect of determining, or the Stress or Power by which Consciousness is self-determined involves, therefore, Veiling, Movement and Presentation.[5]

The two aspects of Revealing and Veiling[6] not only oppose each other but, as ordinary experience shows and illustrates, they tend towards each other. That is to say, what has been revealed tends naturally and gradually to be veiled, and what has been veiled tends naturally and gradually to be revealed; what is undefined and unformed tends naturally and gradually to be defined and determined as forms, and *vice versa*. This mutual play of Revealing and Veiling[7]—which in the Scriptures is often symbolized as the mutual desire[8] of the "Divine Couple" Śiva and

[1] Prakāśa and Vimarśa. [2] Cidākāśa and the Bindu as Stress.
[3] Śiva and Śakti. [4] Prakāśa and Vimarśa.
[5] Tamas, Rajas and Sattva guṇas respectively of Sānkhya and Vedāntic analysis. If veiling be called Āvaraṇa Śakti, Movement and Presentation may jointly be called Vikṣepa Śakti.
[6] Prakāśa and Vimarśa. [7] Prakāśa and Vimarśa. [8] Kāma.

Śakti[1] is rhythmic not only in the particular centres such as man, but in the life of the Cosmos, on account of which there is rhythmic cosmic evolution and involution, just as in man there is alternate waking[2] and sleeping.[3] This fundamental tendency shows itself on the physical plane as expansion and contraction of mass, on the vital plane as anabolism and katabolism and expiration and inspiration, and on the mental plane as knowing and ignoring, owning and disowning.[4] It is fundamental because it underlies the entire scheme of cosmic life, and because we fail to deduce this rhythm as a result or consequence from another law of operation more fundamental than, and therefore antecedent to, itself. It is a primordial law of the Fact to be rhythmically veiled and revealed, defined and undefined.[5] From homogeneity to heterogeneity evolution proceeds; but homogeneity is a condition of implicity[6] which condition gradually changes into one of explicity,[7] and this back into implicity.

It follows that the Veil (that which reduces, contracts, defines, determines the universe of Experience) tends—or in view of the law of rhythm it may be said, swings, or oscillates—between two limits, *viz.*, that of zero and that of infinity. In other words, the Veil tends to completely disappear, and it also tends to infinitely appear. In the former case, when it has completely disappeared, we have experience as the whole[8] or Perfect Experience. In the latter case, when it (*i.e.*, the Veil) has infinitely appeared, we have that condition of experience which is called dissolution[9] or Cosmic Sleep.

Infinity, however, may be either of volume or of mass, either of extensity or of intensity. When Power becomes infinitely intensive or concentrated its condition is called *Bindu* or "Point" (of contraction).[10] Such intensification or concentration presupposes a condition of Power in movement which as "heard" by the Absolute Ear is called Nāda or "Primordial Sound".[11] Energy must constitute a "field", and that field must be subject

---

[1] Hence named Kāmeśvara and Kāmeśvari or the fundamental "Libido". This "erotic" imagery, so objectionable to the prudery from which the Indian as most other ancient peoples were happily free, is not peculiar as some suppose to "the Tantras". So Br.-Up.: "He indeed was just as man and woman in embrace".

[2] Jāgrat. [3] Suṣupti.

[4] Perception is an act of "owning".

[5] See, as to "Elasticity" of Bindu later.

[6] Avyākṛta. [7] Vyākṛta. [8] Pūrṇa. [9] Pralaya.

[10] Sankoca, that is, here potency ready to evolve as the contracted product or universe.

[11] The Śārada Tilaka says that from the Lord issued Power, from Power that state of it which is Nāda, and from Nāda Bindu. This latter becomes threefold as the universe of knower, knowing and known. See "The Garland of Letters".

to an actual straining movement, before it can be supposed to be concentrated into a Point. This is true not merely of so-called physical energies, such as sound, heat or light. Heat or light, for example, can each be focussed, by means of a concave lens, from a more or less diffused condition. In each case, the field must be contracted, the diffused energy must be collected together. And this is true of Experience also—it is a law of Fact-operation which is the basis and model of all actual world-operations on the planes of mind, life and matter. Experience must be given as a continuum or universe, and that universe must be stressed and strained in a given manner, in order that attention may focus itself approximately in a point. If the placid, quiescent condition of the continuum be called *Śiva*, and Movement or Stress be called *Śakti*, then we see that the Continuum in Stress is the active union of the Power-Holder *Śiva* and Power or *Śakti*, and t is perceived why in the Śākta Tantras such active union (depicted, as often is the case, in "erotic" symbolism) is called *Nāda*, and also why it is said (carrying out the same symbolism) that *Bindu* (here Seed) issues from such union.

As an impregnated ovum or germ-cell is the concentrated form of the energies of a male and a female, so *Bindu* is the concentrated form of the substance and energy—if we may speak of them separately—of the entire perfect universe of Experience. It is the Whole[1] whose "mass" has become concentrated into a point. The Point or *Bindu* is therefore a universe, and the Perfect Universe.[1] It is the Universe in a *potential* form—the Seed of the Universe. The scheme of the organism is given in the seed: the plan of the planetary systems is possibly given in the atoms, and this is because all evolution proceeds on the plan of an universe being given in, and evolving out of, *Bindu*.[2]

In man's experience, the Point of Power[3] is given and is constantly active as "I"–ness. His whole experience has crystallized round the nucleus —"I". This is not to say that "I"–ness, above "the threshold line," and the Point[3] should in all cases be identified with each other; the latter is there even when and where the former has not actually appeared, but whenever the former has appeared, it serves as the manifestation and representative of the Point[3] in the growth of the experience of a given

[1] Pūrṇa.

[2] Bindu is called Paramākāśa or "Perfect Ether". Cf. also Chhāndogya-Up., which discusses the "Little Abode" which is also the Perfect Abode, and where there is Supreme Time, Parakāla, which in the former is broken up into the moments of Empirical Time (Kāla). So it is said "Time leads me in time."

[3] Ahantā.

Centre. Besides, the "Self" as the representative of the Point[1] works "sub-consciously" too. Now, t is this "Point" which in man, as well as in other forms of existence, "swells"[2] as the Polar Triangle of the measurer, the measured and the measure or measuring,[3] or Knower, Knowing, Known, and also, as it may be said from another standpoint, as that of "Base," "Index" and "Co-efficient" of the Fact.[4] It further assumes the forms of other Polar Triangles such as Power as Knowing,[5] Power as Feeling-attitude and Interest,[6] and Power as Willing and Volition.[7]

The second Triangle requires explanation. Whenever there is a given experience, analysis shows that it has a "Base" or substratum of immediate, intuitive feeling, an "Index" or superstructure of ideas and memories suggested by the "Base" and a "Co-efficient" or a background or store of possibilities or tendencies[8] which makes the fact change and grow like a crystal in appropriate solution. What is called Base and Index are commonly spoken of in Psychology as "presentative" and "representative" elements, as intuitive and ideational factors. Every perception is thus described as a presentative-representative complex. We hear a name (say *Śankara*) uttered. The base of our experience is not only the immediate, direct cognition of the sound, but it is, as introspection will show, a wide and undefined mass of many other sounds, sights, smells, touches, organic sensations, intuition of being and self and so forth, though all this great mass of feeling is, for the time being, masked under the veil of inattention and ignorance. The sound *Śankara* is the place of emphasis and concentration, but it is obviously not the whole of what we immediately feel or what is directly presented to us now. This whole body of actually given feeling is the Base. The sound *Śankara* calls up certain memories and suggests certain ideas; which memories and ideas associated with the name *Śankara*, constitute the "representative element," and it is by them that the sound becomes intelligible, and conveys a meaning to us; what is a mere sensation becomes a perception to us. This halo or superstructure in, and by, which sensations are supplemented and understood, is the Index. Then again; it is patent to inspection that this complex of impressions and ideas, presentative and representative elements, is not a statical, unmoving, unchanging fact. It is an incessantly changing and growing experience. It changes both at the Bases and at the Index: neither

[1] Ahantā. [2] Uchchūnāvasthā. [3] Mātā, Meya and Mānā.
[4] In "Approaches to Truth," the doctrine is elaborated.
[5] Jnāna-śakti. [6] Icchā-śakti.
[7] Kriyā-śakti. [8] Samskāra.

the mass of sensations nor the halo of suggested ideas ordinarily remains the same for two consecutive moments. Now, the tissue of potentials,[1] commonly lying below the threshold line of pragmatic consciousness, which makes a given experience change and grow like a crystal in a solution of the requisite kind and condition, is the "co-efficient" of the fact. The co-efficient partly determines what the fact shall be at the next moment.

We shall not study here the mutual reactions of the Base, Index and Co-efficient, but note only this that the first refers to the present tense of Time, the second generally to the past, and the last generally to the future. The "triangle" is in this sense three-dimensional in Time.[2]

The "triangle" involves, and is constituted by, veiling. This veiling process can be traced upwards and downwards starting from Perfect Consciousness. Perfect Consciousness veils itself when a Centre or Point of reference and operation appears in it. Consciousness is "partitioned" when it refers itself to and operates through a Centre. It seems to be no longer alogical, absolute and impartial when it so refers and operates. Ether no longer remains homogeneous, even and undivided when a strain-centre appears in it and constitutes a prime atom. By the appearance of such centre the mass as well as the energy of Ether becomes relative—assuming for one moment that they were homogeneous and uniform previously to the appearance of the strain-centres. Similarly, protoplasm becomes relative, both as regards mass and energy, when it assumes the nuclear form and becomes a cell. Lastly, experience becomes relative and partial by reason of the appearance of the ego or "I" in it. To be relative is to become partitioned or divided in a way. The strain-centre in Ether is distinct from, and, in a sense, separate from the rest of ether: it is a kind of hedging round. So in the case of the living cell, and in that of self-referring (either consciously or sub-consciously) experience. Now, veiling or contraction is the name that is given to this principle of hedging round or differentiation.[3] It is that which gives us difference,[4] or duality[5] or separateness.[6] It does so by suppressing or concealing the sameness,

---

[1] Or tendencies—Samskāra, Vāsanā. These have as their supporting and material cause (Śakti) past direct experience.

[2] Kālikopanishad, 5, speaks of the "Trikonam" or Triangle of Kālikā which represents Reality especially as Time (Kālā), and the Devourer of Time ("Kālasya kālī," etc.)

[3] This is variously spoken of in the Śruti as Brahman hiding Itself in a cave, dividing Itself.

[4] Bheda. [5] Dvaita. [6] Vailakṣanya.

unity and impartiality.[1] For veiling we must have therefore two circumstances. First there must be differences, separateness and so on. But only this is not enough. Therefore, secondly, the whole in which the differences exist or appear must be suppressed or concealed in a manner. The whole must retire into a cave. The intrinsic strain-centre in Ether suppresses or conceals the Mother-Ether itself in this sense that it conserves itself, which means that it resists the encroachment of surrounding matter upon itself; resists the tendency to dissolution in the sea of ether out of which it has differentiated itself; and thereby maintains its own individuality as a prime atom of specific mass, constitution and energy. By resisting it maintains its separateness; and resistance is thus avoidance, rejection. The same reasoning applies to the nucleated cell of protoplasm. The nucleus is the physical seat and organ of a Principle of specific operation[2] and control, and such operation and control is possible not merely by acting upon the given mass of protoplasm and the energy contained in it, but also, to a large extent, by resisting the action of the portion of the protoplasm not made into a nucleus.[3]

Lastly, in experience the Ego acts as a Principle of specific operation and control, by reason of which Perfect Experience, like physical ether, is "strained" about a given centre; becomes hedged round or circumscribed, and thereby becomes imperfect, finite individual experience—the experience of the limited embodied self.[4] By being thus differentiated, such experience becomes the accepted and avowed segment of the Perfect Universe or Experience which has been pragmatically veiled, ignored or disowned. Like the nucleus of a cell of living matter, the Ego represents a system of countless tendencies,[5] a system of partialities, of selections and rejections. At every moment of its experience, it selects and rejects. Pragmatically, its experience is not the Perfect Experience, firstly because it is a centre of special differentiation and therefore of circumscription, in the latter; and secondly because it selects in, and therefore cuts up, even that undefinable universe of experience which is its own "Fact". Thus a man may seem to hear a particular sound only in the midst of a given universe of experience comprising many sounds, sights, smells,

[1] According to the luminous definition of Yogarāja or Yogamuni "It is the function of Śakti to negate" (Niṣedha-vyāpāra-rūpaśaktīh) Karikā 4 Comm. on Abhinava Gupta's Paramārthasāra. This recalls the maxim "omnis determinatio est negatio".

[2] This is what is meant by Māyā creating Bheda or Dvaita.

[3] The disintegrating action is often called in Up. as "Mrityu" which, as Brih.-Up. says, assails the "Devas" of the Body and tends to produce "tiredness" in them.

[4] Jīva.

[5] Samskāra.

touches, and so forth; and this given universe is the Perfect Experience strained and differentiated about a given Centre. Man's acknowledged feelings and so forth are therefore doubly removed from the Whole.

A Centre, whether in "dead" Matter, or in "living" Matter, or in Experience represents the metaphysical point or *Bindu:* which means that it is a concentrated, potentialized universe (an infinite sphere whose radii have been infinitely reduced), and consequently that it is a seed out of which a diffused, distended, actual universe is to evolve again.[1]

The *Bindu* is the Perfect Universe in a condition of maximum veiling but infinite potency. If we represent the Perfect Universe or experience by an infinite sphere whose radius stands for infinite presentation or manifestation, then this sphere can be made to represent the *Bindu* when its radius has been infinitely reduced—that is to say, when its manifestation has been completely veiled. Since the sphere is not merely a mathematical sphere, but is dynamic—is a field of operative Power, its infinite contraction means infinite concentration or compactness of Power, so that the Para Bindu[2] or "Supreme Point" may be conceived as infinitely massive Power or Potency,[3] which is also, Power ready to evolve the Universe because, as further explained later, all evolution must start from Energy massed into nuclei or centres. It is as if an infinite coil of wire or spring were compressed infinitely till, in the limit, it became a Point. The more it is compressed, the less become its dimensions and the greater the amount of condensed energy or potency. In the limit, imagined when it has become a Point, its dimensions become infinitely small, but its potency infinitely great.

That such decrease of dimensions and increase of potency can go together, can be shown *a posteriori* from observed phenomena. Chemical action affecting the combination of atoms is, generally speaking, more powerful than physical or mechanical action affecting molar and molecular masses. In fact, greater bulk of operative power in the physical universe is probably derived from chemical action. But even chemical energy, great as it is, is nothing compared with the energy which is stored up in, and sometimes given out, as in radio-activity, by the atom. The atom is small but its store of energy is vast. But neither the atom nor the electron is infinitely small. Hence the energy of the atom or electron

[1] Sarva-Sāropaniṣad compares the "Seed" to that of a Banyan Tree in which the tree lies "hidden".
[2] Also called Īśvara-tattva.
[3] Niratiśaya-ghanībhūta-Śakti.

is not infinitely great. Infinitely vast energy is reached when the metaphysical "Point" or *Bindu*[1] is reached.

It is so because Mass *is* really Energy. Extension of Mass means diffusion of Energy. When the Mass is small, the quantity of Energy per unit area is greater than what it would be per same unit area when the same Mass occupied a larger volume. Mass, in accordance with the highly suggestive pictorial thinking of Faraday, may stand for so many and such and such forms of "lines of force". When Mass occupies a certain volume, we have so many lines of force packed together in a given area; when the volume contracts, the same number of lines of force becomes more closely packed together, so that, area for area, we now have force of a greater intensity. The Atom is matter in which lines of force are very closely conglomerated; in the Electron they must be still more closely packed, till we arrive at the dynamic "Point" in which they are infinitely closely packed, which means that in it force is infinitely intense. The dynamic Point is thus the "limit" in the mathematical sense of the "close packing" of lines of force *ad nfinitum.*[2]

Now, for one moment let us consider evolution as it should be understood in this system.[3] It is a condition of cosmic dis-equilibrium. The stresses of centres do not neutralize one another so long as creative movement goes on. Placed in such a field of disequilibrium or unequal tensions, a Dynamic Point or *Bindu* must tend to expand or swell.[4] That is to say, its infinitely closely packed lines of force (to continue the analogy of Electrical Science) will tend to distend or spread. Which again means that its infinite potency must commence to distribute itself about it as a "field". Such swelling of the Point is illustrated on the different planes of creation. In Matter it is represented by universal radio-activity. Every material particle allows its fount of energy to flow out in streams of radiation: and each material centre becomes surrounded by a field of force.[5] What Science now calls Atom is itself such a field—a little universe of revolving protons and electrons. Even these latter, being of finite magnitude, must

---

[1] It is thus called Ghaṇībhūta or condensed massed Power.

[2] This is carama or niratiśaya ghaṇībhāva of Śakti.

[3] Sṛṣṭi, which is here used in its sense as evolution (Pariṇāma) not of creation whether "out of nothing" or out of pre-existent material. Cosmic Evolution is an unfolding or making explicit of what is implicit in Śakti. The cause remains what it was and yet appears differently in the effect. The difference between this Pariṇāma of Śaktivāda and the Vivartta of Māyāvāda lies in the fact that the former regards the effect as real and the latter as neither real nor unreal.

[4] Uchchūnāvasthā. [5] See Śvetāśvatara-Up., VI. 10.

be of the nature of "fields". In the world of Life, the cell of protoplasm s a field round about a nucleus. In a nutritive solution the cell "swells" and then splits up, divides, subdivides. In this way the cell multiplies itself, and then by integration and co-ordination creates organisms.[1] The material atom also multiplies itself in this sense that, in radio-activity, it gives out radiations each of which is a centre of force ejected from the body of the parent atom. By ejecting such new centres, it creates its field of influence, and slowly recreates itself. In Mind, too, the Self, which represents the "Point", swells and thereby evolves itself—in knowlddge, feeling and action. Apart from such "swelling" or "field", the Self is a point at which countless tendencies[2] are, so to say, infinitely closely packed together. To use another physical analogy, it is the point at which the battery of infinitely condensed mentative energy can be discharged *as well as* that at which it can be charged again. By continuous discharge, it ejects lines of stress, (*i.e.*, action and reaction) in all directions: and through and upon these lines of stress, its world of limited Experience evolves, starting from infancy. By these stresses again the battery or condenser is recharged—new tendencies are impressed. In its discharges upon the physical universe, the mentative force flows out at the point of the Self, and is converted into physical force by the mechanism of the brain centres which, accordingly, may be regarded as "converters". However that be, the Self is like a tap which, pressed in and out, discharges and recharges the infinite condenser or reservoir of Power or *Śakti* which every limited self essentially is. And not only is that self[3] so; organic matter is so; the atom of inorganic matter is so; the living cell of protoplasm is so; in fact, everything is so in which the *Bindu* or Dynamic Point of Power operates and tends to attain to the state of readiness for evolving action.[4] It should be noted further that this tendency, fundamental as it is, is rhythmic; that is to say, there is alternate expansion[5] and contraction[6] of the *Bindu*, in creation and dissolution, in life and death, in waking and slumber. And such rhythm ought on principle to be traceable in the "life-curve" of even the so-called "dead" atom of matter.

It has been already observed that in expansion the Dynamic Point tends to assume the form of the Dynamic Triangle[7]—that is to say, a

[1] That even the formed body or organism is a radiating field of "magnetic" energy is proved by the laboratory researches of Western Scientists. Cf. the well-known passage of Śruti which means that "Hamsa" or Prāṇa radiates out (Śvetāśvatara-Up., III. 18).

[2] Saṃskāra. [3] Jīvātma. [4] Uchchhūnāvasthā.

[5] Vikāśa. [6] Saṁkoca. [7] Trikona.

triangle whose lines and points are not mathematical lines and points only, but are lines and points of force—a circumstance which can be aptly described by calling the triangle a "Polar Triangle".[1] A Triangle in comparison with the Point, is a condition of unveiling manifestation. It becomes a Point again when the boundary lines or sides are made to shrink infinitely. The three poles are drawn infinitely close together, that is, are ultimately made to coincide. The Point or *Bindu* is, in one sense, the condition of maximum veiling or non-manifestation. It is infinitely condensed Power, but so long as it remains what it is, the lines of operation of Power are, so to say, packed up, that is unmanifest. But if by manifestation we mean the condition of being given as Power, the *Bindu* is, as the Perfect Universe, the state of maximum manifestation. It is Complete Being-ness.[2] In it nothing is held back, nothing is incomplete, partial. Since again all operation, all movement, of whatever kind in the world, presupposes and starts from the *Bindu* it really means infinite potency to move and evolve.

In the Upaniṣads *Brahman* has often been described as smaller than the smallest,[3] and larger than the largest.[4] Now, if by *Brahman* we mean Perfect Experience or Universe, then we see how aptly the description applies to *Brahman*, particularly if we are careful to take the *Bindu* for what it really is.

## PURE EXPERIENCE

THE term 'pure' as appended to experience may mean three things. First, it may mean the unbounded Ether of Consciousness[5] in which an infinitely varied world of experience is in the stress of becoming. Whatever is felt and known, hoped and wished, in fact all the varied experiences of the limited self, appear and disappear, rise and fall, like waves in an infinite sea of Consciousness. Like clouds and myriads of heavenly bodies in Ether again, moving and revolving, men's experiences move and change, "live, move and have their being" in a perfectly placid Ether of Consciousness. Man's spiritual existence is never at any moment simply the aggregate

---

[1] *E.g.*, the Kāmakalā of three Bindus, the first (Mahābindu or Paraśiva or "Sun") holding within itself its aspects when polarised as Śiva Bindu ("Fire") and Śakti Bindu or "Moon". See "The Garland of Letters". The triangle is the symbol of unity with diversity as the experiencer, experiencing and the experienced universe of tridimensional matter. The Triangle resting on its base is the Śiva or Power-holder aspect, the reversed triangle is the Śakti aspect and the Hexagon (Ṣatkona) is the union of the two.

[2] Pūrṇa-Sattā. [3] Aṇoraṇiyān. [4] Māhatomahīyān.

[5] Cidākāsa or Ākāsātmā.

of the modes of experience that he may have at that moment. For pragmatic reasons, he commonly ignores many of the modes themselves: he is commonly partial to a few and regards these as all that he possesses at that moment. But these are not all that is ignored; what is generally ignored, though it cannot be even for a single moment effaced or shut out, is the placid background or atmosphere of Consciousness in which all appearances take place. This placid Spiritual-Ether is patent to intuition,[1] though being the Primary Continuum, the fundamental Basis and Light of all lights,[2] or Light of existence itself, it is not capable of being expressed except in terms of analogies which are themselves its inferior forms. Thus it is called Ether, Space, Illumination, and so forth. The Śāstra itself occasionally uses these and other analogies. Now, as man's spiritual being is never simply the sum-total of the modes of experience (as the sea is not simply the sum of its waves, or ether of the physical masses), so, conversely, his spiritual being is not reduced to nothing by eliminating or effacing the modes of experience. Modes may vanish but experience *as such* must remain: waves may die down, but the sea itself will remain placid.[3] This indeed is the quiescent, placid aspect of man's being—the *Śiva* aspect. Against it we have the stressing, dynamical, moving and changing aspect—the *Śakti* aspect. This experience as such, this universal, unlimited, ineffaceable (though commonly ignored) Ether or Mother-stuff of Experience, perfectly placid and homogeneous, impartial and undirected, is Pure[4] Experience.

This Pure and Primary Ether of Consciousness is *immanent* in the ordinary life of experience: it is given and cannot but be given, but it is generally not suspected; it is ignored. General and impartial Consciousness is never suppressed or superseded by particular, and partial "consciousness". It is always patent to intuition. But it is transcendent also. First, in the sense that it is never exhausted, taken up by particular consciousness, like Ether by the physical masses in, and of, it. It goes beyond. Immense or indefinable as the varied world of experience is, it is larger than that immensity.[5] Secondly, it is transcendent in the sense of being the

---

[1] Realizable in what Maitri-Up. calls "manah-kshaya" (melting away of Mind) and the Śākta Tantras and other Tantras calls "Unmanī bhāva,' or Mindlessness.

[2] As Br.-Up., calls it.

[3] Thus in Mahāpralaya which is cosmic slumber all determinations are effaced. all particulars are withdrawn; but consciousness *as such* does not cease to be.

[4] Śuddha.

[5] Mahato mahīyān. Śvetāśvatara-Up., III, 20.

fourth,[1] that is higher than, and going beyond, the three ordinary states of waking, dreaming and dreamless slumber. In this fourth[2] form, apart from the changing modes of the lower three (in which also it is undoubtedly immanent), it can be realized in that form of super-consciousness known to *Yoga*[2] in which Consciousness is realized as such in its non-differentiated, impartial, placid form *only*—apart from all veiling differences[3] or modes or determinations. Even ordinary intuition establishes that it is immanent in the three states of waking, dreaming and slumbering. It therefore always persists, and unchangingly persists; because even in the three states, when Consciousness appears and evolves as the three states, it still remains as the sustaining and illuminating, placid and impartial Ether of Consciousness;[4] because in this aspect it does not change while appearing to change as the world of forms.[5] Accordingly, the *Māyāvāda* of Śankara and of Gaudāpāda[6] his grand-preceptor, which defines 'reality' as absolutely unchanging persistence, regards the Ether of Consciousness[7] alone as the transcendental real,[5] whilst the world which appears and changes in it is pragmatically real,[8] though relative to the transcendent real,[9] "unreal"[10] in the term of non-persistence. This, however, is a matter of definition only.

Pure Consciousness, in the sense of the Primary Ether,[11] is patent to intuition which involves the turning of the light of attention in upon the Self and its experience. Intuition like outwardly directed attention, may be either pragmatic and centralized (*i.e.*, referring to and condensed about a centre), or non-pragmatic and a-centric.[12] The latter is an essay to review and accept the Fact as such, without allowing attention to be restricted to, and therefore concentrated on, particular sections or features therein such as particular sensations or feelings. The latter is not therefore swayed by special interests.[13] It looks upon and orders experience in its concrete entireness. Now, to this a-centric, non-pragmatic intuition, the

[1] Māndūkya-Up. in particular, describes the four "pādas" of Ātman, and correlates them to the four mātrās of Om. The four states are: (1) "Vahih-prajna" (Mind acting through the sense of external perception and action); (2) "Antah-prajna" (when Mind feeds on its own ideas and samskāras); (3) "Ghana-prajna" (consciousness is massive, undifferentiated as in dreamless slumber); and (4) "Śānta" the Supreme State.

[2] Turīya. Nirvikalpa Samādhi.

[3] Viśeṣa. [4] Cidākāśa or Śiva.

[5] Reality as such in contrast with reality as it appears is "Akṣara" and "kṣara".

[6] Cidākāśa. [7] Pāramārthika sat.

[8] Vyāvahārika sat. This is not recognised by Dṛṣṭi-Sṛṣṭivāda form of Māyā-vāda.

[9] Pāramārthika sat. [10] Asat. [11] Cidākāśa.

[12] "Sabīja" and "Nirbija — with or without "Seed". [13] Rāga.

Ether of Consciousness, with a universe of varied experience living, moving and having its being in it, is patent. Then again this Spiritual and Ultimate Ether can be established by the method of Conceptual Limit and that of Perceptional Limit.[1] In using the first we ask ourselves this question: What ultimately, *i.e.*, in the limit, remains when we imagine or think away all modes, all particular determinations from the Fact or Universe of Experience? The latter method is approached and incompletely applied in many normal (*e.g.*, just going to wake, or just falling asleep) and abnormal (*e.g.*, certain kinds of so-called "unconsciousness," anæsthesia and so forth) experiences in which particular determinations tend more or less closely to the vanishing point without vanishing actually and absolutely. This method is said to be perfectly applied—so that the particular determinations of world-experience vanish and the Ether of Consciousness[2] alone remains—in the supreme *yoga* experience.[3] In the process of this *Yoga*, the common "Polar Triangle" of experience contracts into *Bindu*, and this latter dissolves, as an intrinsic strain-centre may be imagined to dissolve in ether, in the strain-less and stress-less Ether of Consciousness.

In the second place, Pure Experience can be taken to mean Experience which is not limited and conditioned and opposed by that which appears to be not Experience. Although really all is experience, yet ordinary experience seems to be limited, conditioned and opposed by what is commonly believed to be not experience, *e.g.*, by matter. There is thus the alien, objective, extra-mental enveloping order for the limited self. It is a system of correlated centres which are not believed to be co-essential with the experiencing self. Its experience is thus the result of the stresses of this external system of centres and those of other centres which are the limited knowing self. Thus duality is involved in the common position in life. The selves are reals entrenching themselves into the spatial, temporal and causal background of a Reality larger than themselves. Each has his own sphere or "field". With respect to the larger Reality, man's sphere, (an indefinable universe though it may be to intuition) is part or section.[4] But suppose we look at the Reality itself disengaging our attention from the sections. Sections are not indeed lost in that case: they lie imbedded in the immense Whole.[5] And what is this immense

[1] See "Approaches to Truth", last section, for its elaboration.
[2] Cidākāśa. [3] Nirvikalpa Samādhi.
[4] Amśa, Kalā. [5] Pūrṇa as Citsvarūpa.

Whole? Experience and nothing but experience. There is no longer an alien, objective order conditioning and opposing Experience. Duality is gone. Reality as the Whole[1] is Pure Experience, not indeed in the first sense explained before, but in this that experience is not opposed by anything, (*e.g.*, matter) which is, or believed as, non-experience.[2] Suppose also, on the other hand, we begin with an individual sphere of experience, and gradually extend its boundary. The "alien" system of mind, life and matter centres which, in their mutual action and reaction on the given centre, constitute the objective order, is recognised as co-essential with the given centre itself, that is, as Consciousness[3] and its Power; Reality in the infinite richness of its expression is recognised as *Cit*, or Consciousness, and in its infinite variety of functioning as the play[4] of *Cit-Śakti* or Consciousness as Power.

Perception is (though we commonly do not suspect it) an act of *owning;* that is, establishing an essential identity between Self and Not-Self, Spirit and Matter.[5] The essential Basis or Common Factor of all existence, whether objective or subjective, is this Consciousness. Every act of perception brings out this common factor, without, however, the action ordinarily suspecting it. Everything is in, and of, *Cit;* the Subject-Centre as well as the system of Object-Centres. In such "knowledge"[6] therefore, experience is the Whole[7] again; and since then there remains nothing other than, and conditioning and opposing, experience, we may call such experience Pure Experience, *i.e.*, Experience and nothing else.

In the third place, 'Pure' may mean 'of one kind or quality'. Perfection of purity in this sense is of course reached in the Ether of Consciousness which is undifferentiated (therefore having no qualitative variations) experience.[8] But apart from this, and in degrees inferior to this, man may have uniform experience which are, therefore, pure in this sense. In his ordinary experience there are, for example, the three poles of Base, Index and Co-efficient explained above. Base stands for immediate, direct perceptions or intuitions;[9] Index for actually recalled and suggested

[1] Pūrṇa as Citsvarūpa.

[2] This is the experience of "Sarvāsmi" or "Brahmāsmi"—I am all: nothing is other than, alien to, Ātman. "Pure Experience" in the first sense would be — "cinmātro'ham" "Niranjano'ham," "Buddha-jnānamasmi" — *i.e.*, I am pure, "undifferenced'' Cit.

[3] Cit.

[4] Līlā of Śakti.

[5] Pramāṇa-Caitanya, Pramātri-caitanya, and Prameya-caitanya.

[6] Jnāna.

[7] Pūrṇa.

[8] See last Chapter but one for further explanation of Śuddha (Pure) and Aśuddha (Not-pure).

[9] Aparokṣa jnāna.

elements, gathering around intuitions and constituting their "halo" of meaning. Co-efficient stands for tendencies[1] by, and in, which the given experience grows and changes like a crystal in the requisite solution. Now, suppose we imagine an Experience which is all Base with no Index and no Co-efficient; that is, an experience which is wholly, in all its elements, actual, direct, immediate.[2] Nothing is, or requires to be, recalled or suggested; nothing which is merely possible (*i.e.*, tendency) is, or requires to be, actualized. Then this is Pure experience in the sense of being of one kind or order. It should be noted in this connection that in dreamless slumber,[3] the Co-efficient is at its maximum, Index is almost nil, and Basis at its minimum, being only a vague, undifferentiated but, as the Śāstra tells us, pleasant[4] feeling of being. In dream[5] all the three poles exist, though the emphasis seems to lie on that of the Index. However that be, Pure Experience which makes the Base the whole of Experience, which is not limited by any unrealized tendencies or possibilities, and which has no admixture of any element that is only a suggestion of another, not directly given, is experience which, in a sense, is whole[6] or Perfect.

Similarly, experience which is only statical or only dynamical will be pure in the sense of being of one kind. The Sānkhyan self[7] or Vedantic Ether of Consciousness[8] is purely statical:[9] it is perfect quiescence. Sānkhyan *Prakṛti* though not recognised as Consciousness-Experience in Sānkhya, is purely dynamical, because it always moves, whether homogeneously[10] or variedly. *Śakti* in Śakti-vāda is essentially Consciousness-Power; and Consciousness, has both a statical, quiescent aspect and a dynamical, stressing aspect. But quiescent Consciousness[12] is also Power,[13] in this sense that Consciousness remains and continues as such (that is, unchanged) by its Power: it persists, it conserves itself. If to suffer a change implies power, not to suffer a change also implies it. In fact, persistence or self-conservation is one of the fundamental expressions of Power—the Power by which Reality or Substance is constituted and held together as such. Hence if we say that *Śiva* in one sense is pure rest, we must say that in another sense He is pure motion or action. A substance that merely

[1] Samskāras. [2] Aparokṣa.
[3] Suṣupti. [4] "Happily I slept. I knew nothing".
[5] Svapna. [6] Pūrna.
[7] Puruṣa, which is neither Kāraṇa (cause) not Kārya (effect) and is cinmātra.
[8] Cidākaśā.
[9] It is the Śiva aspect of the Śākta's Śiva-Śakti
[10] Sadriśa-pariṇāma. [11] Visadriśa-pariṇāma.
[12] Śiva. [13] Śakti.

stops but does not persist, does not continue, is one that is dead and gone. To persist or continue, it must move or act; though, to ensure unchanged continuance, it must be absolutely uniform, invariable or pure action. Its action is analogous to uniform movement of Śānkhyan Psycho-physical Principle.[1] Hence *Śiva* is actionless[2] as well as (as *Śakti*) acting,[3] not merely as, and in the aspect of the changing world but even as Ether of Consciousness.[4] These two aspects (actionless and acting) of *Śiva* in the Ether of Consciousness[4] do not however contradict each other: they do not constitute duality. They are merely two ways (from man's point of view) of expressing one and the same fact. *Śiva*-Experience is therefore really non-dual experience,[5] one essentially indivisible experience, and is, therefore, according to the definition stated, Pure Experience.

Power is both Power to persist and to change. It is the latter which is commonly called Power,[6] though, as we have seen, the former is equally so. Pure action is commonly regarded as no action, pure movement as rest. It is so regarded because commonly and practically man is interested in change or variation. But this is, for reasons above explained, a pragmatic and partial view. In the complete view, rest and pure action can both be predicated of *Śiva* as Ether of Consciousness,[4] because they mean the same thing; they express one non-dual[5] Fact.

On the other hand, Power[6] is that aspect of Consciousness in which it stresses and changes as the world-order. As such changing action is commonly called action or movement, Power[6] is regarded as the moving, acting dynamical aspect of Consciousness.[7] If Consciousness[7] which is the essence of Power,[6] be veiled, that is unrecognised, then Power[6] is the creative Impulse that continuously changes as the world—there being no rest, no endurance, no permanence. Such Power[6] becomes acceptable to such philosophies as that of Heraclitus of old and of Bergson to-day. But it is essentially a power of Consciousness;[7] there is no warrant for going beyond and behind Consciousness[7] in searching for the common root of the world and experience. And though Power[6] is dynamic, is Movement, it cannot but be set against, and sustained by, a quiescent background of Consciousness,[7] the Ether of Consciousness,[8] the Supreme *Śiva*. In fact, an all-change, all-movement view of Reality cannot be assumed without destroying the warrant of experience, the only warrant

---

[1] Prakṛti. [2] Niṣkriya. [3] Sakriya.
[4] Cidākāśa. [5] Advaita. [6] Śakti.
[7] Cit. [8] Cidākāśa. The Mother is Cidrūpiṇī.

and sanction of unimpeachable authority that man possesses. Not only does *Śakti* presuppose *Śiva; Śakti* is *Śiva.* She is that not merely in the sense that She is *Cit* as Power to move, act and change; but also in the sense that She is *Cit* as Power to persist; in other words, *Śakti,* though dynamical, also possesses the essential character of the Ether of Consciousness,[1] of Substance and Reality. As such Ether[1] is statical in one sense (*i.e.*, in the sense of unchanging) and dynamical in another (*i.e.*, in the sense of persisting or continuing), so *Śakti* is dynamical in one sense (*i.e.*, in the sense of moving and changing), and statical in another (*i.e.*, in the sense of persisting as such). *Śakti* is always *Śakti;* She is eternal,[2] in creation and dissolution, in action as well as in rest, in latency as well as in potency; She becomes never other than *Śakti* and is never dissociated from *Śiva* or *Cit.*[3] Even Perfect Power cannot do away with itself—cease to be other than Power. Now, if the experience of such Ether,[1] quiescent and persistent, was pure experience according to the definition given, so must be that of *Śakti,* moving and persisting as such. The latter like the former seems to involve a contradiction in itself—movement and persistence. But, as in the former, the contradictories blend into one non-dual[4] fact in the complete view, having arisen only from the circumstances of man's partial and pragmatic survey. To know (realize) *Śakti* is therefore pure Experience.[5]

## PERFECT EXPERIENCE

Perfect Experience can be best described by the negative method.[6] The Ether of Consciousness[7] as undifferentiated pure Consciousness, is also describable by the negative method. One is, however, not exactly the other. In the first place, Perfect Experience is an Experience of *no* veiling.[8] Veiling treats and disturbs experience fundamentally by setting up Dynamic Points or Centres of strain and stress, whereby Experience becomes referred to, determined and limited by the action and reaction of, correlated Centres. Centralized experience is essentially veiled and cramped experience. Then, secondarily and incidentally, veiling proceeds to create aspects and poles in experience. Thus there arise such distinctions

[1] Cidākāśa. The Mother is Cidrūpiṇī. [2] Nitya.

[3] Na śivah Śakti-rahito, na śaktir vyatirekinī (Śiva Dṛṣṭih III, 23).

[4] Advaita.

[5] Śakti-jnāna is Śiva-jnāna and Brahma-jnāna. The abode of Śakti is the abode of Śiva or Viṣṇu, See v. 44, Ṣatcakra Nirūpaṇa.

[6] Niṣedha, vyatireka, neti. [7] Cidākāśa.

[8] See the explanation of Śuddha-tattvas in the last chapter but one.

as that between actual experience and possible experience, presentations and tendencies,[1] conscious and sub-conscious experience; that between clear, accepted experience, and obscure, ignored experience; actual experience and pragmatic experience; that between the "Fact" and "Fact-Section"; experience and beyond; that between statical aspect and dynamical; changing and unchanging; and so on. Briefly it *limits* experience firstly by setting up separate "universes" in it; secondly by cutting up each universe into aspects and planes such as statical-dynamical, actual-possible, latent-patent; thirdly, by making man partial to sections, pragmatically unmindful of the whole. Now, in Perfect Experience the veil must go in all these three forms. In other words, Perfect Experience cannot be limited to particular "universes," to particular aspects and planes, and to particular sections or features. Conversely, an Experience which is that of a particular Centre operative as such: which is statical only or dynamical only; which is actual in part and possible in part; which is accepted in sections and ignored in the whole;—is not Perfect Experience.

In the second place, Perfect Experience, which is also the Supreme Fact, is alogical.[2] It cannot be reached and expressed by the logical categories. For instance, the Supreme Fact is not a numerical Fact: one and many are categories which do not apply to it. So as regards the categories of Time, Space, Causality. Fact is not now and then, here and there, cause and effect. But, then, two things are to be noted as regards the alogicality of Perfect Experience. First, though transcending all categories, it involves them all. That is, categories of quantity, quality, relation and modality are all immanent in it; arise out of the Power of Consciousness;[4] relate to particular determinations wrought by that Power; and therefore to all "Fact-sections" contained, and even to their sum total.[4] Thus Consciousness,[3] both in the sense of Ether of Consciousness[5] and that of Perfect Experience, is unreachable by thought and discourse.[6] This is the true characterization[7] of Consciousness as Cit.[8] Secondly, we may have nevertheless an approximate characterization,[9]

[1] Samskāras.

[2] Parā Samvit which is Tattvātīta or Beyond the Tattvas or Power defined in a particular way. See *post*, last chapter but one.

[3] Cit. [4] See "Approaches to Truth" for further discussion.

[5] Cidākāśa. [6] Avāngmānasogochara. [7] Svarūpa-lakṣaṇa.

[8] Mahānirvāṇa Tantra, III. 7, gives the "Svarūpa" and III, 9 gives "Tatastha-lākṣaṇa" or Brahman.

[9] Tatastha-lakṣaṇa.

based upon man's experience and thought: that though the categories of judgment do not apply to the fulness and perfectness of experience (which is therefore alogical), yet some concepts come nearer to it than others, and therefore some concepts may be thought as giving an approximate representation of it. It is thus allowable to speak of it as one, immense and infinite, whole and perfect.[1] Nevertheless, in seeking to completely possess and express the alogical by means of logical concepts, we ultimately discover ourselves as dealing in contradictions. To think of the unthinkable, to speak of the unspeakable, involves, *ipso facto*, contradiction. And since man cannot help sometimes thinking and speaking of his Experience, in its perfectness as well as in its segments, his thought does sometimes necessarily involve contradiction. We should expect it rather than be surprised.

For example, we find, in thinking about Consciousness and the World, that *Cit* does not and also does change: that it stresses and changes as the world, and yet it remains unchanged as Pure *Cit*. In trying to cure this logical defect, we commonly do two things. We say either with *Māyāvādā* Vedānta that from the absolute standpoint changing is unreal, that *Cit* does not really change at all; or with *Śākta* and some other forms of Vedānta that changing and unchanging are both real, and that they relate to two aspects of Consciousness.[2] But in either solution the contradiction remains unsolved. The former soon finds that contradiction turned out by one gate inevitably returns by another. *Māyā* or the "hypnotic suggestion"[3] by which unchanging Consciousness[2] appears as the changing world is said to be neither real nor unreal,[4] nor partly real and partly unreal, and hence inscrutable.[5] Contradiction thus reappears in the statement of *Māyā*, and inscrutableness or alogicality is ultimately recognised as the only answer. The crux of the whole problem is this: Though of course the changing world is not real in the sense of 'being persistent in the three tenses of time,'[6] yet it is there in a way: and it can never be said that it does not exist.[7] And this changing existence (call

[1] It is this, together with Sat, Cit, Ānanda, which is commonly given as the Svarūpa-lakṣaṇa which is a definition that always applies to Brahman; and which never becomes contradicted (Vādhita).

[2] Cit. [3] "Indrajāla."

[4] Sadasad-vilakṣaṇā, Tattvā-tattvābhyām anirvacanīya, as Śankara's Commentary has it. See also Sarvasāropaniṣat for definition of Māyā.

[5] Anirvācyā. [6] Kālatrayāvādhitatvam.

[7] Non-existent like the aerial flower, hare's horn, child of a barren woman, etc. The world possesses admittedly not only Prātibhāsika but Vyāvahārika sattā. Compare however the position of the Ekajīva-vādin who recognises only Pārmārthika forms.

it unreal if to change is to be unreal) of the world-experience side by side with unchanging existence of Pure Experience[1] is a Gordian knot which (some may say) we do not either untie by any theory of cosmic hypnosis, or cut by any logical or dialectic weapon. It is best to frankly recognise that Reality (though Consciousness[2] itself) in its wholeness is alogical, and that, therefore, any attempt, direct or indirect, to clothe it in logical concepts must involve us in contradiction.

Neither is the contradiction solved by splitting up Experience into aspects. Aspects help us to imagine pictorially different functionings of one substance; but, as for understanding, they tell us no more than this that the functionings, and therefore, the corresponding powers are different, and that they are experienced as such. Consciousness[2] by its quiescent,[3] mind-transcendent[4] Power[5] remains the Pure Ether of Consciousness[6] or *Śiva;* and by its active, stressing[7] immanent-in-mind[8] or involved Power[5] changes as world-experience. This is, from the point of view of understanding, no more than saying that Consciousness[2] exercises two different (and one may say, opposed) functions, and that we do not know how and why. In spiritual intuition, not swayed by any pragmatic interests whatever, Consciousness[2] is beyond the antithesis of quiescent and moving;[9] beyond the antithesis of active and passive, agent and patient:[10] beyond the antithesis of negation and affirmation;[11] and even beyond "thatness" or the antithesis of this and that, immanent and transcendent.[12] 'Beyond'[13] here means this: Consciousness[2] while presenting to thought the antitheses, polarities or dualities of active-passive and so forth, is not, in its completeness, summed up and expressed by those correlatives. It is Absolute.[14] The correlations are, however, not to be dismissed as mere illusion or an unreal imposition ("unreal" even in *Māyāvāda* means something different); since it is Consciousness[2] itself which, primarily as the Supreme Centre or "I"[15] and secondarily, as Finite Centres or the individual Egos,[16] thinks itself in and as such correlations.

---

[1] In Jāgrat, Svapna and Suṣupti as immanent, in Turīya or Samādhi as transcendent.
[2] Cit. [3] Śānta. [4] Unmanī. [5] Śakti.
[6] Cidākāśa. [7] Sakriya. [8] Samanī. [9] Śāntātīta.
[10] Kriyātīta. [11] Vākyātīta. [12] Tattvāttīta. [13] Atīta.
[14] Iu that form of Sādhanā which is called Kuṇḍalinī yoga, the Ājnā-cakra (the two-petalled lotus at the forehead) represents the last stage of duality or correlativity (which is syurbolized by the fact that it has two "petals"), beyond which is the "place" of Parama-śiva in which Śiva and Śakti unite, which is niṣkala (aspectless) as well as paramakalā (the Supreme Aspect).
[15] Parāhantā. [16] Aparāhantā.

For example, again, let us ask this: is Consciousness--without or with aspects?[1] In *Kuṇḍalinī yoga*[2] we have the "place" beyond the sixth[3] Centre where there is the thousand-petalled lotus representing perfect dynamic[4] Reality, Universe or Experience as well as the perfect static Void[5] which represents pure Reality or Experience.[6] This is to say that contradictions meet here in non-dual[7] experience. So that it is 'beyond'[8] all categories of dual experience[9] *as well as* the "Supreme"[10] of all categories—the "Limit" of all definitions. Thus it is Supreme Reality in its aspect as the source of all which is partial:[11] supreme Time,[12] supreme Ether, supreme Sound, supreme Speech, infinitely concentrated Power, and supreme *Śiva* and *Śakti*.[13] Even ordinary experience, reviewed apart from pragmatic interests, indicates such a solution of contradictories in a way; but for a perfect proving appeal must be made, however, to Supreme Experience—that is, Experience of the *yogi* beyond the sixth Centre.[3] "Supreme"[14] in the above characterizations means an experience which subsumes all dual and imperfect experiences; which, with reference to Centres, becomes dualized and polarized as subjective-objective, active-passive, statical-dynamical experiences.[15] When, for example, it has been said the Experience has both statical and stressing aspects,[16] it remains to be recognised that there is an Aspect of Experience of which both these are dual, polarized manifestations, and which therefore is not in itself completely expressed either by the one or by the other. This fuller Aspect is the Supreme Aspect.[17] So also as regards subjective-objective and other polarities.

Let our next question be this: is Consciousness as *Cit* statical or dynamical ? Whether Western psychologists may or may not agree, it has generally been patent to Indian thought that Consciousness presents

---

[1] Niṣkala or Sakala.
[2] See "The Serpent Power".
[3] Or Ājnā.
[4] Sakala.
[5] Parama Vyoma, or Parama Śūnya : the Niśkala aspect.
[6] Niṣkala, Nirguṇa, *i.e.*, Cidākāśa.
[7] Advaita.
[8] Atīta.
[9] Such as rest (Śānta), action (Sakriya) and so forth.
[10] Paramakalā.
[11] Kalā.
[12] That is transcendent time not split up into sections as is empirical time through the action of sun and moon. Supreme Time is God from the time aspect, sectionless and ever enduring.
[13] Paravyoma, Paranāda, Paravāk, Parabindu, Paraśiva, Paraśakti.
[14] Parama.
[15] See last Chapter but one for evolution of Tattvas; also "The Garland of Letters" and "Śakti and Śākta" on the 36 Tattvas.
[16] Kalā.
[17] Parama Kalā.

two aspects—the unmoving, undifferentiated aspects of "Consciousness-Ether," and the moving, diversified aspect of particularized experiences. Now, Consciousness as Perfect Experience (*i.e.*, in its Supreme Aspect) involves and subsumes both: is alogical and cannot be defined or characterized by either. Any attempt to treat logically (*i.e.*, by categories) the Alogical and Perfect Experience will lead sooner or later to a tangle of thinking. Suppose one were to say first that Perfect Experience is moving evolving *ad infinitum*. But how can Experience be perfect which is in the making, which is unevolved ? How can knowledge be perfect the bounds of which are ever widening and widening ? Shall we say, then, that Perfect Experience is not an "Ideal" merely, realizable in an infinitely distant time, but that it is an actual Fact, that it is completely realized, evolved and statical ? The Perfect[1] has no need to move, and it does not move. It has nothing to add to it: no deficiencies to supply; no ends to realize. Why should it move, or change ? But this view also involves difficulties. The whole[1] does not move; but the parts imbedded in it, the experience of the Centres living in it, do move. Now, how can the whole be imagined to remain unchanged, unmoved, while the parts in it are changing and moving ? To say with *Māyā-vāda* that the parts and their changes are unreal is no solution for those who cannot but accept their reality. To say again that the changes of the parts neutralize one another and do not therefore disturb the equilibrium of the whole is no solution either, for the analogy of physical equilibrium cannot be extended fully to Experience which to be full[1] must sum up the experiences of the parts, must subsume the *changing* experience of the parts. Hence we find ourselves between the horns of a destructive dilemma in attempting to "rationalize" the whole.[1]

The dilemma is this: to say that Perfect experience changes and evolves is to deny that it is Perfect; and to say that experience is unchanging and statical is to deny that it is the whole of Experience as it actually is. But as a whole it must be either moving or unmoving. There is no logical escape from the dilemma.[2] In spiritual intuition, the whole[1] is alogical, and, to the analytic understanding, it presents the two aspects of statical and dynamical. It is known as the whole[1] in spite of all immanent movements; additions and subtractions do not affect it, as expressed by the

[1] Pūrṇa.

[2] This is the meaning of the famous "Tarkāpratishthānāt" in Vedānta. Vedānta Sūtra, II, 1, 11.

mystical saying—"even if the whole[1] be subtracted from the whole,[1] the whole[1] remains."[2]

The question whether Perfect Experience is subjective or not, will be found, if pressed home, to lead to a similar dilemma. By subjective experience is meant an experience that is referred to and "owned" by a Centre or Self. If, therefore, we hold that Perfect Experience is subjective, we must imagine a Perfect Centre or Self as the owner of it. In other words, we must define Perfect Experience as the experience of the Lord.[3] Approximately, that is, to the highest reach of our understanding and expression, it is so, of course. Perfect experience, in so far as it can be owned at all, can be owned only by the Supreme Self.[4] That is to say, after alogical non-dual[5] Perfect Experience has been polarized into the aspects mentioned,[6] there arises the relation of owner and owned, subject and object, and Perfect Experience thus polarized, becomes the experience of the Supreme Subject or Lord. It is obvious from this that the Perfect Experience which is polarized into aspects and the "Perfect" Experience which as one aspect is owned by another aspect, are not logically of the same order. The former is extralogical. The Lord[7] owns and makes an object of Perfect Experience. To express it in other terms, the Lord,[3] is the highest logical construction[8] (not fiction) that man can put upon alogical Perfect Experience. This, however, is not to say that the Lord is "our" construction merely. For the existence of the Supreme Centre and for the Supreme Experience owned by it man, according to Vedānta, possesses as sure a guarantee as he possesses for his own self and his own experiences. It is more than a mere speculative idea. The Lord is the *Brahman* and the mind which conceives Him is the work of His Power.

Before we pass on, it should be observed that "Perfect" and "Supreme" as epithets applied to the Lords' Experience mean perfect or supreme in the logical order or hierarchy in which we, together with countless other centres, are placed. The Lord is the "Limit" or Ideal of local or rational experience. He is thus the Supreme Cause; the Supreme Agent; the Supreme Knower; the Supreme Being as regards Infinite Time[9] and Space[10]

[1] Pūrna.
[2] See Brihadāraṇyaka V, I, 1: Īśa-Up. (opening Mantra).
[3] Paramātmā or Īśvara. For the technical sense of Īśvara-tattva see last chapter but one.
[4] Parāhantā.
[5] Advaita.
[6] Prakāśa and Vimarśa (see *ante*).
[7] Īśvara.
[8] In the Evolution of 36 Tattvas, Īśvara-tattva represents the third "stage". See *post*.
[9] Nitya.
[10] Sarva-vyāpi.

and so on. He is thus the "Limit" of perfection of the logical categories (Causality, Time, Space, etc.) He is thus the perfection of "rational" existence. But as man's own experience, and therefore existence, is not wholly rational or logical, as, in other words, his experience presents two aspects to him (that of the alogical Fact, and that of "Fact-sections" logically treated), so also in Vedānta does the Lord's Supreme Experience. His Experience has a logical or rational aspect, and an alogical or ultra-rational aspect, and, as in man's case, it is the latter which is larger than, subsumes and sustains the former. Man's experience is alogical while it is being logically known, treated or constructed by him. While in his experience a self knows an object, the experience is not wholly either the one or the other. Nor is it merely the sum of the two. So also in the Lord's case, the Lord's Supreme Experience presents to himself and to man's thought the poles of a Supreme Self and a Supreme Object; but it has, and presents to the Lord, another and a "more" supreme aspect,[1] *viz.*, a Whole[2] and alogical Experience or Fact in which, and of which, Supreme self, Supreme Object and the rest are but modes, which is not therefore wholly one of these modes. This indeed does not belittle but really establishes the greatness of the Lord. It says that He has an aspect of being and experience larger than and transcending what He presents to man's thought and belief (*viz.*, the rational or thinkable aspect). As the famous *Puruṣa Sūkta* in Rigveda and Atharva-veda has it: "He is thousand-headed, thousand-eyed and thousand-footed; He, while completely pervading all this, exceeds all this by the measure of ten fingers (so to say)."

Next, we deal with the moral and æsthetic question: Is Perfect Experience (or Being) good or evil, beautiful or ugly ? Does "Perfectness" as applied to experience mean or connote ethical and æsthetic perfection? Undoubtedly it does connote it; but it is more than ("exceeds by ten fingers" so to say) ethical and æsthetic perfection. Good and Beautiful are undoubtedly aspects of it, but we cannot say that Perfect Being is Good and Beautiful *only*. Is it then Evil, and Ugly *also*? Yes, according to the Hindu view, for these are also aspects of it. It means this: Good and Evil, Beautiful and Ugly are categories which are applicable to Experience (=Being) when it has divided and manifested itself as aspects or polarities; it is good or evil, beautiful or ugly *in so far as* aspects or poles exist in it and divide it. But apart from, or without reference to aspects or poles, it is unreachable by either pair of categories. Even while

[1] Parama Kalā. [2] Pūrṇa.

it is taken into poles or aspects, it is agreeable to these pairs of categories in so far as it is taken into aspects or poles; but even then, in its wholeness, "it exceeds all this by ten fingers." The categories belong to the logical, rational or thinkable order; they are therefore applicable when, and in so far as, that order has appeared. And since Perfect Being is of the alogical ultra-rational and unthinkable order even when the logical rational and thinkable has evolved in it, the categories are not applicable to it as the whole.[1]

Well; but are they applicable to it as Experience of the Supreme Self, as Lord's Experience or Being? Is not the Lord's Being perfectly good and perfectly beautiful? Undoubtedly it is. But since according generally to the Hindu conception, the Lord's being is the "Limit" or "Supreme Position" of the logical, rational or thinkable order, we cannot restrict His Being and manifestation to one set of poles only such as good and beautiful, leaving out the correlative poles such as evil and ugly. These latter are also in Him and in His manifestation. Hindu thought has again and again, and boldly, attributed all possible polarities or pairs of opposite categories to the Lord's manifestation. Thus He is at once beautiful[2] and fearful,[3] righteousness[4] and unrighteousness,[5] light[6] and darkness,[7] knowledge[8] and error,[9] and so on. The Mother *Kāli* who holds Her blood-streaming sword and the severed head of the demonic *Asura*, both dispels all fear and gives all blessings. As the supreme synthesis[10] of the logical (*i.e.*, presenting polarities, correlations, aspects) order of experience, the Lord's experience cannot evidently in this view be narrowed down to one set of poles, correlations or aspects only; and not only His experience but His being. A purely ethical God and the existence of Evil (moral and physical) in the world have never been successfully made to fit in with a monistic scheme of the world-order: they have involved an ill-concealed dualism or pluralism. Without however, discussing this aspect of the question, it may be observed that by setting up a God in whom poles and contradictions live side by side, the basis of human morality and religion is not necessarily undermined. Good and Evil both exist in Him, both flow out of Him as streams that variously mingle in the world; but man has, and knows that he has, his law that is the law

[1] Pūrṇa. [2] Śobana. [3] Bhīśana.
[4] Dharma. [5] Adharma. [6] Jyotih.
[7] Tamah. [8] Jnāna.
[9] Bhrama. And so Mārkaṇḍeya Candi salutes the Devi as in the form of Error.
[10] Parākāshthā.

of *his* essential being,[1] given to operate in the line of righteousness; he has his satisfaction and happiness in operating along that line; his progress and ascent in the pursuit of it; and ultimately his liberation, when he again goes beyond the realm of law.[1] To be thus essentially constituted in spite of his apparently being a mixture of good and evil,[2] is part of the Divine outburst, is organic to the cosmic plan. This is, to say in one word, his law of being. Hence the same Power which stands surety for the cosmic plan also stands surety for man's law.[3] There is thus divine guarantee for human evolution.

Summing up we find that Perfect Experience is not in Time and in Space and yet it manifests itself as beginningless and endless cosmic flux and cosmic configuration; it is not Cause, and yet it is the ultimate Basis of causation; it is not a Centre, and yet countless subjects and objects are in varied stress on its bosom; it is not Cosmos, and yet myriads of worlds appear and disappear in it like bubbles on water; it is unthinkable and yet all thought and speech proceed from it; it is the Whole and yet all aspects are Its aspects.[4]

## CONSCIOUSNESS AND REALITY

THE fact which in Vedānta is absolutely beyond doubt is not exactly, as Descartes thought, "I think" but the indefinable universe of experience of which 'I think' is a logical—and by no means an inseparable, adequate and complete—treatment and description, that is, limitation. It is a logical representation of what is presented as alogical. Remembering the definition of Fact given before, we may say therefore, that Fact or Experience is, Reality. This Reality is defined as *absolutely doubtless*[5] *Being Experience*. By "Being-Experience" is meant an experience which does not discriminate between 'thought' and 'thing', and which feels those two aspects or 'poles' as identical. It is the alogical Whole[6] which may, and often does, involve these and many other aspects or poles, but is not partitioned into, and expressible in terms of, aspects or poles. Intuition of the total universe of experience which we have "at any moment" (with-

[1] Dharma. [2] Dharma and Adharma.
[3] Dharma. Dharma and evolution are dealt with in a later section.
[4] Cf. the statements that Brahman is with "four feet", "sixteen limbs or parts", and so forth.
[5] Maitri-Up., VI, 32 (ka)—speaks of Ātman as "the Real of the Real". (Satyam satyasya.)
[6] Pūrṇa. Chānd.-Up calls it "Bhuman"—the Great, or Immense which is also the meaning of Brahman which comes from a root denoting "bigness".

out our commonly recognising, however, that we have it, because we are pragmatic and partial) will, it is said, readily prove that such experience is both being and experience, and absolutely doubtless and undeniable being and experience. This indefinable[1] Whole of experience *is* and it is *Consciousness*—that is it is Being[2] and Consciousness[3] undistinguishably given.[4] This Whole of experience is neither metaphysical nor physical, neither transcendental nor empirical,[5] and yet it is all. It is the Given which may or may not, at any given moment, involve, these and other correlate aspects; and which, under logical operation, yields these and such other aspects.

To be absolute or perfect Reality, Experience must be perfect in the sense of the Whole.[6] That is to say, it must be taken as Supreme Aspect[7] which involves and yet transcends all particular varied aspects[8] and pure or undifferentiated.[9] To narrow Experience down to either of the subordinate aspects is to cut down the perfectness of Reality—is to make Reality *relatively* real. This is the root of the matter.

Thus, suppose, we define with *Māyāvāda* Vedānta Reality[10] as Consciousness[3] in its pure aspect,[9] because this aspect persists in and through all states of experience, and is never effaced or cancelled,[11] and because the other aspect is one of incessant change or flux. We have seen that Pure Consciousness[3] or "Ether Consciousness"[12] is an inalienable feature of experience in all states and forms. If therefore Reality is unchanging persistence or ineffaceable being, then Pure Consciousness[3] is Reality. But, then, how can we be sure that this *alone* is Reality in the sense of ineffaceable being? It is true that Consciousness in the other aspect is stressing and changing; that the consciousness of this moment is not that of the next; and that possibly in ecstasy[13] or in the "fourth"[14] state the stressing and changing aspect may altogether vanish and the pure and quiescent aspect alone may remain. The world of name and form has

---

[1] Brihadāraṇyaka, IV, 2, 4, says—"Sa esha neti netyātmā grihyo na grihyate"—He can be only negatively referred to; he is unreachable by thought and speech, and so, cannot by them be reached.

[2] Sat. [3] Cit.

[4] Chānd. Up., VI, 8, 9, 10......16—"Idam sarvam tat satyam sa ātmā tattvamasi śvetaketo," etc.—which establishes an identity, *viz.*, World=(Idam)=Reality (Satyam) =Consciousness (Ātman)=Self (Tvam).

[5] Chānd.-Up., VII, 25, 1.—"Sa evādhastāt sa uparishthāt"—the Brahman Consciousness is here "below" as well as there "above".

[6] Pūrṇa. [7] Paramā Kala. [8] Sakala.

[9] Niṣkala. [10] Sattā. [11] Vādhita.

[12] Cidākāśa. [13] Samādhi. [14] Turīya, Śānta.

by some been likened to a hypnotic suggestion,[1] a dream, an illusion, so that with the passing of this suggestion or dream, pure changeless and aspectless *Cit* alone abides. Let it be granted for the sake of argument that this may be so. But if *Cit* thus always abides, so also does *Cit* as Power —that is, Power to be and appear in and as different aspects.[2] If *Cit* changelessly persists in all the states by its own Power (and we have seen that to be or to persist is of the essence of Power), it also changes or stresses by its own Power; and in fact to change and persist while changing (it may be as *Māyāvāda* says, apparently), and in ecstasy[3] and liberation[4] to cease to change at all, are all equally undeniable manifestations of *Cit* as Power. Hence this Power—*i.e.*, to be and appear as different aspects and forms—is an inalienable feature of Consciousness,[5] is in fact Consciousness[5] itself; and if the latter is real in the sense of being ineffaceably given, the former is also so. Consciousness[5] as Power projects the world-order remaining itself pure Consciousness[5] all the while; Consciousness also as Power withdraws the world into itself which thus it bursts upon itself, as it were a bubble on the surface of water as *Māyā-vāda* often puts it. It follows therefore that Power *as such*—that is as distinguished from different forms or directions of it—is, even from the Māyāvādin's standpoint, real.

But what, it may be asked, do we gain by discriminating Consciousness[5] from its Power? Do we know anything beyond the fact that Consciousness is and changes; that it changelessly persists while changing and that it may cease to change? Why do we then interpose a Power between *Cit* and this fact? The reply is—we do not interpose anything between them. Our Power is simply the expression of the whole fact. We simply say that Consciousness[5] by itself persists, changes and persists again; that there is nothing else than Consciousness[5] which so persists and changes. *Māyā* of *Māyā-vāda*, on the other hand, has a residual element of unconsciousness[6] and unthinkable alienness[7] left in it, after the attempt has been made to dissolve in non-duality the Sānkhyan *Prakrti* which is absolutely unconscious and alien to *Cit*.

---

[1] Indrajāla. [2] Sakala. [3] Niṣkala.
[4] Sakriya. [5] Cit. [6] Acit Jadatva.
[7] Māyā is neither Brahman nor independent of it. It is taken not as real nor unreal nor partly one and partly the other. To the Śākta Māyā is the Mother-Power—Māhāmāyā—who in Hersef (Svarūpa) is Consciousness and Who by Her Māyā appears to be unconscious.

Again, though an individual Centre may realize Pure *Cit* and the world of distinction and change[1] may cease to exist for him, yet, generally it is admitted that the world-order as a flow is beginningless and endless, though it has a rhythmic life of evolution[2] and involution.[3] During the latter[3] the world is withdrawn into *Brahman* and remains there as potency; during creation it is projected into manifestation again. Now, if by Power we mean nothing else than the fact that cosmic being-experience of itself rhythmically passes into the conditions of seed and fruit, slumber and waking, then we cannot be mistaken in saying that the Power of Consciousness[4] to thus rhythmically change eternally persists, and is, therefore, as much real as Consciousness itself.

Or else, shall we say that the Immense by its own Power veils and finitizes itself and thus becomes the world of varied name or form,[5] of correlated Centres; that the Immense and Immeasurable by its own Power is also gradually unveiling and realizing itself; that the complete unveiling and realizing of itself by itself will mean liberation; and that, therefore, the cosmos can attain liberation only as a whole, there being no actual liberation for individual selves?[6] This is to make *Brahman* the only real self,[7] binding itself and then liberating itself by its own Power. The multiplicity of selves[8] means only so many reflexes or "virtual images" of the one real individual self;[8] so that there is no question of individual antecedence and subsequence in the matter of bondage and liberation. There has been bondage for "all" since *Brahman* has limited itself and there will be liberation for "all" when *Brahman* fully reasserts or reaffirms itself. *Śuka*, *Nārada*, *Vāmadeva*, *Vyāsa*, *Vaśiṣtha* and others are all reflexes with mutual variations, of the one *Brahman*, masking itself by Its own "play"[9] as an individual self,[8] and though possibly, in point of spiritual purification, the persons named have advanced further than other reflexes, they have not yet attained to perfect liberation, because that of which they are reflexes,[10] is still there as *Brahman* masking itself, as the individual self.[8] The principle is this—there is no liberation for individual selves while the individual[8] type is there; there is no vanishing of the reflexions[11] while the original[12] is there and veiling (which like variously shaped and curved mirrors variously reflect) is there.

[1] Nāma and Rūpa. [2] Vikāśa. [3] Laya. [4] Cit-śakti.
[5] Nāma and Rūpa, that is ideas and ideas objectified. [6] Jīvas.
[7] Jīva; the doctrine of Eka-Jīva-vāda. [8] Jīva. [9] Līlā.
[10] *i.e.*, of the Bimba, the prototype or original.
[11] Pratibimbas. [12] Bimba.

Continuing the metaphor we may say that what we have called "reflexes" are double-reflections: we have the first or original reflexion when *Brahman* on the mirror of its own *Māyā,*[1] reflects itself and sees itself as "I am this all".[2] This is the Supreme "Personality,"[3] the first Reflex, the individual Self.[4] Then by variously constituted veiling, the Type is elaborated into infinite variations which are the "double" or secondary reflexes.[5] However this may be, the question which is now pertinent is this: The Immense undoubtedly changelessly persists[6] as Pure[7] *Cit,* even while It thus binds itself and then tends to liberate itself. By veiling and reflection,[8] its essential nature as Consciousness[9] is never for one moment abrogated or effaced. But what about the Power by which it thus binds (*i.e.,* limits) and liberates itself? By 'Power' is meant the *fact* that it does of itself thus limit and reaffirm itself.

Now, having put the question, let us ask: Is this self-denying (or limiting) and self-affirming operation in Time? Is it that *Brahman* limited itself actually in the past and is tending to reaffirm itself in the future? Or shall we say that the temporal determination or scheme is itself a product of the limiting and defining operation,[10] is immanently applicable to all processes and phenomena incidently and subordinate to the fundamental limiting operation; but is *not* applicable either to the fundamental limiting operation as a whole, or to *Brahman* which appears to subject itself to this operation? In other words, the Immense and Immeasurable may not as such have a "life history" of bondage, striving and liberation; and the denying and affirming may not belong to past and future tenses of real Time. Time may be a scheme for the "Reflexes"—the First Reflex as well as the "double reflexions": a Reflex (in the sense of limited Cit, not of unconsciousness[11] appearing as[12] consciousness,)[9] may thus have and think its experience in accordance with the temporal scheme. From its standpoint, therefore, that scheme is real. But the Immense and its fundamental operation of self-limiting may both be alogical, and beyond the temporal scheme.[13] Argument has been offered to show that it *is* so;

[1] Vimarśa as Kāmakalā-vilāsa has it, using the very same metaphor of the mirror—"vimarśa-rūpa-vimalādarśa," [2] Pūrṇāham. [3] Parāhantā. [4] Jīva.
[5] Aparāhantās. [6] Kautasthya. [7] Śuddha. [8] Vimarśa. [9] Cit.
[10] Kāla (Time) is one of the Kancukas. [11] Acit. [12] Cidābhāsa.
[13] Yoga-driṣṭi, and what in the West are now called "Psychometry," "X-ray vision" and so forth, place before us certain phenomena (*e.g.,* reading of the past and the future which is held to be established) which seem to force the conclusion on us that, in reality, past, present and future meet in a point; that they co-exist as a seamless, indivisible tissue of facts which our pragmatic thought and habit (samskāra) takes to pieces. In fact, they meet in the "Bindu".

and if it be so, the Power which thus alogically and extra-temporally denies and affirms itself is a Power that *is*. And once we lay aside the temporal notation (*i.e.*, the tenses) "changeless persistence in the three tenses of Time," which is commonly the *Māyā-vāda* definition of Reality, can only mean being as such. Since the Power of the Immense to Limit itself is as such (we are no longer thinking and speaking in the tenses), and undeniably is, it is Reality. In fact, this is only to say that the Immense is as Pure Consciousness,[1] and is as Power to limit itself as Consciousness. There is warrant for this in pragmatic experience.

But suppose we think as a Reflex must think—that is, logically, and, in accordance with the temporal notation. *Brahman* has made an individual Self[2] of himself, and is tending to liberate himself. When will liberation come? In finite time or infinite? If the latter, then the limiting Power infinitely continues; and since no absolute beginning either can be thought of in relation to the operation of this Power, it eternally continues; and as Power (*i.e.*, apart from modes and directions) it ever is what it is. The definition of Reality is, therefore, satisfied by this Self-limiting Power of *Brahman*. But on the other hand, to remove this prospect[3] of perpetual "bondage," if we say that self-limiting, though perhaps beginningless, has an end, so that the limit may go one day, then also, it should be clearly observed, the eternality of Power as Power is not affected; because, if to limit itself connotes Power, to do away with the limit and to rest in, and as, Perfect Experience also connotes Power. In fact, binding and then unbinding constitute one single fact, though our thought may split it up into two; and if it is agreed to describe the first half of the fact as "Power", there is no reason why we should refuse to describe the second half as Power, Power as such eternally, *is*. It is therefore Real.

But what if we interpret the term "changelessly" rigidly in the sense of the *Māyā-vāda* definition of Reality? Change, like difference[4] may be of three kinds:[5] One thing while remaining essentially the same may change so as to present differences of detail. Thus Power, remaining essentially the same Power, may change from a condition of latency to one of patency. Or else, while Power as a whole remains unaltered, its components may severally vary.[6] Or, Power may change from one form

[1] Cit. [2] Jīva.

[3] Dismal to some though it may be the reverse of dismal to those who see self (ānanda) only in the continuation of the Līlā or World-play.

[4] Bheda. [5] Svāgata, Sajātīya and Vijātiya.

[6] This is Svagata—intrinsic or immanent change.

and direction into another form and direction; but it remains the same kind of Power. Lastly, Power may change into one of a different kind.[1] Now, in all the cases we have mentioned, Power of *Cit* may be supposed to continue eternally as Power; but since in all the cases change from latency to patency, and change of form and direction are involved, we are justified in saying that what eternally persists is power of the same kind (if we do not hold change of form and direction as constituting difference of kind); but we can hardly say that the self-same Power in the same condition persists for all time. If it were so, there would be no creation at all; or there being creation, there would be no dissolution; briefly, no change, apparent or real, in the Given. Power, therefore, while remaining as such, changes its condition. And if it does, it is not changelessly persistent and not, therefore, real.

The objection can be met in two ways. First, we must consider Power as a whole and not in cross-sections. What remains the same Power unchanged is the whole. That is to say, what remains the same Power unchanged in creation, maintenance and dissolution is simply, and nothing less than, Power as creating *and* maintaining *and* dissolving. Suppose we split up this Power into three components or aspects corresponding to these three aspects of the world-process. Then of course we cannot say that Power as creative activity is the same as Power as sustaining activity and this again the same as dissolving activity. The Devis *Brahmāṇī*, *Vaiṣṇavī*, and *Raudrī* are thus different, because they do different kinds of work. But as Primordial Power[2] which now creates, now sustains and now dissolves, it is, and must be, one. Difference is in the sections: non-duality[3] is in the whole.[4] But still we may be told that it involves intrinsic or immanent[5] difference. The aspects or components of Power change. And if they do, absolutely changeless persistence (excluding even immanent variations of form or condition) cannot be predicated of Power considered even as whole;[6] and if not, Power is not real.

Hence, secondly, let us consider this: Is Pure *Cit* absolutely changeless in the sense that its condition remains the same for ever, though it may be now veiled and now unveiled? *Cit* is manifestation itself[7] and

---

[1] These two are Sajātīya and Vijātīya respectively.
[2] Ādyāśakti. [3] Advaita.
[4] Pūrṇa. Brihad.-Up., II, 4, 13; IV, 5, 15.
[5] "Antarlīna" and "Antargata".
[6] Pūrṇa.
[7] Svaprakāśa. Prakāśa-mātra-tanuh as Kāma-kalā-Vilāsa, 1, has it.

yet in ordinary experience—in the three states of waking, dreaming and slumbering—its perfect illumination veils itself in a way, without ceasing to be or being effaced, as intuition, it is said, will directly show. The object of religious striving and its practical method[1] is to raise the undeniable veil. Now, surely, between veiled or ignored "Ether of Consciousness"[2] and unveiled and recognised "Ether,"[2] we must admit a difference of condition. It is undoubtedly a difference that does not affect the Ether as it is in itself.[3] Unveiling here merely means acceptance and recognition of what has been given in consciousness, but practically ignored. Still from veiling to unveiling or *vice versa* is a change of condition. To say that veiling and unveiling are both immaterial, unsubstantial,[4] is not to deny the change. For, in experience, even a fancied change is an actual change of condition. A rope does not indeed become a snake when illusion makes it appear so; but experience of a rope and experience of an illusory snake are not the same experience. Hence though Pure *Cit* remains Pure *Cit* even while it is veiling or unveiling itself, we must admit a difference (whether superimposed or immanent) between the veiled condition and the unveiled. And if we must, what becomes of "absolutely changeless persistence" as assuring the reality of Pure *Cit* alone? We have seen that as regards the Power-aspect of Consciousness, we must admit immanent differences of condition to explain the different conditions of the world process; we now see that as regards the illuminating-aspect[5] of Consciousness also we must admit difference of condition to explain the differences in the four states of waking, dreaming, slumbering and ecstasy[6] and also that between bondage[7] owing to ignorance[8] and liberation[9] on account of "knowledge".[10] "Absolutely changeless" in the definition of Reality is, therefore, in the absolute sense, applicable neither to Power-aspect nor to Illumination aspect.[5] Or else, if we be satisfied with only an approximation, then the definition applies to both. Both are real, and both are one.

We have to be satisfied with an approximation because we have proposed a logical definition (and also pragmatic, for the matter of that) for that which is essentially alogical.[11] The Real is the Whole, the Complete and Perfect Given. This Given as given cannot be doubted, questioned

---

[1] Sādhanā. [2] Cidākāśa. [3] Svarūpa.
[4] Avastu. [5] Prakāśa. [6] Samādhi (turīya)
[7] Bandha. [8] Avidyā. [9] Mukti.
[10] Jnāna. [11] Pramāṇa.

challenged and contradicted. We may indeed pragmatically enquire as to whether a particular section of the "Fact" is, or is not a fact; is or is not evidence.[1] But as Whole[2] the Fact is above the distinction of fact or fancy; beyond the antithesis of true or false. The wildest fancy as part of the Given Universe of Experience *is* experience and has therefore as such absolutely assured being. That it is experience and as such is there, can never be questioned. The 'illusory snake' of Vedānta undoubtedly exists as a mode of consciousness. The illusoriness arises when we pragmatically enquire about the correspondence of this particular mode of consciousness to certain other modes, *viz.*, a group of sensations which Analytic Psychology takes as the representative of a snake. Hence as intuition will readily establish, we touch the absolute ground only in the alogical Given; in any circumscribed portion or aspect of it, we have only the realm of approximation. And a realm of approximation is a realm of doubt, of contradiction.[3]

The so-called transcendental[4] definition of *Māyā-vāda* is really therefore a pragmatic definition[5]—a definition of approximation seeking Reality still in the realm of limitation and doubt. The definition suffers from two defects.[6] We have seen how the fact of Pure *Cit* being ever absolutely changeless is, rationally speaking, open to doubt. If it were so, there could be no veiling and unveiling of it, no ascription[7] of the "magic" of a world upon it as *Māyāvāda* requires. It is of course undeniable that the Ether of Illumination continues uneffaced even while it is being veiled or unveiled, even when the 'magic' is on or off. This is unchanged persistence of an unmistakable nature. But still, as already pointed out, the circumstances of veiling and unveiling, the incidence of the 'magic' and its removal, does constitute a kind of difference. On the other hand, the definition as an approximation is applicable not to the illuminating aspect[8] of Consciousness only, but also to the Power-aspect. It is true that the persistence of the former[8] is more patent than that of Power; that is because the former is manifestation and being itself, and the latter, to man at least, is manifested by the work it does, so that no power is suspected by him when no work is being apparently done. Thus, while to him, Illumination[8] is revelation itself, Power seems to require a revealer.[9] That is why unchanging persistence has been affirmed of the *Cit*-aspect,

---

[1] Pramāṇa.
[2] Pūrṇa.
[3] Apratiṣṭhā and virodha.
[4] Pāramārthika.
[5] Vyavahārika.
[6] Avyāpti and ativyāpti.
[7] Adhyāsa.
[8] Prakāśa.
[9] Prakāśaka, Abhivyanjaka

but denied to the Power-aspect. But this is, absolutely speaking, an unwarranted denial.

Vedānta recognises various orders of Reality. We have referred to the transcendental[1] order already, and explained why the definition must be regarded as a definition of approximation and the order as not the supreme and absolute one which is the alogical Given or Fact called the Whole.[2] The transcendental[1] reality limits us to a "partial" or aspect only of the whole, *viz.*, the Illuminating[3] or Pure aspect. *Māyā-vāda* does so with purpose; realization of the Transcendental[4] aspect of Experience is its objective. The definition is therefore pragmatic.[5] The absolute, supreme Reality can neither be an aspect of the Fact, nor a pragmatic one. It must be above not only thought and speech but use.[5] And this is satisfied by the Complete Fact alone. Reflection will show that the Fact as an unlimited, entire Whole is alogical, and cannot be put to uses.[6] Thoughts can relate to, and motives can be formulated upon, sections only. Only sections can be judged as true or false, valuable and desirable or otherwise. The Supreme Absolute Reality should therefore be called not Transcendental Being[7] but Being which is the Whole,[8] as it is the Supreme[9] That of which Illumination and illumined[10] are both aspects.

Below this Supreme order we have the so-called transcendental[7] order of which the definition (approximately) is—"changeless persistence." We have shown that under this order we must according to the view here dealt with place not only Pure Consciousness,[11] but also its Power aspect,[12] though from man's practical standpoint, the former as Being and Illumination[3] is more patent than Power which is commonly associated with Becoming and manifested by the work it does. But the association of Power with Becoming only is a mistake: Power is Being-Power *as well as* Becoming-Power. And Power finding its revealer in work is also due to man's pragmatic veiling which makes him hide his power in latent capacity and then discover and recognise it in actual work and achievement. Consciousness[11] or Cit as Power to be and to become is therefore

[1] Prakāśaka, Abhivyanjaka. [2] Pūrṇa. [3] Prakāśa.
[4] Niṣkala, niranjana, śānta, saccidānanda.
[5] Vyavahāra. The word artha (purpose or sense) in Pāramārthika implies that.
[6] Vyavahāra. [7] Pāramārthika Sattā.
[8] Parama Satta. It is Pūrṇa. Chhāndogya, VII, 23, 24—calls it "Bhūman, or Immense and it is beyond all specification.
[9] Paramākalā. [10] Prakāśa and Vimarśa.
[11] Cit. [12] Cit Śakti.

transcendental Being.[1] Whatever becomes,[2] does not belong to this order. Whilst Consciousness[3] as "Ether"[4] and as Power to Be and Become "changelessly persists," the world of name and form changes, and it is its nature to change.

Next comes in *Māyā-vāda* Pragmatic,[5] relative, limited Reality. It is pragmatic because such reality is constituted by, and essential to, the uses of the practical living of Centres; it is relative because, as compared with Consciousness[3] and its Power, it changes and may be dissolved in the latter which, therefore, persists even after it (*i.e.*, the changing order) is no longer there; it is limited because, in the first place it is necessarily limited to sections only of the Fact, and because, in the second place, its persistence is limited in time. Thus the world of ordinary experience and its things and processes belong to the pragmatic, relative, limited order of Reality.

This is not to say that the world is an "illusion". Compare the alogical univèrse of "Fact"—even in the veiled and centralized form in which man has it at any moment —with what he *takes* as the world of his practical thinking, feeling and acting. It will be found that the latter is a limited realm accepted out of the much larger and indefinable Given which is, except in the part accepted, ignored; that which in the actual Given all is real as being-experience, in the accepted realm the distinctions of real-unreal, subjective-objective, inner-outer, desirable-undesirable, etc., are set up according as certain sections or features in the realm do or do not satisfy certain practical tests, or do or do not serve certain practical ends. Thus certain features or elements being "thoughts" only and not "things"; certain elements being fancies only and not facts, and so on, arise out of the special disposition of Consciousness[3] Power in the accepted realm; but those distinctions either do not arise in the entire Given itself, or arising, do not affect either the alogicality of the whole Fact, or the reality, in the sense of undeniable being-experience, of the elements thereof. A "fancy" as an element of the Given is as much real as any "fact" in it; it is regarded as a fancy because, compared with a fact, it does not satisfy certain practical tests, or what commonly amounts to the same thing, does not possess certain characteristics (vividness, permanence, requisite

---

[1] Pāramārthika Sattā.

[2] The evolved Tattvas or Principles, the world of Nāma and Rūpa, or the Psycho-physical.

[3] Cit. [4] Cidākāśa. [5] Vyāvahārika Satta.

tone of belief, etc.) which indicate that it will satisfy certain practical tests. The accepted realm is thus an "intentional world," in the defining and constituting of which potential stresses[1] play, however, a greater part than actual stresses which, broadly speaking, are man's "intentions".

The world of experience is not "illusion,"[2] though it is based upon and leads to use.[3] We have said that it is limited Reality in the sense of being limited in time. But here we must draw a distinction. Conventional experience[4] may be eternal or non-eternal.[5] All Scriptures[6] starting from the *Vedas* assert that the world-flow is beginningless and endless; and that the general cosmic scheme or plan (the Types, for example) persists from one cycle of creation or *Kalpa* to another through the intervening "Night" of cosmic slumber.[7] They pass from a state of evolution to one of involution, and this is an unending rhythm. Through this rhythm of evolution and involution they persist; and though such persistence is in a sense changing persistence (*i.e.*, the persistence of alternate appearance and disappearance), and though possibly, the appearance in one cycle may vary somewhat in detail from that in another, still, in a general sense the cosmic plan or scheme is persistent, and as such, is real.[8] The Generals[9] of the *Nyāya-Vaiśeṣika* Philosophy are eternal[10] (as also some other entities); and, from one standpoint, their being[11] is real.[12] Particular things such as a jar have non-eternal reality,[13] unless we subscribe to the theory that the world-order as it is in one cycle repeats itself exactly in another. Nyāya-vaiśeṣika believes in the antecedent non-existence,[14] of a particular thing, and this[14] is beginning,[15] though it may be it has an end,[16] as when that thing actually ceases to exist. That thing, again, when destroyed has an unending destruction.[17] About the non-persistence[18] of particular things, the First Standard raises no difficulties.

The difficulty arises when we come to the Second and Third Standards which agree in equating Cause and Effect, and conceive destruction[19]

---

[1] Samskāras.

[2] Brihadāraṇyaka, 1, 6, 3, calls Nāma and Rūpa "Satyam"; also Brih.-Up., IV, 3, 20, which describes the supreme experience as "Sarvvo'smi"—All is "I am". Also Chhāndogya, VII. 25, 2. "Ātmaivādam sarvamiti," also, Brih.-Up., IV, 5, 7,—"Idam sarvam yadayamātmā".

[3] Vyavahāra. As regards when Vyavahāra is possible and when not, see Maitri-Up., VI, 7; and also Chhāndogya, VII, 24, 1.

[4] Vyavahārā. [5] Nitya or anitya. [6] Śāstras. [7] Laya.

[8] This is Nitya-vyāvahārika sattā. [9] Jati. [10] Nitya.

[11] Sattā. [12] Nitya vyāvahārika. [13] Anitya vyāvahārika sattā.

[14] Prāgabhāva. [15] Anādi. [16] Śānta.

[17] Dvamśa. [18] Anityatā. [19] Vināśa.

as only dissolution of the effect in the Cause. Consistently and rigidly applied, the principle will not admit the absolute beginning or the absolute ending of anything, general or particular : nothing comes to actually exist which did not already potentially exist in its cause; and nothing ceases actually to exist but has again a potential existence in its cause.[1] Not only the twenty-four "Principles"[2] of *Sānkhya* but all their particular modes ought, therefore, according to this principle, to be eternally persistent either patently as effects or latently as causes. We shall not pause here to discuss this question which does not admit of an easy solution.[3]

Cause may be common[4] and uncommon.[5] The Will of God, "Space" and Time[6] and so forth are, according to Nyāya-Vaiśeṣika, the common cause of every phenomenon that takes place. Each phenomenon has also its own special assemblage of conditions which, according to this system, are threefold.[7] Vedānta reduces them to two kinds.[8] Prepared clay is the first in the case of an earthen jar; the putting together of the parts, the wheel and the stick[9] as well as the agent belong to the other group or kind. Now, when an effect is produced, we can consider it in its three elements: (1) its matter or stuff (which may be in some cases mind);[10] (2) its energy, kinetic and potential; and (3) the particular collocation[11] of the matter and energy which constitutes the special form[12] of that effect. In equating Effect to Cause we have, therefore, to equate all these three elements.[13] Of course in seeking to equate we have to consider both Cause and Effect completely and not partially. For instance, it may be necessary to consider the entire antecedent condition of the universe as the cause of the entire subsequent condition of the universe. But even doing so, will it be possible to prove in every case of causation not only that the matter and the energy of the effect were already in the cause, so that there has really been neither addition to them nor subtraction from them (a possibility to which the Physical Theory of Conservation of Matter and Momentum lends countenance), but also that the *special* collocation of matter and energy which makes the special form[12] of the effect was there in the cause, may be latently, and is not, therefore, anything

[1] Nāsato vidyate bhāvo nābhāvo vidyate satah.
[2] Prakriti, Prakriti-vikriti and Vikriti.
[3] See, however, "Power as Causality and Continuity".
[4] Sādhāraṇa. [5] Asādhāraṇa. [6] Dik, Kāla.
[7] Samavāyi, Asamavāyi and Nimitta.
[8] Samavāyi or Upādāna and Nimitta.
[9] The volition of the pot-maker. [10] Antahkaraṇa. [11] Sangyoga.
[12] Rūpā. [13] See "Power as Causality".

new and previously non-existent?[1] Was, for instance, the particular form of the cloth woven existent in the fibres of the cotton, in the spinning and weaving machinery and in the volitions of the spinner and the weaver —distributively or collectively? When a sculptor is chiselling a figure from out of a block of marble, the figure may be supposed to exist as an idea in the mind of the sculptor, and it may be supposed to be "given" latently even in the block of marble. Again it may be thought that, what the chisel of the sculptor does is to knock off the portions which conceal, suppress or fold up the figure given in the block of marble. But this seems to be an apparently strained supposition leading to interminable intricacies. For instance, we must suppose that not only the particular figure in question but every possible figure is latent in the marble like all meanings[2] in a letter as postulated in the *Vyāsa-Bhāṣya* on *Pātanjali's Yoga-Sūtra*. The typal case of evolutionary causation is the seed becoming a plant, though even here variations have to be accounted for. And it is certainly not easy to conform all kinds of effects (*i.e.*, that of production of water by the mixing of Hydrogen and Oxygen; the weaving of cloth from fibres of cotton, etc.) to the seed-model. We do not, however, further discuss this.

Causation is an unsolved riddle; and it must remain so. The world being a manifestation of the Play or *Līlā*[3] of Primordial Consciousness-Power, and the nature of *Līlā* or "Play" being freedom, we can never, except to bring the world-order to any logical account, expect approximately and pragmatically. The Śāstra says that "Even *Brahmā*, *Viṣṇu* and *Rudra* have not understood the Līlā of the Mother-Power". Time in our pragmatic analysis of causation, is a form necessary to the concepts of Cause (which is antecedent) and Effect (which is consequent). But, in reality, they co-exist, and are aspects (arranged by man in the perspective of "before and after") of one single fact. The whole past + the whole present + the whole future = a "Point" or *Bindu*.

But is it a statical, unalterable, *Bindu*? In other words, Is the whole cosmic order (including the Not-yet or Future) absolutely given and determined or fixed? If so, it may be said that it cannot be the manifestation of spontaneity or *Līlā* but of Blind Necessity or "Fate"; and the individual Centres also have no freedom, *i.e.*, no *Karma* properly so called.

---

[1] Prāgabhāva-viśiṣṭa. [2] Arthas.

[3] It is very necessary to distinguish this Trinity and other Divinities of the Māyika world from the Supreme Cause or Mahāmāyā. The supreme Mother-Power which is Consciousness (Cidrūpini) itself is explained later.

It is here that there is a riddle. The Ancients believed and many "psychic researchers" have now come to believe on fresh evidence, that foreknowledge (even as regards details) of the future is possible, which implies the pre-existence of the future in the present; the past also is not in any way lost in the present; which together lead to the conclusion that the Cosmic Order is eternally and unalterably fixed and condensed in a "point" (since the whole can be deciphered from the minutest detail, as for example, when a "medium" is alleged to be able to "read" the past and the future of persons unknown to her and of other persons connected with him, by "looking at" a flower or a piece of paper touched by him). Now, if the Order be so unalterably fixed, what becomes of *Līlā* and *Karma*, both of which imply possible change, and an undetermined future? We can essay to answer this only by supposing that the Cosmic Order is susceptible to change by *Karma*, but that the change in itself, need not be in Time; that is, not a fixed but a changing universe is given in the timeless *Bindu* we have postulated. So that a "medium" *en rapport* with the *Bindu* can "read" an event freely wrought by a Centre, which man's pragmatic, "temporal" thinking must, however, place in the realm of Not-Yet or Future. Imagination doubtless fails to conceive how this may be, as for instance, it fails to conceive Dimensions higher than the third. Analogous is the idea of the *Vaiṣṇava* who believes in an eternal Heaven[1] wherein there is eternal Play.[2]

Pragmatically speaking, the collocation of matter and energy in the effect is either previously existent in the cause (or assemblage of conditions) or non-existent. If the latter, then every moment thousands of phenomena are happening around us which, though persistent in their *types* and also in the quantities of matter and energy involved, are as special collocations new, previously non-existent and ephemeral. These phenomena belong to the transient conventional class.[3] If, on the other hand, the collocation be previously existent as latent in the cause, then, waiving all difficulties to the view, we may again distinguish between two classes of phenomena. There may be certain particulars (not *genera* or types) which as particulars may substantially and actually endure till the end of a *Kalpa* or age of a given cycle of cosmic life or till final liberation is attained; but there are countless others which do not thus actually endure, but are speedily dissolved in their causes, and in the Root Cause[4] during dissolution,[5] to be

[1] Nitya Goloka : Go does not here mean cow but sound and light.
[2] Nitya Līlā. [3] Anitya Vyāvahārika. [4] Prakriti. [5] Pralaya

projected into actuality again during the succeeding *Kalpa*. Thus *Brahmā* and others as particular forms of *Cit-Śakti* have their fixed age to live through; and at the termination of this age a particular *Brahmā* or other ceases to exist, though the type remains. The particular objects of experience have, however, no such prolonged actual life-duration.

Let us pass on to Apparent Reality in Māyāvāda.[1] It is the reality of an illusory perception while the illusion is not suspected as such. It is contradicted and corrected by pragmatic reality,[2] *e.g.*, the rope-snake of an illusion. The rope-snake possesses some marks of reality, but is soon discovered not to possess others which practically settle for us the question of reality of the snake. The tactuo-muscular sense is commonly set up as the judge of reality because practically in the matter of living and self-preserving it happens to be the most important. In dealing with this order of Reality we are introduced to the pragmatic distinction between Right Knowledge or Evidence[3] and false knowledge.[4] In the "Fact" knowledge is simply knowledge and as such undeniably is. The basis of all evidence (even of Perception)[5] and the ground of absolute certainty is Experience as Experience.

With the two other forms of Reality[6]—we shall not deal elaborately. The first is Being-Experience as intuited by each individual Centre for himself.[7] It is the universe of Fact as defined with reference to a given Centre—"You" or "I". It is what you or I totally feel or experience—apart from all pragmatic interests. At this moment I am, for example, pragmatically experiencing the sound of a distant whistle, but actually I have or am an universe of experience comprising many sounds, smells, touches, sights, ideas, etc., of which the particular sound happens to be the prominent element. This universe, though in itself indefinable, is pragmatically defined by myself; and the defining line is a flexible one—now closing, now receding. We may, however, represent it by a circle or a sphere. Then the universe of another Centre is another circle; that of another is a third circle; and so on. In one sense, these spheres all lie outside of one another. What one feels cannot, exactly and in the same relations, be felt by another. What you feel is somewhat like what I have felt. But in another sense these spheres cut one another, and two spheres, A and B for example, have a common element, C. Thus

[1] Prātibhāsika sattā. [2] Vyāvahāra. [3] Pramā. [4] Bhramo.
[5] Pratyaksha. [6] Prātismika Sattā and Anirvacanīya Sattā.
[7] Pratisma.

while A's headache is not in B, or B's idea is not in A, both hear the sound of the distant whistle, see the greenness of the lawn, smell the odour of fresh blossoms and flowers, and so on. In fact, it is the common element that is objectified, and it is there that the different Centres bargain with one another—it is their province of Convention.[1]

It is with reference to this province again that an approximately common standard of Reality is fixed upon by the interacting Centres; it is commonly that which proves the fittest in practice, what is most safely workable in such mutual Experience.[1] Thus: In A there is a wild fancy which is not in B and others. Now, as experience the fancy unquestionably is: its reality in that supreme sense is undoubted. But commonly A does not accept it as reality because it cannot be found in the common province of Conventional[1] being, because, it is not "marketable". There can be ordinarily no practical transaction between A and B on the basis of that fancy. A therefore, defines his practical Reality not as whatever he experiences (which is Reality in the supreme sense), but what he feels in common with others and what, accordingly, can be made a basis of transaction with others. Thus, ordinarily, experiences have "value" for him which have a "currency". Sometimes possible "currency" is enough. A sees the *Mānasa-sarovara* lake in Tibet, and though many others may not yet have actually seen it, he believes his to be a real experience because of its possessing marks of possible currency. The pain of an headache, though subjective and which remains so, yet possesses certain marks which, while not placing it in the first class of experience, makes it a real experience in another way. A actually feels the pain and he cannot wish it away: the feeling appears to have him in possession. A fancy, on the other hand, is also there in him as experience. but it seems to be dependent on his pleasure as regards whether it should be there or not there. We have, therefore, three orders: (1) experience as such which absolutely *is*, and it requires no marks to establish its title to reality; (2) "subjective" experience which possess certain marks such as vividness or "clear tone", relative permanence and independence of the Subject's wish; and (3) "objective" experiences which are approximately common to a group of Centres and also possess certain marks of actual or possible currency.

Marks in the second and third orders are pragmatic marks: they are demanded because certain practical ends have to be served by us.

[1] Vyāvahārā

The demand postulates a condition, raises a question and is formulated as an "if". *If x* possesses such and such marks, it is real, otherwise not: this is how we judge in the second and third classes. Pragmatic reality is therefore conditional, hypothetical reality. The first order is unconditional, categorical. Experience as Experience is unconditionally, unquestionably real. We have called it therefore Fact.[1] It will be seen also that howsoever obstinately man may pin his faith to the pragmatic order of reality (and to a certain extent he cannot help doing it), the first order, that is Experience, as Experience, is still tacitly reserved by him as the ultimate criterion of judgment on questions of reality. A "common" experience is also my experience, or can possibly be my experience.[2] I may commonly waive my right in favour of the experience of an expert some of which I do not now actually have; but the right *is* reserved nevertheless. I could possibly experience that which the expert says he is now experiencing: the reality of *his* experience is admitted subject to his condition. On the other hand, where I have an experience but others not, I certainly expect that, conditions being satisfied others will also have it; but if the conditions be not satisfied and others do not share it, still I feel that I have a right to hold to my own experience as a reality. All this points to where the native soil of Reality is to be found. The *Veda* in the primary sense means Perfect Experience; in the secondary, partial sense — A body of classical experiences obtained by the *Ṛṣis*, and always obtainable by those who are fit to share in them.[3] In matters supersensible,[4] the classics are evidence as direct evidence;[5] but still, so long as it has not been or cannot be verified by my own experience,[6] it remains or belongs to a conditional order—subject to an "if". The relation between experience[7] intuited by each individual centre and complete experience[8] will be further considered when we come to discuss *Cit* and Its Forms.

Inscrutable Being[9] in *Māyā-vāda* Vedānta is the name commonly given to *Māyā* which is the Principle of apparent or unreal change[10] such

---

[1] "Satyasya Satyam." See "The Fundamentals of Vedānta Philosophy", Ganesh & Company, 1961.

[2] Ātmānubhavā.

[3] Yoga Adhikāri. See "The Garland of Letters' for Veda as Perfect Experience. See "The Fundamentals of Vedānta Philosophy", Appendix.

[4] Atīndriya.

[5] Pratyakṣa (like the solar light in the manifestation of rūpa as Śaṅkarācārya puts it.)

[6] Anubhava. [7] Prātismika. [8] Pūrṇa.

[9] Anirvacaniya Sattā. [10] Vivartta.

as that of a rope into a snake in illusion. The snake of illusion has two parts: the apprehension of mere "thatness" or "thisness,"[1] and the suggestion of the characteristics of a snake projected and superimposed upon the basis[2] of the apprehension of "this".[3] The basis "this"[3] is real;[4] that is, in the illusion of rope-snake, the part which is real is the apprehension of this.[4] The superstructure laid upon it is an inscrutable transformation of ignorance[5] the function of which can be analysed into two components: veiling,[6] and movement and imposition.[7] Thus of the real rope before us, the mere "this"[3] part is rightly apprehended, but the special form (and qualities)[8] of the rope is veiled and that of the snake is imposed. This imposed structure of form[7] is the product of the ignorance-tendency[9] (operating, as Western Psychology would say, through association by similarity) and prompted to operate in a particular way by the subjective and objective conditions—dimness of light, defective vision, mental predisposition and so forth—then prevailing. Now, this imposed structure or *Rūpa* which cannot be said either to be existent or to be non-existent or to be partly existent and partly non-existent, possesses inscrutable Being.[10]

A right perception, *e.g.*, that of a real rope is regarded as a transformation[11] of mind;[12] while a false perception as that of the "rope-snake" is regarded as a transformation of ignorance;[13] and the difference between Mind[12] and Ignorance[13] is not one of kind, but of degree—the former being a purer[14] and the latter a cruder[15] form of Māyā. In man this "double" frame-work of *Antahkaraṇa* and *Avidyā* exists, and from them proceeds a double line of transformations—one line giving him "real" perceptions, the other illusions and so forth. We see that the projections of ignorance[13] on the plane of perceptional experience—which look like perceptions but are not really so—are supposed to possess inscrutable being.[16] Now, *Māyā-vāda* seeks to establish a ratio proportion: the world of ordinary experience[17] is to the ultimate experience as Pure *Cit* what an illusion is to ordinary "real" experience. Conventional or pragmatic being[18] is therefore really inscrutable being[19] which is the being[16] of

[1] Idantā. [2] Adhiṣṭhāna. [3] Idam.
[4] See Vedānta-Paribhāṣā (Pratyakṣa-parichcheda). [5] Avidyā.
[6] Āvaraṇa. [7] Vikṣepa. [8] Rūpa. [9] Avidya-Saṃskāra.
[10] Anirvacanīya sattā which is also tuchchha or alīka satta. The term "tuchchha" is given a special meaning sometimes.
[11] Vritti. [12] Antahkaraṇa. [13] Avidyā.
[14] Sattva-prevailing. [15] Tamas-prevailing. [16] Anirvacanīya sattā.
[17] Or the Vyāvahārika order. [18] Vyāvahārika sattā. [19] Satta.

apparent, seeming change.[1] Between the real rope and the "rope-snake" the difference is not one of kind, but mainly of duration. Both are liable to be contradicted and cancelled,[2] one only a moment later, the other perhaps ages after when Pure *Cit* is realized. Illusory being[3] is also inscrutable Being.[4]

But this Māyā-vāda conception of the apparently real will not be found to be free from difficulties. Either all is *Brahman* or all is not *Brahman*. If the latter, then we have a second, independent Principle[5] and the reality of that Principle and its products is not inscrutable[6] in the sense above explained. If the former, then all is *Cit*, all is Being,[7] all is Joy,[8] since *Brahman* is so. It may be that *Brahman* by its own Power appears as other than *Cit* (*i.e.*, unconscious),[9] other than Being[7] (*i.e.*, non-being)[10] and other than Joy[8] (*i.e.*, pain).[11] But it may be asked: Is that Power other than *Brahman* or the same? It must on the monistic hypothesis be the same as *Brahman*. Is the appearance other than *Brahman* or the same? It must be the same again. It follows, therefore that at base the so-called unconscious[8] is *Cit*, the so-called unreal[10] is real,[10] the so-called pain[7] is joy.[11] To the limited, pragmatic review of finite Centre,[12] the antithesis of conscious-unconscious, real-unreal, pleasurable-painful appears and for it counts. But if we start with Being-Consciousness-Bliss,[13] and have never anything else to reckon with, then we cannot really make it end in becoming anything other than itself. A finite, interacting Centre cannot but think in antitheses, poles, dualities. From its standpoint, therefore, a definition of Reality making a distinction between Reality as uncontradicted[14] experience and Reality as contradicted[15] experience —that is, between transcendental being[16] and inscrutable being holds.[17] But this standpoint is essentially a dualistic standpoint. Whatever definition of Reality we may fashion from this standpoint will involve dualism, open or veiled; and, we may point out by way of illustration, that the definition of *Māyā* as inscrutable being[18] does involve veiled dualism. All attempts to define the indefinable will bring us to such a pass. If we

---

[1] Vivartta.
[2] Vādhita.
[3] Prātibhāsika satta.
[4] Anirvacanīya satta.
[5] *E.g.*, a Sāngkhyan Prakriti.
[6] Anirvacanīya.
[7] Sat.
[8] Ānanda.
[9] Jaḍa.
[10] Asat.
[11] Duhkha.
[12] In mutual vyāvahāra.
[13] Sat-Cit-Ānanda.
[14] Avādhita.
[15] Vādhita.
[16] Pāramārthika Sattā.
[17] Anirvacanīya Sattā.
[18] Anirvacanīya (Sadāsad-vilakṣana) Sattā.

must stand by the Absolute one[1] itself, and not tolerate any dualism, open or veiled, then, we must take, that is be, Experience as the Whole.[2] We must not limit ourselves to any aspects or partials; must not set up definitions which partition the non-dual[1] into opposites such as Conscious[3] and Unconscious.[4] And doing this we find that the Whole[2] is inscrutable[5] in the sense of being alogical, indefinable; and also is transcendental being[6] in the sense of being indubitably given, of unquestionable "being". Thus in the Whole,[7] the sense of the two kinds of being,[7] which hold good only in the realm of limitation and convention,[8] are modified; and necessarily so. And since the whole[2] is the basis and synthesis of all "kinds" of being,[7] and yet as the whole transcends all kinds we have called it before (following *Āgama Sāstra*), Supreme, Absolute Reality.[9]

We must be warned therefore against extending the definitions or their senses which are pragmatically valid to that which is above all limitation and all pragmatic use.[8] Thus the transcendental[10] definition approximately applies to one aspect of *Brahman* (lit. the Immense or Whole)[2] as against another aspect. It is a definition that serves while we are the thinker and analyser of *Brahman*. It does *not* serve when the Centre is (in being as well as intuition) *Brahman*. When the Whole has to be consciously *lived*, and not aspects only have to be *thought* and talked about, we must either leave aside all definitions or else applying them, must not employ them in the senses which suggest, and are valid in the realm of, the limited, thinkable and "usable" order of experience only. Here, we must not, for example, define Reality as "changeless, uncontradicted persistence" only; for that at once sets up a correlate Pole, *viz.*, that which changes and is contradicted. Here, Reality is experience as Experience, and since here Experience is all, all is real.[11] So, here, all is at base Consciousness as *Cit* (nothing in itself being unconscious);[12] and all is in essence Joy[13] (since, Pain is impeded, obstructed, limited being); and in the whole[2] there is no impediment, obstruction or limitation. As the *Chhāndogya* Upaniṣad profoundly observes[14]—Immensity[15] is Bliss[16] and littleness or restriction[17] is the negation of Bliss.[18] Experience as *Brahman* or immensity[15] (which the *Chhandogya* goes on to define as Experience

[1] Advaita. [2] Pūrṇa. [3] Cit.
[4] Jada, Acit. [5] Anirvacanīya Sāttā. [6] Pāramārthika Sattā.
[7] Sattā. [8] Vyavāhāra.
[9] Parama Sattā. [10] Pāramārthika.
[11] Sat. So the "Upaniṣad" says—all this is Brahman—Sarvamkhalvidam Brahma
[12] Jaḍa. [13] Ānanda. [14] See *Ante*.
[15] Bhūman. [16] Sukham or Rasah. [17] Alpa. [18] Sukha.

above the relation of knower—knowing—known[1] or pragmatic experience)[2] sees the universe, therefore, not as something in any degree alien to the *Brahman* but as being Divine Mother Herself who is Being-Consciousness-Bliss.[3] It is She who is called *Mahāmāya* and by many another name.[4]

Not only the above pragmatic definition of Reality but other similar variations of it suffer under the same essential disadvantage: they cannot be, in their senses, extended to Whole.[5] Shall we say, for instance, that the Real is that which is universal,[6] and the unreal is particular?[7] The first is defined as what is not limited in space and time:[8] what is everywhere and always. This is also called without exception.[9] The second is limited in space and time—is here but not there, is now but not then. It is with exceptions or limitations.[10]

Now, as before, in having to apply this test to Experience or *Cit*, we must first analyse *Cit* into aspects, reduce the alogical Fact to a logical order amenable to the categories of Time, Space, and so forth. Supreme Being[11] must in this way, be adjusted to our thought or standpoint. After that adjustment, we find that the universe of experience is analysable into five aspects.[12]

Any object, Self or Not-Self, is, known, is pleasant (in some relations or others), has a name, has a defining set of qualities.[13] These are the five "predicables", Of these the first three, are common to all object-experiences.[14] The fourth and the fifth differ from object to object—the name of one and the form[13] of one are not those of another. The first three, which are Being,[15] Consciousness[16] and Bliss[17] respectively, give us the" own form"[18] or nature of *Brahman*, and are, according to the definition real; the rest stand for the world-order,[19] and are said to be "unreal".

That a dividing line can thus be drawn after the first three need not be questioned. Let us assume that a "thing" or object is, and must be, a form of *Cit* or Consciousness. We shall see as we proceed what basis

---

[1] Pramātri-Pramāna-Prameya. This relation is the gist (sangkalitārtha) of Śakti.
[2] Vyāvahāra. [3] Saccidānandamayī.
[4] Lalitā (the player or Creator) Mahātripurasundarī, Mahavaiṣṇavi, Mahakālī and the rest, more than a thousand names being given in the Lalitā Sahasranāmā.
[5] Pūrṇa. [6] Sāmānya [7] Viśeṣa.
[8] Parichchhinna by Deśa and Kāla. [9] Avyavicāri.
[10] Vyavicāri. [11] Parama Sattā.
[12] Asti, Bhāti, Priyam, Nāma, Rūpam. [13] Rūpa.
[14] They are Sāmānya and Avyavicāri. [15] Sat.
[16] Cit. [17] Ānanda. [18] Svarūpa.
[19] Jagat-prapanca.

there is for this. All objective or subjective objects, and the Self amongst them, are then experiences. Now, comparing all modes of forms of experiences we undoubtedly discover some common elements. For example, a tree is, an idea or desire is, an illusion is, void is, nothing is. The names and forms vary, but being or "is-ness" is everywhere and always given, and there is no escape from it even in the case of the void.[1] The void is known or felt as *is*. It is, in this pure sense real[2] and not unreal.[3] Void is the negation of all determinations[4] but is not the negation of "is-ness" as such. That is the fundamental omission of the *Mādhyamikā Bauddha*. In fact between is[5] and is not,[6] the common element is—is.[5] Often this invariable is[5] is there as "this".[7] Thus we feel this tree, this desire, this illusion, this void. Very often again our judgments of facts of experience are not given or stated explicitly as judgments. "Tree is" is an explicit judgment; this tree," suppressing the predicate, is an implicit judgment. Sometimes this[7] also is not explicit there: thus we feel and say—"tree," "desire," "illusion," and so on, simply. But whether this[7] or "is"[5] be explicitly stated or not, the experience of tree and so forth is undoubtedly felt as this[7] or is.[5] It is an inalienable element or rather basis[8] of experience. In some fully explicit judgments both this[7] and is[8] occur.[9]

Next consider *Bhāti* or revelation. Experience means illumination[10] or manifestation.[11] It is manifestation as Consciousness or *Cit*. Thus in the above examples, we have: a tree is felt or known; a desire is felt or known; void is felt or known. The feeling, cognition or consciousness has of course different forms[12] and names[13] in the different examples, but everywhere and always it is *feeling* or consciousness. Even the Void is feeling or consciousness of, or as, the Void. There is no escape from *Cit* as such as there is no escape from Being[14] as such. The *Mādhyamikā Bauddha* has again omitted to recognise this. In slumber or swoon in which nothing seems to be known (possibly because nothing but the sense of blissful sleeping is remembered afterwards) what is, or can be, meant by "nothing" is 'form[12] and name[13] (that is particular determinations); it does not, and cannot, mean feeling or consciousness, pure and bare.[15]

---

[1] Śūnya. [2] Sat. [3] Asat. [4] Viśeṣa.
[5] Asti. [6] Nāsti. [7] Idam. [8] Adhiṣṭhāna.
[9] *E.g.*, in "ayam ghatah asti" (this jar is). [10] Prakāśa. [11] Bhāṇa.
[12] Rūpa. [13] Nāma. [14] Sat.
[15] Māndūkya-Up. calls this state of Slumber—"Ghana-prajna" (massive, undifferentiated consciousness); see Brihadāranyaka, Chhāndogya, etc., for fuller descriptio n of this state.

The common view which looks upon particularized consciousness alone as consciousness, and determined consciousness as no consciousness, is a pragmatic view which sees only what it has interest and need to see. The *Yogācāra Bauddha* whose object, inner or outer, is a mode of experience only, that is, who recognises no "thing" apart from the feeling or thought; and whose experiences[1] are transitory,[2] leaving a real gap between one experience[1] and another, as they succeed one another in time, is also suffering from the Pragmatic Illusion. The so-called experiences[1] are really like the waves moving on, on the surface of a continuous fluid; are like clouds passing in the sky. And this continuous "fluid" or "sky" is, as intuition will show at once, not void[3] in an absolutely nihilistic sense, but *Cit* as *Cit* or Cidākāśa or *Ākāśātma*. This Perfect Ether fills all "gaps', sustains and pervades all modes. The "gap" in every case is born of the non-recognition of Pure Consciousness as Consciousness. The "Light" of *Cit* in, and by which all modes of experience are revealed cannot be extinguished, nor can it be imagined as ever being extinguished.

We have regarded *Cit* as being the essence of "Thing"; so that though there may be extra-mental objects or objects lying outside the pale, or independent of, the individual's ordinary consciousness (thus Matter being as real as Mind), yet we have thought "things" cannot be outside or independent of (1) *Cit* as *Cit*, and (2) *Cit* as "Fact" or the Perfect Universe or Experience. This view disposes of the difficulty that, though illumination[4] is the common element of all objects experienced, it has nothing to do with countless others which are not experienced. For example, a jar experienced is known, is a mode of consciousness; but what about the jar not experienced, or even about the "real" jar which, though experienced, exists in its own right independently of experience ? The jar or the unknown jar is non-illumination[5]—the opposite of illumination.[6] If it be asked is it not so? From the pragmatic and centralized point of view of experience, Yes. From the real and whole[7] point of view, No. From the latter point of view a "thing"—Matter, Mind whichever it may be—is in, and of *Cit*, and as such is *both* "Is" and Illumination:[8] though its beingness,[9] and more particularly, its illumination[10] may be, and often is, doubly veiled or ignored by individual

[1] Vijnāna. [2] Kṣanika. [3] Śūnya.
[4] Bhāti. [5] Prakāśa.
[6] A-bhāti. [7] Pūrṇa.
[8] Asti and Bhāti (because Cit is both asti and bhāti).
[9] Astitā. [10] Bhātitā.

Centres, firstly because they are Centres of specialized function and reference, and secondly, or rather secondarily, because Centres are, owing to their pragmatic interests, apt to limit and narrow down their "Facts" or universes of experience to special aspects or sections only.[1]

Lastly, let us consider *Priyam*, that which is pleasant and gives happiness and which seems to present greater difficulties. The Self presents no difficulty. In fact, the Self is the model of objects as regards the three characteristics—*Asti*, *Bhāti*, *Priyam*. The Self *is*, it is *conscious* of itself and other objects. The Self is supremely *pleasant*[2] to itself. Even in wishing to die and be no more, the Self loves itself, and never ceases to be supremely pleasant to itself; it is only dissatisfied with a certain kind of existence, and chooses death because, rightly or wrongly, it thinks that it will be good, that is pleasant, for the Self to be rid of that kind of existence. A philosophic nihilist may desire to put an end to existence as such, to stop all experience.[3] This is because he thinks that it is on the whole better, that is more pleasant, for the Self not to continue than to continue, since continuance, in any form of existence, is sure to give it a surplus of pain over pleasure. Longer existence is greater pain on the whole; to be extinguished and be merged in nothingness is therefore thought to be the best thing. Best thing for whom ?—The Self. All acts of self-sacrifice, self-abnegation, all altruistic impulses again, have their root of inspiration and their basis of support or sanction and their test or standard of value in a sense of self-satisfaction. Bliss[4] is the substance and expression of the Will-to-be-and-become which, not only the living but all existence is.

The Self conserves itself, or expands and then retires or withdraws into itself; and this Will-to-be-and-become is really Joy,[4] and the activity which expresses it is "Play".[5] Not only the Supreme Self, but every centre down to the "material" particle, has its Joy[4] and its Play.[5] "All things are sustained by a measure of this Joy"[4] which[6] as the Whole[7] is immeasurable. Between the Self and, say, a material centre, the difference is not in essence or in kind, but in the form and degree of veiling. Each is Consciousness[8] and each is Joy,[4] but in the latter, these are veiled to

[1] The unknown jar (ghaṭa) or the so-called independent ghaṭa—that is, independent of Cit—will be found to be a victim of such doubt, ignorance or rejection.

[2] Niratiśaya-premāspada. Love (by the self for the self) in its uttermost limits is Joy (Ānanda). The Essence of the world is that.

[3] Vijnāna, which is Para Nivriti or Para Nirvāṇa.

[4] Ānanda.

[5] Līlā.

[6] Brihadāraṇyaka, IV, 3, 32.

[7] Pūrṇa.

[8] Cit.

such an extent (with reference to man at any rate), that they have the appearance of not being either. Even the human Self is more or less veiled. Hence, though we can be made to perceive that the Self is essentially pleasant,[1] still the great amount of pain and suffering which we have to bear in life, the "unconsciousness" of swoon and slumber, the dull, vapid, indifferent tone of many experiences, the making of sacrifice and the occasional courting of death among other things, would seem to indicate not indeed that existence is pain as out-and-out pessimists, ancient and modern, have contended, but that it is of a mixed nature, and often of an indifferent nature. But, in the case of the Self, it is comparatively easy to see through the appearance of pain and indifference. The difficulty in some respects, is with other objects. But be it easy or difficult, the Scripture says that: The mother is wholly Joy[2] and Play,[3] and all Her creatures, whatever their grade in evolution, must have a share in, and be made of, Joy[4] and Play.[5]

It is the law of veiling first to conceal, then to invert (*i.e.*, change the sense and direction) of a thing. It is the Principle of Polarity[3] in creation. And all pragmatic experience[5] and action[6] is based upon duality.[3] If Being,[7] Consciousness,[8] Bliss,[4] while remaining so, do not also appear as other than so, then there will be no pragmatic experience,[5] no *karma*. Action or movement is to realize the impossible, know the unknown, and attain the unattained joy[4] or get rid of dissatisfaction.[9] That which not yet exists, is not yet known, is not yet satisfaction, is therefore presupposed. If all be displayed and realized, then there can be no play for the Centres, for the play is essentially one of hide and seek. Hence Being,[7] Consciousness,[8] and Bliss[4] are variously veiled and unveiled in the universe of experience. As the Whole[10] and the Immense,[11] Joy[4] is pure and perfect. As soon as a limit is drawn, Joy[4] becomes circumscribed; and it is this bar, this impediment, this restraint which is the seed of all pain.[12] Joy[4] is thus the essence and index of perfect freedom of being and functioning.[13] Since centralized life and existence is necessarily limited, impeded being and functioning, we have pain as an incidence of life. The "throes" or "travail" of birth and the first cries which the new-born babe utters, are symbolic of this. But though limitation imposes

1 Priya.
2 Līlā. A doctrine which Āgama Śāṣtra elaborates and in practice acts upon.
3 Dvaita. 4 Ānanda. 5 Vyavahārā. 6 Karma. 7 Sat.
8 Cit. 9 *i.e.*, impediment to Ānanda. 10 Pūrṇa. 11 Bhūma.
12 The "bar" is Kancuka born of Māya. 13 Called "Sahajāvastha".

pain, it cannot efface the sustaining background of Joy.[1] If that were effaced, the Self, the organ and cells of the organism could not live, for vitality[2] itself is Joy.[3] As at the back of all finite modes of experience the "Ether of Consciousness"[4] remains, so behind all the pain and joy and "indifference" of life, the basis of Joy[5] is given. As the little[6] life is pain, as the great[7] life is Joy[8] (a term which, like *Cit*, is untranslatable). Pain, therefore, may be defined as the feeling of restriction of Bliss.[5] What man calls pleasure and even happiness belong to Pain, with this difference, that while feeling them he attends rather to that which is restricted than to the restriction itself, to what is affirmed rather than to what is denied; he looks to what is within the circle of limitation and not to what is outside. In feeling pain as pain he feels the restriction, the denial, the negation rather than what is circumscribed, given and affirmed. In his bitterest and deepest sufferings, the positive but circumscribed background of joy[5] can be recognized, but then he may be interested in not what is given, but in what has been denied him. By changing the direction of his interest and regard, he can, and sometimes does, touch this ground of joy[5] while he feels himself as being drowned in "a sea of troubles". Feeling of pain, involving as it does, feeling of restriction, can be made to change its quality as well as intensity. Greater regard on the restriction or drawing closer the restricting line, will serve to intensify the feeling; regard on the positive side may change its quality and make it one of pleasure; and finally, merging all restrictions in the Whole[8] itself, will make it Infinite Bliss.[9] Pain is the negation or restriction of something positive. The First and Second Standards defining Liberation[10] as the complete cessation of Pain[11] would seem to imply that Pain is something positive and *Ānanda* merely the negation of this. But Vedānta conceiving Liberation[10] as realization of Supreme Bliss[12] makes Bliss[1] positive; Pain is merely the negation of it due to restriction.[13]

As in cognition it is only the point of pragmatic interest in the total Given which is regarded as the fact cognised and the rest though given in consciousness, is ignored, so in the matter of "affection" (pleasure and

---

[1] Ānanda. [2] Prāṇa.
[3] Ānanda. See Taitirīya-Up., Bhrigu-vallī. [4] Cidākāśa.
[5] Ānanda. The whole process of appearance as given in the scheme of the 36 Tattvas is through increasing contraction or Sangkoca.
[6] Alpa. [7] Bhūma. [8] Pūrṇa. [9] Bhūmānanda.
[10] Mukti. [11] Apāya or Atyanta Nivritti. [12] Paramānandāvāpti.
[13] As Upādhi (Brahma-Sūtra, I, 1, 12, and the Śruti Texts quoted in the Bhāshya thereunder) or Sangkoca.

pain). The ignored parts of the given universe have all the gradations from "self-consciousness" to "sub-consciousness" or "evanescent consciousness". Thus while I am fully conscious of the star Sirius now, I am hardly conscious of the neighbouring stars, of the sounds I may be hearing, of the touches, smells and so forth, I may be feeling, of the ideas and memories I may be entertaining in the mind. All this wealth of actual experience is silently buried in ignorance, because not then useful. It fades into semi-consciousness and subconsciousness. In fact, the dividing line between conscious and sub-conscious or unconscious is due to the habit of selective attention and regard[1] having been so consolidated as to practically operate as an opaque partition or wall between what is attended to and what is not. It is owing to this practical tendency[2] that mental life becomes like a floating ice-berg the greater part of which lies in sub-consciousness. It is thus that experience like an ascending and descending curve, now rises above the "normal line", now goes below it. The "normal" is settled by the tacit consensus of intercentral practice. This practical tendency[3] often acts therefore as a wall to shut out the "not-wanted" in experience, or, from the point of view of the "not-wanted", as a sort of crust more or less completely concealing the fact that it is being experienced. By wanting the not-wanted we can to a degree remove this crust; and by *yoga* this partition between conscious and sub-conscious may be brought as near as desired to the vanishing point.[4]

The same with Bliss.[5] We are practically used to regard as pleasurable or painful such experiences only as lie betewen certain limits. As our eye commonly sees only between certain limits, our ear hears only between certain limits, so experiences affect us as pleasures or pains only between certain limits. Beyond those limits the "affective element or tone" is supposed not to exist. Experience is said to be toneless or indifferent outside those limits. Inherited tendency[2] has erected a wall and built a crust here as it has in cognition. Many experiences or objects experienced are thus thought of as being without "value". Consider, as a typical case, a block of stone lying at the foot of a hill. What has it, we may ask, to do with Joy?[5] To answer this we must raise and decide three issues. (*a*) Is it in itself joy?[5] (*b*) Does it know or feel itself as being so? (*c*) Is it an object of Joy[5] (*i.e.*, *priya* or dear) to others? that is, is it pleasing or pleasant?

[1] Pakṣapāta. [2] Saṃskāra. [3] Vyavahāra saṃskāra.

[4] In Yoga this is called "seeing" the Saṃskāras which are, in fact, subtle (Sūkṣma) presentations or impressions.

[5] Ānanda.

Taking the last issue first, we put two queries: (1) Is it pleasing to ourselves? and (2) Is it pleasing to some other than ourselves? We separate these two because we are commonly so much occupied with ourselves and our own likes and dislikes that we do not care to consider whether a thing, not being useful and pleasing to us, may or may not be useful and pleasing to others. Let us turn up the stone and we shall find that, possibly, many worms and insects live under its shelter, so that that stone is as useful and dear[1] to them as our own sheltering roof is useful and dear[1] to us. And, for anything we know, that stone may be dear[1] not merely to the worms that our eyes may discover there, but to myriads of other unnoticed creatures living on, about, and in the pores of the stone. And we can generalize and say that what is true of a block of stone is true of everything; there is not a thing but is dear[1] to some in some relation or other.[2] In this sense, to be "dear" is a common mark of things. Now, coming next to ourselves, the stone may be dear[1] to us if we have the interest of a geologist or of one who loves the landscape of which it is a part. But let us suppose that apart from such special interests and associations, (and not, moreover, stumbling and getting ourselves hurt by it), we are looking at the block of stone at the foot of yonder hill. Is it dear? This is an important question which, being answered, will lead to a decision as regards the first and second issues raised above.

Let it be considered merely as an object of perception. Now as an object of perception apart from all practical interests, it is a measure[3] of Joy.[4] The play of practical interests will make it either pleasurable or painful; but its nature as Joy[4] is given in perception as such. Since man is not commonly interested in this basis of joy,[4] but rather in the superstructure of pleasure or pain raised on this basis by the "organic" reverberation of "resonance" evoked by that perception, we veil and ignore it, and think as though it were in itself a "toneless" and indifferent perception. But this is a mistake. Suspending for a time all practical interests, and looking up to the blue vault of the sky, or looking at the wide stretch of a field or a mass of water or a forest, we can certainly experience a kind of serene, quiet satisfaction, which is the basis of joy, normally given in every perception, but which is perhaps less veiled in

---

[1] Priya.
[2] *i.e.*, to some in certain "cosmic situations" or Adṛṣṭa.
[3] Mātrā.
[4] Ānanda, as Brih.-Up., IV, 3, 32, has it.

the cases just cited than in others. We can touch and realize this basis more and more closely in proportion as we can rid ourselves of our ordinary practical interests in modes of perception tending to produce organic resonance as pleasures and pains.

Strikingly analogous is the case of sound. We hear a variety of sounds and are interested in them. This prevents our attending to a kind of continuous sound (a continuous *Om*) which is the basis of all sounds, and which some may hear by disengaging their attention from the varieties, and listening in a quiet place and in their calmer moments. In a crowded place, a moment is never quite quiet, for there are then at least "dispersed" sound vibrations in the atmosphere (like dispersed lightwaves during twilight). But in the country-side and in a secluded place, one can listen and perhaps hear the uninterrupted *Om*. A similar experiment may be necessary for verifying the normal basis of Joy[1] given in every perception. "Civilization" however which removes us from life in Nature and according to Nature, removes us from this basis of Joy[1] which is Life, though it may create for us varieties of pleasures and pains. In the *Vedas*, as also in other ancient Revelations, such everyday natural occurences as the rising and setting of the sun, the coming of darkness, rain, thunder-storm and flashes of lightning, and so on, are experiences of intense Joy, but we now almost wonder how it could ever have been so. We have learnt to ignore the normal joy of natural perceptions. In the *Rigveda* and in the *Upaniṣads*, the very wind, earth, water, sun, plants, etc., are perceived to shed drops of "honey";[2] are seen to live, move and have their being in a measureless Joy;[3] are loved as beautiful.[4] In such a view the philosophy of, and outlook on, life and existence is such that death is *not* death to him who sees; old age[5] is not such to him; pain is not pain to him, because he recognises that the Self or *Ātma* is *Sat-Cit-Ānanda* (Being- Consciousness-Bliss), and as such cannot die, age, and be touched by pain and sorrow.[6]

Evil and pain there are in the world, and what man ordinarily calls pleasure may be hardly better than pain. But evil and pain exist by veiling and limiting essential joy which life and existence is; so that even when pain is there, there is also the veiled background of joy prevading it and envelop-

[1] Ānanda.
[2] Madhu Kṣaranti. Cf. The well-known Madhu-vidyā described in detail in Chhāndogya and Brihadāranyaka-Ups.
[3] Ānanda. [4] Sundaram. [5] Jarā.
[6] See in particular, Chhāndogya, VIII.

ing it on all sides. Evil and pain are not, and cannot be in Vedānta, the true word and the last word for man. Consistently with this outlook on life, the *Śāstra* forbids for example, the writing and enacting of tragic dramas: union and joy must be the last word, even in a play, instead of death and sorrow. From witnessing a tragedy we come, on the other hand, laden with sorrow, possessed by evil and sorrow as if these were *the* realities in existence compared with which our pleasures and joys are felt to be "iridescent air bubbles now gay in the sunshine and then broken by the passing wind". A real tragedy thus tends to invert the true order, relation and proportion of joy and sorrow in life and existence; it seems to fill all existence with an unfathomable abyss of pathos on which the so-called joys of life burst like empty bubbles. The Hindu has not countenanced this tendency in his ancient drama, which, though it admits evil and pain as a subsidiary element, has refused to admit it as the fundamental, essential, primary and final theme.

That every object is a measure of Joy is implied in the Vedānta view of Perception. Perception is an act of owning—cognition is recognition—a recognition of the essential identity between the Self which knows and the object that is known. The Self has its own veils of limitation—successive layers, so to say, of the Veil of increasing grossness, from the sheath of Joy[1] to the gross physical body.[2] The "object" has its own "layers" of crust too according to its past action or *Karma* determining its present condition.[3] Both have *Karma* and enjoyment of pleasure and pain,[3] and both have sheaths[4] appropriate to the needs of their special kinds of *Karma* and enjoyment.[3] The latter has its "Self" and Play[5] too, as later explained. Now, when the first perceives the second, there is recognition of the *essential* identity between the two by the first. The crusts of both are so to say pierced in the act of perceiving, the essence of the one coming directly in touch with that of the other, and both being recognised as "the same". This is *owning*. And what is the Self[6] beneath the sheaths ?[7] What is the innermost being of the *Ātman* but Joy ? Hence, there could be no act of owning, and therefore of perceiving, if the Self, in perceiving a block of stone, did not recognise it as essentially Joy also. Perceiving is thus Joy leaping up to joy; one battery of Power

[1] Ānandamaya kośa.
[2] Annamaya kośa. See Taitirīya-Up. for treatment of the five Kośas.
[3] That is Adṛṣṭa or Bhoga. [4] Kośa.
[5] Līlā. [6] Pramātā.
[7] The Īshīka inside the munja as the Kaṭhopaniṣad puts it: Kaṭha-Up., II, 3, 17.

as *Citśakti* sparking out to another. The ancient Vedic practice of producing fire by the friction of two pieces of wood[1] may be treated as symbolic of this.[2] Fire, latent in both, is evoked by friction. So *Cit* and *Ānanda* or Joy, latent in both the self and the stone—may be, more latent in the one than in the other—is evoked by that action which we call sensing and attending. The Vedic parable of two clouds, charged with 'celestial fire,' between which lightning passes, is again suggestive of this. A really unconscious thing[3] could not be known—because it is on that hypothesis, not what the knower and knowledge[4] are, *i.e.*, *Cit*. The third "Pole" of the "Polar Triangle,"[5] *i.e.*, the Known, must be of the essence of the other two.

In many Vedic "parables" *Indra* is described as killing *Vritra* by *Vajra* (commonly translated as lightning). Clouds have gathered but it is not yet raining. Why? Because the minute raindrops forming the clouds are by some hidden influence prevented from gravitating together and forming drops big enough to fall. That hidden influence is *Vritra*. But behold, flashes of lightning begin to pass from cloud to cloud, whereby the resisting power of *Vritra* is overcome; and it now begins to rain. By *Vajra Vritra* has been killed. From rain comes food, from food "beings".[6] This is the meaning on "the physical plane". But it may be made to yield a deeper meaning also. It symbolizes the commonest of facts. In the act of knowing, there is the knower and there is the object to be known. The knower does not yet know it. Why? Because each is encrusted in "ignorance". Because each has constituted itself an alien with respect to the other—because the latter has been, disowned and flung away as unconscious.[7] This Power[8] we may symbolise by *Vritra; Indra* is then *Cit Śakti* functioning as Self and using the mind and the senses. *Vajra* is the attentive direction of the mind and senses by which the coverings of Self and the object are pierced, and one is brought into rapport with the other. Both *Mind* and *Matter* are Joy from which creation proceeds.

In so-called "idol" worship, for example again, the worshipper first purifies himself by the preliminary rite called *Bhūtaśuddhi*.[9] He

[1] Araṇi.
[2] See Aitareya Brāhmaṇa detailing the process (III Ch.) Agni thus produced was called Mathitāgni. [3] Jaḍa. [4] Jnātā and Jnāna. [5] Triputī.
[6] Vrishterannam tatah prajāh. [7] Acit or jaḍa. [8] As Āvaraṇa and Vikṣepa.
[9] This rite is enjoined by the Śākta Tantras as the preliminary of all worship being the purification of the subject about to worship the image or symbol of worship. See *The Serpent Power* and *Śakti and Śākta*.

calls to mind that all Principles[1] and Divinities[2] are in him, have evolved from the Supreme Self,[3] and return again to It. All the Principles and their *Devatās*[4] evolve from and are resolved into the Supreme Self.[5] These two afferent and efferent activities are represented in the *Mantra-Śāstra* by *Hamsah* and *So'ham.*[6] After *Bhūtaśuddhi* comes mental worship,[7] and then finally external worship or worship on the plane of matter.[8] These are the three stages of assimilation of the worshipper to the *Devatā* or Divinity of his worship. In the first, the former calls to mind that he and all else are in ultimate essence—*Sat-Cit-Ānanda.*—The Yogic expression of this is *So'ham* (I am He), Sā'ham ("She I am"). In *yoga* all veils are lifted.[9] In Sādhana (as worship) the Subject and the Object of worship are both invested with the veil of the refined "stuff," that is, "Mind.[10] The worshipper, though he has previously assured himself of the essential identity between himself and the Form worshipped, yet places his Mind[11] in a worshipful attitude with a view to as nearly as possible assimilate it to that of the Divinity or *Devata* which is, *ex hypothesi*, purer and more potent than his. Lastly, comes worship on the vital and physical planes.[12] In this, what has been realized by the worshipper within himself, that is on the higher planes, namely, essential identity as *Sat-Cit-Ānanda*, and assimilation of Mind as nearly as can be to that of the Devatā, is projected on to the vital and physical planes.[13] By such projection, lines of mentative energy (or substance-energy) are made to impinge upon the "matter" of the "Image" worshipped. These lines or streams of mentative and vital substance-energy[14] envelop the matter of the Image, create round about it an aura of "radiant"[15] energy which so acts upon the "material" crust of the idol that, whilst remaining apparently as matter to the senses, it becomes dematerialized for the worshipper in this sense that Consciousness, Mind and Vital Force[16] ordinarily

---

[1] Tattvas. [2] Devatās. [3] Ātmā Saccidānandamaya.

[4] Or controlling Cit-Śaktis. Each Divinity is a special aspect of the one Causal Consciousness.

[5] Sat-Cit-Ānanda as Īśvara and Īśvarī.

[6] See *The Garland of Letters* — "Hamsah". [7] Mānasa-pūjā.

[8] Bāhya-pūjā.

[9] As Maitri-Up., VI, 27 (Ga, Gha, etc.), says, we enter the "Abode of Brahman, by piercing the four sheaths".

[10] Antahkaraṇa (Vijnānamaya and Manomaya Kośas). [11] Antahkaraṇa.

[12] Prāṇamaya and Annamaya Kośas. Vitality is dealt with in the Prāṇapratiṣṭhā rite.

[13] By Nyāsa, Prāṇā-Pratiṣṭhā, etc.

[14] For the "stuff" of mind (Antahkaraṇa) and vital force (Prāṇa) flows out with or as energy (Śakti).

[15] Taijasa. [16] Cit, Antahkaraṇa and Prāṇa.

latent or folded up in it (from the pragmatic standpoint), become evoked, awakened and patent. This is what *Prāṇapratiṣṭhā* or "Life giving" rite means, or is supposed to effect. After this, the Image[1] is no longer to the worshipper "matter" only. It becomes in perception as it already was in reality Consciousness, Mind and Life.[2] And these are not a mere reflex, as the image of the sun in the mirror is a reflex of the sun. The worshipper's Consciousness is not simply reflected in, imaged by something which is unconscious and remains so. In other words, it is not unconsciousness looking like Consciousness.[4] What the projective action of the worshipper does is to cast the "radiant" energy of his own inner being (vastly potentized by *Bhūtaśuddhi* and mental worship)[5] over the matter of the Image thereby evoking, unfolding, "waking up," adjusting the "radiant" stuff and energy folded up in it. This is, so to say, piercing the crust of Matter, evoking Consciousness,[5] Life[6] and Mind[7] in it, and bringing the whole into rapport with the Consciousness and Mind of the worshipper. The "awakened"[8] *Devatā* is thus no mere "creature" of the worshipper, and thus "smaller" than him. The degree to which this can be effected is determined by the extent to which the worshipper has been able to evoke and dynamize himself, spiritually and vitally. The worshipper then sees, after the life-invoking ceremony,[9] not something alien and unconscious[10] in relation to himself, but an embodiment of Power as *Cit*, Power as Mind[11] and Power as Life.[12] The preliminary *Bhūtaśuddhi* rite has enabled him to recognize this essential identity (*So'ham*). To the Divinity he has in part assimilated himself in mental worship.[13] It now stands before his senses as an Embodiment of fuller Power of knowledge, will and action[14] (similar to but fuller than himself which he now worships for the four desirable forms of Good).[15]

This, briefly, is the theory of the practice, as properly understood : whether this theory, and this claim can be substantiated is not so much a matter for speculative argument, as one for experimental proof. But in any case, worship or *Pūjā* is at base a recognition of essential identity and an experimental assimilation, as near as can be, of the form of the worshipper to that of the *Devatā* on the planes of Mind[11] and Life[12] at least,

---

[1] The Pratimā or that which is placed "before" one as the object of worship, not "Idol".
[2] Cinmayī, Manomayī, Prāṇamayī. [3] Achit.
[4] Cidābhāsa. In Śakti doctrine there is no Cidābhāsa.
[5] Cit. [6] Prāṇa. [7] Manas. [8] Jāgrat.
[9] Prāṇapratiṣṭhā. [10] Jaḍa. [11] Manas. [12] Prāṇa. [13] Mānasa-Pūja.
[14] Jnāna-śakti, Ichchhā-śakti and Kriyā-śakti.
[15] Dharma, artha, kāma and mokṣa.

since Matter, being the principle of inertia and solidity," does not easily (though it does, however, upon the necessary conditions being fulfilled) change its form since it is *guru*—that is heavy or ponderous. And what is more important to our present enquiry—the theory of worship[1] is also substantially the theory of Perception. Perception, as Vedānta holds, is an act of assimilation between the Subject and the Object, effected by the Mind[2]—energy of the former going out through the senses to where the object is, enveloping it and assuming its form, and revealing its essential nature as *Cit* and as Bliss.[3] And this is what is supposed to be effective in the Life-giving rite or *Prāṇapratiṣṭhā*. Thus *Prāṇapratiṣṭhā* is perception and perception is *Prāṇapratiṣṭhā*. In both it is seen that what is "here" (*i.e.*, in the worshipper) is also "there,"[4] (*i.e.*, in the image). In the course of worship with a lamp, a fivefold flame of light is waved.[5] This symbolizes the play and offering of the five vital forces[6] as well as of the five senses of perception (as also, the five elements of matter envelopes and so forth).

The Self is, in its substratum, recognized as Bliss.[3] Perception is really the perception of essential identity between the Self and the object, whether in the review and statement of the perception, which are commonly swayed by practical interests, expression be given to such identity or not. In the review of the perception the object may possibly figure as a stranger, as a rival or even as an enemy. But the superimposition of these characters does not destroy the basis of essential identity felt implicitly in perception. It follows therefore that the object of experience, in its substratum, is like the Self, implicitly felt as Joy or *Ānanda*. This conclusion follows deductively from the premises about the nature of the Self, and that of Perception. And it has been shown before that, apart from practical interests and tendencies which variously limit experiences and oppose them to one another, experience of objects, as of Self, is actually and intuitively an experience of bliss,[3] upon the basis of which pleasures and pains may variously intermix and inter-play. Thus the first question we raised before, whether a block of stone is in itself joy[3] is answered. By "thing" we mean of course "thing as experienced".

The second issue raised before *viz.*, whether a block of stone knows itself as Bliss[3] as the Self knows itself, is one which cannot be directly

[1] Antahkaraṇa. [2] Pūja. [3] Ānanda.
[4] As the Vishvasāra Tantra says. [5] Ārati. Panca Pradīpa.
[6] Tattvas—Kṣiti, etc., the five Tanmātras—Rūpa, etc., the five sheaths, kośhas—Annamaya etc., and the five Kancukas.

decided, because here the question is not what the thing may be to us, but what it is to itself. We are driven therefore to infer from signs or marks. We are to proceed either *a priori* or deductively or *a posteriori* or inductively.

In the former case, we begin with a general view of existence (being and becoming) such as is given in these premises; Being is *Cit* or Consciousness. It becomes or evolves as Power. In becoming It finitizes and centralizes Itself as the selves, whereby different Centres with finite "fields" of being appear. These are the Centres of Power as Matter, Power as Life, Power as Mind. But since Cit alone is working as Substance-Energy, these Centres of Matter, Life and Mind are essentially Centres of *Cit Śakti*. And since the *Ātman* manifesting as the Self is not anything other than a Centre of *Cit-Śakti*, the *Ātman* is everywhere—in man, in the amoeba, and in a particle of dust. The forms or "sheaths" of *Cit-Śakti* differ of course in the different cases. But in principle, *Ātman* is everywhere — in an atom of Hydrogen, for example. It is as Power, the Centre-making Principle, and it must be there, where there is a centre of being and operation. A material particle, an amoeba, a plant, an animal, a man—all are *Ātman* which is Consciousness, though in the last named that Consciousness has become evolved to such an extent as to appear as what is called "Self-Consciousness".

Self may be experienced in three forms : sub-consciously as in the amoeba and other low organisms, intuitively as perhaps in some of the higher animals including man; and rationally or logically as perhaps in man alone (excluding for the moment higher Spirtual Beings) who thus formulates his self-consciousness in definite judgments such as "I know this jar," "I will do this action", and so forth. The operation of practical interests and tendencies in man commonly determines him to note and accept life and existence only within certain limits; and sometimes the limits have been imposed upon his organism and his instruments of cognition. Thus the eye, the ear, and so forth can know only within certain approximate limits. Attention also has its limits. These practical limits, so useful in ordinary experience,[1] are responsible for the experience of the "developing" man being graded into three or four orders. Thus, according to one scheme, there are experiences: gross,[2] subtle,[3] and supreme.[4] According to another we have—gross, subtle,[5] causal,[6] and supreme or transcendent.[7] The experience of the developing man deve-

[1] Vyavahāra. [2] Sthūla. [3] Sūkṣma. [4] Para.
[5] Sthūla, sūkṣma. [6] Kāraṇa. [7] Turīa.

lops into these orders to forms. That of the ordinary man is commonly restricted to the gross order or form. Thus it is gross experience to feel that there is "no" life in a block of stone; "no" consciousness and bliss in it or even in the plant which is taken as "living"; "no" self anywhere except in man. Some of the Cartesians went so far as to deny consciousness or feeling even to the higher animals. Thus man is made to stand quite apart from the rest of creation. The denial of consciousness and life to other world-forms is due to man's ignorance and to the fact that he has learnt to commonly recognise and accept the Self only within certain limits. We have given to Self pragmatic definitions which reduce it commonly to the plane of gross and ordinary experience.

Even in ourselves we do not commonly know the Self as a whole but only in a part. Man's Self is really the Presiding Self of a number of selves that are in him. Every cell, every organ, every sense of the body has its own Self[1] which, as such, is the manifestation of the *Devatā* which is the cosmic mode of a particular form of Consciousness as Power or *Cit-Śakti*. The microcosm[2] repeats and involves what *Cit-Śaktis* are at play in the macrocosm: *Āditya* ("the Sun"), for example, is the *Devatā* of the eye.[3] Each *Devatā* in the body has his own sphere[4] of domestic control and economy. The Self of man's Common Self-consciousness,[5] is only the president of a particular collectivity[6] "the united states", each, domestically controlled by its own *Cit-Śakti*.[7] In fact, there is no creation where the polarity of *Cit* as Efficiency Power (*i. e.*, *Cit-Śakti*, technically so called and *Cit* as Material Power *i.e.*, *Māyā-Śakti*) is not involved and repeated. Everywhere there is "material" to be controlled and fashioned and a "Controlling Principle".[8] In every cell, for instance, there is "Matter" undergoing incessant metabolism, and the "Agency" whereby this is done and supervised —which Biology vaguely describes as Vital Power—is a Form of *Cit-Śakti*, a *Devatā*. Now, according to this conception, man's "Self"[9] is only the Chief of the *Devatās*, their *Indra*.[10]

---

[1] Cit-Śakti and its associated Māyā-Śakti. So in Kuṇḍalinī Yoga described in the Tantras each bodily centre (cakra) has its presiding Divinity (adhiṣṭhātrī Devatā). Divinity (Devatā) is the cosmic aspect of individual function. See also the Nāthas described in Introduction to "Tantra-rāja Tantra."

[2] Kṣudra brahmāṇḍa.

[3] See Chhāndogya, Brihadāraṇyaka and some other Ups. Brihadārāṇyaka, V, 5, 2; Chhandogya I, 6, 6, and I, 7, 5, Identify the Devatā in the Sun and the Devatā in the Eye.

[4] Adhikāra.

[5] Jīvātmā.

[6] Sangghāta.

[7] *Cf.* the dispute between Prāṇa (the Chief Devata) and the Devatās of the Eye, Ear, Speech, etc., described in some of the Upaniṣads.

[8] See *Ante* "Power as Life "—Appendix.

[9] Jīvātmā.

[10] Brihadāraṇyaka IV, ii, 2 and 3, place Indra and his wife in the right and left eyes respectively, and explain.

But even the government of this Self is not ordinarily complete. There are many "States" in our organism which, apparently and directly, lie outside its jurisdiction. The activities or affairs of those States, though affecting the general tone and character of experience, are commonly both sub-conscious and involuntary. Several systems of ganglia in the spinal column, for example, are of this type. They may be seats and organs of many race-instincts, individual habits, reflex and automatic actions, and so on. They have their own *Devatās* or Selves. These Selves, though generally co-operating with the "Self", are commonly outside its cognisance and control. If "selective or purposive action" be accepted as the test of *Cit-Śakti*, then, it may be shown by experiment that all nerve-centres are centres of *Cit-Śakti*: all select their action. Those who have experimented with animals in which the cerebral matter has been removed, affirm that such an animal can be made to go through almost the whole round of reflex and instinctively selective actions which constitute the normal life of the animals. The noticeable difference, as William James points out, seems to be increased inertia or loss of spontaneity in its actions. This can be explained by the hypothesis that the lower ganglia have their own Controlling Principle or Self, and though this Self may keep itself somewhat in the background and hide its activity in sub-consciousness while the "cerebral Self" is there, it may rise into prominence and do office for the cerebral Self where or when the latter is inactive or its control ineffectual. In the experiments cited, the "lower" self becomes a substitute for the "higher".

In certain hypnotic subjects again there is effected what may be called exchange or substitution of functions between one sense and another *e.g.*, the sense of sight and that of touch. And since, according to the *Śāstra*, the human birth is preceded by countless other forms of birth, and tendencies of different births are as tendencies stored up, there is in man not only the "cerebral self" and the selves of other ganglia, organs and senses, but the countless selves of the previous births (a few, perhaps, are human or super-human, whilst most are sub-human) brought over and folded up with their characteristic impressions and tendencies.[1] Of the innumerable "groups" of tendencies[1] those only fructify which are pertinent or relevent to the human birth, by the Law of Similars, the rest, though given, do not unfold and make themselves kinetic.[2] In man therefore

[1] Samskāras.
[2] See Pātanjala Darśana, IVth Chapter discussing the whole question.

there is a Plurality of Selves or Personalities. Sometimes two or more "Personalities" may dissociate from each other and each becomes, or tends to become, an independent conscious Personality. Cases are on record in which in hypnotic patients or in mediums or in somnambulists, or else in yogins, Personalities with widely contrasted characters appear and hold their sway.[1] In many forms of practical method[2] again, particularly in Initiation,[3] there is effected superimposition of a higher Self upon a less developed one whereby the latter's development is extraordinarily accelerated.[4] We need not adduce further examples. The point sought to be established is this that of the manifested self[5] as a whole in us we commonly know but little. Our interest is so little and so partial, and our ignorance so deep and so great.

But let us consider the familiar marks of the existence of Personality. A stone or even a dog is commonly to us not a "person"; it is only an "individual". But is this an absolute distinction? Let us try the marks. There are several marks by which we recognise Self in another human person. All these are at the root expressions of one fundamental mark: action springing out of Bliss,[6] that is, free or spontaneous action. Action arising out of bliss[5] is play.[7] Hence the self is what is capable of, and in fact does, play.[7] The Supreme Self or Lord is full of play,[8] the world being His play.[9] The finite Self is a finite reproduction, is made "in the image,"[10] of the Lord. Play[7] is threefold: in creation, in sustenance, in dissolution. Wherever there is Self, we must have evidence there of "Play" in these three aspects. That is, Self must, out of essential bliss[5] create, maintain and destroy. But there is a difference between the Supreme Self and the finite self created by the Veiling Principle which veils and finitizes and conditions Consciousness,[11] Bliss[6] and Play.[7] The Supreme Self is the Lord of *Māyā* (the veiling and conditioning Principle) but the finite Self is subject to it. Hence in every finite Self both Bliss[6]

---

[1] Kāya-Vyūha. [2] Sādhanā. [3] Dīkṣā.

[4] The inner significance of the repeated fight between Devas and Asuras, in which the latter often depose Indra from his lordship over the three worlds (*i.e.*, the three states of experience—waking, dreaming and slumber) and deprive the "gods" of their adhikāras or authorities, but are finally ousted by the grace of the Supreme Power, is in one sense, the fight between co-existent but opposite Personalities in the sādhaka as man.

[5] Vyāvahārika.

[6] Ānanda. [7] Līlā. [8] Līlāmaya.

[9] Līlā. Brih.-Up., I, 3, 3—"Sa vai naiva reme"—Alone He could not enjoy; Also, Maitri-Up., II, 6 (Kha). Brahma-Sūtra, II, 1, 33—"Lokavattu līlākaivalyam."

[10] Kulārṇava Tantra, I—"Tadangaha jīva-sanggakāh......... yathāgnan visphulingakāh." [11] Cit.

and Play[1] are relatively and variously veiled and conditioned. The essence of the Self, which is Bliss and Play, can nowhere be completely suppressed and effaced, however. It may be more veiled and conditioned in A than in B, more in B than in C, and so on. We have accordingly a descending series of Bliss and Play manifestation, starting from the Supreme Self down to the densest or grossest matter.[2] As we descend, we have play[1] more and more veiled, more and more conditioned, till coming to Matter we are presented with the appearance of "insensate" being where behaviour, as physicists believe, is "absolutely" determined. Matter, thus, appears to us as the vanishing point of Bliss[3] and Play.[1]

But it is not really that. In matter an unexhausted residue of Bliss[3] and Play[1] is still left, though ordinarily man has no suspicion of it. Ordinarily he is not interested in looking for Play[1] beyond certain familiar terms of the series referred to. It is said in the *Śāstra* that after gross, solid matter has been created, *Śakti* or Cosmic Power becomes "coiled"[4] or rests. As such, She is given at the Basic[5] Centre which is the centre of solid matter.[6] *Kuṇḍalinī Śakti* is Consciousness, Bliss and Play.[7] Hence in matter too there is an infinite reservoir of Bliss[3] and Play.[1] And part of this fund is patent, kinetic also, though matter may commonly present to us an appearance of absolute lack of spontaneity or freedom. Ascending the series, we come to plants and animals and, then, to man. The lowest type of life, say the amoeba, is noticeably characterized by play.[1] Its behaviour as a whole is unforseeable, incalculable; though it may be only approximately so. Its behaviour generally conforms to that of the type; but every individual speck of protoplasm has a life of its own too; its idiosyncrasy; its play, and therefore, its Self. It has its own slightly, and often unnoticeably peculiar "curve" of life which generally or abstractedly conforms to the general equation of the curve representing the life of the species. It has its "personal equation". A crystal, which grows according to a definite geometrical pattern, has an idiosyncrasy of its own; its own eccentricities; its own play. Deterministic physical explanations are always ultimately faced with a residuum or margin of eccentricities, which, as it is pursued, recedes and recedes like the chased horizon, but never completely vanishes.

---

[1] Līla. [2] Bhūta. [3] Ānanda.
[4] Kuṇḍalinī. [5] Mūlādhāra.
[6] Kṣiti-Tattva. See *The Serpent Power*.
[7] Cinmayī, Ānandamayī and Līlāmayī.

In man, *Māyā*, in the form of subtle tendencies[1] and gross embodiment of tendencies (*i.e.*, the physical body, senses, etc.,) imposes limitations or conditions on his essential being and activity which are Joy[2] and Play.[3] But through all limitations his essential freedom vents itself. In all his actions, however much determined, he is a free agent,[4] whether his freedom may be vented through spontaneity or through volition. His essential freedom is never altogether suppressed; his "empirical determinism" is never absolutely complete. In man we may, however, have grades of freedom. Accordingly, we have three orders of Man : *Paśu*, *Vīra* and *Divya*.[5] The first is in *Pāśa* or bonds[6] (never absolutely so, however), that is subject to the veil;[7] the second is a "hero"[8] who is active to free himself from them that is to lift the veil;[9] the third is a man in whom the *pāśa* has become so light or slender[10] that he is practically a master of himself.[11] The object of ritual and yoga practice[12] is to gain complete mastery over the limiting and conditioning Principle or *Māyā*.[9] The object attained is Self-Rule.[11] It is the consummation of what Kant and other Western thinkers have conceived as the Autonomy of the Self or "Practical Reason".

We have briefly reviewed the ladder by ascending and descending. Now, let us return to our block of stone. *A priori* argument has been given to show that the essential mark of the Self (*i.e.*, play)[3] should be recognisable in it also. *Ahalyā*, the wife of the *Ṛṣi Gautama*, was according to the Śāstra transformed into a stone for a sin she had unwittingly committed. The contact of *Śrī Rāmacandrā's* lotus feet retransformed her into human shape. This, either way, could not be stated to be possible if stone and man were considered to be essentially unlike each other; if, for example, Self which is in the latter were not really, though in a less developed form, given in the former. Similarly, when in worship it is sought to "dematerialize" a piece of stone, and evoke in it *Cit*, Life[13]

---

[1] Samskāras. [2] Ānanda. [3] Līlā.

[4] A Karttā, līlāmaya. The psycho-physical which is a manifestation of the Power of the Ātman is determined but the Ātman itself is ever free (nityamukta).

[5] See for explanation of these terms *Śakti and Śākta*.

[6] Hence called Paśu.

[7] He is subject to the veiling factor of the Psycho-physical Principle as Prakriti or Māyā.

[8] Vīra.

[9] In whom the Rajas guna in the Psycho-physical Principle is active to suppress veiling and to present consciousness.

[10] His bond then being mainly that of Sattva-guṇa.

[11] Svarājyasiddhi. Chhāndogya, VII, 25, 2; also Brih. in some places.

[12] Sādhanā. [13] Prāṇa.

and Mind,[1] success can be had only because, in reality it is so. By practice[2] man only breaks the bonds of his own ignorance and non-realization, and dematerializes that which, chiefly with reference to his veiling *tendencies*,[3] has appeared as dead, senseless, Selfless "matter". By *veiling tendency*[3] we mean a specific form of limiting tendency which is both caused and presupposed by a particular type of practical living[4] in the world. This ignorance[5] is often spoken of in the *Śāstra* as a cave,[6] sometimes as night,[7] and occasionally as sleep.[8] When the Lord of the Veil veils Himself, the veiling, in that aspect, is called yoga sleep. In relation to finite Selves, who are not complete masters of their ignorance[5] or "sleep",[8] the veil is an Obstructing Power.

As in the vedic parable *Indra* or *Āditya,* led by *ushā* (Dawn), first hears the lowing of the cows in the cave, and then proceeds to liberate them; so the Self of the aspirant[10] directed by the drawing perception of Truth,[11] first hears, so to say, the call of the Self shut up in the cave of "Matter," and then recognises that Matter is only another form[12] of *Saccidānanda,* as it were solid masses afloat in the unbounded sea of Being-Consciousness and Joy[13] as Śrī Rāmakrishna Paramahamsa used to say. In fact the cosmic Cause evolves matter through and after Mind[14] which must as an effect involve its cause though in a subtle[15] form. The same operation of "spiritualizing" matter is more systematically tried in *Kuṇḍalinī Yoga*. *Kuṇḍalinī Śakti* or latent causal Power at rest which is at the Radical Centre[16]—the centre of solidity[17]—is the embodiment of all the 36 modes of Reality-Power,[18] the synthesis of all forms of Power,[19] knowing, willing, acting,[20] and the Synthesis of all units of "Sounds".[21] The *Svayambhu-Linga* in the Radical Centre round which Śakti or Power has coiled herself up in "three coils and a half," is the Self or *Ātman* in the Principle of solid matter which is sheathed by the coils of the "Serpent Power" here immanent in Matter in its grossest

[1] Manas. [2] Sādhanā.
[3] Avidyā-samskāra. [4] Vyavahāra. [5] Avidyā.
[6] Guhā. [7] Rātri.
[8] Nidrā. For example, we hear of the yoga-nidrā of Viṣṇu (The "All-pervasive") in the first Māhātmya of Śrī Candī.
[9] Nirodha-Śakti. [10] Sādhaka. [11] Tattva-dṛṣṭi.
[12] Vigraha. [13] Saccidānanda.
[14] Buddhi, Ahankāra etc.
[15] Sūkṣma. [16] Mūlādhāra cakra.
[17] The Prithivī or "earth" Centre. [18] Sarva-tattva-rūpinī.
[19] Sarva-śakti-svarūpinī. [20] Jnānaśakti, Ichchhāśakti and Kriyāśakti.
[21] Sarva-varna-mayī. As to Śabda, see *The Serpent Power*.

form.[1] All this signifies that Matter really involves Self or *Ātman* and the Power whereby this Self is sheathed is really Perfect Power, though "asleep". It is not, therefore, merely what the physicist would recognise as Physical Force or Energy. Mind as *Buddhi* and other forms are all there in it. As the Basal Centre has its *Linga* or Self, so have the other Centres[2] in which other forms of Matter and Mind[3] are represented. The Self of the *Yogī* so acts on these Centres that what is coiled up in them becomes uncoiled, what is latent patent. Thus the Material Tattvas are successively "spiritualized," and are ultimately cast as offerings into the "Fire of Supreme Consciousness and Bliss" in highest realization.

An atom of matter, according to this conception, is not dead, inert, insensate and selfless. In it the Effulgent Person of whom the *Chhandogya* says that He is possessed of golden hair and a golden beard and so forth (who can be seen in the "Sun,"[4] also, on a smaller scale, in the pupil of one's eyes) is in disguise, a disguise due partly at least to the necessity of having to deal with it in specific pragmatic relations of enjoyment and suffering, and, therefore, would not exist in, and as this particular disguise if man's unseen result of Karma,[6] were, or could be made, different. The disguise is relative to the conditions of present practice[7] which set down certain limitations to the functioning of the instruments of apprehension and thinking in man. If one could apprehend the fourth dimension, for instance, a stone would not be to him what it is to us. So again, if one could exercise subtle vision,[8] one might see or hear the actual dance of the particles in a stone – a dance which though it may conform generally to a measure and law[9] might be seen as not wholly determined or bound by it, but as the expression[10] of Joy,[11] even as man's own voluntary actions are so admittedly. This stone, too, has its unseen Karma[6] by which its position and state in the cosmic system are determined relatively to those of other objects. Irrespectively of other objects, therefore, it is not what it appears to be : a block of stone. It is the Whole.[12] This is its *Kaivalya* — that is, its being apart from specific relations to other beings in a stressing cosmic system. Even in actual relations, it is not relatively to one class of objects what it may be relatively to another class.[13] So long as a thing is a member of the cosmic stress-system, it

[1] Prithivī. [2] Cakra.
[3] Prithivī, Ap. Tejas, Vāyu, Vyoma, Antahkaraṇa.
[4] Āditya-maṇḍala. Chāndogya, I, VI. [5] *i.e.*, of Bhoga. [6] Adṛṣṭa.
[7] Vyavahāra. [8] Divya-dṛṣṭi. [9] Chhandah.
[10] Līlā. [11] Ānanda. [12] Pūrṇa. [13] See *Post.*

is a certain thing relatively to man who "is his own measure". Man thus thinks that, relatively to the stone, he is the knower or enjoyer,[1] whilst the stone is known and enjoyed[2] only. But this is veiled thinking. The stone is, according to its unseen karma[3] a knower and enjoyer also. In the case of the sculptor and the stone we have "enjoying" in both, though, in accordance with his unseen *Karma*, the fact may be patent and pronounced in the former, and, in accordance with its *Karma*,[3] it may be latent and hidden in the latter. All that we have a right to say is this however that it is latent and hidden in the latter relatively to our *Karma*[3] or to that of others who are, or are conceived by us to be, constituted and "cosmically situated" similarly to us. It need not necessarily be so, relatively to other constitutions and cosmic situations.

Explanation by an Universal "Over-soul" and Reservoir of Power will not materially affect the position stated above. *Cit-Śakti* in evolving as the World of Forms, divides itself, so to say, into a double line of manifestation — cosmic and micro-cosmic. Thus there are, on one hand, Universal Life, and individual, finite lives, on the other.[5] The Universal is the causal ground of the individual or particular. The individual thus arises out of the Universal, and in dissolution[6] is dissolved in it again. The Universal is therefore not simply the aggregate of the particulars. Thus *Hiraṇyagarbha*[7] is not merely the sum of individual lives[7] and minds.[8] It is their beginning and end. And co-existing with them, it controls them and lies at the back of them as an inexhaustible fund of vital and mentative power. It is also their connecting and pervading "medium" like ether of material bodies. Its control, however, is not determination. And an individual Centre by "closing the circuit" between itself and the Universal Self, can draw upon that general fund of power. In that case, cosmic power flows on into the individual and fills it, just as, on the physical plane, electricity may, through conductors, flow from one body into another and saturate it. As in matter, flow presupposes difference of level, pressure or potential, so in life and mind, flow implies that one object is relatively greater or fuller in power than another. But the lesser thing, though actually or apparently lesser, must have potential capacity, so that it may contain currents of life more than what it ordinarily does contain. That is, even in the case of actual conduction of cosmic power

[1] Jnātā and Bhoktā. [2] Jneya and bhogya. [3] And Adṛṣṭa.
[4] Prāṇa. [5] Antahkaraṇa. [6] Laya. [7] Prāṇas.
[8] Manas. See *The Garland of Letters* where these relations are explained, and particularly, the diagrams.

into a finite Centre, we must presuppose that the latter has potential capacity greater than its actual or seeming capacity; which means that though, practically and seemingly, it is finite and small, yet really and potentially, it is great. And since there can be set no limit to what a "finite" Centre can contain of the Power of the Cosmic Self flowing on into it, we must presuppose that its capacity is potentially indefinitely great or infinite.

Hence in order that Cosmic Power in a large measure may flow into it, its potential capacity must to that extent be kinetized. Otherwise, a well remaining a well will never contain the sea. To contain it it must be sea itself. And it can become the sea because really, though not "in ordinary use," it is the sea. Hence the position that a finite thing, even though material, is merely an empirical[1] form in which the Measureless[2] and Whole[3] appears as Little[4] and Imperfect,[5] and sectional, is not affected by the view that a finite thing's accession to power (physical, vital or mental) is due to the conduction into it of Power from a Cosmic Reservoir. We have seen that such conduction and expansion and filling of the Little is possible, because under the action of the Cosmic Power it can be, more or less nearly, assimilated to the state of the latter; and that it can be so assimilated because potentially it is identical with or similar to the Cosmic Power. In fact, while turning a "finite" face to other centres and in world-experience,[6] it must be conceived as turning an infinite face also to the Infinite Self.

Or the position may be stated thus: It is the Universal Self[7] who, whilst remaining as such, finitizes itself by veiling into a plurality of finite selves; the Universal thus appears in two forms — as Universal and as Particulars which are really the Universal but variously self-veiling. The finite centre's drawing the current of Universal Life really therefore means the Patent and Manifest Universal removing the veil It has put on in, and as, the finite particular. It is really Infinity discovering Infinity in the midst of pragmatic limitations created by Itself. The conduction or "flow" view, therefore, instead of shewing that the little is little, shows that the little is great, the finite infinite. Greatness is not merely "thrust upon" it by an extraneous Agency; it is "born" great, and therefore naturally "achieves," or is made to achieve, greatness. That Mind

[1] Vyavahārika. [2] Bhūmā. [3] Pūrṇa. [4] Alpa.
[5] Apūrṇa. The "disguise" is variously referred to in the Ups.
[6] Vyavahāra. [7] In Prāṇa, Manas, etc.

and Life[1] are given in a block of stone is a position which from this view of things remains unshaken.

But, as on the material plane, we have induction of vital and mental power also, which directly suggests that a "small" thing has a great capacity. In conduction, power actually flows from a source to a receiver, and the amount added to the latter is subtracted from the former. In induction, a charged body by its "influence" evokes a corresponding charge in another body. There is no actual give and take. In induction, Power in the two bodies is of the same sign; in conduction, Power disposes itself in opposite poles in the two bodies. Suppose we take two bodies X and Y of which the former is charged with positive electricity. Now, what happens if Y be brought close to it (but not in contact)? Suppose the faces which X and Y turn to each be A and C respectively, and their respective "backs" B and D. Then, the charge of X will so act upon the neutral condition of Y as to polarize it into a positive charge and a negative charge, and of these, the negative one, which is opposite to the positive charge on A, will settle on C. That is, the two bodies will have their confronting faces, A and C, charged with electricity with opposite signs. Induction, therefore, may be said to reverse the "sign" of power in the influenced body relatively to the influencing body.

Now, consider a stone again. Relatively to the results of previous Karma[2] and the common experience[3] of Self-conscious Man, the direction of Power in a stone is downward:[4] from the evolution of mind, to that of gross matter (in which the former as causal is involved), the curve of Power is a descending one. Man principle represents an ascending current of power as compared with the Matter-principle. This difference of direction can be symbolised by a difference of sign. Now, in ordinary relation, when a man faces a stone, we have this upwardly directed Power facing each other. The former means evolving, unfolding Power; the latter means involved, folded-up Power. The former gives unfolded, manifest, patent being; the latter folded up, unmanifest, latent being. Hence, commonly, a man facing a stone means a self-conscious being facing a thing in which Self and so forth are folded up, latent. Thus the stone appears as neutral, inert. But suppose the man is able to "influence" the stone in the manner before described. The influencing will mean the reversing of the direction of sign of the Power in the stone, that is, making

[1] As Buddhi, Ahaṃkāra, Manas, Prāṇa.
[2] Adṛṣṭa. [3] Vyavahāra. [4] It is adhah-srotah.

it an ascending instead of a descending current, unfolded, instead of folded, evolved instead of involved. That is to say, Self, Mind[1] and Life[2] so long involved in it relatively to the man, will be evolved relatively to him. This change implies, as before explained, a change of Karma[3] of the one relatively to that of the other.

This is Induction in the higher planes which descends, with a special form and name, on the plane of matter. Man's spiritual effort may be through conduction or through induction ("vicarious action") or through both. Some forms of it lay stress on the one, and other forms on the other. The method of Prayer is mainly one of conduction (in which Divine Power flows on into the devotee); the method of *Bhūta-Śuddhi* or *Kuṇḍalinī yoga* is mainly one of induction.[4] But we must not actually separate the one from the other. Every act of perception requires both induction and conduction of Power. And whether it be conduction or it be induction, it has been shown that according to Vedānta a block of stone or a lump of earth, however it may pose itself relatively, to the "potential worths"[3] of other things, is really and potentially the Universal Self, Life and Mind in a certain form of self-limitation; being so, it is always really Bliss[5] and Play[6] as the Self is (for it is none other than the Universal Self); it can be made to appear as a blissful and playful[7] Self only if we can make our "attitude"[8] different and appropriate in relation to it.

The gross view of Matter was the ignorance or nescience of nineteenth-century science, but the present dynamical conception of matter (with which the Indian Doctrine of Power agrees) has gone a considerable way in paving the path for the acceptance of the Vedāntic view above explained. The atom is said to be no longer a "hard billiard-ball" but a sort of miniature universe, with a practically incalculable fund of energy; it ordinarily conserves itself but is, in radio-activity, transforming and evolving; the aspect of Power as *evolving matter*, and that as *dissolving* matter are also perhaps already recognisable in it. Motions and masses in it are calculable only abstractly (that is, after some limitation of the data), but not concretely. Determinism or the 'rule of formula" can never be completely established in its domestic or "foreign" life. The Principle of Relativity

---

[1] Antahkaraṇa. [2] Prāṇa.
[3] And Adṛṣṭa.
[4] See *The Serpent Power* "The Philosophical Basis of Kuṇḍalinī yoga".
[5] Ānandamaya. [6] Līlāmaya.
[7] Ānandamaya, līlāmaya.
[8] See *post*, for further explanation of Adrishta and Karma.

has also been an upsetter of the old bases of calculation. Hence Physics may be supposed to have indicated already that it is a magazine of Power which creates, evolves, conserves and destroys (thus indicating play[1] in all its phases); that it has a system of domestic economy; that it has its own idiosyncrasy; its own "memory," and so on. These indications are, if anything, suggestive of a Self in the atom doing play[1] out of Joy[2] appearing as subject to conditions. What Physics covers or tries to cover by its mathematical formulæ and equations, is an abstract atom representing some only of the conditions; the real concrete atom exceeds these formulæ and equations, and must ever exceed them, because its essence, its driving force is Power which is Joy[2] which expresses itself in spontaneity, freedom and play. Clear-sighted Physicists have long recognized that the nineteenth-century atom is conceptual, abstract, but they must now also recognise that the twentieth-century atom, corpuscle and so forth are no less conceptual in so far as they are supposed to be exactly coverable by differential equations. But the real atom is also slowly disentangling itself from those physico-mathematical bonds.[3] The Self in it has now spoken; evidence of play[1] in it can no longer be mistaken. All this is not to say that the Self in the atom is actually a thinker, a logician, or a judge. A block of stone does not think and judge (by means of categories) its states as we think and judge ours. But this does not affect the position that it has its Self, its experience (however veiled relatively to us) of Joy,[2] and its Play[1] (however determined its behaviour may appear to our abstract calculation).

Thus all the three issues raised with regard to it have been decided according to Śāstric principles. A block of stone is *Saccidānanda* or Being-Consciousness-Bliss veiling itself in a particular manner, but never so veiling as to make its essential nature completely suppressed. Its Self, its Joy[2] may be ordinarily hidden from our practical cognisance which is cognisance within certain narrow, pragmatic limits only.

We began with the *Māyā-vāda* definition of Real as that which is common,[4] not limited by Time and Space, or without exception.[5] Enquiry has shown that of all the infinitely varied objects of experience the common, the invariable element is Being-Consciousness-Bliss or *Sat-Cit-Ānanda.*

---

[1] Līlā. [2] Ānanda.
[3] The dynamical view is a long step already taken towards the "dematerialization" of matter. And "Psychic Research" is furnishing corroborative evidence. See *Post.*
[4] Sāmānya. [5] Avyabhichārī.

This, therefore, is the lasting Real the forms and names not being invariable are "unreal" in the sense of being transient. The fundamental importance of the conception of Experience as being essentially *Saccidānanda* (especially the last)[1] has justified a detailed examination of the matter.

But, as in the other case, *Māyā-vāda*, in thus defining the essence of Reality and Experience, has drawn the veil over, and therefore hidden, something. That essence of experience alone is not Perfect Experience — the Whole.[2] Unless we add to it Power to change or evolve as varied Name and Form,[3] we have "Fact-section" only, not the "Fact". The Real is not the Essence only which is massive Consciousness as Cit,[2] and Bliss,[5] but the Power also by which Joy[5] appears as full activity or play. The Whole[2] is Bliss[5] in itself, as well as Power to manifest as play.[6] One aspect apart from the other is but a fraction.[7]

In conceiving the Whole as Reality (or "Fact"), we must beware of two possible abstractions. To restrict the Fact to the changeless and universal element of experience alone is one abstraction. The other is to restrict it to a sort of statical, unmoving "perfectness". All the *Śāstras* (Vedas as well as Śākta and Advaita Śaiva[8] Tantras) agree in maintaining that there is a transcendental state (immanent in ordinary experience also) of *Cit* which is pure,[9] unveiled,[10] stainless,[11] undivided,[12] quiescent[13] and without a second;[14] that this is changeless and abiding while all forms change, appear and disappear; that this is the Substance, Ground and Root of all world-manifestation; and that liberation[15] can be had by realizing this *Saccidānanda*. *Māyā-vāda* may be justified not only in emphasizing this transcendental aspect of *Cit*, but also (as one method and to some extent), in concentrating the *sādhaka's* thought on this aspect, since without realizing this aspect there is no liberation,[15] and, since according to this method, this aspect should be realized transcendentally first, and then immanently in the varied experiences of the world. That is, *Cit* must first be recognised as differentiated from name and form,[16]

---

[1] The fundamentality of Ānanda is especially treated in Taittirīya Up. (Brigu vallī); see also Brahma Sūtra, I, 1, 12.

[2] Pūrṇa.

[3] Nāma and Rūpa.

[4] "Vijnānaghana, etc., as Brihadāraṇyaka-Up. (IV, 5, 13; III 9, 28; II, 4, 12, etc).

[5] Ānanda.

[6] Līlā.

[7] Kalā.

[8] The Advaita or non-dual position is alone dealt with.

[9] Śuddha

[10] Nirlepa

[11] Niranjana

[12] Akhaṇḍa.

[13] Śānta.

[14] Advaitīya.

[15] Mukti.

[16] Nāma and Rūpa. Expressed by "So'ham".

and then, as identical with the Power evolving them.[1] With this supreme object[2] in view, *Māyā-vāda* defines the transcendental and unchanging aspect as Reality, and the reverse as neither real nor unreal. Let us let alone the unreal, and concentrate our thought on the Real, because that is unchanging, pure, massive *Saccidānanda*, the realization of which is liberation,[3]—this is what *Māyā-vāda* in fact says. Now, assuming the truth of non-dualism no objection can be taken to this as one method of realizing the supreme goal by those suited to this Path. Our interest is naturally in name and form;[4] to transfer it to Pure *Saccidānānda*, we must provisionally discard, and belittle name and form.[4] We have to be persuaded that our interest should lie in Pure *Cit* and not in the forms. And this persuasion is attempted while the Vedantist declares the former as real and the latter neither real nor unreal. From its standpoint *Māyā-vāda* may be right.[5] But still it should be observed that in this we have attempted to define the undefinable, offered as Real that which is an aspect (however fundamental) of the Concrete Whole. Such defining and offering are necessary for the realization of the object in view; but still when it[6] comes to be a question of *living* the full and undivided Reality, we must be careful to recognise that *Cit* as Reality is unchanging, but it is *also* Power to change as the world of name and form;[7] that *Cit* is not Ether-consciousness[8] only, but is also Power in Play[9] manifesting as the world; that *Cit* as Ether[8] only is not Joy[10] but *Cit* in play[9] also is Joy.[10] We have no right to draw a line and say that the Real is here and not there. The Whole and Full is the Fact. Hence the *Upaniṣad* or real name of the *Brahman* is The Reality of Reality.[11]

Nor must we look upon the Fact as a statical, unmoving, "eternally realized" perfectness. That is another abstraction. There may be an aspect of experience in which everything stands manifested in the fullness of its relations to all other things. There is nothing unmanifest, unrealized in regard to such Experience. Here knowing[12] and so forth are eternal.[13] Nothing being here unknown and unrealized, this experience does not evolve. Many western as also Indian thinkers,[14] have conceived such a level of eternally and perfectly realized experience.[14]

[1] Expressed by "Sarvo'smi" [2] Paramārtha. [3] Mukti
[4] Nāma-rūpa or the psycho-physical. [5] *i.e.*, in view of the Paramārtha.
[6] Pūrṇa and Ákhaṇḍa. [7] Namā-rūpa or the psycho-physical.
[8] Cidākāśa [9] Cid-vilāsa. [10] Ānanda.
[11] Brih.-Up., II, 1, 20; Maitri-Up., VI, 32 (Ka). [12] Jnāna. [13] Nitya.
[14] *Cf.* the doctrines of Rāmānujāchārya, Madhvachārya, Vallabhachārya, Nimbāchārya, and others.

It also represents the 26th *Tattva* (Principle), *viz.*, *Īśvarā*, of the Yoga System.[1] He is the knower of all generals[2] and of all particulars.[3] His sound-predicate[4] is the *Mahāmantra Om.*[5] Man's experience has generally been conceived as "a gradual and partial reproduction" of that Spiritual Principle. We do not know, and cannot relate ourselves to, a thing in the completeness of its relations. Hence we know more and more; will and act to place that thing in other and yet other relations to ourselves.

That Consciousness as *Cit*, in evolving by its Power of the world of names and forms, shows a perfect and realized Form (the Supreme Form)[6] and an unending series of less and less perfect and less realized forms, yet remaining as it is in itself always and everywhere, whilst veiling and limiting itself variously as it descends from the Supreme Form and Name[7] to the lower levels, is a position which is assured by the very nature of evolution itself. Evolution means this. A Supreme Form or Ideal, as actual Reality, involves or folds itself up progressively by its veiling and finitizing Power; but the Supreme Form possesses supreme *elasticity*[8] (as the imperfect forms, material or otherwise, possess their elasticities by which when strained they stress to regain their own forms; whereby in and through all strained, that is veiled and finitized, forms, it again tends to regain its Supreme Form). This is Cosmic Elasticity and it is at the root of Evolution. It is analysable into two factors—a downward or forward sweep and an upward or backward sweep; an outgoing current and a return current;[9] an ejection and an absorption. One of the *Śāstric* symbols is the Divine Tortoise[10] who projects and withdraws His limbs, and Who is described as having borne on His back the *Vedas* (*i.e.*, the highest form of Experience together with all sounds)[11] in the "Causal Waters" during Dissolution. The movement of the Divine Tortoise as the symbol of Cosmic Elasticity by which finite forms, etc., are projected from the Supreme Form (representing the "strains"), and are again withdrawn into it. The factors of the Cosmic Elasticity are concurrent, but one factor may have a cyclic or rhythmic ascendency over the other factor. That is, in the cyclic life of the world the two factors appear alternately as the dominant and the recessive respectively. This being

---

[1] Pātanjala-Sūtra — concept of Īśvara.
[2] Sarvajna. [3] Sarva-vit. [4] Vācaka.
[5] "Tasya vācakah pranavah" — Pātanjala-Sūtra. [6] Īśvara.
[7] The Supreme Śabda-Artha-Pratyaya, which is the Lord Īśvara.
[8] See *post* for further explanation.
[9] Pravritti and Nivritti Mārga. [10] Kūrma. [11] Śabdas.

the meaning of evolution, we must hold that the Supreme Form as actual Reality is at the root of the process; and that it is a partial and incorrect view to say, with many of the western evolutionists, that the very lowest and simplest forms only are at the start, and that the higher and more complex forms are progressively evolved, with occasional reversions to lower forms, the tendency being on the whole towards the realization of perfect forms which perhaps cannot be realized under existing circumstances in finite time. This gives us a side view and a distorted view of the matter. The Supreme Form[1] and the higher Forms[2] are in the beginning as actual realities, who supervise, as *Cit-Śaktis* or Controlling Principles, the downward sweep which gradually involves the higher forms as well as the upward sweep which gradually evolves them. The Supreme Form or *Īśvara*[3] is thus given in the process not merely as an unrealized, infinitely distant Cosmic Ideal, but as a Reality present in, and controlling, the whole cosmic process.[4]

But the Supreme Form must not be offered as being alone the Reality. It is an aspect or Form of Reality, as Pure *Cidākāśa* is an aspect. The Full Reality[5] or "Fact" is *Cit* which, while remaining by its Power the Pure Ether which is *Saccidānanda* or *Śiva*, yet evolves by its Power, the World-Mother, as the world of forms. The Supreme Form[1] involves Itself into lower and lower forms and also evolves these again into higher and higher forms until in dissolution they are withdrawn into Itself to be projected again during creation. *Being-Consciousness-Bliss as both Power to Be* and *to Become or evolve is therefore the Reality Whole.*[6] Time, Space and Causality are born in its womb;[7] that is, in itself It is *Mahākāli*, which means not only that *Mahākāla* or *Infinite* Time is the Power, but that She "stands upon" *Mahākāla* who, as the symbol depicts, is "at Her feet".

---

[1] Īśvara.

[2] Such as the Prajāpatis, Mānasa-putras, Manus. It is interesting to note that practically all ancient traditions make History start with Manu. India, Manu; Egypt, Manes of M'na; Crete, Minos; Lydia, Manes; Phrygia, Manis; German, Mannus; and so on.

[3] In the scheme of "36 Tattvas" Īśvara-tattva is given a special meaning.

[4] The doctrine therefore does not favour any theory of "God in the Making." Śruti very often uses the epithets "sarvādhyaksha," etc., meaning that He is the Supreme Lord, Overseer, etc.

[5] Pūrṇa.

[6] Pūrṇa (Parama-Kalā). This fundamental doctrine is evidenced by the association of Śiva-Śakti on all planes and their unity. They are never, even in dissolution, apart from one another.

[7] Kāla-Śakti is one of the Kancukas. Cit as Power becomes in evolution Kāla-Śakti.

She is the Mother as also the Consort of *Mahākāla* — a truth which is now understood. She produces Time, and having produced, plays with, and as, Time. Such play is Her play,[1] Her love-joying.[2] She is the Supreme Principle[3] evolving as, and transcending, the 36 Tattvas or Stages of involution and evolution. The Pure[4] *Cit* of *Māyā-vāda* and also the eternal Whole with attributes[5] are both Her aspects: She is both above the factors[6] of the radical psycho-physical potential[7] and their support,[8] and is both without and with attributes constituted of such Factors.[9] She is the Supreme without aspects, as well as with aspects.[10] We cannot define Her by anyone of Her aspects. In Herself She is the Whole which manifests as the Universe of Parts existent within It.

## CONSCIOUSNESS[11] AND UNCONSCIOUSNESS[12]

In the previous Section we have dealt with *Cit* as Reality. But, whether tacitly or explicitly, we have, throughout the discussion, proceeded on the basis that there is no *Acit*[12] or unconsciousness, no "thing" independent of Consciousness. We must now briefly examine that basis. The previous discussion has already sufficiently prepared the ground for such examination.

Unconsciousness[13] may mean three things: (1) Objects known by Consciousness and yet believed to exist by their own right outside of Consciousness, *e.g.*, a block of stone we now see or touch; (2) objects believed to exist by their own right of which we have no consciousness at all; and (3) anything which is, or can be, made an object of knowing,[14] and which therefore can be distinguished from the "I" or subject or principle of knowing[15] as "This."[16] The second class of objects may be of two kinds: (*a*) Objects which, though themselves conscious, are yet outside and independent of our consciousness; and (*b*) objects which are outside and independent of our consciousness and are believed to be unconscious in themselves, *e.g.*, unknown material objects. Now Vedānta does not recognise the first two classes (1 and 2), as unconsciousness,[13] though, pragmatically, it may sometimes call them so. There is nothing

[1] Līlā. [2] Ramanānanda. [3] Pūrṇa-Tattva.
[4] Nirguṇa.
[5] Nitya-Pūrṇa-guṇa-viśiṣta. The Cit of Viśiṣtādvaita, for instance.
[6] Guṇātīta. [7] Prakṛti Śakti. [8] Gunāśraya.
[9] Guṇamayī. [10] Niṣkala as well as Sakala.
[11] Cit. [12] Acit is 'not Cit'. [13] Acit or Jaḍa.
[14] *i.e.*, Jneya. [15] Aham, Jnāta. [16] Idam.

outside and independent of Consciousness as such; nothing existing by a right which is not the supreme right of Consciousness-Being; hence there is no unconsciousness[1] in the first two senses. Consciousness should not, however, be taken to mean veiled, individualized Consciousness which means Consciousness so limiting itself as to have other "consciousnesses" and things existing outside its or their limits. Thus a block of stone even while it is being seen and touched by a Subject A, is believed to exist independently of A's Consciousness; and that belief is correct, and Realism is justified, in a certain sense. An unknown object, far away in the heavens, or far below in the interior of the earth for instance, may thus really exist outside of the consciousness of A or B. But still it never exists independent of Consciousness as such or Cosmic Consciousness which is the unveiled form or state of Consciousness. Even, with regard to A's consciousness, it is outside and alien in so far as A's consciousness is A's and not B's or C's; that is, in so far as it is veiled consciousness setting up the pragmatic walls of the sub-conscious and unconscious about it. Cosmic Consciousness is Consciousness *minus* these walls and partitions. Every object is in it, and of it.

Consider an unknown star so far distant that its light neither reaches the eyes nor affects a sensitive photographic plate. It is thus outside of, and alien to, A's consciousness. But what part of it? That it is outside the inner ring of A's consciousness which is the accepted and recognised portion (commonly called the consciousness) is clear. But what about the outlying zone of gradually thickening and darkening sub-consciousness? Many things, not recognised in the "broad daylight" ring, can be by means of the "searchlight" discovered in the darker zones—in the realms of "twilight" for instance, which some western psychologists call the "fringe of consciousness". Now, is the unknown star here? In other words, has it really been known without our noticing it—recognising that it has been known? No; the searchlight does not discover it. Has it no place in the semi-conscious and sub-conscious zones then? We can never be sure that it has not.

The universe is an infinite stress-system. All centres, near or distant, are in constant interaction. For instance, if a lump of matter be suddenly created or annihilated now in space thousands of billions of miles away from us, that event will certainly affect the entire stress-system of the universe, of the earth and of A's organism for the matter of that. The

[1] Jaḍa.

effect may be inappreciably small, if the event in question be small, or too far away. But this only means that our sense-organs and perceptive machinery have been so constituted and adjusted that they ordinarily do not record disturbances (sound, heat, light and the like) which do not come within certain limits of intensity, duration, and so forth. But this does not mean either that the distant event has failed to influence our organism and machinery at all, or that, having influenced it, it has not contributed its share to the general, vague, massive feeling, partly semi-conscious and partly sub-conscious, which always clings to and constitutes a sort of "background" of all definite and recognised feelings or perceptions that we may have in life. In fact, it must follow *a priori* from our position in the cosmic stress-system (which has no "watertight compartments") that every move in this cosmic dance must produce a corresponding tremor in the chords of our feeling, and that the "clear notes" which one hears from those chords are always set in a background of half-tones and subtones—a general, massive, indiscriminated, unrecognised chorus of notes—to which the movement of any corpuscle anywhere in boundless space must have borne its share. The clear note is gross;[1] this background of sub-notes represents the realm of subtle,[2] variously graded. The first with the second is the concrete whole of feeling; it is an abstraction and unreality without the second.

Our searchlight does not commonly reveal everything in this background because it is a pragmatic searchlight, ordinarily so fitted and adjusted as to reveal objects within certain limits only. But by *Yoga* this searchlight can be made to approach as near as possible to perfection.[3] By its means the subtle background of our experiences can be made to come into clear relief. Thus a *yogī* may know by meditation[4] a subtle,[2] obstructed,[5] distant[6] object or event, because it was already in his feeling, though unperceived and unrecognised. To say that he discovers it not by exploring his own experience but by drawing upon a perfect bank of experience which is Cosmic Consciousness is only a different way of stating what has been above formulated. The difference between his own experience and that of the Lord and Mother is a difference of veiling or ignorance only; so that the same act (meditation and so forth) by which he "explores" his own experience and discovers a previously un-

[1] Sthūla. [2] Sūkṣma.

[3] This includes what is now cultivated in the West as "X-ray vision" or as Clairvoyance, or "Psychometry," etc.

[4] Dhyāna. [5] Vyavahita. [6] Viprakriṣta.

known element in it, is also the act by which he lifts the veil drawn over his own knowledge and assimilates his mind to that of the Lord.[1] His exploration becomes productive of new discoveries in proportion as this unveiling and assimilation progresses. Finally, when perfect assimilation is effected, his experience becomes the Experience of the Lord[1] which is Perfect *Veda* or *Veda* in the limit to which man's *Vedas* and even those of the *Ṛṣīs* are more or less distant or near approximations. To bring oneself in perfect rapport with the Perfect *Veda* is to become It.[2] Clairvoyance and like faculties in which things subtle, far distant in time and place, are perceived, is thus the recognition of the unrecognised in our experience, or otherwise stated, the projection on the lighted white screen of the seer's consciousness of the things that are in the Cosmic Consciousness. This being the position, it is clear that things (known or unknown) which are believed to exist objectively to, or independently of, A's consciousness, really do so if A's consciousness be restricted to what he and others accept as such; but if A's consciousness, including the realms of the semi-conscious, sub-conscious and "unconscious," be so unveiled and lighted as to become identical with Cosmic Consciousness, then there is, or can be, nothing existing independently of it.

A material thing, for instance, is independent of the "normal" consciousness of A, both as regards the primary and the secondary qualities. But does it exist exactly as a copy of A's perception? No. A's cognitive faculty being limited and conditioned by his tendencies,[3] he knows a part only of the thing as a whole, and that part too, to some extent in his own way. Even in perception each person has his idiosyncrasy, his "personal equation". Thus A's perception is not exactly equal to B's; B's not exactly equal to C's. The inspection of the Scientist or the meditation[4] of the *yogī* gives a fuller picture; but these fuller pictures also more or less differ. The question therefore arises; What is the standard perception or the cognition of the thing in the perfectness of its qualities and relations? This standard perception may again relate either to the pure type[5] of the thing or to *all* the details or particulars in their correlation. The former is the General[6] and the latter the Particulars.[7] Both

[1] Īśvara and Īśvarī according as we regard the Śiva or Śakti aspect of the Whole.
[2] And so it is said "To know Brahman is to be Brahman (Brahmavid Brahmaiva bhavati)". The kind of "Knowing" is Jnāna svarūpa as contrasted with Knowing in the subject-object relation" or Jnānakriyā.
[3] Samskāras. [4] Dhyāna. [5] Jāti or Sāmānya or ākriti.
[6] Tanmātra. [7] Viśeṣa.

are cognised by the Standard Mind which is the Lord Who, in respect of the former is called "Knower of all generals,"[1] and in respect of the latter, "Knower of all particulars."[2] Hence what exists really independently of A's normal consciousness is the Standard Thing as cognised by, and as existing in, the Lord.[3]

Common Realism objectifies A's perceptions; they are objective not only as regards their exciting cause or ground but also as regards their primary and secondary qualities; but not simply in the sectional view which A, by reason of his limited capacities, takes of it, nor in the more or less "coloured" view which A by reason of his idiosyncrasy or special tendencies[4] forms of it. Even the scientist relying on his artificially extended capacities of perception has to neutralize these idiosyncrasies and so forth; hence his real thing is what is perceivable by a "mean or average" observer with the help of "perfect" instruments. Both are ideal conditions. The "average" man does not actually exist; and no earthly workshops can of course turn out "perfect" instruments. For the "mean" man with perfect instruments we substitute the Standard Mind, and though this latter may be beyond mathematical measurement ("Science is measurement"), it is within the possibility of realization, being the unveiled "that which we are in ourselves."[5]

Vedānta thus does not recognise unconsciousness[6] in the first two senses set forth above. Where it uses the term, it does so in the third sense, that is, the *known* represented by "This".[7] Briefly, according to this conception, Illumination[8] is *Cit* or Consciousness, and that[9] which is made an object of the former or revealing is, as such, object, unconscious. The Mind[10] and the limited Self produced through its operation[11] are thus unconscious because both can be, and are, known as "this". But, be it noted that, they as well as the so-called Matter are unconscious[12] only in this sense, that as being the object of the conscious Ego they are therefore as such object not conscious. Apart from this sense, and in themselves, they are consciousness. The point is that *Cit*, makes unconsciousness of itself by making an "object" of itself. There is nothing but *Cit*, object or no object. There is even in fact no such thing as seeming or "reflex" consciousness.[14] There is nothing other than *Cit*,

---

[1] Sarvajna. [2] Sarva-vit. Mundaka-Up., I, 1, 9; II, 2, 7. [3] Īśvara.
[4] Samskāras. [5] Svarūpa. [6] Acit, Jaḍa.
[7] Idam. See Shārīraka Bhāshya, Upodghāta. [8] Prakāsha.
[9] Vimarśa. [10] Antahkaraṇa. [11] As Ahamkāra.
[12] Jaḍa. [13] Acit. [14] Cidābhāsa.

lucid or opaque, on which the "Light" of *Cit* can reflect itself, thus making that object to look like something luminous. To say that there is really an unconscious thing,[1] which looks as though it were conscious owing to its association with *Cit*, is Sānkhyan Dualism, and in Monistic[2] doctrine no relic of that Dualism can be suffered to remain.

Mind[3] is at base really *Cit*, though, pragmatically, it may be called unconscious[1] on account of its being an "object" of knowledge, and its having a varying veil, measure and movement. It never ceases to be other than *Cit*. It is *Cit* limiting and defining itself as Mind as distinguished from Matter,[4] for instance, which is *Cit* limiting and defining itself in Matter.[5] Vedānta does not countenance any essential dualism of Mind and Matter. It maintains unmoving, unveiled, unmeasured aspect of *Cit* as well as a moving, veiled, measured aspect. The latter is Mind, Matter, Space, Motion and so forth. Hence it does not hesitate to conceive Mind as something having a variable measure (sometimes expanding, sometimes contracting), a variable structure owing to the variable mixing of the three Factors[6] of the Principle of Contraction and a variable movement even in Space (as in Perception, and so forth).[7] It is really *Cit* moving in *Cit*, existing in *Cit* and functioning in *Cit*. If there be Extension, Inertia, Movement, Impenetrability, etc. (the usual marks of Matter) in the world, it is because *Cit* has so defined itself as to be extended, inert, mobile, impenetrable and so forth. Western philosophers sometimes look askance at thought-movement and so forth, because they hold to the dispaiity of Mind and Matter. And, usually, they do not distinguish between Mind and Consciousness. Consciousness as such does not come and go, but Mind as psychic process does.

There has been, both in India and elsewhere, much controversy about the question whether there may be "unconscious ideation" or unconscious experience. It seems hardly open to doubt, however, that many common places of experience as well as many "abnormal," extraordinary and "occult" experiences cannot be satisfactorily accounted for at all except by maintaining that there is a "normal" or "threshold" line of consciousness in man in respect of which his curve of experience is partly above and partly below. Habit, Memory, Instinctive thinking

---

[1] Jaḍa [2] Advaita. [3] Antahkaraṇa.
[4] Antahkaraṇāvacchinna-caitanya.
[5] Prameyāvacchīnna-caitanya as Vedānta-paribhāṣā defines.
[6] Śvetāśvatara. Up., III, 18; Brih. – Up. IV, 3, 7; Chhānd. – Up., VIII. 6, 5.
[7] Guṇa.

and action, dreaming which has been said to involve repressed, unsatisfied desires, and the like as also many "uncommon" experiences presuppose a continuous curve of experience part of which is "subliminal," and which, therefore, like a floating ice-berg is not all what it looks. The explanation by "cerebral vestiges," without having recourse to subliminal depths, is not sufficient and cannot cover all cases. The brain may not be a necessary organ of the mind, and in so far as it is an organ, its stresses may correspond to, run parallel to, without wholly causing, the stresses of the mind. Vedānta not being afraid of Matter, is not, therefore, afraid of the brain. It is prepared to maintain a real interaction between the brain and the mind; which is not simply a parallelism between psychosis and neurosis. But still the mind may have a life larger than, and in some cases, and to a certain degree, independent of the brain. The "cerebralist," on the other hand, makes the life of the brain larger than, and independent of, that of the mind. Thus brain-activities may go on without there being accompanying mental states; and brain-vestiges may remain without there being actual mental "seeds," and tendencies.[1]

A stronger position is that mental states, after their intensities or interests sink below a certain "mark", persist as subliminal forms and stresses which are tendencies,[1] and when these tendencies press themselves beyond a certain mark, they again become "conscious" presentations. Between a presentation and a "tendency," the difference is really one of degree; the latter is a veiled or subtle kind of presentation. That certain "mark" is approximately determined by the needs and interests of "normal" life — it slightly varies with different people, and can be varied considerably by hypnosis, trance, *yoga*, etc. Thus a man searching into the subliminal depths of his consciousness may "see" the subtle presentations. The transition from "normal" consciousness to "unconsciousness" is not abrupt — there are different shades according to degrees of veiling. The so-called "sub-conscious" and "unconscious" are only modes of consciousness which cannot be restricted to what little may be practically accepted in the indefinable vastness of actual personal experience. So one may not be prepared to admit the sub-conscious and unconscious as orders of experience different from the conscious. They are the veiled, ignored, non-accepted, unnoticed zones in consciousness itself. Thus the Śāstra takes up a position which is not either that of

[1] Saṃskāras. See Chap. on Consciousness and Brain, "The Fundamentals of Vedānta Philosophy" by Swami Pratyagātmānanda Saraswati.

the "cerebralist" who would confine experience to "normal" consciousness only and explain memory, habit and so forth by brain vestiges or brain-dispositions, or that of the common type of the philosopher of the Unconscious who, while admitting experiences below the threshold line, regards such experiences as really sub-conscious, thus setting the threshold line as the boundary of consciousness itself (his consciousness being, therefore, not other than "normal", pragmatic consciousness which is but a section of actual consciousness). As the cerebralist in the Vedāntic view commits the mistake of regarding mental life (or experience) as a structure raised on the wider and more enduring basis of cerebral life, so the "sub-conscious thinker" is in error in regarding consciousness as structure raised on the wider, deeper and more abiding basis of sub-conscious experience. Consciousness as *Cit* is the basis and there is no other. *Cit* is not "normal" or pragmatic only.

In the *Śānkhya* Philosophy, experience,[1] being a mode of the Psycho-Physical Principle[2] (which is unconscious)[3] is also unconscious;[3] and it is only when the Unconscious "reflects" itself on, or catches the "reflection" of the Conscious,[4] that it becomes conscious experience. Thus experience has two forms—conscious and unconscious, of which the former is a reflex or imposed form. This apparently comes near to the position of the western "subconscious thinker," but, fundamentally, it is a different position inasmuch as its consciousness is not a variable "accident" of experience only, but an independent Principle existing by its own right. Thus though experience may be conscious or unconscious (as the western sub-conscious thinker holds), yet Consciousness is neither a proprium nor an accident of anything other than itself. It is eternal,[5] changeless, pure, though it may variously reflect the character and complexion of the mind[6] with which it may be associated.[7]

This position is only a "stopping short" of the final position which is taken up by Vedānta. Analysing experience we find Illumination[8] and illuminated;[9] *Cit* which reveals and the "Stress" which is revealed. Experience as joining together these two aspects is the Fact; each is an abstraction considered by itself. Now, *Śānkhya* makes a substance of

---

[1] Buddhi-vyāpāra.
[2] Prakṛti which is a Real independent of Consciousness as the Selves or Puruṣas.
[3] Acit. Sāmkhya-Kārikā, 11. [4] Pūruśa which is Cit.
[5] Nitya. [6] Buddhi, etc.
[7] See *Power as Mind*. [8] Prakāśa. [9] Vimarśā.

each of the two abstractions. The underlying principle of this procedure is this: Illumination[1] cannot make an "object" of itself; on the other hand, an "object" cannot be its own revealer[2] or cogniser. In the Vedāntic view it is a plausible principle without being a valid one; and if man did not normally deal with pragmatic Fact-sections or abstractions, he would have discovered that the principle is invalid.

The *Bhatta*[3] School of interpretation in the *Pūrvamīmāmsa* (of Jaimini) also proceeded upon this principle and conceived the *Ātman* as possessing a dual character—being conscious in one part, and unconscious in another. The *Ātman* was compared to a glow-worm which now shines and now does not. *Ātman* was *cit* as knower[2] and *acit* as known, as object,[4]: *cit* as seer[5] and *acit* as seen.[6] *Śānkhya*, as we have seen, stows apart what are thus juxtaposed and made to co-exist in one and the same substance. Vedānta identifies in essence the Illuminator[2] and the Illuminated;[4] the *Bhatta* school differentiates them and places them side by side like the two seeds in a grain of gram; *Śānkhya* takes them quite asunder. The first is for non-difference;[7] the second for difference, non-difference;[8] the third for difference.[9] The invalidity of the second and third positions lies in this: the revealer[2] does not make a revealed[4] of itself; nor does the revealed[4] become its own revealer.[2] It is *Cit* simply which by Its Power is the Revealer[2] as well as becomes the Revealed.[4] By its power, or rather, as Power.[10] It is thus polarised.

The *Prabhākara* school of Pūrva-Mīmāmsa, as also the Nyāya-Vaiśeṣika School, makes the *Ātman* unconscious[11] in itself, its consciousness[12] being a separable property which is existent in it only when certain conditions are fulfilled, and which is non-existent otherwise. Just as a leaf may be the support of a particular tint of colour which may not always exist in it, so the *Ātman* is the support of the quality of consciousness.[13] In dreamless slumber, for example, there is (it is supposed) no consciousness as evidenced by the subsequent recollection — "I was asleep; I knew nothing." This, however, is a mistake. "I knew nothing." means of course "I knew nothing in particular". During slumber there is this positive knowledge of knowing nothing in particular, and also, as the

---

[1] Prakāśa. [2] Prakāśaka.
[3] See Śloka-vārttika (Śūnya-vāda, Ātmavāda) of Kumārila-Bhatta.
[4] Prakāśya. [5] Driśi. [6] Driśya.
[7] Abheda. [8] Bhedābheda. [9] Bheda.
[10] Commonly we speak of the Power of Consciousness but Power is in itself Consciousness. And so the Devī or Mother-Power is Chidrūpinī.
[11] Acit. [12] Caitanya. [13] Jnāna or Caitanya.

*Śruti* maintains, a veiled consciousness of amorphic Bliss.[1] As regards the general position that *Ātman* is unconscious,[2] and becomes conscious only conditionally, that is when linked up with mind and its object, we need observe merely this that in this position *Cit* is recognised only as "normal or pragmatic" consciousness which is a section only; that this pragmatic consciousness, which is one of "interesting" particulars, is mistaken for consciousness as such, so that when in slumber particulars or forms do not exist, it is thought that consciousness as such also does not exist. Not perceiving that the essence of Substance-Energy is *Cit*, it wrongly makes an attribute[3] of *Cit* which sometimes inheres and sometimes does not in a Substance[4] which in itself is different from its attribute,[3] and is unconscious[2] when the attribute[5] does not exist in it.[6]

But is the essence of Substance-Energy *Cit*? Cannot *Cit* be an attribute[3] only? It need not be an "epiphenomenon", a "by-product," as the Materialists and *Lokāyatas* (followers of Chārvāka) say, of Matter. It may not either be a separable phenomenon like the consciousness[7] of the First Standard *Ātman*. But should we not regard it as a phenomenon still — as distinguished from the Noumenon or Thing-in-Itself? Even the *Yogācāra Bauddha* to whom the universe (subjective and objective) is merely a beginningless succession of transient[8] "pulses" of experience,[9] as modern psychologists might call them, and various grouping or clustering together of such pulses;[6] who breaks up the apparently continuous flow of "Self" consciousness into a series of rapidly succeeding but discrete apperceptions (perceptions of Self or "I"), and distinguishes this series[10] from the series of object-perceptions (in the "mind" or outside it)[8]; — even he would not make these pulses of experience, succeeding one another and grouping together, the Substance or Reality as many western Empiricists have done. No "thing" exists of course as other than the knowing[11] (this is denial of Realism); but even the knowing does not "exist" — that is, the knowing[11] is of, and in, the Void.[12] The *Vaibhāshika* and *Sautrāntika Bauddhas* believed in things independent of experience (the latter making them directly perceived,[13] the former making them indirectly or inferentially known); but here also, the Basis of things is not *Cit* but the Void.

[1] Ānanda or Sukham. Māndūkya, Up., I, 5. It is said in the sūtra "Happily I slept and knew nothing." That there was bliss is shown by the recollection of it on waking. For there can only be remembrance of that of which there has been experienee (anubhava).
[2] Acit. [3] Guṇa. [4] Dravya. [5] Cit-Guṇa.
[6] In Śānkhya-Vedānta, Ātmā is Nitya-Caitanya; in Nyāya-Vaiśeṣika, it is Āgantuka-Caitanya. [7] Jnāna. [8] Kṣanika. [9] Vijnāna.
[10] Ālaya-vijnāna. [11] Pravritti-vijnāna. [12] Śunya. [13] Pratyakṣa.

But what is it really? What constitutes the essence of Thinghood? Consider again a block of stone. It is seen, touched, pressed, lifted, pushed and pulled, and so on. We have just a group of "experiences" succeeding one another—the experience[2] as above explained. Is it merely the aggregate of these actual experiences and certain others that may be possible? Either it is or it is not. If it is, then the experiences[2] coming and going in a "medium" or "ether" or *Cit* make that block of stone nothing but a structure of experiencing[3] raised upon the basis of *Cit*. Reflection will show that the succeeding "pulses" of feeling require at least two permanent Principles: a self-distinguishing Subject called the "witness"[4] which notes the pulses as coming and going, as before and after, as related in this way or that and which therefore must not itself come and go, be past and future, be related in this way or that. To know for instance that A, B, C have succeeded one another, there must be a Knower who has remained above the succession so as to correlete them according to a certain temporal scheme. He must abide and witness, and distinguish himself from the changing phenomena. This "I"[5] or Witness cannot itself be broken into rapidly succeeding pulses of "I" feeling;[6] for, who knows and says that the "I" feelings are succeeding? We require a Self behind these fleeting "selves". Who, again, remembers that when C is, A and B are no more but that they were before?[7] To say that the Series[8] knows and remembers itself, is to forget that what actually exists as experience[2] at any moment is not a series but a particular experience[2] and that the series does not, and cannot, exist as series except to a Witness who is not in, and of, the series. To say again that the last term of the series that is C, as an actual experience[2] remembers, sums up and judges the past experience,[2] is to assume that past and non-existing experience[2] can yet exist in a manner in the present pulse, C; that C can somehow involve a thought of B and A which are no more.

But suppose this assumption is correct; C does remember and judge A and B. But what is this C — this so-called present "pulse"? If we do not pragmatize and ignore the given whole of experience, we shall see that C is not a pulse at all, but the indefinable, alogical universe of

[1] See Sarva-darśana-sangraha.
[2] Vijnāna. [3] Vijnānas.
[4] Sākṣi Caitanya. Mundaka-Up., III, 1, 1; Śevetāśvatara-Up., IV, 6.
[5] Aham. [6] Aham-pratyaya.
[7] In other words who is responsible for Smriti, Pratyabhignā, Anuvyavasāya, etc.?
[8] Vijnāna-santāna.

experience, (*i.e.*, Fact) which, in order to suit our practice and our theory, we are cutting up into "pulses" coming and going, judging and remembering, and so on. Experience is an indefinable universe in which we accept certain aspects or sections only, and in which those sections are correlated by us or by our tendencies[1] temporally, spatially and causally, thus giving us thoughts and things succeeding one another in time, co-existing with one another in space, and causally affecting one another. "Pulses" are thus born of "ignorance". In fact we have the continuum of experience; and this continuum, which in an alogical way whilst remaining such continuum, yet, as *Cit*, variously stresses into correlated forms. This *Cit* as Continuum is at the back of all pulses, and all experiences[2] which Buddhistic Philosophy has often looked up to as the great Void. Hence the fleeting-states or pulses to be known and remembered as such require not only a permanent Witness[3] but a permanent Continuum also.[4]

Of these two the latter is the more fundamental; because while the Witness is indispensable to experience treated as a logical order (*i.e.*, in the thinking and reviewing of experience), the latter is indispensable to experience both as logical and as alogical. As a matter of fact, in intuitive, as distinguished from thinking and judging, life, the Self as "Subject" is often in abeyance; the Subject-witness presupposes a thing or object witnessed—that is, a polarity.[5] In non-polar[6] experience the Subject-witness as witness therefore need not exist.

Thus we cannot according to Vedānta do without *Cit* as a substantive background, even if we agree to regard a block of stone as a cluster of actual and possible "sensations". Sensations are the outcome of a three-fold ignorance and abstraction. Sensations are abstractions from perceptions which are relatively more concrete; perceptions are abstractions from the entire universe of experience at a given moment; and the universe of experience at a given moment is a temporal cross-section and abstraction of the real "Fact" which is *Cit* as Power stressing and constituting as such an indefinable, alogical Whole involving Time, Space, and so forth.

But let us, in the alternative, regard the stone as not an aggregate of actual and possible sensations, but as the objective ground and cause of sensations (as Realism holds). But how can we be sure that the "objective ground" really exists? We firmly believe that it does, but evidently the

[1] Samskāra. [2] Vijnānas. [3] Sākṣi Caitanya.
[4] Cidākāśa. [5] Dvaita. [6] Advaita.

belief also is a part of our experience and thought, and, therefore, cannot carry us beyond to anything outside and independent of experience and thought.[1] But then why should we believe that which is not the fact? And there are marks which indicate that the belief is well-grounded. Perceptions and "objective experiences" by reason of their independence of our wish and insistence on our attention, and so forth, constitute an altogether different order pointing to an objective order of realities. Their relative permanence, independence in being and becoming, resistance and insistence, objectification and localization, vividness and interest, and the like are the important distinguishing marks, of which the first four are the most important.

We may concede, without further discussion, that if Solipsism and Subjectivism cannot explain away these marks or explain them satisfactorily, on the other hand it is difficult to make an out-and-out Subjectivist answer any outside knocks or calls once he has bolted all his doors and windows and locked himself in.

So a block of stone is there permanently, unlike a feeling or idea in the mind; it is there though we may wish it away; it is and changes according to its own laws; it resists our movement and will; it thrusts itself upon our mind when the senses and attention are near and not otherwise engaged; it is more vivid and interesting than a corresponding image in the mind; and so on. Hence it exists by its own right. It does; but where and how? Its existence is, in some essential respects independent of the particular Centre's experience and thought; but can it exist independently of Experience or *Cit* as such? No. It exists and is a mode of Perfect *Cit* in the fulness of its relations, which a limited Centre knows gradually and partially — that is, accepting in part but ignoring as a whole. The ignored realms are the realms of the "objective"; every imperfect perception is an act of partial owning; perfect perception is perfect owning in which the distinction between subjective and objective, as we have it, disappears. But why should not a thing exist apart from Experience, imperfect or perfect.

This, for long, has been a point of dispute between the so-called "Idealists" and "Realists". Vedānta is Idealism in so far as it makes Being or *Sat* identical with Consciousness,[2] and that, in its essence, the same as Bliss.[3] Vedānta is Realism in so far as it makes objects or things

---

[1] As was argued by the Vijnāna-vādins.
[2] Cit. [3] Ānanda.

independent of a specialized Subject's modes of consciousness: a thing is not thus in the Mind, it is actually outside it. Matter is thus every whit as real as Mind. Both, however, are in, and of, *Cit*.

These following grounds are offered by Vedānta as the main lines of proof:

(*a*) No rational theory of perception is possible without postulating essential identity between the Self and Matter. Perception is an act of "owning," and there can be no owning where the object is absolutely foreign to the Subject. Attempts to explain the "agreement" between "Cit" and "Matter" by the theories of Occasional Cause, Pre-established Harmony, Parallelism and Materialism have led either to an evasion of the real problem, or to failure to solve it (as in the case of gross Materialism). In the Indian view the only possible explanation is by a doctrine which makes Spirit or Consciousness in the sense of *Cit* (and not in the sense of Mind)[1] the ground as well as the activity of both Mind and Matter. Such fundamental identity between Mind and Matter being given, we can well conceive a direct interaction between the two; as also their operation according to certain fundamental laws which apply to Matter as well as to Mind.[1] Thus Mind[1] being acted on by Matter through the senses *reacts* by going out to where Matter is, "envelops" it and makes a "mental double" of it in Space;[2] we can conceive even the assimilation of one to the other, and the transformation (in part, generally) of one into the other. It is, therefore, not Materialism to assert that the mind[1] moves, expands or contracts like matter; and that the one kind of Substance Energy is convertible into the other.[3] The difference between Mind and Matter is this that whilst the Root-Substance Energy (*Cit*), appearing or evolving as Mind,[1] appears in a comparatively subtler form and operates according to laws which restrict to a lesser extent its essential nature[4] (indicated in Play),[5] it appears in a grosser or cruder (*i.e.*, less elastic and dynamic) form as Matter, and operates according to the laws which restrict to a greater extent its Being-Consciousness-Bliss. The latter form and the latter operation being only less perfect (as regards expression and dynamic "coefficient") than the former, the difference between

---

1 Antahkaraṇa.

2 See the Vedānta view of Perception described in "Power as Mind". See also P. N. M.'s "The Fundamentals of Vedānta Philosophy".

3 Cf. Chhāndogya-Up., VI, 5, 1, etc., describing how the "finest elements" of the food eaten go to constitute "Manas," etc.

4 Being (Sat), Consciousness (Cit), Bliss (Ānanda).

5 Līlā.

Mind and Matter is a difference in degree and "stage of evolution" only; so that Matter is comparatively "rigid" or "dense" Mind, and the Laws of Matter are comparatively "stereotyped," inelstic forms of the Laws of Mind.

(*b*) The action of Will on Matter (directly or through Matter organised as the brain) is inexplicable without such essential identity being given. Causation or activity in its fundamental nature is not easily understood; still it is easier to conceive causation or interaction between two similar forms of Substance-Energy than between dissimilar forms. Modern scientific explanations of the interaction between Mind and Brain tend either (1) to deny all causal activity to Consciousness (making the chain of physical causation a "closed curve," like that of the evolution of the radical Psychophysical Potential[1] in the Sāngkhyan doctrine which though denying direct action of the consciousness[2] on such Potential,[1] yet granted the existence of a kind of "catalytic action"), or (2) to "parallelism" which, in its turn, tends either to Materialism or to Spiritualism.

(*c*) To these ordinary psychic phenomena must now be added others[3] which many investigators in the West have recognised and called *Parapsychic*[4] that is, mental facts, well established, which cannot be explained by the known laws of Physiology and Psychology. These phenomena, now investigated under the three heads of *hypnotoidal*, *magnetoidal* and *spiritoidal*,[5] seem to point to the essential affinity between Mind and Matter, and between Vital Force and each of the other two—an affinity which shows Matter-Energy, Vital Energy and Thought-Energy in an ascending order of dynamism,[6] and, therefore, of fundamentality.

Telepathy or Thought-transference, "Psychometry" (which Dr. Maxwell[7] defines as "the faculty possessed by certain persons of placing themselves in relation, either spontaneously or, for the most part, through the intermediary of some object, with unknown and often very distant things and people"), "Levitation" (or the lifting of material objects in the air without touching or handling them), "Materialization" (or the condensation of "Psychic forces" into apparent grossness), "Exteriorization" (or the projection out of the body of the motor and sensitive forces)

---

[1] Prakṛti. [2] Puruṣa.
[3] For long studied and experimented upon in India.
[4] Prof. Emile Boirac, La Psychologie inconnue.
[5] Bhūta-Śakti, Prāṇa Śakti, Mānasī Śakti. [6] Śakti.
[7] Qoted by Maurice Maeterlinck in his "The Unknown Guest" (p. 49), 3rd Ed.

"Dissociation" (or the act of separating certain psychical elements from the body through psychological methods and processes), "Astral Projection" (or the act of projecting by the action of the will, consciously or unconsciously, the human "double"), and many other phenomena, now under serious investigation in the West, require for their explanation a basis which cannot be supplied by the "orthodox" views on Spirit, Life and Matter (making each separate from the others and each being regarded as consisting of discrete units only). If Spirit and Matter be ontologically or substantially distinct, it cannot be understood or even imagined how a person touching a material object (say, a flower or a sheet of paper) may leave "the impress of his personality" on it, which that object may bear for an indefinite length of time, and which makes it possible for a "medium" to "read" the whole history of that person, and of others connected with him, by merely handling the object once touched by him. It is supposed that the object touched by a person becomes "impregnated with his fluid" (or, as Dr. Osty[1] says, "the object can latently register the human personalities which have touched it"). But what is this human "fluid", and how can a "material" object be impregnated with it, and carry it for an indefinite length of time? And how can the "register" thus kept by the object be deciphered again by a proper Subject? The Dualistic view of Mind and Matter fails to go to the root of the matter in trying to answer these questions. A sheet of paper so touched may be likened to a gramophone record where a whole musical composition lies latently registered; but there the forces making the "register" are physical forces, and the mechanism by which that record may be deciphered is also a physical mechanism. We have not, therefore, to leave the physical plane at any step. But the system of ideas (conscious and subconscious), thoughts, feelings, desires, and so forth, of a person which constitute his personality are not physical forces; and these are the first link of the causal chain; at the other end of the chain we have the "latent register" in the sheet of paper touched; the act of touching is an intermediate link in the chain, and it means a vital motor activity. In this case, it appears that Vital Force[2] negotiates between "Soul"[3] and Matter[4] (*viz.*, the sheet of paper). Assuming such Power[5] is established, how can this be understood from a dualistic or pluralistic position?

---

[1] Author of Lucidite et intuition. [2] Prāṇa. [3] Antahkaraṇa. [4] Jaḍa.

[5] In India generically described as *Siddhi*. A considerable portion of the Tantras deals with these supernormal faculties. This so-called "Magic" is an extension of normal faculty and natural.

Then, again, in what is now called "Psycho dynamism" — exemplified in such phenomena as levitation, materialization and the like — we must admit an essential identity between the forces which constitute matter and those which constitute the *psyche* or soul; the moment which we see at the outer end (*e.g.*, in the table raised in the air) presupposes at the other and inner end also something which is analogous to movement. And if that which is at the two ends are each capable of movement, it is reasonable to suppose that they are similar, substantially and dynamically —that is, as being and as energy.

These "parapsychic" or metapsychic (often called "occult") facts as well as the facts of common psychology require for their explanation a basis, deeper and wider than what we have above indicated. They presuppose not merely affinity between Spirit and Life and between Life and Matter (1) as regards substance, and (2) as regards dynamic operation; they presuppose at their very root a universal Spiritual Stuff or Substance-Energy which, while evolving as a system of correlated Spirit-centres, Life-centres and Matter-centres remains as the Mother Energy-Stuff, sustaining, nourishing and connecting all its numberless evolutes. The Mother Substance-energy does not cease to be Itself in evolving as an infinite system of centres: the centres would not be centres if it were so; and, no unfoldment of the centres and no interaction among them would be possible if it were so. The Mother Substance-Energy perpetually abides as the universal background of substance and evolution and interaction for every centre, whether "material" or otherwise. Behind and overlapping the "Self" of man, the cell of a plant and the "sphere" of a material corpuscle, there is, therefore, the unbounded and unfathomed Being-Energy or *Mahāmāyā* which has evolved those centres, and which remains as an infinite reservoir of energy of all these centres to draw upon in their being as well as in their becoming or evolving. The part of the energy which a material or a living centre ordinarily stands for and uses constitutes, from the standpoint of that particular centre, its kinetic energy. The infinite reservoir at the back or root of its being is, for all common purposes, latent, dormant. And this infinite dynamic potential has been called *Kuṇḍalinī Śakti*, (or, cosmically speaking, *Mahā-kuṇḍalinī Śakti*) in the Śākta Tantras of the *Āgama Śāstra*. Thus conceived, not only the human body, but every form of centre (say, an atom of Hydrogen) must have *Kuṇḍalinī Śakti* given at the "heart" or base of its being, its radical centre.[1]

[1] Mūlādhāra Cakra.

Not to speak of parapsychic or occult phenomena, even such a commonplace as an act of perception or volition, cannot be probed to the root without revealing the background of the Mother Substance-Energy in which and of which the perceiving agency and the object perceived are both imbedded and interlinked centres; which makes it possible for the energy of the one to pass to the other, and "assimilate" that other to itself (which is the essence of perception).

In the case of "psychometry" through an intermediary object (for example, a sheet of paper touched by a person not now present), the suggestion put forward by Dr. Osty is probably well-founded: "This object has no other function than to allow the medium's sensitiveness to distinguish a definite force from among the innumerable forces that assail it." The obvious implication, in the words of Maurice Maeterlinck,[1] is this: "It seems more and more certain that, as the cells of an immense organism, we are connected with everything that exists by an inextricable network of vibrations, waves, influences or nameless, numberless and uninterrupted fluids. Nearly always, in nearly all men, everything carried along by these invisible wires falls into the depths of the unconscious and passes unperceived, which does not mean that it remains inactive. But sometimes an exceptional circumstance.......... suddenly reveals to us, by the vibrations and the undeniable action of one of these wires, the existence of the infinite network."

The infinite network we have (following Śākta Vedāntism) otherwise expressed as the Universal Stress-system in which all objects, spiritual or "material," great or small, are centres. A material atom, an organic cell, a Self,[2] or Person thus represents a definite but not isolated strain-and-stress-centre.

But this strain-and-stress-centre must be in, and of, something. That something-in-itself must be unbounded, unfathomable Being.[3] It must be Power (*Śakti* manifesting as Soul-Energy, Vital Energy and Matter Energy) since the essence of everything is in its dynamism.[4] And this Power must be fundamental in relation to Thought-Energy, Vital Energy and Matter-Energy.

And that fundamental Power is *Cit*, an untranslatable word, commonly translated as Consciousness. The so-called *Acit* or Unconscious,

---

[1] *The Unknown Guest.* [2] Jīva. [3] Bhūman.

[4] In Śākta doctrine Power or Śakti in the ultimate Real of which the Universe is the manifestation.

arises from a pragmatic limitation of *Cit*, from the veiling or ignoring of *Cit* by itself, thus concealing its essential nature of Being-Consciousness and Bliss. (*a*) All objects must be necessarily known and conceived in terms of "modes" of consciousness, or to express it more rigidly, as particular strain-forms in Consciousness; the opposite is conceivable. This, however, does not mean that things must be known as subjective "representations" or ideas. (*b*) All objects at the root are Power; and Power must be known and conceived as Consciousness: Power (such as we experience in volition, attention, mental effort and the like); the opposite is, in reality, inconceivable. "Blind" physical energy, "unconscious" vital or mentative force have been supposed to exist and work; but they cannot be actually conceived as other than Consciousness-Power. Blind and unconscious forces are born of veiling and abstraction. (*c*) Perception and volition involve a belief in the Not-Self existing by its own right; the Subject perceiving requires at the other "pole" an independent Object perceived; and the agent acting requires not only a patient acted upon, but an independent agent reacting. This is Realism, and it is perfectly valid. But Realism does *not* require that the Not-Self and the independent agent must be essentially different from, or dissimilar to, the Self or Conscious Power operating in, and as, ourselves. On the contrary, if we could lay aside the pragmatic attitude which we commonly take in our actions and perceptions we should discover that the actual implication of our realistic belief is that the external agent is a centre of Consciousness-Power such as we are ourselves. It is our practical attitude in relation to them which makes some of them appear to be, or present themselves to us, as unintelligent, unconscious, blind—in fact, as devoid of Consciousness[1] and Bliss[2] and its expression, Play.[3] Commonly we are *not* interested in taking them as forms of Consciousness-Power,[4] as incarnations of Bliss[2] and as capable of Play.[3] In relation to our practice,[5] and therefore factor conditioning karma[6] which underlies it, they have put on a veil and a disguise. This pragmatic view of things has naturally affected Science and Philosophy in a way which they have not found it easy to shake off.

To Vedāntism, and the *Śākta* form of it in particular every object down to the material particle is a Divinity or *Devaṭā*, which means that

[1] Cit. [2] Ānanda. [3] Līlā.
[4] Cit-Śakti. [5] Vyavahāra.
[6] Adṛṣṭa which stands for past karma.

it is a form of Conscious-Power, whose being is Joy and whose life or activity is Play.[1] A particular thing, A, by virtue of its position in the Stress-system[2] in relation to another thing, B, may behave as though it were devoid of Consciousness, Bliss and Play (*i.e.*, free, spontaneous action); but this does not mean either that A is in itself (that is, irrespectively of its relation to B in the Stress system) devoid of these, or that it is necessarily devoid of them in relation to a third centre, say, C. C may recognise it as *Devatā* while B does not. Whether A will manifest itself as Consciousness,[3] Bliss[4] and Play[1] or not, will, in fact, depend upon two co-efficients or determinants: its past action[5]—assigning its place in the cosmic stress-system, in Space, Time and Causal chain, and tending to hold it there;[6] and its play[1]—changing or tending to change its place in the cosmic stress-syetem, therefore tending to move and evolve it.[7] Now, A's position[5] can be regarded from three points of view: (1) A's position considered in relation to a Perfect Centre, that is position as it is in the cosmic stress-system as a whole; (2) its position in relation to its own point of view (therefore, more or less limited or restricted); and (3) its position in relation to B, C, D, and others. It is obvious that the position[5] in relation to A, B, C, D, etc., are different. So that while to A, B, D and others, A's being appears as "dead", "inert" and "material," it is possible that to C, it may appear as Life, Mind, Consciousness and Bliss including Play.[8] C, therefore, may have a truer and deeper intuition of its being.

*Adṛṣṭa*[9] is static power in the sense that though it may also move things, it moves them in a fixed, determined line; Play[1] is dynamic power in the sense that it tends to make things depart from any line that may have been predetermined for them by the total assemblage of conditions. It implies, therefore, freedom, or power transcending the causal chain of necessity. Every object in creation possesses the power, since it is an incarnation of the Supreme Power which is Being, Consciousness, Bliss and Play.[10] The result, accordingly is, that the world does not move in an absolutely fixed line; and the so-called causal chain of necessity is an outcome of abstract analysis of physical and *quasi*-physical science.

[1] Līlā. [2] Adṛṣṭa which stands for past karma. [3] Cit.
[4] Ānanda. [5] Adṛṣṭa determining present condition. See Text *post*.
[6] This in its statical aspect of Dik Śakti.
[7] Kāla Śakti of which that which moves things on or the vital urge is a component.
[8] Prāṇamaya, Manomaya, Vijnānamaya and Ānandamaya (including Līlamaya).
[9] Compare it with "Niyatī," one of the 36 Tattvas (See *The Garland of Letters*—The Tattvas).
[10] Saccidānandamayī and Līlāmayī.

In its actual manifestations, that Power has however, chosen to subject itself to varying limitations, or as it has been often put, clothed itself with "sheaths"[1] of varying density. This is a precondition of the evolution of a world of infinitely varied forms, or as we have put it, a system of countless strain-and-stress centres. There would be no such world of varied forms if the Fundamental Power were to remain undifferentiated and undivided, or else, divided as a system of undifferentiated points only.

Evolution and history have become possible because the Power has manifested itself as Centres. A Centre is Cosmic Power or Potency condensed into a point[2] in a certain stage of evolution; it therefore presupposes a relative disposition or ratio of latency and patency of the Perfect Potency,[2] and readiness to create, whose evolute it is. Thus in a given centre, A, the ratio of latency and patency of Power may be different from that in another centre, B. Apart from this ratio, A=B=Bindu= Perfect Power. It is the ratio which constitutes the difference. The ratio may be otherwise expressed as the ratio of determination[3] and freedom.[4] In every object these two factors co-operate. Now, centres may be arranged in order of evolution or progress according as the latter factor prevails over the former; in other words, according as freedom or self-determination prevails over "other determination". Centres are higher in which spontaneous activity[3] is more manifested, and determination less insistent. Matter, Life and Mind constitute, from this standpoint, an hierarchy, because the co-efficient of free play[5] is more and more manifested as we pass from the first to the second, and from the second to the third. The "matter" of Physical Science appears to be wholly determined without the least suggestions of freedom: but this is only an approximate truth. According to Vedānta, freedom to act must be there in it because the free *Cit* is its essence. The very smallness of the atom seems to be a strength instead of a weakness: its energies are vast, and its atomic motions incredibly rapid. It also is a world. If its behaviour seems restrained and uniform and lacking in self-conscious direction, it is not because it is in fact unconscious mechanism but because the *Cit* which is its essence has freely so determined to present itself. Whatever be the form it takes, self-determination is free determination.

[1] Kośa or Kancuka. [2] Bindu. See *ante*. [3] Adṛṣṭa.
[4] Līlā. Or Karma.
[5] Līlā.

Moreover, a lump of matter, with reference to our pragmatic attitude and factor conditioning action,[1] appears as (approximately) dead, inert and determined; but we are not permitted to generalize and say that it must be so (1) to itself, or (2) to other beings whose attitudes, tendencies[2] and factor conditioning action[1] are markedly different. To the Seer[2] for instance, its common crust of inertness may break away revealing it as consciousness[3] instead of earthiness.[4]

Every centre is, therefore, *Bindu* subject to the varying ratio of determination[5] and freedom.[6] It does not appear as perfect Being and Power (which *Bindu* is in absolute condensation) because of its special relative disposition of determination[5] and freedom.[6] It is this which constitutes the difference between an atom of Hydrogen and an amoeboid cell and the soul of a Śankara. If we take into account both what is latent and what is patent, what is actual and what is possible, then the first = the second = the third = Perfect Being and Power. Not only does Perfect Being and Power lie at the root and background of all things, but all things are, in the complete view (as distinguished from the partial and pragmatic view which we commonly take), Perfect Being and Power—that is *Brahman*. It is owing to man's pragmatic veiling and "ignorance" (determined by his action[7] and position in the cosmic scheme,)[5] that they appear and behave as finite, circumscribed specific objects.

*Brahman*, or *Śiva* (or in Its dynamic aspect, *Śakti*) thus works the greatest of all miracles which is this: while evolving as the world of infinitely diversified names and forms, It does not suffer Its own immensity, fullness and perfectness to be narrowed and whittled down in the process. Its immensity and infinity inalienably abide in, and through, all things, great or small: particular, finite things being only the practical ignorance of that Immensity and Infinity.

That Immensity and Infinity has two aspects: the infinite[8] aspect, and the infinitesimal[9] aspect. The former is the aspect of infinite expansion, diffusion and manifestation[10] the latter is the aspect of infinite or ultimate condensation.[11] Now, *any* finite Centre, apart from its ratio of determination[12] and freedom[13] (which does not allow its recognising

[1] Adṛṣṭa. This determines the psycho-physical subject to freedom of choice of the essentially free self.

[2] Tattva-darśī or Sūkṣmadarśī who unlike the Sthūladarśī, sees the subtle nature of things.

[3] Cinmaya. [4] Mṛṇmaya. [5] Adṛṣṭa. [6] Karma as Līlā.

[7] Karma. [8] Virāt or Mahat. [9] Kṣudra or Aṇu.

[10] Abhivyakti. [11] Avyakta. [12] Adṛṣṭa. [13] Karma.

and accepting its being in all its dimensions), involves Power both in the infinite and the infinitesimal aspects above explained. It is *Brahman* which is greater than the great,[1] and smaller than the smallest.[2]

The infinitestimal is not infinitely small in respect of Being or Potency: it is infinitely small in the sense of not being further divisible into more elementary dynamic components (hence called "*Bindu*" or "Point"). It is called "small" also because of its appearing to us as subtle and condensed[3] and unmanifest.[4] In reality, however, it is, as we have seen, Perfect Being and Power.[5] And, if we call condensed Power "Potency," then it is Perfect Potency.[6] The electric corpuscle or "vortex-ring" in ether which builds the chemical atom, the nucleus of the germ or seed of the animal and plant, are approximate representatives and compounded forms of the true Dynamic Point or "Bindu". It is the condition of Consciousness-Power operating to create and evolve: because, whether on the whole or in detail, there is no creative process without Power massing itself[7] into Points. Diffusion is the condition of dissolution[8] as concentration is that of creation.[9]

Matter, Life and Mind are the threefold manifestation of Mother-Power. Centres of each are centres (in the sense above explained) of the Mother-Power as a whole. In the Matter-aspect, the Mother-Power is Ether;[10] a matter-particle is, therefore, a strain-centre in Ether, which means, and implies that it is a centre at and through which the stress-system of Ether operates in a given manner. In the Life-aspect, Mother-Power is *Prāṇa* or *Āditya* in the sense these terms are understood in the Upaniṣads.[11] A particular living cell is a centre of this Vital Power,[12] which as the Maitri-Upaniṣad explains, is not summed up by

[1] Mahato mahīyān.

[2] Aṇoraṇīyān. Śvetāśvatara, III, 20. Metaphysically the first is the Ether of Consciousness and the Second Bindu. Physically the first is the Ether and the second the atoms of matter in it. Those who, like many of the present-day Relativists, discard the Ether, may substitute Space-Time Continuum.

[3] Sūkṣma. [4] Mṛṇmaya.

[5] It is, not in itself subject to the Spatial and Temporal Orders but involves them. It is, in one aspect, connected with the Space-Time Continuum out of which our relative spaces and times are evolved. See for discussion of this question P.N.M.'s *Fundamentals of Vedānta Philosophy*.

[6] It is also Perfect Readiness to create or evolve. See *ante*.

[7] "Cidghana": Ghanībhūtā Śakti. [8] Laya. [9] Sṛṣṭi.

[10] Ākāśa. Or Space-Time Continuum. For a particular modern presentation of this concept in relation to Deity one may instance the speculations of Prof. Alexander and others in the West.

[11] See Maitri-Up. in particular.

[12] Prāṇaśakti or Āditya-Śakti.

the apparent solar energy, but diffused throughout the universe. In the mind-aspect, the Power is Cosmic Mind which in the Vedānta is called *Hiraṇyagarbha.* An individual Self is a centre at and through which the Cosmic Mind operates in a given manner; which does not exclude determination and freedom for the individual, because the individual is the Cosmic-Mind, accepting its infinity being and potency only in part, and operating in a specific manner.

Sound,[1] Object[2] and Thought or Idea[3] are another threefold manifestation of Mother-Power. The Power in its Sound aspect is the most generic and fundamental "Sound" whose "approximate acoustic equivalent" is what is heard by gross ears as the *Mantra, Om.*[4] All particular "Sound"[5] are particular modes and manifestations of *Om.* In the object-aspect, Power is the Cosmic Form or Order—the relative disposition or configuration of the elements of the world-system. Any particular object is and represents the Cosmic Order[6] in a particular way. It is no wonder, therefore, that a material atom is "a miniature universe": everything, structurally and dynamically considered, must be so. Each body is a "little universe",[7] So that a "Seer" can see "folded up" in every object the whole Cosmos; and he who is competent, can evolve all things out of everything.[8] The dynamic graph or the diagram of forces by which anything (say, a magnet) can be represented—the picture of the constituent forces—is called the *Yantra* of that thing. And though of course each particular object must have its own peculiar *Yantra* (as also *Mantra*), it is to be observed that its *Yantra* must only be a modification or particular form of the *Mahāyantra*,[9] (analogous to the *Mahāmantra, Om*) which stands for the Cosmos as a whole. In the thought-aspect, every object, even a grain of matter, must be a mode of Cosmic Consciousness-Power (with Its three components of Power as Will, Knowledge and Action)[10] which is the essence of both its peculiar being and dynamism. Every being—

---

[1] Śabda. [2] Artha.

[3] Pratyaya. See *The Garland of Letters* as to these terms.

[4] See *The Garland of Letters.* [5] Viśeṣa Śabda.

[6] Virāt or Viśva-rūpa. [7] Kṣudra brahmāṇḍa.

[8] "Sarva-smādeva sarva-samudbhavah. A version of the Hermetic doctrine relative to the Macrocosm and Microcosm (Mahā brahmāṇḍa and Kṣudra brahmāṇḍa) is given in the Viśvasāra Tantra as follows: "What is here is elsewhere. What is not here is nowhere; (Yadihāsti tad anyatra Yannehāsti na tat kvacit.)

[9] Study the famous Śrīyantra of the Devī Tripura-Sundarī which sums up all Tattvas and their evolution: and also, other yantras. See *Tantrarāja Tantra*, Introduction; and *Kāmakalāvilāsa*.

[10] Icchā-Śakti, Jnāna-Śakti and Kriyā-Śakti.

since it is a mode of Cosmic Consciousness-Power, that is, uncircumscribed Consciousness-Power—must in the Vedāntic view involve, whether latently or patently, Consciousness-Power in its threefold division; that is to say, even a grain of matter must involve Power as Knowledge, Will and action [1] though these may appear to be latent in relation to man's present condition. And if what is latent and what is patent, what it veils and what it reveals, be added, then, in a grain of matter we must have as its stock the Whole as Consciousness-Power.

This last aspect of Power (*viz.*, Consciousness) is the fundamental aspect of which Sound[2] and its meaning[3] are side-aspects or derivates. Because while all things and processes (including sound[2] and meaning)[3] are sustained in, reducible to, and perceived and conceived in terms of, Consciousness, there is nothing else which can be conceived as the sustainer of Consciousness, nothing else to which Consciousness itself can be reduced, and nothing else in terms of which Consciousness itself must be known. Consciousness, therefore, is the basis of all being and all power. It being given, a thing is; it being not given, a thing is not. Things being given, it is; things not being given, it still is; which is Pure Experience, which the Buddhistic system called *Śūnya,* the Void.[4] Further, it being given, all else can be perceived and conceived; whilst, its not being given, can neither be perceived nor conceived. We do sometimes conceive "unconsciousness" in ourselves, or in matter; but this is abstract, pragmatic, symbolic and approximate thinking. Concretely and really, the "unconsciousness" in us or in matter is simply not the sort and tone of consciousness which we have in practice, learnt to accept as "our conscious life," extended over a narrow area, and expressed in certain pragmatic responses and signs. Beyond that area, and in default of those signs and responses, we "see" nothing but unconsciousness.[5]

The Subconscious Mind, or the "Subliminal Consciousness" is now requisitioned to explain many common psychic as well as many "parapsychic" phenomena. Like an iceberg floating in water, "nine-tenths" of mental life is said to lie submerged in subconsciousness. "It (subconsciousness) has been likened to an immense block of which our personality is but a diminutive facet; to an iceberg of which we see a few glisten-

[1] Icchā-Śakti, Jnāna-Śakti and Kriyā-Śakti.
[2] Śabda. [3] Artha.
[4] Śūnya. The term is also used in Hinduism, not always in the sense of nihilism but of indetermination of being.
[5] Acit.

ing prisms that represent our life, while nine-tenths of the enormous mass remain buried in the shadows of the sea. According to Sir Oliver Lodge, it is that part of our being that has not become incarnate; according to Gustave Le Bon, it is the 'condensed' soul of our ancestors, which is true, beyond a doubt but only a part of the truth, for we find in it also the soul of the future and probably of many other forces which are not necessarily human. William James saw in it a diffuse cosmic consciousness and the chance intrusion into our scientifically-organized world of remnants and vestiges of primordial chaos. Here are "a number of images striving to give us an idea of a reality so that we are unable to grasp it."[1]

Psychometry, "X-ray vision," and "mediumistic phenomena" generally, would seem to require not only that a subconscious background of our "conscious life" exists, but that it must be credited with potentialities of knowing and acting which exceed the limits of man's common intelligence and will, and which therefore, in that way and to that extent, should rather be called Super-consciousness. It may be that the so-called subconsciousness is really cosmic consciousness—all seeing, all-knowing and all-powerful—hidden from our ordinary conscious life by a pragmatic veil which, when "accidentally" lifted, gives us what the Psychic Research Societies of the West are now studying as "occult" phenomena; and, when lifted by suitable practical methods,[2] gives the higher psychic powers[3] and vision[4] to which every individual can attain (since, Supreme Spirit[5] being connected with every individual spirit, psychic powers, and so forth cannot be an exclusive possession), provided he cares to train himself properly in accordance with those methods.

Hindu System of Philosophy, and the Vedānta in particular, have recognised this Supreme Spirit[5] of which, and in which, all particular Spirits[6] are; and Vedānta has held that a particular Spirit[6] is the Supreme Spirit, separated by a veil of practical "ignorance" or non-acceptance; so that it realizes itself as the Supreme Soul, in knowledge and in power, in proportion as, by effort,[2] it can raise the "veil" between itself and its Prototype. The veil gone, it is, and realizes itself as, the Whole.[7] This consummation can be made available to all who care to go through the necessary discipline. Revelation is not merely a past historic fact. It is a present possibility.

[1] Maurice Maeterlinck, *The Unknown Guest*, p. 321 (3rd. Ed.)
[2] Sādhanā. [3] Siddhi. [4] Sūkṣma-dṛṣṭi.
[5] Paramātmā. [6] Jīvātmā.
[7] Pūrṇa-Brahmaiva bhavati.

In the West "the laboratory methods" applied to the study of these phenomena have produced admirable results so far as the testing, recording and ordering of facts are concerned. But hypotheses such as will explain them are still vague, hesitating and unsatisfactory,[1] and there seems to be as yet little suggestion of courses of systematic discipline by which one who is not "by nature" a medium, and so forth may develop the higher psychic potentialities, and with perseverance, may even, ultimately, bring them to perfection.

M. Ernest Bozzano, whose article in the *Annales des Sciences Psychiques* (September, 1906), M. Maeterlinck cites (*The Unknown Guest*, 3rd Ed., p. 324) says: "It does not seem that it is possible to cultivate or develop them (occult faculties) systematically. The Hindu races in particular, who for thousands of years have been devoting themselves to the study of these manifestations, have arrived at nothing but a better knowledge of the empirical methods calculated to produce them in individuals already endowed with these supernormal faculties." The Hindu position however is that it is possible to cultivate and develop these "faculties" systematically, and bring them to perfection; that it is possible to arrive at a knowledge of the principles, not merely of the "empirical" methods (which therefore, are not purely empirical); and that, the methods can be applied, and if properly applied and pursued, success can be attained, by all individuals.

In India, the Vedāntic doctrine has afforded a wide and firm basis for the understanding of our common as well as "occult" experiences, and that doctrine is clear in its main outlines. On the practical side, too, the Indian genius has been remarkable for the courses of *Sādhanā* or discipline it has evolved, suited to the varying temperament and competency[2] of men, leading by steps to the highest stages of realization—"I am the Whole."[3] Human personalities alone are not in, and of, the Supreme Spirit, but all things conceal beneath their apparent cramped existences mines of unbounded subliminal Power (which is ultimately Consciousness-Power). The so-called "instincts" (*e.g.*, the instinct of direction) of animals, particuarly of ants, bees and many insects, show this unsuspected Power at work, and doing things which man's intelligence cannot, in some cases, do at all, and in others, do but haltingly and imperfectly. It has been claimed that the famous Elberfeld horses in Germany trained by Krall proved two things—first, that rationality is, ordinarily,

[1] *The Unknown Guest*, by M. Maeterlinck, p. 259.
[2] Adhikāra.
[3] Pūrṇo'ham, Brahmāsmi, Sarvo'smi.

only dormant in the lower animals, or passes unobserved; second, that even animals can, acting under proper circumstances and stimuli perform wonderful intellectual feats, particularly in the domain of abstract numbers which human intelligence, has so long regarded as peculiarly its own. For instance, an Elberfeld horse could extract the fourth root of a number of six figures (involving in actual calculation 31 operations), in five or six seconds, "that is to say, during the brief, careless glance which he gives at the black-board on which the problem is inscribed, as though the answer came to him intuitively and instantaneously."[1]

The "lower" animal has his share in the occult phenomena also. M. Ernest Bozzano[2] has collected 69 cases of telepathy, presentiments and hallucinations of sight or hearing in which the main parts are played by animals. The Hindu scriptures are replete with stories in which, not only Animals, but "Stocks and Stones"[3] also, are shown as possessing a Consciousness, ordinarily latent in them, but becoming patent under certain relative circumstances of Kārmic condition. The substance of these myths is in accord with the fundamental position of Hindu Thought, which holds that *Cit* and the Vital Principle (really one) not only pervade all creation, but that all objects are forms and modes of *Cit*, both substantially and dynamically.

As regards these stories it is to be observed that a careful study of the so-called "earlier" as well as "later" *Śāstras* shows that, behind the veil of its sensuous manifestation every object was believed to be a mode of *Cit-Śakti* technically called "Presiding Deity".[4] Every object is, therefore, naturally addressed as a *Devatā* or Divinity or Consciousness-Power, and the *Sādhaka* is taught to bring himself into "living" contact with the Power embodied in them, and to make that Power available for the furtherance of his desired ends.[5]

In fact, according to Vedāntic conceptions, all things or centres, though essentially they are Being-Consciousness-Bliss,[6] present varied aspects to one another by virtue of their varying action and factor conditioning it. Hence, a given thing, A, may seem and behave, for all practical purposes, as totally or partially "dead" and "unconscious," in

[1] *The Unknown Guest*, p. 259, by M. Maeterlinck.

[2] In an article on Les Perceptions Physiques des animaux (Annales des sciences psychiques, August, 1905).

[3] To the upper and lower fire-producing sticks (Araṇi) which in Rigveda appear in the role of lovers (X, 95), male and female are called Ūrvashī and Purūravāh (Yajurveda Mādhyandinī c, 5, Kaṇḍikā 2).

[4] Abhimāninī Devatā. [5] Pūruṣārthas. [6] Saccidānanda.

relation to B, or even to itself. Now, this "unconsciousness" is only consciousness veiled or ignored and such veiling has degrees.

Man's own "unconsciousness" and "subconsciousness" are thus veiled, unaccepted, unrecognised forms of Consciousness itself. Or if we are likely to create confusion by using the word "Consciousness" (which is used in a limited and pragmatic sense in the West) we must employ the Vedāntic term *Cit* itself which means the Reality-Whole. We should then say that "unconsciousness" and "subconsciousness" are modes of *Cit*.

It has been shown in previous chapters that man's Experience is really a Universe; that for practical reasons he ignores the immensity of experience, and seizes upon particular features only which happen to interest him, and thus carves a portion out of the Infinite Given, and regards this portion alone as his consciousness of the moment. In reality, no bounds can be set to the Given which is the alogical Whole, and, is therefore, all-inclusive: It is *Brahman* and the Immense.[1] Dynamically, it must be so: since men are centres in an infinite Stress-system, the stress (which is the basis of its experience) of a given centre must involve, and be connected with, the entire system. As the forces producing experience cannot be in themselves hedged round, so experience cannot be hedged round. If we hedge it round, it is because our tendencies[2] and factor conditioning[3] action do not require the whole. This limiting is due to the so-called ignorance.[4]

Conversely, by knowledge (chiefly, "spiritual" intuition or "vision"), the limits of the given experience can (it is claimed) be indefinitely pushed back, and the whole Universe, past, present and future, can be "discovered" in it, since it *is* the Universe. Sub-consciousness, in that consummation reached by degrees, becomes Super-Consciousness and Perfect Consciousness.

---

[1] Bhūman; both terms have the same meaning.
[2] Avidyā.
[3] Vidyā. Both Vidyā and Avidyā are Powers of the one Divine Mother. By the first she frees, by the second as Cosmic Māyā, she binds, that is, involves herself as Consciousness in Mind and Matter. The being of the centre thus produced is a form of Avidyā.
[4] Bhūman; both terms have the same meaning.

## CIT AND "CENTRES"

WITH the aid of the explanations given in the foregoing sections we can attempt to formulate an approximate idea of *Cit*—approximate because *Cit* as the Whole[1] is alogical, and therefore, indefinable.[2] It can be thought about and defined only in aspects or sections.[2] Now, *Cit* is the Reality-Power which is fundamentally the Consciousness in us, but which as such is infinitely larger than what is commonly and pragmatically accepted as our "conscious life"; stretching over, and remaining as, the realms of the "sub-conscious" and "unconscious"; evolving and manifesting as Vital Power and Forms,[3] and as Material Power and Forms;[4] in other words, evolving and manifesting as the Universe which we regard and treat in Time, Space and Causality (which does not mean that these are only Forms of Thought), but which has an aspect transcending these categories also.[5]

Further, *Cit* in evolving and manifesting as this universe of multifarious forms, in some of which its essential nature as Consciousness and Joy seems to be veiled or even reversed,[6] never ceases to be the Perfect Reality-Power that it is. That is, Cit as Perfect Being-Consciousness-Bliss[7]—(*a*) becomes the World of finite forms; (*b*) is immanent in the World of finite forms; and (*c*) is transcendent in relation to the World of finite forms. It never ceases to be (*b*) and (*c*) in being (*a*).

The unchanged Perfect-Reality-Power, as underlying, and yet distinguished from, the changing world-forms, has, again, two aspects; (1) the absolutely great,[8] diffuse and undifferentiated aspect which is the Ether of Consciousness[9] and (2) the absolutely small[10] condensed, "potentized" aspect which is *Bindu* of which "Self," living "Germ," material "Atom" or corpuscle are lower forms and evolutes. As the Perfect Continuum[9]

---

[1] Pūrṇa. [2] Āvāng mānasa gochara.
[3] Prāṇa-Śakti. [4] Bhūta-Śakti.
[5] Rig-veda and Atharva-veda, Puruṣa Sūkta; Śvetāśvatara Up., III, 14, 15, 16.
[6] Vādhita. [7] Sat, Cit, Ānanda.
[8] Paramamahat. [9] Cidākāśa. [10] Parama-aṇu.

has a tendency to evolve as a series of Lower Continua in which it still remains immanent (and also, transcendent), so the Perfect Dynamic Point[1] has a tendency to evolve as a series of Lower "Centres," and yet remain as the "Point" at the base of them all: it is thus, "the Centre of all centres". It is also transcendent in this sense that a given Centre, say, a material atom or a living cell, ordinarily manifests and draws upon a part of its infinite dynamism or potency.

As the Ether of Consciousness[2] is the direction of Unity and Undifferentiation, so the Point[1] is the direction of Plurality and Heterogeneity. That is, *Cit*, in having to become many and varied, must begin as *Bindu*, so that *Bindu* is the start of the creative and evolutionary process as the result of the Desire "may I be many".[3] *Bindu* contains within itself "seeds" of multiplicity, illustrated by the desire of the Self to multiply or reproduce itself in generation and creation by the vital impetus in the "cells" towards cell-division and multiplication; by radioactivity and other phenomena showing how matter continually tends to split and rebuild itself into new kinds of matter starting, as physicists now generally believe, from one fundamental kind of matter. By reason of this fundamental tendency to multiplicity, we have the Prime Bindu[4] splitting into a multiplicity of Points[5] which become the starting nuclei of the world of correlated centres.

*Cit*, which is immense Power, condenses itself into the *Bindu* for purposes of creative evolution. By this operation, as *we* must think, magnitude or "field" of being is infinitely contracted, but Power is infinitely massed—which is infinite Potency and Readiness.[6] *Bindu*, therefore in our conception, is the "Limit" of strain (*i.e.*, change of dimensions), as also the "Limit" of Stress (*i.e.*, power involved in the change of dimension, *e.g.*, in a rubber ball pressed by the hand, or in a stretched bowstring; and also the power by which it tends to regain its natural dimensions or form). "Limit" means here "the ultimate point or extent beyond which a thing or energy cannot be contracted and condensed (*i.e.*, strained)—perfect condensation or compactness; it is also Perfect Stress in the sense that it is endowed with perfect Power to regain its original Form, *i.e.*, *Brahman* as immense kinetic, manifest Power. In a limited way, this is illustrated by a germ or seed, when, by its inherent

[1] Bindu. [2] Cidākāśa. [3] Bahu syāng prajā-yeya.
[4] Parama-Bindu as Supreme Self.
[5] Bindus or limited selves (Jīva or Puruṣa).
[6] Ucchūnāvasthā.

power, it tends to grow into an animal or a plant. Bindu's inherent power to evolve may be otherwise expressed by saying that *Bindu* possesses Perfect elasticity. Ordinary centres have imperfect strains and stresses (for practical purposes), so that their elasticities too are imperfect.

As *Bindu* is at the base or "heart"[1] of all cosmic Centres, its elasticity is the basis of the differing elasticities of different centres on account of which they grow, tend to push back and outgrow their constraints, and gradually evolve towards perfection. The reason of cosmic stressing and evolution is, therefore, given in the elasticity of the *Bindu* which must "swell".[2]

Thus we have a fundamental cycle or "circuit" involved in the very fact of creation: *Brahman* as the Kinetic Immense infinitely strains (*i.e.*, condenses) into *Brahman* as Immense Potential (which is *Bindu*); this Immense Potential by reason of its perfect Elasticity swells into Immense Kinetic or Manifest again. Here we have cyclic movement which requires that (1) the cosmos as a system of centres must have cyclic life; and (2) individual centres and groups of centres (*e.g.*, species of animals, communities, nations and so forth), must have cyclic life too. The factor of Bliss and Play[3] ensures, however, that this cyclic life is not a mere mechanical spinning round and round in an eternally fixed groove.

Elasticity, as we have seen, involves both Strain[4] and Stress.[5] The correlate "pole" of the illumined[6] is illuminator.[7] The latter (or *Śiva*) "projects" out of Itself Its own creative Power (with which It is in indivisible unity): this Primary action is the illumined;[6] then, the latter reacts on the former[7] by "reflecting itself on it," *i.e.*, by making itself an Object

---

[1] Śakti or Power is called the "Heart of the Supreme Lord" (*hṛdayam Parameśituh*).

[2] A state called Uchūnāvasthā. It is interesting to note how this idea of "swelling" and dynamic, rhythmic expansion and contraction (Samkoca-vikāśa) of Bindu is coming to be recognised recently as essentially the idea of the Atom, which is a representation of Bindu in the material plane: "According to Bohr, the emission of light from an atom is not a single process but takes place in two distinct stages. The first stage is the energising of the atom, in other words, its passing over from a normal or non-luminous condition into a new state of higher energy content. The second stage is the return of the atom to a condition of lower energy accompanied by the emission of light......", From the Presidential Address, Indian Science Congress, 1928. Whatever the explanation of the phenomenon be, the phenomenon itself (*viz.*, the expansion and contraction of the energy-content of the Atom) now appears to be established.

[3] Ānanda and Līlā.

[4] Samkoca.

[5] Vikāśa-Śakti. According to Śāstra, Samkoca-Śakti + Vikāśa-Śakti = Vimarśa-Śakti. Elsewhere we have used "Stress" in the sense of Power acting and reacting in *all* its phases; *e.g.*, in the conception of the World as a Stress-system.

[6] Vimārśa.

[7] Prakāśa.

of Illumination or Consciousness. Thus arises the Supreme Cosmic Self-Consciousness or Supreme Self[1] which is the state of Supreme *Bindu.*[2] From this last, by multiplication, correlation and co-ordination, the World (often compared to an *Aśvattha* Tree) sprouts into manifestation. In the plane of Mind, the *Bindu* is represented (perfectly in the case of the Lord, but approximately in our case) by the Ego or Self; in the plane of Life, it is represented by the "cell-nucleus" (which is also "Self" veiled); and in the plane of Matter, it is represented by the "central electric charge" (as known to physicists so far)—which is "Self" still further veiled. Self, therefore, is—and according to the Cosmic plan above explained, must be—in every form of being. Modern physiologists generally restrict consciousness to the cortex of the brain: so that actions of the sub-cerebral centres are sub-conscious or unconscious. But from the premises which have been submitted, and also from other scientific and *quasi*-scientific considerations which we have previously partly stated, it should on a Vedantic view follow—(1) that Consciousness and Self cannot be restricted to the life of the cerebrum; (2) that all Centres of the organism (down to the cells or even their elements) must have their own consciousnesses and selves, which are, generally, "ejective" (in the sense in which William James used the word)[3] in relation to central consciousness and our ordinary self; and (3) that these selves, though they may be mutually ejective, co-operate for the purposes of the enjoyment and action[4] of the organism.[5] The Body (gross and subtle) is thus a corporation of *Devatās* or Divinities. What is true in this case, is true in the case of all Things constituted. There is no unconsciousness, or unconsciousness appearing as consciousness[6] to be controlled only by *Cit*. *Cit* is both the Material and Efficient Cause.

As we have seen, the appearance of *Bindu* and its derivate centres, implies Power operating as a contracting Force.[7] The result of such contraction is called *Kancuka* or envelope.[8] Diversity of Centres implies divergent working of such envelope;[9] a higher Centre is that in which the constraint[7] is comparatively more relaxed. *Parameśvara* or Supreme Self is the Lord of such constraints.[9] In point of relaxation these constitute

[1] Para-ahantā. [2] Para-Bindu.
[3] Principles of Psychology. Vol. 1. [4] Bhoga and Karma.
[5] Or the Piṇḍābhimānī Self of Jīva.
[6] Acit and no Cidābhāsa. As in Sāmkhya and Māyāvāda.
[7] Samkoca.
[8] See *The Garland of Letters*—"Kancukas" in which Māyā is the Primordial Kancuka, referred to before.
[9] Kancuka.

an ascending order of higher and higher Centres. Its operative arrangement in a given Centre constitutes its system of "sheaths". All Centres have "sheaths". In man, their operative arrangement is given by the system of the "five sheaths".[1] According to another scheme, the arrangement is represented by the "seven planes";[2] according to another, it is the "seven Centres".[3] Planes, sheaths and so forth are, however, not peculiar to human constitution; they are involved in all things, though, possibly, in varying degree "folded up".

The World shows Centres in different stages of growth: they appear to constitute an hierarchy from "dead" matter to the highest Spirit. It both means and requires that their positions in the cosmic dynamic system are different, and their actions or *karmas*, that is, more or less spontaneous activities by which those positions are sought to be altered, are different. *Adṛṣṭa* is often substituted by its equivalent, *Samskāra* ("tendency" or "predisposition"), and *Karma* by its expression, *Bhoga*, (enjoyment of Pleasure and Pain, etc.). *Bhoga*, is the expression of *Karma*, because *Adṛṣṭa*, though apparently a factor conditioning *Karma*, and therefore *Bhoga*, is itself the result of previous *Karma*. At the root, we can have nothing but *Cit* "elaborating" its Bliss by Play; no particular Centre can, therefore, have its action absolutely determined. Practically, however, *Adṛṣṭa* and *Karma* constitute what is called "cyclic causation" in which the latter is conditioned by certain pre-existent tendencies. Two Centres, A and B, are different; because, their *Adṛṣṭa* and *Karma* are different; these latter are different because the elasticities of A and B have been different; that is, A's power to modify its strains has been different from that of B. And, in our temporal thinking, there is no absolute beginning in time of these differences in the elasticities of Centres: in *Laya* or "Cosmic Sleep" these differences must be imagined as still persisting as "seeds".

Differences are infinitely various yet Centres may be grouped together as Matter, as Life and as Mind. We have seen that there is, in a certain sense, an antithesis between *Adṛṣṭa* as presently determined condition and *Karma* which essays to change and master it; and that *Karma* is essentially the expression of *Joy* and *Play*.[4] Now Matter is that in which *Adṛṣṭa* predominates, and *Karma*, from man's standpoint

[1] "Annamaya", etc., of Vedānta; see in particular, Taittirīya-Up.
[2] Loka. See *The Serpent Power* for explanation of these matters.
[3] Cakra of the spinal column (merudaṇḍa).
[4] Ānanda and Līlā.

at least, in the sense of autonomous action, is almost completely disguised. Mind (as Self-Consciousness and Self-determination) is that in which *Karma* predominates. Life, in the plants and animals, regarded from Man's standpoint again lies midway between these two. In fact, the greater its co-efficient of *Karma*, involving control of *Aḍṛṣṭa*, and the greater, therefore, its manifestation of Joy and Play,[1] the higher is the place of a Centre or group of centres in the Scheme of Beings.

Matter moves, but its "career" is traced in almost (it cannot be absolute) fixed curves and expressed in nearly fixed rounds or routines, covered by the physicist's formulæ and equations. The "life-curve" comes to be less and less fixed as we proceed from Matter to the lower forms of Life, and from these to the higher forms; because the factor of *Karma* more and more asserts itself. The lowest forms of life seem to be endowed with power of spontaneous action: Life is seen to seize upon the atoms of C, H, N, O, build by means of these materials the cell of protoplasm, which it then proceeds to differentiate and integrate with a view to reproduce a certain species or kind. This power of construction for an end is even more marked in the activities of the Self working through, and as, Mind.[2] This power, which is natural in man, can be developed by self-discipline and development,[3] so that the limited self may progressively become controller and creator of wider and wider phases of creation, until at last it becomes identified with[4] the Supreme Creator and controller[5] Himself.[6] Śāstra, therefore, holds—*first*, that any Centre, by appropriate *Karma*, can raise itself to the level of the Highest Centre, because it carries, as manifestation of Power[7] the potentiality of the Immense or *Brahman; secondly*, that *Manu*, *Dakṣa* and other Higher Powers who preside over what are called their respective jurisdictions,[8] are Centres who have attained their high altitude by *Karma* : and *thirdly*, that aspects of the world-process, as a whole presided over by the Supreme Centre, are presided over by "deputies" in detail—an arrangement which, while ensuring the rational direction of the creative process, does not annul the possibility of *Karma* on the Part of subordinate Centres. *Karma*, implying freedom, is the "birthright" of every Centre; it is not "delegated";

[1] Ānanda and Līlā. [2] Antahkaraṇa. [3] Sādhanā.
[4] Sāyujya-siddhi. [5] Prajāpati or the Lord.
[6] In fact, Manu and others, who are credited with having started and presided over different aspects of creative evolution, are Centres who by disciplined fervour (*tapasyā*) have raised themselves to their high level of creative efficiency.
[7] Bindu-Śakti. [8] Adhikāra.

it cannot, therefore, be taken away. On the other hand, evolution does not proceed on a footing of "fortuitous modifications" and "chance conglomerations". It is a directed and "supervised" process.

If the world-process were to proceed on purely mechanistic and deterministic lines, its curve of history would be absolutely and eternally fixed: things and processes would go on spinning in eternally fixed cycles. On the other hand, if *Karma* were to work absolutely independently of *Aḍṛṣṭa*, (*i.e.*, the total assemblage of conditions), the curve would most likely be a "whimsical" one, not amenable to law and order. As a matter of fact, the curve has reference to collective *Aḍṛṣṭa* as well as to collective *Karma;* so that the world-process, though generally cyclic, moves to change also. And, in order that such movement may on the whole be towards betterment or "progress," collective *Karma* must include *Karma* by some Higher Centres who know the road to real betterment and are competent to direct the *Karma* of others, without compulsion, to and along that road. This shows the place of *Manu* and others in the economy of world evolution.[1] The *Karma* of Centres makes the curve of history not a mere cycle, which *Aḍṛṣṭa* left alone, would make it. The control of Higher Centres makes the curve, so to say, *spiraline*,[2] that is, one in which the movement of rotation is combined with a movement of upward (and from man's limited point of view, sometimes downward) translation. But for this control, the *Karma* of ordinary Centres—not generally characterized by any clear and sure intuition of the True, Good and Beautiful—would, in the resultant, be either mutually destructive (truths and falsities, good and evil intentions neutralizing one another), or be precarious and unsteady (that is, not steadily making for an ideal).

From man's pragmatic point of view, the Cosmic Spiral[3] is generally hidden as a whole, and manifest only in parts, sections or aspects. He, therefore, sees now upward phases, and now downward phases—in his own life history, in the history of groups, and, as he thinks, in the history of the world as a whole. Hence there is both progress and "reversion" (or degeneracy) in the career of a Centre of a group of Centres. In the complete view, all such upward and downward phases are seen to be "elements" of the continuous World-Spiraline Movement.

---

[1] This Indian Doctrine appears to be represented in Theosophy by its teaching regarding the "Masters". [2] See *The Garland of Letters.*

[3] The Six Centres through which the "Serpent Power" (itself "spiraline") ascends to the highest, are seen to be arranged spirally, shewing the Cosmic Plan of Movement and, possibly, also Constitution.

The Spiral, as we have seen, combines translation with rotation, the former being due to *Karma*, especially those by the Higher Centres. Any *Karma* done affects, therefore, the aspect of translation; both as regards magnitude and duration. A good and wise *Karma* contributes to upward translation or progress[1] being greater and more rapid; a bad and foolish act tends to make it less and delayed. By ignorance and sin man falls. This fall may, in the long run, raise him, through repentance and expiation after several births if not in the same birth, higher than where he had been before he fell.[2] This shows that there is progress even through falls and lapses. But the path would assuredly be both straightened and shortened if man could, at the critical moment, develop Power or *Śakti*, in knowledge and will, so as not to fall. Hence the spiraline (or cosmically progressive) nature of the world-curve does not warrant that any Centre should merely drift in order to reach the highest point. Since the current is towards the highest end, it could reach it by drifting along the current; but it could not reach it, even in that prodigious age which is called *Kalpa* (counted in thousands of billions of human years), but, so far as man can see in nothing short of infinite time; and, during that unending course, it would have to pass through countless ups and downs spelling untold miseries. In order to cut short this protracted career, in fact, in order to dissociate himself from the mazes of the Spiral, "the Wandering"[3] itself, man must be up and doing, and be a devotee and striver or *Sādhaka*, and "tap" the potentiality of infinite knowledge and power and bliss which is contained in his being.

Any discipline[4] which is calculated to straighten and shorten its career in the Spiral is called the *Dharma* or Law of Form (incompletely translated as Religion) of a given Centre; by following it, its "lifts" are assured and multiplied, and its "fall" prevented and minimized. The result is called progress.[5] When, ultimately, the Centre, by realizing itself as the whole Consciousness Power,[6] can dissociate itself from the Spiral itself, having no further need of specialized effort and movement, the consummation reached is called Liberation.[7]

Where the co-efficient of *Karma* is, practically, very small, as in the case of the Matter-centres, *Dharma* is Power as Law summing up and

---

[1] Abhyudaya.

[2] The Kulārṇava Tantra says that man should learn to raise himself by that which causes his fall through abuse of natural function.

[3] Samsāra. [4] Sādhana. [5] Abhyudaya.

[6] Pūrṇa, Cit-Śakti. [7] Nihśreyasa or Mokṣa or Mukti.

describing the routine of their behaviour. In the case of higher centres, there is no "routine" strictly so called; so that *Dharma* is Power as Law ("regulative" or "normative" without being binding) relative to the conservation[1] of those Centres essentially as such as well as to the progress and liberation[2] (in the senses above explained) of them.

It has been seen that voluntary control of evolutionary movement especially by the higher Centres (from Man upwards) is not only possible, but it exists. We have to consolidate and intensify this control—which is *Sādhana*. In this process, intellect, feeling and will are at work to prepare the aspirant for *Yoga*[3] directed for the attainment of the Supreme End.[4] This *Yoga* effects the transformation of the "Little Self"[5] into the "Supreme Self"[6] by removing the veil of ignorance[7] which alone separates the one from the other; the Yogi leaves behind his "little" intellect, feeling and will, as tools of practical deliberation and selection (therefore, tools that limit, dissect and define), in entering into the realm of the super-consciousness,[8] and Alogical. All forms of *Yoga* agree in placing the Supreme Experience beyond the reach of "Mind" and "Speech". In the last stages, therefore, the Method is Intuition and Ecstasy.[9] The enveloping[10] and thus limiting powers which confine a Centre to its "little sphere" of pragmatic life must be removed in order that it can realize itself as *All*. In the progress of this liberating process, the Centre subsumes and extends its control over the elements of matter.[11]

Essentially and dynamically the same, Matter-centres, Life-centres and Mind-centres are not only correlated in the Cosmos, but are interchangeable; that is, a Matter-centre can, under proper conditions, "transmute" not only into another kind of matter, but into life and mind; and *vice versa*. Any Centre, in its beginningless career, may have, therefore, passed through all these forms, which means that "sheaths" and "instruments" of the imperishable *Cit* have only varied.

Since *Cit-Śakti*, which is the essence of all centres both as regards being and as regards evolving impetus, is imperishable, it follows that

---

[1] Sthiti. Dharma comes from the root Dhri "to maintain".

[2] Abhyudaya and Nihśreyasa.

[3] This term is commonly used to denote both result as unity and the process which achieves it.

[4] It is often unknown that Yoga may be done to achieve any end but Yoga simply ordinarily denotes a "spiritual" process and end.

[5] Jivātman. [6] Paramātman. [7] Avidyā.

[8] Pūrṇa. Cit-Svarūpa. [9] Samādhi. [10] Kancuka.

[11] Bhūtajaya.

all centres, considered as modes of Being-Energy, are so. The particular *forms* ("sheaths" and "instruments") of the centres are continuously changing, however, according to the varying ratios of their *Karma* and *Adṛṣṭa*. Even during what is called a single "lease of life" or birth, the sheaths and instruments of a centre are changing from moment to moment; and what is called the "personal identity" of a centre is only pragmatic identity which, strictly speaking, is not identity. This is true not only of "Selves" and living organisms, but also of material corpuscles which physics has now discovered to be "systems" (and even the Electron, being of finite mass and energy, ought to be so). But in the midst of all this continuous flux, a centre has its endurance or persistence assured in two important respects: (*a*) a centre is in reality the whole Being-Consciousness-Bliss Power, and as such is absolutely imperishable; and (*b*) that Power wills to evolve and "live" as a particular centre; so that this "will" is the "seed" and "root" of that particular centre manifestation; and this seed also is (conditionally) imperishable, that is, as long as the Basic Will lasts. From the latter position it follows that the seed and principle of a given centre must persist through cycles of creation and dissolution, being variously evolved during the former and involved or latent during the latter. The seed of a centre is not destroyed through all these changes of condition—of sheaths and instruments: the "will" of *Brahman* to be and become such centre remaining all through. A centre ceases to be such when it realizes itself as the Whole; therefore, when the Basic Will of *Cit* to be and become *this* particular centre goes and therefore the root of this particular manifestation "dies".

Of the "sheaths" and "instruments" of a Centre, all are not susceptible to change and disintegration to the same degree. The principle which determines susceptibility to change and disintegration is this: A form of Power which evolves (integrates and organises) another form, and controls the latter when evolved, is more persistent than the latter *e.g.*, Vital Power which evolves protoplasm out of C, H, N, O, and elaborates this into a living organism, is more persistent than the "material vehicle' so organised and controlled by it; so that, it will persist after the material body has disintegrated. The Self (represented by *Ahangkāra* or "I-making" Principle) which, according to the views here explained, evolves and controls vehicles or sheaths subtler than the gross body, and, through these subtler vehicles the gross body also, is more persistent than all its vehicles, subtle or gross. Power as *Bindu* is the most fundamental form of Power in relation to the evolution of centres; hence, *Bindu* must persist even after a centre has disintegrated in *all other* forms. Finally, Consciousness-Power as Whole or Perfect Experience is absolute persistence, since It evolves the *Bindu* itself and involves it again.

So that we have an hierarchy of persistent forms, having at the bottom material vehicles or bodies, and at the top, *Bindu* if we exclude the Whole which is absolute persistence. The subtle forms of Power are thus more "vital" and enduring than those that are relatively gross.

The death of the physical body does not according to this view, mean the death of Life and Soul and Spirit. Death separates the subtle vehicle of a Centre from its gross vehicle, and, though these may continuously change by *Karma*, yet they are relatively persistent (*i.e.*, do not disintegrate) through countless births, till by realization, the Centre transcends its own limited self, and becomes merged in the Perfect Whole itself which is absolute deathlessness.

Whether Power as a Centre does or does not evolve and provide itself with a sensuous material vehicle depends on its *Karma* (and *Aḍṛṣṭa*). Its existence as such Centre does *not* depend upon its having evolved a gross material vehicle; so that, it may exist with or without (as the case may be) of a gross vehicle having been evolved and associated with it. Thus Centres may be incarnate or embodied, disincarnate or disembodied.

In its beginningless career a Centre may describe its curve of life according to the "equation' of its varying *Karma* on a board which is infinite Space and Time. And this curve may exhibit it in all possible positions—now embodied, now disembodied; now a "god", now a material thing; now a man, now an amoeba. In its passage it meets with no "forbidden tracts" and "reserved compartments". Fulfilling the *Kārmic* conditions, it can become anything from a Creator of the worlds down to a blade of grass or a particle of dust. And we have seen that all these Centre-Forms are essentially transmutable into one another, all being in essence Consciousness-Power. Of these countless forms, the Human form possesses some advantages in respect of further evolution; since, this form has a mixed experience of pleasure and pain, good and evil acting as an incentive to betterment, and self-consciousness and self-determination to a requisite degree to think out a path and take to it.

Since the curve is described by *Karma*, we may say that a Centre in its ages-long career ever becomes what it *chooses* to become. It is a Centre of Power the essence of which is Joy and Freedom. Its "littleness" as well as its "greatness" are due to its action—its bondage and liberation; its degeneration and progress. An individual Centre may enter, when the ratio of its collective *Karma* and *Aḍṛṣṭa* so requires it, a given and relatively fixed line of character-attitude in the world which is called a Type, Kind, Species, Race or Caste; but by *Karma* again it can leave that line, and pass into another, higher or lower; and by suitable spiritual effort, in can assimilate itself to the *Summum Genus* which is *Cit* as Whole and Perfect. This consummation is *Yoga* or "Union".

The *Śākta* Doctrine thus makes *every* Centre a Magazine of free and undying Power—essentially Perfect but pragmatically limited, that is, veiled and ignored.

## CIT AND ITS INVOLUTION

THE study of Perfect Experience has necessarily to start on the basis of man's own experience, and it is no false "anthropomorphic" metaphysics which models the Cosmos essentially on the lines discoverable in himself. In metaphysics no more ultimate and surer basis can be thought of. "What is here is there".[1] Apart from spiritual intuition giving direct apprehension of the Reality-Power, what is open to logical thinking is, first to attempt a faithful rendering and analysis of man's own consciousness (so far as this may be possible), and thereupon form an idea of the Reality-Power as manifesting in and through ourselves; and then, secondly, to extend and apply this conception of Reality to the interpretation of Life, Matter and the World-system generally. Now, the conception of Reality thus extended either suits (*i.e.*, explains) the World-Order, or does not suit it. If it does not suit, the inference is not that metaphysical enquiry has failed because it has started at the wrong end (*i.e.*, the Self and its experience), but that there has been superficiality or other defect in the rendering and analysis of Self-experience, so that, the premises being vicious have vitiated the conclusions. In fact, the enquiry, to be final, has, according to this doctrine, to be started at one end only, and that end is the Self. We may indeed begin with Life or with Matter or with Force; but the enquiry will yield results neither intelligible nor final, till it be tested, revised, supplemented and understood by an enquiry into the experience of the Self. That experience is the ultimate and unquestioned "Fact"; everything else has to make good its title by its bearing upon that Fact;

[1] Yadihāsti tad anyatra, *ante*.

apart from such reference, actual or possible, atoms, ethers, forces and the rest, howsoever perfectly they may be expressed by mathematical formulae, are nothing else than abstract ideas "without local habitation and name".

It is in man's self that he touches the foundations of the view that Reality is ultimately Consciousness as *Cit* which by its own Power makes an object of itself, and elaborates this object into a world of correlated Centres of Matter, Life and Mind; and that in such elaboration *Cit* does not suffer its essence, that is, Being-Consciousness-Bliss[1] to be either abrogated or changed. That is so in man's own experience: *Cit* becoming varied experience and yet remaining Pure *Cit* always.

It is, again, in his own experience that man must find the key to discover the meaning of the Cosmic Principles called *Tattvas.* Principle is one and it is *Cit:* but it has different phases and aspects of world-manifestation, such as unveiled and veiled; alogical and logical; extra-temporal and temporal; and so on. With reference to such phases, and in describing and explaining them, we have one Principle "evolving" as many. The Philosophy of Śākta Vedāntism and Śaiva non-dualism is the enunciation and statement of the mutual relationships of what are called the Thirty-six *Tattvas.*[2]

Now, the Principles, in their broad outlines, can be discovered in normal experience, and, in detail, can be known and verified by *yoga,* or supernormal experience, which is not an absolutely new order of experience, but is experience more unveiled, more fully recognised and "accepted" than man's normal, pragmatic experience.

Experience is an alogical, undefined Universe. It is Pure Consciousness, but is not only that : it has a varied content. It is subjective, but is so only when, and in so far as, it as been "dissected" by a logical operation. It involves all categories or Forms of Thought, but, in its fullness, is not covered by any of them. It is pragmatic, that is, having reference to practical ends, but is so, only as considered as a "section", not as the complete "Fact". Correct intuition will not even allow our saying that "*Cit* is in us"; the fact is that we, as centres of specific action and reaction, are in *Cit* which by its Power appears as such centres.

Man for the sake of the ends of his pragmatic life, disowns his Self which is *Cit.* But suppose he essays to be it. Then it is, and recognised

---

[1] Sat-Cit-Ānanda.

[2] See *Śakti and Śākta* and *The Garland of Letters* (Chapter on Tattvas), in which the evolution of the "Principles," from the psychological as well as mantra standpoint, has been dealt with, and authorities cited.

as, Alogical, the Whole[1] beyond the six Limitations,[2] and transcending all categories, though involving them. It is so, and is so recognised or intuited, if man is able to completely withdraw the Veil,[3] and so, do away with all pragmatic limitations, even what is called "central reference."

Now, what is the import of the revelation of this Experience ?

(1) Since it is unveiled and free from all limitations, it may be called both Pure and Perfect. It is the Whole[4] and absolutely pure.[5]

(2) Since it is alogical and indefinable, it cannot be called a *Tattva* which means Reality-Power defined in a particular way, that is, as regards a phase or aspect. It is therefore beyond[6] (though involving) all (*i.e.*, 36) *Tattvas*.

(3) It is Being, Consciousness, Bliss,[7] but the aspects are not "sundered" or thought apart. It is the manifesting Principle[8] as well as object and manifestation,[9] *Cit* as well as Power, but these are in indistinguishable unity. Something reveals and something is revealed, but there is no logical separation of the one from the other. It is *Parā Saṃvit* or *Cit* which is Perfect Experience of which the Ether of Consciousness[10] is an undistinguished phase.

Suppose, now, we proceed to think about this alogical Whole of Experience. We ask ourselves; What is it? What is there in it? We see that it is Consciousness stressing as a universe of experience. This is the fullest account we can render of the Fact. We see also that Consciousness and Its Stress or Power is one and not two, though we think them apart. Consciousness, in our review, is the Manifesting Principle,[11] and Its stressing is the content or object of manifestation.[12] But the former is also Power, and the latter is also manifestation (since it is abstraction to say that manifestation is one thing and its "content" or object is another; and though it may be possible in *yoga* to have experience as Pure Manifestation without any special content,[13] in that case, Manifestation becomes its own content; and in other cases where there is special content,[13] this latter as manifested is the indivisible concrete fact which abstraction splits into manifestation *and* manifested). Hence *Śiva-tattva* and *Śakti-*

---

[1] Pūrṇa. [2] Kancukas.

[3] *i.e.*, Māyā of which the other five Kancukas—Niyati, Kāla, etc., are born. See *The Garland of Letters* ("Kancukas") in which the matter is explained, and authorities are cited.

[4] Pūrṇa. [5] Śuddha. [6] Tattvātita. [7] Sat-Cit-Ānanda.

[8] Prakāśa. [9] Vimarśa; Antarlīna-vimarsha. [10] Cidākāśa.

[11] Prakāśa, called Śiva-tattva.

[12] Vimarśa, called Śakti-tattva. [13] Vishesha.

*tattva* are one. And yet now, from the standpoint of our thinking, manifestation[1] and manifested[2] exist like two seeds contained in a grain of gram.[3] It is also pure[4] because though our thinking has now distinguished the indistinguishable and thought about the alogical and unthinkable, (1) it has not yet set apart one aspect from the other aspect and looked upon them as distinct Principles (*i.e.*, there is as yet no duality), (2) nor has it yet hedged round and veiled the Complete Fact, accepting parts only and rejecting or ignoring others.

The manifested[5] is the fact of Consciousness being a content or object and making a content or object of itself. (This is depicted in the symbolism of the *Kāmakalāvilāsa*[6] as the reflection of the Self in a mirror).

Suppose next, we essay to give to ourselves a summary statement of the illumining-illumined, this *Śiva-Śakti* experience. What is the most general category under which we may (approximately of course) subsume the experience? By what name may we call it, though absolutely unnamable it be ?

The category which most nearly subsumes and expresses the whole of man's experience is—"I" (*Aham*). This "I" should, however, be distinguished from what is pragmatically known and used as "I" which is but a comparatively limited section of experience, referred to a centre, *i.e.*, Ego, and sharply contrasted with a vaster non-ego or not-self, known and used as "*Idam*" or "This". What it may be asked is all this manifestation as experience? And the first and most comprehensive answer is—It is "I".[7] In this, Consciousness or Manifestation makes a content or object of Itself—the Primary Object. And since we have called this fact the illumined,[8] the Primary Object may be called the I-experience.[9] Its logical correlate is, of course, "This,"[10] but in the primary stage, the This is as yet latent, implicit: we know and describe our entire Being-Experience as "I", and nothing but that. In pragmatic thought, "I" is Subject in relation to "This" as Object; but in the primary representation of Experience, "I" as concrete consciousness makes an object of itself, as, relatively speaking, in the pragmatic sphere also, we sometimes make an object of "I" or Ego. And since in the primary presentation, "I" is

[1] Prakāśa. [2] Vimarśa.
[3] Canaka. [4] Śuddha Tattva. [5] Vimarśa.
[6] A work by a Śaiva author on the great Śrī Yantra of the Divine Mother Mahātripura-Sundarī.
[7] Not to be confounded with empiric or Pragmatic Ego or Self: it is Transcendental Self, whose object is the universe as itself and not as in the case of the limited self as non-self.
[8] Vimarśa. [9] Aham-vimarśa. [10] Idam-vimarśa.

all-inclusive, leaving no margin for a correlate "This", Power as *Vimarśa*, in so far as it functions to present this latter, may be supposed to be *negative*.[1]

*Śiva-tattva* is then the presentation (primary in the logical line, but approximate and secondary in relation to *Para-Samvit* which is alogical) of Experience as an exclusive "I," the associate *Śakti-tattva* so operating as not to present the other logical pole—"Idam" or "This". It is "pure" in the sense that though experience is not here partitioned into "I" and "This," the Whole (with nothing veiled or subtracted) is thought of as "I". The province of "This" not being rejected, is covered by the all-inclusive concept, "I".

Next, in the seamless experience thus intuited as "I," a seam or fissure is seen to appear—the Polarity of I[2] and This,[3] but the latter "Pole" is as yet, very faintly or hazily, folded up with the "I". There is as yet (1) no clear differentiation or projection of the latter Pole;[3] and (2) no distinct blossoming[4] of it. The 'This'[3] is faintly perceived by the "I"[5] as part of the one Self, the emphasis being therefore on the "I" side of experience.[6] There is representation of, and warrant for this in man's own ordinary experience. This second logical stage is called *Sadāśiva-Tattva*. It is the stage of the subject relation.[7] The This is however here the self and not non-self, in which the stress is on the first. It is also pure[8] (approximately so, when compared with *Parā-Samvit* or the alogical *Whole*), in the sense that, though polarity is here introduced, experience is still intuited as a whole and not in this aspect or that only. The limitations (*Māyā* and "her progeny" contracting experience) have not yet commenced to exist and operate.

An appeal to normal experience will show that when the above stage has been reached, attention or regard swings from "Fact conceived as "I" to "Fact conceived as This". This, evidently, is not the Fact (*i.e.*, the Universe of Experience) becoming veiled in one "section" or aspect, and revealed in another. The Fact as a whole was there (approximately, because we were logically operating on the alogical) in the state of I-emphasis,[9] as it is now in the state of This-emphasis.[10] But of the two

---

[1] Niṣedha-rūpa.
[2] Aham.
[3] Idam.
[4] Sphutatvam. Yogamuni says the function of Power is to negate (Niṣedha-vyāpāra-rūpā śaktiḥ). This is said as regards Śakti-Tattva specifically so called; is applicable to all forms of Śakti.
[5] Aham.
[6] *The Garland of Letters.*
[7] Aham-Idam-Vimarśa.
[8] Śuddha.
[9] Aham-Vimarśa.
[10] Idam-Vimarśa.

polar concepts, "I" and "This," the former was emphatic in the first, and latter emphatic in the second. The emphasis or regard plays between these poles. The same complete "Universe" is differently regarded (*viz.*, as "I" and as "This") in the two cases. The Universe has not been sectioned yet, and has not been laid upon any "basis" other than consciousness. There is as yet no double framework, one for the Self and the other for the Not-Self. This is *Īśvara-tattva.* It also is pure.[3]

Then, as a preliminary to the "disruption" of the Universe of Experience into Self and Not-Self, *Puruṣa* and *Prakriti*, thought of as independent of each other, we have a state of experience in which the "Universe, still remaining (approximately) entire and still regarded as laid upon the one[3] non-dual basis of Consciousness, is conceived both as 'I' and 'This',[4] the emphasis being laid on both. In normal experience, too, the like of this is seen when man's "Fact" is equally and indifferently regarded as "I" and "This". "I" and "This" here are not the "I" and "This" of ordinary pragmatic thought which refers to different "sections" of experience, and, in the case of external perception, lays them upon a dual and independent basis (*e.g.*, Mind and Matter).

This is *Sadvidyā* or *Śuddhavidyā Taṭtva.* It is also pure[2] and the last of the pure Tattvas.[5]

After this the operation of *Māyā,*[6] *Kancukas* and duality[7] begins, concealing and limiting the dimensions of the Universe, and sharply dividing it into Self[8] and Not-Self,[9] setting them up as independent Principles. Commencing from this stage, their reign extends over the evolution of the lower *Tattvas;*[10] and we have, further, the emergence of the order of Time and that of Space, which prior to this were not evolved.

Broadly speaking, then, we have two aspects and two stages in the second aspect: (1) the aspect as Alogical Whole; and (2) that of the transcendentally[11] logical *Śiva-Śakti-tattva* and its unmanifested[12] stages down to *Sadvidyā-tattvā;* and (3) the empirical pragmatic manifested stage of the Psycho-physical Potential[9] down to solid matter.[13] The Sāmkhyan Prakriti is one but in Advaita Śaiva philosophy, many. Between (2) and (3) there is a transitional, dual-non-dual[14] or difference-and

[1] Adhikaraṇa. [2] Śuddha. [3] Advaita.
[4] Aham and Idam. [5] Śuddha Tattvas.
[6] See *Śakti and Śākta* and *Garland of Letters*—Māyā Tattva. [7] Dvaita.
[8] Puruṣa. [9] Prakriti. [10] Called Śuddhāśuddha and Aśuddha.
[11] "Transcendental" logic, because the categories here dealt with are the transcendental Aham and Idam, and not pragmatic, empirical Self and Not-Self, Subject and Object.
[12] Adṛṣṭadṛṣṭi. [13] Pṛthivī. [14] Advaita-dvaita.

not-difference[1] stage during which *Māyā* (the Principle of Difference),[2] the five "Sheaths"[3] and *Puruṣa* or the individual self are evolved.

The main outlines of the order or stages of Cosmic Evolution,[4] are, as indeed they must be, traceable in the evolution of man's own experience, if he essays to uplift, as far as possible, the Veil hiding from his pragmatic eye, the real and total content and import of his life and existence. The more he removes the veil, the larger and deeper become the content and import of *Cit* operating in, and as, himself. The question, evidently, is: What is that content and that import of *Cit* in the "limit," that is, when the veil has been completely uplifted? That "limit" is Consciousness as It is in Itself or *Parā-Saṃvit.* The main "lines" of the evolution of the microcosm are also, in the "limit," the lines of the evolution of the macrocosm. Those "lines," are: (*a*) A neutral, undifferentiated, non-polarized condition (the Alogical); (*b*) a condition of potential differentiation, or polarization, in which the Substance still remaining undivided, there is emphasis on one "pole" or on the other (the condition of Fundamental Movement);[5] and (*c*) the condition of actual dissociation of the poles, and resultant splitting up of the non-dual Substance into dual and manifold. The Supreme Point[6] must be implicit in the second stage, since we cannot have "poles", potential or differentiated, and stressing upon and between them, without Power focussing itself into a Point.[7] *Bindu* is manifestly operative in the third or differentiating and multiplying stage.

Now, Matter (believed to be constituted by Positive and Negative charge of electricity) may be and by some has been, conceived as evolving from the Mother Stuff (*e.g.*,Ether) substantially in the manner described in (*a*), (*b*) and (*c*)—a neutral state; a potentially polar (but undissociated) stressing state; and a dissociated (though configurated), stressing state of electrons and protons constituting an atom of Matter. The non-nucleated protoplasm; the nucleated protoplasm in which the sex-difference is still implicit; the organised plant or animal tissue in which the sexes gradually dissociate themselves (in some plants, for example, though the sexes are dissociated, they are still parts of the same organism); these prove the "lines" or stages in vital evolution. Or, without reference to sex-difference, we might trace the "lines" more simply thus: first, non-nucleated protoplasm in which the nucleus may be implicit; second, the nucleated proto-

[1] Bhedābheda. [2] Bhedabuddhi. [3] Kancuka. [4] Tattva.
[5] Of Spanda, Para Śabdā or Para-Nāda. [6] Para Bindu. [7] Cidghana.

plasm often involving another nucleus within itself, stressing, under the conditions of nutrition, etc., to "divide" itself; third, the divided cell of protoplasm, each with its own independent nucleus. In experience, too, knowledge begins with an undifferentiated state; evolves the poles (first associated and co-substantial) of "I" and "This"; dissociates the poles and makes independent substances of them. The study of even a common act of perception, if not allowed to be swayed and cramped by pragmatic considerations, will show that this is so. Man's experience has three broad forms. Cognition, Feeling-attitude and Volition; each is, or tends to become, polar; thus cognition is of this object or of that; feeling is either pleasure or pain; volition is either attractive or repulsive.[1] Now, intuition is relied on to show that a neutral, non-polar condition is the basis and background of each of these three pairs of poles. Cognition of this or that is based upon, and branches off from, a generic cognition;[2] pleasure and pain are based upon, and shoot out from, a "mother-stuff" of feeling which is veiled bliss;[3] and attraction and repulsion[1] presuppose, and may reveal, a placid background of quiescence.[4]

So the "lines" of the Grand Cosmic Evolution, as traced before, are repeated in the details of creation.

And, all that exists, all whether as Mind, Life and Matter, are forms and products of the one fundamental Substance Power which is *Cit-Śakti*, or unlimited Being-Consciousness as Power which is also Bliss.

## RETROSPECT AND CONCLUSION

THERE is no finality in human science, and its conclusions are, and are apt to remain, for the most part dubious. Yet, the results and hypotheses of science in the domains of Matter, Life and Mind (including what are called "parapsychic phenomena") as they now stand, and also regard being had to what they now point to, appear to be not antagonistic to the principles of *Śākta Vedāntism;* nay, they appear, so far as they go, to fit in with those principles. The modern dynamic view of the constitution of Matter—a view that has tended to dematerialise Matter; a view that sees in the atoms of Matter a vast magazine of Power; a view that is faced with a residual element of the inexplicable in all its mechanistic explanations; a view that sees in radio-activity the drafting of new and

[1] Rāga or Dveṣa.
[2] Sāmānya jnāna.
[3] Ānanda.
[4] Śāntabhāva.

practically inexhaustible energy into the hitherto-supposed closed and constant realm of physical energies; —already shows that Physical Science has taken vast strides towards the *Śākta* position which (*a*) makes Power to be the essence of everything; (*b*) makes Power in reality immeasurable in everything and in the universe for the matter of that; and (*c*) makes the "Dynamic Point" the Perfect Magazine of Power (hence making the "atom" also a vast magazine). As regards the further and higher view of *Vedānta* that this Power manifesting as Matter is essentially Consciousness-Power which is measureless Joy expressed in unrestricted Play, Physical Science has, as such nothing to say at present; but if one were logically to work out what is now implicit in its position, and imagine the promise contained therein fulfilled, particularly in consonance with the results and promises of Biological and Psychical Sciences, one might feel that Science has, unconsciously, taken even a longer stride than one would imagine towards the final position of *Śākta* Vedāntism. To see this, the results and indications of one Science should not be reviewed by themselves alone; but they should be correlated to, co-ordinated with those of the Sister Sciences—because, Science is one. As it is, Physical Science within her own province has steadily, and now very closely, approached the ideal of unification and correlation. She has tended more and more to reduce all kinds of Matter to one kind, and all forms of Energy to one kind; and has, further, tended to reduce Matter and Energy to a Common Root. So that the physical universe has now become a universe of Stress-systems, not of gross stresses only but subtle stresses (as evidenced by X and other invisible rays, and the Hertzian waves of the wireless among other things), not limited and calculable but practically unlimited and incalculable (as evidenced by radio-activity), not forming a "closed curve" but in subtle and constant action and reaction with other kinds of forces—vital and psychic.

The Vital and Psychic Sciences, in their turn, are helping this grand unification and the universal linking up of forces and phenomena. Though the "living molecule" is now even a greater mystery than it ever was, the gulf between the living and the non-living is steadily narrowing rather than widening, and already there are indicators of the characteristic responses of the living being, in a veiled way, discoverable in the so-called non-living matter; and, within the province of the living itself, the supposed absolute difference between plant life and animal life is in the course of being gradually effaced, not of being accentuated. Evolution is now sought to be explained less and less on mechanistic lines or in terms of "fortuitous modifications," and more and more in terms of an "original impetus," free and not determined, given in the constitution of things and at the root of phenomena to change and evolve (a position from which one can have a vision of Vedāntic Joy and Play—the basic factors of world evolution and involution). And Biologists, no less than Physicists, are now on the way to perceiving that the path of world-evolution is not traced by an "upward movement" only, but that it is a curve showing rhythms and cycles—making the world's history one of evolution and involution and then evolution again.

Within the living organism itself Biology, so long content to explain its phenomena on quasi-mechanistic lines in terms of nerve-stimulation, cell-disturbance, and so forth, has now unexpectedly stumbled upon a new and mysterious factor whose action on the organism is found to be more profoundly "vital" than that of any other known agency: the, mysterious glands ("pituitary," "pineal", "thyroid," "adrenal," "interstitial") and their mysterious secretions ("hormones"). Descartes, it is true, had suggested the pineal gland as the "bridge" between the Mind and Matter in us; but he was never taken seriously until quite recently.

Correspondence between Science and *Śākta* Doctrine should be understood in the full depth of its import. It shows that as in radio-activity, Science has discovered the physical atom to be a magazine of Power whereby its constitution as well as its "evolution" (or transmutation) is determined, so in the case of the cells of these glands and their subtle secretions (analogous to the radiations of the radio-active atom) she has now discovered a magazine of Power and its workings whereby the constitution of the body and its growth, etc., are regulated. In Physics she has discovered the vast potency and efficiency of the smallest thing—the atom, and of its unseen emanations; in Biology she has discovered the wonderful potency and efficiency of the smallest constituents of the gland and of their subtle secretions. Apparently the smallest is thus being perceived to be really and dynamically the greatest—a perception which is preparing the way for a final recognition of the "Dynamic Point" of the *Śākta* Doctrine, which is "smaller than the smallest and greater than the greatest".

As regards the position that Consciousness merely accompanies and "lights up" some of the processes of the nervous system (*viz.*, the cerebral processes), it has been shown before that the actual evidence before us does not warrant the conclusion (1) that Consciousness is simply an onlooker and revealer exercising no causal influence on the cortical phenomena which by themselves form a "closed curve"; and (2) that Consciousness as such, that is as distinguished from that part of it which is pragmatically accepted as *the* Consciousness is limited to the cerebral centres and line only, not having anything to do with other centres which are commonly taken as subconscious or unconscious. On the contrary, on two grounds at least Consciousness must be believed to possess causal efficiency (not merely as a directing force or "switcher" but as a supplier of new energy)[1] over the whole range of man's nervous mechanism: (*a*) the fact that a very slight stimulus (*e.g.*, the reading of a line of a message that a beloved friend is seriously ill) provokes an enormous and complicated response (in emotion, idea and action) out of all proportion to the physical nature and intensity of the provoking cause; and (*b*) the fact that the activity of every nerve-centre whether in the cerebrum or in the spinal cord, is in the nature of an overflow of energy and selective operation (suggesting, therefore, Joy, Play and Choice). Besides these, there is also the indisputable evidence of self-consciousness showing Consciousness—to be an ever-active operative Power—not merely in the so-called "motor" phenomena of conscious experience as attending, striving and willing, but also in what are called the "sensory," cognitive and affective phenomena—knowing, imagining, thinking and feeling. Consciousness as operative Power is a matter of direct and constant experience.

Mental Science, in dealing with ordinary psychic and the "para-psychic" phenomena, is steadily veering round to a position whence one can have not a very distant view of the ultimate truth as held in, Śākta Vedāntism. Mental Science is coming to recognise (1) that ordinary, pragmatic consciousness is only a part of a larger Consciousness which it now calls "sub-consciousness"; (2) that this larger Consciousness is not only a Power but the Power which seems to contain within itself the whole mystery and wonder of Life and existence; (3) that this larger Consciousness is one in which all individual pragmatic consciousnesses "live, move and have their being"; that it is to the individual Centres what the Ether is believed by many to be in relation to the strain-and-stress centres in it; (4) that to this larger Consciousness, Matter and

[1] As the physical doctrine of Conservation of Matter and Energy has now ceased to be looked upon as an "axiom" or "first principle" in view of radio-activity and the dynamic and evolutionary view of Matter, the fact that Consciousness is a supplier of new energy is no challenge to an "established" law of Matter and Energy.

Force are not alien, but they seem to be its evolutes, products and dependents; and finally, (5) that Time and Space also are not alien to, and independent of, it; that these are its own ways of representing itself to the centres involved in it. The fourth point is being steadily established by the accumulation of phenomena collected under the general heading, "psychodynamism"; and the fifth by the phenomena of "psychometry," "X-ray vision," and so forth, in which spatial determinations such as "here and there," "near and distant," as well as temporal determinations such as "now and then," "past and future" all appear to be, not only "in the melting pot," but meeting in a "point".

Referring to certain genuine cases of pre-vision of the future (Dr. Maxwell's, Professor Flournoy's, Mrs. Verrall's ....) M. Mæterlinck writes.... "Under the erroneous idea we form of the past and the present, a new verity is living and moving, eager to come to light. The efforts of that verity.... strike to the very roots of history. We soon lose all inclination to doubt. We penetrate into another world and come to a stop, all out of countenance. We no longer know where we stand; before and after overlap and mingle, we no longer distinguish the insidious and factitious but indispensable line which separates the years that have gone by from the years that are to come. ....We discover with uneasiness that time, on which we based our whole existence, itself no longer exists.... it alters its position no more than space, of which it is doubtless but the incomprehensible reflex. It reigns in the centre of every event; and every event is fixed in its centre and all that comes and all that goes passes from end to end of our little life without moving by a hair's breadth around its motionless pivot.... yesterday, recently, formerly, erstwhile, after, before, to-morrow, soon, never, later, fall like childish masks, whereas to-day and always cover with their united shadows the idea which we form in the end of a duration which has no sub-divisions, no breaks and no stages, which is pulseless, motionless and boundless."

The "to-day and always" without subdivisions and breaks and stages is rather the "now and always"—showing Duration[1] in the aspect of "Point" (now) and in that of boundless "Continuum" (always); that is to say Duration which has no beginning and no end and breaks is also wholly condensed into a "Point," and this latter aspect is referred to above as the "centre of every event" or phenomenon, "its motionless

[1] This is Parakāla, or supreme Time, as opposed to Kāla which only comes in "with moon and sun".

pivot". But though the centre or pivot is "motionless" in this sense that the whole of Duration or History is condensed into, and as, it (so that to be at the centre is also to be and have the whole), it is also dynamic in the sense that the centre or "Point" does expand as a sphere, and an ever-widening sphere, which is the Experience of Duration—the beginningless and endless History with past, present and future. If the "Point" were to remain statical, there would be no experience of Duration or History as it actually is (involving past and future); on the other hand, if Duration or History were not wholly condensed into, and given in and as, the Point, the pre-existence of the future in the present, and therefore, foreknowledge of the future (either Divine or human—that of the "seer") would not be possible; but since this is said to be not only possible but is, already to some extent, a fact, so it is claimed, perfect foreknowledge and perfect recollection must be believed to be possible also; and that is possible only if the Future and the Past in their entireness co-exist and meet at a Point.

The same reasoning will apply to Space also. If the "X-ray vision" with respect to a spatially remote thing or event be a fact, then, we must believe that Space too, like Time, has the twofold aspect of "here and everywhere"[1] —the former aspect (here) containing as a "Point" the whole of Space regarded as a boundless "Continuum" ("everywhere"). And the "Point" is dynamic in the sense above explained.

The Dynamic Point, as we have seen, occupies a very prominent place in the Śākta-Vedānta : It is the Consciousness-Power regarded as Perfect Potency to evolve; and It is also a Perfect Universe in the sense that whatever is to evolve as the world in Time, Space and Causal concatenation, is contained in the *Bindu* which is the seed of everything. It is thus the centre of every being and every event : the centre "swells"[2] into every being and every event, and every being and every event is reabsorbed, folded up into the centre. Time, Space and Causality are "forms" or modes of such "swelling" and "shrinking"[3] of the Dynamic Point. Hence to be consciously in touch with the *Bindu* is to know whatever exists or goes on in the spatial, temporal and causal scheme of the universe.

---

[1] *Cf.* the verse (before quoted in Viśvasāra-tantra): "What is here is everywhere, and what is not here is nowhere."

[2] Ūchchhūnatā.

[3] Samkochaprasara. *Cf.* The modern dynamic view of the Atom as outlined by Bohr and others, and the Quantum Theory of Radiation (the "Compton Effect" in particular).

The possibility of foreknowledge (perfect or partial) does not, however, require that the world-order is unalterably fixed and determined leaving no margin for free play. The world is a free play;[1] every being is an incarnation of Joy; and every act and event is a play out of Joy. Joy and Play are the "birthright" even of the so-called material thing, and, there is no reason to suppose that it has entirely forfeited that right. Actions are, more of less, free or undetermined in every instance. No foreknowledge of them is, therefore, possible if, and so long as, we take actions and events in the ordinary temporal way—arranging them according to the scheme of past, present and future : what is not yet determined cannot now be known. But in the Dynamic Point where all times and spaces meet (in an alogical and unthinkable way), what is not yet co-exists with what has been and what is. So that there the undetermined future co-exists with the determined past, and with the present determining itself. Here, therefore, foreknowledge of a still undetermined future becomes possible, because here Time itself is annulled or transcended. A "seer" placing himself in rapport with this "Point" Universe may, therefore, (it is said) "see" exactly how a person "will" act or an event "will" happen, though the acting and the happening are, wholly or partly, free and undetermined.

This "mystic sense" is, of course, inexplicable. But we may suppose that the seer may, after seeing the free and undetermined act in the timeless and spaceless Point, decipher his mystic knowledge back into temporal and spatial terms, and predict that so-and-so will act thus or do this at that particular moment and that at that particular place. The case is in a way, analogous to the "deciphering" by the motion of the machine itself of a gramophone record where a song is given and inscribed in co-existent scratches back into the singing of the song in which the notes succeed one another. The analogy, however, is partial, because, though the record contains an order of succession transformed into an order of co-existence, it is not the "Point" transcending both Time and Space; and so what the machine does is apparently to retranslate a song already determined and spatially inscribed into a rehearsal of the song in the usual temporal way.

Whilst the *Saṁkhyan* Doctrine makes the evolution of the world a process of actual change of the Root Principle, and *Māyāvāda* makes it

[1] *Cf.* the saying of Dionysius—"He, the very cause of all things, becomes ecstatic, moves out of Himself, by the abundance of His loving Goodness," etc.

one of seeming change of *Brāhman*, the *Śākta* Doctrine combines the two views recognising in each a partial truth. The Root changes as the evolving world, and yet, It changelessly abides—an insoluble logical contradiction for which however, man has, in his own experience, sufficient warrant. The corollaries to this Principle of Evolution are important:

(1) Pure and Perfect Consciousness, in evolving by Its own Power as finite and particular consciousnesses (*i.e.*, consciousness of varying modes, degrees and limits), does never cease to be Pure and Perfect Consciousness; so that restricted consciousness, "sub-consciousness" and "unconsciousness" are imbedded in a never-failing background of Pure and Perfect Consciousness.

(2) Consciousness as Pure and Perfect Bliss-Joy and Freedom-Play remains as such, never ceases to be other than Itself, though, as finite centres, It evolves as infinitely varied pleasures and pains, actions and their determining conditions. Just as in the first case, the Universe regarded as Experience is not merely the sum total of restricted, particularised consciousness, subconsciousness and unconsciousness, but is like an unbounded sphere of Pure and Perfect Consciousness within which these are included as smaller spheres, so also in the second case, Pure and Perfect Bliss-Joy and Freedom-Play is not the sum total of the particular pleasures and pains, actions and conditions of the particular centres, but, (*a*) includes these and is immanent (as an unfailing background) in these, and (*b*) exceeds these as Perfect Bliss.

(3) Its condensation as the Dynamic Point does not efface the immensity of Its Being-Power; hence, the Point = the whole *Brahman* or *Śiva-Śakti*.

(4) The Point also, in actually "swelling" and "shrinking" (as evolution and involution of the world), does not cease to be the Perfect *Bindu*.[1]

Each of these corollaries, it will be observed, involves the insoluble logical contradiction above referred to.

---

[1] The fact that Matter and Energy are both of "granular structure," coupled with the fact that Life also is now recognised, (*e.g.*, in Arrheneus' theory of *Cosmozoa* or *Panspermia* which posits "atoms" of Life), as "atomistic," together with the fact that Mind and Soul are widely believed to exist and operate as "atoms" of Energy, shows that the Bindu as such is at the root of all existence and operation. It is now further recognised that both in the creation of "atoms" of matter and their disintegration, enormously concentrated Energy is required; and that high concentration of Energy is required also for the evolution of organic from so-called inorganic matter. Concentrated Power is an approximate representation of Bindu.

In the scheme of 36 Principles outlined in the previous chapter, it has been noted that *Īśvara-tattva* has a place especially assigned to it, and that, considered in that technical sense, it is not the highest category. The highest category in the logical line is *Śiva-Śakti*, beyond which there is *Para-Samvit* which is alogical, beyond the scheme of Principles, and therefore, not Itself a category. It will thus be perceived that what western metaphysic and religion regard as the highest category of Being and Thought (*viz.*, God) cannot be identified with the *Īsvara* in the above scheme: It corresponds rather to *Śiva-Śakti*. The *Śāstra*, however, does not require that the "higher" and "lower" in the above scheme should be taken in a rigid and absolute way, especially in that part of the scheme which shows the evolution of what are called "Pure" Principles. In the domain of the "impure" Principles—where *Māyā* and the Envelopes hold their sway—"higher and lower" as also "before and after," "cause and consequence" have ordinary, pragmatic meanings; but in the realm of Pure Principles, each *is* the Whole with the emphasis of logical representation laid on a special aspect (such as "I" or "This"). Hence, *Śiva-Śakti* is also usually spoken of as *Maheśvara-maheśvarī* or as *Parameśvara-Parameśvarī*—usually with the epithets *mahat* (Great) or *Parama* (Supreme) prefixed to the term *Īśvara*.

Now, *Śiva-Śakti* is Being-Consciousness-Bliss. This Supreme Principle veils and finitizes Itself in, and as, the world of finite Centres. As a consequence we have not only different modes of finite being but even so-called "non-being"; different modes of particular consciousnesses but even so-called "unconsciousness"; and different modes of joy and pleasure but also "pains" and "sorrows". Thus also, God who is Pure Act becomes in, and as, the finite Centres, actions-and-reactions, conditional actions; Who is Perfect "Energy," becomes in and as, such Centres, mixtures of potential and kinetic power—in which Power is neither, wholly kinetic nor wholly potential, and therefore, imperfect energy. But in evolving as all this, the Supreme Principle remains Supreme Being-Consciousness-Bliss, Pure Act and Perfect Energy: we have thus an alogical mingling of change and changelessness in the Life of the Perfect Being-Power.

There is much actual pain and sorrow in the world. Since the Supreme Experience of God includes all this, how can it be said that the Supreme Experience is all Bliss? The Supreme Experience (1) sums up all particular pains and sorrows as also all particular pleasures and happinesses, and (2) involves each particular pain or pleasure as such. Now, in the first case, it need not be supposed that the grand total of all pains and pleasures must be a prodigious pain *plus* a prodigious pleasure. As two sets of opposing forces may produce in the resultant not motion this way or that but rest or quiescence; as again the sum of all particular sounds is, according to *Mantra-Śāstra, the Mahāmantra Om:* as, also, in the realm of colours, the synthesis of all the colourbands is white light; —so it may be reasonable to suppose that the grand total of all pleasures and pains is not a dual experience of great pleasure *and* great pain, but a non-dual alogical experience of something which is akin to man's feeling of quiescence. And this feeling of quiescence is embedded in an undiminished Bliss-Consciousness which as the *Śāstra* maintains, perpetually abides even while finite Centres of Expression appear in It.

In the latter case, particular pleasures and pains as such enter into the Supreme Experience. But even that does not make that Experience other than an Experience of Bliss-Joy. In the first place, each particular pleasure or pain is not there in Divine experience in a veiled, isolated and disconnected way, but in the fullness of its relation to other feelings and to the whole; and as a particular note, discordant in itself, may not be so when it forms an element of the harmony of a symphony, so a feeling, painful when its relations and background are veiled, may not be so when it is consciously set in its relations to the whole. Hence, Divine Consciousness, though It involves and knows all particular feelings of particular Centres, involves and knows them as "elements" of an infinite whole of Experience, so that their effective tones as veiled and disconnected particulars do not remain when seen as elements of a Grand Harmony which is Divine Life. Pain is feeling of bar or constraint which is created by veiling or ignorance. In Divine Experience there is no ignorance, and therefore, no bar: particulars exist in it but not veiled away from the whole. In such Experience, therefore, there can be no pain as such.

In the second place, the Supreme Being having by His own activity evolved as particular Centres and their particular experiences of pleasure and pain, knows in, and as, such Centres all their pleasures and pains. In fact, their pleasures and pains are His pleasures and pains. Hence, as such Centres, He feels pleasure as pleasure and pain as pain. Therefore, we have four forms: (1) Divine Life as transcendent-immanent Being-Consciousness-Bliss which is unchanged in changing as the varied world—this guarantees a background and "atmosphere" of Bliss-Joy for all particular feelings of whatever kind; (2) Divine Life as the grand total of all particular feelings, which is a Life of Bliss and Quiescence, though the particular constituents may be variously pleasurable or painful; (3) Divine Life as the grand Harmony in which particular feelings without coalescing and neutralizing one another are "seen" in their proper and true relations like the notes of a symphony; and (4) Divine Life as the Life of the particular Centres with their particular pleasures and pains. In the last case, pleasures and pains are "seen" as such, but since the Supreme Being, in becoming a particular Centre, does not (*a*) cease to be Supreme and (*b*) pure Bliss-Consciousness, it follows that the "seeing" of particular pleasures and pains of particular Centres by God means their being reflected on a pure and perfect Bliss-Consciousness, imbedded in an unbounded mass of Pure Joy:[1] It is infinite Joy and Bliss looking finite pleasures and pains in the face.

Such reflection of man's pleasures and pains on Cosmic Bliss-Consciousness renders divine compassion and grace possible. And it should be noted that *Śākta Vedānta*, in its practical aspect, is not the Path of Effort and Action[2] only, or the Path of Contemplation and Meditation[3] only, but is also is the Path of Devotion and Love.[4] It is not simply an Art that achieves, a Science that knows, but it is also an Aesthetic awakening in the aspirant of spiritual thirst and feeling, making him love and worship the Divine Mother whose play it is to bind and whose grace it is to liberate. As on the speculative side this doctrine is a synthesis and harmony of partial, and sometimes warring truths, so on the practical side it is a summing up and reconciliation of divergent methods of realization.

As the Doctrine of Power it looks upon every Centre as a veiled Cosmic Power and makes its emancipation the realization by it that it is the Cosmic Power. Naturally the greatest emphasis is laid on active Effort in the practice of realization. It rightly recognises that complete self-surrender to God and absolute reliance on God's grace is not at all a negative and passive attitude signifying lack of will and power, but it is, really, perfect self-exertion and heroism, and "conquest" of divinity: that if to strive after divinity connotes exertion of Power, surrender to and reliance on divine grace, to the exclusion and inhibition of all little, ordinary self-seekings and self-adjustments, also connotes it. This doctrine lends no countenance to such methods as are really calculated to diminish

[1] Ānanda-Śraya.
[2] Karma-Yoga.
[3] Jnāna-Yoga.
[4] Bhakti-Yoga.

the efficiency of human will and endeavour, such as really spell lack of vitality. As on the speculative side the essence of Reality is Power, so on the practical side the essence of spiritual endeavour is dynamism.

Accordingly, it is not a cult of false asceticism and excessive mortification of the "flesh". Since all is manifestation of Bliss-Consciousness-Power and every object of creation, however apparently "lowly" and insignificant is an incarnation and magazine of such Power, the highest end of realization cannot be achieved by fleeing from or rejecting the world of objects, but by removing the veil of practical ignorance which has concealed from men their true nature of Bliss-Consciousness-Power. When the veil is removed, the Experience of realization will be of the form "All is *Brahman*"[1] as well as of the form "Thou art It".[2] It is man's use, or rather abuse, that has made things—in reality, "True, good and beautiful"—lowly, bad, ugly, evil and so forth. There are other things, too, which, in man's use, are high, good, beautiful and so forth; but they are finitely and relatively so. To realize "All is *Brahman*," these latter must be perceived to be infinitely and absolutely so—that is, each object must be realized as Mother *Saccidānanda-mayī* Herself. More essential and more difficult becomes the task when the former objects—lowly, ugly and evil—have to be so realized. And they must be so realized—else, "All is not *Brahman*" —there will be duality of Good and Evil and so forth. Hence, greater emphasis should be laid on this latter task: the aspirant must know that it is ignorant abuse that has made these things evil and ugly and that he can reach his goal of non-dual Perfect Experience only by seeing, realizing the *Brahman* in and through them. This is the true principle of the psycho-physical ritual in the *Śāstra*. It is the effort of the Hero,[3] and not of the ordinary man in his bonds of convention.[4] The purification of the five "tattvas"[5] means or should mean the casting off of their pragmatic sheaths of abuse and ignorance in which they masquerade as lowly and ugly and evil; when these sheaths are cast away, they are as much true, good and beautiful as the Self of the aspirant, and then, they can be assimilated, the result being the Self and the Not-Self assimilated to each other in, and as, the Whole.

As to the question whether *Śākta* Doctrine affords a sure and sufficient basis for man's belief in a Personal and Moral God, it may be observed

[1] Sarvam Khalvidam Brahman. [2] Tattvamasi.
[3] Vīra. [4] Paśu.
[5] See "*Śakti and Śākta*", "The Pancatattva".

only this that though the Reality-Whole = Perfect Experience = Alogical = beyond all duality such as moral-non-moral, personal-impersonal, and so forth, yet the most fundamental expression of the Supreme Reality-Power is the Supreme "Joy"[1] = Supreme Person = God. God, therefore, is quite secure in this Doctrine, though it does not allow the defining and circumscribing of a Reality which is indefinable and immeasurable. The Supreme Being-Power is a Personal and Moral God, but personality and morality are attributes that do not exhaust the immensity of Supreme Being.

Further, since this Doctrine in solving the world-problem suffers no residue, overt or covert, of duality to remain, since, therefore, according to it, the "lowliest" object is really the Mother who is *Saccidānanda-mayī* Herself, it follows that physical, moral and aesthetic evil exists only in ignorance and non-acceptance of the Whole, and that in the eyes of him who sees the Whole, the Mother showing Herself in an infinite variety of expression (which finite Centres may know pragmatically as good or bad, true or false, beautiful or ugly and so forth) never goes out of Her Being-essence which is Being-Consciousness-Bliss.

The Cosmos being the theatre of Divine Play provides the arena in which the Centres must interplay and ultimately realize the Divinity playing in, and as, them. The scheme of creation and the principles on which it is run are calculated to lead progressively to the end or purpose of the world-scheme.

As the belief in Universal Power has been the basis of all ancient human faiths, so a body of "mysterious" rites (called "magical") has been at the basis of all ancient human religious practices. The nature of "magic" has been commonly misunderstood; but modern thought is slowly coming to recognise that it is not "meaningless"; that it is a kind of "primitive science" whereby the primitive man, still in the lower grades of culture, has essayed to propitiate the powers by which he thinks he is encompassed and turn their influence to his own best account. The definition is substantially correct, if we drop the terms by which the cult of magic is thus evaluated as "primitive", "lower", and so forth, and if we drop also the distinction commonly made between magic which is supposed to involve no sense of man's dependence on higher Powers and no element of worship and religion which involves both. *Tāntric* ritual (whether we call it magic or not) is based upon the Science that

---

1 See the explanation of Śiva-tattva with its associate Śakti-tattva in the preceding chapter. It is the highest in the "logical line."

the World is Power which is the same as the Consciousness-Power in man, that the Cosmic Power can be linked up with Man-Power by worship and other means, giving effectiveness and success to man in the pursuit of his ends, in the world or as liberation therefrom.

This linking up is held to be possible, for at root man's power is the Cosmic Power. The Kulārṇava Tantra says that in Śākta doctrine world-enjoyment may be made *Yoga*.[1] Power may be realised in a two-fold way; man may wish to remain man, to perfect himself as man, and to have such worldly enjoyment as he may lawfully desire.[2] He then cultivates those powers which are the Mother in Form. Or he may desire to be one with the Formless Mother Herself. This end also may, (according to the system) be achieved on the path of world-enjoyment provided that it be realised that the individual life is a part of the divine action in nature and not a separate thing to be held and pursued apart for its own sake only. In the Vedās enjoyment is the fruit of sacrifice and the gift of the gods. The higher sacrifice is to the Mother-Power of whom all deities and all men are inferior forms. When this is known and man unifies himself with that Cosmic Power, enjoyment becomes *Yoga* and passage is made to that state in which there is neither sacrifice nor sacrificer. This is the Supreme Experience which is the Mother-Power in Her own formless nature. As the Creatrix of forms the Divine Mother is *Māyā*, and as the produced individual form *Avidyā* (ignorance). As Liberatrix from the ignorance of the forms which are of Her making She is *Mahā-Māyā*.[3] In the Śakti Sutras of Agastya all is spoken of in terms of Power, which is the essence of Reality as World, and which is the Real, both as God and God-head.[4]

[1] Bhogo Yogāyate.

[2] In the Puruṣārtha, Dharma or law and morality, is a governing factor both in the case of Kāma and Artha, on the world-path (Pravritti mārga).

[3] Literally, the term means "The Great Measurer". It includes, therefore, Māyā, and is, sometimes, regarded as this latter cosmically considered. In some places, too (*e.g.*, in some of the verses of the Kālikā and Devī Purāṇa) the term is taken to mean the Veiler even of the Creator, Sustainer, and Destroyer of the World. But, fundamentally, She is, according to Śastra, the Whole Reality-Power, both in Its veiling and revealing, binding and liberating aspect, emphasis being, often, laid on the latter aspect. As the Supreme Veiler She is commonly referred to as Mahā-mohā, and as the Supreme Revealer She is called Mahā-vidyā. In her aspect as Māyā, She is, generally, described as the veiler, creating and drawing the veil over all particular existences; and, according as this veil makes for Bhoga or for Yoga, She is called Bhoga-māyā or yoga-māya. For a comprehensive conception of Māhā-māyā, see, in particular, Śrī Candī, Chap. I, 54-87. Verses 55 56 show Her as the Supreme Veiler, and verse 57 as the Supreme Revealer ("Paramā vidyā"; "mukter Hetu-bhūtā sanātanī"). Verse 58 calls her the Root of the Samsāra (World) Bond, and also, the Lord of the Lord of All ("Sarveśvareśvarī").

[4] In Māyāvāda God is only pragmatically real. Though the Śakti-Vāda Brahman has a transcendent aspect, yet it, in such aspect, only, exceeds but does not exclude its aspect as Lord.